Language and Society

Language and Society

An Introduction

Andrew Simpson

Oxford University Press is a department of the University of Oxford. It furthers
the University's objective of excellence in research, scholarship, and education
by publishing worldwide. Oxford is a registered trade mark of Oxford University
Press in the UK and certain other countries.

Published in the United States of America by Oxford University Press
198 Madison Avenue, New York, NY 10016, United States of America.

© Oxford University Press 2019

All rights reserved. No part of this publication may be reproduced, stored in
a retrieval system, or transmitted, in any form or by any means, without the
prior permission in writing of Oxford University Press, or as expressly permitted
by law, by license, or under terms agreed with the appropriate reproduction
rights organization. Inquiries concerning reproduction outside the scope of the
above should be sent to the Rights Department, Oxford University Press, at the
address above.

You must not circulate this work in any other form
and you must impose this same condition on any acquirer.

Library of Congress Cataloging-in-Publication Data
Names: Simpson, Andrew, 1962– author.
Title: Language and society : an introduction / Andrew Simpson.
Description: New York, NY : Oxford University Press, [2019] |
Includes bibliographical references and index.
Identifiers: LCCN 2018038473 (print) | LCCN 2018050574 (ebook) |
ISBN 9780190210670 (updf) | ISBN 9780190940201 (epub) |
ISBN 9780190210663 (paperback : alk. paper)
Subjects: LCSH: Sociolinguistics.
Classification: LCC P40 (ebook) | LCC P40 .S493 2019 (print) |
DDC 306.44—dc23
LC record available at https://lccn.loc.gov/2018038473

1 3 5 7 9 8 6 4 2

Printed by WebCom, Inc., Canada

Contents

Foreword for Instructors — vii

1. Languages and Dialects — 1
2. Languages with Special Roles: National and Official Languages — 27
3. Languages under Pressure: Minority Groups and Language Loss — 67
4. Diglossia and Code-Switching — 109
5. Pidgins and Creoles: The Birth and Development of New Languages — 142
6. The Globalization of English — 181
7. Language(s) in the United States — 222
8. Bilingualism — 264
9. Language and Thought: The Linguistic Relativity Controversy — 311
10. Language and Gender — 352
11. Language Variation and Change — 406

References — 455
Index — 473

Foreword for Instructors

This volume is intended to have a primary use as a textbook for general education-type courses aimed at students from a variety of majors and backgrounds who have little or no prior knowledge of linguistics and no necessary commitment to studying linguistics beyond the general education level. While there are a number of fine introductions to sociolinguistics available for use with students majoring in linguistics, much fewer resources are available for teaching courses on language and society to students who are engineers, architects, business majors, medical students, and anthropologists. This book sets out to fill such a gap and to introduce a broad and exciting array of topics in the interaction of language and society in a clear, non-specialist way to undergraduates who may perhaps take only one course in linguistics during their time at university. The book has evolved from materials developed during the author's teaching of general education-type classes on language and society for over twenty years in the University of Southern California, UCLA, UC Irvine, and the University of London, and is organized into eleven major topics which the author has regularly found to be enjoyed by students coming to the study of linguistics for the first (and sometimes last) time.

When used as a textbook for general education courses (or as introductions to language and society for focused anthropology and sociology majors), the eleven chapters can be adapted for either a 16-week semester or a 10-week quarter/term, by selectively using the materials in each chapter, or by utilizing some but not all of the chapters. The chapters have all quite deliberately been written on the long side in order to provide instructors with flexibility in their teaching and the opportunity to selectively customize how individual courses are structured and taught. Given the amount of information that is present in each chapter, it is unlikely that all of the material in the textbook should be presented in any single course, and instructors should consider how much of each chapter to cover in each course, adjusting this to the time available and the interests of both students and instructors themselves. Each chapter offers a very broad introduction to a particular topic, and provides support and exemplification of the key points being discussed with additional detailed background information and contextualization which can be made use of as felt appropriate, either brought into lectures, assigned as further reading, used by teaching assistants in group discussion, or alternatively omitted if time is limited, without this causing any negative impact on students' understanding of the core ideas present in the book. The chapters also all include a final set of suggestions for further reading, discussion, and simple research activities that students can be asked to engage in relating to the topic matter of each chapter, suitable for private study or use in TA-led discussion sections. A brief overview of the eleven units is now given, chapter by chapter, in order to familiarize potential instructors with the general contents of the book.

The first chapter of the book, *Languages and Dialects*, discusses how the important term 'language' is applied to certain varieties of speech and writing, and 'dialect' to others. The chapter shows how language-dialect divisions may often be made for socio-political rather than linguistic reasons, and explains how the imposition of such terminological distinctions may have important consequences for people's everyday life. A broad range of examples is used to illustrate the often arbitrary divisions made between 'languages' and other varieties, and how the classification of varieties as 'languages' or 'dialects' is sometimes manipulated for political ends.

Chapter 2 examines *Languages with Special Roles: National and Official Languages*—languages which are promoted with particular symbolic or utilitarian functions during the establishment and development of independent states. The chapter describes processes of language planning and the different kinds of national and official language policies pursued in ethno-linguistically complex states around the world. An extensive set of case studies from different countries illustrates how language planning decisions can either help unite a population or alternatively lead to civil unrest, conflict, and calls for independence. Instructors may choose to focus on a subset of these case studies and outcome types, or simply highlight the generalizations which each study provides. The social, historical, and political background described in each case is included to help students understand how the different language situations have arisen, and is not information that students should normally be expected to learn for examinations. Students should rather be encouraged to focus on the broad lessons for governmental language planning which emerge from the policies adopted in different countries. Chapter 2 also includes discussion of linguistic assimilation and the suppression of languages, the symbolic and utilitarian power of different scripts/orthography, language purification, and the ways that languages create new words and expand their vocabulary.

Chapter 3 considers how the promotion and growth of larger languages has effects on linguistic minorities and the maintenance of their languages in *Languages under Pressure: Minority Groups and Language Loss*. The first half of the chapter describes typical cross-generational patterns of language shift and loss among immigrant minorities and the factors that regularly cause people to abandon their heritage languages. The second part of the chapter then turns to language endangerment among indigenous minority groups and the rapid increase in the disappearance of smaller languages in the 20th and 21st centuries— 'language death'—which may perhaps affect as much as two-thirds of the world's languages during the course of the present century. Positive responses to global language endangerment, such as language documentation and language revitalization programs, are also described with illustrations of their results in various countries.

Knowledge and the use of two or more languages in special ways by many speakers in different parts of the world is the topic of chapter 4: *Diglossia and Code-Switching*. The first part of the chapter looks at situations of stable bilingualism in which people use their two languages for different purposes, the occurrence of 'diglossia' in countries such as Switzerland, Paraguay, and the Arabic-speaking world. The remainder of the chapter then describes the widespread phenomenon of 'code-switching', in which speakers mix their two languages in single conversations, and often within single sentences, in different ways. The chapter explains what the common social, stylistic, and linguistic causes of code-switching are, how code-switching is perceived as a form of linguistic behavior both positively and negatively, and how code-switching is used by speakers as a way to increase solidarity and express personal and group identity, or occasionally to project a more confrontational stance to others. Examples of code-switching from a broad range of languages are used to illustrate the patterns being discussed.

Having described the disappearance and loss of older languages in chapter 3, chapter 5 investigates situations in which *new* languages frequently come into existence: *Pidgins and Creoles: the Birth and Development of New Languages*. This chapter describes the interesting pidgin-to-creole life cycle and how early pidgin languages develop into stable pidgins and creoles in different ways, as a result of the social situation such languages are used in. The chapter also reviews different explanations which have been offered for pidginization, creolization, and the similarities existing among such languages around the world, which attribute their development to patterns of first- and second-language acquisition and the possibility of a single historical origin. Although reference is made to a number of different morphological, syntactic, and phonological properties of pidgins and creoles in the chapter, this is done in ways that can be easily understood by students with no previous exposure to linguistics.

Chapters 1–5 all highlight interactions between languages of different sizes and official statuses. Chapter 6 turns to focus on the *Globalization of English* and the phenomenal spread of knowledge of English around the world, now understood and used by more speakers than any other language present or past. The chapter asks what factors have caused knowledge of English to be so widespread in the 21st century, what negative consequences might result from the emergence of a 'global language', and also considers what may be predicted about the future of English as a world lingua franca. The chapter discusses attitudes that exist toward English among second-language speakers, how a variety of localized 'world Englishes' are coming into existence, and what factors may influence the future development of English as a common, international language.

Chapter 7, *Language(s) in the United States,* focuses on the interplay of linguistic and social forces in the United States, where English has come to have a heavily dominant role in almost all domains of life, despite the presence of many other languages brought to the USA by immigrants building up the population of the country. The chapter is divided into two major parts. The first part examines how English established such a powerful position in the USA relative to other languages, and why the settlement of different ethnic groups in the United States did not result in any widespread bilingualism and the sustained maintenance of other languages. The text describes the tensions which continue to exist between movements attempting to promote the official status of English and English monolingualism, and those who attempt to defend multilingualism and encourage the learning of heritage languages as additions to knowledge of English. The second part of the chapter is a concentrated study of the most researched and discussed non-standard variety of English in the USA—African American Vernacular English (AAVE). This variety has regularly been at the center of discussions on how to help young speakers of English which is different from Mainstream American English (MAE) be successful in schools where MAE has been used as the default medium of education, and to overcome difficulties often caused by differences between home-spoken dialects of English and MAE-based academic English. The chapter includes discussion of the 1996 Ebonics controversy and more recent 'code-switching' approaches to language teaching in schools with students whose home variety of English is significantly different to MAE. While the chapter may naturally seem to have greater relevance for students living in the USA, parts of the chapter can also be added to classes taught in other countries as illustration of the difficulties which exist more widely in the world when students' home languages are different from the language used in school.

Chapter 8 presents an extended profile of *Bilingualism* and how the majority of the world's population manages to successfully acquire and make use of two (or more) languages in their everyday life. While chapters dedicated to the development and maintenance of bilingualism are less common in other introductions to language and society, such a chapter has been included in the current volume because students regularly seem to enjoy learning about the bilingual mind and how people acquire and manipulate their abilities in two (or more) languages. A significant portion of the chapter looks at different ways in which bilingualism is established in both younger and older speakers, including discussion of simultaneous and sequential bilingualism, the Critical Period Hypothesis, bilinguals' mental lexicons, language attrition, and the various linguistic and cognitive advantages of becoming bilingual. The chapter also considers how research into bilingualism can help shape language policy in education and improve learning outcomes for children from language minority groups. As with certain other chapters in the volume, instructors can customize their use of the chapter on bilingualism and select various portions for presentation in class, and assign other sections as further background reading. The level of technical discussion in some sections of chapter 8 is higher than in various of the other chapters, but still within the reach of engaged students coming to linguistics for the first time. Interest in the topic matter of this chapter has often led students in the author's classes to seek out further courses in linguistics, particularly in the areas of language acquisition and cognitive linguistics/psycholinguistics.

One of the topics discussed in chapter 8 is how words link up with concepts in the minds of speakers, and how these connections may be organized in people who know more than one language. Chapter 9, *Language and Thought: The Linguistic Relativity Controversy*, considers how language in general relates to thought, and whether it can be concluded that the language a person speaks may influence his/her ways of thinking and behavior. The first part of the chapter introduces early ideas about linguistic relativity and criticisms raised against it which caused a downturn in interest in the theory during the 1970s–1980s. Research into linguistic relativity revived strongly from the 1990s to the present, as new techniques were developed to probe how language can influence non-verbal behavior and provide better empirical support for the hypothesis of linguistic relativity. The second part of the chapter looks at some of the key neo-Whorfian experiments carried out in recent years on phenomena which have been argued to show the effects of language on perception. The chapter also considers the interaction of linguistic relativity and bilingualism and how an individual's way(s) of thinking may be impacted by the knowledge of two different languages, linking the chapter back to the theme of chapter 8. As with chapter 2 and chapter 8, instructors may choose to present a subset of the various (experimental) case studies presented in the chapter, rather than ask students to familiarize themselves with all of the empirical patterns described in the second half of the chapter. The chapter on linguistic relativity was included in the volume as it is another broad topic which students are often very interested in, and recent neo-Whorfian experimental work enables an interesting reassessment of the original Sapir-Whorf Hypothesis.

The final two chapters in the book look at variation that occurs within individual languages, rather than between different languages. Chapter 10, *Language and Gender*, considers qualitative and quantitative differences in the ways that many male and female speakers use the 'same' language, and what such patterns might be taken to indicate about men's and women's relation to each other and to society in general. The chapter reviews different theories of male and females groups' use of language, and the issue of contextualized variation *within* men's and women's language. While much of the first part of the chapter is concerned with gender-related language use in the West, the second part of the chapter adds a focused coverage of gendered language use in Japan as a contrast and balance to the emphasis on Western language patterns. The chapter also includes a section on the phenomenon of sexism in language. While studies on language and gender have been evolving rapidly in new directions in recent years, the goal of chapter 10 is principally to provide students with a foundation in work on this topic over the past several decades, as a way to engage students in this growing area of study and to equip them with knowledge of the broad development of the field up to the present time and its more recent post-modern emphasis on gender performance and variability in male and female language. The chapter offers suggestions for further reading, leading students to a range of additional topics that will add to their understanding of issues in language and gender.

Chapter 11 closes the volume with an overview of ground-breaking and interesting recent research on *Language Variation and Change* among different speech communities, and the sociolinguistic causes and consequences of such change. The chapter begins with a consideration of two classic, pioneering studies of language variation carried out in the 1960s, which set the scene and standards for much subsequent work on ongoing change, and then moves on to examine a diverse set of more contemporary projects, each of which brings into focus a different aspect of language change and its relation to society, ranging from '*uptalk*' and '*vocal fry*', through the international spread of quotative '*be like*', to very recent lexical creativity in forms such as '*big-ass car*' and the question-marker '*innit*'. Due to the prime, intended use of the book, most of the illustrations of language variation described in the chapter are patterns of change occurring in the English-speaking world, as readers may find it easier to appreciate these examples and in some cases may have opinions and intuitions about the actual patterns themselves and an understanding of the attitudes that commonly exist toward speakers using them. Additionally, examples in the second half of the chapter all relate to language patterns innovated and used predominantly by younger speakers—teenagers and young adults—as these patterns may be familiar to students using the book. As with chapter 10, the level of chapter 11 has been kept very accessible for all readers and does not include reference to any heavily technical aspects of language analysis or require knowledge of phonetics, statistics, or other skills often applied in research on language variation and change.

It is hoped that the volume, however used by instructors, students, and other readers, will stimulate a new awareness and interest in the many different kinds of interactions language has with structures in society, individuals and their identities, and forces affecting the use, rise and decline, and re-growth of languages around the world. Coming to understand the complexities of language and its functions in society is both exciting and challenging at times. Hopefully the selection of topics included in the book and their mode of presentation will communicate to 'newcomers' some of this sense of amazement and awe that the sociological study of language regularly gives rise to.

1

Languages and Dialects

Introduction

The word 'language' will be used very frequently throughout this book, and will sometimes be used in contrast to other terms such as 'dialect', 'style', 'register', and 'code'. The purpose of this first chapter is to look closely at the term 'language', and the associated term 'dialect', and consider what such terms refer to and how they may be defined. Although we might take it for granted that we know what is meant by the word 'language', and how it is commonly used, it will become clear in the course of the chapter that the application of the term 'language' to a way of speaking and writing is actually not straightforward, and is heavily influenced by the way that societies organize themselves politically. It will also be seen that there are important consequences affecting people's everyday life due to the designation of certain forms of speech as languages, and others as dialects. The first part of the chapter will focus specifically on the term 'language' and its application to ways of speaking and writing in different parts of the world. The second part of the chapter will then turn to examine the term 'dialect', which needs to be defined and understood in direct relation to the term 'language'. We will consider what properties dialects are regularly assumed to have, how these properties may or may not be different from those associated with ways of speaking recognized to be languages, and how the language-dialect division may sometimes be quite controversial, manipulated for political ends, and in various cases disputed.

What is a language and how are languages defined?

The *Oxford English Dictionary* (*OED*) provides a broad range of definitions for the word 'language', characterizing its varied use both now and in the past. Among these, the following three descriptions occur:

> *Definitions given for the term 'language' (adapted from the OED online)*
> (a) The system of spoken or written communication used by a particular country, people, community, etc., typically consisting of words used within a regular grammatical and syntactic structure.

(b) The method of human communication, either spoken or written, consisting of the use of words in a structured and conventional way.
(c) The form of words in which something is communicated; manner or style of expression.

The characterization found in (b) picks out the use of 'language' in a very general way, as a specifically human ability, in sentences such as 'Language is normally acquired by children successfully in the first few years of their lives.' The description in (c) refers to an individual's speech or writing in a particular instance—his/her chosen style in an act of communication—as heard in sentences such as 'John's language gets absolutely foul when he has had a few drinks with his friends.' In this chapter, we will be focusing on the use of the term 'language' approximated in definition (a), where it occurs as a noun referring to a system of communication attributed to a particular population of speakers. In this sense, we find the word language occurring in sentences such as: 'There are nine languages spoken on the island of Fiji', and 'Warlpiri is a language of northern Australia with approximately 2,500 speakers.' The question we will be asking here is why certain systems of spoken or written communication are viewed and recognized as languages, while others are accorded the status of dialects, and is it the case that a single, objective set of criteria are consistently made use of in applying the term 'language' to distinctive ways of speaking in different populations and societies.

Before approaching such questions more closely, it is useful to flag ahead of time why such terminological issues are potentially important and therefore worth probing and trying to understand, i.e., why we might really care about this issue of the application of a simple word. What is potentially at stake here is the power of a particular label to help generate benefits for certain members of a population in their everyday life. It has been observed widely throughout the world that if a variety of speech is officially recognized as a language rather than a dialect or just a style of speaking, this may often accord its speakers particular linguistic rights and privileges, sanctioning use of the 'language' in certain significant areas of life where the use of other dialect forms is not legitimized in any similar way. For example, certain 'languages' may be approved for use in education (schools and universities), courts of law, and government administration, so that speakers have the right to use and be addressed in their 'language' in such domains, but it is very rare to find that 'dialects' are officialized for use in such spheres of life. Similarly, employment opportunities may often require knowledge of and abilities in languages, giving natural advantages to their speakers, whereas forms of speech determined to be dialects rather than languages seldom become listed as professional requirements. Languages but not dialects are also commonly provided with special linguistic resources such as dictionaries, the development of literature, and the expansion of vocabulary, specifically designed to help the growth of languages and their ability to be learned and used by more people in a full range of communicative situations. The categorization of a certain form of speech as a distinct language may furthermore engender various attitudes among its speakers, such as increased confidence and pride in their speaking of the language, while speakers of dialects may sometimes experience more negative feelings toward their speech and an induced belief that it is hierarchically inferior to other forms recognized as languages. Much therefore may result from the way that different forms of speech are classified by the terms 'language' and 'dialect', making it relevant indeed to ask why such distinctions are made, and how a particular set of forms is to be identified as a language rather than as a dialect, register, style, or other way of speaking.

Following a linguistic practice common since Petyt (1980) and Chambers and Trudgill (1980), we will now frequently make use of the additional term '*variety* (of speech/writing)' as a way to refer neutrally to certain forms of speech, without needing to choose between use of the words 'language' or 'dialect' in certain instances. Petyt (1980: 27) describes 'variety' as a term available to refer to 'any form of language considered for some purpose as a single entity.'

Turning to use of the term 'language' now, a first question we can ask is the following: When a variety of speech is classified as a language, is this done so purely on *linguistic* grounds, and if so, how? Two different approaches to the identification of 'languages' in virtue of the linguistic properties that a variety has can be considered here. A first possibility is to assume that a language should be taken to be the combination of a set of vocabulary and grammatical rules shared and used in the same way by a particular community. For example, if we declare that a language named 'Kutuku' exists, we might assume that speakers of Kutuku all use a specific set of words and a grammar in the same way. We can call such an approach the 'invariant system hypothesis':

The Invariant System Hypothesis
A language consists in: (a) a set of words (a vocabulary) and (b) a set of rules of grammar, both used in an identical way by a sizable population of speakers, e.g. the French, the Greeks, etc.

However, this is actually an idealistic and unrealistic way of trying to define the notion 'language' because we find that in reality no two individuals actually do possess the same set of vocabulary items and the same set of grammar rules—there are always certain differences present in the speech of people we can compare. Sometimes these differences may be quite salient and obvious. For example, many speakers of English use a double negation form in casual speech, as illustrated in (2), in contrast to the more standardized single negation equivalent in (1), and other speakers produce double modal forms as in (4), which are different from the more widespread single modal patterns seen in (3).

(1) a. I didn't do anything.
     b. They haven't seen anything.

(2) a. I ain't done nothing.
     b. They didn't see nothing.

(3) a. We might need to tell him.
     b. A chainsaw would be able to cut it easily.

(4) a. We might should tell him.
     b. A chainsaw would could cut it easily.

In the area of past tense formation, variation is found among speakers of English in different places, with some using strong irregular forms, and others simply adding -ed to the stem of a verb, as with most verbs in English:

(5) a. He dove into the water.
    b. He dived into the water.

(6) a. We grew potatoes for a while.
    b. We growed potatoes for a while.

(7) a. We snuck into the movie house.
    b. We sneaked into the cinema.

(8) a. I clumb right up the tree.
    b. I climbed right up the tree.

Vocabulary items are also different in various instances among speakers of English in different countries, as illustrated with the word pairs in (8) commonly used in the USA and the UK:

(9) | US English | UK English |
|---|---|
| gas | petrol |
| trash | rubbish |
| trunk | boot |
| flashlight | torch |
| cookie | biscuit |
| fries | chips |
| eraser | rubber |

Of course, it might be objected by some that forms such as (2) and (4) (and some of 5–8) are not 'correct' English and that the rules which lead to (2) and (4) are not rules of the English language—and therefore that speakers who produce sentences like (2) and (4) are not speaking English but some other language which resembles English a lot, but is technically a different language. There are, however, many more areas where speakers differ in what they say, and it becomes extremely difficult to reach any full agreement on what is 'grammatical' in English. For example, some speakers use a subject pronoun 'I' in sequences such as (10a), whereas others insist that the pronoun should be 'me' here, as in (10b), because it follows a preposition. Another instance of disagreement occurs in the placement of adverbs—many people use adverbs after the infinitive marker *to*, as in (11), while others may argue that this is 'ungrammatical':

(10) a. between you and I
     b. between you and me

(11) a. I want you to carefully read this report and then destroy it.
     b. These are the voyages of the Starship Enterprise, its 5 year mission: to explore strange new worlds, to seek out new life and new civilizations, to boldly go where no man has gone before. (*Star Trek*, original series)

Further, very subtle differences occur in the speech of people who self-identify as speakers of the same language, and these differences may not be widely noticed. For example, speakers of American English may say forms such as (13a) in response to a question such as (12), whereas British speakers will regularly produce the form in (13b):

(12)   Are you going to the party tomorrow?

(13) a. I might.
     b. I might do.

Just focusing on the 'English' spoken in one country, the USA, a massive survey carried out in the middle of the 20th century, the American Linguistic Atlas Project, asked significant numbers of people around the country about their speech patterns and reported that no two speakers gave exactly same set of responses to questionnaires about their everyday language use; hence all exhibited certain differences in the way they spoke from others questioned in the survey.

The bottom line is that each individual speaker in a population has a somewhat different exposure to language and will consequently develop a somewhat different rule system and vocabulary, and a partially idiosyncratic way of speaking. Linguists have coined a term for this variation and refer to the distinctive, unique characteristics of the language of an individual speaker as his/her *idiolect* (see Fromkin et al. 2011: 430). The end result for the Invariant System Hypothesis of language is that although it might be possible to formulate a single set of rules and call them characteristic of 'English', it will turn out that almost no one follows these rules *completely* and therefore that most people in the USA, the UK, Canada, Australia, and New Zealand do not speak 'English' but some other related language. Quite generally, if a language is defined in the way of the Invariant System Hypothesis as consisting in a *single* set of rules and an associated vocabulary used in the *same* way by a community of speakers, it would have to be concluded that everyone in the world actually speaks a different language.

But such a conclusion seems to be wrong and to go against the common intuition we have that there are in fact languages such as English, Russian, and Korean, which have many speakers. So, what are our everyday intuitions about languages really based upon? A second, rather less stringent linguistic approach that has been proposed for the definition of languages is the suggestion that speakers need not share *identical* rule systems and vocabularies in order to be viewed as speakers of a single language, but they must be speakers of varieties which are *mutually intelligible*. It is suggested that if two speakers are able to understand each other when they use somewhat different varieties of language, they can be said to speak variant forms of a *single language*. This can be formalized as the Mutual Intelligibility Hypothesis:

The Mutual Intelligibility Hypothesis
(a) If speakers of two varieties of language, A and B, can understand each other when they speak, then A and B can be considered to be varieties of a single language C.
(b) If speakers of a variety X and a variety Y cannot understand each other when they speak, then X and Y cannot be considered to be varieties of a single language Z, and therefore must be independent languages X and Y (or varieties of separate languages).

The criterion of mutual intelligibility is a naturally appealing one. It allows us to say that speakers who use forms such as (1–13) above all speak the same basic language—English. It also clearly allows us to state that, for example, English and French are different languages because someone speaking English will not be able to communicate with and understand a French speaker if neither of them speaks the other's language. However, further thought shows us that, in the world around us, mutual intelligibility is not always the critical property used to divide up different linguistic varieties into languages, and there are many varieties that are accepted as languages which fail to satisfy the criteria of the Mutual Intelligibility Hypothesis.

The counter-examples to the Mutual Intelligibility Hypothesis are of two types. In some instances, we find that speakers of two (or more) varieties can understand each other quite well when they speak, and so these varieties should be classified as dialects of a single language according to part (a) of the Mutual Intelligibility Hypothesis. However, it is found that these varieties are officially recognized as distinct languages. Illustrations of this will shortly be given. In other instances, we find that speakers of two or more varieties cannot understand each other when they speak, and so one would expect these varieties to be categorized as distinct languages, according to part (b) of the Mutual Intelligibility Hypothesis, but in reality it is found that these varieties are classed as dialects of a single language.

There are many classic examples of the first kind of situation that have been noted in the literature. One example frequently given is the case of **Hindi** and **Urdu**, both of which are spoken extensively in India, with Urdu also being used by many speakers in Pakistan. These two 'languages' are actually very similar, the differences essentially reducing to a different script being used for writing Hindi and Urdu (devanagari script for the former, Arabic script for the latter), and certain differences in vocabulary, with Hindi containing more Sanskrit-origin words, and Urdu making use of more words that have their origins in Persian and Arabic. The difference in vocabulary is, however, not extremely significant and is similar in degree to the vocabulary differences present in British and American English (for example, *lift* vs. *elevator, flat* vs. *apartment*, etc.). These differences do not impede understanding, especially at the level of colloquial, non-formal speech, and Hindi and Urdu generally have a very high degree of mutual intelligibility. They consequently should be classed as variants of a single language according to the Mutual Intelligibility Hypothesis, yet they are commonly referred to as different languages and are treated as separate languages in a whole range of ways. Hindi and Urdu are officially listed as individual languages in the Indian constitution; they can frequently be studied as separate languages in universities in Asia, Europe, and North America; there are separate dictionaries, grammatical descriptions, and language-learning materials available for Hindi and Urdu; and speakers of these varieties will often emphatically insist that they are indeed two formally separate languages. Hindi and Urdu now also occur listed as distinct languages in *Google Translate*. And yet, these two varieties are extremely close in their colloquial forms, and sometimes are indistinguishable—when spoken, example (14) would be identical in both Hindi and Urdu, and speakers of both varieties would recognize it as a sentence of their language:

(14) ye   larkii bahut lambii hai.
     this girl   very   tall   is
     'This girl is very tall.'

A second, frequently noted example of a situation in which part (a) of the Mutual Intelligibility Hypothesis seems to clearly be disproved as a universal criterion comes from Scandinavia. **Danish**, **Swedish** and **Norwegian** are all officially recognized as separate languages, both in Scandinavia itself and elsewhere in the world. One can buy separate dictionaries of Danish, Swedish, and Norwegian, study these varieties as separate languages in academic institutions, and find separate entries for Danish, Swedish, and Norwegian in all regular lists of the world's languages. However, speakers of Danish, Swedish, and Norwegian by and large can engage in successful communication and understand each other quite well when they speak (Chambers and Trudgill 1980), which should suggest that they are speaking the same single language, according to part (a) of the Mutual Intelligibility Hypothesis. The examples given in (15) show how similar Danish, Swedish, and Norwegian frequently may be. Despite some differences in pronunciation, vocabulary, and minor differences in orthography, these varieties do not seem to be different languages for the purposes of mutual understanding among speakers.

(15) 'The book is on the table.'
     Danish: Bogen er på bordet.
     Swedish: Boken är på bordet.
     Norwegian: Boken er på bordet.

The fact that Danish, Swedish, and Norwegian nevertheless are recognized as separate languages indicates that the Mutual Intelligibility Hypothesis is not made use of in various cases of language classification.

Further instances of counter-examples to part (a) of the Mutual Intelligibility Hypothesis can be given from different parts of the globe. In Eastern Europe, **Russian**, **Belarusian**, and **Ukrainian** have been characterized as being largely mutually intelligible, but they are officially distinguished as separate languages. In South Africa, the same is true of **Zulu** and **Xhosa** (Mesthrie et al. 2003); in Southeast Asia, **Malay** and **Indonesian** are mutually intelligible varieties that are recognized as different national languages; and in South America, **Quechua** and **Aymara** have been described as being linguistically close enough to be mutually intelligible, but they are officially classified as distinct languages.

There are also many well-known instances of counter-examples to part (b) of the Mutual Intelligibility Hypothesis—situations in which speakers of two varieties cannot understand each other when they speak, although their varieties are classified as being dialectal variants of a single language. One good example of this is the relationship of different forms of **Chinese** to each other. In China, it is commonly declared and believed that Mandarin, Cantonese, Shanghainese, Hokkien, and other regional varieties are dialects of a single Chinese language, not different languages. The Mandarin Chinese word for 'language' applied to officially recognized languages such as French, German, and Japanese is *yuyan*, but the different term *fangyan* (literally 'place-speech') is used to refer to Cantonese, Hakka, Hokkien, and other regional varieties, in a way that parallels the use of the English term 'dialect' (more on this term in the next section). However, these regional forms of 'Chinese' are most certainly *not* mutually intelligible. A person who speaks Cantonese will not understand a speaker of Hokkien or Shanghainese (unless s/he has studied these varieties) and vice versa—the forms of these varieties are often very different indeed, as illustrated with a simple example of everyday speech:

(16) 'She is very good-looking.'
    Mandarin: ta hen piaoliang
    Cantonese: keoi ho leng
    Hokkien: ee jin swee
    Shanghainese: ee ho khu de lay

(17) 'I don't know.'
    Mandarin: wo bu zhidao
    Cantonese   ngor m jee
    Hokkien: gwa m zai
    Shanghainese: ngoe va showtta

Consequently, according to part (b) of the Mutual Intelligibility Hypothesis, Cantonese, Hokkien, Mandarin, and Shanghainese should all be categorized as different languages, yet both Chinese people and the Chinese leadership do not wish to label these forms as different languages in the way that English and Japanese are considered to be different languages, and when foreign linguists such as Leonard Bloomfield referred to these varieties as different languages in the 1930s, stating that 'the term *Chinese* denotes a family of mutually unintelligible languages' (Bloomfield 1933: 44), such a classification resulted in considerable criticism from authorities and academics within China.

A very similar situation to that in China is present in the **Arabic**-speaking world. Varieties which are commonly referred to as forms of Arabic are spoken throughout North Africa and much of the Middle East, for example: Moroccan Arabic, Egyptian Arabic, Lebanese Arabic, Iraqi Arabic. If such forms of speech are simply regional varieties of a single 'Arabic' language, it would be expected that they should be mutually intelligible, but this is not the case. If a speaker of Moroccan Arabic attempts to communicate in this variety with a speaker of Lebanese, Egyptian, or Iraqi Arabic using his/her regional variety, there will be a failure in communication, as the regional forms of Arabic are in many ways very different from each other and not mutually intelligible (see further discussion on the history and modern use of Arabic in chapter 2), as illustrated in the simple examples in (17) and (18) below.

(17) 'The house may be big.'
    Standard Arabic: min almomkin anna albayt yakunu kabiran
    Moroccan Arabic: d-dar təqdər tkun kbira
    Lebanese Arabic: lbeet byiʔdir ykuun kbir
    Egyptian Arabic: il-bit yimkin yib'a kbiir

(18) 'He will study.'
    Standard Arabic: sawfa yadrus
    Moroccan Arabic: ɣadi yəqra
    Lebanese Arabic: raħ yidrus
    Egyptian Arabic: hayzakir

Part (b) of the Mutual Intelligibility Hypothesis, which suggests that a lack of mutual intelligibility should correspond to a classification of different varieties as distinct languages, is again contradicted by the way that colloquial speech in Morocco, Egypt, Iraq, and Lebanon is regularly referred to as constituting different regional forms of a single language, Arabic.

Further counter-examples to part (b) of the Mutual Intelligibility Hypothesis, in which mutually unintelligible varieties are commonly grouped as dialects of a single language, can be given for regional forms of **Italian** and **German**. In both such cases, there is a wide range of geographically dispersed varieties which are extremely different from each other and not mutually intelligible (for example, Swabian and Bavarian German, and Napoletan and Venetian Italian). A strict application of the Mutual Intelligibility Hypothesis should lead to the classification of these varieties as distinct languages, but, again, this is not commonly done.

So, if many instances of the classification of a commonly spoken form as a 'language' are not made on the basis of mutual intelligibility and purely linguistic properties, what factors do result in the division of different varieties of speech into 'languages' and 'dialects' and why are certain varieties classed as 'special' and referred to as languages? The simple conclusion arrived at by considering many officially recognized languages around the world is that the division of different forms of speech and writing into 'languages' and 'dialects' is frequently done on the basis of *socio-political* grounds, due to a variety of reasons and motivations. Political events and situations, sometimes interacting with social, cultural, and historical factors, very frequently lead to the formal recognition of certain varieties as languages, and the classification of others as dialects, as will now be illustrated with discussion of a representative range of examples.

As noted earlier, colloquial **Hindi** and **Urdu** are mutually intelligible to a very high degree and sometimes indistinguishable. These varieties have come to be called different languages primarily due to the interaction of politics and religious factors during the course of the 20th century. Each variety is associated with a different religious population. 'Urdu' is primarily spoken by Muslims in India and Pakistan, while 'Hindi' is spoken by Hindus in India. The division of a single form of speech into two formally recognized 'languages' occurred largely during the early half of the 20th century, when the leadership of Hindu and Muslim political factions set about emphasizing differences between the varieties they used. Prior to the 20th century, the terms 'Hindi' and 'Urdu' were both used, interchangeably, along with the third term 'Hindustani', to refer to a general colloquial form of speech which had developed in north and central India. In the early part of the 20th century, it was realized that the Indian subcontinent would at some not-too-distant point achieve independence from British colonial rule. This growing awareness of likely future independence led to politicization and polarization of the population along religious lines, and the formation of Hindu and Muslim political parties. The former then began to use the term 'Hindi' to refer to their speech and writing, and the latter emphasized increasingly that what they spoke and wrote was 'Urdu'. When independence came to the subcontinent in 1947, British India underwent partition into two new states, India and Pakistan, and massive population movements took place, with large numbers of Muslims moving from India into Pakistan, while Hindus from the area of Pakistan moved into India. As Pakistan emerged with a new Islamic identity, Urdu was declared its national language, reinforcing the connection between use of the term 'Urdu' and Muslims in South Asia. This choice of 'Urdu' as Pakistan's new national language was largely symbolic, as at the time of the creation of Pakistan, only around 7% of the population of the state could actually speak Urdu well.

Consequently, as a result of political developments relating to religion, a single way of speaking increasingly became associated with two different names in the course of the 20th century, 'Hindi' used by Hindus to refer to their variety of speech, and 'Urdu' used by Muslims, with both Hindi and Urdu being officially recognized as distinct languages in the Indian constitution, despite being mutually intelligible. While the written forms of Hindi and Urdu make use of different scripts, and very formal Hindi and Urdu utilize certain different vocabulary items sourced in Sanskrit and Persian/Arabic, informal, colloquial Hindi and Urdu remain very close, and movies produced by the large Bollywood film industry are regularly made in the mutually intelligible variety, for consumption by both Hindu and Muslim audiences. Viewed in purely linguistic terms, Hindi and Urdu should still be seen to be alternate names for a single language, but a division into two 'languages' has occurred for non-linguistic, politico-religious reasons.

In southeast Europe, in the states of Croatia, Bosnia-Herzegovina, Serbia, and Montenegro, ethnic and religious divisions among a population with a broadly uniform way of speaking have resulted in this being officially characterized in different ways at different times, for political reasons. In the 19th century, there was a common 'Illyrian' view that the mutually intelligible speech of the Serbian and Croatian population of the Balkans instantiated regional variants of a single language, referred to as **'Serbo-Croatian'** in a grammatical description published in 1867. From the late 19th century up into the first half of the 20th century, the idea of a unified language spoken by Serbs and Croats continued on, despite the existence of certain differences between the Serbian and Croatian forms of the language in the area of vocabulary and pronunciation, and larger differences in the way that Serbs and Croats wrote. In the 19th century, Serbs made use of a highly artificial style of writing, almost a language in itself, which did not resemble any Serbian dialect (Greenberg 2011). In

1926 the government of Yugoslavia affirmed that 'in spite of many statements to the contrary, 'Serbian' and 'Croatian' are one and the same language' (Carmichael 2000: 237), and during the 1930s, the Kingdom of Yugoslavia encouraged the growth of a single Yugoslav identity among Serbs and Croats by means of language, publishing a manual of writing for the unified language. Following the declaration of the Federal People's Republic of Yugoslavia in 1946, the long-term president of the Republic, General Tito, heavily stressed the unity of the language of the Serbs, Croats, and Montenegrins, and was committed to the development of a shared written form of Serbo-Croatian. In 1954, a meeting of Serb and Croat linguists resulted in the important Novi Sad Agreement, which stated that 'the national language of the Serbs, Croats, and Montenegrins is a single language, with two variant forms, an eastern and a western form' (Carmichael 2000: 226). Widespread agreement therefore existed among Serbs and Croats in the new communist Yugoslavia that they spoke a single language, with some regional variation.

However, in the 1970s/80s, ethnic pressure between the Serbs and Croats conspired to weaken the unity of Serbo-Croatian, and in 1974 the new Yugoslav Constitution conceded that each of the constituent peoples of the state had the right to use its own language, and four regional variants were recognized as standard or semi-standard forms: Croatian, Serbian, Bosnia-Herzegovinian, and Montenegrin. With further ethnic nationalism growing through the 1980s, the Federal Republic of Yugoslavia finally collapsed and broke up in 1991, splintering into a number of separate states: Croatia, Slovenia, Bosnia-Herzegovina, Macedonia, Serbia and Montenegro. With the disintegration of Yugoslavia, the ethnic populations of each new state (or, at least, their nationalist leaders) set out to emphasize their distinct national identities through assertions of the distinctness of their language, and the single, unified Serbo-Croatian language became renamed as Serbian in Serbia and Montenegro, as Croatian in Croatia, and as Bosnian in Bosnia-Herzegovina. In the latter state, it is recorded in the 1991 census that the majority of Muslims claimed that they spoke Bosnian rather than Serbo-Croatian, following the urgings of the Muslim Party of Democratic Action to identify their speech as such (Greenberg 2011), and in Croatia, the government of Franco Tudjman attempted to foreground the special properties of 'Croatian' by purging the language of words that sounded Serbian, and finding new words to replace them from Croatian regional dialects and historical sources, often introducing obscure forms unknown to many speakers. In Serbia, similar acts of differentiation were initiated, and use of the Cyrillic script to write 'Serbian' was promoted as a marker of Serb identity by nationalists, even though use of the Latin alphabet among the Serbs had actually been gaining much acceptance.

Significant changes in the political make-up of an ethnically complex population have thus been direct causes of changes in the way that the term 'language' has been applied to largely stable varieties of speech over time. For a considerable period of time, the mutually intelligible ways of speaking made use of by Serbs, Croatians, and Bosnian Muslims were viewed and then officially categorized as a single language, when this was perceived to help stimulate and mirror political unification. Later, when this political unity fractured and disappeared, and new polities came into being, nationalist leaders decided to refer to the same set of variants of the single language Serbo-Croatian as three fully distinct languages—**Serbian, Croatian**, and **Bosnian**—and when Montenegro later asserted its independence from Serbia in 2006, this new state also began to declare that its population spoke a separate language, **Montenegrin**, not Serbian, even though many Montenegrins have been skeptical about calling their variety a different language. The official division of a set of related varieties of speech into distinct 'languages' has consequently clearly been made on the basis of political not linguistic grounds, powered by ethnic and religious differences in the former Yugoslavia. While it is true that there are certain differences in the vocabulary of Serbian, Croatian, and to a lesser extent Bosnian, as the Catholic Croats borrow words from Latin, while the Orthodox Serbs borrow words from Greek and Russian, and the Bosnian Muslims now incorporate new words from Arabic and Turkish, it has been estimated that lexical variation between these varieties is only of the order of 3–7% (Carmichael 2000: 236), and not a serious impediment to communication. From a linguistic viewpoint, then, and the Mutual Intelligibility Hypothesis, the speech of Serbs, Croats, Bosnian Muslims, and Montenegrins should still be taken to be dialectal variants of a single language (and this is what foreign linguists tend to do), but for political reasons in the Balkans it has officially been decided that they are different languages.

The examples of Hindi/Urdu and Serbian/Croatian/Bosnian/Montenegrin are instances in which socio-political factors have led to a range of mutually understandable speech forms being categorized by political leaderships as formally different languages. There are also various cases in which a set of mutually unintelligible ways of speaking have been classified as variants of a single language, for heavily political reasons. One good example of this is the situation with **Chinese**. As noted earlier, varieties such as Cantonese, Hokkien, Shanghainese, and Mandarin are mutually unintelligible and so might be thought to be different languages. They certainly would be characterized as separate languages by linguists using the Mutual Intelligibility Hypothesis as a way to distinguish languages from other forms of speech such as dialects, and linguists often speak of the 'Chinese languages' in a similar way to the 'Romance languages' or 'Bantu languages'. However, there has been a tradition within China itself to stress the links that exist between varieties of Chinese and their speakers and to justify the treatment of Chinese as a single language in virtue of these connections. Culturally, it has been emphasized that Chinese people feel united in sharing a common long history and system of social organization. Linguistically, it has been noted that the grammars of different varieties of Chinese are actually very similar, and that Chinese writing is carried out by means of a shared, very distinctive system—the use of Chinese 'characters'. The political and intellectual leadership of China has suggested that such properties can be taken to support the idea that Chinese is a single language, rather than a family of languages. Objectively speaking, though, the linguistic arguments given to promote the single-language view of Chinese are not especially strong. The similarities in grammatical structure between different varieties of Chinese are not significantly greater than those between closely related varieties recognized as different languages in groups such as the Romance languages, and the radically different pronunciation of Cantonese, Shanghainese, and Hokkien makes such varieties appear further apart, linguistically, than separate languages such as Spanish and Italian. The observation that speakers of different varieties of Chinese utilize the same form of writing is also somewhat deceptive and needs care to be correctly understood. Due to the historical dominance of a particular way of writing Chinese throughout China (classical Chinese) and its evolution in the modern era, speakers from all parts of China do indeed write in a single way, but what such speakers are now uniformly writing and reading is Mandarin Chinese. Hence a person from, for example, Fujian province will speak Hokkien in everyday interactions but carry out all reading and writing in Mandarin Chinese, and a person from Guangzhou will speak Cantonese but typically read and write Mandarin. What is therefore shared among people throughout China is knowledge of written (and now very frequently spoken) Mandarin Chinese.

It is not the case that speakers from different parts of China make use of a single writing system, Chinese characters, to write down their own regional varieties of Chinese, and the use of Chinese characters to represent non-Mandarin varieties of Chinese has been extremely limited (for example, in the case of Cantonese being restricted to advertising billboards, cartoons, some folk literature, and not accepted as appropriate for any 'serious' writing). The link that exists among speakers of Chinese in the area of writing consequently relates to the use of written Mandarin Chinese, and it is not the case that regional varieties of Chinese are closely bound together by an exclusive use of Chinese characters.

Considering the case for presenting all forms of Chinese as constituting a single language, ultimately one may conclude that it has been above all a strong political desire to foster and preserve unity among the population of China, through history, which has upheld the single-language view of Chinese despite the mutual unintelligibility of its different varieties. Where language divisions are acknowledged to exist, there lurks the possibility that ethnic divisions may grow or be deliberately cultivated, and those focused on maintaining the political unity of the Chinese population have consequently been keen to emphasize the linguistic unity of the Chinese people, and resist suggestions of the existence of multiple Chinese languages. Socio-political rather than purely linguistic reasons can therefore be said to be the principal factor motivating the characterization of Chinese as one language, and concerns of schism within the Chinese population which might receive encouragement from the recognition of Cantonese, Hokkien, etc., as different languages have regularly led to their categorization as dialects rather than individual languages.

A second case in which the fostering of political unity among a population can be seen as a major driving force in the classification of mutually unintelligible varieties of speech as dialects of a single language is found in Japan. In the very southern part of Japan, there is a series of islands where people speak different forms of **Ryuukyuan**. The Ryuukyuan islands originally constituted a separate country from the 15th to the 17th century, when they became dominated by a Japanese clan, and were eventually incorporated into Japan in the 19th century. Shibatani (1990: 191) notes that from a historical perspective, the varieties of Ryuukyuan spoken in today's Okinawa prefecture can be considered to be members of an independent Ryuukyuan language, and it is well-observed that all varieties of Ryuukyuan are mutually unintelligible with any dialect of Japanese, though there are various systematic similarities in grammar and vocabulary with Japanese. Chamberlain (1895) has also suggested that the linguistic differences which exist between Ryuukyuan and Japanese are similar in scale to those which are found between Spanish and Italian, or French and Italian. However, despite the obvious differences between Ryuukyuan and Japanese, and their mutual unintelligibility, it has frequently been claimed that Ryuukyuan should be classed as a set of dialects of Japanese, rather than varieties of a separate language. The linguistic status of Ryuukyuan within Japan as a dialect of Japanese or as an independent language has potentially significant consequences. During much of the 20th century, Japan emphasized an image of itself both to its own population and outsiders as a monolingual, mono-cultural and mono-ethnic country, quite different from other countries, with a uniquely Japanese national character, culture, and language. With the Ainu ethnic group in northern Japan having almost fully lost its language and distinct cultural traditions, the only remaining indigenous challenge to the image of a fully homogenous Japanese society, as ardently projected by nation-builders at various times, would have been a recognition that the Ryuukyuan islanders were ethnically and linguistically not Japanese. Such considerations have consequently added pressure to interpret the linguistic 'facts' in a certain way, and see the Ryuukyuan islanders and their language as being Japanese, and not 'foreign' in a way that might impinge on and threaten the image of a fully homogeneous nation.

The examples of Chinese and Ryuukyuan are useful illustrations of a very general observation made about the division of varieties of speech into 'languages' and 'dialects'. We often find that it is those in some position of authority—the political and intellectual leaders of a population—who dictate and inform a population where the divisions between 'languages' and other forms of speech lie, and decide which varieties are officially to be considered languages, and which do not have language status. In many instances such divisions of a range of related ways of speaking into language and dialects are not occasioned by purely linguistic criteria, but result from political and social pressures to promote certain varieties as symbols of broader socio-political organization. Once made by those with some kind of authority and power, decisions relating to language/dialect divisions tend to be accepted by general populations, who may not consider themselves qualified to dispute the categorizations of those assumed to have better, relevant knowledge. In many instances, as we have seen, this leads to the establishment of linguistically artificial borders separating or conjoining different varieties as languages, erected as a means to support other aspects of national or group identity. The arbitrary way that divisions between languages and dialects is often made, and the fact that it is those in power who frequently impose their view of language/dialect classifications on others in subservient positions, is highlighted in the following, famous saying attributed to the linguist Max Weinreich:

'A language is a dialect with an army and a navy.'

This quip, which was initially made by an anonymous audience member to Max Weinreich following one of his presentations and then repeated by Weinreich himself, emphasizes the point that the only real difference that may exist between varieties recognized as languages, and those seen to be dialects, is that the former may often be associated with groups having greater resources at their disposal, and the power to elevate their own way of speaking to language status.

Further examples of governments dictating the official classification of different varieties of speech as either 'languages' or 'dialects' can briefly be added from Spain, Greece, and India. In Spain under General Franco's rule, only Castilian Spanish was recognized to be a language, and all other non-Castilian varieties such as Catalan and Galician were referred to as dialects, as Franco's regime sought to impose a single Castilian-dominated national identity on the population of Spain. Later on, in a different political climate, the official categorization of these varieties changed again, and the Spanish constitution came to recognize Catalan and Galician as languages like Castilian, not dialects, although linguistically the non-Castilian varieties had not changed in any way—they just came to be classified in a different way as the political situation changed in Spain (Mar-Molinero 2000).

In Greece, too, towards the end of the 20th century, politicians have attempted to impose their own politically motivated classification of languages and dialects on the Slavic minority population in the north of the country, who identify themselves as speakers of Macedonian. Concerned that these speakers might develop strong ties with the neighboring population of the Republic of Macedonia, established in 1991, due to being speakers of the same language, politicians in Greece have taken to denying that Macedonian exists as a separate language, and have claimed that it should be viewed as merely a dialect of Bulgarian (Trudgill 2000). In this way, the attempt has been made to dampen any nationalistic desires for independence and secession among the Greek Macedonians which could be stimulated by the use of Macedonian as a strong common symbol of ethnicity. Referring to Macedonian as simply a dialect of another larger language and ethnic group—Bulgarian and the Bulgarians—potentially weakens its ability to serve as a force to rally all Macedonians together as a separate nation distinguished by its own special language.

Finally, one can note that manipulations of the terms 'language' and 'dialect' have sometimes been made for political gains, and not for valid linguistic reasons, in government population censuses investigating language and ethnicity. One example of this is the census of languages carried out in India shortly after it received independence. At this time, the new political leadership of the country was keen to identify and establish a national language for independent India, and Hindi was viewed as the most viable indigenous candidate, as it was spoken by more people than any other Indian language, although still not by a majority of the population. In order to claim the highest possible number of Hindi speakers and help justify the choice of Hindi as the new national language, certain clear liberties were taken in the construction of the census which reported on language use around the country, it was later reported. For example, when people in the large state of Rajasthan were asked by the census-makers which language they spoke as their mother tongue, replies such as 'Marwari', 'Dhundhari', and 'Harauti' were received. However, such responses were often not accepted by the government officials carrying out the census investigation, and speakers were informed that these varieties were just dialects of Hindi, so they would be recorded as being speakers of Hindi, thus artificially inflating the total number of Hindi speakers arrived at in the census. Again we see that those in authority have the power to decide what counts officially as a language, and what is to be classified as a dialect, and such categorizations may frequently not correspond well with real linguistic divisions between varieties of speech, and instead may be driven by political motivations.

Summing up this section, the important conclusion to be drawn from all of the observations noted here is that the division of varieties of speech into languages and other varieties not recognized as languages is often rather arbitrary and made on socio-political rather than pure linguistic grounds. While reference to the linguistic properties of a variety may play some role in official recognitions of certain varieties as languages and others as dialects, those in positions of authority who may decide on such matters do not consistently (or even frequently) use the Mutual Intelligibility Hypothesis as the decisive criteria, unlike the majority of (politically neutral) linguists, and there is consequently a common mismatch between the numbers of languages officially recognized by a state, and those which linguists may objectively recognize as being present in a state, using the Mutual Intelligibility Hypothesis. For example, the 2011 Census of India records the presence of 122 languages in the country, while the *Ethnologue* website (ethnologue.com), which provides extensive linguistic profiles of all of the world's countries, suggests that there are currently 447 living languages in India. Similarly, the government of Mexico recognizes 68 languages within its borders, whereas *Ethnologue* estimates there to be 283 distinct languages. Further significant differences in official and linguistic observer opinion can be found for most of the countries surveyed by *Ethnologue* and other organizations whose linguistic studies are not influenced by the politics of language/dialect divisions. Before moving on to consider how the term 'dialect' is applied, and how dialects are described, it is important to stress again a point made at the outset of this chapter, that the issue of language vs. dialect terminology is an important one as it has real life consequences that can affect people's lives in significant ways. If a variety is officially recognized as a language (not just by linguists/*Ethnologue*, but by local and national governments), this status can be very meaningful and can lead to the accordance of linguistic rights in the areas of education, employment, the legal system, and government administration, as well as potentially increase economic opportunities open to individuals who are able to demonstrate competence in the language. The recognition of certain varieties as 'languages' and others as 'dialects' also frequently has psychological effects on speakers, with more positive feelings often being associated with varieties recognized as languages than those classified as dialects. In the second part of this introductory chapter, we will now look at issues relating to the identification of dialects, and how linguists attempt to map out divisions between different dialects present in a country.

Dialects: properties and patterns

What are the typical characteristics that dialects have, which lead to use of the term 'dialect'? There are three properties in particular which are often taken to be necessary characteristics of such varieties, as described in the following, and we will shortly add a fourth property after some further discussion.

[1] 'Dialect' is a 'relational term'. Referring to a particular variety of speech as a dialect infers that it is related to some other variety which is formally recognized as a language. If a person says, for example, that 'Brentish is a dialect,' one can legitimately ask 'What is Brentish a dialect of?' and some answer must be possible. A dialect is a sub-variety of a language, a way of speaking (and much less commonly writing) that is not itself recognized as a language, but which is systematically related to some variety that is accorded language status.

Because of the necessary relational nature of the term 'dialect', this term cannot be applied to varieties which are not related to any other varieties/languages at all, 'language isolates' such as Basque in Europe or Ainu in Japan. Such 'linguistic orphans', which have no genealogical links to other languages, are always categorized as individual languages rather than dialects, even if they do not have the full set of resources that languages are often provided with, such as writing systems and extensive vocabularies, as in the case of Bangime in Mali, and Kusunda in Nepal.

[2] Dialects typically exhibit three types of linguistic differences from other dialects and standard forms of the language they are associated with: (i) differences in pronunciation, (ii) differences in grammar, (iii) differences in vocabulary. If a particular variety differs from other related varieties only in terms of its pronunciation, but does not show significant grammatical or lexical differences, the term 'accent' rather than 'dialect' is used. Thus one may refer to the 'Brooklyn accent' (of US English) or the 'Birmingham accent' (of UK English), where such varieties have a very distinctive sound to them, but do not exhibit much in the way of grammatical or vocabulary variation from other forms of US/UK English.

[3] Dialects are most commonly assumed to be associated with a particular geographical region. For example, the Isan dialect of Thai is spoken in a broad area of northeastern Thailand, and the Kantō dialect of Japanese characterizes the speech of the eastern part of the country. In recent years, the term 'dialect' has sometimes been applied to non-regional forms of speech which are variants of a particular language, using the phrases 'social dialect' and 'ethnic dialect', but the most widespread use of the term 'dialect' is to refer to speech which varies by geographical region. Consequently, if a person states, for example, that 'Xhaba is a dialect of Swahili', the assumption that hearers will most naturally make, or first entertain, is that there is a specific region/place known as Xhaba where the Swahili is spoken in a distinctive way, rather than there is a social or ethnic grouping of people collectively known as the Xhaba who speak Swahili in a special way, no matter where they live within East Africa (which would mean that their 'dialect' is not defined by location but by membership of a particular ethnicity or social grouping).

A further socio-linguistic phenomenon frequently observed to be found with regional dialects is that such varieties are often perceived to be less prestigious than the standard forms of the languages they are related to. Hence speakers of more standardized forms of a language, and even some speakers of dialect forms themselves, may consider that dialects sound less educated and refined than use of a standard form of a language, and that greater social status is projected by use of the standard form of a language. This observation should certainly not be assumed to be a necessary feature of dialects—a variety need not be held to be weakly prestigious in order to be classified as a dialect—and it is also found that certain languages may be subjectively held to be less prestigious than other languages in multilingual societies (more on this in chapters 2 and 3). The linguist Peter Trudgill has also pointed out that people's attitudes toward dialects may be different toward those spoken in rural areas and those heard within towns and cities. Trudgill

(1983: 196) writes that '[t]here is, in fact, a widespread tendency to regard *rural* dialect forms as acceptable (if somewhat quaint) but to treat *urban* dialect forms simply as "errors"'. Variation away from standard forms of a language is thus often felt to be linguistically 'legitimate' in rural speech, but simply ungrammatical when occurring in accented urban varieties.

We can now illustrate the typical properties of a dialect described in [1–3] with a number of examples from the Devon dialect of British English. This dialect is spoken in rural areas of the county of Devon in the southwest of England; hence it is associated with a particular area, and it is systematically related to other dialects of British English. Variation in Devon English is found, as expected, in the areas of pronunciation, grammar, and vocabulary. In terms of pronunciation, it is found that many standard English words have their sounds reshaped in Devon English, as seen in the examples in Table 1.1.[1]

TABLE 1.1 **Pronunciation Variation in Devon English**

Devon English	Standard English
ansum	handsome
booty (my booty)	beauty (my beauty)
ockerd	awkward
onwriggler	unregular
purtickly	particularly
urch	rich
iggerant	ignorant

Special grammatical forms have developed in Devon English which are different from those in standard English, as illustrated in Table 1.2.

TABLE 1.2 **Grammatical Differences in Devon English**

Devon English	Standard English
er	he, him, it
subject 'us': 'Us be in the kitchen.'	we: 'We're in the kitchen.'
ee	you
twadden	it was not
bist	(you) are
baint	not going to/not be
sentence-final 'you': My, 'tis cold you!'	emphasis: 'It's really cold!'
invariant 'be': 'John be in the garden now.'	is/are: 'John is in the garden now.'

1. Examples here are taken from Downes (1986) and the author's personal experience in southwest England.

There are also many vocabulary items which are different in Devon and standard English. In some instances, superscripted with [M] in Table 1.3, the *meaning* of a standard English word is quite different in Devon English. In other cases, superscripted with [N] in Table 1.3, there is a different, *new* word that has evolved in the Devon dialect.

TABLE 1.3 **Vocabulary Differences in Devon English**

Devon English	Standard English
clever [M]	in good health
near [M]	miserly, mean
frightened [M]	surprised
call home [M]: 'Us can't call him home.'	remember: 'We can't remember him.'
proper [M]	very
manful [M]	powerful
terrify [M]: 'I do like to terrify boys.'	tease: 'I do like to tease boys.'
nang [N]	hit
grockle [N]	tourist (pejorative)

Rural speech in Devon thus shows variation across all three areas: sounds, grammar, and words, and is therefore aptly referred to as a regional dialect of English.

The existence of such differences between Devon dialect and standard English raises a general question about dialects—should varieties classed as dialects of a single language be assumed to be mutually intelligible? Specifically, in the case of Devon 'dialect', do the differences in pronunciation, grammar, and vocabulary perhaps result in a variety that is no longer understandable to outsiders who speak more standardized forms of English? The answer to the latter question is that mutual intelligibility is to some extent a matter of degree, and in the case of Devon dialect, outsiders are actually likely to understand most of the speech heard within the area of Devon, but in certain instances, understanding may falter a little. There will consequently be a high degree, but not perfect understanding of speakers of Devon dialect. Similar instances of misunderstanding may in fact sometimes occur between speakers of more standard forms of English when one speaker makes use of very technical jargon or obscure vocabulary items, but they are normally not significant enough to lead to a major breakdown in communication, unlike situations in which monolingual speakers of two different languages attempt to talk with each other. It has also been observed that not all speakers of a dialect will necessarily make consistent use of all of the features noted to be characteristic of the dialect. Trudgill (1983) notes that the greatest degree of dialect use is typically found among speakers from lower socio-economic backgrounds, and that lower quantities of dialect words and dialectal grammatical structures often occur in the speech of those from higher socio-economic groups living in the same dialect area. Consequently, while differences such as those noted in Tables 1.1–1.3 establish the way of speaking in Devon as clearly distinct from standard English in many ways, in practice the differences found among speakers of Devonshire forms are not so great as to warrant treating their variety as a distinct language.

On a very general level, if the Mutual Intelligibility Hypothesis is taken to be the most useful means of distinguishing languages from other forms of speech such as dialects, when two varieties are not mutually intelligible, they should be categorized as different languages (or as dialects of different languages—see part (b) of the Mutual Intelligibility Hypothesis). Most linguists do indeed assume such an approach and believe that varieties described as dialects of a single language should have the property of being mutually intelligible. For example, Chambers and Trudgill (1980) note that it has been common to assume that 'a language is a collection of mutually intelligible dialects'; Fromkin et al. (2011) state that dialects are 'mutually intelligible versions of the same basic grammar, with systematic differences among them'; and Petyt (1980) offers a similar characterization. Following such a 'strict' objective approach to dialect and language differentiation, we can therefore add a fourth property of dialects to those already listed in [1–3]

[4] The dialects of a single language should be found to be mutually intelligible, to at least a considerable degree. Where two varieties are not mutually intelligible, they should be viewed as belonging to or instantiating different languages.

Determining the distribution of regional dialects

The study and description of regional dialects is carried out by linguists who are known as 'dialectologists', and those who focus on establishing the physical distribution of dialects in order to produce dialect maps are called 'dialect geographers'. Using the internet, one can find dialect maps which have been created for many countries—just try typing 'dialect map of Italy/Korea/France etc.' into any search engine, and this will produce a range of images indicating where the various dialects spoken in a country are located. Dialect geographers create such maps by investigating the distribution of individual linguistic features believed to be present in a dialect. These features may be aspects of grammar, vocabulary items, or special pronunciation forms. Dialect geographers travel around the area in which the dialect is spoken and try to track down where the borders of the dialect may lie, by asking local people questions about their speech. For example, investigating whether the Devon dialect of English is restricted to the actual county of Devonshire or also occurs in adjacent areas, the dialect geographer will attempt to determine where people use Devon dialect words such as *nang* and *grockle*, and special pronunciations such as /boi/ and /moi/ (rhyming with 'toy') for the words 'buy' and 'my', and then plot this on a map, along with information about other features of the dialect. This may result in the dialect geographer being able to draw a line on the map which divides those people who use a particular dialect feature such as *nang* or *grockle* from those in adjacent areas who do not. The name given to such a demarcation line is an 'isogloss'. Linguists will set out to determine: (a) whether clear isoglosses for each dialect feature can be created, and (b) whether the isoglosses for all of the features mapped out coincide and establish a neat dialect border.

In many instances, it may indeed be possible to create neat isoglosses for the features of a dialect, but in some cases the distribution of dialect words can also be rather messy. For example, in creating the American Linguistic Atlas, investigators were able to establish that the dialect word '*darning needle*' (meaning 'dragonfly') was used in the northern part of the USA, allowing for the creation of an isogloss extending from just north of Atlantic City on the eastern seaboard to the area of Cleveland on Lake Erie (Kurath 1949). Similar isoglosses were also established for the words '*pail*' (for 'bucket') and '*whiffletree*' (a piece of farmyard equipment). However, the distribution of many other words was reported to be 'spotty', according to Kretzschmar (2004), so that neat isoglosses could not be drawn. It was furthermore found that the isoglosses which could be created for dialect words did not necessarily all follow the same routing and establish precisely the same borderline for the northern, southern, and midland dialects of the USA. Hence the isoglosses for *darning needle, pail,* and *whiffletree* coincide well for a distance of 300 miles, but then show some deviations for the remaining 200 miles. Let's consider another, similar example, from Japan. Linguists mapping out features of the Kansai (western) and Kantō (eastern) dialects of Japanese observed the distribution shown in Figure 1.1 for five pairs of linguistic variables, from Shibatani (1990: 197). As can be seen, four of the five isoglosses coincide well from the northern coast until about 70 miles east of the city of Nagoya, and then they split apart.

In order to produce a map indicating where dialects are located in a country, one ideally needs to find that the set of isoglosses created by linguists coincide fully, in their entirety. This occurs most frequently when there are major geographical features such as mountain ranges and large rivers separating neighboring populations. Such natural boundaries inhibit communication between adjacent groups, resulting in less language transfer between groups, and the development of different, distinctive dialects.[2] However, in the absence of physical impediments to communication between neighboring groups, one finds that some dialect features may spread further geographically than others, causing aberrations from the 'ideal' pattern of a set of fully overlapping isoglosses. The neat dialect maps we may access on the internet and linguists' detailed descriptions of dialects therefore are often idealizations of a somewhat more complicated distribution in which the boundaries of certain forms (dialect words, grammatical structures, types of pronunciation) show some variation, and it is challenging to define the precise set of features that distinguish one dialect from another. Nevertheless, such best possible idealizations are, for the most part, still useful guides to the different regional varieties of speech found in a country, and highlight in a very broad way the distribution of individual dialects in virtue of their most prototypical features. Furthermore, while it may be tricky to provide exhaustive definitions of the features of many dialects, people generally find it rather easy to identify typical speakers of different dialects in their native country and will often be able to name the dialect that they speak (see chapter 11 for reference to an experiment showing that British speakers could distinguish and name nine different regional forms of British English with considerable accuracy). The divisions seen in

---

2. For example, the existence of a large swampy area known as the 'Fens' in England made north-south travel and contact difficult in earlier centuries, and resulted in a dialect boundary. People living north of the Fens came to pronounce their vowels in different ways from those living south of the Fens, so that words such as 'laugh' and 'butter' were pronounced as 'laff' and 'booter' in the north of England (Trudgill 1999; Seargeant and Swann 2012).

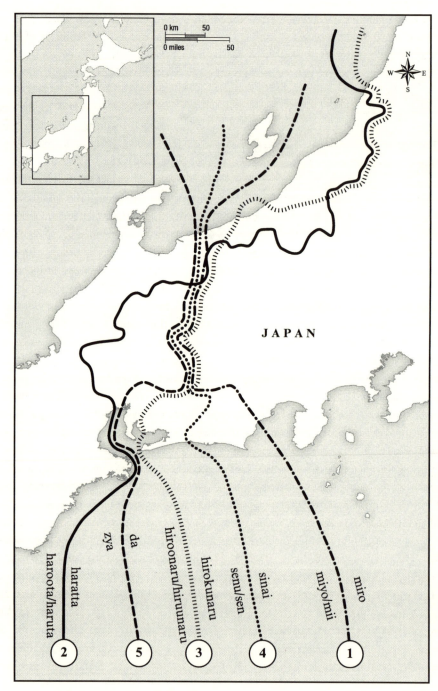

FIGURE 1.1 Bundle of Isoglosses Separating the Western and Eastern Dialects of Japan (adapted from Shibatani 1990: 197).

dialect maps and described by linguists consequently have a clear psychological reality for many speakers and do represent what speakers seem to believe about the (approximate) distribution of regional speech.

An additional phenomenon which dialect geographers have noted as a recurrent property of dialect groups in many parts of the world is the occurrence of 'dialect continua' (singular: 'dialect continuum'). This refers to the observation that there may not seem to be any really strong dialect boundaries present among populations stretched out over certain large geographical distances, and adjacent dialects may just seem to blend into each other without any major breaks, although a comparison of speakers at either end of the continuum would reveal many significant differences in speech, and the varieties spoken at the two ends of the continuum may well be mutually unintelligible. This patterning can be illustrated by means of a hypothetical journey taken from Austria to the Netherlands. Supposing you were to start a long and slow journey by road from Vienna northwestward to Amsterdam, if you knew how to speak the Viennese dialect of German, you could probably understand people speaking a slightly different form of Austrian German to the west of Vienna in the province of Lower Austria. As the differences between Viennese German and Lower Austrian German are not very great, one might not feel that there is an obvious dialect division here. If you were to learn these small differences, staying a while in the western part of Lower Austria, you would then be able to communicate with people speaking German further to the west in Upper Austria. The differences between Lower and Upper Austrian German again being small, one would not perceive there to be two clearly different dialects. Having acquired a knowledge of the slightly different dialect forms in Upper Austria, you would then be able to understand Austrians living further west in Salzburg, and then Germans over the border in Bavaria. This process could go on and on until you reached Amsterdam. At each point in your journey you would just learn a few small differences in the local way of speaking and this would allow you to continue your trip onward, being able to communicate well with people living along the route. If you took your time on such a journey, familiarizing yourself gradually with the slightly different words and pronunciations used in each area, you would most probably not feel that there was any major dialect boundary between Vienna and Amsterdam. There is, instead, a continuum of minor changes in the dialectal speech of neighboring populations. At either end of the dialect continuum, the forms spoken may be extremely different and mutually unintelligible (as with Dutch in Amsterdam and Viennese German), but it is difficult to specify exactly where any major dialect boundary and change occurs between these endpoints. This situation is rather different from that with national standard languages, which will be considered more in chapter 2. When a person crosses a border into another country, it is found that most signs, radio and television, and so on, *immediately* change into the standard language of that country, and there is consequently a major shift from one national language into another.

Dialect continua have been noted to occur quite pervasively in Europe (Chambers and Trudgill 1980). In addition to the West Germanic continuum between Austria and the Netherlands, there is a West Romance dialect continuum, which extends from the coast of Portugal through Spain and France and into central Belgium—hence one could make a slow journey from Lisbon in Portugal to Charleroi in Belgium, learning small differences in the local forms of Portuguese, Spanish, and French along the way, without becoming aware of a major dialect boundary (noting that the Portuguese and Spanish spoken either side of the Portugal/Spain border are mutually intelligible and don't seem like different languages, and the same goes for the dialect forms of Spanish and French either side of the border of Spain and France). In the eastern portion of Europe, there is a North Slavic dialect continuum, linking speakers of Russian, Belarusian, Ukrainian, Polish, Czech, and Slovak, and a South Slavic continuum between Slovenia and Bulgaria. A Scandinavian dialect continuum is additionally present in the north of Europe, connecting Denmark, Sweden, and Norway. Outside Europe, similar patterns have been noted to occur, for example the North Indian speech continuum stretching 1,500 miles from Pakistan through India to Bangladesh (Gumperz 1971; Mesthrie et al. 2003). In all of these cases, except for Scandinavia, the languages/dialects spoken at the endpoints of the continuum are mutually unintelligible, but no sharp dialect boundaries are found along the continuum.

The occurrence of dialect continua is a further illustration of the potential fuzziness of dialect borders, and might seem to call into question whether different dialects can actually be recognized along such a continuum. In practice, linguists do make regular reference to varieties taken to be dialects which are found at points along dialect continua, for example Bavarian, Middle German, Frankish, and Alemannic along the West Germanic continuum, so one might wonder how such apparently discrete entities are effectively identified. The optimal way to understand such categorization is in terms of the prototypical features that a dialect is described as having, and in terms of an opposition between the center of a dialect area and its edges. 'Typical' speakers of a dialect are those who produce close to a full range of the prototypical properties described for a dialect and are likely to be located in the central portions of the dialect area. If such typical speakers of Bavarian German are compared with typical speakers of Middle German, there most certainly will be salient differences in their speech and the perception that two different dialects are being spoken. If, however, speakers from the adjacent outer peripheries of the Middle German and Bavarian dialect areas are compared, such speakers will make use of significantly less of the prototypical features of the dialect as spoken at the center, and sound much more closely related. Descriptions of dialects consequently tend to be characterizations of the speech of prototypical speakers living away from the messy border areas, and focusing on such speakers does lead to descriptions of clearly different dialects, even where these are also part of a broader dialect continuum. Similar considerations furthermore hold for dialects which are not in any continuum, but which exhibit 'untidy' border areas, such as mentioned for the Kansai-Kantō dialect division in Japan, where isoglosses for certain features distinguishing the two dialects do not always line up in a consistently clear way. Descriptions of the Kansai and Kantō varieties of Japanese list features typically found together in the speech of the majority of people who live in the central parts of the dialect area, and not the small proportion of speakers located in the transitional border zone. Concentrating on the properties of prototypical speakers in this way, rather than on those who may have certain mixed features from adjacent varieties, allows dialectologists to produce descriptions of dialects which characterize the speech of significant numbers of speakers in various regions, despite the linguistic 'confusion' and merging of dialects found among many border populations.

Concluding our examination of the various properties of dialects, the following points can usefully be emphasized:

- A dialect is a variety of speech which relates in a systematic way to the standard form of a language, with differences occurring in vocabulary, grammar, and pronunciation.
- The dialects of a single language are commonly assumed to be mutually intelligible by (most) linguists. If two varieties are found to be mutually unintelligible, they should be classed as distinct languages (or varieties of two distinct languages).
- Socio-political rather than purely linguistic reasons may often underlie the recognition of certain varieties of speech as 'languages'. However, the identification of dialects is based solely on their linguistic properties, and it is extremely rare to find political factors driving categorization of the dialects of a language to be made in a particular way. There is generally no 'political agenda' associated with the description of dialects, in contrast to the recognition of languages.
- The presence of major geographical boundaries (mountains, rivers) tends to cause sharp divisions between dialects. Where no such physical boundaries divide a population, dialect boundaries are sometimes fuzzy and less obvious.
- Regional dialects are often perceived to be less prestigious than the standard form of a language, but may be valued by their speakers as symbols of belonging to a particular community.

A final question about dialects that we can ask here is whether regional dialects may be weakening and disappearing under the influence of increased urbanization and the spread of media such as television and cinema featuring speakers using more standard forms of a language. At least in countries which have undergone rapid recent modernization, it would indeed seem that the strongest forms of regional dialects are no longer as vibrant as they previously were, and are not being used by rising generations in the same way as their parents and grandparents. What is particularly being lost among younger generations appears to be knowledge of the rich vocabulary of many dialects, and use of their more unusual grammatical structures. Young people are experiencing increased pressure to acquire competence in the standard forms of a language in order to succeed in education and employment, and this may cause abandonment of local dialects. There may also be status-related factors that cause young speakers to favor use of the standard form of a language rather than a regional dialect. However, interestingly, one aspect of regional speech appears to be surviving quite well, despite all the pressures of the modern world. Rather surprisingly, it has been noted that local accents continue to remain strong in both rural and urban areas, and Labov and Ash (1997) report that accents found in cities in the USA are 'more different from each other than at any time in the past' (quoted in Kretzschmar 2004: 39). While standard pronunciations of a language may convey higher social status and education, and so may be targeted by many speakers, others seem to value the ways in which speaking with a distinctive local accent can project a desirable image of solidarity with fellow members of a local community. Still other speakers may become 'bi-dialectal' and regularly switch between regional and standard speech depending on the situation and with whom they are engaged in talking (more on all of this will come in subsequent chapters). Regional speech may therefore be sustained into the future in various ways despite increasing changes in the ways our lives are organized in modern times.

Suggestions for further reading and activities

1. Read and discuss the following chapter, which examines how dialects interact with social class:
   Macaulay, Ronald. 2008. Regional dialects and social class. In Virginia Clark, Paul Escholz, Alfred Rosa, and Beth Lee Simon (eds.), *Language: introductory readings*. New York: Bedford/St. Martins, 383–397.
2. Familiarize yourself with the development of regional dialects in the USA and read more about the 'alignment' issue of isoglosses in pages 39–48 of:
   Kretzschmar, William. 2004. Regional dialects. In Edward Finegan and John Rickford (eds.), *Language in the USA*. Cambridge: Cambridge University Press, 39–57.
3. Access the *Oxford English Dictionary* online and consider the full set of entries it gives for the word 'language' and discuss these. How many of these uses are you familiar with?
4. Using the Internet, research the term 'social dialect' and see what examples and definitions of this term you can find.
5. Find dialect map images online for any country you are interested in, and compare the maps with each other. To what extent do they 'agree' on dialect names and divisions within the country?
6. Access the *Ethnologue* online entry for three countries in different continents and see which languages are listed as being spoken in each of these countries. Then try to find online official government descriptions of the languages present in these three countries, and consider whether the government list of languages corresponds well with the *Ethnologue* list or not.

2

Languages with Special Roles
National and Official Languages

Introduction

In chapter 1, we saw that some varieties of speech have been recognized as languages, and others are referred to as dialects, and it was noted that dialects are often felt to be less prestigious than varieties classified as languages. In this chapter, we will see that some languages are given special roles and functions in the establishment and development of states, and often come to be associated with higher status, desirability, and more pragmatic value than other languages present in a country—languages that are referred to as 'official' and 'national languages' (Holmes 1997; Spolsky 2004).

Most countries specify which language(s) may officially be used in certain important areas or 'domains' of life, such as government administration and debate, courts of law, and education. A language which is formally sanctioned for such practical everyday use is an 'official language', and the set of domains which a particular language can be used in will be specified legally by a government. The geographical area in which a language has official status also has to be determined—this may be the entire area of a country, or perhaps a smaller portion such as a regional state or province, where this is seen to be appropriate. In India, for example, Gujarati, Bengali, and Tamil are recognized as official languages within the states of Gujarat, West Bengal, and Tamil Nadu, respectively, but do not have official status throughout the country. Similarly, Hawaiian has official language status in Hawaii, but not in other states in the USA.

Countries which hope to stimulate strong feelings of unity and loyalty among their populations may also attempt to exploit the symbolic power of language to project group identity, and promote one or more languages as linguistic representatives of the 'nation', designating such languages as 'national languages'. It is assumed that if people feel connected to each other and their country by speaking a language that distinguishes them from other neighboring populations, this will help the growth of a special national identity and will bind a population together in beneficial ways.

In many instances, the language which seems best suited to serve official language functions in a country may also be the most natural candidate for the role of national language, and just one language is therefore recognized as having a special status, fulfilling both utilitarian-official and symbolic-representative roles. This typically occurs when the population of a country exhibits a high degree of ethnic homogeneity, as for example in Japan, France, Iceland, Poland, and Slovakia. However, in a considerable number of other countries, particularly in Africa and Asia, populations are ethnolinguistically complex, and it is not so easy to determine which language(s) should serve as official language(s), and which as national language(s), and various countries have opted to recognize different languages in these roles. Holmes (1992) writes the following about the distinction between national and official languages, and provides examples of states which have made different types of choices for these roles, as represented in Table 2.1. As can be seen, certain states have opted to recognize more than one official/national language in a range of different configurations, whose general rationale will soon be discussed.

> A national language is the language of a political, cultural and social unit. It is generally developed and used as a symbol of national unity. Its functions are to identify the nation and unite the people of a nation. An official language, by contrast, is simply a language which may be used for government business. Its function is primarily utilitarian rather than symbolic. It is possible, of course, for one language to serve both functions.
>
> (HOLMES 1992:105)

TABLE 2.1 **Examples of National and Official Languages**

Country	Official Language(s)	National Language(s)
Paraguay	Spanish	Guaraní
Tanzania	Swahili, English	Swahili
Democratic Republic of Congo (DRC)	French	Lingala, Tshiluba, Kikongo, Swahili
Singapore	Malay, Mandarin, Tamil, English	Malay
The Philippines	Filipino, English	Filipino

The formal process which establishes and develops languages in national and official language functions is one very important application of the general activity of 'language planning', in which linguists analyze language-related problems and situations and devise practical solutions to structure and frequently change the language habits of a speech community. In this chapter, we will first outline the general steps involved in operations of national and official language planning, and then consider a range of actual implementations of language policymaking and its consequences, seeing how certain decisions have been very successful in bonding together ethnically mixed populations, while others have had heavily negative effects, leading to civil disturbance, independence movements, and even secession from a country.

Language planning for national and official languages

Language planning, as applied to the development of national and official languages, involves a number of different activities, which will be described here.

The term '**status planning**' refers to efforts to change the function and use of a language in a particular society by formally assigning it a special status/role. The **selection** of a variety as a national or official language is a typical instance of status planning. Determining whether a country can best develop if regional official languages are also established, or special legal rights are provided to protect certain linguistic communities, is also part of status planning. In each instance of such planning, the new role given to a language must be clearly defined. If a language is recognized as having an official role, it must be specified which areas of life it may or must officially be used in, and whether this ruling applies to the entire country, or just a geographical sub-part.

'**Corpus planning**' refers to activities which describe the norms of use of a variety (the way its grammar, pronunciation, and vocabulary are typically used), and then often attempt to establish a standard form of the language. Linguists who set out to describe or '**codify**' a language regularly find that speakers of the language will use different grammatical rules and words to some extent, depending on where they live and with whom they interact. In creating precise descriptions of a language, which can subsequently be used to promote it further, linguists need to decide which forms are to be recorded as the standard forms of the language. This process of language **standardization** will result in the creation of **grammatical descriptions** ('grammars') and **dictionaries** so that there is a clearly identified common set of forms that people can learn, both inside and also sometimes outside the speech community (as when 'standard English' or 'standard French' is taught and learned in non-English- or non-French-speaking countries). In certain instances, it may be the case that a language selected for a particular role does not have an established or standardized way of writing the language. If so, attempts will commonly be made to develop a standardized written form that can be used by speakers in a uniform way. In some cases, when a language has never before been written down, it will be necessary for language planners to consider which type of **orthography** is best suited to the language, for example, whether writing should be carried out by means of the Roman/Latin or Cyrillic alphabet, or Arabic script, or perhaps with Chinese characters. Decisions on which script to use for a language—'**graphization**'—should consider which type of writing can best represent the special linguistic features of the language (for example, not all orthographies have symbols that can represent the range of sounds found in certain languages). Later we will see that there are also clearly political issues which influence the choice of script adopted by speakers of a language.

Corpus planning is additionally involved in helping the vocabularies of languages develop further and generate new words, so that they can be used in all domains of life, for example when interacting with government officials, in courtrooms, scientific discussion, and commerce, and in schools and universities. Consequently, a large amount of new vocabulary may need to be coined for use in these different areas, and decisions will need to be made on how new words should be created. This issue is considered later in the chapter. We will see that the way that **lexical expansion** is carried out in a language may often be influenced by the desires of political leaders to maintain a strong national identity with the help of language.

Two further steps in the development of national and official languages need to take place in order for their establishment to be successful. Once a language has been selected for a new national or official language role and then standardized, knowledge of the language needs to be spread among the population which is expected to adopt it for regular use. The **promotion** of new national and official languages may be achieved in a variety of ways. The use of such languages in mass, public education is normally an effective way to teach a new national and official language to the younger members of a population, and in some countries, extensive adult education campaigns have helped older segments of society acquire a proficiency in new national/official languages. Radio and television programming are also useful ways of spreading knowledge of a new national or official language among a population, although this generally creates passive understanding of the language rather than the ability to speak it, and over time, newspapers and magazines may switch to exclusive use of the new national/official languages. The promotion of new national/official languages may additionally be stimulated by governments offering special incentives for individuals to improve their abilities in these languages, for example by making promotions or getting jobs dependent on proficiency in the national/official language, or by offering bonuses to those who can demonstrate mastery of the national/official language. More negatively, some states have attempted to introduce fines and punishments for those who fail to use the national or official language in certain specified domains (normally the place of work, schools, and government buildings). Propaganda in various forms has also often been used to induce people to speak a certain language being promoted by a government.

Finally, governments promoting new national or official languages must regularly work on the psychological challenge of **winning acceptance** of these languages in their new roles. For the spread of a new national/official language to be truly successful, the language must be willingly accepted by those who are intended to speak it. This may involve considerable effort in positive promotion strategies by the government to stress the value and usefulness of the language. The population of a country must be encouraged to take pride in a new national language and to see it as prestigious, and to appreciate the utilitarian value of a new official language.

The typical steps in establishing a language in a new national or official role can be illustrated with the example of **modern Japanese**, which emerged as the result of vigorous language planning initiatives during the 20th century. Pre-modern Japan had been divided into regions ruled by local clans and little travel was allowed, restricting communication between the inhabitants of different regions in the country. As a result, no common language had become well established, and regional dialects and differences in speech remained strong. Toward the end of the 19th century, it was realized that Japan direly needed to develop itself as a modern nation in order to compete with the growing presence of Western powers in Asia, and to ward off any threats of colonization. This required Japan to undergo significant modernization in the organization of a range of institutions. In addition to reforms relating to its system of government and political structure, and the development of modern military and naval forces, the drive toward nationalism involved the establishment and spread of a common form of Japanese which could be used to unite the population of the country and facilitate other aspects of nationwide modernization and growth. After much careful consideration, the variety of Japanese which the National Language Research Council ultimately selected to be the model for the new national language in 1916 was the dialect of educated middle- and upper-class speakers living in the Yamanote area of western Tokyo, which was felt to be a desirable representation of Japanese for the entire nation. Following its selection and codification, knowledge of the new standard form of Japanese was then successfully spread throughout Japan by means of the growing public school system, national radio broadcasting, and its adoption in newspapers and by writers of popular novels. Having won widespread acceptance of the new national language during the 1920s and 1930s, attention to the psychological promotion of modern Japanese subsequently continued through the postwar period, and in the 1960s, a new form of cultural nationalism emphasized the special qualities of the national language, arguing that the language was so unique and different from other languages that it established a 'linguistic moat between Japan and the world' (Gottlieb 2007: 193). Standard Japanese has thus come to be appreciated as a strong linguistic 'boundary marker', separating the population of Japan from outsiders, unifying the nation, and providing a highly effective means of communication for all Japanese people.

The choice of a variety of Japanese as the new national language was a fairly uncomplicated decision for language planners in Japan, as Japanese was clearly the dominant language spoken in Japan, and the country's population was extremely homogenous, and ethnically (almost) all Japanese. The development of standard Japanese as the nation's single promoted language is an example of a **unilingual** national/official language policy, in which only one language is recognized to have a special national or official language role. In many other countries, the task of selection of national and official languages is often much less straightforward, due to the presence of much more mixed populations, and multiple languages being spoken in a country. This problem has been especially acute in Africa, and also parts of Asia. In Africa, a considerable majority of the continent's modern states exist in their current territorial shapes as the result of earlier European colonial expansion, and the artificial creation of countries with extremely mixed populations. When these states finally achieved independence, the result was a huge challenge for the new leaders of these states, who had to figure out how to construct an equitable and effective national/official language policy which would gain the enthusiastic support of the speakers of all the languages present in the population. In order to appreciate the degree of ethnolinguistic complexity in many African states, consider Table 2.2, which plots the approximate numbers of languages spoken in four representative states against population size in millions. As can be seen, a tremendously large number of languages is often spoken by a relatively small population, when compared with ratios of language to population in the countries of Europe. Given such massive linguistic diversity, and the observation that none of the languages in these and most other African states was spoken by a majority of the population at the time of independence, how can one fairly select a single language to represent the nation and win its acceptance as national or official language? Whichever language is selected for such a special role, this would seem to give automatic advantages to one ethnic group (its native speakers) over all others and would be resented as a language policy by members of other groups.

TABLE 2.2 **Language Numbers and Population Size in African States**

Country	Population (in millions)	Numbers of Languages Spoken
Sudan	28	140
Tanzania	60	200
Cameroon	16	250
Nigeria	140	400

Similar ethnolinguistic complexity is present in various states in Asia, peaking at high levels in India, Indonesia, and the Philippines, and there are few countries in Asia with the uniformity of population found in many European states (the primary exceptions being Japan and Korea). As a result, leaderships in Africa and Asia have often avoided attempts at unilingual national language policies, despite the received wisdom from European nationalism that each nation should (ideally) be represented by a single language ('one nation, one language'), and a variety of **multilingual** combinations of national and official languages have been experimented with, as already previewed in Table 2.1 (which also includes the combination of national and official languages selected in the South American state of Paraguay).

There are advantages and disadvantages to the pursuit of both unilingual and multilingual policies with national and official languages. With regard to national languages, it has become widely believed, since the philosophical writings of Herder in the 19th century, that the national identity of a country can be most effectively developed if just one language is promoted as a national language, representing the identity of its population. However, where there is great complexity in a country's population, it often seems that according national-language status to a single language is not (or cannot be made to appear to be) genuinely representative of the nation, and this may lead governments to consider selecting more than one national language, as seen with the Democratic Republic of Congo, in Table 2.1, which decided to recognize four different national languages, each being a language spoken widely as either a first or second language in a major region of the country. While such a multilingual policy may successfully avoid the problems which can arise if a single national language is selected, and recognizes a broader section of the population at the national-language level, it also weakens the essential binding role that national languages are intended to have, uniting populations in a single, shared identity. With the declaration of multiple national languages, there is a risk that multiple national identities will be perceived to exist within a population, and people may fail to develop feelings of being linguistically bound together as a single nation. The more languages that are declared to be national languages, the less meaningful this concept and its everyday usefulness becomes. In Cameroon, overwhelmed by the difficulty of identifying a national language for the state when it became independent, the government decided to proclaim that all 250 of the countries indigenous languages were to be considered national languages. Clearly such a 'policy' reduces to being a purely symbolic act of recognition of the state's linguistic diversity, and has little practical force to help unite the population through the common use of a shared language.

In instances where a language that is chosen to be a national language is not well-suited to serve official language functions, normally due to a lack of vocabulary items available for use in all domains of life, governments may choose to recognize an additional language as the official language of the state. This is what occurred when Pakistan and Malaysia became independent in the 20th century. It was felt that Urdu and Malay were not sufficiently well developed in the area of scientific, technical, legal, and other formal vocabulary to allow them to be used with ease in all of the activities and domains that official languages need to be used in. Consequently, both countries decreed that English would serve as the official language of the state for a period of years, while the national languages Urdu and Malay were further developed, and that the national languages would eventually replace English in all official language roles. Such an approach produces a multilingual policy in which one or more national languages are combined with a separate official language, the latter often being a European language such as English, French, or Portuguese. There are also instances in which governments decide to declare more than one language to be official languages of the state for various reasons. Three such cases will be described later in the chapter—Singapore, Canada, and Cameroon. The natural advantage to having multiple official languages is that this allows different segments of a complex population to use its language (or a language its speakers know better than other languages) in all official language domains. There are, however, also potential disadvantages and challenges which face the maintenance of multiple official language policies. One of these is financial. If a country declares that it will have two official languages, all of the costs associated with supporting an official language will automatically double—support for the language in government administration, education, legal documentation, etc. Multiple official language policies are therefore expensive, if correctly and fairly implemented, and impose an extra burden on the taxpayer. Such financial considerations do not affect the maintenance of purely national languages in the same way (if a state also has a separate official language), as national languages are not intended for use in government services, schools, and other formal domains.

A second potential challenge for states attempting to maintain multiple official languages is that this requires constant, very careful attention and monitoring to ensure that each official language is supported in the same way, and there is no imbalance in the way the official languages are treated. As we will see in the later short studies of Singapore, Canada, and Cameroon, in all three of these states there have been difficulties in balancing support for the state's official languages in a way that is perceived to be fully equal, and the communities associated with these languages have often complained that there is unfair treatment of 'their' official language. Unilingual and multilingual national and official language policies consequently all have certain potential disadvantages, as well as advantages, which language planners need to be aware of when initiating any type of policy for a country.

A final type of unilingual language policy which can be mentioned here, before we begin to consider individual case studies of language planning in more depth, is the situation in which a state only has a non-indigenous official language (frequently English or French), and no national language. Such a situation has arisen quite frequently when it seems impossible to select and promote any variety in a national language role, as has been the case in many multi-ethnic states in Africa, for example Nigeria, Guinea, Togo, Gabon, and Zambia. The prime advantage of such a policy is that the selection of a non-indigenous, well-standardized language such as English or French as sole official language is seen to be an ethnically neutral choice which does not result in any particular group being favored more than others, because the language is not the mother tongue of any ethnic group within the country. Additionally, languages such as English and French have long been standardized and so require no further corpus planning work before they can be employed as official languages. The primary disadvantage to such a policy is that the opportunity to use language as a means to symbolically unite a nation is not utilized, as a non-indigenous language cannot be suggested to be representative of a nation's special identity. It therefore cannot be promoted into national as well as official language functions. Furthermore, it may be the case that learning a non-indigenous language may be a challenge for many in the population, as its linguistic structure and vocabulary will be quite different from that of other indigenous languages in a country. Despite such drawbacks, and as a way to avoid inter-ethnic conflict arising from national language-related issues, governments of newly independent states have in many instances opted for a single non-indigenous, Western language as sole official language, and have abandoned attempts to find a workable national language policy.

Before continuing to examine language planning decisions in different states and their positive and negative consequences, we need to clarify a terminological issue. The question is what term a country should use to refer to a single language that fulfills both national and official language functions, for example French in France, Japanese in Japan, and Hungarian in Hungary. Should it be called both a 'national language' and an 'official language', or a 'national official language', or given some other kind of designation? Linguists tend to prefer the term 'national official language', but governments are sometimes inconsistent in the way they apply terms, some using 'official language' and others 'national language' to refer to a language that serves both official and national language functions in a country. For example, in Slovakia and Poland, Slovak and Polish are referred to as official languages, but clearly serve the national language function as well, while in Japan, Japanese is referred to as the national language, although it fulfills all official language functions as well as those of a national language. The lesson to be drawn from this is that sometimes one needs to examine quite carefully what functions a language actually serves in a country before accepting the formal official or national language designation it is given by a state. In the remainder of the chapter, wherever there is any divergence from the ideal usage of the terms 'national language' and 'official language' in the cases being considered, this will be duly noted.

Problems arising from the selection of a national/official language

Our first two case studies highlight instances in which the unwise selection and promotion of an indigenous language into a very prominent, dominating role resulted in severe ethnic discord in a country, in one instance leading to the break-up of a newly independent nation into two different states, and in the other being the root cause of extended civil disturbance and war.

Pakistan and Bangladesh

Pakistan was created as a homeland for Muslims in South Asia in 1947, and originally consisted of two geographically separate entities with quite different populations—the very mixed West Pakistan (modern-day Pakistan), where a variety of languages were spoken, and the much more homogenous East Pakistan (formerly East Bengal, now Bangladesh), where Bangla/Bengali was spoken by over 90% of the population. Because Urdu was symbolically associated with Muslims in South Asia, forces in West Pakistan insisted that the new state of Pakistan adopt Urdu as its national language as a linguistic projection of the state's Muslim identity, and that Urdu subsequently be used throughout both West and East Pakistan in official business, giving Urdu an official language role as well (with English being recognized as a secondary official language for temporary use in certain formal domains). In terms of the population of Pakistan at independence, Urdu was in fact known only by a quite small proportion, around 7%, most of these being the 'Mohajirs' or 'refugees' who had flooded into the area of Pakistan from India at the time of the partition, many settling in the West Pakistan province of Sindh. However, the selection of Urdu as Pakistan's national language had the concrete result of conferring an important advantage on the Urdu-speaking minority present in the country, allowing the latter easier access to better government-related employment, and disadvantaging the majority of the population who spoke a range of other languages. In the Sindhi capital, Karachi, where many Mohajirs had settled, Sindhi speakers actually became a minority and were obliged to learn Urdu to get jobs in the government, but the Urdu-speaking Mohajirs were not seen to make any efforts to learn Sindhi. Although Sindhi itself had a long literature and was viewed by its speakers with pride as a prestigious language, Urdu also replaced Sindhi as the language of higher education, upsetting many Sindhi speakers. In order to protest against the local dominance of Urdu in Sindh, a Sindhi language movement emerged, but it was denounced by Urdu speakers as being anti-patriotic and anti-Islamic. Some concessions were made to the use of Sindhi, but they were not perceived as giving equality between Urdu and Sindhi, and dissatisfaction among Sindhi speakers at the sidelining of their language resulted in violent riots.

With regard to language and relations between the two geographically separated parts of Pakistan, at the time of independence there had actually been suggestions from East Pakistan that Bangla/Bengali be used as the national language of the country on account of the large proportion of native speakers of Bangla present in Pakistan—44 million out of a total population of 69 million for West and East Pakistan. However, this possibility was rejected by the West Pakistani leadership, as were more modest calls for Bangla to be made a co-official language of the nation, along with Urdu and English. The aggressive dismissal of the request for Bangla to be recognized as an official language of the new nation led to considerable agitation in East Pakistan and disillusionment with the union with West Pakistan. When several protestors were killed by police during a demonstration calling for Bangla to be accepted as an official/national language of Pakistan, this agitation heightened further and became widespread, engendering a language movement which subsequently grew into a more general liberation movement calling for independence from West Pakistan. Fueled by other perceptions of unfair treatment of East Pakistan by those holding power in West

Pakistan, Bengali nationalists finally declared East Pakistan to be independent as the People's Republic of Bangladesh, and achieved formal separation from West Pakistan in 1971, following a bitter nine-month civil war. Bangladesh thus seceded from Pakistan as the result of disputes whose foundation lay in language policy, and the common, binding factor of religion was not strong enough to keep the two parts of Pakistan together. It is also significant to note that after several years of confrontation over language issues during the first decade of Pakistani independence, in 1954 it was actually conceded that Bengali could become a joint national/official language of Pakistan. However, the population of East Pakistan perceived that this declaration did not result in an equal treatment of Urdu and Bengali in reality, hence the late, partial satisfaction of the initial claims for national/official language status came too late and were not implemented well enough to make those in East Pakistan feel that they were equal language partners in the state of Pakistan.

With East Pakistan having declared independence as Bangladesh, problems connected with the selection of Urdu as national and official language continued in (West) Pakistan, as the government failed to spread knowledge of Urdu effectively and evenly throughout the country. Together with the problem that English rather than Urdu continues to be dominant among many of the elites in the country, this has produced a situation in which Urdu maintains a considerably weak position as national language, and government linguistic policy has not only failed to bring about a strengthening of the nation, but actually increased language-related ethnic problems and dissatisfaction. Ayres (2003) even goes so far as to suggest that the government's language policies have alienated every province's sense of identity in Pakistan. Instead of supporting a collaborative project of building a new homeland for Muslims, the policies are argued to reflect the degree to which all but the most privileged are prevented from participating in the process of nation-building, and rather than helping unify the population and facilitate national cohesion, the state's language policies have exacerbated ethnic divisions and have led to instability and violence.

Sri Lanka

Sri Lanka achieved its independence from the British in 1948, with an imbalanced population made up of a large majority (75% of the population) of speakers of Sinhala, an Indo-Aryan language of north India, and a sizable minority (the remaining 25% of the population) of speakers of Tamil, a south Indian Dravidian language. Prior to independence, and for much of the time of the British occupation, English was a third language with a significant presence in Sri Lanka, and it was the language which dominated government and the civil service. Due to the Tamil population's rather accidental, higher level of exposure to English due to missionary activities carried out in Tamil areas, a disproportionate amount of Tamil speakers with a proficiency in English had come to occupy jobs in the civil service, which was a cause of discontent among the Sinhalese. In the years leading up to independence, there were moves to decrease the use of English in government offices, and to allow for Sinhala (and in theory Tamil) to increasingly replace English in formal domains. However, for the Sinhala speakers, this process of replacement did not seem to be taking place rapidly enough, and it appeared to many in the Sinhalese population that Tamil speakers were continuing to take advantage of their English skills to gain access to better jobs. In the first democratic elections held in Sri Lanka following independence, in 1956, language issues became extremely important in the campaign for electoral support mounted by the Sinhalese United National Party (UNP) led by S. W. R. D. Bandaranaike. The UNP campaigned with the phrase 'Sinhala only, and in 24 hours', pledging to make Sinhala immediately the unique official language of Sri Lanka, which would return the linguistic advantage to speakers of Sinhala in the seeking of government jobs, as well as in a range of other domains. Bandaranaike and the UNP won the elections with a very large margin, and went through with their pre-election promises, making Sinhala into the country's single official language.

The imposition of Sinhala as the single official language of the country in 1956 triggered a rapid deterioration in relations between the minority Tamil population and the majority Sinhalese, who were seen as symbolically excluding the Tamils from a united and equally shared future in the nation through the formal promotion of Sinhala over Tamil, as well as threatening their economic future via new requirements that only Sinhala be used in central government administration. In 1956 there were initially peaceful protests from the Tamil community, but then riots when confrontation with Sinhala speakers occurred, leading to the deaths of 150 Tamils. In 1958 riots again occurred, resulting in the deaths of several hundred Tamils, as the Tamil community began to call for autonomy for the Tamil-speaking areas of Sri Lanka and equal status for Tamil and Sinhala. Attempts at a compromise solution initiated by Bandaranaike and the UNP were successfully blocked by other militant Sinhalese, and Bandaranaike was assassinated. Subsequent elections in 1960 were strongly anti-Tamil and led to bans on the import of Tamil books and films from India, and Tamil civil servants were informed that they would need to learn Sinhala and start to use it at work within three years or lose their positions. Furthermore, government workers who were native speakers of Sinhala were relocated in Tamil areas to ensure that the Sinhala-only policies came into effect. Combined with the introduction of other important language-specific restrictions on university entrance which seemed to favor Sinhala speakers, and the formal recognition of Buddhism (practiced by most of the Sinhalese but not by Tamils, who were either Hindus or Muslims) as having a privileged position in Sri Lanka, such government-initiated measures led to a gradual worsening of ethnic relations through the 1960s and to the coalescence of a new Tamil nationalist movement, particularly supported by alienated Tamil youths who saw increasingly fewer opportunities for Tamils to advance themselves. Interactions between Tamils and Sinhalese then began to escalate out of all control into violent conflict and a disastrous situation of civil war that has still not reached a fully peaceful conclusion (DeVotta 2003; Dharmadasa 2007).

In Sri Lanka, just as in Pakistan, language issues have consequently been at the very root of serious civil unrest and have significantly evolved into wider movements of dissatisfaction and resistance. Additionally, it can be noted that after the lack of attention to initial language-related problems has led to broader secessionist-type movements, the momentum of the latter is difficult to halt with simple changes in language policy. In Sri Lanka there actually was a procrastinated recognition of Tamil in the same kinds of roles that Sinhala had—first in 1978 as a joint national language of Sri Lanka, and then in 1987 as an official national language with the same status as Sinhala. However, such apparent rectification of the initial linguistic cause of discontent significantly came too late to repair the damage done to ethnic relations or to avoid the further widening of major fault lines within the nation, just as was the case in Pakistan with the late recognition of Bangla as joint national official language prior to the secession of Bangladesh from West Pakistan.

Successful selection and promotion of a single official language in a multi-ethnic state: Indonesia

While Pakistan and Sri Lanka provide good lessons in how the imprudent selection and imposition of a national/official language can lead to major problems in a society, a consideration of Indonesia in its post-independence years shows how language planning can also be highly successful in a complex ethno-linguistic state, with the development of an indigenous language that offers equal opportunities to all of its population, and stimulates the growth of national identity.

In Southeast Asia, various multi-ethnic states have been faced with clear challenges when attempting to institute a single national language, and have arrived at solutions with differing degrees of success (see the collection of studies in Simpson 2007a). The populous state of Indonesia became fully independent in 1949, after several years of armed struggle against the former colonial power, the Netherlands, and had to engage in language-planning decisions for its very mixed population, which consisted of many different ethnolinguistic groups scattered around a large island nation. Even before officially achieving independence, the nationalist leaders of Indonesia had in fact collectively determined what they wished would be the future official language of the country. The nationalists did not want to adopt Dutch, the language of the colonial rulers of Indonesia, as the official language, as Dutch was very much a foreign language, and was associated with outside domination of the country. Javanese, which was the language of the largest ethnic group in Indonesia and also the language of much of the nationalist leadership, was also magnanimously rejected, because it was realized that the choice of Javanese as official language would have conveyed an unfair advantage to the Javanese group in the future development of the country. The leadership instead supported the promotion of a much more ethnically neutral language for this role, and selected a form of Malay that was used in trading situations between members of different groups. This was renamed and developed considerably, through careful standardization and the creation of new vocabulary, as 'Indonesian' ('Bahasa Indonesia'—the Indonesian language).

There were many good reasons for this choice. First of all, Bahasa Indonesia was, and still is, viewed as an ethnically neutral language not identified with any major group in Indonesia, and this has helped tremendously in its becoming widely accepted. Prior to independence it had functioned as a 'link language' or 'lingua franca' (a language used for communication between members of different language groups) in the Indonesian archipelago of islands, and was only the mother tongue of a relatively small ethnic group on the island of Sumatra, who were not politically or economically dominant. Consequently, the choice of Indonesian as official language did not seem to favor any existing, strong ethnic group over others—almost all the population of Indonesia were native speakers of other languages, and all had to learn the new official language in the same way. Second, Malay/Indonesian had already been introduced in the educational system to some extent prior to independence. It was also used in a growing number of periodicals and in the development of popular novels read throughout the Indonesian archipelago. Third, most of Indonesia's indigenous languages are Austronesian languages, and Malay/Indonesian as an Austronesian language therefore was appropriate as a symbol of broad local linguistic identity—its linguistic structure and vocabulary bore similarities with many other languages in the country. Fourth, Indonesian had come to be used in meetings of the nationalists campaigning for independence since the 1930s. Consequently, it had positive nationalist prestige associated with it. As Bahasa Indonesia has developed over the decades since independence, its increasing ability to be used in the fields of science and academic discussion has further boosted its prestige. Currently, it can be said that Indonesian clearly unifies its speakers in Indonesia, and equitably does not offer special advantages to any one major group over others, as it is not the first language of a single major ethno-linguistic group. It allows all Indonesians the advantage that they can use the language to communicate with others throughout the country, and is increasingly identified with modernity and progress in a very positive way.

Indonesia is therefore one of the clear success stories of indigenous official language planning. The development of Bahasa Indonesia as an official language was carried out without any repression of other indigenous languages, and the result is a very healthy state of stable bilingualism, in which people use Indonesian as a common language across the nation and to access science, technology, and areas of higher education, but continue to learn and use other regional languages of Indonesia at home and in most informal, local communication. With its establishment of a well-liked language linking up the nation and enabling effective communication in all official domains, and its tolerance for the continued use of other home languages, Indonesia has achieved and maintains a well-balanced configuration of multilingualism, and language issues have not figured as the causes of ethnic disturbance among the large and very mixed population (for further description, see Bertrand 2003; Simpson 2007b).

In Holmes's (1992: 115) discussion of national language planning in Tanzania, which represents another very successful instance of the selection and implementation of an indigenous national and official language in a complex population, she highlights the importance of four functions that a national language should ideally fulfill, drawing on work in Eastman (1983), Haugen (1966), Rubin and Jermudd (1971), and others. Holmes's description of these four functions is as follows:

- *Unifying*: it must unify the nation, and offer advantages to speakers over their dialects and vernaculars.
- *Separatist*: it must set the nation off from surrounding nations.
- *Prestige*: it should be recognized as a proper or 'real' language with higher status than other local dialects and vernacular languages.
- *Frame-of-reference function*: the standard variety serves as a yardstick for correctness.

(Holmes 1992: 115–116)

While Indonesian is formally referred to as the official language of the state, it actually fulfills more than a purely utilitarian, official role, and has helped quite significantly in the development of a new Indonesian national identity, therefore serving a national language function as well. As an official + (unofficial) national language, Indonesian can be concluded to serve at least three of the ideal national language functions very well, and to satisfy the fourth 'separatist' function quite well, once one understands a little more about the languages spoken in Indonesia's neighboring states. First of all, as already noted, Indonesian unites the mixed population of Indonesia very successfully and offers opportunities for inter-ethnic communication that other local languages do not. This satisfies the unifying function. Second, Indonesian is most certainly recognized as a 'real' language, and people in Indonesia are very proud of the language, and acknowledge that it can be used in a greater range of domains than other local languages, due to the expanded vocabulary which has been developed for it. The prestige function is therefore well fulfilled. Third, due to the careful codification of Indonesian over many years, it now serves as a very effective standard and model for learning, satisfying the frame-of-reference function. Finally, if one considers the separatist function that national languages ideally should fulfill, distinguishing speakers of one nation from those of other surrounding nations, it might be thought that Indonesian does not satisfy this function particularly well, because Indonesian was developed from a form of Malay, and Malay is spoken both in neighboring Malaysia and Singapore. However, while speakers of Indonesian acknowledge obvious similarities and earlier close links with Malay, they will also generally confirm that, in their minds, Indonesian is now quite different from Malay, and maybe even 'better' than Malay in certain ways. Certainly, Indonesians are generally very proud that Indonesia established Indonesian as the official language of the nation before Malay was given a similar status in Malaysia, Indonesia achieving its independence several years before Malaya (subsequently renamed Malaysia). Psychologically, then, Indonesian does fulfill the separatist role, too, being felt to be very distinctive of Indonesia, and significantly different from other surrounding languages. Indonesian, therefore, has come to serve not only as a very effective official language for the country, but is also now fulfilling typical national language functions. The careful language planning carried out by the Indonesian government at and following independence has consequently been very successful, and demonstrates that a policy promoting a single indigenous language into a dominant role is indeed possible in an ethnically mixed country, if managed with care and continued toleration for other local languages.

Attempts at multilingual policies: the challenges of linguistic pluralism

Having examined cases where a single indigenous language is promoted over other indigenous languages into an official/national language role, we will now consider instances of attempts at linguistic pluralism—multilingual policies that promote more than one local language into an official/national language role. This kind of language policy brings with it different kinds of challenges from those with an essentially unilingual approach, as we will see.

Singapore: enabling equal opportunities for all

The small Asian state of Singapore represents one of the most concerted attempts anywhere to nurture a pluralist multicultural national identity in an ethnically mixed population. In such an endeavor, multilingualism and the establishment of a complex official/national language policy have been central to the government's direction of the state since its independence from British colonial rule, and have helped create an integrated new nation almost entirely free from inter-ethnic conflict.

When self-government (though not full independence) was achieved in 1958, the Singapore leadership pondered how to bring together the different ethnic groups of the territory, which had largely been isolated from each other under British rule. Around 75% of the population were ethnically Chinese, 17% Malay, 6% South Asians/Indians, and the remainder 2% other 'Eurasians'. Instead of privileging any one of these groups over the others in the development of a new national identity for the future independent Singapore, the government decided to promote a policy of multi-racialism and declared that Mandarin Chinese, Malay, and Tamil would all be co-official languages of the state, enabling a representative official language for each of the three major ethnic groups, and English would be recognized as a fourth official language for its pragmatic value and use in business and inter-group communication. For purely political reasons, Malay was symbolically recognized as Singapore's single national language, in order to send a signal to Singapore's much larger and more powerful Malay-speaking neighbors (during a period of tense international relations) that Singapore saw itself as part of this larger Malay-anchored world. This special status accorded to Malay has remained largely symbolic and is generally restricted to purely ceremonial use (for example, singing the national anthem). For all other important activities of everyday life, including education, government, and the media, the four official languages were guaranteed equal treatment, and the government promoted the importance of equal rights and opportunities, and economic growth, as critical for the nation's future development.

In order to improve communication between the different ethnic groups, the government introduced an ambitious plan for mandatory bilingual education, in which every student would select two languages from among the four official languages as mediums of education. The first language selected, 'L1', was referred to as the mother tongue, and would be used as the language of instruction for 60% of a student's classes, while the second language, 'L2', would be used for the remaining 40%. The very noble integrative intention of the bilingual education program was that students would learn languages of the other ethnic groups in Singapore, and so improve their understanding of their neighbors from different backgrounds. However, an unexpected complication seriously impeded this outcome, and it was found that students increasingly selected English as their 'mother tongue' L1, and the language closest to their ethnicity as their L2. Hence a Cantonese-speaking Chinese student would declare English as his L1, and Mandarin Chinese as his L2, and a Malayalam-speaking Indian student would select English as her L1, and Tamil as her L2. Consequently, rising generations in Singapore did become bilingual (or trilingual), but generally only in a combination of their home language, the official language associated with their ethnic group, and English, and not in a language from another of Singapore's major ethnic groups. Such was the movement toward English, selected purely for its value in securing better future employment, that the government ultimately reorganized the entire school system, making all of Singapore's schools L1-English schools, and eliminating schools offering Mandarin, Malay, and Tamil as an L1. While this essentially just recognized the reality of the evolving situation in Singapore, with less than 1% of new students selecting either Mandarin, Malay, or Tamil as L1 in 1983 before the change, it nevertheless triggered a negative reaction from part of the Chinese community, who saw it as officially undermining equal support for Chinese and as giving preferential treatment to the growth of English. The fact that Singapore's Nanyang University, the only Chinese-language university in Southeast Asia, had been converted into an English-speaking institution in 1980, merged into the new National University of Singapore, and that educational qualifications in Chinese as L1 were not valued by employers as much as parallel qualifications with English emphasized to many in the large Chinese community that the government was becoming biased in its management of languages in Singapore, and discontent set in.

The government, in response to complaints that it was failing to support the upkeep of Chinese, announced two new initiatives to attempt to address this perception and placate the Chinese community. The first of these was a 'Speak Mandarin Campaign', which encouraged ethnic Chinese to switch from speaking other home varieties of Chinese, such as Hokkien and Cantonese, to the use of Mandarin Chinese, as a way to improve knowledge of Mandarin in Singapore and to unify the Chinese population with a single common form of Chinese. The government provided free classes and instructional materials in Mandarin for adults who had not previously studied Mandarin Chinese, and it began to require Chinese government employees, taxi drivers, bus conductors, and market sellers to make use of Mandarin in their interactions with Chinese clients and customers, and not other forms of Chinese. Such pressures and encouragements to speak Mandarin, which targeted new domains of life each year, resulted in a significant increase in abilities in Mandarin Chinese among the population, when assessed several years later, and established Mandarin as the regular form of communication among Chinese from different linguistic backgrounds (a role which might have been taken over by English, had knowledge of Mandarin not been strongly cultivated). The Speak Mandarin Campaign also went some way toward satisfying members of the Chinese population that the government was sensitive to its desire to maintain the vitality of Chinese in Singapore. A second Chinese-focused initiative helped strengthen this impression, and the government announced the creation of a new series of Special Assistance Programs to allow gifted Chinese students to achieve high levels of Chinese/English bilingualism.

Such language-sensitive issues and the government's reaction to them provide a flavor of the potential volatility of a system which attempts to guarantee and maintain equitable treatment of multiple official languages, regularly necessitating adjustment when unexpected developments occur to affect perceptions of their parity. A further example of an unexpected side effect arising from an adjustment to the bilingual education policy occurred in the 1980s, when the government announced it was going to reduce the L2 language requirements for entrance to university in Singapore. Many otherwise gifted students had been struggling to master two languages to the high levels specified for university entrance, and found it necessary to apply to universities in other countries as a result. In order to stem this flow of talented young people out of the country, the government announced it was going to lower the L2 scores required for entry into the National University of Singapore. Such an adjustment certainly helped students hoping to attend university in Singapore, but resulted in renewed complaints from the Chinese community that a lowering of required L2 proficiency in the entrance exams would lead to a drop in the standards of Chinese in Singapore. The government therefore felt pressured to institute new measures to appease the Chinese community, this time promising that new courses in Chinese history and society would be added in schools, as a way to increase knowledge of Chinese culture among younger generations.

Assessing Singapore's attempts to foster linguistic pluralism over the first fifty years of its independence, it can be said that the state's well-intentioned policy of multilingualism in which rising generations would learn the languages of other ethnic groups in Singapore has actually *not* directly resulted in integration of the country's mixed population, due to the complicating strong attraction of young people to learning English in place of a second Asian language. However, the state's official multilingualism, providing language resources and rights for each of the three major ethnic groups in the population, has helped create the conditions of social stability to allow for the growth of a unifying national identity based on multiculturalism, and the government has been able to help people in Singapore become familiar with the culture of other groups in the state through means other than language (for example, regular media promotion of cultural activities of the three major ethnic groups, specially designed school textbooks highlighting aspects of Chinese, Malay, and Indian culture). As a result of such efforts, recent surveys have found that people of all groups identify strongly with Singapore as a nation and have a very positive sense of belonging to and loyalty toward a single multicultural nation. While maintaining a policy of linguistic pluralism, in the form of multiple local official or national languages, is unquestionably challenging, requiring constant attention and adjustments to balance the interests of different groups and to preserve equality, the case of Singapore demonstrates that it is both possible and potentially very successful, helping to weaken the potential for linguistic issues to be major causes of inter-ethnic strife, and facilitating general attempts at social integration (Simpson 2007c).

Multilingual policies in other states

Other states which have ambitiously attempted to recognize more than one official language in a multilingual policy have experienced challenges which are similar in ways to those occurring in Singapore. In **South Africa**, following the end of the apartheid era in 1994, the government decided to develop a policy of linguistic pluralism and recognize eleven official languages—English, Afrikaans (a mixture of Dutch and African languages, developed among white settlers in South Africa), and nine other African languages, the latter being the mother tongue of 99% of the black African population. The new constitution declared that measures should be taken to elevate the status and advance the use of all of the country's official languages. In the time since this initial statement of intent, new resources for the nine less well-developed African languages have indeed been created, but the post-apartheid period has been dominated linguistically by the growth of English at the expense of other languages, and English has come to be used significantly more than all the other official languages in government administration, higher education, the law courts, and other domains, including business, and increasingly in social interactions (Mesthrie 2008). As in Singapore, the perceived utilitarian value of English (combined, in South Africa, with positive historical associations of English with the anti-apartheid movement) has led to a marked imbalance in the way that the state's official languages are actually used in everyday life, and although a number of languages have been formally recognized as having equal official language status, in practice one language, English, features much more prominently than the others in formal daily interactions, and is viewed as having higher value than the African official languages.

An imbalance in the use and treatment of co-official languages has also been perceived in certain countries with a much more restricted set of official languages, for example **Cameroon**, where it might be thought that equal support for each language would be easier to maintain. Cameroon has two official languages, French and English, resulting from the fact that France and Britain both administered different parts of the country during colonial times, but it is reported that the Anglophone minority (those who speak English or identify with English rather than French) feels that there is unfair and unequal governmental emphasis on the French language (Biloa and Echu 2008). Perceptions of being discriminated against by a Francophone majority (those who speak French or identify with French rather than English) have caused people in the Southwest and Northwest provinces of the country to unite and develop a strong new English-centered Anglophone identity, and have resulted in the creation of Anglophone nationalist movements calling for independence for the two Anglophone-majority provinces. The important lesson from Cameroon is therefore that it is not sufficient to declare multiple languages official; governments must constantly work to see that equality of treatment of such languages is maintained in the eyes of the people. Quite similar rumblings of discontent relating to the status of English and French as imbalanced co-official languages have also periodically been heard in northeast Canada in the Francophone province of Quebec, where a secessionist movement has called for independence from the rest of the country, citing linguistic, as well as economic and cultural, reasons. This has occurred despite attempts by the government to better integrate and accommodate Anglophone and Francophone parts of Canada by means of the Official Languages Act of 1969, which declared French and English to be official throughout the country (Bonvilain 2007).

Regional multilingualism

Multilingualism has also been pursued as an explicit policy below the national level in various countries with declarations that certain languages are official in regions or individual states of a country. A good example of this is **India**, where the government reorganized the borders of the country into 'linguistic states' between 1956 and 1966, in which twelve major regional languages became official. Hence, for example, Bengali became official in the new state of West Bengal, Tamil became official in Tamil Nadu, and Gujarati was recognized as the official language of the new state of Gujarat (Amritavalli and Jayaseelan 2007). Reorganizing the provincial boundaries previously created by British colonial rule in a way that matched up much more naturally with the distribution of major Indian languages, and making these languages official within their respective states, facilitated the carrying out of any activities relating to local government offices for much of the population, and also helped the development of the regional languages themselves, as they came to be used extensively in education. The establishment of multiple regional official languages consequently reduced the likelihood that linguistic issues might cause discontent and lead to civil unrest among the ethnically mixed population of India.

In other states, governments have not actually empowered regional languages with any official role, but have nevertheless encouraged or shown great tolerance for the maintenance of regional or minority languages in addition to national and official languages. In Indonesia, from 1987 onward, the government placed increased emphasis on the value of local languages, in addition to the national official language, Indonesian, and encouraged their use in education again. It was reasoned that the maintenance of regional culture and traditional values via language might be beneficial for individuals' personal development and might strengthen their general sense of pride in a local ethnic identity in a way that would also be beneficial for the state. The preservation and valuation of an ethnic or regional identity and its associated language was thus not felt to be a threat to the growth of national identity, and was in fact suggested to be helpful for the nurturing of the latter (Bertrand 2003). It is certainly possible that the spread of the new national official language, Indonesian, was so successful in part because there was no attempt by the government to have it replace the use of local languages in informal domains. In **China**, too, the state has overseen a form of unofficial multilingualism, referred to as 'pluralistic integrity' (Chen 2007: 161). It is held that the nation is structured in two levels—a lower pluralistic base made up of the country's many different ethnolinguistic groups (55, in addition to the main Han Chinese group), and a higher national level consisting of all of the state's population—and that the preservation of an ethnic identity and language is fully compatible with an individual also holding a national identity and being a speaker of the common language of the state, Mandarin Chinese.

Quite generally, it can be noted that the recognition of regional official languages, or the simple encouragement of local language and culture, does not necessarily lead to the development of local independence movements, contrary to the beliefs of many politicians (Brown 2003). If a state is well-organized and there is equitable treatment of its citizens, minority groups will typically not think of secession, as the benefits from continuing to belong to an established, successful state are likely to seem more attractive than the uncertainties of what might result from any departure from the state, and people will only develop thoughts of seeking independence from a state if they are badly treated and discriminated against. For example, the Khmer people in eastern Thailand have never agitated for independence from Thailand in order to join the Khmer population in neighboring Cambodia, as conditions for the Khmer in Thailand are not oppressive in any way, and they are free to maintain their language and culture as they like in Thailand, and may also feel that they benefit from Thailand's more developed economy and stability (Smalley 1994). National and other regional or ethnic identities are therefore quite compatible, and language planners should bear this important point in mind. As we will see later in the chapter, unfortunately, the leaderships of certain countries have at various points engaged in policies of active oppression of local languages and cultures in attempts to assimilate populations to a new national identity, understanding the former to be a threat to the development of the latter.

Finally, in closing this consideration of pluralist approaches to language planning, we can observe that multilingual policies most commonly do seem to benefit populations and governments when they are managed well with adequate resources, but there are also some instances in which multilingualism has actually been stimulated for negative political reasons, to divide (and subsequently rule) a population by emphasizing distinctions between different ethnolinguistic groups. A divide-and-rule approach has been a clear feature of language planning attempts in apartheid South Africa, Burma, and the USSR. In South Africa, the apartheid government imposed strong ethnolinguistic divisions on the black African population, which in fact did not correspond to really major differences in language and culture, as a way to support the separation and relocation of the black population into a set of poorly resourced, small 'homelands', where (primary) schooling was subsequently carried out in different local languages. While such a policy certainly seemed to be supporting the use of multiple languages in a positive way, the motivation behind such a 'pluralist' approach was to deliberately fragment the black population and exert control over it in different enclaves, frustrating any potential attempts to develop a unified resistance to the government (Mesthrie 2008). In Burma, the military government in the 1990s similarly promoted the maintenance of multiple minority languages, but not in order to help benefit their speakers. Rather, it was worried that its political opposition, the National League for Democracy (NLD) had begun to establish good relations with various of the country's ethnolinguistic minority groups, and the government tried to block this through encouraging the revival of certain minority languages, hoping this would prove an impediment to communication between these groups and the NLD (Callahan 2003). In the Soviet Union, before its disintegration, there was an initiative to promote the status of smaller regional languages and dialects. This was carried out with the aim of hindering the development of larger regional linguistic identities which might arise if a single non-Russian language came to be spoken in any large region. Soviet strategists reasoned that if a large number of minor languages were spoken within an area, then the different ethnic peoples in such an area would not come to unite under any of the larger regional languages, and in the absence of any widespread regional language in each state, the government could insist that Russian be used as a common link language, strengthening its role throughout the Soviet Union (Wardhaugh 1998). It can thus be seen that even language-planning strategies which would seem to heavily favor the linguistic rights and opportunities of minority groups can be adapted as means to politically control populations and the development of democracy, although fortunately most attempts at multilingualism do have more altruistic motivations.

Having focused on issues relating to status planning (the selection of national and official languages) and implementation(spreading the use of these languages), we will now consider certain aspects of corpus planning in more depth, looking specifically at the ways that new words are created in different languages, and how this may be directed or controlled by political forces in a country, and how the role of script choice (graphization) is involved in the projection of national identity.

The expansion of vocabulary and its symbolic effects

When a language is selected to have a special role, such as that of a national or official language, it may need to be developed further so that it can be used effectively in all domains of life. One area that language planners frequently focus their efforts on in corpus planning is the creation of new words to help enlarge the lexicon of a language. Cross-linguistically (that is, when we look at languages from different parts of the world), there are different ways that a language can expand its vocabulary when it needs to build new words, and the kind of word-creation strategy and source of words adopted by a population may well reflect its orientation toward the outside world and the way it hopes to define a specific national identity. There are two broad ways in which new words can be established in a language, making use of either internal or external linguistic resources, as described in the following.

Language-internal sourcing of new words

Most languages make at least some new words from creatively re-cycling words or sub-parts of words which already exist in a language, in three ways. First, an old word which may have gone into disuse may be reactivated with a new meaning. For example, the Old Chinese word *shēngjì* [升济] which meant '(Buddhist) salvation' was given the new meaning of 'economy' in modern Chinese, and in Hausa (West Africa), the word *jakaadaa* which meant 'important palace messenger' in earlier times was adapted to mean 'ambassador' in the modern world (Mesthrie et al 2003).

Second, words only used in certain regional dialects may be added to the standard form of a language, sometimes with new meanings. In the development of a new standard form of Korean in North Korea during the 1960s, many dialect words were used as replacements for existing words that the government wished to eliminate, for example the common term *hwangso* ('ox') was replaced with the dialect word *twungkulso*, and *okswuswu* ('corn, maize') was replaced with *kangnayngi* (King 2000; see also the section on language 'purification' later in this chapter).

Third, in very many instances, new words are created from making novel combinations of words or parts of words which already exist in a language. For example, English 'compact disc' and 'hard drive' are compound words which name new items of technology with original combinations of other common words. French '*portefeuille*', (literally 'carry sheet/leaf') was created to mean 'wallet', and German '*Fernseher*', (literally 'far see-er') was coined with the meaning 'television'.[1]

Language-external sourcing of new words

Instead of creating new words from language-internal resources, languages may also 'borrow' words directly from other languages. Hence, when new items of technology are invented and named in a language by those who created them, these terms may simply be imported into other languages, perhaps with some slight adjustments in pronunciation, as for example with the words 'computer', 'video', and 'telephone', which have been borrowed from English into various other languages. Such 'borrowings' are regularly referred to as 'loan words'. All languages seem to have made significant use of borrowing at some time or other in their history. For example, as much as two-thirds of the vocabulary of Modern English may be the result of earlier borrowings into English from other languages, in particular French and Latin. While

---

1. A rather 'extreme' example of a new word formed from many other words in a language is the term reportedly coined in German for military tanks, when they first appeared in warfare in 1917— *Schützengrabenvernichtungspanzerkraftwagen*—literally 'protective digging annihilation panther strength vehicle', later commonly shortened to *Panzer* (panther).

English has borrowed very extensively from other languages in previous times, now English has become a major source of loan words that are borrowed into other languages.

Borrowing may take place either from languages which are currently widely spoken, such as English, French, or Russian, or from languages which no longer have any (or extremely few) living speakers, but which are felt to be prestigious, such as Latin, Ancient Greek, and Sanskrit. With the former type of borrowing, there may be a psychological effect that (certain) speakers will feel their language is inadequate or being underutilized and dominated by outside forces if it simply adopts loan words from other living languages in place of coining new words from its own resources, and there may be some resistance to the importation of large numbers of loan words from other contemporary languages. However, borrowing from classical 'non-living' languages such as Ancient Greek or Sanskrit is commonly perceived in a different way, and often is viewed as educated and elevated in style, due to the high prestige associated with these languages of ancient civilizations. While English, French, and other western European languages all continue to create words from Latin and Ancient Greek sources, in South and Southeast Asia, Hindi, Thai, and Cambodian all borrow and create new words from Sanskrit, a language spoken many centuries ago in India. For Hindi, adding new words from Sanskrit has the function of emphasizing the Indian nature of the language and distinguishing it from Urdu, which tends to borrow much more from Arabic and Persian, giving it more of an Islamic identity.

Considering the two broad routes in which new words ('neologisms') enter a language, either via internal or external sources, the use of internal sources may commonly dominate in countries focusing on developing and maintaining a distinct national identity, as this stresses the individual nature of the language and helps fulfill the separatist function of national languages. Extensive borrowing from other languages may be more frequent in countries which are happy to accept a certain amount of 'linguistic coloring' and influence from other countries and cultures. In East Asia, the neighboring countries of China and Japan make use of these strategies in different ways. Modern Chinese seems to strongly favor creating new words from Chinese-internal sources, while Japanese is currently adding many new words through external borrowing, above all from English. These tendencies can be illustrated with the words used for 'elevator' and 'computer' in the two languages. Note that the Japanese borrowings from English are adjusted to make the English words easy to pronounce in Japanese. The literal meaning of the words in Chinese is added in following parentheses:

English	*Japanese*	*Chinese*
elevator	erebetaa	dianti ('electric raise')
computer	konpyutaa	diannao ('electric brain')

In Japan, the strategies used to coin new words have actually fluctuated, depending on the political climate of the time. While foreign-sourced loan words freely came into the new national language when it was first developing in the beginning of the 20th century, during the ultra-nationalist period of the 1930s there was a strong move against the acceptance of borrowings from other languages, and English-sourced words such as *beesobooru* ('baseball' accommodated to a Japanese pronunciation) and *haikingu* 'hiking' were replaced with 'real'

Japanese words *yakyuu* and *ensoku*. As strong feelings of nationalism faded in the second half of the 20th century, it again became fashionable to borrow words from other successful countries and their languages, with the majority of these coming from English and the USA, and being associated with modernity, technological progress, and departures from traditional culture.

Presently, it is estimated that approximately 10% of the Japanese lexicon consists in English loan words. While this clearly represents a certain openness to external influences, there is also an interesting originality to the way that English words are incorporated into Japanese, which illustrates well how borrowing may not always involve just a blind copying of words from another language. When words are borrowed into Japanese, they are adapted to conform to the language's sound system and certain other word-formation constraints. One of these constraints is that Japanese tends to avoid using nouns that have many syllables. Another restriction is that many of the sequences of sounds which occur in other languages are difficult for Japanese speakers to pronounce. Because of this, Japanese frequently tends to add extra vowels between groups of consonants in borrowed words to break them up into manageable sound sequences. Japanese also requires most words to end in a vowel. The combination of these constraints often causes words which are borrowed into Japanese to first get lengthened, with extra vowels inserted between pairs of consonants and following final consonants, as shown in the second column in Table 2.3, and then get shortened so that nouns are not very long, resulting in the final, commonly used forms in column 3. As can be seen from a comparison of column 1 and column 3, in many cases this process results in a considerable distortion of the original borrowed word, which may no longer be easily identifiable in the new Japanese form.

TABLE 2.3 **Borrowing of English Nouns into Japanese**

1	2	3
Original English Word	**Vowels Inserted**	**Shortening of Length of Words**
strike	sutoraiki	suto
super-market	suupaa-maaketto	suupaa
platform	puratto-foomu	foomu
personal computer	paasonaru konpyuuta	pasu-kon
word processor	waado purosessa	waa-puro
sexual harassment	sekusyaru harasumento	seku hara

Adapted from Loveday (1986).

The borrowing of foreign words into Japanese has also sometimes been noted to result in a change of the meaning of the original word (Loveday 1986). For example, *dorai* borrowed from English 'dry' means 'business-like' or 'unsentimental', *handoru* from 'handle' means 'steering wheel', and *miruku* from 'milk' only refers to condensed milk. New words are additionally created from English sources which do not occur in English, for example *sukin-shippu*, 'skinship', meaning 'physical closeness'. The changes which are regularly applied to foreign-sourced words give rise to words that, in many cases, might not be viewed as simple borrowings from other languages, but rather as new Japanese-styled words inspired by other languages. Assessing the large-scale borrowing of English words into Japanese from the point of view of national identity and its projection through language, it could be suggested that Japanese is not somehow becoming linguistically 'subservient' to foreign languages through its adoption of many foreign-origin words, but is making use of other language resources in a creative and distinctively Japanese way to enrich the development of Japanese. As commented by Carroll (2001: 161):

> Words are not taken in 'lock, stock, and barrel', but are altered phonologically, morphologically and semantically, in a process of cultural assimilation that 'Japanizes' foreign words to meet the needs of Japanese society.

While the expansion of vocabulary via external sources (borrowing) may at times be perceived as a foreign linguistic 'invasion' which needs to be resisted in order to safeguard the distinctive character of a national language (as will soon be discussed), such critical distinctiveness may also arise during the actual process of borrowing and adaptation, as seen here with Japanese, with the result that loan words take on an original domestic character of their own.

Language purism, purification, and protectionism

All languages continually need to coin new words, as new commercial products and inventions are created, and words are required to refer to these novel items. In the expansion and also the day-to-day maintenance of a language and its vocabulary, two particular activities are often observed among nations which are either in the process of developing a new national identity, or keen to defend an image previously established through a national language—language '**purification**' and '**protectionism**'.

During periods of nationalism and the emphasis or creation of symbols representing a nation, it is not uncommon to find that national languages are subjected to policies of '**lexical purification**'. Politicians direct linguists to 'purge' a national language of words which seem to be foreign in origin and so restore the language to an original, 'pure' state. This allows it to be promoted as the genuine, unadulterated linguistic spirit of the nation, strongly fulfilling the separatist function of national languages. During the purification process, foreign borrowings are replaced with new words coined from within the language, past and present. A sampling of cases in which the pursuit of **language purism** for political reasons has led to heavy purging of foreign-sourced words and their replacement with native words is briefly described in the following, with a more extended description of this process, its motivation and consequences, in the interesting case of North Korea.

Greece

Greece came into existence as an independent nation-state only in 1832. Before that, for most of the preceding 400 years, it was part of the Ottoman Empire, whose dominant language was Turkish, and over time spoken Greek incorporated many words from Turkish, and also from Italian. Once independence was achieved, many nationalists attempted to eliminate all Turkish, Italian, and other borrowings from Greek so as to create a national language that would genuinely represent the Greek nation and its former glory. This resulted in the creation of the 'purifying' form of the Greek language—'Katharevousa' Greek—one of two varieties of Greek that would compete for status as the country's official language into the 20th century (Mackridge 2010).

Italy

During the period of pre–World War II fascism in Italy, words of foreign origin were purged from standard Italian, especially where these occurred in the names of towns, hotels, surnames, public signs, and advertisements, and people who had German and Slovene names were forced to replace these with Italian names, with this practice even extending to the replacement of names on tombstones (Ruzza 2000).

Czech Nationalism

In the 19th century, Czech nationalists in the Kingdom of Bohemia set about creating a standardized form of Czech that could be promoted as a new national language for an independent Czech state. This involved the purging from Czech of all foreign words, including many 'Germanisms' (German-influenced words)—even those which had become widespread in other languages and so had an international rather than just German flavor, for example words such as *tyatr*, 'theater' (Törnquist-Plewa 2000).

Croatia

As noted in chapter 1, when Croatia became an independent state in 1991, the government of Franco Tudjman set about purifying 'Croatian' and eliminating all words that sounded Serbian, as a way to try to maximally distinguish Croatian from Serbian and to establish it as a separate language which would be the national and official language of Croatia. This process caused 'Croatian' to begin to diverge from 'Serbian', as new Croatian words were introduced that did not occur in the speech of Serbs (Greenberg 2011).

North Korea

From the 1960s onward, a major initiative was launched in North Korea to develop a new standard form of 'pure' Korean, free from words borrowed from European languages, Japanese, and also Chinese. This was directed by the leader of North Korea, Kim Il-sung, who made various important speeches on the role that language should play in developing a strong socialist state. In speeches given in 1964 and 1966, Kim Il-sung declared that the Korean language was important as a powerful weapon in the development of the nation's economy, culture, science, and technology, that standard Seoul Korean had become 'polluted' by foreign language words and was not fit to be used as the country's national language, being an impure mixed language—'a jumble filled with Western, Japanese, and Chinese elements due to American imperialists and their followers' national language erasure policy' (quoted in Sohn 1999). North Korea therefore had a duty to create a new standard language to replace the 'bastardized' impure form of speech used in South Korea, with all its English and Japanese borrowings (King 2007). The new standard Korean that Kim Il-sung proposed was to be based on Pyongyang speech, the capital of the North, and was named *munhwao*, 'Cultured Speech'.

In creating *munhwao*, thousands of foreign-origin words were eliminated and new Korean replacements were created from words in North Korean dialects, such internal-sourcing of new words being part of the leadership's more general strategy of self-reliance (*chuch'e*) in all areas of life in North Korea. Due to the personality cult surrounding Kim Il-sung, all of the words he used, and new words suggested by him, were immediately added to *munhwao* dictionaries, and Kim Il-sung's speech was taken to be a model for the new standard Korean developed in the North.

The massive purging of foreign words from Korean carried out in North Korea, along with other measures changing the language relating to writing and style, provides a striking example of how language planning can be utilized for the development of nationalist ideology (King 1996, 1998). The North Korean leadership specified how language would be shaped so as to conform to socialist principles and the planned cultural growth of North Korea, and the population and national institutions were then strictly controlled to make sure that they used only the language prescribed as the new standard of the state.

The wholesale changes made to Korean in North Korea during the 1960s and 1970s not only allowed North Korea to maintain that its language had become free of foreign, imperialist contamination, but also created a new form of Korean which was significantly different from the language used in South Korea. Currently it is estimated that the lexicon in South Korean consists in 35% native Korean words, 60% Chinese-origin words ('Sino-Korean' words), and 5% Western loan words. Purification activities in North Korean *munhwao* have, in strong contrast, produced a language whose lexicon is now over 90% native Korean, so there are very large portions of Korean vocabulary that are now different in North and South Korean. When contact occurred between representatives of the North and South for the first time since the Korean War in 1972, officials from the South were very shocked by the language they heard used by the North Koreans, and said that they could not easily understand the Northerners' speech, because it had changed so much. The far-reaching changes to North Korean, arising from 'purification', combined with the continual borrowing of foreign loan words in South Korean, has led to heavy **divergence** in the language, and the possibility that 'Korean' in North and South Korea might become mutually unintelligible and develop into two different languages.

Linguistic protectionism is a process in which new words in a language are either heavily encouraged or required to be created via language-internal resources, rather than borrowing. Such an ongoing policy toward the creation of new words does not necessarily require the elimination of all earlier foreign borrowings and so is generally less extreme and disruptive than the types of purification referred to in the preceding paragraphs. A good example of a nation with a heavy protectionist policy toward its language is **France**. In France it has at times been the law that new words be made from genuine French sources, and those who worked in government offices and schools risked having to pay fines if they did not follow directives on the use of newly coined words. The French Academy, which is responsible for many aspects of the direction of the French language, is strongly against the use of

English-borrowed words, such as *le weekend, le sandwich, le drugstore,* and *le computer,* and attempts to impose the use of French equivalents.

Similar national language organizations and policies of protectionism are present in Israel (for Hebrew), Slovakia, and Iceland, among other states. **Iceland** is now the only example in Europe of a linguistically homogenous nation-state—all of the population of Iceland speak Icelandic as their first language and use it in all domains of life, and Icelandic is not spoken by any population outside Iceland. The language therefore is a strong symbol of national identity, and fulfills all the primary functions of a national language, as well as serving the official language role (Vikør 2000). Despite the fact that Icelandic is an almost ideal national official language, it is perceived that Icelandic is regularly threatened by the influence of other languages, initially Danish, and now English. Because of this, there are vigorous attempts to protect the language from words coming in from other languages, and new Icelandic-sourced words are constantly being created whenever necessary to name new concepts and technology. Such proactive linguistic protectionism is reported to be enthusiastically supported by the public, much more so than in certain other countries such as France, where the use of words borrowed from other languages (in particular English) is generally not objected to by the majority of speakers, and only is focused on negatively by a (highly vocal) minority, some in positions of power and influence (Judge 2000). In Iceland there are also concerted efforts to restrict the occurrence of English in the media, business, and science contexts, by means of formal legislation, so as to protect the primacy of Icelandic further.

Issues relating to graphization and orthography

The languages of the world are written in many different scripts. Some of these are shared by a number of different languages, for example the Roman/Latin alphabet, the Cyrillic alphabet, and Chinese characters. Other scripts are only used by a single language, for example Korean *hangul*. The selection and promotion of a particular writing system/script for a language is an area of corpus planning that has sometimes been deliberately manipulated for political reasons relating to national identity and the enabling or restricting of communicative links with other states and populations. Here we will consider a range of examples that illustrate well how script choice is important in different sociolinguistic ways, establishing relations between languages and speakers' social and political identities.

Our first three examples highlight the symbolic value and perception of script forms among different populations, and how the perceived value of a particular script may change over time and also vary across different populations utilizing it.

In **Japan** during the 1930s, when nationalism was at its height, and the Japanese language was strongly perceived to be an embodiment of the soul of the Japanese nation, in a philosophy known as *kotodama*, the central focus of linguistic veneration was for the written form of the language, and its script in particular (Gottlieb 2007). Although the characters used to write Japanese were Chinese in origin, they had been used for so many centuries in Japan that they were seen as a crucial component of Japanese national cultural heritage, and enjoyed a semi-sacred position among the Japanese intelligentsia. Consequently, when certain reformers proposed adjusting many of the characters, simplifying their complex shapes in ways that might help make them easier to learn, such proposals were stridently rejected as attacks on the defining symbol of Japanese national identity. Traditional Japanese script, in the form of (Chinese-origin) characters, was accorded an almost spiritual importance. Interestingly, at the same time that Japanese nationalists were outraged by proposals to tamper with 'Japanese' characters, in order to potentially improve learning of the written language, in China quite different sentiments were being expressed toward the same writing system. Frustrated that the complexity of Chinese characters made them difficult for common people to learn, intellectuals involved in China's modernization and development in the 1920s and 1930s called for drastic measures to be taken with the script, so as to spread knowledge of written Chinese, and many advocated completely doing away with Chinese characters, and replacing them with a new alphabetic form of writing Chinese. The General Secretary of the Chinese Communist Party, Qu Qiubai, expressed the strongly negative feelings that were felt by many in the leadership toward characters at the time, claiming that 'Chinese characters are like the filthiest, most abominable, most wicked, medieval night soil cesspit' (quoted in Chen 2007: 151). As Chen (2007) notes, in China, pragmatic needs to educate the massive population of the country won out over any idealistic attachment toward the traditional script as a symbolic representation of Chinese culture.

Korea provides a second good illustration of how the symbolic value attributed to a script may vary, but this time within a single nation over time. For many centuries, Korean was written primarily by means of characters borrowed from Chinese, and although an alphabetic script known as *hangul* was invented for Korean in the 15th century, it was considered socially inferior for those with status and education to write with it, causing the use of *hangul* to be heavily restricted until the end of the 19th century. When modernizing nationalist movements grew in Korea in the early 20th century, however, the status of *hangul* radically changed in a very positive way, and now *hangul* is viewed with tremendous pride in both South and North Korea as an outstanding, superior writing system, whose 15th-century creation by King Sejong is celebrated each year on a special day, which for many years was also a public holiday. The changing status of *hangul* shows that attitudes toward script forms can be very strong (positive and negative), and also can undergo change as the sociopolitical situation in a society and country evolves in different ways.

Our third example of variation in attitudes toward a writing system comes from **Vietnam**, which is another East Asian nation that made use of Chinese characters for much of its pre-modern history. While writing carried out by government officials and those in high society was done with Chinese characters until the 20th century, French missionaries in Vietnam created an alphabetic representation of Vietnamese in order to spread Christianity, named *quốc ngữ*. This script form was subsequently promoted by the French colonial government through the 19th and into the 20th centuries, but was rejected by Vietnamese intellectuals and political leaders in resistance movements, as it was strongly associated with French colonial domination. However, after some time, independence activists in the 20th century began to appreciate that *quốc ngữ* was a much more effective script for spreading knowledge of written Vietnamese, and as their political struggle for an independent Vietnam depended on the dissemination of written forms of anti-French propaganda, the negative symbolic perception of *quốc ngữ* was replaced with a positive view of its high pragmatic value, and *quốc ngữ* came to be adopted by Vietnamese nationalists (Lo Bianco 2001; Lê and

O'Harrow 2007). Now, in the 21st century, *quốc ngữ* would seem to be an indispensable component of Vietnamese linguistic identity, with its very distinctive appearance, making use of a combination of the Roman alphabet and a special set of diacritical marks to represent tones and other aspects of the pronunciation of Vietnamese. As with *hangul* and the different views of Chinese characters in Japan and China in the 1930s, we see that a single script form can stimulate both strongly positive and negative attitudes in different political situations.

A second, broad observation that can be made about the importance of script choice and use is their function to distinguish different 'languages'. In a range of cases, two varieties which are mutually intelligible, which thus should really be treated as dialects of a single language, are actually presented as different languages, for the kinds of sociopolitical reasons already discussed in chapter 1. In various instances, the use of different scripts by the two related varieties helps enforce the perception of greater linguistic differences between such varieties than would be felt if only spoken forms of these 'languages' were taken into consideration. As described in chapter 1, **Hindi** and **Urdu** are mutually intelligible when spoken colloquially, but are treated as different languages due to their political association with different religious groups during the course of the 20th century. While the strong similarity of spoken forms of Hindi and Urdu naturally questions their distinction as separate languages, the use of different scripts to write these varieties—the Devanagari script for Hindi, and Perso-Arabic script for Urdu—helps embed the plausibility in speakers' minds that they are really using distinct languages. A similar situation exists with the separation of Serbo-Croatian into two different languages, **Serbian** and **Croatian**. While these varieties remain mutually intelligible to a high degree when spoken, suggesting that they should still be treated as dialects of a single language, the insistence of Serb and Croat leaders that Serbian and Croatian are separate languages is assisted by the fact that different scripts are commonly used in their writing—the Cyrillic alphabet for Serbian, and the Roman alphabet for Croatian.

A third example of the power of a different script form to distinguish varieties as different languages in the minds of those assessing the status of such varieties can be given from India and the recognition of **Punjabi** as a distinct language. Earlier in this chapter we mentioned the creation of 'linguistic states' in India, with regional languages being accorded official roles in these states. As this process took place under the direction of the government, peaceful attempts by certain populations to argue for the recognition of a number of official state languages were made and submitted to the government. A notable example of this was the Sikh-led petition for the recognition of Punjabi as the official state language of the Punjab in northern India. In 1953, the States Reorganization Commission rejected such a petition on the grounds that 'Punjabi' was not a distinct language, and was simply a dialect of Hindi, which should therefore remain as the official state language. However, the Sikh leadership continued to make the case for Punjabi as a separate language, and designated the Gurumukhi script, which was otherwise used for writing the Sikh scriptures, as the Punjabi script. Such an identification of a 'dialect' with a particular, distinct script, together with other linguistic arguments which were made more forcefully than before, finally convinced the government to recognize Punjabi as a separate language and as appropriate as the official language of the state of Punjab, the Sikh homeland. In this way, 'Punjabi' was officially born as a discrete language strongly linked (within India, but not in Pakistan) to the Sikh religious group. Whereas most other attempts to have 'dialects' of Hindi recognized as independent languages with linguistic rights for their speakers were unsuccessful, the combination of a particular dialect with a unique religious identity and a distinct writing form was enough to help achieve linguistic independence for Punjabi (Amritavalli and Jayaseelan 2007).

A final illustration of the application of two different scripts to a broadly uniform way of speaking can be given from the **Wa** language in Asia. The Wa people live in an area that straddles the international border between Burma (Myanmar) and China. Previously, Wa was only a spoken language, and had never been written down, but more recently language planners in Burma and China have provided the Wa with a way to write down their language. Because part of the Wa group live in China, and the remainder are in Burma, and language planners in the two countries were under pressure to impose Chinese/Burmese characteristics on their standardization efforts, the writing developed for the Wa people makes use of a different script form in the two countries—Chinese characters for the Wa in China, and an adaptation of the Burmese alphabet for those in Burma. The result is a situation in which Chinese and Burmese Wa people cannot share written forms of their language, which is clearly a negative consequence of the uncoordinated language planning which has taken place on either side of the border. Both countries have prioritized a desire to territorialize the Wa people within their borders through the marking of the respective national scripts—Chinese characters 'claim' the Wa to the east of the border for China, and Burmese script marks the Wa to the west as politically being very much part of Burma. Once again, politics becomes mixed up in language planning, and what linguistically might have been best for the standardization of a single language—a single writing system—has been displaced by a perceived imperative to 'brand' a people in two distinctive ways with different scripts. While oral communication continues to be successful between the Wa in China and those in Burma, the establishment of different ways of writing has the potential to hinder future growth of the Wa as a single ethnolinguistic group living in adjacent areas, and could indeed lead to language divergence if writing assumes a more important role in the everyday life of the Wa.

Language planning by intrusive state governments has led to the manipulation of script as a way to restrict inter-group access, in a way that highlights another aspect of the sociopolitical importance of script. Contacts between speakers of different but related languages that might be facilitated through the use of a common orthography (i.e., writing these languages with the same alphabet, as for example Italian and Spanish) can be made significantly more difficult if a major difference in script type is introduced. Speakers would have to learn a quite different script, in addition to other features of a language (differences in vocabulary and grammar), in order to be able to read any materials written in that language. This kind of access control via the control of script occurred with repeated frequency in the former Soviet Union, when the central government involved itself in linguistic issues in various of the Asian republics located in the USSR. A good illustration of the kinds of changes in official policy on script imposed by the Russian government can be given from the switches in script use that occurred in **Azerbaijan**. Prior to the incorporation of Azerbaijan into the Soviet Union in 1920, the Azeri language spoken in Azerbaijan had been written for thirteen centuries by means of Arabic script, as the result of early contact with Arabs and Islam. When Azerbaijan formally became part of the Soviet Union, the Soviet government began to encourage the use of the Latin alphabet to write Azeri, and then in 1925 required that all newspapers and official documents use Latin script. By requiring a switch from Arabic to Latin script, Soviet language planners intended to weaken the population's identification with Islam and the neighboring Azerbaijani people in Iran, and with people in other Islamic countries making use of Arabic script in their languages. A law was subsequently passed prohibiting the importation of any materials printed in Arabic script, and books written in Arabic script in Azerbaijan were destroyed, in an attempt to eradicate the population's links with their Islamic past. The form of the Latin alphabet promulgated by the Russian government was known as the Unified Turkic Latin Alphabet, and had certain extra characters to allow for its use to represent not only Azeri but all the other Turkic languages spoken in the Soviet Union. Then in 1928 Turkey itself adopted the use of the Latin alphabet, as a replacement for Arabic script, and this prompted fears that a pan-Turkic identity movement might arise among the Islamic republics in the Soviet Union, linked with Turkey, as use of the same script form now made communication and the sharing of written materials easy among speakers of all the Turkic languages. In order to block access between Turkic people in the Soviet Union and those in Turkey, in the 1930s, it was decreed that all languages in the Soviet Union should switch to the use of Cyrillic script for writing (the script form used to write Russian), and each republic was invited to customize the Cyrillic alphabet with additional symbols and diacritics to enable it to represent the special features of each Turkic language. This latter 'encouragement' was designed to create impediments to language-sharing among the Soviet Turkic republics, and so help break down ethnic Turkic links and identity (Hatcher 2008).

When independence finally came to Azerbaijan in 1991, the Azerbaijani people were finally free to decide which script they would like to use for the writing of Azeri. The Cyrillic script was strongly rejected, despite its familiarity, due to negative associations with the Soviet period, and discussions continued between those promoting a return to Arabic script, in order to project an Islamic identity for Azerbaijan, and others advocating the use of the Latin alphabet again, as a way to enable connections with other now independent Turkic-speaking states from the Soviet Union, which had decided to switch to the use of Latin script. In the end, an enthusiastic decision to re-adopt Latin script was made, and this now serves to enable links with other Turkic-speaking nations and to stress the Turkic component of Azerbaijani national identity. Choice of script is therefore very meaningful and has the potential to open up or shut down international connections, as well as signal aspects of a nation's targeted identity.

As a final illustration of the way that writing may potentially be controlled in order to support a particular ordering of society, the failure to provide a population of speakers with a means to write their variety can be used as a strategy to hinder the growth of 'language' status claims for a variety, and stimulate its continued treatment as a simple dialect. In China in the 1930s and 1940s, the nationalist government banned the use of the Latin alphabet–based system *Latinxua sin wenz* for the writing of Chinese 'dialects' as a way to both promote strong unity behind a single Chinese language, written in a uniform way, and preempt the emergence of any strong regional identities that might have coalesced around southern varieties such as Cantonese and Southern Min, had these established their own written forms. If a variety has its own writing system, this helps support its perception as a distinct language, but if it cannot be written down, there is a greater psychological pressure among people to consider it a dialect (especially if a closely related form is regularly written down—as with Mandarin Chinese). Some form of script and writing is frequently felt to be essential for groups considering themselves to be independent language groups.

Linguistic assimilation and the suppression of languages

When governments seek to control the language habits of a population, and direct people to the spoken use of a new national or official language, we sometimes find a very forceful imposition of such a language, accompanied by the suppression of other languages, in policies of linguistic and cultural assimilation. The attempt is made to promote the exclusive use of a certain language in various domains of life by forbidding people to use other languages (frequently their mother tongues) in those same domains. The goal of such a policy is normally to try to force the growth of a unique shared identity, in which the ethnolinguistic differences present in a mixed population are either eradicated or heavily reduced, and all people living in a state assimilate culturally and linguistically to a single national identity. Three examples of this very domineering kind of language engineering will be described as illustrations of the unwelcome pressures that people may sometimes be subjected to in instances of language planning: Taiwan in the 20th century, Nepal during the Panchayat regime (1960–1990), and the changing treatment of the Ainu minority in Japan from the 17th to the 20th centuries.

Taiwan

The history of Taiwan in the twentieth century is a revealing tale of a population which was deprived of self-determination for a period of ninety years, forcefully encouraged to adopt different national identities in part through the imposition of repressive language policies, but where neither the forced learning and use of Japanese from 1895 to 1945 nor that of Mandarin Chinese from 1949 to 1987 was successful in creating loyalty to the national identities associated with these languages; instead, such language policies actually served to unite and harden opposition to the dominating power.

Following China's military defeat by Japan in 1895, the former ceded Taiwan to the latter as part of the Treaty of Shimonoseki. The island of Taiwan thus became an overseas territory of Japan until 1945, and the Japanese government of Taiwan attempted to instill feelings of loyalty to Japan as new members of the Japanese empire. Prior to the Japanese occupation of Taiwan, the island had had a very checkered past and was a mixed and lawless place, with no cohesiveness in the population of different Chinese and Austronesian groups. In its attempts to mold a new loyal Japanese population on Taiwan, the Japanese government engaged in a replacement of all forms of Chinese and Austronesian languages in the education system and introduced requirements that only Japanese be used in a variety of public places, such as government offices, banks, and schools, and in newspapers, though there were no attempts to force the use of Japanese in private, home environments. For those who were ethnically Chinese, the fifty-year period during which new generations were unable to acquire knowledge of written Chinese and accessibility to Chinese writing was severely curtailed resulted in a major loss of contact with Chinese culture. The goal of the Japanese language policy was to achieve a severing of ties between the Chinese on Taiwan and mainland China and to cultivate a new Japanese national identity. In actuality, however, the hardships suffered together under Japanese rule in fact served to bring the previously disconnected Taiwanese groups together, feeling united in shared adversity, and the learning of Japanese ironically provided a common language for the first time that allowed these groups to communicate successfully with each other, enabling the beginnings of a new Taiwanese rather than Japanese identity. The repressive language policy of the Japanese period consequently failed to achieve its objective of creating new loyal Japanese citizens, and ultimately helped coalesce a different, local identity where none had previously existed.

At the end of World War II, Japanese forces withdrew from Taiwan, and the Chinese nationalist army, which had been engaged in conflict with communist Chinese forces in mainland China, arrived to occupy the island. In 1949, after further defeats at the hands of the communists on the mainland, the nationalist army fully retreated to Taiwan, adding 2.5 million people to the existing Taiwanese population of 5–6 million. The nationalist army and its political wing, the Kuo Min Tang (KMT), assumed full control of Taiwan and also continued to project its claim to be the only legitimate government of all China. In order to maintain such a position, it was felt that Mandarin Chinese, which was referred to in Chinese as the National Language (*guoyu*), should be imposed in all formal domains of language use in Taiwan, as a constituent part of China. Consequently, just when those on Taiwan had the expectation that they would finally be able to make use of their home languages in public places again, having been 'liberated' from the Japanese military, Mandarin Chinese was instead imposed in all the domains that Japanese had been, and other varieties of Chinese and Austronesian were again disallowed as means of communication in government offices, banks, schools, etc. Prior to the arrival of the Chinese nationalists on Taiwan, very few on the island understood or spoke any Mandarin Chinese, which was a northern variety of Chinese. The pre-1949 Chinese inhabitants of Taiwan instead primarily spoke Hokkien and Hakka varieties of Chinese, which are mutually unintelligible with Mandarin when spoken. The new requirement that Mandarin be used by all those working for the civil service had the effect that initially very few Taiwanese could compete with 'Mainlanders' for jobs in the government and education, causing widespread resentment among the Taiwanese. Coupled with the occurrence of harsh and sometimes violent confrontations with the KMT police and military, this created severe alienation among many Taiwanese toward the general Chinese national identity that the KMT government was hoping to instill in those on Taiwan. In its place, a Taiwanese vs. Mainlander distinction grew stronger in the minds of many in Taiwan, and as with the Japanese occupation of Taiwan, the use of an overly forceful language policy clearly failed to help implant a new sense of identity in the population of the island.

When the repressive language measures were eventually lifted in 1987, and genuine democracy was permitted with the promise of general elections and the tolerance of opposition political parties, this resulted in a vibrant open resurgence of the use of languages which had publicly been stifled for many decades, in particular Hokkien Chinese, which then became (over-zealously) presented as 'Taiwanese' by new Taiwanese nationalists. Currently, in the post-nationalist, stabilized era of democracy in Taiwan, a new Taiwanese identity has emerged which is finally not so strongly based on particular languages and divisions between Mandarin (associated with the foreign mainland Chinese) and 'Taiwanese' languages, but on a broader linguistic pluralism and a commitment to a common future together. All in all, a consideration of Taiwan and its turbulent history in the twentieth century shows that language issues are at their most explosive when accompanied by other forms of unequal treatment, and that the attempted imposition of specific languages as a way to stimulate the adoption of new identities is likely to fail when other expected individual rights and opportunities are denied the inhabitants of a territory (Simpson 2007d).

Nepal

Nepal is a country in the southern Himalayas with a very mixed population, having around one hundred different Indo-Aryan and Tibeto-Burman languages. The country was unified politically in the 18th century, but this did not result in any national bond among the population, who continued to be fragmented into many different groups. Linguistically, the Nepali language spread as a common link language (a lingua franca) used between speakers of different languages, and knowledge of Nepali increased significantly with the introduction of widespread education in the 20th century.

In 1960, the king of Nepal took away all power from the country's parliament, and began a thirty-year period of autocratic royal rule, which heavily promoted nationalism in Nepal through the media and education. At the center of this nationalism was emphasis on the belief that Nepal should develop a monocultural, unilingual national identity, as characterized in the political slogan 'one country, one dress, one language', and for all of its thirty years, the Panchayat regime 'presented the image of a country united by a strong, shared nationalist sentiment symbolized by the sole national language (Nepali)' (Chalmers 2007: 95). As Nepali was vigorously pressed on the population as a way to stimulate national unity, this led to fewer opportunities to make use of other languages, and increased pressure to assimilate to an overarching Nepali identity.

The Panchayat regime eventually fell in 1990, and when this occurred and multi-party democracy was introduced, there was an unexpected, massive resurgence of pride in ethnolinguistic diversity. Although many groups had adopted Nepali as their primary language during the Panchayat years, as a result of the government's campaigns of promotion and coercion, newly democratic Nepal saw a renewed celebration of the country's many minority languages, and a clear rejection of the monolingual nationalism imposed by the government from 1960 to 1990. This came as a major surprise to the Panchayat political leadership and outside observers alike, who believed that the repression of ethnic identity and minority languages had been 'successful' and had eliminated the possibility that the population would return to embrace more local identities and languages once again. However, this is precisely what happened, and the recognition of linguistic diversity in the country became a central issue in political discussion after 1990, with demands for minority languages to be sanctioned for use both in official domains and in education, and for linguistic and cultural pluralism to be acknowledged as a cornerstone of the nation's identity. The new constitution declared in 1990 duly incorporated this view of the Nepali nation, declaring it to be multi-ethnic and multilingual, and that while Nepali would continue to have the status of official language of the country, other languages would henceforth be recognized as national languages (Chalmers 2007: 93). Interestingly, as with Taiwan, one sees that heavy-handed attempts to force a unified national identity on a diverse population through the promotion of a national language and the repression of other languages were not able to achieve their purpose, and other language-related identities which were forcibly subdued for several decades have now bounced back with amazing energy, as people enjoy renewed freedom of linguistic and cultural expression. Policies of assimilation and language suppression are consequently neither commendable nor practically effective ways to coerce a long-lasting stable national identity, though when applied with sufficient force for a significant period of time, they do have the power to eliminate speakers' abilities in their ancestral languages, as we will note in our third example, from Japan.

The Ainu in Japan

The Ainu are a minority group who mostly live in the northern Japanese island of Hokkaido, which was incorporated into Japan in 1869 when borders with Russia were officially established. Prior to this, trade between the Ainu and the Japanese had flourished between the 15th and the 17th centuries, and the Japanese restricted their contacts with the Ainu to this commerce, feeling no desire to involve themselves culturally with the Ainu. The fact that the Ainu looked and dressed themselves quite differently from the Japanese and spoke a different language suited the Japanese worldview of the time, which emphasized distinctions between the center of the Japanese world and its periphery. As this notion of Japanese center vs. foreign periphery became increasingly stressed, concerted attempts were made to actually exaggerate the exotic nature of the periphery, and the Ainu were accordingly forbidden to learn and speak Japanese or to wear Japanese-style clothing, in a policy of active *dissimilation*.

Somewhat later in the 18th century, Russian traders and soldiers began to become more of a presence in the Kurile islands north of Hokkaido, where Ainu people also lived, and the local Ainu there were quickly becoming being 'Russified', starting to wear Western clothing, adopt Russian names, and take up Orthodox Christianity. As a response to this undesired Russian encroachment into the Japanese periphery, and to strengthen the northern border area, it was decided that the Ainu living there should be made into Japanese people. The Ainu were consequently encouraged to adopt the use of Japanese clothing, shave their beards and tie up their hair Japanese style, live in Japanese-style houses, and study and use the Japanese language. Certain traditional Ainu ceremonies were suppressed, and other, official ceremonies were introduced in which Ainu who were deemed to have assimilated well were displayed and presented with 'assimilation medals' (*kaizoku pai*) (Morris-Suzuki 1996: 55). Cultural and linguistic dissimilation were thus replaced with assimilation, as a means to achieve a political end, the firming up of Japan's border zones.

Later still in the 18th century, the Russian threat was seen to recede, and all attempts to assimilate the Ainu were discontinued. In the early part of the 19th century, to their surprise and bewilderment, the Ainu were ordered to stop wearing Japanese clothing and give up attempts to learn and use Japanese. The policy of assimilation was changed to one of dissimilation again.

The ever-fluctuating story of the Ainu's apparent use as political pawns, at times claimed to be part of Japanese society, at other times presented as external markers of the periphery of Japan, continued further in the 19th century, when the island of Hokkaido was officially acknowledged as being part of Japan, in a treaty with Russia. This triggered renewed efforts to 'Japanize' the Ainu, which were more assiduous than earlier attempts. What powered this second push toward assimilation of the Ainu was the growth of a much more dynamic and encompassing vision of what it meant to be 'Japanese' than in the past, with heavy emphasis on the fully homogenous nature of the Japanese population. This desire to see full ethnic homogeneity meant that all deviations from the important ideal of a uniform population and culture had to be removed through assimilation of the periphery populations both in the north (the Ainu) and the south (the Ryuukyuan islanders). A key component of this renewed, vigorous policy of assimilation was a requirement that all of the Japanese nation speak Japanese, so the Ainu found themselves pressured to give up speaking Ainu and to adopt Japanese. Curiously, in order to justify assimilation of the Ainu (and the Ryuukyuans in the south) and to claim these groups as part of an ethnically uniform nation, the idea was developed that the Ainu and the Ryuukyuans were not foreigners at all, but actually were Japanese in their underlying ethnicity—Japanese who simply had been separated from the rest of the Japanese nation at some earlier point in time, causing apparent differences to arise in their language and culture (Morris-Suzuki 1996: 64). Linguistic and cultural 'assimilation' of the Ainu and Ryuukyuans was therefore simply a form of guidance back to the Japanese nation and their origins.

The idea that the Ainu were originally Japanese has no independent support, and was simply used as an excuse to impose linguistic uniformity across the nation. So rigorous were the 20th-century efforts to substitute Japanese for Ainu that the Ainu language has now all but disappeared, with only a few language enthusiasts (who are mostly ethnic Japanese, not Ainu) having any ability to speak the language. The 1997 official government recognition that the Ainu are a distinct ethnic minority and not ethnically Japanese came too late for the decline in Ainu to be turned around, and this instance of sustained pressure on a language has been so intense that there is almost no chance that it will revive, despite the cessation of attempts to suppress the language and its associated culture. Unlike the situation in Taiwan and Nepal, where languages suppressed by policies of assimilation have now been restored to their earlier vitality, sadly the Ainu language seems doomed to disappear as a living language, as the Ainu people are no longer able to speak it. In the next chapter we will see more of this phenomenon of language endangerment and death, which is becoming very widespread in modern times, due to a range of factors and pressures.

The benefits of doing nothing: how a hands-off 'policy' can be successful

As a way to end our consideration of different cases of language planning on a rather more positive note, we can briefly mention a 'policy' which is the complete opposite of assimilation and language suppression, and how it may be surprisingly successful—the decision *not* to promote a language into any official/national role, and to let it grow naturally among a national population.

In the West African state of **Senegal**, the most widespread of the country's indigenous languages is called **Wolof**. This language is the mother tongue of 40% of the Senegalese population, and is spoken as a second language by a further 50%. McLaughlin (2008) notes that the growing use of Wolof in Senegal has established it as dominant to such a degree that it is 'clearly functioning as a de facto national language', and in fact it is regularly referred to as the national language of Senegal, although officially it has no higher, more special status than Senegal's other indigenous languages. Additionally, any proposals to formally give Wolof a special role have been strongly resisted by various politicians. McLaughlin (2008) suggests that the remarkably successful growth of Wolof—what she refers to as 'the creeping Wolofization of the state'—is largely due to the government *not* giving it any higher status than other languages. As there has been no special privileging of Wolof at the governmental level, people cannot legally dispute its increased use, and Wolof has continued to develop naturally throughout Senegal. Wolof is consequently an interesting case of a language which is coming to be a successful national language and symbol of Senegalese identity without any official assistance, and it may well be developing so effectively because there have been no explicit attempts to privilege it above other languages. In **Mali**, a similar situation has been developing with the language **Bambara**, which is spoken by 40% of the population as their first language, and by a further 40% as a second language, such growth having occurred without any official language planning. A hands-off policy of letting languages develop naturally into new roles binding populations together and facilitating widespread communication may be a useful way to avoid language-related conflict in multi-ethnic states, though the direction of such growth is clearly unpredictable and cannot be assured.

Conclusions and review

In both emerging and long-established states, language has the ability to play an important symbolic role as the national language of a state's population, and also a major utilitarian role as its official language. Whenever languages are officially promoted into such roles, the question of equity arises—whether or not the selection and widespread promotion of a particular language results in a fully inclusive sharing of opportunities in everyday life and participation in a targeted national identity. This chapter has highlighted a range of approaches to the planning of national and official languages instituted by governments in different countries, and how these policies may impact the development of independent nationhood in both positive and negative ways. Examining the kind of patterns that frequently occur, we find that different population and language configurations may lead to different kinds of attempts to deal with the national/official language issue, as summarized in the following.

In largely homogenous populations such as Japan, Italy, Iceland, Somalia, and Bangladesh, the choice of a single national official language is straightforward and therefore has the potential to be quickly exploited to generate strong feelings of national identity and belonging to a single, distinct nation. In certain cases, a national language may even become the most important marker of national identity for a people, as with the Slovak language, which, in the 20th century, was used as the primary means to drive Slovak nationalism in the absence of other strong markers of shared national identity such as the historical occupation of a single independent territory (Törnquist-Plewa 2000; see also the similar case of Polish, described in the same work).

In multi-ethnic states where a single large majority ethnic group is present, such as Thailand or Vietnam, where over 90% of the population is ethnically Thai and Viet, there is often a broad pragmatic acceptance by other smaller minorities that the majority language may have a natural position as the official or national language of the state, and minorities typically learn the majority national/official language as a means to gain better access to resources such as education and government employment, just as smaller minorities may learn and make use of regional languages or dialects in large countries such as China and India. In multi-ethnic states where the most numerous single ethno-linguistic group does not constitute such a proportionally large majority in a population, and perhaps does not even make up 50% of the population, it might be expected that a single-language model (unilingualism) might be avoided due to issues of potential inter-ethnic competition and jealousy. However, the strong desire to implement a single-language model has in fact also led to various attempts to promote the language of significant but non-majority indigenous groups as the single national and official language of a country. As we have seen, these initiatives have frequently met with much less success and have been seen to provide unfair advantages to mother tongue speakers of the language, as in Sri Lanka, Pakistan, and Taiwan under the KMT (see also India's post-independence attempt to install Hindi as the country's national language, described in Amritavalli and Jayaseelan 2007, and the promotion of Pilipino/Filipino in the Philippines, discussed in Hau and Tinio 2003, Gonzales 2007). By way of contrast, the most successful single-language policies developed in states with no very large majority group have often been those in which leaderships have selected as national/official language the language of a smaller indigenous group with relatively little power, as in Indonesia with Malay, and Tanzania with Swahili (Topan 2008), both cases where the promotion of a budding trade lingua franca as national official language has been seen to offer good new equal advantages to all the population.

An alternative to the single-language model in other states has been the ambitious pursuit of linguistic pluralism and the parallel extension of elevated linguistic privileges to a number of languages in an attempt to accord equal status and linguistic rights to a range of large minorities. Good examples of such a policy are Singapore, Switzerland, and India (with its recognition of many regional languages as local official languages).

A further attempted solution to the challenge of establishing and spreading a common language among ethnically mixed populations, mentioned in our discussion of unilingual policies, has been the selection of a non-indigenous language such as English or French as an ethnically neutral official language, this being particularly common in post-colonial Africa. The success of language planning in states with extremely complex populations needs to be measured in different ways from that in ethnically more homogenous states, where national languages can be used to vigorously stimulate the growth of a unifying national identity. When the choice of a single indigenous language as national official language does not seem to be possible, and a non-indigenous language is instead recognized as a state's single official language, the goals of language planning are rather different, and primarily focus on maintaining peaceful relations among a population and reducing the possibility that language-related issues can lead to internal conflict, while feelings of belonging to a single nation are gradually developed by a range of means. To the extent that the pragmatic selection of English, French, or another non-indigenous language as the official language of a heterogeneous state helps minimize ethnic discord and offers equal opportunities to all its groups, such a policy can be considered a successful instance of language planning, achieving more modest, but realistic goals than may be possible in ethnically homogenous populations. The choice of a non-indigenous language for a prominent official role is also one which brings with it challenges relating to the difficulty of learning a non-indigenous language with different kinds of linguistic structures, and the symbolic connections that Western European languages may still have to memories of previous colonial powers and foreign dominance. In certain instances, such policies may additionally result in the development of local elites who are monolingual in the official language, and are perceived not to be in touch with the rest of the nation, being unable to speak any indigenous language, as has occurred, for example, with English in Pakistan (Ayres 2003) and Singapore (Simpson 2007c). However, an interesting post-word on the use of languages such as English or French as neutral official languages is that such languages may over time undergo a process of indigenization, absorbing words and intonation patterns from local languages and developing away from standard English and French into highly distinctive, non-European 'national' forms of these languages, such as Ghanean English (Anyidoho and Kropp Dakubu 2008) and Abidjanais French in Ivory Coast (Knutsen 2008). Although foreign in origin, with the help of local 'mutations', such languages in many places are showing signs of beginning to help signal new national identities and are increasingly being viewed by their speakers as local, not outsider languages. We will have more to say on highly adjusted localized forms of English—'World Englishes'—and how these are being appropriated as indigenous languages by other populations in chapter 6.

Finally, and relating to the symbolic goal of using language to engineer broad new loyalties to states as their identities develop, the overviews of Taiwan in the 20th century and Nepal under the Panchayat regime confirm that coercing a population to adopt a language, even for long periods of time, frequently does not eradicate the desire to rekindle the wider use of publicly suppressed home languages, or deeply embed a new national identity associated with an imposed language, and 'forbidden' languages may well bounce back with great vigor once equal linguistic rights are made available to a population. National language policies are therefore only as effective as a means to stimulate cohesiveness in a population as the degree to which other rights and opportunities are also offered equally to the citizens of a state.

In closing the current chapter, one general consequence of the establishment of official and national languages that can be usefully highlighted is that such a process creates a hierarchy of languages—official and national languages are privileged with having roles and statuses that other languages (and dialects) in a state do not have. In the next chapter will see how the growth of certain languages in major roles may have a significant impact on the maintenance of smaller languages and may lead to changing patterns of language use and loss, even contributing heavily to the full disappearance of languages—'language death'.

Suggestions for further reading and activities

1. Try to find out more about Switzerland's policy of multiple official languages. How does this system work in everyday life? In which domains are its official languages recognized for use (government administration, education, law, etc.)? As far as you can ascertain, is there fully equal treatment of all four of Switzerland's four official languages? Have there ever been problems with Switzerland's policy of linguistic pluralism?
2. Find out more about the idea of 'language/linguistic rights' using the following reading:

    Spolsky, Bernard. 2004. Language rights. Chapter 8 in *Language policy*. Cambridge: Cambridge University Press, 113–132.

3. Consider the following list of ten words, which have all come into the English language in modern times. Pick any two languages and find out what words these languages use to refer to the items in the list. Then try to figure out, using your small sample, whether the languages you have picked seem to favor the use of language-internal or language-external sources to create new words.

camera	*computer*	*elevator*	*telephone*	*television*
drone	*microwave*	*hamburger*	*selfie*	*jeans*

4. Read the following chapter and discuss the role of Spanish and indigenous languages in official uses in countries in Latin America. What types of language policy trends in Latin America does the chapter describe?

    García, Ofelia, López, Dina, and Carmina Makar. 2010. Latin America. Chapter 22 in Joshua Fishman (ed.), *Handbook of language and ethnic identity*. Oxford: Oxford University Press, 353–373.

5. Use the internet and sources you can find there to research the term 'elite closure'. What does this term refer to?
6. Nation-building can make use of a number of different ways to build and strengthen national identity: emphasis on a shared language, adherence to a common religion, belonging to a single ethnicity/race, and/or the historical or present sharing of a common territory. Which of these do you think can be best made use of to distinguish a population's national identity, and why?
7. Read about language planning in sub-Saharan Africa in chapter 4 of Ayo Bamgbose's 1991 book, *Language and the Nation*, and discuss the kinds of policies proposed in the chapter.
8. National language planning in the Philippines is commonly considered not to have been successful. Familiarize yourself with the background of the selection of Pilipino/Filipino as the country's national language (and one of its two official languages) in Hau and Tinio (2003) Gonzales (2007). Then, using the knowledge you have gained in this chapter, try to develop your own national language planning proposal for the Philippines back in 1946, when independence was achieved. In other words, imagine you could go back in time and substitute a different policy for the policy adopted and developed following independence—what would this policy be? Justify your choices with support from other instances of language planning that have been discussed.

3

Languages under Pressure
Minority Groups and Language Loss

Introduction: common patterns of language shift in minority groups

This chapter considers changing patterns of language use among comparatively small linguistic communities located within larger language majorities. Typically, such configurations lead to the occurrence of 'language shift' and language loss, sometimes even leading to the full disappearance of languages—'language death'. The term 'language shift' refers to the observation that people frequently shift their daily speech away from the dominant or regular use of one language into the increased use of a different language. Language shift very often occurs with members of ethnolinguistic minority groups, and results in speakers using less and less of the language historically associated with their minority group, the 'ancestral' or 'heritage language' of the group, and switching to more frequent use of the language of some other larger group they are regularly in contact with—a local majority-group language.

An ethnic group may come to be a minority within a larger majority population in different ways. One common way in which minorities arise is through the voluntary physical relocation of members of a group away from their homeland into a different country or region where a larger group is present—the *migration* of speakers of one language into a concentrated population of speakers of another language. Such movement from an original homeland into a country or region dominated by a different ethnic group frequently occurs for economic reasons, as people seek better employment opportunities in a different location. It is also sometimes occasioned by political reasons, as members of one group flee persecution or conflict in their home country and seek asylum in a second country perceived to be more stable. This process of relocation gives rise to the creation of *immigrant minorities* in the country/region moved to, and frequently results in a situation in which the heritage language of immigrants (their mother tongue) is different from the language of the new local majority group, as for example when Italian and Polish migrants first came to the United States, or when Turkish people emigrated to Germany, or Koreans moved to Japan (prior to World War II), all as economic migrants. Language shift then commonly occurs among such immigrants, as will shortly be described.

A second way in which ethnolinguistic groups may come to be minorities within a larger majority population does not result from migration or movement of the minority groups themselves, but from expansion of the territory controlled by a neighboring larger group, engulfing and absorbing the homeland of other smaller groups. Where such incorporation of smaller ethnolinguistic groups into a surrounding state established and dominated by a more populous group has occurred, the term *indigenous minority* is commonly used, recognizing the fact that such groups have long lived in their current location, now territorially absorbed into a larger new state. Indigenous minorities have arisen around the world wherever the power of an expanding group has led to a significant growth in the territory it controls and subsequently populates, as, for example, when the Han Chinese empire grew and incorporated the lands and populations of many non-Chinese ethnolinguistic groups, when European-American settlers expanded their control over areas inhabited by Native American tribes, and when the Japanese nation claimed the island of Hokkaido with its Ainu population to be officially part of Japan. In all such instances, speakers of the new minority languages have either been drawn or pressured to use the newly established majority language, and have experienced a shifting away from use of their original heritage language, to different degrees.

A third way that new ethnic minority groups are created within larger populations without any movement of the former is through the realignment of two nations' borders, sometimes occurring as the result of peace settlements and treaties concluded after a war between two countries. A victorious nation may occasionally demand a portion of territory from a defeated neighbor as a 'prize' following a war, resulting in the transfer of both a region and its population from one country to another. Where the dominant languages spoken in the two countries are different, the inhabitants of the transferred region will become a new minority in the country they have been added to, as, for example, when a portion of Hungary was reassigned to Austria following World War I, and the Hungarian-speaking population of this area became a new linguistic minority within German-speaking Austria. A second example of such a process is the ceding to the United States of Mexican territory corresponding to California and six other present-day states in the Treaty of Guadalupe-Hidalgo in 1848, which transferred a Spanish-speaking population into a larger English-dominant nation, creating a (sizable) Hispanic minority in the Southwest of the USA.[1] This additional way in which new minority groups arise is in some respects similar to the creation of indigenous minorities via the territorial expansion of a more dominant group, such as the Han-Chinese occupation of lands belonging to other non-Chinese groups, but also different from this in one important way. When, for example, the Ainu were incorporated into Japan and the Navajo became absorbed into the USA, the entirety of these groups became part of a larger national population, and the size of the full Ainu- and Navajo-speaking groups was relatively small in comparison to the size of the Japanese- and English-speaking populations

---

1. The fact that the Hispanic population in the Southwest of the USA is long settled in this area has been neatly captured in the observation that: 'We [Mexican-Americans] didn't cross the border. It crossed over us.' Such a remark has frequently been repeated in contexts of the political discussion of immigration and attitudes toward Mexican Americans, and famously occurred in the Oscar-winning movie *Crash* in 2004.

which engulfed them. However, when part of Hungary was ceded to Austria in 1918 and part of Mexico to the USA in 1848, a large population of Hungarian- and Spanish-speakers still remained in Hungary and Mexico, respectively, and the total populations of Hungary and Austria and Mexico and USA were much closer in size than those of the Ainu versus the Japanese, or the Tibetans compared to the Han. The Austrian annexation of a portion of Hungarian-speakers and the transfer of part of Mexico's population of Spanish-speakers to the USA thus established these groups as new minorities in Austria and the USA, but ones which spoke the same language as a large adjacent population just across the realigned border, potentially creating a rather different dynamic from the case of indigenous minorities like the Ainu who have no links to other larger populations of the same ethnic background. In this third case of minority creation, it is, however, again found that language shift occurs, though sometimes masked by new patterns of immigration, as we will later see in the case of Spanish in the Southwest of the USA.

The three-generation pattern of language shift and loss

When people migrate to other countries and find themselves surrounded by a new language spoken by a longer-established majority of the local population, the mother tongue language of immigrants frequently undergoes decay and gradually becomes lost, as the linguistic dominance of the majority population asserts itself. The speed at which this process of language shift and loss occurs across generations is significantly fast, and quite predictable in many instances, having been found to take place in highly similar ways through three successive generations of immigrant minority groups (Fishman 1966; Veltman 1983).

Generation 1 speakers of a particular language move to a new country/region, often for economic or political reasons, and frequently learn small amounts of the local majority language, developing 'survival' language skills—enough of the majority language for them to be able to function successfully in everyday life and work. At home and with family and friends, Generation 1 speakers will typically continue to use their mother tongue, the heritage language, and so will not develop a strong proficiency in the local majority language for use in social relations. They will consequently not be fully comfortable using this language other than when necessary.

Generation 2, the children of generation 1, born in the country/region migrated to, often become bilingual and are able to understand and speak both the heritage language of their parents and the local majority language. Proficiency in the former comes from regular communication with their parents (and other similar Generation 1 speakers) in the heritage language, as members of Generation 1 prefer to use their mother tongue for acts of social communication. An ability to speak the local majority language results from constant heavy exposure to this language in school and with same-age friends and acquaintances who are monolingual speakers of the local majority language.

Generation 3, the grandchildren of Generation 1, often fail to acquire a strong competence in the original heritage language of Generation 1 and become heavily monolingual in the language of the local majority. This generation knows that its parents are good speakers of the local majority language, and so feels that it does not need to learn the heritage language to communicate successfully in the home. As a strong, native-speaker ability in the local majority language arises naturally through its use in school and in interactions with same-age friends from other ethnic backgrounds, young members of Generation 3 often fail to see any reason to learn and use the original heritage language, and may only use whatever abilities they do have in this language for communication with their grandparents, whose proficiency in the local majority language may have remained low. Frequently it is reported that members of Generation 3 have difficulties communicating with Generation 1, when skills in the heritage language have not been acquired by the former, and the latter have not become fluent speakers of the local majority language.

A simple illustration of this three-generation pattern of language shift and loss can be given with the example of speakers of the Southeast Asian languages Cambodian and Hmong, who relocated to the USA in sizable numbers in the latter half of the 20th century, following the Vietnam War. After their arrival in the USA, these new immigrants learned survival language skills in the local majority language, English, for use in work, which in many cases was relatively low-paid employment not requiring fluency in English. The children of these immigrants, born in the USA and educated through English grew up regularly as bilinguals, using Cambodian and Hmong in the home with their parents, and English in most activities outside the home (though visits to places of worship and businesses owned by older speakers of Cambodian and Hmong may naturally have led to the some use of the heritage language outside the home). Typically, in virtue of acquiring a strong, native-like ability in English from interactions in school, English developed in many second-generation Cambodian- and Hmong-Americans as the preferred language for acts of communication with similar aged friends and acquaintances, even if the latter might be proficient speakers of the same heritage language. Siblings therefore often chose to communicate with each other in English, despite being bilingual in English and Cambodian/Hmong. The grandchildren of the original Cambodian and Hmong immigrants, born in the USA and raised with English all around them in their daily life and with parents who are able to speak English well, have largely developed as monolingual speakers of English, with little ability to speak Cambodian or Hmong. Knowledge of the heritage language has consequently been lost to a high degree in the course of three generations, in a pattern that has been observed to be very common among immigrant groups in all parts of the world.

With regard to indigenous minority groups, patterns of language shift and loss have also regularly been observed, in some instances with drastic effects, leading to the complete disappearance of a language, as we will see later in this chapter. However, the rate at which language shift occurs in indigenous minorities is often less predictable than with many immigrant groups, where a three-generation cycle of shift and loss frequently occurs. Indigenous minorities, such as the Tibetans or Mongolians in China, or the Sami in Finland, are long-established communities with many speakers living together, and such communities may not necessarily be greatly disturbed by incorporation of their territory into a larger country. How swiftly and significantly patterns of language shift occur in such groups will depend on the degree to which traditional ways of life, including language and culture, are intruded upon by the surrounding majority population and their political leadership, and this may vary from country to country, causing different rates of language maintenance and loss. By way of contrast, immigrants who undergo relocation to a new country find themselves suddenly living in a different, new world where there may not be a large community of speakers of the same heritage language, and many aspects of life, including the securing of employment, immediately have to be carried out in a new language. It is this sudden, dramatic change which causes rapid, cross-generational language loss in an almost inevitable way, as just described. Where variation in the common three-generation pattern of language shift and loss sometimes occurs, this is due to the potential influence of a range of factors which interact with language use, in some cases serving to accelerate the speed of loss, so that members of Generation 2 may fail to develop native skills in the heritage language, and in other instances helping to slow it down, so that Generation 3 is actually still able to communicate quite well in the language of its grandparents. We will now consider these primary influences on language maintenance and shift, noting that the presence and force of such properties is also relevant for the study of language shift in indigenous minority groups.

WHICH GENERATION DO I BELONG TO?

If at some point in the past your family relocated to where you now live from another country, you might want to clarify which particular generation you belong to, in order to compare your experiences with the 'typical' three-generation pattern of language shift and loss. The following is a simple guide to help figure this out for prototypical Generations 1–3, imagining that you now live in the USA (substitute other countries for the USA where relevant).

Generation 1	*Generation 2*	*Generation 3*
You were born outside the USA.	You were born in the USA.	You were born in the USA.
You now live in the USA.	You currently live in the USA.	You currently live in the USA.
	Your parents were born outside the USA.	Your parents were born in the USA.
		Your grandparents were born outside the USA.

Example I: Shelley was born and grew up in the USA, but her parents were both born in Rome and grew up in Italy, moving to the USA before Shelley was born. Shelley is a second-generation Italian-American.

Example II: Paul and his parents were all born in the USA. Paul's grandparents were born in Shanghai and grew up in China before moving to the USA as young adults. Paul is a third-generation Chinese-American.

> **Further distinctions.** Some linguists and sociologists studying patterns of language shift among immigrant populations have suggested that it is useful to assume a finer range of categorizations than simply three different generations (i.e., Generation 1, Generation 2, and Generation 3). It is now increasingly common to read of studies of young people referred to as members of '**Generation 1.5**', who immigrated to a new country at an early age, before their teen years (Kang 2004; Rumbaut 2004; Lao and Lee 2009). According to the strict three-generation categorization just presented, such people should be described as members of Generation 1, having been born overseas, but because of the fact that they spend a significant portion of their early life in the country their families have emigrated to, they are not like typical members of Generation 1, and develop much stronger skills in the local majority language than members of Generation 1 who arrive in a new host country after adolescence. They also tend to experience a much stronger sense of cultural integration in the host country than is felt by prototypical Generation 1 members, though the situation is complex, and we will return to consider this in a little more detail later in the chapter.
>
> It has also (less frequently) been proposed that those who immigrate to a country at a very early age, between 0–5 years old, should be referred to as **Generation 1.75**, as their behavioral patterning is very close to prototypical members of Generation 2, while those who arrive as immigrants in their middle to late adolescence, between the ages of 13–17, can be categorized as belonging to a **Generation 1.25**, as they are closer in their linguistic and cultural behavior to Generation 1, though their skills in the local majority language are still more advanced than typical members of Generation 1. If such a finer range of distinctions is adopted, the term Generation 1.5 can be reserved for young people settling in a new country between the ages of 6–12.

What causes members of a minority group to shift away from (or retain) use of their mother tongue?

Certain forces and factors present in the sociolinguistic environment inhabited by minority groups serve to accelerate language shift and loss, while other aspects of an individual's personal situation may help slow down the rate of such processes. We will first note a range of factors which have negative effects on heritage language maintenance in the presence of a dominant majority language, and then consider what may stimulate the maintenance of a minority language across generations in more positive ways.

Factors undermining the maintenance and transmission of minority languages
Official discouragement or suppression of minority languages

In order to attempt to promote unity in a country and to control the power of smaller ethnic groups, a government may actively discourage or, in extreme cases, outlaw the use of minority languages, either totally, or in certain key domains of life, such as in schools, the media, and government-run buildings. We have already seen several examples of this dominant control of smaller languages in chapter 2, when we examined Taiwan, Nepal, and the case of the Ainu in Japan. Many further instances of the suppression of minority languages for political reasons have occurred around the world at different times and in different places, each time reducing the opportunities for the speakers of such languages to use and transmit learning of their heritage language or dialect to subsequent generations. Additional examples of official attempts to disrupt the use of non-majority languages include the following:

(a) The US governmental initiative during the 19th and early 20th centuries to replace knowledge of Native American languages with English through the forced placement of young Native Americans in boarding schools where only English was allowed to be spoken, with punishments meted out for any use of Native American languages.
(b) The closure of schools teaching Chinese to ethnically Chinese people in Thailand and Indonesia during portions of the 20th century, in attempts to assimilate Chinese minorities to a fully Thai/Indonesian national identity.
(c) The suppression of non-standard, regional varieties of French during the French Revolution, from 1794 onward, in order to enforce the use of Parisian standard French throughout the French population.
(d) The denigration of non-Castilian varieties of Spanish (and also Basque) during General Franco's period of rule in Spain in the 20th century, as a way to promote the national use of Castilian Spanish.

Social pressure to discontinue the use of a minority language

In order to 'fit in' to surrounding society and be accepted, young people in particular may feel a pressure to use the language of the majority group where they live. This is especially so in the case of immigrant groups. When immigrants join a longer established population, they may often feel that they need to conform to the new society in which they live, so as not to stand out as 'different' and be the target of prejudicial treatment. One obvious way of conforming is to learn and use the language of the new society and give up the use of an ancestral language. Indeed, children from minority groups going to schools where most other students speak only the local majority language often report that they deliberately do not speak their heritage language with others from the same minority background in school, for fear that this will single them out for mockery, social exclusion, and bullying. Use of the heritage language therefore becomes restricted to contexts in which it is absolutely necessary for communication, and the majority language is spoken at all other times, as expressed in the following comments from young Chinese children in the USA in Zhang and Slaughter-Defoe (2009: 90): 'I don't want to [speak Chinese]. I don't want to because my friends are going to hear me talking Chinese and they will kill me.' 'I only speak Chinese when I have to.'

An example of an entire ethnic minority group which has experienced heavy language shift and loss due to earlier pressure to disguise its ethnicity is the population of Japanese-Americans and Japanese-Canadians present in North America. During World War II, Japanese citizens of the USA and Canada were placed in internment camps until 1945, and subsequently switched to a dominant use of English after being released so as not to be identified with the previous 'enemy' in the war. Currently, as a result of this self-imposed suppression of its heritage language, ethnic Japanese are the most linguistically assimilated of all the major East Asian heritage groups in the USA and Canada, with much less general proficiency in its heritage language than Chinese- and Korean-Americans.

Quite generally, speakers of minority languages of all ages may be made to feel ashamed of their mother tongues, as these are often suggested to be low in value and inferior to the majority language of a society, with the result that immigrants and other indigenous minorities develop negative feelings toward their ancestral languages and use them less and less.

Switching to increased use of a majority language for reasons of employment

In order to get a job, it may be necessary to speak another language. People often shift either language or location in order to get work, and a shift in location will often naturally result in a shift of language. For example, Zapotec speakers in Mexico may find that they can receive a better rate of pay if they accept a job which requires communication to be in Spanish, and there may in fact be relatively few jobs that permit only the use of Zapotec. The majority of a person's working day may therefore need to be carried out with Spanish, embedding this language further among minorities such as the Zapotec and potentially weakening a person's command of his or her heritage language, which may become confined to use in the home if the majority language, Spanish, is also used in other domains of life such as commercial activities and interactions with government officials. Alternatively, Zaptoec speakers may migrate away from their home villages to larger cities located outside areas speaking Zapotec in order to find work, and find themselves in a fully Spanish-speaking environment, which will again serve to erode their spontaneous abilities in the heritage language, especially if the decision is made to settle permanently in a Spanish-dominant city. Employment-related reasons for language shift are observed to be very common and conspire with other changes in a person's environment to reduce the opportunities a person has for use of a minority language.

Switching to increased use of a majority language for reasons of social status

Another factor which has the power to decrease the use of a heritage language and increase daily use of a local majority language is the projection of personal status in society which results from language use. Larger, majority languages such as English, French, Spanish, Russian, and Mandarin Chinese are regularly associated with higher levels of social prestige than smaller minority languages, and people who show themselves able to speak such languages are often perceived to be more successful and to sound more educated than those whose speech is restricted to the use of a minority language. Where ambitious-minded members of a minority group are anxious to claim higher social status through the use of language and to project an image of being successful, this frequently leads to increased use of a majority language not only in the place of work (or education), but also in social interactions where language choice is fully free. Such a trend toward more frequent use of a majority language for image-related reasons has been found to be particularly common among young members of minority groups who may be focused on creating a more affluent life for themselves than that enjoyed by typical older members of the heritage language community. As an illustration of this, it has been observed that young people in China living outside of the northern Mandarin Chinese belt in areas traditionally dominated by other regional forms of Chinese are now switching to the use of Mandarin Chinese in all areas of life because Mandarin is strongly associated with modernity, with being educated, and with having the potential to get ahead in life. As young people increasingly substitute Mandarin for other regional varieties of Chinese in their social interactions, their proficiency in the mother tongue variety of their parents is being significantly weakened, and, in all likelihood, this may not get transmitted well to their own children in future years.

Families of mixed ethnicities and languages

If the parents of children come from different language groups, and one of these is the language of the local majority group, and the other a minority language, it is uncommon for the heritage language to be learned well by the children of such families. Most frequently, the language used at home between a married couple of mixed language background will be that of the local majority. For example, where Korean immigrants in Japan have intermarried with local Japanese people, they and their children almost inevitably use Japanese as the standard language of the home. Elsewhere, in the USA, the first wave of Korean immigrants in the early 20th century, mostly men settling in Hawaii, regularly engaged in intermarriage with local non-Koreans who spoke English and Hawai'i Creole, and this resulted in rapid language shift and a failure to transmit Korean to their offspring. This can be contrasted with the second major occurrence of Korean immigration to the USA from the 1970s onward, when both men and women settled in different parts of the USA (the West, the Northwest, the South, and North Central areas) and intermarriage with non-Koreans was less common. Due to more frequent marriage between Koreans in the USA in recent decades, Korean language maintenance rates have been significantly higher than in earlier times. The occurrence of intermarriage between members of a minority group and members of the local majority-language group therefore often speeds up the process of language shift and breaks the transmission of heritage languages to subsequent generations, unless great efforts are made to help facilitate this.

The influence of school

Even if a mother makes a major effort to teach her children a language which is different from the local majority-population language, children will be heavily influenced by the language they hear and use in school and normally switch to that language as their first language over a period of time. Indeed, in many families where parents speak a language different from the local majority language, the latter first spreads into the home environment via the children, as they learn and use the majority language in school. Typically this leads to the parents using the majority language together with the children over time, especially if the parents have to use some of this language in their place of work. Parents may also often feel that speaking the local majority language with their children in the home will help their children become more proficient speakers of the majority language, which will benefit them in school, and later help them compete well for better employment opportunities. As a consequence, use of the heritage language in the home may fall into disuse once children are regularly attending schools where classes are taught through the local majority language.

Why should I learn Chinese? Children failing to understand the value of a heritage language

In instances where parents make considerable efforts to speak to their children regularly in their heritage language, and also provide them with opportunities to learn the heritage language outside the home, it is often reported that children fail to see the relevance of the heritage language for their lives, and complain that learning the heritage language is a time-consuming chore with no obvious rewards. If children know that their parents have at least some proficiency in the local majority language, and they can communicate with their parents in this language, children often simply don't understand why they should also learn a second language, whose use is apparently much more restricted. A lack of personal motivation to acquire a minority language among children is an additional reason why the transmission of heritage languages is often difficult and unsuccessful.

Factors helping the maintenance and transmission of minority languages

While it is common for minority-group languages to be lost among immigrant families across three generations, as young members of the third generation shift heavily into use of the local majority language, there are certain factors which can help slow down this process and assist in a better rate of transmission of heritage languages to rising generations.

Size and concentration of minority groups

Language shift occurs more quickly in smaller minority groups. Where there is a significantly large minority group concentrated in a single city/area, it may be able to maintain its language longer than the otherwise typical pattern of three generational loss. For example, the large Chinatown areas in San Francisco and New York, and Koreatown in Los Angeles, remain strong as centers of Cantonese and Korean, whereas other speakers of these languages who live apart from each other may often switch to English as a replacement for Chinese or Korean significantly faster. One late 20th-century study carried out in Los Angeles, San Francisco, and New York established that almost all ethnic Koreans living in the Koreatowns in these cities still used Korean as their primary home language.

A further good example of a high concentration of speakers of a particular minority language in one geographical area is the Garden Grove community in Orange County, California, where a large number of ethnically Vietnamese people live in close proximity to each other. This clustering has resulted in knowledge of Vietnamese being comparatively good among younger generation speakers born in the USA. The continued transmission of Vietnamese is facilitated by a number of factors: the possibility of finding work in local businesses where an ability to speak Vietnamese is valued, the availability of Vietnamese-language television broadcasts and newspapers, Vietnamese Parent-Teacher Associations, community cultural events (such as Vietnamese New Year), and the use of Vietnamese in local churches and temples. While an ongoing shift to English has still been observed among young inhabitants of Garden Grove, the rate of shift is significantly slower than in smaller, more isolated Vietnamese communities.

Fresh blood in the community: the arrival of new monolingual immigrants

The continued arrival of new immigrants with native speaker languages skills helps maintain the buoyancy of heritage languages in many communities. Many new immigrants may be largely monolingual speakers of a language of their country of origin, while others may come with some ability in the majority language of the country they have moved to. All such immigrants will probably prefer to use their mother tongue in interactions with others who have some ability in this language, and hence stimulate second- and third-generation members of the minority group to use their heritage language skills. As we will see later in this chapter with two short case studies of the Mirpuri Pakistanis in northern England and the Hispanic population in Los Angeles, the addition of new first-generation immigrants to long-established minority groups is one of the most important ways in which use of a heritage language is kept well alive.

Keeping one's distance: language retention in medium-sized isolated communities

When speakers of minority languages live far apart from each other among populations who only speak the local majority language, language shift is very fast. For example, Cantonese-speaking Chinese who have settled in rural towns in the United Kingdom to set up restaurant businesses may be quite isolated from other ethnically Chinese people, and not have the opportunity to use Cantonese much outside the family. Second-generation members of such groups will quickly switch to very dominant use of the majority language, English. However, being isolated in rural areas can sometimes also be highly beneficial for the transmission of a heritage language to younger generations, if there is a sizable enough community of the heritage language in one location. Being cut off from larger populations of majority-language speakers in the countryside can help a community function without much need for the majority language in its daily life, and succeed in passing its minority language on to children growing up in the community. For example, in the USA, the Amish people have been very successful in maintaining and passing on 'Pennsylvania Dutch', due to isolating themselves in rural areas, and similar success in the transmission of minority heritage languages has occurred in rural communities of French-speakers in northern Vermont, New Hampshire, and Maine, and Spanish-speakers in Texas, New Mexico, and Arizona.

Media availability in the minority language

A dramatic increase in the number of television channels and radio stations that can easily be accessed has been extremely advantageous for many minority groups, who can now frequently enjoy programming in their heritage language, both via new local television stations and, for immigrant minorities, also often via satellite, receiving television broadcasts in their ancestral language from the home country. For less prosperous, smaller indigenous minorities, whose community does not have the means to establish television programming in their language, radio stations are often a less expensive way to provide broadcasts in the minority language to members of the group and to reinforce understanding of the language through daily exposure to it in news and light entertainment programs. Similarly, the growth in (often free) heritage language newspapers and other forms of print media helps maintain the literacy of immigrant minorities able to read their ancestral language, and sustain the presence of the language among the immigrant group (though sadly a common feature of second- and third-generation immigrants is a low rate of literacy in their heritage language, when compared with their abilities to speak it—often learning to read and write in the heritage language is a low priority for immigrants, especially when this involves needing to master a different form of script or alphabet, and is seen as much less important than the ability to speak the language).

Family visits to the home country

Another useful mechanism for the reinforcement of heritage languages among immigrant minorities is the making of regular trips back to visit family relations in the home country originally emigrated from. Where such extended family members and other local people encountered in the home country are monolingual speakers in the language of the ethnic group, and unable to speak English, French, or whatever language dominates in the country immigrants have moved to, the latter will be obliged to make use of their heritage language to communicate. This provides important practice in the heritage language at the time of such visits, and also motivation to maintain heritage language skills when at home in anticipation of making trips back to the country of their ancestors and relatives.

Parents committed to the transmission of heritage languages to younger generations

It is absolutely critical for the success of language transmission from one generation to the next, especially from the second, bilingual generation of immigrants on to subsequent generations, that parents are committed to and enthusiastic about their children acquiring knowledge of the heritage language. Where parents have a strongly positive attitude toward their heritage language and are pro-active in communicating this to their offspring, children growing up exposed to a dominant local majority language will have a much better chance to develop a competence in the heritage language, and potentially do this even when being members of the third (or a later) generation of an immigrant family.

Parents from immigrant minority language groups who make efforts to help their children learn the group's heritage language typically do this for three types of reasons. First of all, many parents stress the *connection between language and ethnic identity*, and emphasize that is important for children to grow up with a knowledge of their group's culture and traditions. Learning and using the heritage language of the group is seen as a vital means for children to understand and appreciate their ethnic roots, and in various communities, such as the overseas Chinese, proficiency in the heritage language may even be held to be the most important symbol of belonging to an ethnic grouping (Liu 2008). With groups such as the Chinese and Koreans living in the USA and other countries, many parents feel that knowledge of the group's ethnic language is such an important expression of being Chinese or Korean that parents 'lose face' in front of others if their children are seen to be unable to speak and understand their ethnic languages—parents are perceived to have failed in their duty to raise their children with an appropriate awareness of their ethnicity (Shin 2005; Liu 2008). A second reason why children should make efforts to learn their heritage language, according to the parents of a number of immigrant groups, is its potential *value as a resource* to help secure better employment in the future, when children eventually graduate from school or college. It is stressed that being bilingual in the heritage language and the local majority language opens up a wide range of job opportunities which require a person to serve as an interface between members of the different language communities. Third, many parents in immigrant minority groups, and particularly first-generation immigrants, emphasize that knowledge of the heritage language is important for building and maintaining *family cohesion*. As the initial immigrants to a foreign country often do not develop very strong language skills in the local majority language, their only way of communicating in a deep and meaningful way with their offspring will be if their children become proficient in the heritage language and use it regularly in the home.

Different groups may possibly each place a different emphasis on these three important functions of a heritage language for rising generations, with certain different effects. For example, a study of ethnically Japanese parents in the USA revealed that they found family cohesion to be the most important reason for children to learn the heritage language of their parents, and not its value as a resource. Because of this, children were not pressed to learn written Japanese, as all that was needed in the home to maintain cohesion among family members of different generations was the ability to communicate in the spoken language. Similar attitudes have been found among other groups who are less focused on the outward, public projection of identity, and who do not prioritize the language-as-resource function of heritage languages.

Opportunities to learn the heritage language in school

Heritage language maintenance needs to be supported in the home, through regular interactions between parents and their children in the language, but it can also potentially be stimulated and further advanced through children's attendance at schools which teach the language, or use the language as a medium to teach other subjects. Some immigrant communities are able to send their children to schools offering bilingual education, which may lead to children developing a high level of proficiency in both the local majority language and their heritage language (more on this in chapter 7). In other communities, where bilingual education is not available, children may attend special schools focused on the heritage language and culture which hold classes either at weekends or in the evenings, after children have come home from their regular day schools which use the local majority language. Children attending such evening or weekend classes will practice and advance their abilities in the heritage language, and also have the opportunity to develop friendships and bonds with other children from the same ethnic background, which helps nurture a sense of shared cultural identity.

Despite the potential benefits of heritage-language schools, many children going to such schools indicate that they find it tiresome to have to go to further classes after regular school, and that they only do this in order to please or obey their parents. Such children fail to understand why learning the heritage language might be useful for them in a variety of ways, and may be resentful that these classes take up part of their leisure hours (Zhang and Slaughter-Defoe 2009). Interestingly, such rather negative attitudes often seem to undergo change with age and maturity. Although younger children from immigrant families may not be very enthusiastic about learning the heritage language and culture in evening and weekend classes, as these children become a little older and enter high school and later university, it is frequently noted that they develop a much stronger interest in their ethnic culture and identity, and turn into eager language-learners. In one representative study of ethnically Japanese students carried out in a high school in Los Angeles, Chinen and Tucker (2005) found a greater sense of Japanese ethnic identity emerging among the older pupils and concluded that

> ... the formation of ethnic identity requires a certain time for 'gestation' and even social maturity. One of the students we interviewed said, 'Compared to before, I have more Japanese friends, and I know more Japanese stuff. I feel like I'm becoming more Japanese. Next year, I may be even more Japanese.' (Chinen and Tucker 2005: 38)

Similarly, a report on ethnically Chinese students at university attending Chinese heritage language classes described in He (2006) notes that such students often said they disliked taking Chinese lessons when they were young, and at that time they were not at all interested in exploring their family background. However, later in early adulthood, they experienced a clear change in attitude and became very keen to find out about their cultural heritage and learn the language of their parents (see also Lee 2002 for parallel remarks on Korean students at university).

The Generation 4 Effect

In addition to the maturity effect on heritage language learning among members of younger generations, in which interest in heritage language and culture typically increases in late adolescence and early adulthood, there is also an influence of economic standing and security which impacts rising generations' interest in and engagement with their ethnolinguistic background, which can be referred to as the 'Generation 4 Effect.' Earlier in this chapter we noted that significant language shift frequently takes place across three generations among immigrant families. Generation 1 is heavily monolingual in the heritage language; members of Generation 2 are very often bilingual in the heritage language and the local majority language; and Generation 3 becomes dominant in the local majority language and may have little ability in the heritage language. Because of this poor knowledge of the original heritage language that Generation 3 speakers have, they commonly fail to pass the language on well to their own offspring. Generation 4 therefore grows up regularly with no home-cultivated knowledge of the language of its original ethnic group. Economically, however, due to the increasing integration into the local workforce that Generations 2 and 3 achieve with their competence in the local dominant language, Generation 4 often grows up with a higher degree of home prosperity than that enjoyed by previous generations.

Raised in such an environment of stabilized economic security, but aware of having a second ethnic identity, the children of Generation 3 may often be critical of their parents for having 'lost' the heritage language of their grandparents and try to set about learning this language where suitable means are available (normally, classes in the language offered by universities and community colleges). Consequently, once economic stability is achieved by a community, there is a common desire among its adolescent and young adult members to reconnect with and learn about their original ethnic identity, and because language is such an important component of ethnic identity, Generation 4 is often found to have a very positive attitude toward learning its group's heritage language. Economic security and personal maturity work together to produce individuals who are well-disposed toward heritage-language maintenance and revival.

Economic factors relating to stability and prosperity have also been found to affect indigenous minorities' attitudes toward maintenance of their ethnic languages. King (1999) studied two minority communities of the Saraguro people in Ecuador whose ethnic language is Quechua. One group lives in the district of Lagunas, next to the Pan-American Highway and a large town and commercial center populated by 'white' monolingual speakers of Spanish, where the Saraguros regularly find work. The other group lives in a more isolated area, Tambopamba, further away from other urban development, and is predominantly involved in agriculture. Language shift from Quechua to Spanish has occurred in both communities, but because the Saraguros in Lagunas have had much more contact with Spanish-speakers than those in Tambopamba, the loss of Quechua and switch to Spanish has been faster in Lagunas.

Previously, Quechua was highly stigmatized and often insultingly referred to by Spanish-speakers as the 'language of animals'. Although this induced negative feelings among the Saraguros toward Quechua in the past, and stimulated language shift into Spanish, in Lagunas the situation is now changing. As the Saraguros in Lagunas have had access to Spanish for a long time now, they have become fluent in the language, and Lagunas itself has over time developed into a prosperous and well-educated community. Now that economic and social security has been established, and abilities in Spanish are taken for granted, the status of Quechua in Lagunas has become quite different. Quechua is now viewed very positively as an important symbol of ethnic identity by the Lagunas Saraguros, who are proud of their ethnic origins and do not wish to assimilate to the 'white' population. Speaking Quechua is associated with holding 'hip' and progressive political views, and as most young adults who know Quechua have learned it through university courses, Quechua is also positively associated with the most highly educated and successful young members of the community. Due to such attitudes and renewed pride in Quechua, there are conscious attempts to revive the use of Quechua in Lagunas and make it more a part of everyday life. In Tambopamba, by way of contrast, there has been no similar economic success for the community, and Quechua is still associated with being rural, uneducated, and of low status, and Spanish is viewed as the desired language of socioeconomic development. As a result of this different perception of Quechua in Tambopamba, the use of Quechua in this community is different and is not being consciously revived in the way it is in Lagunas. A comparison of these two communities and their different attitudes toward their heritage language thus shows that positive attitudes toward language maintenance and revival may be closely tied with personal confidence (in this case, in Lagunas, the Saraguros' knowledge that they can speak Spanish fluently when necessary) and economic security. Heritage-language maintenance may thus thrive best when speakers have developed a comfortable, secure level of prosperity and the maturity to value their ancestral language as an important symbol of ethnicity.

This point can be usefully echoed still further with reports of the differing experiences of language transmission among immigrant communities in the USA. In He (2006) and several other studies, it has been observed that if a heritage language is spoken in the home between Generation 1 and Generation 2 because the former are unable to speak the local majority language well, members of Generation 2 are likely to perceive the heritage language as 'limiting rather than enriching' (He 2006: 19), meaning that use of the heritage language is forced by circumstances and not freely chosen in virtue of any positive 'enriching' qualities it may have. In other homes where parents have developed bilingual abilities yet choose to speak the heritage language with their children, rather than the local majority language, young learners tend to see the language in a more positive light and are more willing to use it with their parents.

All of the preceding factors have effects on the successful maintenance of heritage languages and speakers' shift into larger majority languages. While several highlight quite specific issues, a number of them relate very directly to the three 'pillars' of a general overarching theory of language maintenance known as the '**Capacity-Opportunity-Desire**' framework (Grin 1990; Lo Bianco 2008), which has been used to analyze the success rate of many communities in the retention of ethnic languages. 'Capacity' refers to the abilities that individuals develop in a heritage language, through formal teaching in schools and colleges and informal interactions with family members and friends. 'Opportunity' refers to the availability of areas and activities in daily life where the heritage language can naturally be used—for example, in local stores, places of worship, restaurants, and communal sporting activities. 'Desire' is simply the eagerness speakers experience to use a heritage language for various reasons—for example, the desire to communicate with older family members, the desire to explore one's ethnic identity, the desire to use a heritage language in business or education. What is particularly distinctive and important about the Capacity-Opportunity-Desire (COD) framework is that it argues that *all three components* are necessary for the successful maintenance and transmission of minority languages across generations. Whereas some communities may think that providing regular classes in a heritage language in schools may be sufficient to help younger generations become speakers of the language, the COD approach argues that (extensive) opportunities for the use of the language outside school must also be enabled—adults must be prepared to speak the language at home with their children, communal activities using the language must regularly be arranged—and a positive desire to use the language must be cultivated among young learners. Otherwise, if all three COD components are not facilitated, it is predicted that language transmission and revival will not be effective or sustainable for long. Consequently, while we have listed a range of factors that may positively encourage the maintenance of a minority language among rising generations (and other factors that may hinder this), it is useful to remember that minority communities should really attempt a 'broad spectrum' approach to language maintenance and make efforts to see that classroom learning and home learning are combined with increased public use of heritage languages in the community and the careful cultivation of positive attitudes toward the language.

The COD framework is also helpful to make use of when trying to understand why heritage language transmission is thriving in certain instances, or alternatively not progressing well. Here we can see how it can be applied to distinguish the differing heritage language transmission rates in two overseas South Asian communities—the large Mirpuri community from Pakistan settled in the north of England and the fast-growing population of Hindi-background speakers now living in the USA (see also the 2013 Winter edition of the *Heritage Language Journal* for the application of the COD approach to the maintenance of a wide range of languages by immigrant and indigenous minorities, including German, French, Russian, Japanese, and Native American languages).

The maintenance of Mirpur Pahari in northern England

Over 75% of the sizable Pakastani community in England originates from an area in Pakistan called Mirpur, and speaks a distinctive Mirpuri variety of the Pahari language. With a population of 500,000 to 600,000 speakers, Mirpur Pahari is actually the second most common mother tongue spoken in the UK, after English. In Lothers and Lothers (2012) it is noted that Pakistanis in general maintain stronger links with their homeland than most other immigrant groups, which is reinforced by the widespread maintenance of a number of cultural practices involving trips back to Pakistan. One of these is the strong tendency for Pakistani parents in England to arrange marriages for their offspring with a spouse in Pakistan, rather than with a Pakistani born in England. This is done in order to foster traditional conservative Pakistani values, and has the effect of increasing the Pakistani population in England, as the newly married couples subsequently settle together in England. Overseas Pakistanis also follow the practice of burying their family members who die in England back in Pakistan, and frequently make visits back to Pakistan to visit ailing relatives there.

Assessing the state of heritage-language maintenance among the Mirpuri in the UK, Lothers and Lothers (2012) report that language shift and loss are slow, and Mirpur Pahari is well maintained and well transmitted to new generations born in the UK. A range of factors help stimulate this buoyancy of the language. First, Mirpur Pahari is used extensively in the home, even when second-generation speakers also know English. To a significant degree, this is aided by the practice of transcontinental marriage with spouses from Pakistan, who have limited English skills when they arrive in the UK. Young mothers will typically raise their children using Mirpur Pahari, and Mirpur Pahari will be used to converse with older generations present in the household, who may not understand English well. Second, Mirpuris in the UK live in large communities that encourage the use of Mirpur Pahari in cities such as Manchester, Sheffield, Bradford, and Leeds. Here many neighborhoods are heavily Pakistani and schools are filled with young speakers of Mirpur Pahari. In the community, Mirpur Pahari is regularly used with neighbors, shopkeepers, friends, and in visits to the mosque. Third, there are very strongly positive attitudes toward Mirpur Pahari among its speakers, who see it as an important expression of their ethnic identity, so much so that most siblings who are bilingual in Mirpur Pahari and English will frequently use the heritage language with each other as a way of stressing their shared ethnicity. Mirpuri adults also emphasize that they desire their children to grow up being able to speak Mirpur Pahari, as well as English, and they are confident that this will also happen, as most communication with young children in the home is carried out in the heritage language. Fourth, as already noted, Mirpuris maintain regular contacts with Pakistan and feel that fluency in Mirpur Pahari is necessary for the trips they make back to visit relatives in Pakistan.

In sum, the minority heritage language Mirpur Pahari is surviving well across generations in the UK, and seems to be much more resistant to patterns of shift and loss than many other minority communities are. Characterized in terms of the Capacity-Opportunity-Desire approach to heritage-language maintenance, it can be noted that all three COD components are well satisfied in the Mirpuri community. Young Mirpuris are learning the language well in the home, as their mothers (who may often be monolingual speakers of Mirpur Pahari recently arrived from Pakistan) raise them with this language—their *capacity* in the heritage language is thus well developed. Mirpuris of all ages also have ample *opportunities* to use their heritage language in the community, in the home, and in trips to Pakistan. Finally, Mirpuris commonly have very positive attitudes toward their heritage language, and so have a strong *desire* to speak it, in order to express solidarity with other Mirpuris in the community. As all COD components therefore support knowledge and use of the heritage language, Mirpur Pahari continues to have a very robust presence in the Mirpuri population living in the UK.

Hindi language maintenance in the United States

A consideration of Hindi in the USA results in a different picture of language maintenance than with Mirpur Pahari in England. South Asians in the USA are now the fastest-growing and second-largest immigrant group, after Mexicans, recently surpassing the number of immigrants from China, the Philippines, and Vietnam. The South Asian population in the United States has grown extremely rapidly, from around only 12,000 in 1960, to its current size of over 2,000,000, principally due to changes in legislation in the 1960s which made it easier for highly skilled immigrants to settle in the USA (Zong and Batalova 2015). Among the various languages brought in as mother tongues by immigrants from South Asia, Hindi is the most widely spoken Indian language used in the home, with over 500,000 speakers. Despite the existence of such a large population, heavily concentrated in California and four other states, Hindi language transmission to second- and third-generation family members is not very effective, and there is significant shift into English, with corresponding loss of Hindi. Members of the second generation may be able to understand Hindi, but are generally not becoming bilingual and are quite limited in their abilities to speak Hindi. While Hindi may sometimes be used in a restricted way to communicate with grandparents and in trips made to India, members of the second generation typically speak with their parents in English, and almost always use English with their siblings and friends (Simpson and Thukral 2015). Language loss among members of the third generation is even more advanced, and the prospects for subsequent generations to acquire a strong proficiency in Hindi and use it in the home and the community are not good.

There are various reasons why Hindi is not being successfully transmitted down the generations of Indian immigrants in the United States. Considering the issue of *capacity*, and the learning of Hindi, Generation 1 parents who are fluent in Hindi are not strongly helping their children to develop Hindi language skills. To a considerable extent, this is because of differences between recent first-generation immigrants from India and those from other countries. The large numbers of immigrants settling in the USA from India since the 1960s are, for the most part, highly educated and know English well on arrival (due to its presence and use among educated classes in India). Because of this, Generation 1 parents usually do not enforce use of Hindi in the home and may regularly speak English with their children, and may even use English with each other, alternating with Hindi. As their parents are very capable speakers of English, unlike most other first-generation immigrants, their children feel very comfortable using English with them, and Hindi is not necessary to ensure family cohesion. As for *opportunity*, Gambhir and Gambhir (2013) stress that Hindi is not widely used in the communities where South Asians live, not in restaurants, stores, temples, or community centers, and English is instead made use of as a neutral language that can be understood by speakers of different South Asian languages. The use of Hindi outside the home is consequently severely limited, restricting the opportunity that younger speakers might have to practice their language skills. Investigations of the attitudes held toward Hindi and the maintenance of Hindi among second-generation South Asians show that there are actually very positive feelings about the heritage language, and a strong *desire* to be more proficient in the language, and to have rising generations develop good abilities in Hindi. However, as emphasized in the Capacity-Opportunity-Desire approach, it is necessary for positive desires to be combined with acquired abilities (capacity) and ample opportunities to use a heritage language in order to prevent language shift and loss, and in the case of Hindi in the United States, the capacity and opportunity aspects of language maintenance are significantly lacking, leading to the likely full replacement of Hindi by English in subsequent generations of South Asian Americans, despite the presence of very positive attitudes toward the language.

Generation 1.5: caught between two worlds and two languages

The three-generation pattern of language shift and loss described at the beginning of this chapter indicates what kinds of changes in language abilities typically happen with immigrant minorities, and we have also seen what kinds of factors interact with heritage-language transmission to either speed this process up, or slow it down. In addition to the typical outcomes found with generations 1–3, studies of immigrant families have found that young people who migrate to another country between the ages of 6 and 12 (approximately) often have a different kind of experience of language and cultural identity which sets them off from typical members of both Generation 1 and Generation 2. Here we will consider the interesting case of Generation 1.5, who frequently suggest that they feel caught between two worlds and fully belong to neither.

A typical member of Generation 1.5 is someone who began the early years of elementary school in the country where they were born, before moving with their family to another country, where they complete elementary school, and then progress into middle and high school (Kang 2004; Rumbaut 2004). By the time they graduate from high school, they will have spent about half of their life in one country and its society and culture, and the other half in a second country. Early classifications of such individuals have viewed them either as members of Generation 2, because their parents are typical members of Generation 1—new immigrants often struggling hard to learn the language of the country migrated to—or, alternatively, as members of Generation 1, because they were born and grew up for many years in a different country, prior to migrating with their parents to the new host country, where they spend their teenage years. However, young people who resettle in a new country between the ages of 6 and 12 are significantly different from typical members of both Generations 1 and 2. Linguistically, members of Generation 1.5 develop as fluent bilinguals, being able to speak both the heritage language and the majority language of the country migrated to, after several years there. They are generally stronger in the heritage language than many members of Generation 2, and certainly more proficient in the local majority language than their parents and other Generation 1 members. However, it is frequently reported that the language skills that members of Generation 1.5 develop in both the heritage language and the local majority language are not the same as other native speakers. When they speak the heritage language, they may not have the full vocabulary of regular native speakers, and lack many of the words needed to talk about aspects of science, learning, and other formal topics of discussion. When they speak the local majority language, they may lack the full range of idiomatic expressions that same-aged monolingual native speakers are familiar with, due to fewer years of exposure to the language.

Culturally, members of Generation 1.5 are immersed in the customs, beliefs, and way of life of the heritage language group during the first half of their childhood, and then are thrown into the new local majority culture in the second country for their teenage years. While this normally establishes a good familiarity with both sets of traditions, there will also be many cultural 'gaps' in the experiences of young people in Generation 1.5. Arriving in a new country between the ages of 6 and 12, members of Generation 1.5 will miss out on various aspects of life that are typically absorbed by children in that country during their early years, and having departed from their country of birth before middle adolescence, they will not participate in typical teenage experiences in the culture of the heritage country. As these early and late childhood experiences of life may be important for the development of cultural identity, members of Generation 1.5 may find that they fail to relate completely to young people who have grown up entirely in the local majority culture, and also feel distanced from their peers back in the home country, when they make visits there, due to their incomplete knowledge of the heritage culture. Members of Generation 1.5 may therefore struggle a little to build up a social identity that they are fully confident in and comfortable with, sometimes feeling neither fully accepted as equal-status members of the population they have joined in adolescence, nor viewed as genuine insiders by others living back in the country of birth. The experience of an interrupted childhood spent in two different societies and languages may therefore be a challenge for members of Generation 1.5, as well as providing them with the potential richness of a bilingual, bicultural upbringing. While members of this generation are likely to remain strong speakers of two languages during their life and not undergo significant language loss, they may regularly be confronted by complex questions of personal identity and belonging.

The second major portion of this chapter's examination of language maintenance and shift will now move on to consider *extreme cases of language loss*, where whole societies shift into other languages and endanger the continued existence of their ancestral languages.

Endangered languages and language death

Continued large-scale language shift can often eventually lead to **language endangerment** and **language death**—the full disappearance of a language. An important difference between language shift and loss in immigrant communities and the occurrence of similar processes with indigenous minorities is that, in the former, a language is only lost in one local environment by one group of its speakers. However, when members of an indigenous minority who are the only speakers of a particular language all lose their ability to speak this language, it is fully lost and will no longer be spoken anywhere. For example, if Korean speakers who have migrated to Japan lose their ability to speak Korean, this will not result in the global disappearance of Korean—there will still be large numbers of Korean speakers elsewhere, in North and South Korea. But, in many other cases where long-term language shift occurs among speakers of a language in their native area/country of origin, this may well result in languages fully dying out—'language death'. For example, in Ireland, Irish is now classified as 'endangered', and may lose its last speakers in the course of the 21st century, as may Ainu in Japan and many other minority languages in countries throughout the world.

Examining the current extent of language death and language loss

How serious is the current situation of language endangerment? In recent years, due to significant increases in the data available on the world's languages, linguists have come to the realization that very large numbers of languages are now endangered due to growing pressures in the modern world, and may disappear within several more generations unless positive action is taken to change their ongoing, sometimes very rapid decline.

In trying to establish how many of the world's languages may be in danger of extinction, it is important to study both population size and patterns of language shift and language death to figure out how many speakers a language may need in order to be 'safe' from dying out. There is a widespread assumption among non-specialists that it is only languages with small numbers of native speakers that are in danger of extinction. However, patterns of language shift suggest that we should not be so confident about this. Supposing a language has as many as 10,000 speakers, this might suggest that it is safe for the present, but possibly not necessarily out of danger in the near future. In fact, linguists working in certain areas of the world have argued that a language should be considered to be endangered if it has fewer than 20,000 speakers. Languages with *apparently* large numbers of speakers can therefore still be in danger, and in the 20th century there are many cases where languages have fallen from having very many speakers to significantly fewer. One example from France which can illustrate this is the situation with Breton, a language which is spoken in the northwest of the country. In 1905 there were 1.4 million speakers of Breton in France. At the end of the 20th century, according to UNESCO, there were only 250,000, and the language may now be losing 10,000 speakers each year (Hooper 2011). If this downward trend continues—and there is no reason to think it won't, unless actively stopped—then it can be expected that Breton will probably die out at some point in the next 100 years.

What one therefore needs to examine is downward *trends* and patterns of language loss. Once a language goes into clear and serious decline, it is highly likely that it has started out on the common path to extinction and that language death may follow within a few generations, unless efforts are made to reverse the downward pattern.

David Crystal, in an excellent book on language death published in 2000, offers a useful perspective on the vitality of the world's languages and language endangerment, looking at the situation initially in terms of statistics on languages and speaker populations. It is first pointed out that most of the world's population actually speaks one of a very small number of languages as its mother tongue. There are eight 'super' languages in the world that have more than 100 million mother tongue speakers (i.e., speakers for whom these languages are the first language they learned in the home):[2]

Languages with over 100 million native speakers:
Mandarin Chinese, Spanish, English, Bengali, Hindi, Portuguese, Russian, Japanese

Speakers of these languages make up approximately 3 billion of the world's population of 7 billion. If the list is extended to include just the top twenty common languages in the world (in terms of native speakers), this results in a total of 3.7 billion—over half the world's population—and if the analysis is continued downward, it is found that just 4% of the world's languages are spoken by 96% of the world's population. Turning this statistic the other way around, it can be realized that

96% of the world's languages are spoken by just 4% of the world's population.

Rather than there being an even distribution of languages across the world's population, a majority of the world's languages have relatively small speaker populations, and other dominant languages have very large numbers of speakers. This is important to keep in mind when thinking about language endangerment. Approximately half of the world's languages are spoken by populations of 10,000 speakers or less, and as many as 25% of the world's languages have fewer than 1,000 speakers, with many of these languages now reduced to very small populations—at the beginning of the 21st century, 500 languages were noted to be down to less than 100 speakers.

Current estimates of the total number of languages in the world vary between 6,000 and 7,000. This variation in numbers is the result of different views of language vs. dialect

---

2. Note that 'Arabic' does not figure here, due to the fact that different regional varieties of Arabic are mutually unintelligible and so do not constitute a single language, if the Mutual Intelligibility Hypothesis is adopted as a way to distinguish languages from dialects.

distinctions, as discussed in chapter 1, leading to certain disagreement as to which varieties should be classified as languages, and which as dialects. A fairly common view held among linguists (though by no means all linguists) is that there are around 6,000 languages in the world, and this is the figure we will make use of here. If it is assumed that having fewer than 20,000 speakers puts a language in danger of extinction within a few generations, then the startling conclusion from a consideration of language population size is that as many as two-thirds of the world's languages may currently be endangered (or about 4,000 languages) and may die out during the course of the 21st century. Some linguists have put the figure even higher, with the most pessimistic estimate being Michael Krauss's suggestion that 90% are endangered, in his 1992 paper 'The World's Languages in Crisis'.

Different stages of endangerment have been recognized by linguists attempting to quantify the extent of ongoing language loss around the world. UNESCO, in its online *Atlas of the World's Languages in Danger* (www.unesco.org/languages-atlas/), suggests a six-level set of categories for languages ranging from 'safe' to 'extinct', as follows:

SAFE: language is spoken by all generations; intergenerational transmission is uninterrupted;
VULNERABLE: most children speak the language, but it may be restricted to certain domains (e.g., home);
DEFINITELY ENDANGERED: children no longer learn the language as mother tongue in the home;
SEVERELY ENDANGERED: language is spoken by grandparents and older generations; while the parent generation may understand it, they do not speak it to children or among themselves;
CRITICALLY ENDANGERED: the youngest speakers are grandparents and older, and they speak the language partially and infrequently;
EXTINCT: there are no speakers left.

Brenzinger (2007) additionally identifies nine core factors that can usefully be employed to assess the endangered status of languages, including questions about population size, the domains that languages are used in, and whether languages are being transmitted to rising generations:

Factor 1. Intergenerational language transmission
Factor 2. Absolute numbers of speakers
Factor 3. Proportion of speakers within the total population
Factor 4. Loss of existing language domains[3]
Factor 5. Response to new domains and media[4]
Factor 6. Material for language education and literacy

---

3. This factor examines whether the language is now being used in a smaller set of domains than in the past.

4. This asks whether the language is being used in new domains that become available for communication, such as the internet.

Factor 7. Governmental and institutional language attitudes and policies, including official language status and use

Factor 8. Community members' attitudes toward their own language

Factor 9. Amount and quality of documentation.[5]

Both the UNESCO categorization and Brenzinger's assessment framework reference the important issue of whether languages are being passed on to new generations by older speakers—whether there is 'intergenerational language transmission' (Factor 1). As soon as this ceases to occur, a language passes from a safe or vulnerable status into being endangered, and it is classed as being '**moribund**'. Estimates are that well over half the world's languages are currently moribund and are not being effectively passed on to the next generation. This issue is important. Although many languages may have reasonable numbers of older speakers and therefore may seem to be 'healthy' in terms of total numbers of speakers considered, they are not being handed on well to younger generations. In North America, 80% of the Native American languages there are now moribund, as young children switch into using English and sometimes French, and parents no longer actively engage in using their ancestral languages in the home with their children (Krauss 1992). In other populations, the proportion of children who learn a heritage language from their parents is continually decreasing, so that languages are on the verge of becoming fully moribund. A study of Canada's native Indian population published in 1998 (Norris 1998, quoted in Crystal 2000) indicated that 60% of those aged over 85 were native speakers of an indigenous language, but only 20% of children under the age of 5 were. If this downward trend does not change, when present younger generation speakers become the new older generation, the total number of speakers of many languages will be *dramatically* less, and there may be no new younger generation speakers learning many of Canada's indigenous languages. The Canadian government has in fact suggested that only 3 of the country's 50 native Indian languages has large enough populations to be currently secure from extinction occurring at some point in the not-too-distant future.

Another complication affecting language transmission among indigenous minorities is that when the primary linguistic activities of the younger generation are carried out in the local majority language, even where a minority language is being passed on from older to younger generations it is often simplified in the process, and younger generation speakers acquire a form of the language which is not really the same as the language spoken by their parents. In many instances, younger generation speakers may significantly simplify their parents' ancestral languages and subconsciously allow their ability in the local majority language to influence their speaking of the heritage language. For example, young heritage speakers of Navajo in the USA who have English as their first language may produce a form of Navajo which is not as 'genuine' and close to native-speaker Navajo as that of their parents and grandparents. Sometimes the changes made will simply be lexical substitutions of English words for Navajo words that the speaker may not have learned, but in other cases

---

5. This considers whether the language has been well described or not.

there may be a 'transfer' of English grammar into the 'Najavo' produced by a speaker. When these effects are consistent and strong among younger generation speakers of endangered languages, the result is that languages are passed on in forms which are increasingly different and less like the original language.

Considering where language endangerment is at its most acute in the world, investigations have concluded that the situation seems to be at its very worst in the Americas and Australia, where an extremely high proportion of indigenous languages are endangered, and many languages have already disappeared. South Asia is now also coming to be affected very significantly by language endangerment. The situation is somewhat more stable in Africa, where the proportion of languages currently threatened is lower, when compared to the large numbers of African languages that are still deemed 'safe'. However, all continents have been found to be experiencing rapid patterns of language shift and loss among their immigrant and indigenous minority groups, so that the global future for smaller languages presently looks very bleak, and while languages have certainly died out in the past, and hence language death is not a new phenomenon, the rate at which this is now occurring is quite unprecedented and much, much faster than in any previous times.

Reasons to be concerned about the loss of languages

Most people are quite shocked to hear that thousands of the world's languages may die out during the course of the present century. Linguists who are now focusing their energies on the alarming spread of language endangerment regularly emphasize a range of reasons why there should be concern about the imminent, massive loss of languages around the world.

Most important of all is the value of ancestral languages to heritage communities themselves, and the deep sense of loss of identity that typically ensues among a community if its language disappears (Grenoble 2011). Languages, perhaps more than any other aspect of culture, encode the identity of different ethnic groups, and the loss of one's native language may correspond to a significant loss of cultural identity, particularly if a language fully disappears and there are no living speakers left. Such feelings are constantly repeated by members of small minority groups whose languages are being threatened by outside influences and pressures, as voiced in the following declarations from two speakers of endangered indigenous languages of North America:

'Language is a great part of your culture and a great part of identity and of who we are as people. Each breath you take without your language, you might as well be dead.'
Nora Vasquez, Chemehuevi Indian, Arizona, speaking in *The Linguists* (2008).

'To lose your language is to lose the soul of your culture, and when the language is gone you are forever disconnected from the wisdom of ancestors.'
Lilikalā Kameyeleihiwa, Hawaii, quoted in Aguilaria and LeCompte (2007: 11).[6]

6. Closely relating to these concerns about the connection of cultural identity and language, it has been noted that in many technologically less advanced societies whose languages are not written down, the history of many ethnic groups is actually handed down from generation to generation via spoken language, in purely oral accounts. If such languages are lost at some point, the full history and understanding of the ethnic group's past may also be suddenly and irrevocably lost, both to themselves and to the outside world.

Second, it is often stressed that where individual languages are lost, general cultural diversity in the world is also lost, as languages are an essential means for expressing culture. Many people see this as a very negative development, leading to the increased global homogenization of culture, and a decrease in the existence of traditional, local communities and different outlooks on the world. Crystal (2000: 36) quotes the Russian writer Vjaceslav Ivanov, who expresses this widely felt concern:

> Each language constitutes a certain model of the universe, a semiotic system of understanding the world, and if we have 4,000 [6,000] different ways to describe the world, this makes us rich. We should be concerned about preserving languages just as we are about ecology.

The message such writers and many linguists want to communicate is that diversity in language may be held to be as healthy and natural as diversity in nature, and that we should try to protect the world's languages, just as ecological diversity is protected.

Third, and in connection with the global loss of cultural diversity, it is noted that we may be able to learn a great deal about human civilization and culture in general through the preservation and study of the world's many different languages, as each language reflects a distinct and unique interpretation of life and the world around us, instantiating a wide range of different and valuable knowledge systems. The view that languages are each special reflections of the way that speakers perceive the world will be examined in more detail in chapter 9 on the Sapir-Whorf hypothesis and linguistic relativity.

Finally, it is observed that much information and learning about the physical and biological world which the inhabitants of isolated areas have amassed over time may only be encoded in their heritage languages, for example, information gained about the special medicinal uses of plants not known elsewhere. If the languages of such peoples disappear, this may also result in the loss of much useful knowledge about the unique properties of the physical environments they have lived in.

People who share these concerns about the negative consequences of language death and are moved to do something positive about this may engage in two main kinds of action aimed at helping with problems caused by language endangerment—programs of *language documentation* and *revitalization*. We will shortly consider exactly what these two activities involve, but first consider briefly what the primary factors are which cause language endangerment and death.

Reasons for language endangerment

There is no single cause of language death, and languages become extinct for many of the same reasons that there is language shift in migrant communities, as already discussed. Here we highlight again the most important, recurring causes of language loss and those which have a particular relevance for small, indigenous minorities.

The growth of official languages and domain reduction of smaller languages

As modern states often select and promote a single language for universal official use, this naturally causes non-official languages to be used less, and to be used in fewer *domains*. Official government business, commerce, and education may all be carried out in the official language of a country, and other languages may become restricted to use within the family and with friends. The increased reduction in domains of use—Brenzinger's (2007) Factor 4—initiates language shift and is a significant first step on the downward path toward language loss.

Negative attitudes toward minority languages

The creation of official state languages also has wider *psychological effects* on speakers of other minority languages so that speakers become discouraged from using their heritage languages. When a single language is recognized as being official and promoted for use in all the 'important' areas of life, other languages seem to their speakers to be less 'important' and less worthy. Because of the mental association created between official languages and social prestige, speakers may tend to speak official languages more and more, and consider their own native languages inferior and to be avoided in many circumstances. The existence of negative attitudes toward one's own native language due to the existence of other more dominant locally spoken languages is one of the most important causes of language loss and death. People frequently give up using their native language due to considering it backward and a hindrance to social and economic progress, and when such opinions are widely shared in a linguistic community, the ultimate death of a language is likely to happen, even if the number of native speakers is in fact quite large. It should be noted that in many cases negative attitudes of this type are also encouraged from outside the indigenous language group. There are many cases where children going to school have been forbidden to speak their mother tongue and have been punished in various ways if they used any language other than the official state language. Adults, too, are also frequently made to feel badly about their heritage language use by speakers of more dominant languages. The following two quotations are from speakers of the Siberian language Chulym in a powerful segment from the film *The Linguists*. The speakers talk of how they regularly felt humiliated by Russians' reactions to their use of Chulym, and largely came to stop using the language as a result:

'He'd say: "What are you saying, black ass?" Chulym was viewed as a gutter language.'
'It was horrible. Since first grade we were ashamed to speak the language.'

Economic reasons

As observed in the earlier discussion of language shift among immigrant minorities, it may often be advantageous for speakers of less widespread languages to switch to a more dominant local/national language in order to find work. When indigenous minorities find that certain other languages become increasingly dominant in a single country and are required in order to obtain employment of certain types, they may regularly switch into these larger languages and decide not to transmit the heritage language to their children, so as to help maximize the chances that their children will have for economic success.

Globalization and urbanization

In recent decades, there has been a huge increase in global population, travel, and communication linking people of different linguistic backgrounds. This has naturally led to the increased need for languages which can be used for communication with people who have different language backgrounds—'*lingua francas*'—creating further pressure on less widely spoken native languages.

Additionally, heavy urbanization in many countries has resulted in many speakers of local indigenous languages leaving their rural areas and moving to new cities. Such population movements have resulted in a reduction of speakers of smaller languages in the countryside, as well as language loss among the children of those who move to the cities (who frequently end up speaking mostly the language of the dominant majority in a city).

Invasion and colonization by outsiders

Smaller language groups may often become surrounded by a more dominant population of speakers of a different language due to invasion, colonization, and large-scale immigration of members of the larger group. For example, late 20th-century Chinese immigration into Xinjiang province in northwest China has now resulted in Turkic-language speakers becoming minorities in this part of China, although groups such as the Uyghur and Kazakhs were previously local majorities. Such flooding of the areas inhabited by relatively smaller groups with members of a dominant majority dilutes the use of local heritage languages within their home regions and stimulates their decline—Brenzinger's (2007) Factor 3, which emphasizes that the proportion of heritage language speakers to others within a population has a clear effect on the maintenance of a heritage language.

Physical causes

Another cause of language loss among smaller ethnic groups may be the occurrence of natural disasters such as earthquakes, tsunamis, and flooding, which sometimes have the power to kill or disperse much of the populations of minority groups. If such groups are forced to split up and move to different areas to live, it is likely that this will put their native language under serious pressure as they become immigrants in other communities.

A further significant physical cause of language loss is the effect of imported disease on indigenous populations. For example, it is reported that diseases brought by European colonizers and their livestock to the Americas caused as much as a 90% reduction of the indigenous population in North, Central, and South America over the course of two hundred years (McNeill 1976; Crystal 2000).

All the preceding factors may cause or conspire with each other to induce language shift and endangerment, leading to the full loss of languages. The interaction of economic factors and a change in the proportion of minority to dominant population, due to immigration of the members of latter into the homeland of the former, can be illustrated with a review of the fate of the Oroqen people in northwest China, who have succumbed to typical processes of language shift as their lifestyle has undergone changes which in many ways might otherwise seem to have improved the comfort of their lives.

The Oroqen people in Northwest China

The Oroqen people of northwest of China were by tradition a nomadic group.[7] As communist forces took official control of all territory in China from 1949, the government introduced measures to improve the living conditions of ethnically non-Chinese minority groups in the country, providing them with health care and schooling opportunities for their children. A significant consequence of this policy was that nomadic minorities were obliged to settle in one place, in order for their children to receive education. Consequently, the Oroqen gave up their nomadic life and settled in villages constructed for them in the 1950s. Shortly after this, large numbers of ethnically Chinese workers entered the region to work in the new mining industries being set up there by the government. This led to the Oroqen quickly becoming a small minority, surrounded by Han Chinese people. With the construction of new roads and the influx of a large new population in the area, the Oroqen soon found it difficult to live by traditional hunting methods and came to adopt different ways of making a living in more settled, modern ways. Their children also received free secondary education and benefited from special quotas guaranteeing minority nationalities a certain number of places in universities (an 'affirmative action' policy). As a result, a relatively high number of the Oroqen went through the educational system to high levels.

The Oroqen also benefited from being exempt from the one-child per family policy in China,[8] and as a further incentive to settle down, the government provided them with good quality housing. These advantages gave the Oroqen a better standard of life, in many ways, than Han Chinese living in the area, and attracted Han Chinese settlers to marry with Oroqen people, as a way to gain a higher standard of living. Intermarriage has subsequently resulted in the Oroqen being dissolved as a group and has led to large-scale language shift from Oroqen to Chinese.

When the Oroqen became aware that their language was no longer being learned by the younger generation, attempts were made to teach Oroqen in schools and to have Oroqen broadcast on TV, but these have not been a total success due to disagreements over the form of Oroqen that is used—there are many dialects and no agreed-upon standard form of the language. The decline of Oroqen thus represents a Catch 22–type dilemma common among many minorities. In order to protect and revive a group's endangered language, it may be best for the group to isolate itself and shun the use of regional/national majority languages, but this may cut it off from the resources made available by contact with speakers of larger languages and the means toward economic advancement. The loss of a heritage language is therefore a highly likely outcome of increased heavy exposure to speakers of more dominant languages,

---

7. Information on the Oroqen comes from Whaley (2002), as presented in Wright (2004).

8. This official policy was an attempt to keep population growth in China under control, and allowed ethnically Chinese families to have only one child in urban areas.

unless careful, advanced bilingualism can somehow be established and maintained, and this has sadly not been the case with the Oroqen and their interactions with the Han Chinese.

Positive reactions to language endangerment: documentation and revitalization programs

There are two broad kinds of activities that are initiated to help with endangered languages and their populations in a positive way: (a) language documentation, and (b) revitalization programs. Although these activities can be carried out independently of each other, it is common that the results of language documentation are made use of by subsequent efforts to revitalize languages. We will outline what is involved in each kind of initiative, and then consider a number of cases where attempts at revitalization have met with success and have helped communities reactivate the use of their heritage languages.

Language documentation

'Language documentation' refers to activities aimed at describing a language, its grammar, vocabulary, pronunciation, and stylistic uses. Language documentation is normally carried out by linguists who have acquired skills in analyzing unfamiliar languages and in interacting well with linguistic informants (speakers of the language being documented). A superb and very lively introduction to the work and experiences of 'field linguists' who visit endangered language communities and attempt to document their languages can be seen in the film *The Linguists* (2008, Ironbound Films).[9] This documentary follows the interactions of two young professors of linguistics with speakers of endangered languages in India, Siberia, Bolivia, and the USA (Arizona), and shows how they set about learning about, analyzing, and recording these languages, as well as dealing with sometimes quite challenging situations and conditions.

In many cases of the documentation of small endangered languages there may be no materials available which describe the languages in any way, and so documentation efforts will need to start at the very beginning, and build up basic descriptions of the words and grammar used in the language. Additionally, if a language has never been written down before, it will be necessary to devise a way of writing the language in some script which can accurately represent the pronunciation of the language's words. In various other cases, writing conventions and certain descriptions of a language may already be available, and these can be used to create more advanced profiles of the language. The physical products of sustained language documentation will normally be books/monographs which describe the grammar and usage conventions of the language, dictionaries which list as many of its words as possible, and how they are pronounced, and frequently also audio and video files providing further information on the way the language is spoken. Such materials can then be used in attempts to re-energize actual

---

9. Kramer, Seth, Daniel Miller, and Jeremy Newberger (directors). 2008. *The Linguists*. Garrison, NY: Ironbound Films.

use of an endangered language in a community and revitalize knowledge of the language among its heritage speakers.

Language documentation activities may be carried out by individuals working alone or by small teams of linguists with different specialties in language analysis (syntax, sound structure, word structure, etc.), and may frequently be coordinated and assisted by governmental or privately funded centers or university departments with a focus on endangered languages. Some of the larger organizations of this type which support documentation (and often revitalization) work around different parts of the world are listed following this paragraph. Many more also exist in individual countries and concentrate on the languages present in these countries (for further listings and useful links, go to: www.livingtongues.org/links.html). Several of this growing number of organizations set up to help document the world's disappearing languages provide training in the special linguistic and technical skills needed for carrying out language documentation, and help with the archiving of materials produced by different projects. While it may frequently be linguists from outside an endangered language community who initiate the documentation of a language with the skills they have acquired in special training programs, it will be optimal for the sustained creation of materials documenting the language if such outsider linguists can pass on their skills to members of the community themselves, and help train them to be able to continue to describe further aspects of their language and to create more detailed information about its vocabulary, grammar, and pragmatic use.

Organizations that support the documentation of endangered languages include the following:

> Foundation for Endangered Languages: http://www.ogmios.org
> Endangered Language Fund: http://www.endangeredlanguagefund.org/
> Society for Endangered Languages: http://www.uni-koeln.de/gbs/e_index.html
> Summer Institute of Linguistics: www.sil.org/
> Endangered Languages Documentation Program: www.eldp.net/
> Documentation of Endangered Languages: http://www.mpi.nl/DOBES/.

Language revitalization

For many linguists and members of endangered language communities, the ultimate goal of the documentation of such languages is to provide a foundation for the revitalization of threatened and dying languages, and help members of an endangered language community revive its use, where there is a positive desire among the community (or a clear portion of it) to do this.[10]

---

10. Without a positive attitude toward language revival being present in a community, it is very unlikely that efforts at revitalization will be successful, so it important for linguists to establish what kinds of feelings a community has about its heritage language at the outset of documentation projects ultimately aimed toward revitalization initiatives. There are many minority communities who are extremely keen to keep their heritage languages alive and to help them be used more by all generations of speakers, and it is in these communities that language revitalization efforts have the greatest possibility of achieving progress.

When there is enthusiasm and a willingness to work toward the re-energization of a threatened language, revitalization efforts may be initiated in a number of diverse forms, tailored to different situations and degrees of endangerment, and focusing on the young and adult members of a community via different strategies.

Teaching of the heritage language may be introduced in schools for rising generations, in three formats, depending on how much time children are asked to study/use the language, and the depth of resources that are available in the language. If the latter are relatively limited, and documentation projects have simply been able to produce new textbooks introducing the language, the heritage language can be **taught as a subject**, meaning that it will be studied for a few hours per week, as a foreign language such as French or German might be studied in other schools. If a broader range of pedagogical materials have been prepared, communities may start **bilingual education** in their schools, with both the local majority language and the heritage language being used as **mediums of education** to teach other subjects. Hence schools in Brittany, France, for example, might use French to teach children mathematics, history, and literature, and Breton to teach geography, chemistry, and music classes. Most ambitious of all efforts to jump start and embed knowledge and fluency in the heritage language in children at school are (full) **immersion programs**, which only use the heritage language to teach all subjects for the first several years of schooling, with the local majority language being very gradually introduced as a medium of education in later years. Both immersion and bilingual education programs require that a large amount of teaching materials are prepared in the heritage language, whose quality will probably need state approval, so it is challenging to launch such programs at the beginning of efforts at revitalization. However, immersion programs are the most successful way to rapidly help young children achieve fluency in a heritage (or other) language, and bilingual education programs will help children become speakers of the heritage language a lot more effectively and more swiftly than programs which simply teach the language for a few hours per week as a subject. Although the latter kind of program will not establish high levels of fluency in children due to the limited hours of classes, the language conservationist Leanne Hinton points out that

> Teaching the language as a subject has done a lot in many communities to help erase the shame that generations of people have felt about their language and has created a readiness and eagerness in young people to learn their language and develop more intensive programs for revitalization. Hinton (2001: 7)

Hinton goes on to add that children can become extremely proud of their linguistic heritage through such introductory classes, in contrast to the negative feelings experienced by their parents at the same age, and teenagers may often even state that it is 'cool' to know the heritage language. Even teaching a heritage language for a few hours a week can therefore have very positive effects in a community and can help build a new generation who will take revitalization of the language further in the future.

Each community will ultimately have to select a form of heritage language education that can be supported by the breadth of materials it has available, and as more teaching materials are created, more ambitious levels of incorporation of the language in schools can be attempted. All programs introducing an endangered language into classrooms in schools will also need qualified teachers who are speakers of the language, which is difficult in some communities, where the only speakers of a disappearing language are older people, who may not have teaching qualifications. In such instances, measures will need to be taken to help create new adult speakers who can serve as teachers, and if these adults are not initially fluent, strong speakers of the language, it is likely that bilingual education and immersion programs may take longer to develop, and the language will initially have to be taught as a subject.

Two other kinds of language initiatives have been made use of to teach heritage languages to children. A number of communities set up **summer language camps** which provide intensive language exposure to children for several weeks, as a way to supplement what children have already learned of the language in school. Because such camps operate independently of schools and are therefore free from restrictions imposed on schools, they can make use of elders and other adults in the community who are good speakers (and therefore good models) of the heritage language but have no official teaching qualifications. A second, innovative stratagem increasingly used to help even younger children gain an exposure to the heritage language outside the home (where parents may perhaps not be native speakers of the language) is the enrollment of children in pre-school '**language nests**', a kindergarten-like experience focused on use of the heritage language, which was initiated in New Zealand, and then spread to other countries. In language nests, fluent speakers of a heritage language, who are generally older members of a community and sometimes the last remaining speakers of an endangered language, come to preschools and speak the ancestral language with children throughout the day. The preschools' regular teachers tend to the children's non-linguistic needs, either using the ancestral language, if they can, or interacting with the children without language (Thomason 2015). The heritage language will therefore be the only form of linguistic communication used in the classroom during the day, and language nests are a form of early full immersion which creates heritage language fluency in children from a very young age.

Linguists and community members involved in language revitalization have regularly observed that heritage language programs in schools and preschools are likely to be successful in the long term only if supported by additional regular use of the heritage language outside schools with parents in the home. Thus most school-based programs also attempt to build a family component in which parents are encouraged to learn and then use the heritage language with their children in the home, to help reinforce the skills developed by children in schools. Adult learning of heritage languages is typically carried out by attending evening classes in the language. In addition to such after-work classes, there is a special type of program aimed at adults of all ages who have limited abilities in their ancestral language and want to quickly learn more. This is a late-age immersion method known as the **Master-Apprentice Language Learning Program**, initially developed in California and now effectively spread to many endangered language communities around the world (Hinton 2011). The master-apprentice approach pairs up a fluent speaker of the ancestral language, the 'master' (typically an older member of the community, as with language nests), with an 'apprentice' who is focused on improving his/her abilities in the language. Master and apprentice spend at least ten to twenty hours each week working together and only use the heritage language with each other, even if this creates difficulty in communication when the apprentice doesn't understand certain words. The use of non-verbal communication, gestures, pointing, and facial expressions are all encouraged to help avoid using other languages, and the activities engaged in by master and apprentice should all be real-life situations requiring interaction and speech, mimicking the way that languages are naturally learned by younger people.

There are consequently a number of different methods for helping young and adult members of endangered language groups reactivate language use within the community, and each heritage language group can select a means appropriate to the resources it has available and the existing state of knowledge of the language among different generations. What is particularly important is that **realistic goals** for revitalization should be set by communities, once an assessment of resources has been made. In various instances, where languages have become severely endangered, the setting of more modest goals may initially be wiser, such as trying to have all members of a community begin to use some of the ancestral language again, without expecting the swift achievement of across-the-board fluency among all generations. Being able to successfully attain shorter-term, moderate goals can bring important rewards to a community, and can help develop enthusiasm for the identification of more ambitious, longer-term plans to re-establish use of its ancestral language (Grenoble and Whaley 2006). When suitable goals are identified, and members of a threatened (or even extinct) language community are motivated and keen to participate in revitalization programs, much can be achieved to stem the decline of an endangered language, as will now be illustrated with examples of several languages which have been revitalized to different degrees.

Reviving 'extinct' languages: Hebrew, Cornish, and Miami

Perhaps the most startling case of successful language revitalization is the full revival of Hebrew in the 20th century, as Hebrew had not been used as a spoken language for almost two thousand years, since the dispersal of the Jews following the destruction of the second temple in Jerusalem in 70 C.E. From this time right up until the early 20th century, Hebrew had no native speakers and was only used for religious purposes in services and prayers and as a literary language, with young men learning to read Biblical Hebrew in order to read the Torah.

In the late 19th and early 20th centuries, a movement to establish a new Jewish nation through settlement in Palestine was accompanied by the idea of reviving Hebrew as a modern spoken language, initially led and inspired by the language activist Eliezer Ben-Yehuda, who arrived in Jerusalem in 1881. Progress in revitalizing Biblical Hebrew as a colloquial language for everyday life was extremely slow to begin with, as it lacked words to refer to many aspects of day-to-day life, and these words had to be gradually created by Ben-Yehuda and others. For example, the American poet Solomon Blumgarten, visiting Palestine in 1913, famously asked a teenage girl for the Hebrew names of some flowers he saw one day, and was given the reply, 'Flowers have no names', as words for flowers had not yet been coined in Hebrew at that time (Harshav 2009: 27). The revival and modernization of Hebrew was reported to be a very challenging and difficult process for all those involved in it, requiring great commitment. However, over time, the vocabulary of the language was significantly increased and Hebrew came to be used in schools, establishing new, young native speakers, as parents made efforts to raise their children speaking only Hebrew. Subsequently, Hebrew appeared in newspapers, translations of works of Western literature, new works of fiction, and scientific books, and came to be used regularly in public activities and in social interactions. Today, amazingly, Hebrew has millions of mother-tongue speakers and is used in all domains of life among the Jewish population of Israel, including formal domains such as higher education, modern science and technology, and government administration, as well as in informal, colloquial speech. The language has become fully 'safe' and its 'dormancy' has been completely reversed, showing that, with great determination and (importantly) time, even languages with no native speakers can be revived very successfully if there are some records of the language.

The successful revitalization of Hebrew has been an inspiration for many other attempts to revive endangered and extinct (or 'dormant', 'sleeping') languages which have no native speakers. While Hebrew has been a major success, resulting in a very large population of native speakers following decades of revitalization work and commitment to reviving the language, there are also many noteworthy smaller success stories of languages that have lost all their speakers now beginning to be revived. A brief consideration of the ongoing revival of **Miami** and **Cornish** emphasizes the importance of three factors that can generally help with the revitalization of endangered languages: (a) the existence of records of a language (language documentation), (b) the presence of centers which can serve as hubs for revitalization efforts, and (c) governmental recognition of an endangered language as having a certain official status.

Miami (also known as Myaamia) is a Native American language whose tribal members live in the states of Indiana, Kansas, and Oklahoma. Due to various pressures on the language through the 19th and 20th centuries, Miami became moribund and by the late 1980s had no more native speakers. Language 'reconstruction' work was initiated with a 1994 PhD dissertation study of Miami[11], whose important achievement was to gather together a wide range of records of Miami from different parts of the United States where the Miami people had lived. This collection of descriptions laid the foundation for members of the Miami tribe to start reviving their language, and work began on the production of teaching materials and the staging of summer programs, which helped both children and adults learn some of the Miami language. A major boost to the Miami revitalization efforts came in 2001, when tribal leaders made contact with Miami University (in Ohio) hoping to establish a center in the university that could help support the ongoing efforts at Miami language revival. After many years of cooperation with faculty in the university, the Myaamia Project was officially recognized as a Miami University center in 2013. The Myaamia Center now helps transmit knowledge of Miami language and culture to the tribal community by means of educational programs and online resources (http://myaamiacenter.org/). Its presence on campus has also helped increase the enrollment of young tribal members in Miami University, where they are required to take courses on Miami language, history, and culture, in addition to their regular classes. This is reported to have had a strongly beneficial effect on both young Miami students'

---

11. Costa, David. 1994. *The Miami-Illinois Language.* PhD dissertation, University of California, Berkeley.

self-esteem and their educational achievements. Baldwin (2014), in his overview of progress made in Miami language reclamation, stresses that the establishment of the Myaamia Center in Miami University has been of tremendous importance to the Miami tribal community and their attempts to revitalize their language and pass on knowledge of their traditions and culture to new generations. From being completely without speakers in recent times, Miami is now used regularly as a second language by tribal members, and children are once again being raised to be speakers of the language. Tribal publications, formal meetings, prayers, and new online resources all make use of Miami, and use of the language is expected to increase steadily as work on revitalization continues (Baldwin 2014: 213).

Cornish is a Celtic language that used to be spoken in the southwest of England. Severely endangered already in the 18th century, the last native speaker of Cornish died in 1891, and the language became dormant for sixty years. In the 1950s, a revival movement was initiated, and in 1967 the Cornish Language Board was set up to help promote the revival of Cornish, publishing educational and other reference materials in the language. The revitalization movement subsequently grew through the 1980s, and Cornish is now taught in schools, universities, and adult evening classes, and a population of fluent speakers has come into existence who regularly use the language in their daily lives. Grenoble and Whaley (2006) note that this a remarkable comeback for a language which had ceased to be used or known by anyone for a long period of time. In assessing the progress that has been made with the revival of Cornish, it is pointed out that the efforts of the Cornish community to re-establish use of their heritage language were assisted greatly by an official government act of recognition in 2003, which acknowledged that Cornish qualified as a language for the purposes of the European Charter for Regional or Minority Languages. This official classification of Cornish as a minority/regional language on a par with Welsh, Irish, Basque, and Catalan gave its budding speakers enormous new psychological encouragement in their efforts to revitalize the language and greatly stimulated the feelings of pride in Cornish that had begun to spread again in the southwest of England. As noted in Crystal (2000, ch. 5), the official state recognition of a minority language in a country is a mechanism which symbolically can increase the prestige of the language in the minds of its speakers and their neighbors, and potentially also offer more power and protection to speakers as they attempt to revive a language in distress. Achieving such recognition can therefore be a milestone in revitalization progress for any endangered language community.

Maori in New Zealand

When languages are endangered but still have populations of native speakers, revitalization efforts can generally make swifter progress than when a language has lost all its mother tongue speakers and has become 'extinct', or is viewed as 'dormant/sleeping'. In New Zealand, where Maori was spoken by all of the population prior to the arrival of European explorers in the 18th century, large-scale settlement of English-speakers in the 19th century, combined with the effects of disease and warfare, resulted in the Maori people becoming a minority group in the country (now making up around 15% of New Zealand's population), and their language going into decline. In 1867 the Native Schools Act enforced the use of English in all schools, and Maori children were subsequently punished for speaking their mother tongue in schools. English also became the language of government and official writing, although literacy in Maori had previously become very widespread and had resulted in a large body of written works. The use of Maori subsequently retreated to the home, religious services, tribal meetings, and other informal, colloquial interactions. In these domains, however, Maori continued to remain strong, and a 1930 survey of Maori children showed that 97% spoke only Maori in the home with family members (May 2010).

The serious and swift decline of Maori began to occur after World War II as rapid urbanization turned a 90% rural Maori population into an 80% urban one, putting heavy pressure on maintenance of the language as Maori-speakers became increasingly intermixed with English-speakers in the towns and cities. As more and more parents stopped speaking Maori to their children, so that they could develop better English skills and obtain better jobs and enjoy higher social prestige, the domestic use of Maori plummeted, and by 1960 only 26% of children reported using Maori in the home. By the end of the 1970s, forecasts were that the language would fully die out in future generations if ongoing downward patterns of maintenance and transmission carried on.

The realization that Maori was in such a threatened state triggered a positive defense of the language from the 1980s onward, and the initiation of a very active Maori language revitalization movement. When Maori leaders and teachers met to discuss how best to revive use of the language, it was proposed that this could be achieved most successfully and swiftly if older members of the Maori community, typically grandparents, were to speak Maori with young children for several hours each day in preschool centers, and the innovative idea of language nests was born and put into action. The first language nest opened in 1982, and this was quickly followed by many more, growing to a peak of over 800 such centers in the mid-1990s, when nearly half of Maori children of preschool age were attending language nests and achieving early fluency in the language. Parents of children attending language nests helped further with this process by speaking Maori with their children in the home as much as possible, though the majority of parents were not very confident or proficient speakers.

The language nest experience was judged to be so successful and beneficial for preschool children that parents asked for Maori to be utilized as a medium of education in primary schools, and this led to the development of independent, full-immersion primary schools with classes held in Maori (Spolsky 2009). Following this, Maori immersion was developed and spread to all levels of education, including high schools, and was made use of in both state and independent schools. The result of such continuous Maori-medium education has been the successful creation of a new generation of native speakers of Maori, who are now in a good position to pass the language on effectively to their children (King 2001).

The revitalization of Maori through the educational system and increased use of Maori in the home was given additional general support by the government of New Zealand, when it decided to acknowledge Maori as an official language of the country in the 1987 Maori Language Act. The government also helped fund the use of Maori in radio and television programming, and established a Maori Language Commission to help promote the learning of Maori and support its use as an official language.

Spolsky (2009) notes that four decades of revitalization efforts have now managed to rescue Maori from the heavily endangered state it had slipped into in the 1960s. There are now many more speakers of Maori than before, and most importantly, there are many new, young speakers, who can help transmit the language further. The outlook for Maori is therefore now clearly positive, and the future of Maori through the 21st century seems to be relatively secure, thanks to the sustained efforts of the Maori language movement and positive assistance from the government. The particular innovation at the heart of the revitalization of Maori—the creation of language nests—has also been an inspiration for other language groups searching for ways to reverse language shift in younger generations, as we will see in a final case study of language revitalization in Hawaii.

The revival of Hawaiian

The movement to revitalize the Hawaiian language has become well-known as another very successful community-based effort to turn around a language in severe decay. Hawaiian was previously very widely known and used on the Hawaiian islands, until the end of the 19th century, and was spoken not only by ethnic Hawaiians but also by the children of immigrants who settled in Hawaii from other countries such as Japan, China, and Brazil. In 1893, the Hawaiian monarchy was overthrown by a force of US marines, responding to a request for support from the small but economically powerful Anglo-American community which owned large sugar, coffee, and pineapple plantations, and in 1900 Hawaii was officially incorporated into the United States. As 'Anglos' thus came to dominate Hawaii, English was heavily promoted and Hawaiian was suppressed. The use of Hawaiian as a medium of education in both public and private schools was forbidden, from 1896 until 1986, and Hawaiians were pressured to use English in place of Hawaiian in their daily lives and even in the home. Use of any language other than English by students or teachers in schools resulted in heavy punishments. However, young people were actually not able to develop a good proficiency in English for some time, as their teachers were not good speakers of English, and what emerged as a common new speech form was a mixture of English and Hawaiian, also absorbing influences from other immigrant languages such as Japanese and Chinese. This became known as Hawai'i Creole, and was also known locally simply as 'Pidgin' (chapter 5 will later consider 'pidgin' and 'creole' languages in some depth). During the first three decades of the 20th century, Pidgin replaced Hawaiian as the language most frequently used by people in Hawaii, and the use of Hawaiian became restricted to various religious activities and communication with the elderly (Wilson 1998). The language consequently went into heavy decline, with new generations initially shifting into Pidgin, and later into English.

The revitalization of Hawaiian began in the 1970s, when a general 'Hawaiian renaissance' occurred, establishing a widespread re-emergence of interest in Hawaiian culture. Initially this interest was focused on reviving Hawaiian music and dance, but later extended naturally to language, and many ethnic Hawaiians found a new enthusiasm for learning Hawaiian. Introductory courses in Hawaiian offered by the University of Hawaii increased greatly in number, Hawaiian-language student and teacher organizations came into existence, newsletters in the Hawaiian language appeared, and Hawaiian was promoted in sports, camping trips, and other social activities (Wilson 1998). This all helped produce a new wave of second-language speakers of Hawaiian, able and motivated to assist with further revitalization of the language.

In 1978, the grassroots movement to revive Hawaiian achieved a significant victory when Hawaiian was declared to be an official language of the state, along with English, and the constitution mandated that the state make new efforts to promote knowledge of Hawaiian culture, history, and also language (Warner 2001). Some years after these positive developments, in 1982, a group of language activists, who were mostly graduates of the University of Hawaii at Mānoa, met to discuss how to strengthen the momentum of the revival of Hawaiian and broaden popular use of the language. It was concluded that the future of Hawaiian could only be assured if a new generation of native speakers of the language were to come into existence, and so attention was turned toward the issue of language learning among the young. Quite fortuitously, one of those present at the meeting had just returned from New Zealand, where he had become familiar with the successful program of language nests initiated there, and after some discussion it was decided to adopt the New Zealand model for Hawaii. The Hawaiian Organization of Language Nests was subsequently established and helped set up many independent preschool centers which only used Hawaiian, beginning the process of creating new mother tongue speakers of the language.

When the official ban against Hawaiian as a medium of education in schools was finally lifted in 1986, language activists petitioned for the extension of immersion education in Hawaiian to primary schools, and then to high schools, and successfully established the availability of Hawaiian-language immersion programs for all twelve grades of public schooling. They also developed a college dedicated to Hawaiian language at the University of Hawaii at Hilo which enables students to make use of Hawaiian in their studies up to the PhD level. Such efforts to embed Hawaiian within all levels of education were assisted by substantial federal funding from 1990 onward, and the establishment of a new state requirement that Hawaiian be taught in some form in all public schools (Wilson 1998).

The results of Hawaiian-language revitalization have been very significant. Hawaiian is the only Native American language which can be used to take classes through the entire educational system, from preschool to graduate programs, and the performance of young people going through Hawaiian-medium immersion schooling has been found to be extremely good, resulting in a higher high school graduation and college admission rate than students who attend mainstream English-medium public schools (Wilson 2014: 223). This high level of academic success has served as an inspiration to others, and has caused more parents to raise their children speaking Hawaiian in the home and to send them to Hawaiian-medium schools. Adults are also being drawn to learn and use Hawaiian again, as best they can, and there are now community language courses available in evening classes, churches, and family groups which have been enrolling thousands of late language learners. Hawaiian has a new presence in television, radio, and newspapers, and across the board there has been an enormous increase in the use of Hawaiian, with the proportion of those reporting use of Hawaiian in the home having grown by 90% between 1990 and 2000 (Wilson 2014: 224).

Because of all this positive movement back to the Hawaiian language, the revival of Hawaiian represents the most successful instance of language revitalization in the United States. Grenoble and Whaley (2006: 97) observe that a very important factor helping this strong regrowth of Hawaiian has been the tireless work of a group of people dedicated to the language and winning its re-adoption and development in the education system.

They emphasize that this is a crucial point for the success of language revitalization efforts in general, and one which should be borne in mind by all attempts to revive endangered languages:

> Few programs have any hope of succeeding without an individual or individuals who are willing to sacrifice greatly over many years' time. While outside support in the form of money, expertise, or moral support can be valuable, it does not make revitalization happen. (Grenoble and Whaley 2006: 98)

Rather, it is members of the community determined to reverse language loss who will ultimately be decisive for the success of language revitalization in the majority of instances, and it is such individuals who also need to be recognized for their contributions in the global struggle against language endangerment.

Final remarks

The second half of this chapter has focused on language loss among indigenous minority groups and the disappearance of smaller languages. We have noted that the world is currently experiencing a massive and rapid decline in the number of languages that are spoken as people shift from use of their ancestral languages into larger, more dominant languages. Having highlighted predictions about the extent of language death which is anticipated to occur during the 21st century, we saw how various attempts are now being made to reverse the loss of languages, and to revitalize languages that have become endangered. We will now close the chapter with a question which naturally arises given such observations, and then make two final points about language maintenance and revitalization which are important as general, take-home messages and lessons.

First, if there is now an awareness that at least half of the world's languages are endangered (maybe even two-thirds or more), and if we now also have an understanding of what is involved to rescue a language and successfully revitalize it, is it going to be possible to save all the languages presently identified as moribund and endangered? The simple answer to this question is that this is not likely to happen, and large numbers of languages will almost inevitably die out over the next hundred years, unfortunately, as the resources and conditions necessary to engineer their revival are often not available (existence of a positive-minded community, dedicated core of language activists, language documentation, etc.), and some minority groups are still unaware that their languages are slipping away as rising generations fail to acquire them. However, it is also clear that many endangered language communities around the world are now fighting back against heritage language loss and are revitalizing their languages, and these efforts are giving hope and inspiration to others whose languages are similarly threatened. Modern efforts to reverse language loss therefore are having a very positive impact, and communities present on all continents are being helped by revitalization initiatives. This more positive perspective on reactions to language endangerment now brings us to the first of two final points.

All documentation and revitalization work is potentially valuable

There is sometimes an attitude that only the full revival of an endangered language can be considered a success for its speakers. However, it has repeatedly been found that almost all documentation and revitalization work has value and can benefit a community, bringing its members together and rekindling feelings of enthusiasm and pride in the heritage language and cultural identity of the group. Such positive effects may result even from the renewed use of greetings and other simple expressions in the ancestral language and do not necessarily arise only when a language has been completely revitalized. What is important, as mentioned earlier, is that a community sets itself realistic goals to achieve and is able to make some steps toward using its heritage language again. Full revitalization of an endangered language regularly takes several generations to come about, as new native speakers are raised and mature within a language community, but positive attitudes and the foundations for more extensive revival work can very usefully be laid by modest, initial targets of language documentation and use.

Speakers of endangered languages do not need to abandon their heritage languages in order to speak other, majority languages

A very common reason given by adult speakers of minority languages for deliberately not passing on their heritage language to rising generations is that they want their children to become proficient speakers of a local majority language, so as to have access to better possibilities of employment. The assumption generally made by such well-meaning parents is that children need to avoid acquiring the heritage language in order to become fluent speakers of the larger language. However, this assessment is simply incorrect and assumes that children must be monolingual, either learning to speak the heritage language or a different, majority language, and that one must be sacrificed for the other to develop. Yet bilingualism in individuals is in fact extremely widespread throughout the world, and the majority of the world's population are proficient speakers of two or more languages. It is therefore not necessary for heritage languages to be abandoned simply to enable access to other economically advantageous languages, and children can become effective speakers of both an ancestral language and a second, majority language, if sufficient input from the two languages is provided (see chapter 8 for more discussion of the achievement of bilingualism). The eminent linguist Joshua Fishman, who has devoted his life to studying language and ethnicity, along with many other language conservationists, has regularly stressed that functional bilingualism should be the goal of endangered language communities, maintaining (or reviving) their ancestral language for the benefits it provides in cultural identity and community pride, and acquiring fluency in whatever other larger language offers the best economic and academic opportunities to its speakers. Stable bilingualism exists in many countries and populations, as we will see in chapter 4, and it can certainly also be encouraged and cultivated as a practice among speakers of threatened languages.

Suggestions for further reading and activities

1. Select an *immigrant minority group* in the country where you live (or some other country you are interested in) and try to find out the extent to which it has been able to maintain its heritage language and pass it on to rising generations, or has been experiencing language shift and loss. Which of the factors typically causing language shift discussed in the chapter seem to be most relevant for the group you are considering?
2. Create a profile of an *indigenous minority group* in the country where you live (or some other country), describing the history of the group and how it came to be a minority. Has the language of this group been documented and described in dictionaries and grammar books, and does it have a written form and literature? What attitudes do members of this group have toward their language?
3. Use the internet to find out more about Generation 1.5 and its experiences of belonging to (or feeling disconnected from) the two cultures it has connections with.
4. Watch the film *The Linguists* and discuss which sections you found most interesting. Did watching this film make you feel more or less supportive of efforts made to revitalize languages?
5. Read chapter 11 of Sue Wright's (2004) book *Language Policy and Language Planning*, published by Palgrave Macmillan (New York). Section 11.1 reviews a range of arguments that are commonly given as reasons why people should be concerned about language loss. Discuss which reasons you think are most convincing, and which might seem to you to be less important, or even questionable.
6. Welsh is a Celtic language which is frequently presented as a very successful case of language revitalization. Irish, by way of contrast, is a Celtic language which is reported not to have responded well to attempts at revitalization. Find out more about Welsh and Irish and why there seems to be a difference in the way that these related languages are currently surviving in their communities.
7. Access the UNESCO online *Atlas of the World's Languages in Danger* (http://www.unesco.org/languages-atlas/), pick a continent or a particular country, and find out about the ongoing state of language endangerment in that part of the world. You can find further very useful information at *The Endangered Languages Project* interactive website: http://www.endangeredlanguages.com/#/3/33.945/70.494/0/100000/0/low/mid/high/unknown
8. Mark Abley's book *Spoken Here: Travels among Threatened Languages* (published in 2003 by Hougthon Mifflin) is a vivid depiction of the author's journey through different endangered language communities around the world. Pick one of the chapters from this book to read, and discuss the experiences Abley describes. Does Abley suggest that there is hope for the survival of the languages he comes in contact with, or are they likely to die out?

4

Diglossia and Code-Switching

Introduction

At the end of chapter 3 it was noted that members of endangered language communities who wish to reap the economic benefits made available by knowledge of dominant local languages without abandoning their heritage languages can be advised to cultivate functional bilingualism and the use of different languages in different domains of life. Heritage languages can be maintained for primary use in the home, with family, friends, and the local community, while a larger, majority language can be used to gain access to better-paid employment and higher education. In the first part of this chapter, we will see that there are in fact many countries and populations where people make use of two distinct languages or two distinct varieties of a single language for different purposes and activities, a linguistic situation which has become known as '**diglossia**'. It is consequently quite plausible and indeed common for stable bilingualism to involve the application of a person's two languages to different areas of life, and we will consider what kinds of division of domains typically occur in diglossic situations. In the second part of this chapter, we will focus on another phenomenon found in many bilingual communities: the mixing of languages in single conversations and within sentences, as speakers combine words and structures from two (or more) languages in their speech, a pattern of behavior known as '**code-switching**'. Our study of this widespread language habit will examine exactly how speakers alternate between different languages within short stretches of discourse, why they frequently engage in this intermixing of languages, and what kinds of attitudes are held toward code-switching by members of bilingual groups.

Diglossia

Diglossia is a term popularized in a very influential article by Charles Ferguson in 1959 and used, prototypically, to refer to the use of *two varieties of the same language* by members of a single speech community in different, mutually exclusive situations. In developing his description of diglossia, Ferguson refers to four countries/regions in which alternations between two forms of a single language regularly occur, depending on the speech context and setting: (German-speaking) Switzerland, Greece (until the 1970s), Haiti, and Arabic-speaking states of North Africa and the Middle East. In these and many other instances where diglossia is observed, the following properties are commonly found to characterize the 'diglossic' situation:

A. **Two distinct varieties of the same language occur**. In diglossic situations, members of a single population regularly make use of two clearly differentiated varieties of a single language. One of these is conventionally referred to as the H or 'high' variety by linguists, and the other as the L or 'low' variety. In the four case studies focused on by Ferguson, the H and L varieties are as follows:

Switzerland (German-speaking areas)
H variety: Standard German
L variety: Swiss German

Haiti
H variety: French
L variety: Haitian Creole

Greece (during most of the 20th century)
H variety: Katharévousa
L variety: Dhimotikí

Arabic-speaking countries
H variety: Classical Arabic
L variety: local varieties of Arabic
(e.g., Moroccan Arabic, Egyptian Arabic)

The H and L varieties are distinguished from each other in the words they make use of in many instances. This is illustrated with examples from Greek and Arabic, which show that even very common words may be significantly different in H and L.

	Greek			Arabic	
	H	L		H	L
house	íkos	spíti	*nose*	anshun	manaxir
water	ídhor	neró	*what*	mā	ʻēh
but	alá	má	*now*	ˈalˈāna	dilwaˈti

There may also be differences of grammar and phonology in H and L.

B. **Two distinct sets of functions separate H and L**. The H and L varieties are used for quite different functions, with very little overlap. The two varieties occur in 'complementary distribution'—they complement each other in their use. In certain domains of life the H variety but not the L variety is appropriate, and in other domains there is almost exclusive use of the L variety, and the H variety is not utilized. Ferguson (1959) gives an illustration of the typical division of linguistic labor found with H and L varieties in the following sample listing of possible situations, which shows which variety would be used in each domain.

	H	L
Sermon in church or mosque	✓	
Instructions to servants, waiters, workmen, clerks		✓
Personal letter	✓	
Speech in parliament, political speech	✓	

	H	L
University lecture		✓
Conversation with family, friends, colleagues		✓
News broadcast	✓	
Radio 'soap opera'		✓
Newspaper editorial, news story, caption on picture	✓	
Caption on political cartoon		✓
Poetry	✓	
Folk literature		✓

C. **Acquisition of H and L.** The L variety is the form of language everyone learns first, when they are young. It is acquired at home in interactions with parents and other family members. The H variety is only learned later, through formal education in school. Because of the different ways that H and L are acquired, speakers are normally much more confident, natural speakers of L, and may frequently be less spontaneously fluent in the H variety.

D. **Use/non-use in everyday speech.** No one uses the H variety in everyday informal conversation. Only the L variety is used for such purposes. The H variety dominates all formal domains of communication, and using it in informal interactions would immediately strike people as unnatural, pretentious, and completely out of place.

E. **Codification/standardization.** The H variety is normally highly codified and standardized—there will be grammatical descriptions of a standard form of the language and dictionaries listing its vocabulary. It is uncommon to find any formal descriptions of L varieties, almost as if they do not really exist, or are not felt worthy of being described in grammars and dictionaries. There is always a standardized way of writing the H variety (i.e., an accepted script form and spelling conventions), whereas there is often no commonly agreed-upon way to write L, and L is very infrequently used for writing, if at all.

F. **Literature.** The H variety of a language is often associated with a substantial amount of high-status literature (novels, drama, poetry) and other non-fiction writing (scientific, legal, and educational texts). If the L variety is ever used for writing, this will normally be restricted to low-status uses in cartoons, advertising and folk literature.

In addition to the four cases which Ferguson presents as prime examples of diglossia, he also mentions three other clear instances of diglossia from different parts of the world. In South Asia (India and Sri Lanka), the Dravidian language **Tamil** is noted to occur in a typical diglossic situation. The H variety, used for writing, in literature, and all very formal purposes, is 'literary Tamil', while informal acts of communication are always carried out in the L variety, 'colloquial Tamil'. Literary Tamil is learned in school, whereas colloquial Tamil is acquired in the home, and the two varieties differ from each other to a considerable degree in their grammar and vocabulary.[1] In medieval Europe, **Latin** and the early **Romance languages** which emerged out of Latin were used in the manner typical of diglossia, with the H variety Latin occurring in the domains of writing, very formal speech, religious services, and church literature, and a range of vernacular L varieties (very early forms of French, Italian, and Spanish, developing from Latin) being used in everyday speech. In East Asia, **Chinese**, for much of its history, also figured heavily in a diglossic relation, as writing and speech made use of different, though related forms of the language. The H variety in this case was *wenyan* 'literary/classical Chinese' and the L varieties were a large number of regional forms of colloquial Chinese, very different from the highly stylized Chinese used for writing (Chen 1999).

Extended diglossia

Following Ferguson's initial work on diglossia, other linguists have proposed extending the way this term is used, to cover related and very similar instances where speakers make use of two different forms of language in different domains (see Fishman 1967, in particular). One way in which 'extended diglossia' is suggested to occur is when H and L are not varieties of the same language, as in 'strict diglossia' (according to Ferguson), but actually are different languages. A classic example of this is the language situation in Paraguay, as reported by Rubin (1968) and others. In this South American country, knowledge of both Spanish and the indigenous language Guaraní is widespread among the population, and the two languages are used for different purposes. Spanish is the H variety/language, used in formal domains (government offices, church, business meetings), while Guaraní is the L variety/language, occurring in acts of informal communication with friends, family, and members of the local community.

Triglossia

Further research has also revealed that there are complex language situations in which three languages (or varieties) are regularly used in distinctive ways that resemble the functional division of language use in simple diglossia, where just two languages/varieties are involved. Such situations have been referred to as instances of 'triglossia', and it is often reported that there may be two languages/varieties that have H functions, and one that is used in a typical L role. Putative examples of triglossia have been suggested to occur (or have occurred) in the following countries:

Luxembourg
H varieties: German and French
L variety: Lëtzebuergesch
(Hoffman 1981)

Tanzania
H varieties: English and Swahili
L variety: regional tribal languages
(Mkilifi 1972)

---

1. The differences between colloquial and literary Tamil are so significant that this has sometimes posed problems for young heritage language learners in places such as Singapore, who grow up acquiring English as their mother tongue, and then later try to learn Tamil in school. As literary Tamil is considered to be the prestige form of the language, this is the form students are taught in schools. However, a knowledge of literary Tamil does not allow young people to communicate effectively with older generation speakers of Tamil who only know and speak colloquial Tamil, as the two forms of the language are quite distinct. See Sravanan (1998) for an interesting discussion of the factors relating to colloquial and literary Tamil that are causing language shift away from the language among South Asians in Singapore.

Early medieval England
H varieties: Latin and French
L variety: English
(Crystal 2004)

Morocco
H varieties: Classical Arabic and Middle Moroccan Arabic
L variety: vernacular Moroccan Arabic
(Youssi 1995)

Considering both examples of diglossia and triglossia, it is natural to wonder how such unusual situations develop, and why a community of speakers would come to use two or more distinct varieties or languages for different activities in life. Each case of diglossia may in fact evolve historically in a somewhat different way, and there is no single path of development which typifies every emergence of this phenomenon. Here we will explore two of Ferguson's classic cases of diglossia in a bit more depth to illustrate how such patterns may come into being in a society: the stories of Arabic and modern Greek.

Arabic
The early development of Arabic

The label 'Arabic' first referred to a range of varieties of speech centered in Arabia and the Syrian desert before Islamic times, (the first written record of Arabic being dated 512 B.C.E.), forming a dialect continuum which had no clearly sharp borders and merged into Aramaic in the north. However, each major tribe in the broadly Arabic area was associated with a particular dialect. In addition to this, a shared lingua franca form of Arabic occurred and was used in poetry and in the writing of the Qur'an (Koran), the most important event in the development of Arabic. When the Qur'an was proclaimed by the prophet Mohammed and subsequently written down in the 7th century C.E. in the common form of Arabic, mixed with features of Mohammed's own regional variety of Arabic (the dialect of Mecca), this established it as a fixed model of the language which has been revered, copied, and preserved without change to the present. Qur'anic Arabic is commonly referred to as Classical Arabic, or sometimes Literary Arabic. It is still learned in school as the prestigious and *only* way to write Arabic throughout the Arabic-speaking world.

Shortly after the writing of the Qur'an in the 7th century, the Arabic-speaking tribes of Arabia and the Syrian desert spread out much further in the Middle East and managed to conquer large amounts of territory both in the Middle East and North Africa (and also in the Balkan area of eastern Europe, and southern Spain), spreading both Islam and Arabic as this process took place. As Arabic came into contact with other languages, for example Berber in the area which is now Morocco and Algeria, and Coptic in Egypt, it developed local dialect forms with distinctive features, and different speaking conventions evolved which ultimately resulted in the creation of a wide range of forms of colloquial spoken Arabic, including modern colloquial Moroccan Arabic, Egyptian Arabic, Lebanese Arabic, and Iraqi Arabic. This development from Classical Qur'anic Arabic to the modern regional dialects has been likened to the emergence of the Romance languages from Latin in western Europe.

Differences between Classical Arabic and modern colloquial forms of Arabic

Classical Arabic and modern, colloquial forms of Arabic differ in many ways:

(a) Pronunciation: regional forms of Arabic may make regular use of certain different sounds.
(b) Grammar: colloquial forms of Arabic have simplified aspects of the grammar of Classical Arabic (for example, eliminating subject/object/possessor markings on nouns).
(c) Words: a major difference between Classical Arabic and colloquial varieties is in the lexicon—many words in colloquial varieties are different from those in Classical Arabic.

Diglossia

The diglossic division of Arabic into H(igh) and L(ow) forms is extremely important and has been very important for much of the history of the language. Classical Qur'anic Arabic is the H form—highly prestigious and widely perceived throughout the Arabic-speaking world as being logical and clear in its design, beautiful in its mode of expression, and generally superior to all colloquial forms of Arabic. Such strong feelings about Classical Arabic are reported to be held among those with education and the non-educated/illiterate alike.

In recent decades, the lexicon of Classical Arabic has been developed further to include words to refer to new inventions and ideas of the modern world. Such words have been coined very carefully, making use of the resources of Classical Arabic so as not to radically alter its basic linguistic nature and orientation, and have resulted in what is referred to as **Modern Standard Arabic (MSA)**. MSA has the grammar and lexicon/words of Classical Arabic augmented by new words for concepts which did not exist in earlier centuries.

In all Arabic-speaking countries, there is a common difference in the forms of Arabic used in formal and informal domains of life. Almost all forms of writing are carried out in MSA, including informal notes to family members and friends. The only exceptions to this are certain folkloric plays and poetry which may be written down in colloquial forms of Arabic. Otherwise, all books, newspapers, magazines, and letters are composed with MSA, not with colloquial Arabic.

In spoken language, by way of contrast, it is regional, colloquial forms of Arabic which predominantly occur, regardless of the level of society (i.e., both among the educated and those who have not received much education), and the use of MSA is highly restricted, occurring just in religious sermons, TV news-reading, university lectures, and some political speeches (especially those of more fundamentalist politicians). Films and TV shows which are imported from other countries are also commonly dubbed into MSA, so that they can be broadcast to a wider international audience of Arabic speakers. Otherwise, in TV soap operas, chat shows, and in instances of discussion at all levels of education (also in seminars in universities), it is the local colloquial form of Arabic that is used by all speakers.

Colloquial Arabic is the language form that all speakers learn as their first language, and it is the variety that all speakers will use with their family, friends, and also at work, even to seniors to whom respect is due. Colloquial forms of Arabic are never taught in school, though they are regularly used in classrooms, between teachers and students. Classical Arabic and MSA, on the other hand, are both acquired by formal learning in schools, and MSA is learned primarily as a written rather than a spoken form of Arabic, so that very few speakers become able to sustain a long conversation in MSA. When it is stated that Arabic is the official language of a country, this naturally refers to use of Classical Arabic/MSA and not the local colloquial form of Arabic. Normally constitutions state that 'al 'arabiyyah' is the official language, where this term translates simply as 'Arabic' but is conventionally used to refer (somewhat ambiguously) to both Classical Arabic and MSA. The term 'al fushā' exists to refer to colloquial forms of Arabic.

A clearly delineated diglossic situation in Arabic-speaking countries thus became established many centuries ago, as spoken forms of Arabic developed in different ways under the influence of other, local non-Arabic languages, but written Arabic remained unchanged since the 7th century, because the structure, style, and words in Qur'anic Arabic were deemed to be sacred in nature, and should not be adjusted in any way to mirror changes occurring in local spoken varieties.

Greek

The development of diglossia in Greece in recent times has followed a different social path than Arabic-diglossia, and is heavily associated with public disagreement over language use and with political controversy. Greece itself came into existence as an independent nation-state only in 1832. Before that, for most of the preceding 400 years, it was part of the Ottoman Empire, whose dominant language was Turkish, with some additional use of Persian and Arabic. Concerning the Greek language, as Ancient Greek developed over the centuries into New Testament Greek and then Byzantine Greek, the written and spoken forms of Greek became more and more different from each other. Spoken Greek borrowed and made regular use of many words from Turkish and Italian, while written Greek made extensive use of Classical Greek words. This separation of the spoken and written forms of Greek thus resulted in a situation of diglossia, with speakers using two different varieties of the same language for different activities—oral and written communication.

In the late 18th century, as a new movement for Greek independence began to grow, it was seen as a problem that there was such a gap between written and spoken forms of the language. To try to solve the problem, various solutions were proposed (Trudgill 2000). Some Greek nationalists suggested that there should be a return to the past, and Greeks should start writing and also speaking Ancient Greek again. However, this was an unrealistic option and never had much chance of practical success. Others took the colloquial form of Greek which was widely spoken at the time and tried to purify and purge it of all Turkish and other foreign loan words so that it became more genuinely and fully Greek, in their eyes, and free of foreign influence. This resulted in the creation of the 'purifying' form of the Greek language known as Katharévousa. A third position advocated by many in Greece was that people should make more widespread use of colloquial Greek and also use it in writing. This view championed the spread of a spoken form of Greek which had developed from a number of dialects in the Peloponnese area and then became dominant in Athens, subsequently being referred to as Dhimotikí (or 'demotic Greek').

When Greece achieved independence in 1832, those who came to govern the country were uneasy with the thought of using a form of colloquial Greek as the new official language of the country, to be used for all writing, and so favored Katharévousa. Katharévousa was therefore made into the official language of education, government, and the media, embedding diglossia more deeply within newly independent Greece, with the use of Katharévousa in formal domains contrasting with the use of a quite different form of Greek in everyday, informal speech.

However, many people were unhappy with the enforced use of Katharévousa in formal domains, as Katharévousa was difficult to learn and seemed like an artificial, archaic language form. This led to increased support for extensions of the use of Dhimotikí toward the end of the 19th century, and many intellectuals took to creating new works of literature with Dhimotikí. The 20th century then saw an extended battle to end the diglossic situation which had evolved in Greece, with proponents of Dhimotikí campaigning for its use in education and other formal domains dominated by Katharévousa. The struggle to achieve this involved much bitter confrontation between different political factions. Katharévousa was associated with right-wing nationalist elements and reviving the purity of the Greek language. Dhimotikí, on the other hand, was associated with left-wing politics and the defense of democracy. The Orthodox Greek Church supported Katharévousa, as it was closer to the Greek of the New Testament, and proposals for Dhimotikí to replace Katharévousa in written contexts were represented as attacks on the church, as a betrayal of the Greek nation, and as support for foreign enemies (Trudgill 2000). In 1903, when a translation of the Bible appeared in Dhimotikí, this actually resulted in public riots, led by indignant supporters of Katharévousa, and the deaths of eight people in the rioting in Athens. Performances of classical plays in Dhimotikí also led to angry mobs marching in the streets protesting against the use of the spoken language for high-prestige functions.

As the course of the 20th century unfolded, there were frequent changes in the ways that Dhimotikí was allowed to intrude into formal domains previously restricted to use of Katharévousa. In some years Dhimotikí was permitted as the medium of education in schools, in others Katharévousa was strictly reinstated. After many disruptive changes extending over several decades, ultimately Dhimotikí achieved the upper hand and became established as the official language of all formal domains, developing into what is now called Modern Standard Greek. To some significant extent, the final victory of Dhimotikí in the late 1970s was connected with the fall of a very unpopular military government in 1974, which had strongly supported Katharévousa. Popular sentiment rejected Katharévousa, along with the military regime it was associated with, and welcomed Dhimotikí as a full replacement for the archaic H variety of the language (Mackridge 2009). Viewed over the whole trajectory of developments through the 18th–20th centuries, Greece presents an interesting example of diglossia in which an L variety, initially restricted to typically informal uses, has incrementally rid itself of restrictions on its use in formal domains, and over time has acquired new uses in areas normally dominated by H varieties—literature, education, government administration, and written media. This elimination of an original, stable situation of diglossia was achieved only with great personal commitment to the elevation of a colloquial form of language and a fight against deeply entrenched attitudes among much of the population which venerated the H variety as the only rightful form of language for certain acts of communication. Such feelings that H varieties have special linguistic properties which positively distinguish them from L varieties in terms of prestige have frequently been reported for diglossic situations (Ferguson 1959), as we will now briefly discuss.

Prestige values of H and L

In his 1959 introduction to diglossia across languages, Charles Ferguson lists 'prestige' as an additional feature that H varieties commonly have, and suggests that speakers may find the H variety superior to the L variety in a number of ways, believing it to have greater inherent beauty, logical structure, or expressive power as a language, even in instances when a person does not have a strong proficiency in H, and uses the L variety most of the time. This kind of respect for the H variety has been well attested in a range of diglossic situations, and in certain cases there is a clear connection with religion, the H variety being the language long used in religious texts. For example, Classical Arabic is the language of the Qur'an, and Katharévousa is perceived to be very close to New Testament Greek. Any attempts to present sacred religious messages through the medium of the L variety may be strongly resisted, even where this may allow for more people to understand the meaning of such texts. Hence, there have been very strong rejections of suggestions that the Qur'an be translated into modern Arabic dialects, and in the late Middle Ages many objected violently to translations of the Bible into English in replacement of Latin.

While it might therefore be concluded that the H variety is regularly attributed more prestige than the L variety, and that L varieties are accordingly viewed as being low in prestige value, further investigations have shown that attitudes toward H and L are more complex than this, and it is not always predictable that there will be strongly positive attitudes towards H and less positive or even negative attitudes towards the value of L. In discussing the situation in Greece in the 19th century, we noted that many leading intellectuals found Katharévousa highly artificial and not well suited for writing Greek, and similar attitudes toward classical Chinese were present at the beginning of the 20th century, leading to the *baihua* language reform movement, which effectively ended diglossia in China in a way similar to what transpired in Greece (Chen 1999). Additionally, the existence of genuine admiration and respect for an H variety does not necessarily imply an absence of positive feelings for L. Indeed, many people may indicate that the L variety is the best way to express their feelings and value it highly for this property. In Paraguay, for example, people are reported to be very proud of and attached to Guaraní, the L variety, and generally prefer it in domains which stress solidarity. In Switzerland, too, there are highly positive attitudes toward the L variety, Swiss German,[2] as it allows the Swiss to project a specifically Swiss identity and distinguish themselves from their northern neighbors, the Germans. Similar positive attitudes have been documented in many diglossic communities, though such feelings are not always expressed openly and directly by speakers when asked—the 'prestige' which L forms have is

---

2. 'Swiss German' is actually a term which picks out a range of Swiss dialects of German. Each of these serves as an L variety, paired with standard German as the H variety.

often somewhat concealed and 'covert' (see chapter 11 for discussion of differences between the notions of 'overt' and 'covert' prestige).

Summary

As has been outlined in this first part of the chapter, diglossia is a situation in which two distinct varieties of a single language, or sometimes two distinct languages (extended diglossia), are made use of by the members of a speech community, and are used in everyday life for different functions. One of these varieties, the L(ow) variety, occurs in simple conversation between family, friends, and acquaintances in the home and the community, while the other variety, the H(igh) form, is made use of in formal domains, such as education, government business, newspapers, and the creation of works of literature. L and H varieties occur in complementary distribution with each other, with very little overlap in use, and no one in the speech community makes use of the H variety for regular, informal communication. As the H variety is generally learned in school, people are often much less confident speakers of H, and would find it difficult to sustain any kind of long conversation in H, even with formal topics of discussion.

One final note can be added about the term 'diglossia' and how it applies. It has frequently been pointed out that a distinction needs to be made between situations of diglossia and somewhat similar, very common situations of bilingualism involving a 'standard (language) and dialects'. In a number of countries, it is found that a standard form of a particular language is used in formal domains, and related dialects are used in informal communication. Examples of this kind of situation are present in Germany, Italy, and modern China and might initially seem to call for use of the term 'diglossia'. However, when we compare Germany, Italy, and modern China with the situation in Switzerland and Arabic-speaking countries, there is a key difference. In the latter, diglossic situations, no speakers regularly make use of the formal H variety for everyday informal speech. However, in a 'standard and dialects' situation such as Germany, Italy, and modern China, a large number of speakers do use the standard language in informal interactions as well as in formal communication, and it is their basic 'mother tongue' variety of speech, learned at home.

Code-switching

In addition to diglossia, there is another phenomenon involving alternations between two (or more) languages which is frequently observed in multilingual societies: the occurrence of 'code-switching', which refers to the switching between different languages or varieties *within a single conversation*, with alternations taking place either between sentences or actually inside sentences in many instances.

The following exchange is an example of code-switching in a Quechua/Spanish community in Ecuador from King (1999). The speakers begin their conversation in a store with greetings in Quechua, then switch to Spanish as the customer asks to purchase some goods, and finally Quechua is returned to in some small talk before the customer leaves. Note that in this example, Spanish is represented in italic script, and Quechua in non-italic script. The translations to the right retain this italic/non-italic difference to highlight the alternation between the two languages.

Storekeeper:	Alli chishi.	Good afternoon.
Customer:	Alli chishi. Imashinalla?	Good afternoon. How are you?
	A ver, una media libra de azúcar y cuatro pancitos.	Let's see, a half pound of sugar and four rolls.
Storekeeper:	Ya. Novecientos. Imata rura canpac hijo? Caipichu?	All right. Nine hundred (sucres). What is your son doing? Is he here?
Customer:	Mana caipichu. Paica Yacuambipi.	He's not here. He's in Yacuambi.

Code-switching like this is very common in situations which involve greetings and small talk, mixed together with some kind of business transaction. The use of Quechua establishes a feeling of group solidarity between customer and storekeeper as members of the same Quechua-speaking community, and is juxtaposed with Spanish, which is more widely spoken in this particular community due to the process of language shift and loss described in chapter 3.

A second example of code-switching from the speech of a Japanese-Canadian in Nishimura (1997) shows how a speaker alternates between two languages, Japanese and English, within a monologue, with switches occurring in multiple places between and inside sentences:

B.C. *ni iku toki, hikooki de yomou to omotte kara*, I bought it.	When I flew to B.C., *as I thought I would read it*, I bought it.
I haven't finished it yet, and its hard, because me-*nanka, moo hon nanka yomu to* cover-to-cover *yomanakattara*,	I haven't finished it yet, and its hard, *because someone like me, if I read a book if I don't read (it)* cover-to-cover,
if I stop *doka-de*, I forget the story.	(and) if I stop *somewhere*, I forget the story.
One week later, *yomu desho*, I've got to go back.	One week later, *when I read (it)* I've got to go back.

We will shortly begin to consider first *how* code-switching occurs linguistically in a number of different ways, and then *why* speakers may engage in such alternations, and what kinds of attitudes people have toward code-switching as a general practice. Before we do this, it will be useful to highlight certain of the properties which distinguish code-switching from diglossia.

Diglossia and code-switching compared

Diglossia: Different varieties/languages are used almost automatically in different domains. Speakers do not have any real choice as to which language they use in any particular situation. The causes of alternations between languages are very clear and due to the formality of the speech act, and the H variety is never used in informal interactions. When a particular activity (giving a sermon, news-reading, writing, informal conversation, etc.) triggers the use of either the H or the L variety, this variety is used throughout the activity, often for an extended period of time, with no switches back to the other variety.

Code-switching: In code-switching, there is considerably more spontaneous switching between two languages/varieties. Speakers have much more freedom to choose how they use their two languages and alternate between them, and are not constrained to use only one variety in a particular situation. Both of the languages known by a code-switching speaker will often be used in informal conversation. Switches between languages may be frequent and may occur within short periods of time. The causes of alternations between two languages in instances of code-switching are quite varied and sometimes more complex to understand than in diglossia, where it is normally obvious what motivates the use of the H and L varieties.

Types of code-switching

It is often suggested that there are several different 'levels' of language-mixing which should be recognized when considering code-switching phenomena, corresponding to the position of breaks that are made between two languages. Four main alternation points and styles can be identified in the code-switching of speakers from different backgrounds.

Level 1. Sentence-boundary code-switching

The most basic and linguistically least complicated mode of switching that speakers of two languages can carry out within a single conversation is to alternate languages between sentences, producing each sentence entirely in one language, with breaks occurring between sentences. This was already seen in the Quechua-Spanish example, and is illustrated again in the following French-English monologue .

Hier j'ai rencontré Jean et sa nouvelle copine à Toronto.	*Yesterday I met Jean and his new girlfriend in Toronto.*
You know, I think it's really too much.	You know, I think it's really too much.
He's only just divorced.	He's only just divorced.
Alors, il m'a dit qu'il va te visiter demain.	*So, he said to me he's going to visit you tomorrow.*

This kind of alternation in which switches are made at sentence junctures will be referred to as '**sentence-boundary code-switching**'. It is very common, and avoids the difficulties of combining words and grammar from two languages inside a single sentence. The following diagram provides a schematic representation of this kind of code-switching. Each box represents a full sentence, with L1 and L2 standing for language 1 and language 2—the two languages being used. Alternations between the two languages may occur after entire sentences in one language have been completed.

Level 2. Extra-sentential code-switching/'tag-insertion'

This form of code-switching occurs at the *periphery* of sentences and involves the insertion of 'tag'-like elements such as '*You know . . .*' and '*I mean . . .*' into a sentence. Such tags, which may either precede or follow the main body of the sentence, are in one language, while the rest of the sentence is in the second language. Because they occur at the edges of sentences, words and short phrases functioning as tags can be easily inserted, as they do not interrupt the grammatical structure of the second language used in the rest of the sentence.

'I mean, *c'est un idiot, ce mec-là!*'	English/French
'I mean, he's an idiot, that guy!'	
'I'm going to take the car now, *daijoobu daroo*?'	English/Japanese
'I'm going to take the car now, ok?'	

Extra-sentential code-switching can be represented in the following way, with small additions from either L1 or L2 occurring at the beginning or end of sentences.

Level 3. Clause-boundary code-switching

When speakers make switches between two languages at *clause boundaries* within a single sentence, with one clause being in one language, and the following full clause being in the second language, this will be referred to as *clause-boundary code-switching*. As such switching requires more attention to the internal grammatical structure of a sentence than is necessary for Level 1 and Level 2 switching, it is often more challenging than simple sentence-boundary and extra-sentential code-switching, especially if typologically different languages are mixed.[3] Clause-boundary code-switching requires greater fluency in both languages than tag-insertion, or sentence boundary switches, as major portions of a single sentence must conform to the rules of distinct languages.

---

3. The forms of code-switching which are here being referred to as *sentence boundary code-switching* (Level 1) and *clause boundary code-switching* (Level 3) are elsewhere often grouped together and both referred to as instances of *inter-sentential code-switching*. This term is used in works such as Poplack (1980) to pick out not only sentence-internal switching at clause boundaries, but also switches at sentence boundaries, where the alternation between two languages is not sentence-internal. Here we separate out these two cases of code-switching as they show certain differences. Switches at sentence boundaries are syntactically the easiest to produce, as there is *no* integration of the two languages with each other inside a single sentence, and this kind of switching is therefore more common than switching inside sentences, either in sentence-peripheral positions (extra-sentential code-switching) or at sentence-internal clause boundaries, and produced by more speakers than the higher levels of code-switching.

'*Johann hat mir gesagt*, that you were going to leave.'   German/English
'*Johann told me* that you were going to leave.'

'*Chigum ton-i opsoso*, I can't buy it.'   Korean/English
'*As I don't have money now*, I can't buy it.'

'*Jokhon Mini bari eshechilo*, Ram was watching TV.'   Bengali/English
'*When Mini came home*, Ram was watching TV.'

This form of alternation between languages can be given the following representation, where the switch between L1 and L2 occurs at a clause boundary:

Level 4. Intra-sentential code-switching

This term refers to switching which occurs *within clause boundaries*. Intra-sentential switching requires much bilingual skill and may be avoided by all but the most fluent bilinguals. In order to switch swiftly and congruently between two languages (often multiple times) within clauses, speakers must have a very high level of proficiency in both languages, and intra-sentential code-switching is generally only observed in bilingual speakers who are fully fluent in both of the languages they know. Ironically, outsiders who criticize this kind of language mixing frequently suggest that it is done because speakers are confused about the two languages they use and are not fully competent in either, but the opposite is in fact true—only the most advanced bilinguals who have had much practice in intra-sentential code-switching can carry out such mixing with confidence.

'*Women zuotian qu kan de* movie was really amazing!'   Mandarin/English
'The movie *we went to see yesterday* was really amazing!'

'*Il a envoyé* the book you gave him *à sa mère*.'   English/French
'*He sent* the book you gave him *to his mother*.'

'*khaw khuan ja* communicate all that *nai phasaa thai*.'   English/Thai
'*He should* communicate all that *in Thai*?'

Intra-sentential switching may often seem to take place for no apparent reason, and there may frequently be no obvious change in topic, hearer, or setting which would trigger the switches. In this sense, intra-sentential switching may be different from other bilingual language switching, which can sometimes be attributed to changes in the topic of conversation and the people being spoken to. Sometimes intra-sentential switching is given the special term **code-mixing** to distinguish it from other forms of code-switching.

> **Code-mixing**: where switching between languages takes place inside clauses and within the main core of a single sentence (i.e., not just at the periphery—tag insertion), and in the discussion of a single topic.

Following are two further examples of advanced code-mixing from speakers of English and Spanish, and English and Japanese:

> 'But I used to eat the *bofe*, the brain. And then they stopped selling it because *tenian, este, le encontraron que tenia* worms. I used to make some *bofe! Después yo hacía uno d'esos* concoctions: the garlic *con cebolla, y hacía un mojo, y yo dejaba que se curate eso* for a couple of hours.' (Poplack 1980)

> 'But I used to eat the *bofe*, the brain. And then they stopped selling it because *they had, uh, they found out that it had* worms. I used to make some *bofe! Then I would make one of those* concoctions: the garlic *with onion, and I'd make a sauce, and I'd let that sit* for a couple of hours.'

> '*Sore da kara*, anyway, *asoko de* smoked salmon *katta no yo*.'
> '*So*, anyway, (we) *bought* smoked salmon *there, you see*.' Nishimura (1997)

Intra-sentential code-switching/code-mixing can potentially look as follows, with multiple switches between L1 and L2:

L1   L2   L1   L2   L1   L2   L1

While it might perhaps seem that intra-sentential code-switching allows for two languages to be mixed up with each other in any random way, studies have established that there are grammatical constraints on where switches between languages may occur which are sensitive to the syntactic structures of the two languages being intertwined. When breaks between L1 and L2 are made in certain places, speakers who regularly code-mix reject such forms as ungrammatical and unnatural. Intra-sentential code-switching thus requires a very fine understanding of the grammar of both languages and which syntactic junctures will allow for language alternation to take place naturally (see Gardner-Chloros 2009, chapter 5, for discussion).

Borrowing vs. code-switching

All languages borrow and incorporate words from other languages at some point in their history, and in most languages the borrowing of loan words continues to occur, as new products of technology and new concepts need to be named (see the discussion in chapter 2). The borrowing and incorporation of a word from another language is a process that is different from the use of a word from another language in instances of code-switching. Borrowing occurs widely in language groups who do not engage in code-switching at all, and borrowing makes a loan word a permanent new member of the vocabulary of a community, rather than a 'temporary loan' when a bilingual speaker accesses words from one language while speaking another. When genuine borrowing does occur, because of its long-lasting nature, and the fact that speakers of the 'host language' (i.e., the language being borrowed into) may not be speakers of the 'donor language' (the language from which a borrowed word originates), various changes to borrowed words typically occur, integrating them into the pronunciation norms and grammar of the host language.

Loan words are commonly adapted to have the regular phonological and morpho-syntactic properties of words in the host language. For example, when Chinese words are borrowed into English, they are stripped of the tones (distinguishing pitch contour) that each syllable normally carries, and various other adjustments to pronunciation may be made. The Mandarin Chinese word *gōngfu* which refers to a popular martial art form, and which has a high level tone on its first syllable, is adjusted to become English *kungfu* with no high tone and a different initial consonant and vowel sound. Cantonese *Bāk-kìng*, with a low-level tone on the first syllable and a high falling tone on the second syllable, lost both of these tones and certain other sound properties as it was borrowed and adapted into English as *Peking*, the old name for the northern capital of China.

Code-switching, by way of contrast, is generally the *unadapted* use of elements from one language together with those of another language. In code-switching, two different language systems are being used, with all of their special properties, and it is not the case that elements from one language are adapted to conform to the linguistic properties of a second language when mixing occurs. This difference allows one to distinguish cases of borrowing from code-switching among bilingual speakers in instances where a single word from one of the speaker's languages occurs embedded within words from the other language, as schematized below.

If the L2 word is pronounced with patterns of pronunciation typical of L1, this identifies it as a borrowing. However, if this word is pronounced in the way it would be pronounced in monolingual use of L2, this signals that is a (very short) instance of code-switching. Two actual examples will help make this clear. Consider the sentence '*Tomorrow I'm going to Paris with Sue.*' The place name in this sentence can be pronounced in two different ways. There is the English-style pronunciation in which the final –*s* is clearly heard, and there is a second French-style pronunciation in which the final –*s* is 'silent' and the word sounds as if it were spelled '*Paree*'. If a bilingual speaker uses the English-style pronunciation, this is the use of *Paris* as a borrowed and adapted word, but if the same speaker pronounces it with French pronunciation, this represents an unadapted code-switch. A parallel example from Chinese-English borrowing and code-switching might involve the pronunciation of the place name 'Hong Kong'. In Cantonese this is pronounced as '*Hèung Kóong*' with a falling and then a rising tone. If one hears this pronunciation in a sentence that is otherwise fully in English, it will be a code-switch, whereas if a Cantonese-English bilingual pronounces it as '*Hong Kong*', this will be the borrowed form.

Code-switching consequently can apply just to single words, and care is needed to distinguish such short switches from the use of related borrowed words. In addition to the pronunciation differences just discussed, it has also been noted that borrowed and code-switched words may show distinctions in the way that morphological affixes are attached. The generalization is that borrowed words are expected to allow for the attachment of appropriate affixes, whereas code-switched words which are only temporarily imported into a sentence produced in another language may not allow such attachments. Consider the following example relating Japanese to English. In English, a noun such as '*apple*' will require the attachment of a plural suffix –*s* in instances such as: 'John bought apples.' The word *apple* now also occurs in Japanese. It has been borrowed and adjusted to Japanese phonological patterns, being pronounced as '*appuru*', which clearly makes it sound quite distinct from the original source word '*apple*'. Now suppose that a bilingual Japanese-English speaker produces the form *appuru* in a basically English sentence. Given its pronunciation, this will be an instance of code-switching, and one might expect it would not necessarily allow attachment of the plural suffix –s, which is otherwise regularly used on English nouns and nouns borrowed into English. This is what is found, and one would naturally hear 'John bought appuru' rather than 'John bought appuru-s.' A convergence in adaptation is therefore often observed in borrowing (and absent from code-switching)—when a word is borrowed from one language into another, it will be phonologically adjusted and allow for the attachment of regular inflections, whereas code-switching will not affect the original pronunciation of a word, and may not qualify it to take affix attachments that are normally used within the second language.[4]

Analyses of code-switching: alternation and insertion

Linguists investigating the general phenomenon of code-switching have suggested that two rather different mental processes may be involved when languages are mixed in the ways described here. In one analysis, it is proposed that one of a bilingual speaker's two languages is mentally 'selected' and fully 'switched on' for language production, and serves as the 'base' or 'matrix language'. The second language is not fully activated, and only its vocabulary is accessed occasionally. Words and small phrases from this language, the 'embedded language', are selected and inserted into the grammatical structures created by use of the matrix language. Such 'insertional code-switching' is represented in the following diagram, in which the horizontal solid line indicates that L2 is fully switched on as the matrix language, and L1 (the embedded language) is only periodically accessed for vocabulary items inserted into the L2 base.

Insertional code-switching

This kind of modeling is taken to be appropriate for instances of code-switching in which just single words or small phrases from one language appear in sentences which are otherwise fully constructed with a second language.

---

4. For further discussion of the difference between borrowings/loan words and code-switches, including the contentious issue of spontaneous, one-time 'nonce borrowings', see Shana Poplack's 2018 book *Borrowing: Loanwords in the speech community and in the grammar*. Oxford: Oxford University Press.

A second analysis of code-switching, which is argued to be a more accurate modeling of Level 3 and Level 4 instances of code-switching in which no single language is obviously maintained as a base/matrix language throughout a sentence, is referred to as 'alternational code-switching.' This assumes that both L1 and L2 are periodically switched on and off and alternate as the base language for a sentence, as schematized below.

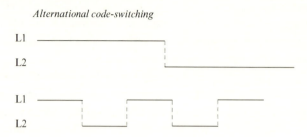

Alternational code-switching

It is plausible that both kinds of analysis are correct, and apply to different types of code-switching, with the insertional model capturing a speaker's mental language production in Level 1 and Level 2 code-switching, and an alternational analysis being correct for Level 3 and 4 alternations.

What causes people to code-switch?

Having described how code-switching may structurally occur in a number of ways, with alternations and insertions at various points typically creating a range of different styles and levels of code-switching, we will now consider why bilinguals actually engage in this kind of language mixing and what causes such a special type of linguistic behavior. We will see that there is, in fact, a range of reasons why people in different bilingual communities adopt one or another form of code-switching, and there is no single factor responsible for all instances of code-switching. Following much cross-linguistic investigation of mixing phenomena, the underlying, fundamental causes of code-switching can broadly be categorized into three separate sets of factors: (a) consequences of differences in the L1/L2 language abilities of bilinguals, (b) factors relating to language style and variety of expression, and (c) causes relating to the projection of personal identity through language and the manipulation of social relations with others.

Code-switching as a result of speakers' imbalance in knowledge of their two languages

As will be discussed further in chapter 8 (Bilingualism), most people who know two languages well have developed somewhat different abilities in these two languages, L1 and L2. While bilinguals may be confident, fluent speakers in their two languages, it is likely that the vocabularies that speakers have built up for each language are not identical, and speakers will know some words in one language that they will not know in their other language. Often this is a result of the way that many bilinguals acquire their language skills when young. In many bilingual communities, one language may be acquired in the home, among the family, and used with same-age friends, their 'L1', while the second language 'L2' is learned some years later when going to school. Such a common experience will regularly result in a young person having a stronger L2 vocabulary for talking about subjects relating to their studies in school—for example, science, politics, and history—but have a longer-developed habit of talking about home-related issues and their feelings in their L1. The differences in language ability that a bilingual speaker has can frequently trigger a switch from one language to another when the topic of conversation undergoes a change and the speaker finds it easier to talk about the new topic in a different language. In Taiwan, for example, where much of the population is bilingual in Mandarin Chinese and Taiwanese, the latter variety is generally acquired in the home, whereas the former is frequently learned (early on) in school. As a result of this, speakers often feel that certain topics—typically formal or official matters—are discussed more easily and effectively in Mandarin, while other topics relating to the home and countryside may be better expressed in Taiwanese. Additionally, as all reading and writing in Taiwan is done in Mandarin Chinese not Taiwanese, people may naturally use Mandarin to discuss the kinds of materials they read in newspapers and magazines. If a conversation begins in Taiwanese with talk about the family and home but then moves on to discuss recent international events read about in newspapers, or described in television news, the *ease of communication* factor may naturally cause a switch into Mandarin.

In many instances, speakers may wish to refer to a particular object or idea but either temporarily forget the appropriate word (perhaps due to not using it often in one of their two languages) or not know the word at all in the language they are currently speaking, due to never having learned it in this language. If, however, they do know the word for the object/idea in their other language, and this is also mentally quite easy to recall/access, due to regularly being used, it will be natural for a code-switch to occur, inserting the word from this language into the ongoing speech. For example, due to their particular life experiences in the USA in the mid-20th century, second-generation Japanese Americans came to learn a range of English words for which equivalents were never learned in their Japanese, such as *relocation center, minority race,* and *evacuation* (Nishimura 1997). When speaking Japanese and wishing to refer to such concepts, members of this group code-switch into English to import these words before continuing on in Japanese, as in the following sentence, which was part of a conversation mostly in Japanese (Nishimura 1997):

'Evacuation-*ga 1942 made deshita*.'
'The evacuation *went on until 1942*.'

Using a word from one language within another in this way, when a speaker forgets or does not know the word in the language he/she is currently speaking, is referred to as the use of code-switching for the '*filling of lexical gaps*'.

While speakers may simply code-switch a single word when necessary to fill a temporary or permanent lexical gap, and continue in the other language serving as matrix language, in some cases the use of a single word from the second, non-matrix language can actually cause a full switch into this language for the remainder of a sentence, and even longer. This effect of single-word code-switches occurring to fill lexical gaps has been referred to as '*triggering*'—the use of one word from the non-matrix language may be enough to cause speakers to switch completely into that language, as illustrated in the following Cantonese-English example and its accompanying schematization, where a speaker cannot remember the Cantonese word for 'hard-drive', makes use of the English word, and then continues in English:

'*Ngoh kam-yat maai-joh yat-goh* . . . <u>hard drive</u> . . . and today I'll have to install it.'
'*Yesterday I bought a* . . . hard drive . . . and today I'll have to install it.'
Cantonese → English

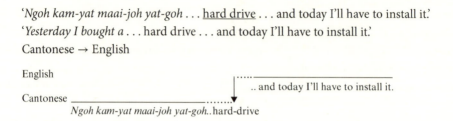

The effects of an imbalance in a speaker's proficiency in his/her two languages may also affect the general the type of code-switching that is commonly produced. If a speaker is significantly stronger in one language, but still engages in switching between the L1 and L2, it has been observed that this code-switching is much more likely to be Level 1 or 2 switching, rather than the more advanced patterns found with Level 3 and 4 alternations. However, bilinguals who have developed very strong abilities in both their languages may sometimes actually prefer to use the more challenging Level-4 type code-mixing, for reasons which we will shortly come to (Poplack 1980).

Finally, there may be situations in which a bilingual speaker is aware of how a common word or phrase in one language can be expressed in his/her other language, but avoids using it in the second language for non-linguistic reasons, and this sometimes causes a switch so that the word/expression can be produced in the language which is felt more appropriate for its use. An interesting example of such switching which relates to an imbalance in the regular *use* of equivalent words in L1/L2, not their potential availability, is discussed in Chung's (2006) study of Korean-English bilinguals. Chung observes that Korean adult males may regularly switch from Korean into English in order to produce expressions which they would feel uncomfortable producing in Korean. These are principally expressions of strong emotion and open affection toward their children and spouses, such as the words 'I love you' and requests for a hug at children's bedtime. While such things certainly can be said in Korean, they are regularly inhibited by a traditional cultural norm, in which Korean men are not supposed to show overt affection toward their offspring and wives with very direct speech. Switching into English allows men to somehow free themselves of the psychological bond imposed by the use of Korean in such situations, and to benefit from the more common occurrence and social acceptability of these expressions among English-speakers, both female and male.

Code-switching for stylistic reasons, general and specific

Gumperz (1982) and others note that various instances of code-switching seem to be made for discourse-related **stylistic reasons**. Frequently speakers may switch between two languages simply to vary the style of their speech and add variety, as for example, in the switch from Taiwanese to Mandarin Chinese in the following:

'gwa kam-kak hit-khaon-e tai-chi *ku-zao-wu-wei*, hoⁿ. (Mandarin Chinese in italics)
'I feel that things like that are *dry and boring*.' (Shih and Song 2002)

People who code-switch often freely admit that the mixing of two languages gives their speech a lively, modern, and desirably 'young' feeling which is felt to be more interesting stylistically at times than simply using one language. Such a shift away from a more conservative single-language style can be compared with the use of special language forms in instances of monolingual *texting* rather than the use of more standard language—monolingual speakers will frequently say that using abbreviations, acronyms, and special symbols in texting makes this form of communication more fun and lively than if standard written language is used in texts, tweets, and other forms of online interactions.

In addition to the use of code-switching as a *general* style of language, switches between two languages are also regularly found to occur for certain *specific* reasons relating to discourse style, three of which will be mentioned here. First, it has been suggested that code-switching may sometimes be used as a stylistic mechanism to simply represent a different *point of view* in a discourse (Romaine 1995). For example, when bilingual speakers are engaged in story-telling or the recounting of events, it has been observed that speakers may switch into a second language when they present *reported speech* (i.e., the speech of another individual), as for example in the following French to English and German to English switches:

'*Et puis le gars est entré et il dit que* John wasn't there.'
'*And then the guy came in and says that* John wasn't there.'

'*Er meinte:* 'We should leave now.'
'*He said:* 'We should leave now.'

It is not necessarily the case that the reported speech has to be in the language that was used by the actual speaker. In the following excerpt, the persons whose speech is 'quoted' actually spoke in Japanese, but here it is represented by the story-teller in English in order to highlight these as quotations:

Midori: *Denwa kakeru desho* 'How's the weather down there?' 'One hundred degrees.' So, I says 'Goodbye!' *Moo*, traffic-*ga erai kara yo,* 100 degrees *dattara yo.*
'*I called her* "How's the weather down there?' 'One hundred degrees.' So, I says 'Goodbye!' *Really,* the traffic *would be terrible if it is* 100 degrees.'
(Nishimura 1997)

Consequently, code-switched quotations do not necessarily occur for simple 'authenticity' reasons to report the original language used. What the code-switch does is mark a change in point of view, so that we may switch to seeing things from the point of view of the person referred to in the discourse or perhaps from some other angle. Sometimes the precise effect of such switches is difficult to pin down and be fully clear about, but monolingual speakers also use devices to change the perspective and orientation of their speech in subtle ways. For example, a monolingual speaker of English recounting a series of events may switch from using a simple past tense form to the present tense to vividly portray some past event. This switch presents the past event in a way as if the hearer were also present (due to use of the present tense) and so in this way marks a subtle switch in perspective and point of view, as for example in:

> 'I was just about ready to go out and then the doorbell rang. I <u>open</u> the door and suddenly there <u>is</u> this old woman standing there with a little girl and she <u>asks</u> me if she <u>can</u> use the phone.' (present tense forms are underlined)

Second, alternations between two languages sometimes occur for reasons of *emphasis*, to underline or make clearer the meaning of a message. Such switching often involves *repetition*—a speaker says something in one language and then repeats the same thing in the second language for emphasis. In the following two German/English examples, a mother uses one language to give instructions to her children, and then repeats these commands in the second language to stress her commands:

> Mother to child: 'ced*Setz dich hin*. Sit down!'
> '*Sit down*. Sit down!'
> 'Come here. *Komm mal her!*'
> 'Come here. *Come here!*'

In the following English-French repetition pair, a market-seller states the price of an item first in English and then repeats it in French, for added clarity:

> Customer: 'How much is one kilo?'
> Market seller: 'Two francs fifty. *Deux francs cinquante.*'
> 'Two francs fifty. *Two francs fifty.*'

Third, code-switches have been observed as a strategy which sometimes marks a distinction between the *topic*-like part of a sentence (the person/thing that a sentence is about) and the *comment*-part (something new said about this person/thing). So, a topic may be first introduced in one language and then commented on further in a second language, as in the following examples. In this pair of examples from Nishimura (1985), the Japanese topic-marker element *–wa* is attached to the topic *Yano-san* 'Mr. Yano' and 'she', and this is followed by a full switch into English, giving further information about this topic:

> '*Yano-san-wa*, he was speaking in English.'
> '*As for Mr. Yano*, he was speaking in English.'

> 'She-*wa* took her a month to come home *yo.*'
> 'As for her, it took her a month to come home, you know.'

The following French-English example similarly introduces a topic in one language and follows this with a comment in the second language:

'*Les ivoiriens*, they are really rich.'
'*As for people from the Ivory Coast*, they are really rich.'

Such style-related code-switches have interestingly also been noted to occur in written language. Although code-switching is less common in writing, as writing is in many instances a more formal mode of communication, it does occur frequently in informal email communication and in newspaper headlines in some communities. In Taiwan, for example, it is quite common to find Mandarin and Taiwanese mixed with each other in creative ways in newspaper headlines, and this is done for a variety of reasons (Shih and Song 2002): to attract readers' attention, for humorous effect, to add 'local flavor' to the basically Mandarin text, to highlight quotations, and to increase the expressive power of a headline, as in the next example, where a typically Taiwanese expression enhances the preceding Mandarin words in a colorful way.

'Guo-min-dang jin-hou bu shi *nng-kha-he*!'
'The KMT party will no longer remain a *feeble-legged-shrimp* (i.e., remain incompetent)!'

Code-switching for identity-related reasons

The language that individuals choose to use with others can serve as an important expression of personal identity, both in multilingual and in monolingual societies, when different languages and styles are selected. The projection of identity through the use of code-switching is a common reason why language-mixing is utilized by bilinguals, and manifests itself in various ways.[5]

Code-switching is made use of by many bilinguals in order to signal membership in a particular group, and to stress 'solidarity' and closeness with other members of the group. Code-switching thus becomes a style of language that people within a particular community of speakers all use with each other, identifying them as insiders with similar backgrounds and personal links, and distinguishing them from outsiders who do not engage in code-switching in the same way. In some societies, the regular mixing of two languages in any way at all is sufficient to signal speakers as different from other bilinguals who do not code-switch and from monolinguals who only speak one of the code-switched languages. In Hong Kong, for example, many local, ethnically Chinese people regularly mix English words with Cantonese to produce a code-switched style of language that is felt to distinguish them in positive ways from neighboring Chinese people in Canton province to the north, who do not mix English with their Cantonese. Bilinguals in Hong Kong often suggest that speaking purely in Cantonese sounds too traditional and like 'mainlanders' (those who live

---

5. The term 'identity' here is used with the common, non-specialist interpretation regularly given to it in everyday life. Following Cameron (2010: 209), we can say that each individual's 'sense of identity' refers to the sort of person he or she is or wants to be seen as: who an individual feels he/she is like, and who he/she feels he/she is different from. With regard to the larger phrase 'projection of identity', recent, post-modern approaches to language and identity argue that identities are actually not attributes that speakers 'project', but rather constructs produced through practices that speakers engage in. While such a reassessment of the notion of 'identity projection' may well be justified (and interesting), the text will nevertheless continue to make use of phrasings such as 'the projection of personal identity' for its common, familiarity value and traditional ease of understanding.

in China proper, north of Hong Kong), and that speaking purely in English sounds artificial for Chinese people. The 'solution', in order to project a special identity of being from Hong Kong and feeling connected with others living in this territory, is to mix a certain amount of English into a Cantonese base, and code-switching has become a regular style of communication for a significant proportion of the population in Hong Kong, particularly so among the young, educated, and middle class.

In other communities, it may be the case that different segments of the community all code-switch to some extent, but in different ways, and it is the particular way that one group mixes two languages that sets it apart and establishes cohesion among the group. This has been reported in a study of the ethnically Japanese population living in Toronto and San Francisco in Nishimura (1997) which focuses on the language habits of second-generation Japanese-Americans and Japanese-Canadians, who are known as '*Niseis*' (literally 'second generation-ers'). The Niseis are bilingual in Japanese and English and have speech patterns which are distinct from those of their parents, the *Isseis*—first-generation Japanese immigrants, and the *Sanseis*—third-generation offspring of the *Niseis*, although code-switching in fact occurs with all three generation groups to some degree.

The Niseis themselves adopt three distinct patterns of speech when talking with members of different generations. With the Isseis, who are much stronger speakers of Japanese than English, the Niseis often use a pattern which is referred to as 'the basically Japanese variety', which is mostly Japanese, but includes extra-sentential code-switching patterns ('tag-insertion' tokens of English at the periphery of sentences such as '*You know* . . .', '*I mean* . . .', '*Well* . . .', '*Lets see* . . .', etc.), and the frequent insertion of English nouns, but generally not other kinds of words. With the Sanseis, whose command of Japanese is not very good, the Niseis use a 'basically English variety'—an English base with Japanese words sporadically inserted into it.

The third form of Nisei speech is called 'the mixed variety', which involves frequent switches between Japanese and English, and no constant 'base language'—i.e., both Japanese and English are often used in equal amounts. It is this form of code-mixing that the Niseis use with each other, signaling their special Nisei identity, which is part Japanese, part Canadian/American, and different from the more dominant Japanese identity of the Isseis (first-generation Japanese North Americans) and the more dominant Canadian/American identity of the Sanseis (children of the Niseis). The Niseis as a group thus successfully emphasize solidarity with each other by means of a particular, heavily mixed form of code-switching which is different from that used with other Japanese-Americans and Japanese-Canadians.

Code-switching in Hong Kong and among the Niseis in Toronto and San Francisco involves the use of a 'we-code' (Gumperz 1982)—members of a particular group confirm their membership in the group by using the same forms of speech with each other. Code-switching is also sometimes used as a mechanism to narrow social distance *between* different groups. Two examples of this can be given. One is the use of code-switched French and English in Ottowa-Hull, described in Poplack (1988). The adjacent communities of Ottowa and Hull in Canada are dominated by different languages. Ottowa in the province of Ontario is largely English-speaking, while Hull, lying across the river Ottowa in Quebec, is dominated by French. Poplack reports that speakers from one community may use a code-switched variety of English/French to interact in empathetic ways with members of the other language group. Mixing of the two languages is a way to express friendliness to people belonging to an outsider group, acknowledging their language and identity through switching into the former. This kind of behavior is an instance of linguistic '**convergence**'. The speaker adjusts his/her language so that it converges more with that of the person being spoken to (or their preferred, home language) and helps reduce the social distance that typically arises when people come from different language groups. Modifying one's behavior in any way that brings it closer to that of another person who is being interacted with is also known as '**accommodation**'—we may alter our speech or non-linguistic behavior in ways that cause it to be more similar to others around us—for example, a speaker of British English might acquire an Australian accent through spending time in Australia, and visitors to Japan may start to bow to others as a form of greeting in place of extending a hand for a handshake. The code-switched use of English/French in Ottowa-Hull is an example of 'partial accommodation'—adapting one's native language partially to that of a speaker of a different language ('full accommodation' would be to switch fully into the other person's language rather than mix parts of it into one's own language).

A second example of convergence and partial accommodation where code-switching establishes a closer link between two groups is the language alternation that occurs in speeches given by politicians campaigning for votes in multilingual countries. In order to reach out to and attract the votes of a particular ethnolinguistic group, a politician campaigning for office may attempt to speak to this group in its own language, indicating that he/she cares for and has a connection with the group. If the politician is not a fluent speaker of the group's language, this may result in code-switching and use of words, phrases, and perhaps some sentences from the group's language mixed into the primary language spoken by the politician. For example, in Taiwan, Mandarin Chinese is now widely known throughout the island, but the home language for many people living in the south of Taiwan is actually still Taiwanese (they will mostly be bilingual, but favor the use of Taiwanese for friendly informal interactions). Politicians from the north of Taiwan who are first-language speakers of Mandarin Chinese are often observed to use some Taiwanese in their speeches at political rallies in the south of the island, as a way of building a connection with their audiences there. Typically, small portions of Taiwanese will be mixed into Mandarin in order to symbolically stress the politician's concern for Taiwanese speakers and their interests, and other politicians who do not attempt to code-switch in this way may be viewed as disinterested outsiders, not really focused on people in the south of Taiwan. Highly similar patterns of language mixing have been reported in the speech of politicians elsewhere in parallel situations, and code-switching has come to be a frequent tool in politicians' arsenals in linguistically mixed populations.

While the switching between two languages can therefore be used in essentially positive ways, to establish and maintain solidarity, in other instances one finds that language alternation within a conversation is associated with much more negative effects and the emphasis of distance between individuals. Importantly, what occurs in such cases is not code-switching in the speech of a single person, as we have regularly been describing so far, but an alternating pattern of language use among bilinguals in which one person uses one language, and attempts to establish this as the language of the conversation, and a second person consistently replies in a different language. This results in a kind of '**linguistic dueling**', in which people who are able to speak two languages refuse to use the language that someone else addresses them in, in a typically defiant and often rude way. An example of such an exchange is the following interaction from Heller (1992). In a provincial government office in Montreal, an Anglophone Canadian (a person whose mother tongue is English) comes to take a test in French proficiency (which is required for members of certain professions), and asks for directions from the Francophone receptionist (whose mother tongue is French). The latter refuses to switch into English and pretends not to understand what is being said. Both individuals in the situation are in fact able to understand and speak the other's language, but show clear signs of not wishing to use it, and instead want to use just their mother tongue.

Man:	Could you tell me where the French test is?
Receptionist:	*Pardon?* [What's that?]
Man:	Could you tell me where the French test is?
Receptionist:	*En francais?* [In French?]
Man:	I have the right to be addressed in English by the government of Quebec according to Bill 101.
Receptionist:	*Qu'est-ce qu'il dit?* [What is he saying?]

Such non-cooperation in switching to use the language in which another person initiates a conversation is an example of speech '**divergence**', the opposite of accommodation and convergence. In divergent speech, speakers seem to deliberately try to make their speech different from the language of the person they are speaking to, normally in a confrontational kind of way.

A second example of such a situation can be given from the situation in Taiwan in the late 1980s, when the government lifted restrictions on the use of Taiwanese after decades of repressing the language (see chapter 2). When this happened, taxi drivers, particularly in southern Taiwan, often tried to insist that their fares speak Taiwanese to them, in an aggressive move to reassert the presence of the language. Sometimes, this encountered resistance from those who actually preferred to speak Mandarin Chinese. In the following example, the potential passenger refuses to try to use Taiwanese with taxi driver, and the latter pretends not to understand the Mandarin spoken by the passenger, although both understand Mandarin and Taiwanese (which is represented in italic script).

Taxi driver:	*beh khi tuhwii?* [Where do you want to go?]
Passenger:	wo qu Dan Shui ye-shi. [I want to go Dan Shui night market.]
Taxi driver:	*gwa tia^n buh.* [I don't understand]. *kong taiwanwe!* [Speak Taiwanese!]
Passenger:	wo bu yao shuo Taiwanhua. (I don't want to speak Taiwanese.) wo qu Dan Shui ye-shi. (I want to go Dan Shui night market)
Taxi driver:	*gwa tia^n buh.* [I don't understand] (pops door open) *li yong tsao-e khi!* [You can just run there then!]

A third, frequently occurring scenario in which two speakers each make use of a different language in a conversation and do not switch from use of their own preferred language to that of the person they are speaking to comes in instances of **inter-generational communication** between parents and their children. This can be illustrated with a study of a Chinese community in northern England in Li et al. (2000). There it is noted that different generations of immigrants may have different attitudes toward the languages they are familiar with. Chinese communities in England arose for the most part as a result of immigration from the province of Canton in southern China. The first families to arrive frequently established catering businesses and restaurants in different cities and towns in Britain, and although there were communities of Chinese throughout the UK, these communities were never large, and would characteristically only consist of a few hundred speakers who had irregular contact with each other. The early immigrants were generally keen that their children should enter more highly paid professions and so encouraged their children to enter schools and universities where they mixed predominantly with non-Chinese-speaking people of their own age. Investigations of the current speech abilities and preferences of the Chinese communities in northern England in Li et al. (2000) show that second-generation Chinese born in the UK are fully fluent in Chinese (normally Cantonese), but show signs of dispreferring Chinese as a medium of communication. This contrasts with the older generation, who prefer to use Chinese whenever possible. When younger and older speakers are found together, it often occurs that older speakers will try to speak to their children in Cantonese, but the younger generation will consistently reply back to them in English, as represented in the following exchange:

Parent: *Nei yau mo heui baakfogungsi a?* ['Did you go to the department store?']
Son: Yes, I went this morning.
Parent: *Gam, nei maai-jo matye a?* [So, what did you buy?]
Son: A pair of jeans.

Younger generation speakers therefore sometimes do not wish to switch into their heritage language when addressed in this by their parents because they do not have very positive attitudes toward it, or they simply feel more comfortable speaking a local majority language. Young speakers in Li et al.'s study were also found to use English frequently when they wanted to disagree with their parents or reject offers from the latter:

Parent: *Oy-m-oy faan a? Ah Ying a? Ho sik ge-a!*
['Do you want rice, Ah Ying? Its very tasty!']
Ying: I don't want any.
Parent: *Gam, nei sik di choi a!* ['Then eat some vegetables!']
Ying: No, I won't.

This pattern of refusing to switch languages when giving largely negative responses (rejecting invitations and requests and expressing disagreement) seems to occur predominantly among the young when interacting with older generations, and has been observed in many other bilingual communities.

While the lack of language accommodation in parent-child communication may occur frequently in various groups and in certain situations of conflict, such behavior is not present in intergenerational exchanges in all bilingual groups. Within the large South Asian community in Britain, it is noted that Punjabi and Bengali are regularly spoken between younger and older generations, and younger speakers seem quite willing to use their heritage language with their parents and grandparents (though they nevertheless may choose to speak English with same-age friends and siblings). Attitudes toward using a heritage language with members of older generations may indeed relate to the size of a community. For example, in Los Angeles with its large Spanish-speaking community, there are often reports of younger speakers saying they would actually like to be able to speak *more* Spanish with their older generation relatives rather than less. This tendency is probably due to the positive attitudes toward Spanish that are generally held among Spanish-speakers in Los Angeles.

Finally, we can mention how code-switching may often be used for identity-related purposes in interaction with *expectations about language use* in certain contexts. In each discourse situation within multilingual communities, speakers may expect to hear a certain type of language—the default language commonly used by people in certain places and for the discussion of certain topics. For example, in multilingual Kenya in East Africa, it is common for people to use Swahili with each other in banks, post offices, and government offices and on public transportation such as buses and trains. In the home and with family and friends, it is more natural and common for people to use a tribal language, and in certain much more formal situations, such as in higher education/universities, company board meetings, and corporate business discussions, English will regularly be used. The term frequently used to refer to the language which is expected by default to occur in a particular situation is '**the unmarked language**'. If speakers choose to switch away from the unmarked language into a different language which is not commonly used in a certain domain—into a '**marked language**' (i.e., unexpected language)—this may achieve various discourse effects, and a manipulation of the use of marked and unmarked languages is a strategy that speakers have been observed to use effectively in many ways. Much interesting work on this phenomenon has been carried out by Carol Myers Scotton, in studies of multilingual interactions in Africa.

In her observations of language choice and code-switching in Nairobi, the capital of Kenya, Myers Scotton (1988, 1993) documents interactions between Kenyans in a variety of public places. Here we will introduce two of these exchanges which involve departures from the use of the unmarked language in a situation. Both take place on public buses, where, as noted, the unmarked language is Swahili. In the first sequence, a passenger deliberately uses his tribal language Lwidakho to speak to the bus-driver in place of Swahili. The passenger does this in order to try to persuade the driver to give him a cheaper, reduced fare on the bus, as he knows that the driver is also a Lwidakho-speaker. The passenger is thus attempting to stress tribal solidarity in order to win the favor of a reduced fare, and although the use of Lwidakho is rejected by the driver, who replies in Swahili, in the end the driver does give the passenger a discount, indicating that the use of their shared tribal language actually has been effective. Lwidakho is represented in italic script, Swahili in non-italics. As this is an extended dialogue, for simplicity, we use English words to represent the two African languages—italic script for Lwidakho, and non-italic script for Swahili. For the original Lwidakho and Swahili words, see Myers Scotton (1998: 167–168).

Passenger: (speaking in a loud and joking voice in Lwidakho):
    'Dear brother, take only 50 cents.'
(Laughter comes from the driver and the other passengers)
Passenger (again in Lwidakho):
    'Aren't you my brother?'
Driver (speaking in Swahili):
    'No, I am not your brother. If you were my brother, I would know you by name, but I don't know you or understand you.'
Passenger (switching from Lwidakho into Swahili):
    'Just help me mister. The life of Nairobi has defeated me because the price of everything has gone up. I live at Kariobang'i, and have to pay a lot of money for the bus fare there.'
Driver: 'I have only taken 80 cents from you.'
Passenger: 'Thank you very much. I am thankful of your pity, brother.'

In a second exchange heard on a bus in Nairobi (Myers Scotton 1998: 168), a passenger switches from the neutral, expected language, Swahili (represented with English words in italics), into English. This is done in an attempt to encode authority and educational status, not solidarity. Here the passenger is concerned that he is not going to get his change back from the money he has given to the driver for a ticket, and switches into English in a semi-threatening way to indicate that he is an educated person who cannot be deceived. In this situation the driver responds by using English back to the passenger, showing that he will not be intimidated by the passenger and that he is a person who is able to use English too:

Passenger: *'I want to go to the post office.'*

Driver: *'That's 50 cents.'*
(The passenger hands over a shilling, from which there should be 50 cents in change.)

Driver: *'Wait for your change.'*
(The passenger says nothing until a few minutes have passed and the bus nears the post office where the passenger will get off.)

Passenger: *'I want my change.'*

Driver: *'You'll get your change, mister.'*

Passenger (switching from Swahili into English):
    'I am nearing my destination.'
Driver (also switching into English):
    'Do you think I could run away with your change?'

In both the preceding instances, the switch away from the unmarked language into a second 'marked' language is surprising and thereby achieves a special effect. This switch can either be 'downward' to a more intimate language form (Lwidakho in the first example), spotlighting membership of the same tribe and petitioning solidarity, or 'upward' to a more formal variety (English in the second example), stressing the speakers' level of education. Code-switching is consequently made use of in both cases to emphasize an additional component of the speaker's identity which would otherwise not be revealed if only the unmarked language Swahili were to be used—the speaker's tribal background and his personal sophistication.

The manipulation of marked and unmarked languages has been found to be a widespread phenomenon in multilingual communities and occurs for various reasons. The expression of *anger* and *disapproval* has often been found to lead to switches away from the language normally used in informal environments to a more formal language that is otherwise felt to be out of place in family situations and in conversations with friends. Switching into such a marked language can immediately create social distance in a speech situation, as the speaker temporarily assumes a different identity in moments of anger, no longer friend but critic and opponent.

Bilingual parents have also been observed to switch languages sometimes when they attempt to discipline their children (Holmes 1992: 47). Interestingly, even if children do not understand the second language used by their parents in such instances, sometimes the switch away from the friendly home language to a foreign-sounding non-home language may effectively underline the seriousness of a parent's words and cause children to pay greater attention. Again, in such interactions, the transition from the unmarked language of the home to an outsider-language allows a speaker (here, a parent) to adopt a different identity for a brief moment, and to take advantage of that adjustment to achieve a particular effect (have the child change its behavior).

Quite generally, then, the projection of personal identity turns out to be a very important factor underlying the phenomenon of code-switching and is frequently the reason why speakers alternate between different languages. Code-switching has the potential to communicate a range of meanings which result from the choice of a language making salient an aspect of a speaker's social identity relative to other speakers and is triggered by the particular context a speaker is in, with the notion of 'unmarked/expected' language playing a significant role here. In the course of this section, we have seen that code-switching may also often occur for other purely stylistic reasons which do not necessarily have any direct social significance, and sometimes additionally result from an imbalance in the ability that speakers have in the two (or more) languages they know. We will now close this chapter with some brief reflections on the attitudes that people hold toward code-switching as a form of linguistic behavior, and note that these vary quite considerably from positive to negative feelings.

What do People Feel about Code-Switching as a Language Habit?

Attitudes toward code-switching are far from uniform. Some people have very negative feelings about the mixing of languages in a single conversation or sentence, while others are much more positive about it as a practice. Differing attitudes toward bilingualism in general and the role it plays in establishing a speaker's identity may play a part in determining the amount and the type of code-switching a speaker engages in. At one end of the scale, it has been reported that Puerto Ricans in New York evaluate bilingualism and code-switching positively, and the Puerto Rican community is known to engage in Spanish-English code-switching extensively and with significant skill. One important property of code-switching is that the most proficient bilingual speakers can switch between their languages without there being any perceivable pauses in the transitions from one language into another, i.e., one language alternates with the second without one hearing any clear hesitations or intonational breaks. The Puerto Rican community in New York is particularly skilled in such fast, pauseless code-switching.

Other bilingual speakers may not have such positive attitudes toward mixed speech and instead see it as impure, faulty speech, believing that a bilingual's two languages should be kept strictly apart. Mixing is viewed as a linguistic weakness, showing that a person is not able to speak either of his/her languages in a pure, 'unadulterated' way. This is a perception which has been found among bilingual speakers of English and Punjabi in Britain who engage in code-switching, as recorded by Romaine (1995: 122) in the following passage. This passage involves switches between English and Punjabi. In both the original speech and the translation/rendering of this passage into English words, the sections which the speaker produced in Punjabi are represented in italics.

> 'I mean I'm guilty too, in the sense *ke ziada usi* English *i bolde fer ode nal eda hunda ke tuhadi jeri zaban e, na? Odec har ik* sentence *ic je do tin* English *de word honde* ... but I think that's wrong. I mean, *ma khad cana ma ke, jado Panjabi bolda e,* pure *Panjabi bola usi* mix *karde raene a*. I mean unconsciously, subconsciously, *kari janee*, you know, *par* I wish, you know *ke ma* pure *Panjabi bol saka*.'

> 'I mean I'm guilty too, in the sense *that we speak* English *more and more and then what happens is that when you speak your own language, you get two or three* English words *in each* sentence ... but I think that's wrong. I mean, *I myself would like to speak* pure *Punjabi. We keep mixing*. I mean unconsciously, subconsciously, *we keep doing it*, you know, *but* I wish, you know *that I could speak* pure *Punjabi*.'

Further down the scale of proficiency in code-switching than the Puerto Ricans in New York (and also Punjabi-English bilinguals in Britain) one can find bilingual speakers who switch between languages but do this much less skilfully than speakers in other communities. For example, in Canada it has been noted that many speakers who switch between French and English do not always make very smooth transitions between the two languages, and show hesitations, repetitions, and special intonations in their mixing. They have also been observed to comment in a critical way on their switching.

The ability to carry out code-switching is therefore not shared equally by all speakers who do switch between two languages, and this may correlate with feelings about code-switching as a mode of communication. Some speakers may have very positive attitudes toward switching and be very skilful at it, showing extensive code-switching of all types, Levels

1–4. Other speakers may show more restricted switching, either Levels 1–3 or just Levels 1–2, and have less positive attitudes toward switching. There are also speakers who engage in code-switching in ways that are not very smooth and who are strongly critical of the mixing of two languages. To the extent that it is possible to make generalizations about attitudes toward code-switching among different groups, it seems that code-switching is more likely to be positively evaluated in larger bilingual communities where speakers have a high level of proficiency in both languages that are mixed, and speakers code-switch regularly and without obvious pauses between the languages that are being combined. On the other hand, code-switching is likely to be less positively perceived in smaller bilingual communities, where speakers are not so equally balanced in the skills they have in their two languages, tend to code-switch less often, and mostly use lower levels of mixing. Additionally, one finds that code-switching is more frequently disapproved of by older, tradition-minded members of a community rather than the young and the more modern-minded and outward-looking, and by those who may be bilingual but choose not to code-switch at all.

As with most generalizations, however, one still finds exceptions to such tendencies and differences of opinion within single communities. The following assessments of code-switching were all given by people in Hong Kong, where Cantonese/English codes-switching is very common in everyday life, in the film *Multilingual Hong Kong Kong: A Sociolinguistic Case Study of Code-Switching*.[6] As can be seen, there is a mixture of positive and negative opinions, and interestingly all these statements were produced by relatively young speakers proficient in both Cantonese and English.

> 'It's our culture. We start doing it as soon as we are born. We're used to living with it.'
>
> 'I don't accept it. It's awful. As much as possible, I'll use only Cantonese or only English. You mix two languages because you don't know either of them well, so you use both to compensate.'
>
> 'I don't think there's a problem. Language is for communication. As long as you can express your meaning, mixing is not a problem.'
>
> 'Sometimes, I can't control myself! I'm just so used to it. Everyone mixes, I hear it, and then I do it. Sometimes it's hard to control.'
>
> 'Mixing can express your meaning, but it isn't pure.'
>
> 'It doesn't matter, as long as the other person accepts it. Mixing a little English can lighten the mood. It can be fun.'

Having considered here both how and why people in bilingual communities creatively mix languages in patterns of code-switching, in the next chapter we will investigate how new languages may actually arise as mixtures of other languages and over time become the primary means of communication in emerging populations—the intriguing development of new 'Pidgin' and 'Creole' languages.

---

6. Produced by Films for the Humanities and Sciences, Princeton, NJ: www.films.com. Note that the quotations given here are English translations of the Cantonese words produced in interviews with speakers in Hong Kong.

Suggestions for further reading and activities

1. Find out more about the situation of extended diglossia in Paraguay and how it arose historically, by consulting Rubin (1968) or other sources you can find online.

    Rubin, Joan. 1968. *National bilingualism in Paraguay*. The Hague: Mouton.

2. The generalizations about diglossia presented in this chapter originated in Charles Ferguson's classic 1959 paper 'Diglossia' which appeared in the journal *Word* 15: 325–340. Ideas relating to diglossia were subsequently developed further in Joshua Fishman's 1967 paper 'Bilingualism with and without Diglossia; Diglossia with and without Bilingualism' in the *Journal of Social Issues* 23: 29–38. Read Fishman's paper and compare it with Ferguson's descriptions. In what ways are the two approaches different in the ways they define diglossia?

3. Do you or any of your classmates engage in code-switching? If so, describe what kind of code-switching you produce (what levels), what kind of bilingual community you are part of, and what your attitudes toward codeswitching are.

4. Use any resources available to you in libraries and on the Internet to try to find out what is meant by the terms '*situational code-switching*' and '*metaphorical code-switching*' and how they are assumed to differ.

5. Watch the film *Multilingual Hong Kong Kong: A Sociolinguistic Case Study of Code-Switching* (Films for the Humanities and Sciences, Princeton, NJ: www.films.com). What reasons do people give for code-switching in this film, and what type of people regularly code-switch in Hong Kong?

6. Another influential article by Joshua Fishman on multilingual language use is 'Who Speaks What Language to Whom and When?' Originally published in 1965 in the journal *La Linguistique*, this article is now more easily available in *The Bilingualism Reader* (2000, edited by Wei Li for Routledge Press, London). Read Fishman's influential article and find out what importance he attributes to 'group, situation, and topic' as causes of shifts between languages used by bilinguals.

7. Code-switching has been made use of increasingly in rap music in different, multilingual countries. Use the Internet to try to find examples of this and learn why singers decide to mix different languages together.

8. If you live in a multilingual community, see if you can find examples of written code-switching used in commercial advertisements and on public billboards and signs. What kinds of products do companies advertise with code-switched language, and is code-switching ever present in written information and signs produced by the government?

5

Pidgins and Creoles
The Birth and Development of New Languages

Introduction

In chapter 4, we saw how two special kinds of linguistic patterns may emerge when speakers in multilingual societies are familiar with two (or more) languages—code-switching and diglossia. In this chapter, we will consider another interesting kind of outcome which may arise in situations where speakers of different languages are present and in regular contact with each other—the development of *new* languages known as 'pidgins' and 'creoles'. Such languages are regularly created in certain situations by speakers of multiple, mutually unintelligible languages who have a need to communicate with each other on a daily basis but have no common language and no real opportunity to study and properly learn the language(s) of other speakers. In order to achieve a basic level of inter-group communication, a very simple variety of language is initially established which, to a degree, is a spontaneous *mixture* of parts of all of the languages spoken by those in the environment, but typically dominated in its vocabulary by words borrowed from one particular language, whose speakers have greater socio-economic power or positions of authority than others present in the contact situation. Such 'pidgin' languages are able to facilitate simple communication between speakers of different mother tongues in the workplace or in trading situations, but, to begin with, are highly variable and rudimentary in their structure, and limited in the topics they can be used to talk about. With the passing of time, however, pidgins may become increasingly sophisticated and linguistically complex until they can effectively be used in all domains that 'standard' languages are used in. When pidgins develop to such a stage and also acquire *native speakers*, they are classed as 'creole' languages, and are regularized as the primary means of communication of whole communities.

Pidgin and creole languages raise a number of very interesting linguistic and sociolinguistic issues. Speakers of such varieties may often perceive them to be impure, sub-standard forms of speech which are not worthy of being labeled 'languages', and such an attitude toward pidgins and creoles is also frequently held by speakers of other, longer-established languages. However, it can be shown that expanded pidgin and creole languages actually have the same degree of linguistic complexity as 'regular' languages, and also seem to exhibit the same fundamental 'design properties' as older languages (to be explained and illustrated later). This raises interesting questions about the *universality* of human language—if newly created languages show many features found in other, older languages, does this show that human languages always have to conform to some common set of linguistic structures and principles of grammar? Pidgin and creole languages which have come into being in different parts of the world and in contact with very different languages also show many striking similarities which need to be explained in some way. Should these rather mysterious similarities perhaps be attributed to the historical development of all modern pidgins and creoles from a unique early pidgin source, or do they arise naturally as a result of universal principles of first- and second-language acquisition operating in the same way whenever new languages are established? We will begin to consider these issues by first giving a broad introduction to the nature of pidgins and creoles and how they develop through a common type of language 'life cycle'. We will then examine various ideas about the possible origins of pidgins and creoles and theories which have been constructed to explain the links which exist between pidgins and creoles in different geographical areas. The chapter will also consider the socio-linguistic status of well-established pidgins and creoles and how such varieties may come to take on important roles in ethno-linguistically complex societies, even being considered in certain states as potential new national and official languages.

Basic properties of pidgins and creoles

Pidgin languages characteristically arise when speakers of multiple, different languages experience new needs to communicate with each other and there is an imbalance in power among the groups which are interacting with each other, with those who speak one particular language having a dominant role in the contact situation, for example as the employers or overseers of migrant or indentured laborers from different language backgrounds. This unequal social relation among those trying to initiate a new, common means of communication regularly influences how the latter may develop in two distinct ways. First, it is repeatedly found that the words which are made use of in the new pidgin language are principally sourced from the language of the dominant group. Second, it is often the case that there is limited daily contact between members of the more powerful group and individuals who belong to the other, socially subordinate groups. This causes transmission of the language of the dominant group to be incomplete and largely restricted to just the words of this language, and not its syntactic, semantic, and pragmatic properties. Members of the subordinate groups will have limited daily access to speakers from the more powerful group and so will not be able to learn their language via more regular routes of second language acquisition, which require frequent individual practice with native speakers.

The social and linguistic dynamic involved in a typical context of 'pidginization' can usefully be illustrated by means of the development of plantation pidgins in the Americas in earlier centuries. One recurrent situation in which pidgins have arisen in the past was in communities of slaves forced to work on large plantations in the Caribbean and mainland North America during the 18th and 19th centuries. As slaves imported to these areas were taken from a wide variety of different tribes in West Africa which all had different languages, they generally had no common language to use with each other or with the white plantation owners when transported from Africa to the Americas. Consequently, in order to establish some form of communication, words taken from the language of the plantation owners were frequently used, in many cases these being English words (and French, Portuguese, and Spanish in other areas). In the earliest stages of development of such contact 'languages', there was normally very little in the way of clear grammatical structure, as slaves working on plantations had infrequent one-on-one interactions with native speakers of English and other European languages, and therefore little opportunity to absorb more than just words from the languages of those owning and managing the plantations. However, once words from such 'donor' languages were acquired among the slave population, they would subsequently be used by the slaves in communication with each other, as no other shared language was generally available. Linguistic interactions of this type, between individuals of equal (lack of) power, have been termed instances of *'horizontal interaction'* or the occurrence of *'horizontal relations'*—slaves (and common laborers in various other situations) have equal status relative to each other, and their relations can be conceptualized as taking place on a horizontal plane. Where the members of a subordinate group communicate with those of a dominant, more powerful group, this is known as *'vertical interaction'*, or the occurrence of *'vertical relations'*—connecting individuals anchored to a subordinate, horizontal social plane with those occupying a second, higher level of power. In imbalanced, highly structured societies such as those constituted by slaves and their managers/foremen, horizontal communication among slaves occurred with much greater frequency than vertical interactions with those in positions of power, and it is this common language use among non-native speakers which has regularly given emerging pidgins their special character, only weakly and infrequently guided by the influence of mother-tongue speakers of English, French, and other donor languages.

What results from initial vertical interactions providing a source of vocabulary and then daily use of such words by non-native speakers with each other is an unstable, variable pidgin language, apparently based on the language of the dominant group in the contact situation, but also very different from this in many ways, with little evidence of fixed grammatical rules. To begin with, pidgins emerge to handle communication needs in a very restricted range of domains, and are used for quite focused purposes such as trading or simple work-oriented tasks. Their use is therefore to communicate factual information and instructions relating to the situations that speakers find themselves in, and early developing pidgins have generally not been used by speakers for the purposes of simple social conversation. Indeed, it is often only when pidgins later come to be used in more social ways that they start to stabilize and develop grammatical rules, as we will later see.

Around the world, new pidgin languages have arisen in a variety of contact situations. The four most frequently occurring contexts which have produced pidgins are as described in the following, with the first two of these scenarios giving rise to the bulk of the world's documented pidgins.

1. **Plantation and other workplace pidgins**. Many pidgins come into being when a workforce consists of speakers of different languages and no common language is

known by workers and their managers/foremen. A pidgin arises to facilitate the communication which is necessary in the workplace. This occurred repeatedly in a massively traumatic way among communities of African slaves torn from different language groups and forced to work together on plantations with no shared language. Guyanese, Ndjuka, and many other pidgins arose from such a situation during the time that it held in the Caribbean and North America. Elsewhere, plantation pidgins have also come into existence in less heavily abusive circumstances among linguistically mixed laborers migrating from their homelands to seek work in places such as Hawai'i and Queensland (Australia), where Hawaiian Pidgin English and Melanesian Pidgin were established during the 19th and early 20th centuries. Additionally, various non-plantation enterprises employing workers from different linguistic backgrounds have resulted in pidgins coming into existence as new languages spoken by a particular workforce, as for example in South Africa, where Fanakolo was created as a workplace pidgin among communities of miners.

2. **Trading pidgins**. Pidgins have often developed as languages of trade along coastal areas or in inland regions, as traders encounter and interact with speakers of a number of different languages. A pidgin is frequently established which allows traders from other areas to buy and sell goods with a range of different language groups (for example, West African Pidgin, Bazaar Malay, Chinook Jargon, and Chinese Pidgin Russian, used respectively in West Africa, Southeast Asia, Washington/Oregon, and Russia).

3. **Maritime pidgins** (also known as nautical pidgins). In earlier times (up until the 19th century), the crews working on ships involved in long-distance travel were often made up of speakers of many different languages. In order for communication to occur on board ship, pidgins would be created. In many instances these were not given any specific names, but one widespread maritime pidgin used on ships in the Mediterranean area from the Middle Ages on was known simply as 'Lingua Franca' (discussed more in a later section on the origins of pidgins and creoles).

4. **War zone/occupation pidgins**. In various instances in which foreign soldiers have interacted with local civilians during a period of war or post-conflict occupation of a territory, temporary pidgins have come into existence to assist in these interactions. This occurred during extended periods of conflict in Vietnam, Korea, and other war zones (with the Korean War giving rise to a pidgin known as Korean Bamboo English, a development of Bamboo English which had come into being among US soldiers stationed in Japan following World War II).

In terms of their **geographical distribution**, a large proportion of the world's pidgin and creole languages have been noted to be spoken along coastal areas due to the contact situations which result from sea trading. These are above all clustered around the coastal regions of West Africa, Southeast Asia, the South Pacific, the Caribbean and adjacent areas of South America, and parts of the Indian Ocean.

Regarding the **language base** for pidgin languages, we have thus far used the term 'donor language' to refer to the language which supplies the majority of words in an emerging pidgin, in almost all cases this being the language of the most powerful or numerically dominant group in the pidgin contact situation. Two rather more technical terms are commonly used by linguists to refer to such 'word donor languages', and will be employed during the rest of the chapter. These are the terms '**lexifier** (language)' and '**superstrate** (language)'. Both are used in the same way to refer to the language which is the primary source of words in pidgins and creoles as they develop. Hence, for example, French was the lexifier/superstrate for Haitian Creole, a French-based creole in the Caribbean island of Haiti, and Spanish was the lexifier/superstrate for Papiamentu, spoken on a group of islands just north of Venezuela.

A very considerable amount of the world's pidgins have been found to relate to a small number of European superstrate languages. These are:

- **English**   • **French**   • **Spanish**   • **Portuguese**   • **Dutch**

In addition to these five major lexifiers of pidgins and creoles, it has been observed that other pidgins have arisen with superstrates that are *not* European languages (a point which is significant for certain theories of the origins of pidgin languages, as will be discussed later in the chapter). A brief selection of pidgins which have come into existence with words sourced from non-Indo-European languages is given here:

Pidgins with superstrates other than European languages

Pidgin	*Superstrate*	*Location*
Nubi	Arabic	Uganda/Kenya
Chinook Jargon	Chinook/Nootka	Washington/Oregon, USA
Fanakalo	Zulu	Southern Africa
Eskimo Trade Jargon	Inuit	Northern Canada

An additional technical term which is important in the description of pidgins and creoles is '**substrate** (language)'. This is used to refer to the languages spoken by those in (pidgin-producing) contact situations who are in subordinate positions of power relative to speakers of the superstrate language. For example, in Hawai'i during the late 19th and early 20th centuries, speakers of the substrate languages Portuguese, Chinese, Japanese, and various Filipino languages were all involved in the creation of Hawaiian Pidgin English, which had English as its superstrate, and in the Caribbean, West African languages such as Twi, Wolof, Igbo, and Hausa were substrate languages spoken by slaves working on sugar plantations where English and French superstrate pidgins emerged. Substrate languages commonly provide certain items of vocabulary (though significantly less than the superstrate), and may also influence the development of the grammar of pidgins/creoles in subtle ways as these languages become more complex over time. Research into various pidgins and creoles have shown that aspects of the evolving grammar of these languages which cannot be attributed to the superstrate language may come from one of the substrate languages (as will be illustrated in a later part of the chapter). Pidgins and creoles are therefore often clearly found to be a *mixture* of languages; in many cases European superstrate languages provide most of the initial vocabulary of a pidgin, while other non-European substrate languages add a smaller proportion of words and potentially affect the grammatical structure of pidgins as this develops.

The pidgin-to-creole cycle

The linguist Robert Hall (and then many others after him) has described pidgins as typically going through a **life cycle** of development, from very elementary and variable language forms in their early stages to much more regularized and complex language systems as expanded pidgins and creoles. Creoles are the linguistic descendants of pidgins which have become the first language (mother tongue) of a new generation of speakers. Pidgins are always originally spoken as a new *second language* by people who have some *other* language as their mother tongue. When later generations grow up making use of a pidgin as a *first language/mother tongue*, the pidgin expands further into a creole stage. This expansion occurs in the area of vocabulary and grammatical complexity and allows speakers of the creole to use it effectively in all domains of daily life. In certain situations, such complexity may also be achieved during a late pidgin stage, when a pidgin has become widely adopted as a lingua franca by a community that has used the pidgin for a considerable period of time.

Not all early pidgins actually reach the creole stage of development, as pidgins only persist as long as they are needed by the contact situation which originally caused them to be created. If this situation changes dramatically or disappears, as, for example, when a war is terminated and foreign troops return home, or trading between different groups ceases for certain reasons, the pidgin may itself simply disappear, if it has not become established as a creole with mother-tongue speakers. Three trading pidgins that were developed to help communication between different Native American tribes and also European settlers, but which all disappeared as regular interactions between these groups were significantly reduced, are Delaware Pidgin, Mobilian Pidgin, and Chinook Jargon. However, if there is no major change in the need for a common language in a multilingual situation and a pidgin has come into existence to serve this function, a number of stages of development may characterize the pidgin as it increases in complexity and potentially acquires native speakers, moving through the following steps:

early pidgin/'jargon' → *stable/stabilized pidgin* → *expanded pidgin* → *creole*

In a broad study of *Pidgin and Creole Linguistics* published by the linguist Peter Mühlhäusler in 1986, it is suggested that the route from early pidgin/jargon to creole may actually proceed in three different variant forms of the life cycle outlined above, with pidgins in various situations undergoing a more rapid pidgin-to-creole transformation than in other communities. Certain pidgins are argued to undergo a very swift transition from early pidgin directly to a creole stage as young second-generation speakers immediately convert a largely unstructured initial pidgin into a complex language system which becomes their mother tongue. In other communities, it is suggested that the transition from pidgin to creole may extend over several generations before native speakers come into existence. The three types of pidgin-to-creole passage described by Mühlhäusler for different languages are the scenarios schematized as follows:

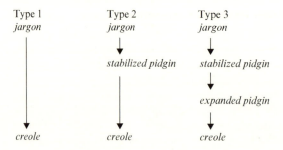

In the sections to come, we will outline what kinds of linguistic properties pidgin/creole languages may have at these different stages of development, and also consider a further possible step in the pidgin and creole life cycle when certain creoles undergo a process of 'de-creolization'.

Attitudes toward pidgins and creoles

People often have rather negative attitudes toward pidgins and creoles and think of these ways of speaking as random, flawed, imperfect forms of superstrate languages such as English, French, etc., which speakers make use of because they are unable to speak 'proper', grammatical English, French, or Spanish. Speakers of pidgins and creoles are sometimes thought to be cognitively deficient in a certain way and possibly not able to speak a 'regular' human language. Additionally, it has been suggested that speaking in pidgin or with a creole is actually detrimental to a person's mental processes and may inhibit people from thinking in 'normal' ways. This kind of view is uninformed and potentially harmful, leading to prejudice and attitudes of superiority. Stabilized pidgins and creoles should *not* be confused with any kind of defective language impairment, and clearly do have their own rule systems, as will be shown shortly, which can be just as complex as the rules which govern older language varieties. When people first hear pidgins and creoles being spoken, they may sometimes think that these can be spoken by anyone who just tries to randomly simplify their speech. However, this is not the case, and stabilized pidgins and creoles have their own very particular rules of grammar, just like other languages. Stigmatization and lack of respect for pidgins and creoles are nevertheless quite widespread, especially in communities where the lexifier of a pidgin/creole continues to be spoken by some members of the community, as this frequently leads to direct comparisons of standard English, French, and other superstrate languages with the pidgins they have lexically helped come into existence. In various instances, negative psychological attitudes held by speakers toward pidgins and creoles are so deeply entrenched and strong that, unfortunately, they may hinder the use of pidgins and creoles in roles that they would otherwise be well-suited to, for example as mediums of education and as official languages in countries where a pidgin is the most widely known form of local language. This point will be returned to later, in a section on further outcomes of the pidgin-to-creole life cycle.

Summary of basic properties

Before moving on to look at specific linguistic properties of pidgins and creoles, let's summarize the major points of what has been discussed so far and review some of the terminology that has been introduced to describe features of these languages.

Pidgins arise as new systems of communication in **multilingual contact situations**, most frequently involving speakers of **more than two languages** who have to interact with each other regularly in the **workplace** or in **trading** and **commerce**.

A **superstrate/lexifier** language spoken by a **dominant group** in the contact situation provides most of the words for a new pidgin. A much smaller proportion of words enter the pidgin from the **substrate** languages spoken by others present from (typically) subordinate groups.

Vertical interactions between the superstrate and substrate speakers are less frequent than **horizontal interactions** between substrate speakers. Because of **limited access** to the superstrate language, substrate speakers do not learn the superstrate directly, but borrow words from this language to create a new system of communication, a pidgin.

Pidgins are always either developed or learned as **second languages** by their speakers, and are never speakers' first language/mother tongue.

Emerging **early pidgins** are unstable and do not make use of fixed grammatical rules. The **life cycle** of pidgins which survive beyond the early pidgin stage may lead to a **stable pidgin** stage, an **expanded pidgin** stage, and **creolization**, as pidgins become increasingly complex and acquire native speakers as **creoles**.

Although pidgins and creoles are functionally very useful languages, people often hold **negative attitudes** toward them because they are viewed as impure mixtures of other 'real' languages.

'EXCEPTIONS TO THE RULE'

While most pidgins have arisen in situations where multiple languages are spoken by members of a community, sometimes pidgins have also developed where there are speakers of just two different languages. Russenorsk and Chinese pidgin Russian are two good examples of this rather less common pattern (Hall 1966).

Russenorsk was a pidgin that was created when Russian sailors and Norwegian fishermen came into contact with each other along the Arctic coast of northern Norway from the 18th century to the early 20th century. In addition to being a pidgin formed from the contact of just two languages, Russenorsk is atypical in its development as a pidgin because the two groups present in the contact situation were social equals rather than being in any kind of superordinate-subordinate power relation. It has been noted that this social parity may have resulted in the vocabulary of Russenorsk being much more evenly split than is normally the case with pidgins, which have a single major lexifier. The pidgin Russenorsk was composed of both Russian and Norwegian words, in almost equal measure, and was not strongly dominated by either language as superstrate.

Chinese pidgin Russian was a pidgin that was spoken when Chinese traders visited Russia from the early 18th century to the mid-19th century. As there was an official ruling that Chinese visitors were obliged to know 'Russian', but there was little opportunity for Chinese people to study and learn standard Russian, a pidgin arose primarily lexified with Russian words. This case of pidginization is again one in which the two groups in contact were not distinguished by any major difference in power (although the Russians were *numerically* dominant in the trading exchanges, which took place within Russia).

Interestingly, in both of these cases, the pidgins were felt to be so different from the lexifiers that speakers were under the impression that they were using a quite different language. When Russenorsk was spoken, it is reported that Russian sailors thought they were actually speaking Norwegian and Norwegian fishermen believed they were speaking Russian, and when Chinese pidgin Russian was spoken by Russians with Chinese people, the former imagined they were actually speaking Chinese. This is a good indication of how distinct pidgins may be from their lexifier languages, despite many borrowed words being familiar.

The linguistic properties of pidgins and creoles

Pidginization (the creation of a pidgin) commonly involves the *simplification* of many properties of a superstrate language: the elimination of word endings (morphological affixes on words), a reduction in the number of sounds used in words in the language (its phonological structure), a simplification of the grammatical rules which speakers normally follow (its syntactic structure), and a reduction in the number of functional domains the language is used in (hence pidgins are not regularly used in education or writing). **Creolization** (the development of a creole), on the other hand, involves linguistic *expansion* of a pidgin's morphology and syntax, and an increase in the number of domains the language can be used in. These processes can be observed to be at work during the pidgin-to-creole life cycle, beginning with early pidgins/jargons, and progressing through subsequent stable and expanded pidgin stages and then creolization.

Early pidgins/jargons

The earliest forms of pidgins and creoles are very simple '*jargons*' which seem to show a lot of variation in the way they are spoken, the use of short phrases and sentences, very little fixed grammar, and the communication of messages mainly via the meanings of words and not as a result of the syntactic structure of sentences. Early pidgin speakers typically make use of many physical gestures to reinforce the intended meaning of their words, and are very restricted in what they can successfully talk about.

A range of processes seem to be used by speakers trying to develop a simplified version of complex superstrate languages, and these establish the basic character of early pidgins.

Elimination or reduction of 'functional words'

All languages which have been spoken for some time develop specialized grammatical words, such as auxiliary verbs (English 'have/be', and 'will' used before other verbs), determiners (English 'the', and 'a'), and complementizers (English 'if', 'whether', and 'that'). Such 'functional words' are regularly eliminated/not made use of in early developing pidgins, so that speakers' sentences essentially consist in just 'content words' (nouns, verbs, and adjectives).

Superstrate	Early pidgin version
The doctor is a good man.	*Doctor good man.*
I did not go to the market.	*I no go bazaar.*

Simplification of superstrate morphology

Nouns, verbs and adjectives in common superstrate languages regularly change their shape and add endings to encode tense and subject agreement on verbs, case, and number (singular vs. plural distinctions) on nouns, and gender, number distinctions on adjectives. However, nouns, verbs, and adjectives in early pidgins based on English, French, Dutch, and Portuguese are regularly 'bare' and have a single shape, not altered in any way to represent differences in tense, number, case, or gender. For example, whereas English has the affixes –*ed* and –*s* for verbs, and –*s* for nouns, these are regularly eliminated from verbs and nouns in developing pidgins:

English superstrate	Early pidgin version
Jim walk<u>ed</u> home already.	*Jim walk home already.*
Jo stay<u>s</u> here.	*Jo stay here.*
ten cat<u>s</u>	*ten cat*

Reanalysis of words

In emerging pidgins it is common to find that some words borrowed from the superstrate language are interpreted in new ways which are different from their normal use in the superstrate. For example, in Melanesian pidgin, the name 'Mary' has been reanalyzed to mean simply 'girl, woman', and is also used as an adjective meaning 'female' (so *hos meri*, literally 'horse Mary/female' means 'mare', and *pik meri* 'pig Mary/female' means 'sow'), and English 'him', pronounced as *em*, has been reanalyzed as a pronoun allowing for any of the following meanings: 'he, him, she, her'. In a similar way, the word 'long' has also been reanalyzed as a general preposition which can substitute for a wide range of English prepositions, including 'to, at, on, in, for'.

Vocabulary size

Speakers of early pidgins often make use of a small vocabulary, possibly just 200–300 words. This figure can be compared with the large total of 50,000 words which speakers of a superstrate language such as English are estimated to be familiar with. The vocabulary of pidgin grows as the pidgin develops, but is very restricted in the early stages.

Phonology/sounds

In terms of their pronunciation, pidgins tend to be simpler than any of the languages which are involved in their creation. For example, whereas standard English has approximately 14 distinct vowel sounds, pidgins lexified by English commonly make do with a 5–7-vowel system. The set of consonant sounds used in pidgins is also simplified in a way which typically follows a principle called '**convergence**'. When a particular sound occurs in both the superstrate and substrate languages, this sound will generally be maintained in the resulting pidgin. For example, many languages make use of a 'd' sound and a 't' sound at the beginnings of words. When superstrate and substrate languages share these sounds, they will be maintained in the pidgin. However, when a sound occurs in the superstrate but not in the substrates, the tendency is that this sound will be eliminated from the new pidgin. Two sounds that occur in English but which are quite uncommon in other languages are the 'th' sounds in words such as 'this' and 'thing'. Many speakers of English-superstrate pidgins will pronounce sequences such as 'this thing' as 'dis ting', converting the 'th' sounds to other sounds which are common in the substrate languages. Pidgins therefore tend to *converge* on sounds which are commonly shared by the substrate and superstrate languages, and avoid unusual sounds which occur in only one of the base languages. When sounds not shared by the superstrate and substrates are eliminated (or not produced) in the pidgin, this is also referred to as '**leveling**'—the unusual, non-matching parts of the superstrate and substrate sound systems are 'leveled out' to leave just a simple, reduced core set of sounds. Other common instances of leveling in English-lexified pidgins are the elimination of the 'sh' and 'f' sounds in English, and their replacement with 's' and 'p' sounds, which are more widespread (hence English 'ship' becomes 'sip', and 'fish' becomes 'pis'). At the ends of words, when English may have a pairing of consonant sounds such as 'nd' in 'hand' and 'pt' in 'kept', but substrate languages do not allow such complex final sequences of consonants, it is found that pidgin speakers simplify the superstrate sequences and reduce them to a single consonant sound, often simply eliminating the final consonant in the pair, so that 'hand' is pronounced as 'han', and 'kept' as just 'kep'.

Word order

In all of the major superstrate languages, the order of words plays an important role in communicating meaning. In English, French, and Portuguese, for example, the noun which occurs before the verb is regularly interpreted as its subject, the person who carries out an action, and a noun which follows a verb is interpreted as the verb's object, and understood to undergo the action of the verb. A sentence such as 'Mary helped the doctor' is therefore unambiguous, and only interpreted as meaning that Mary was the person doing the 'helping', and the doctor was the person being helped (even though it is common for doctors to help other people—here the word order instructs us how to interpret the sentence). In early pidgins, the order of words in sentences is very variable and not a good indication of how to interpret sentences. There often seems to be no consistent ordering of nouns, verbs, and other words, and meaning often results simply from guessing at what the combination of the meanings of the individual words could signify when used together. For example, the meaning of 'Sara cooked yams' might be communicated in a number of ways:

> *Sara cook yam.*   *Yam cook Sara.*
> *Yam Sara cook.*   *Sara yam cook.*

Consider also the following example, produced by a Japanese speaker of Hawaiian pidgin English, quoted in Pinker (1994: 33) from interviews carried out between pidgin speakers in Hawai'i and the linguist Derek Bickerton in the 1970s.

> *Me cape [coffee] buy. Me check make.*

It is noted that the speaker meant to communicate that 'He bought my coffee. He made me out a check.' However, given the lack of grammatical words and the variability of word order in this speaker's basic pidgin, the sentence is quite ambiguous and could be used to communicate a range of other meanings, such as 'I bought coffee. I made him out a check', or 'I will buy coffee. I will make him out a check', or various other possibilities. Early pidgins are thus quite vague, and additional contextual help is often essential to interpret what speakers intend to mean.

Stabilized pidgins

Not all pidgins survive and move past the initial early period. Pidgins arise for specific needs, and if these needs are fully met by just a very basic-level language, there may be no need for the pidgin to develop further. It also happens that the situation which called for the creation of a pidgin sometimes disappears, and so the pidgin dies away naturally, again without developing past the early pidgin/jargon stage. In other cases, however, early pidgins do undergo further changes, entering into a more stable state in which the pidgin is used in a wider range of activities, and becomes much less ambiguous as a form of communication. Stabilized pidgins are distinguished from early pidgins in two broad ways, relating to word order and vocabulary.

Word order stabilization

When speakers use a pidgin regularly as a second language for a significant amount of time, it is found that much of the variability in early pidgin speech is reduced, and conventions or 'norms' emerge which speakers start to follow quite regularly. Whereas early pidgin speakers seem to 'experiment' a lot when using their language and create sentences in idiosyncratic ways through (apparently) random, spontaneous simplifications, grammatical rules later emerge and guide all speakers to produce sentences in similar ways. A stabilized pidgin is a form of language which needs to be *learned* by speakers, in order to speak like others in the speech community, while an early pidgin is much more of a free-form mode of speech, with each individual speaker inventing new ways to express meaning without any single set of grammatical rules ever coalescing and being adopted by all speakers. With the extended use of a pidgin, one important feature of its stabilization is the establishment of a fixed ordering of words. Thus, without any explicit agreement or obvious planning, speakers appear to converge on the use of a single way of sequencing the major syntactic constituents in a sentence, such as subjects, verbs, and objects. In some stabilized pidgin groups, this may give rise to a consistent *subject > verb > object* [SVO] ordering, while in others a different ordering may be adopted, such as *subject > object > verb* [SOV], or *verb > subject > object* [VSO]. To some extent, it may be that the substrate languages spoken by members of the pidgin community exert an effect here and influence the kind of standardized word order that emerges in the stable pidgin stage, hence if the substrate languages are all VSO languages (as in some areas of the South Pacific), this might become imposed as the new, common order in the pidgin, while SVO and SOV substrates would influence the word order of stabilizing pidgins in different ways. What is important is that out of the extreme variability and linguistic 'chaos' present in early pidgins, clear new patterns of some type emerge and become consistently and commonly used by speakers, decreasing the ambiguity and context-dependent nature of early pidgins and improving speakers' efficiency in communication.

Vocabulary growth

As speakers come to use pidgins in an increasing range of domains of life, they develop words to refer to a wider set of objects and experiences, so the vocabulary of stabilized pidgins increases quite significantly. This growth in words and in the ways that words can be used and interpreted is achieved in various ways.

Compound formation

Compounds are new words which are formed from novel combinations of two independent words. In many instances, the meaning of a compound cannot necessarily be guessed from simply knowing the meanings of the two (or more) words combined in the compound. For example, in English, the meanings of the compounds 'greenhouse', 'wetsuit', and 'walkman' cannot be predicted from the interpretations of the words being put together to form the compounds (a 'greenhouse' is not 'green', and a 'walkman' is not a type of 'walking man', etc). Pidgins very frequently use the process of compounding to create new items of vocabulary. In situations where English and the other major superstrate languages might have quite distinct words for different objects or concepts, pidgins tend to recycle the limited number of words which are available in the pidgin and compound these to make new words, as in the following examples, formed in Tok Pisin, one of the Melanesian pidgins.

Pidgin compound	Words used in compound (in English)	English meaning/equivalent
kilman	kill man	murderer
daiman	die man	corpse
ranaweman	runaway man	fugitive; refugee
stilman	steal man	thief
trikman	trick man	magician

Pidgin compound	Words used in compound (in English)	English meaning/equivalent
haus buk	house book	library
haus dring	house drink	bar
haus ka	house car	garage
haus kuk	house cook	kitchen
haus mani	house money	bank
haus pepa	house paper	office
haus sik	house sick	hospital
tok pait	talk fight	argument, quarrel
tok orait	talk all right	agreement
tok sori	talk sorry	condolence
tok win	talk wind	rumor

Polysemy

Many words in pidgin languages have more than one meaning. In instances where standard English might have several distinct words, an English-based pidgin may have only one:

Kamtok	English
hia	hear
hia	sense
hia	understand

In Kamtok (Cameroon, Africa), the single word *hia* is used in situations to communicate the meaning of the three distinct words, 'hear', 'sense', and 'understand', in standard English. This phenomenon is known as 'polysemy'. The use of a language's existing vocabulary items can be expanded to provide reference to an increased number of objects and experiences by allowing existing words to have multiple meanings (for example, in English, a 'mole' can either denote an underground animal or a spy, and a 'crane' can be a bird or a piece of lifting equipment used on a construction site).

Multi-functionality

Words in pidgin languages frequently seem to be able to function as if they belonged to a variety of different syntactic category types. This increases their versatility and the ability of a pidgin to use its restricted number of words in more contexts than might regularly be possible in older, superstrate languages. For example, the Kamtok word *bad* can function as an adjective, as a noun, as an adverb, and also in a verb-like way.

Used as an adjective:	*tu bad pikin* 'two bad children'
Used as a noun:	*We no laik dis kain bad.* 'We don't like this kind of badness'
Used as an adverb:	*A laikam bad.* 'I like it very much'
Used in a verb-like way:	*Di pikin bad.* 'The children are bad.'

(More) reanalysis

As in all stages of pidginization and creolization, reanalysis of superstrate words occurs, creating new words and uses of words in stabilized pidgins which increases the ways that pidgins can be used and also improves their clarity in various instances. For example, as verbs in early pidgins do not occur with any inflections indicating past, present, or future tense, the intended time reference of sentences is often very ambiguous, and a sentence such as 'Jim buy medicine' could potentially refer to a past action 'Jim bought medicine' or a future intention 'Jim will buy medicine', or a presently occurring event 'Jim is buying medicine.' Stabilized pidgins begin to develop means to eliminate this ambiguity by means of 'time adverbials' which help indicate when an event takes place. Some of these time adverbials are produced via the reanalysis of superstrate words and their adaptation as specifiers of temporal relations. As an illustration of this, Bakker (1994: 37) notes that the English word 'before' was reanalyzed in Chinese pidgin English as a temporal adverb indicating a past time reference for an event, in a way that substitutes for a past tense inflection on the verb:

Before my   sell   um   for   ten   dollar.
PAST   I   sell   it   for   ten   dollar
'I sold it for ten dollars.'

Creolization

When a pidgin acquires young native speakers who use the pidgin in *all* domains of life as a first language, its syntax becomes more complex, its vocabulary increases dramatically, adding new grammatical and descriptive words, and a variety of other changes occur which make it into a much more sophisticated language form, as will soon be described. In various cases, creolization may occur after a pidgin has stabilized from an early pidgin/jargon stage and has been used for a time as a stable pidgin with regularized word order patterns and an increase in vocabulary, as noted in the previous section. In certain other instances, there may, however, be 'abrupt creolization' and a much more rapid transition from an early pidgin/jargon stage directly to a creole stage, as the children of early pidgin speakers swiftly convert a very rudimentary, variable jargon into a structurally much more advanced creole. Alleyne (1971) notes that creoles which developed on slave plantations in the Caribbean may have lacked a stable pidgin stage in this way, and proceeded directly from jargon to creole (see also Romaine 1988).

A third possibility which has been reported is that a somewhat slower path of development occurs, with stable pidgins changing into 'expanded pidgins' before acquiring native speakers and being creoles, hence the pidgin-to-creole cycle would consist in four broad steps: early pidgin → stable pidgin → expanded pidgin → creole.

An extended pidgin is the primary language of a substantial community of native speakers of other languages. Due to regular, daily use by a large number of speakers over a significant period of time, it becomes syntactically more developed than a stable pidgin, and potentially has much more of the striking complexity of creoles developed and spoken by native speakers. Examples of creoles which have had extended pidgin stages are the three Melanesian Pidgins: Bislama, Pijin, and Tok Pisin. Many generations ago, Melanesians were recruited to work in plantations in Queensland, Australia, and then in Samoa and Fiji. There a broad Melanesian Pidgin was developed among the workers from different language backgrounds, and this stabilized pidgin was later brought back home by workers returning to their countries of origin. This pidgin then continued to develop in different ways as a result of the influence of the local languages, becoming Tok Pisin in Papua New Guinea, Bislama in Vanuatu, and Pijin in the Solomon Islands. As the speakers of these pidgins all had other mother tongues which they used at home and in their villages, reserving the pidgin for communication with people from other tribal groups, the development of the pidgin was steady but not rapid, and entered into an extended pidgin stage, becoming increasingly complex in its structure. In recent years, changes in traditional marriage patterns have been occurring more and more, and young people are increasingly marrying outside their original tribal groups, especially in urban environments. When intermarriage between speakers of different local languages takes place, pidgin is the form of communication that husband and wife will generally share and use with each other, and pass on to their children. New generations of mother tongue speakers of Tok Pisin, Bislama, and Pijin have therefore come into existence, bringing these extended pidgins further into a creole stage (Siegel 2009). There are, however, still many people who learn Tok Pisin, Bislama, and Pijin as a second language rather than as a mother tongue—in fact, as many as 90% of those who use Tok Pisin in Papua New Guinea are non-native speakers. For these speakers, Tok Pisin therefore still technically counts as a pidgin, as the term 'creole' is only used, by convention, for the speech of mother tongue speakers of a variety that originated as a pidgin. In such a situation, where there are both native and non-native speakers of a pidgin/creole, the language can be characterized as having a dual status within a population, being both an extended pidgin and a creole, for different segments of a speech community (and the pidgin/creole will probably be spoken in somewhat different ways across the community, with native speakers being more advanced and confident in their speech than non-native speakers, just as in other societies where second-language learners are less proficient in a language than those who acquire a language as their mother tongue).

In what follows, we will describe linguistic changes that may occur as early pidgins and stable pidgins become substantially more complex as creoles (or as extended pidgins which lead into creoles). For the sake of simplicity, we will regularly refer to these changes as being typically representative of the creole stage of development, but it should be remembered that at least some of the properties being described may well start to occur during an extended pidgin stage, before a community actually produces the first native speaker generation of its pidgin.

New grammatical/functional words

As pidgins develop into creoles, they regularly acquire many more grammatical words. These often serve a variety of different functions, and impose more structure and precision on the language.

New markers of tense and aspect

Creoles tend to develop a much clearer encoding of time distinctions through the use of special tense markers similar to words like 'will' in English (for example: 'John will leave tomorrow.'). Other markers occur with verbs that add further information about how an event occurs—for example, whether it is instantaneous, or occurs stretched out over a period of time (as in the use of the English *be verb-ing* construction: 'John was reading a book.'). Such functional words are known as 'aspect' markers and are frequently made use of in creoles. Two sets of examples of new tense and aspect particles are given in the following, one from Bislama (Vanuatu) and the other from Krio (Sierra Leone). The development of such elements distinguishes creoles quite markedly from early and stable pidgins, which do not have particles encoding tense and aspect.

Bislama (examples from Crowley 1990)

Past tense marker '*bin*'	Mi bin kaekae wan krab.
	'I ate a crab.'
Future tense marker '*bae*'	Bae hem i go.
	'He will go.'
Habitual/progressive aspect marker '*stap*':	Hem i stap toktok.
	'He talks/is talking.'
Completive aspect marker '*finis*'	Mi go finis.
	'I have gone.'

Krio (examples from Jones 1968 and Romaine 1988)

Past tense marker '*bin*'	A bin rait.
	'I wrote.'
Progressive aspect marker '*de*'	A de rait.
	'I am writing.'
Past + progressive combined	A bin de rait.
	'I was writing.'
Completive aspect marker '*don*'	A don rait.
	'I have written.'
Past + completive combined	A bin don rait.
	'I had written.'

New tense and aspect particles have been found to occur in all creoles, and often develop quite clearly from the reanalysis of superstrate words. For example, the markers of past tense in creoles lexified with English words is frequently derived from the word 'been'—*bin* in Bislama, Tok Pisin, Krio, Hawai'i Creole, and Guyanese Creole, and *ben* in Jamaican Creole. The Krio marker of completive aspect *don* is a reanalysis of English 'done', and the Bislama equivalent *finis* is derived from English 'finish'. These new particles must obligatorily be used by speakers of creoles to specify the time reference of events, indicating that creoles are establishing new grammatical rules that must be followed by speakers. In earlier pidgin stages, by way of contrast, the use of most words is not governed by syntactic rules, and speakers are quite variable in the ways they build sentences together.

The development of 'predicate markers'

In creoles of the South Pacific, a new grammatical particle *i* preceding and marking the predicate in a sentence (the verb and its object) has regularly arisen. This is illustrated with examples from Tok Pisin and Bislama.

Fred i bin go long pati.   Tok Pisin
'Fred went to the party.'

Man ya i stilim mane.   Bislama (example from Crowley 1990)
'This man stole the money.'

The predicate marker *i* is derived comes from the English word 'he', but syntactically it corresponds to predicate markers which occur in the Austronesian substrate languages of South Pacific pidgins and creoles. Many of these languages have a parallel predicate marker, and it seems that creole speakers import this aspect of the substrate languages when they develop the grammar of the creole further. When they do this, they do not borrow the actual predicate markers present in the substrate languages (which, for example, in Arosi is *a*, and in Kwaio is *la*: Crowley 1990: 87), but develop an English word for use in this grammatical role, reanalyzing 'he' as the new functional particle *i*. Such a process is known as 'functional transfer'—a word is borrowed from the superstrate/lexifier language and is given a function which corresponds to a grammatical element present in the substrate languages.

The development of determiners

When pidgins initially come into existence, definite and indefinite determiners (words equivalent to English 'the' and 'a') are eliminated from the superstrate input, with the result that nouns are often ambiguous in their interpretation. For example, a pidgin sentence such as 'Jim eat papaya' is in many ways ambiguous, and in addition to the ambiguity caused by a lack of tense inflection (so that the timing of the event could be in the past, the present, or the future), the referential properties of the object are unclear, and the sentence could mean any of the following sentences in its lexifier, English.

'Jim ate the papaya.'
'Jim ate a papaya.'
'Jim ate papayas.'

Creoles reintroduce determiners so that the vagueness present in early and stable pidgins is removed and creoles are more precise in their properties of reference. A definite determiner is either borrowed directly from the lexifier language or created from some other source via reanalysis, re-establishing equivalents to 'the' and parallel words in other superstrates. In French, Spanish, Portuguese, and German, determiners change their shape according to the gender, number, and (in German) case of a noun. Hence Spanish has 'el' as 'the' before masculine singular nouns, 'la' before feminine singular nouns, 'los' before masculine plural nouns, and 'las' before feminine plural nouns. When determiners are recreated in creoles, they occur in one form, and do not change their shape. Typically, one of the set of definite determiners will be borrowed from the superstrate to represent a definite interpretation of all nouns it is added to. For example, in German, determiners have many different forms depending on whether the nouns they combine with are masculine, feminine, or neuter, singular or plural, and whether the noun functions as the subject or the object in the sentence it occurs in. In German-based creoles, however (such as Rabaul German Creole in the South Pacific), a single form of the definite article 'the' is used for all forms. In the following example, 'der' is used for both nouns, whereas standard German would use neuter 'das' for 'Baby' and feminine 'die' for 'Mama' (example from Romaine 1988).

> *Wenn der Baby weinen, der Mama muss aufpicken*
> when the baby cry the mama must pick-up
> 'When the baby cries, the mother must pick it up.'

Creoles have interestingly been observed to introduce finer referential distinctions with their new determiners than are present in the common lexifier languages. All the most frequent superstrate languages have a definite article such as 'the', which is used with nouns whose reference is known to both the speaker and the hearer, and an indefinite article like English 'a', which is used with nouns whose reference is not known to the hearer. Creoles have regularly been found to create a more advanced three-way system of reference. An equivalent to 'the' is created for definite reference, and there are *two* ways of referring to a noun whose identity is not known to the hearer. If its identity is known to the speaker (but not the hearer) an indefinite article (often sourced from the superstrate word for 'one') is used, whereas if neither speaker or hearer is aware of the identity of an object, it occurs as a simple bare noun, as illustrated in the following example of Hawaiian Creole English:

> *da cat* 'the cat' – known to speaker and hearer (definite reference)
> *wan cat* 'a cat' – known to speaker but not hearer (specific indefinite reference)
> *cat* 'a cat' – known to neither speaker or hearer (non-specific indefinite reference)

Creoles are thus able to move beyond their lexifiers and develop highly sophisticated systems of reference, becoming even more informative and clear about the reference values of nouns than in older superstrate languages.

The creation of new specialized pronoun forms

During the early and stable pidgin stage, pronouns (equivalent to English 'he', 'me', 'you', etc.) are quite basic, but when creoles develop, more complex forms are often found to emerge. For example, in creoles of the South Pacific, there are two forms for the English pronoun '*we*' (and '*us*'). One of these is called an 'inclusive we' and is used to refer to the speaker and the listener(s), like English 'we'. The other type of 'we' is called an 'exclusive we', and refers to the speaker and other people who carry out an action with the speaker, but does *not* include the listeners, as seen in the following two examples from Tok Pisin.

Yumi mas painim pik.
you-me must find pig
'We (the two of us) must find a pig.'
yumi = INCLUSIVE 'we'

Mipela mas painim pik.
me-fellow must find pig
'We (me and certain others not including you) must find a pig.'
mipela = EXCLUSIVE 'we'

Vocabulary size

When an early or stable pidgin develops into a creole, the number of distinct words in the language becomes much larger, allowing speakers to talk about a very wide range of topics in a way that is not always possible during earlier pidgin stages. This vocabulary increase is achieved by the kinds of word-building strategies which occur in the stable pidgin stage (very frequently via compounding) and supplemented by an additional word-repetition process which only occurs in creoles and not early or stable pidgins. This is known as '**reduplication**'. A word is simply produced twice in quick succession in order to encode some new kind of meaning, often (but not always) involving an intensification of the meaning of the original word. The following are some examples of this from Kamtok and Tok Pisin. Where English (or some other superstrate) may have a completely different word to represent an intensification of the meaning of a verb or adjective, reduplication produces this effect in creoles without the need for creating a completely different word.

Kamtok:	*big* – 'big'	*big big* – 'enormous'	
	luk – 'look'	*luk luk* – 'stare at'	
	krai – 'cry'	*kraikrai* – 'cry continuously'	
Tok Pisin:	*hol* – 'hold'	*holholim* – 'to hold something/someone tight'	
	tok - 'talk'	*toktok* – 'to chatter on'	
	go – 'go'	*gogo* – 'to walk fast'	
	ask – 'ask'	*askaskim* – 'to ask persistently'	
	sing – 'sing'	*singsing* – a party, festival	

The creation of syntactic constructions

As pidgins undergo creolization, there is a clear increase in the complexity of syntactic constructions, and forms such as relative clauses and embedded clauses begin to develop and occur as in other, older languages. This allows the creole to express much more complex linguistic relations within sentences than in the earlier pidgin stages. The following is an example of a new relative clause construction embedded in a sentence in Tok Pisin from Romaine (1988) (the relative clause is represented with underlining in the English translation):

Dispela man i slip, em i papa bilong mi.
this fellow-man he sleep him he father belong me
'The man who is asleep is my father.'

Word order: global convergence on SVO patterns

In the early pidgin/jargon stage, the ordering of words in sentences is often quite random and not fixed in any clear way, and speakers do not seem to be following any obvious rules when they string words together in their utterances. As pidgins undergo stabilization, however, speakers are observed to adopt a systematic way of ordering the major elements in sentences, subjects, verbs, and objects, but may do this in a variety of ways, either consistently following an SVO pattern, or an SOV order, or a VSO sequencing. Speakers of stable pidgins therefore establish a fixed word order in their speech, but what this order is may vary from pidgin to pidgin. When pidgins become creoles (or extended pidgins), it is interesting that there is a clear, new cross-linguistic convergence on SVO as the regular word order used by speakers. An SVO order is the neutral and most common word order in English, French, Spanish, Portuguese, and Dutch, the major superstrate languages. It is also an order which is common in many of the West African languages which were spoken by slaves brought to the Americas—the frequent substrate languages of pidgins and creoles arising in the Caribbean, the northern part of South America, and in the USA. Consequently, it is not surprising that this order should turn out to be the favored order in pidgins and creoles (a potential occurrence of *convergence*—as both superstrate and substrate languages share the same basic word order patterning, this is maintained in the pidgin and creole which is formed from these languages). However, an SVO order also seems to develop regularly in instances where the superstrate and substrate languages have a *different* word order, for example an SOV or a VSO order. While such word order patterns may be used during the stable pidgin stage, when pidgins advance further in their life cycle and become extended pidgins and creoles, it has been observed that SOV, VSO, and any other patterns that speakers have regularly used give way to and are replaced by an SVO ordering.[1] This global establishment of the same SVO word order in creoles whose superstrate and substrate languages have different kinds of word order is an observation that needs some explanation, and one which has led to various theories about the kinds of linguistic forces that determine the ways creole languages may develop, as we shall shortly see.

---

1. Some exceptions to this broad generalization might seem to be present in parts of Asia, but it has been suggested that these non-SVO patterns have resulted from influences of local languages *after* the creole was formed, for example, Sri Lankan Creole was originally SVO but later became SOV under the post-creole influence of Sinhala and Tamil, both of which are SOV languages. A similar situation is suggested to have occurred in the Philippines, as SVO patterns in creoles there were replaced by VSO sequences under sustained influence from local VSO languages (Bakker 2008). If this is the correct historical analysis of these patterns, the generalization that creoles all make use of an SVO word order pattern may indeed be without exception, and a 'universal' property of creole languages.

The development of morphology

Early pidgins are regularly found to eliminate occurrences of inflectional morphology from the words which they borrow from superstrate languages, and early and stable pidgins do not utilize affixes on words, unlike the major lexifier languages. When early and stable pidgins develop further, however, as extended pidgins and creoles, they often start to produce new instances of inflectional morphology and the use of new affixes on words. One example of this is the addition of a suffix *-im* to the end of *transitive verbs* (i.e., verbs which have objects) in creoles spoken in the South Pacific area. Compare the following pairs of sentence. In the first sentence of each pair, the verb does not have an object, and the verb is not given any suffix ending, but when an object is present, in the second sentence of each pair, the verb has to occur with the suffix *-im*.

Mi bin rit. *Mi bin rit**im** buk.*
I PAST write I PAST write-im book
'I wrote.' 'I wrote a book.'

Masket i bin pairip. *Mi bin pairip**im** masket.*
gun *i* PAST fire I PAST fire-*im* gun
'A gun went off/was fired.' 'I fired a gun.'

This suffix *-im* is referred to as a 'transitivity marker' and derives from a reanalysis of the English word 'him'. Most probably it developed in creoles in the South Pacific due to influence from substrate languages in the region which have similar markers on verbs; for example Kiribati has a transitivity marker '*-a*' attached to verbs with objects, and in Anejom '*-yic*' is suffixed to transitive verbs (Crowley 1990: 87). This is another case of functional transfer, similar to the development of the predicate marker *i* considered earlier—a creole language reanalyzes a word from the superstrate language in a way that matches a grammatical morpheme in its substrate languages.

The same suffix *-im* has also been added by creole speakers to *adjectives* to convert them into verbs in a way that is very similar to the way English uses the ending *-en* to make adjectives into verbs:

English: adjective to verb conversion with *-en*
'red' → 'redden'
'black' → 'blacken'
'white' → 'whiten'
'She whitens her face every day with an expensive powder.'

Tok Pisin adjective to verb conversion with *-im*:
doti 'dirty' → *dotiim* → 'make something dirty, to soil something'
brait 'wide' → *braitim* → 'widen something'
bik – 'big' → *bikim* – 'enlarge, make something big'

Thus we see that creoles begin to make words morphologically complex through the development of new affixes, which are common features of older languages established for much longer periods of time.

Faster speech and the reduction of word size

In stable pidgins, new words are often compounds whose meaning is sometimes quite clear from the words involved, as in the following Melanesian pidgin example:

wara bilong skin – 'water belong skin' = 'sweat'

During the creole stage, however, many of these compounds are shortened by speakers, as in the following:

wara bilong skin → *skinwara*

In various instances, such *reduction* in the size of words will result in the meaning of creole words being less clear than in the pidgin stage.

Other related occurrences of word reduction take place in creole speech. This is a result of the fact that creoles are *mother-tongue/first* languages of their speakers, and because of this, creoles are spoken more confidently and fluently than pidgins, and generally *faster* than in the pidgin stage. The increased speed at which creoles are spoken causes words to be contracted, just as in other languages. In English, for example, contractions occur with sequences of 'I' and 'am' becoming 'I'm', 'he' and 'would' reducing to 'he'd', and 'we' and 'have' being pronounced as the shortened form 'we've'. In creoles, similar reductions are made by speakers, contracting words that were produced in longer forms during the pidgin period. For example, in the stable pidgin stage of Tok Pisin, future time reference was indicated by the sentence-initial time adverb *baimbai* derived by reanalysis from English 'by and by'. In its development into an expanded pidgin and creole, a series of changes have occurred, ultimately resulting in a highly reduced form *ba-*, which is pronounced as if it were part of the following verb (i.e., like a tense inflection in non-creole languages—another instance of creoles developing new morphological affixes). In fact, the heavily reduced form *ba-* will become even smaller when preceding a verb beginning with a vowel, and be pronounced simply as *b-*, hence pidgin *baimbai* over time has become simply *ba-* or *b-* in creole speech. The following paradigm is from Sankoff and Laberge (1973), repeated in Romaine (1988) and Holmes (1992), and shows how the full-form *baimbai* changes over time to *ba-* as the language develops from a stable pidgin into an extended pidgin and creole.

(i) *Baimbai mi go.* 'I will go.'
(ii) *Bambai mi go.* 'I will go.'
(iii) *Bai mi go.* 'I will go.'
(iv) *Mi bai go.* 'I will go.'
(v) *Mi bago.* 'I will go.'

The following Tok Pisin examples from Romaine (1988) are further illustrations of reductions resulting from faster rates of speech. The new forms are no longer 'transparent' in meaning in the way that they used to be during the stable pidgin stage:

'of'	*bilong* → *blo*
'of them/their'	*bilong em* → *blem*
'behind him'	*bihainim* → *beinim*
'one person ('fellow')'	*wanpela* → *nla*
'this fellow'	*dispela* → *disla*
'you-two-fellows'	*yutupela* → *yuta*
'future-marker'	*laik* → *la* (or *l'* before a word beginning with a vowel)

Similarly, in Bislama, Crowley (2008) notes that the preposition *long* now becomes just *l'* before a word beginning with a vowel:

in the next afternoon	*long nekis aftenun*
in the afternoon	*l'aftenun*

The faster speech that speakers of creoles typically use thus has a significant effect on the shapes of words, often disguising their superstrate origin, and making creoles seem increasingly different from the languages which initially lexified them as pidgins.

Summary

What we have seen in looking at the changing linguistic properties of pidgins and creoles is that there is a typical progression through a cycle of development. First, in the early pidgin stage there is radical simplification of the linguistic input sourced (primarily) from the superstrate languages, and much variability in the way that pidgins are spoken. Following this, there is often a period of pidgin stabilization when some common conventions begin to be observed by speakers, and pidgins have to be learned rather than spontaneously improvised most of the time, but stable (non-extended) pidgins still remain very basic in their syntactic and morphological structure. As communities of speakers find more regular needs for the use of a pidgin, however, and extended pidgins and creoles develop further, there consistently occurs a dramatic increase in structural complexity, either very swiftly through creolization and 'nativization' of the pidgin, as native speakers are established and rapidly develop a pidgin as their native language (so that the pidgin becomes a creole), or somewhat less abruptly over the course of one or two generations as extended pidgins expand their ability to be used in all domains of life.

Massive simplification of linguistic forms at the outset of the pidgin-to-creole life cycle thus leads to a gradual and then fast renewal of the kind of complex formations of syntax and word structure that are present in much older languages, such as the original lexifiers of pidgins. There is more to describe in this intriguing cycle of language development, and further outcomes that may occur with creoles as they potentially undergo de-creolization or standardization, stabilize in diglossia, and lead to re-creolization. We will examine all these phenomena a little later. First, we are going to consider what many creolists have suggested is the greatest challenge for studies of pidgins and creole languages—accounting for the many clear similarities observed among pidgins and creoles around the world, regardless of their lexifiers and their substrate languages. Various theories have been proposed to explain how pidgins in different parts of the world regularly develop similar linguistic properties, but there is still no strong agreement about how to account for this observation, and the apparent links which seem to exist between geographically unrelated pidgins and creoles is a topic which has caused much interesting discussion of the foundations and universality of human language.

Theories of the global similarity of pidgins and creoles

It is clear that pidgins and creoles all lexically relate to some superstrate language (i.e., the primary vocabulary stems from a particular lexifier language), and that there are also lexical and some grammatical influences from various substrate languages. This varied contribution of superstrate and substrate languages may tend to introduce certain differences among pidgins and creoles. However, what has really impressed and puzzled linguists comparing pidgins and creoles from around the world is the *striking similarities* that these languages repeatedly show to each other in terms of:

(i) their *basic syntactic structure*, which seems to be extremely similar in all pidgins and creoles. Again and again, it is found that creoles develop the same kinds of grammatical constructions, so that creoles which have evolved in different continents appear to be as close to each other in their grammatical properties as 'old' languages which are geographically very near to each other and descended from a single language family, such as Spanish and Italian.

(ii) *aspects of their lexicon*: many grammatical words occur in highly similar forms in different creoles, and pidgins and creoles in different parts of the world curiously seem to have words of Portuguese origin, even when the (obvious) superstrate language is not Portuguese. Words from Portuguese which commonly occur in both English and French pidgins and creoles are (i) *savi/save/sabi* meaning 'to know', derived from Portuguese 'saber', and (ii) *pikin* meaning 'small' or 'child', derived from Portuguese *pequeno*.

There are several theories which attempt to account for the unexpected similarities which have constantly found among pidgin and creole languages. The two most influential types of hypothesis in linguistic studies of pidgins and creoles are:

(a) approaches which suggest that all European-superstrate pidgins historically relate back to a *single language source*;
(b) models which attribute the cross-linguistic similarities in pidgins and creoles to *universal mechanisms of language acquisition*.

Theories of 'monogenetic origin'

Some linguists have suggested that the linguistic similarities observed in pidgins and creoles throughout different parts of the world are due to a *common ancestry*, and that pidgins throughout the world are actually *genetically related* to each other. The most prominent 'monogenetic' theory of this type suggests that all pidgins with European language-lexifiers derive from a Portuguese-origin maritime pidgin which was spoken by multi-national sailors and established in the 15th century. This pidgin is hypothesized to be directly related to a language form used by multilingual sea traders active in the Mediterranean area during the Middle Ages and by soldiers from different nations participating in the Crusades. The name given to this early trading language was Sabir, and it was also sometimes simply known as 'Lingua Franca'. An interesting property of Sabir/Lingua Franca is that its vocabulary was different when it was spoken in different areas, but its grammatical structure remained the same. One of the different language forms of Sabir was spoken with Portuguese word substitutions, and it is suggested that this particular version of Sabir was spread along trade routes around the world by the crews of Portuguese ships as they traded and interacted with local people living on the coasts of West Africa, India, Southeast Asia, and the Far East. As the Portuguese were the first European traders to reach many parts of Africa and Asia, Portuguese-lexified Sabir would therefore have been the first European contact language learned by Africans and Asians. However, other European nations later overcame the Portuguese and took their place trading in areas where the Portuguese pidgin had been learned by local people.

To begin with, English, French, and Dutch maritime traders would have needed to use the Portuguese pidgin to communicate successfully with the Africans and Asians they met in coastal regions. But over time, it is assumed that English, French, and Dutch words were gradually added into the pidgin, making it into a 'language blend', part Portuguese, part English/French/Dutch. With continued contact, the vocabulary of the pidgin would have come to be increasingly dominated by English/French/Dutch, as substitutions from these languages ousted earlier Portuguese words, leaving behind just a few Portuguese 'fossils' in the language as it became spoken with different superstrate words in various parts of Asia and Africa (Romaine 1988). Such an almost complete change in the word base of a 'single' language from using the words of one language to using those of another language, while maintaining the original grammatical structure, is referred to as the '**relexification**' of a language (and characterized by Hall 1966: 183 as 'substitution of vocabulary items for others with the maintenance of a stable syntactic base'). Relexification is a process that has occurred with a considerable number of languages, making it plausible as part of a monogenetic origin theory of pidgins and creoles. Here we can note just a few examples of languages that have undergone this phenomenon of vocabulary change, in which words from one language are substituted by words from another without this changing the syntax of a language:

- In the Gansu Province of China, Uyghur speakers heavily borrowed Mandarin words into the grammatical structure of Uyghur, creating a new Chinese relexified form of the Turkic language Uyghur (Lee-Smith 1996).
- In Ecuador, certain Quechua-speakers have relexified Quechua with (90%) Spanish words, converting it into a new mixed language known as 'Media Lengua', in which Spanish content words are combined with Quechua functional morphemes (Holm 1989).
- Relexification has also been documented with various pidgin languages. For example, in New Caledonia an English-superstrate pidgin called Beach-la-Mar was heavily relexified

with French words when France took over control of this territory in the 19th century, and in Suriname in the Caribbean, a pidgin known as Saramaccan which was originally formed with Portuguese vocabulary later underwent relexification with many English words (Romaine 1988).[2]

The assumption that relexification has frequently occurred to an original Portuguese pidgin derived from Lingua Franca/Sabir provides a way of potentially accounting for the many connections that seem to exist among pidgins and creoles in different part of the world. Relating all European-language-based pidgins to a single early source is suggested to explain why there is so much similarity in the basic grammatical properties of pidgins with different superstrate languages—these properties are attributed to the original Portuguese source and are assumed to have been maintained as the Portuguese pidgin was later relexified with English, French, Dutch, and German words. Hypothesizing that the first pidgin was formed with Portuguese words also allows for an understanding of why Portuguese words appear in pidgins and creoles whose vocabulary is primarily sourced from other languages—the Portuguese words are relics left over from an earlier period in the life cycle of these pidgins. Finally, the suggestion that it was an initial *maritime* pidgin that was spread around the world in newly relexified forms offers some insight into the observation that many pidgins have words of *nautical* origin, which have now developed broader uses. For example, words such as 'capsize', 'cargo', and 'galley' are common in pidgins in the Pacific and Atlantic, but with modified meanings—equivalents to 'capsize' often mean to 'spill or knock something over', 'galley' in pidgins may regularly refer to kitchens in houses, and 'cargo' is used to refer to any load, however this is transported—carried in the hand, on the head, or in any form of transport, not just in ships (Todd 1990).

While the monogenetic origin and relexification hypothesis is thus able to offer a possible account of the similarities found in different pidgins and creoles, and the presence of Portuguese and maritime vocabulary, it has not been accepted by everyone. A number of linguists have argued that this kind of theory is actually implausible, because it is unlikely that a single language (the Portuguese form of Sabir) would be carried by maritime traders around the world and simply relexified without the occurrence of other major grammatical changes which would make the relexified pidgins increasingly different from each other—yet the grammar of pidgins/creoles has been found to be oddly similar wherever these occur. In other words, if there were to be just a single historical source for all pidgins, one might expect that this language would undergo many changes when brought into contact with differently

---

2. An interesting case of an individual whom Smith and Tsimpli (1995) describe as having relexified his mother tongue, English, multiple times is the polyglot Christopher Taylor, a 'language savant' who is linguistically very gifted, apparently being able to learn quite unrelated languages very quickly. Christopher's special aptitude seems to be above all in phonology, as he learns words from different new languages and pronounces them perfectly, but combines them with what is essentially a grammatical structure provided by English, hence he largely relexifies his English with words from Hindi, Arabic, Turkish, Swedish, and many other languages (over twenty), and gives the impression of having fully mastered all these languages. However, what Christopher has actually been producing is to a great extent a repeated relexification of English, rather than genuine full copies of Hindi, Arabic, etc., spoken with the grammar of these languages as well as their vocabulary.

structured languages in different continents, but pidgins and creoles all over the world still maintain a strikingly high parallelism in their grammatical structure. Given what is known from language change among 'regular' non-pidgin languages, it is unlikely that such a parallelism (in pidgins and creoles) would have been so well maintained over the centuries if it originated from a unique early source. Elsewhere it has commonly been observed that languages undergo significant grammatical changes when they come into contact with other languages of different types, and there is no reason to suppose that pidgin languages should be an exception to such a patterning. Consequently, it is argued, their strong similarities should be attributed to some other kind of explanation. Additionally, it is pointed out that there are pidgin languages whose origins *cannot* be linked back to any European trading language such as Sabir, for example Chinook, Delaware, and Mobilian Jargons, spoken among North American Indians, and Hawaiian Pidgin English which was only created 100 years ago. The North American pidgins nevertheless show the same common properties that other pidgins regularly have.

The role of language acquisition mechanisms in pidginization and creolization

Studies of pidgins have frequently suggested that these languages resemble the speech of young children in certain ways—similar kinds of simplifications are made in both early pidgins and children's language in their first years, with few grammatical words being used and very little or no inflections/affixes occurring on nouns and verbs. A second prominent theory of the development of pidgins which has arisen from such observations is that pidgins, and later creoles, result from processes of language acquisition which operate in the same way in pidgin-creating environments as they do with young children acquiring language in non-pidgin situations. It is suggested that humans, both young and old, make use of the same mechanisms to simplify complex linguistic input heard from others and develop new abilities in language, and that the universal nature of these strategies causes very similar linguistic structures to come into existence, both in situations involving pidginization, and when children go through the stages of regular early child language acquisition. The common resemblance of pidgins to each other in different parts of the world is, in such a learning-based approach, attributed to humans simply applying the same mental processes to language development whenever this is necessary, and languages with typical pidgin-type properties and structures are viewed as an inevitable result of this shared mode of language acquisition applied to complicated input.

Two rather different versions of such an acquisition-grounded account of pidgin and creole similarity have been proposed by linguists, varying in their perspectives on the mental processes involved in first- and second-language acquisition and in their primary focus on either pidginization or creolization.

The second-language acquisition (SLA) approach

A number of researchers have focused their attention on the creation of early, stable, and expanded pidgins. Pidgins are first established and then developed further by adults who are mother-tongue speakers of some other language (one of the substrate languages). What is involved in pidginization is therefore the development of a new second language among mixed adult populations, and pidginization has been compared to the general phenomenon of second-language acquisition (SLA), which takes place when speakers of one language set out to learn another language, normally after early adolescence through into adulthood.[3] As mastering the complexities of an unfamiliar language may initially be somewhat overwhelming to second-language learners, it is common to find that learners make certain simplifications to their production of the target language. Hence when speakers hear a new language and attempt to copy it and speak it themselves, they will typically make a number of adjustments and produce a simplified version of the language in certain respects. In second-language acquisition, it is frequently suggested that speakers make use of *general cognitive principles* to analyze, learn, and reproduce a new language, applying the same generalized analytical techniques that would be used in other instances of *non-linguistic* problem-solving (in other words, speakers approach the task of learning a second language with the same mental tools they would use when trying to understand other logical puzzles which don't involve language). A second-language acquisition approach to pidginization consequently assumes that humans make use of *universal cognitive mechanisms* to simplify complex input data, and when applied to superstrate languages, such mechanisms create simplifications in the same basic kinds of ways, regardless of the particular language that serves as the superstrate. Consequently, whether the superstrate language in a multilingual contact situation is English, French, Dutch, or Portuguese (or any other language), the results of the simplification processes are expected to be very similar, producing 'stripped down' pidgins that resemble each other structurally wherever the process of pidginization actually takes place. The striking similarity of pidgins around the world is therefore attributed to parallel cognitive strategies being used whenever second-language acquisition is attempted.

One potential challenge for such an SLA approach to pidgin similarities which has been noted in the literature is that second-language acquisition in non-pidgin contexts normally results in speakers developing a form of the targeted language which clearly resembles it and is mutually intelligible with it despite certain mistakes which speakers make. Pidginization, however, often establishes a new language form which is very significantly different from the superstrate language, and in many instances not mutually intelligible with it. In this regard, pidginization might seem to be quite different from typical second-language acquisition, bringing into question whether the SLA model is in fact an appropriate way to explain the similarities found across pidgins. In order to reconcile this apparent inconsistency between typical SLA and pidginization, it is emphasized that the latter process is inhibited in operating in the way of fully regular second-language acquisition because speakers developing pidgins have much less frequent access to hearing the 'target language' and practicing

---

3. When younger children acquire a second language through regular exposure to it before adolescence, this frequently results in them becoming bilingual, and when children have become native speakers of two languages, this is normally not considered to be an occurrence of second-language acquisition. The term 'second-language acquisition' is usually reserved for attempts to acquire an additional language which take place either during a person's teenage years or adult life, often through studying a particular language and normally without this leading to full native-speaker proficiency in the language. Chapter 8 presents discussion of the phenomenon of bilingualism and attempts to acquire a second language at different stages in a person's life.

with native speakers than is common in other instances of regular second-language acquisition. This is because substrate speakers often have few opportunities to interact directly with superstrate speakers due to the typical power differential that exists between these speakers, as described earlier in the chapter. It is therefore the unusually restricted nature of access to native speakers and their language that is suggested to cause the major differences between pidgins and superstrates, and it is argued that the similarities observed among pidgins can indeed still be attributed to universal properties of SLA, with the SLA process simply being hampered by less-than-normal amounts of primary-language data.

Universal Grammar and the Bioprogram Hypothesis

A second acquisition-based account of the similarities of pidgin and creole languages relates these to Noam Chomsky's Innateness Hypothesis and the workings of 'Universal Grammar'. In Chomsky's view, humans are all born with a part of the brain that is dedicated to the understanding and production of language, and this both assists and also constrains the process of language acquisition in young children. When new human languages are developed, such as pidgins and creoles, the claim is that they will necessarily resemble each other to a highly significant degree, because they will have to be produced by the same neurological 'hardware' that all humans have available for language-related activities. It is hypothesized that there is a 'universal blueprint' of specific language design properties hard-wired into the part of our brains which deals with language, and when this is applied to create a new language, it will impose restrictions on the kind of structures that can be developed. Due to the assumption that this set of architectural restrictions on language-building is the same in all humans (we are born with this language specialization—it is an 'innate' part of our cognitive abilities), when new languages such as pidgins are developed in special contact situations, clear similarities are expected to emerge—they are the output effects of the application of 'Universal Grammar', the innate, universal rules of (human) language construction.

A second relevant aspect of Chomsky's Innateness Hypothesis is that our ability to make use of Universal Grammar is stronger when we are young. This means that people are generally much better at learning and also creating new languages in their early years, up until the early teens. After this time, we can apply our language abilities to acquire new languages, but less effectively—hence people tend to find it harder to learn new languages the older they get. Concerning the development of pidgins and creoles, the effect of such assumptions is as follows. Adults who first create a pidgin will establish a linguistic system that is much more primitive and less sophisticated than any new language developed by children. Pidgin languages in their early stages are therefore less complex and advanced in their syntax and morphology than creole languages. According to advocates of a Chomskyean approach to creolization, such as Derek Bickerton and his 'Language Bioprogram Hypothesis', it is critically when pidgin languages acquire native speakers, who are regularly the children of the first pidgin speakers, that pidgins rapidly develop into complex creole languages which not only resemble each other to a high degree, but also show many of the classic design properties of other, older languages. What is taken to allow for this accelerated progress and conversion of pidgins into complex creole languages is children's enhanced connections to the part of the brain specialized in controlling language and its development, links which are believed to deteriorate over time and to be significantly weaker among adults.

The application of Chomsky's ideas about language in Bickerton's Language Bioprogram Hypothesis (Bickerton 1981, 1984) attributes the special properties of pidgin and creole languages and their life cycle to the differences that are assumed to exist in first- and second-language acquisition. For Bickerton, pidgins result from second-language acquisition and are simple linguistic systems because adults are restricted in their access to Universal Grammar, whereas creoles are produced by first-language acquisition among children, and become much more complex than pidgins because children still have privileged access to the part of the brain that enables the development of language. The similarities that are observed to occur in creole languages around the world are taken to be due to the principles of Universal Grammar applying in the same way to all new language development led by children, constraining the production of new linguistic systems in highly particular ways.

Comparing the two acquisition approaches to pidgin and creole similarities and differences, one may wonder which (if either) is more likely to be a better explanation of the repeated patterns which have been observed. The two different perspectives can be summarized as follows. The *second-language acquisition*–based hypothesis primarily focuses on the similarities in *pidgins* (early, stable, and extended), and suggests that these are due to the application of *general, but universal cognitive mechanisms* to restricted linguistic input from a superstrate language, in similar multilingual situations (plantations, ships, etc.). The *Bioprogram/Chomskyean approach* focuses more on similarities among *creoles* and attributes these and the complexity of creoles to properties of *first-language acquisition* in children, which are determined by the innate structuring of a part of the brain dedicated to language production (hence not simply general modes of analysis made available by the brain, but really language-specific mechanisms anchored in a particular location in the brain, most commonly the left hemisphere). It is actually possible that the SLA model and the Bioprogram approach might *both* be correct, but for different cases of pidgin/creole development. The Bioprogram Hypothesis is aimed to explain cases of *abrupt creolization*, where there is a very dramatic and sudden increase in the complexity of a language as it acquires a community of native speakers and enters the creole stage. Such cases would indeed seem to require a special role for children in the rapid change of an early or stable pidgin into a much more sophisticated creole, and the Bioprogram Hypothesis is well placed to explain the important potential role of native speakers in creolization. However, criticisms of the Bioprogram Hypothesis have noted that there are other paths of pidgin development which do not show any swift and sudden growth in syntax and morphology, as occurs in abrupt creolization, but a clear increase in the complexity of pidgins nevertheless appears to take place. This is suggested to arise more gradually, over the course of several generations of pidgin speakers, and is most commonly manifested in extended pidgins which have not yet developed native speakers. Where such more *gradualist* cases occur, and *nativization* cannot be appealed to in order to explain the changes in complexity that occur, they may best be captured by an SLA-type model in which adult second-language learners can *over time* help a pidgin achieve similar levels of complexity as children native speakers may do within shorter spaces of time, in situations of forced abrupt creolization. To the extent that both types of development may genuinely occur—gradual second-language growth of pidgins to a sophisticated extended pidgin stage without native speakers (either monolingual or bilingual), and rapid transition from an early or stable pidgin stage to advanced creole status—both types of acquisition models may perhaps be justified as accounts of pidginization and creolization, and as potential explanations for the similarities that exist among pidgins and creoles in different parts of the world.[4]

Whatever the correct account of pidgin/creole similarities might ultimately be, linguists will continue to be captivated, puzzled, and inspired by the phenomenon of these new languages, which can become just as complex as older languages within relatively short periods of time (either during one or two-to-three generations), spontaneously developing syntactic structures and morphological features that are not only shared across expanded pidgins and creoles, but are also re-creations of many classic linguistic properties of long-established languages, such as the development of tense and aspect systems, relative clauses, subject and object agreement morphemes, and a variety of other patterns common to languages which have very long histories. This is much of the special fascination of pidgins and creoles—they demonstrate the emergence of fully new languages and a potential window of insight into how languages may originally have been created. Because of this special property, they will certainly continue to be studied and to generate controversy for much time to come, as researchers probe their properties and paths of development and attempt to understand both how new languages can come into existence, and why such new languages regularly seem to end up heavily resembling other, older languages.

NICARAGUAN SIGN LANGUAGE: PIDGINIZATION AND CREOLIZATION AT WORK IN NON-VOCAL COMMUNICATION

In Nicaragua, no sign language existed prior to the 1970s, and deaf people had no real regular contact with each other. This changed when the government set up schools for the deaf from 1977 onward, and a community of mostly young deaf Nicaraguans came into being for the first time. The new schools initially attempted to teach young people spoken language and lip-reading skills, but were not very successful in this. However, as the students interacted with each other outside class in playgrounds and on buses going to school, they started to make use of signs as a form of communication, both creating new signs and using gestures they had developed earlier in their life at home. What emerged from these new sign-based acts of communication was very much like an early pidgin language—a lot of individual variation occurred in the signs, and there was little consistent, systematic use of the signs that were produced. The children who established this new early sign pidgin were all aged ten and over, and many were in

---

4. It should also be added that both language acquisition-based accounts of these similarities will need to be supplemented by the assumption that some cross-linguistic borrowing of Portuguese words has somehow occurred, in order to account for their frequent presence in pidgins and creoles.

their mid- to late teens. What is particularly interesting is that when younger children were admitted to the schools for the deaf, and started to participate in signing with other children, a quite different signing system emerged, which has been characterized as creole-like—it is much more regularized, appears to follow distinct rules, has developed an extensive vocabulary of signs, and can be used to communicate advanced abstract thoughts, as well as complex stories and emotive information. Thus almost as soon as the new pidgin sign language came to be used by young, pre-teenage children as a primary form of communication (a new native language), the pidgin appears to have been developed into a creole stage, just as spoken pidgin languages are creolized when they acquire young native speakers. Pinker (1994) notes that Chomsky's approach to language acquisition has a natural way to describe this very impressive progression (see also Kegl 2002, and Kegl, Senghas, and Coppola 1999). The Innateness Hypothesis claims that children have a much stronger and direct access to Universal Grammar than adults do, and so can apply this to the task of language creation in a much more effective way than adults and children in their mid- to late teens can. In Nicaragua, when teenage children began to communicate with each other by means of signs for the first time, they were unable to develop these interactions into a complex, stable system, and a pidgin sign language came about. Younger pre-teenage children, however, achieved quite different results, and very quickly seem to have created a grammatically sophisticated language which is very similar in its fundamental design properties to other longer-established sign languages.[5]

Further outcomes

This chapter has highlighted how pidgins and creoles may pass through a life cycle with various stages of development, beginning with an early pidgin/jargon period and continuing on until creolization potentially occurs and a high level of linguistic complexity is attained. When pidgins do reach the creole stage, there are various further outcomes that may be observed and additional uses to which a creole may be put. These are described in the following paragraphs and will complete our study of the pathways that pidgin and creole language typically take in the societies where they are established.

Stable diglossia

If a creole is spoken in a country/area where the official language is not the superstrate language associated with the creole as it emerged in its pidgin state, one further outcome for a creole is that it continues to exist alongside the official language in an extended diglossic situation, the creole serving L variety functions, and the official language being used in common

---

5. Note that an important assumption in Chomsky's theory is that Universal Grammar is a 'medium-independent' blueprint for language construction, hence an abstract set of linguistic principles which can be used to build and understand human language whether this is conveyed through the medium of voice or physical gesture. The theory can therefore be applied to sign languages in a simple way, and even leads to the expectation that there should be pidgin and creole languages that are signed as well as spoken.

H variety domains. For example, supposing an English-based creole were to be spoken in a territory where Dutch came to be the current official language, as in Suriname in South America, these two varieties might continue to exist alongside each other with no further development (the actual name of the creole in Suriname is Sranan, and this fulfils L variety functions, while Dutch is used for formal interactions as the H variety).

De-creolization

A second, regularly attested outcome of the pidgin-creole life cycle is a process referred to as de-creolization, in which a creole changes further and becomes more and more like the original superstrate language, increasingly resembling this language over time. This occurs when two conditions are met:

(i) The superstrate language continues to be used in the same region/country as the creole, often as an official language.

(ii) There is no clear social separation of creole-speakers and those whose primary language is the superstrate (English, French etc). Speakers of the creole have regular social interactions with speakers of the superstrate.

What happens in the process of de-creolization is that the distinctive vocabulary, syntax, and morphology which have developed in the creole tend to be increasingly replaced with words and grammatical structures and morphology from the standard language which served as its superstrate, as creole speakers are influenced by regularly hearing the superstrate and consciously or sub-consciously take to imitating it more in their own speech. Hence, for example, an English-based creole may become more and more like standard English as speakers of the creole introduce more patterns and words from standard English into the way they speak. In typical situations of de-creolization, there is in fact quite often a *continuum* of creole types, forming a range of varieties between the original creole at one end, called the 'basilect', and the standard superstrate at the other, referred to as the 'acrolect'. Intermediate varieties between the basilect and the acrolect are called 'mesolects', and the full range of forms has been termed a 'post-creole continuum'. Such changes to creole speech have been observed in Jamaica, Guyana, and a number of other places, and were first documented in detail in DeCamp (1971). The following examples illustrate some of the range of variety which may exist between basilect and acrolect in a typical post-creole continuum.

Post-creole continuum with Guyanese Creole (McWhorter 2008)

Creole basilect
↓
English acrolect

Mi bin gee am wan.
Mi di gi ee wan.
Ah did give ee wan.
Ah gave im wan.
I gave him one.

Post-creole continuum with Jamaican Creole (Siegel 2008)

Creole basilect
↓
English acrolect

Im a nyam im dinner.
Im a eat im dinner
Im eatin im dinner.
Him is eatin him dinner.
He is eating his dinner.

If de-creolization takes place over an extended period of time, and speakers use more of the mesolect varieties in place of the original basilect form, a creole can potentially 'hide its tracks' over time and may no longer be recognized as a creole, just seeming to be a minor dialectal variation of the standard form of a superstrate language such as English, French, or Dutch.

Promotion into a national or official language role and use in education

A creole may sometimes be standardized as a national or official language in the ways described in chapter 2—grammars and dictionaries are written, a single norm is established, and the creole becomes used in written form in newspapers, official documents, and eventually literature. This has occurred with Sango in the Central African Republic, Seselwa/Seychellois Créole in the Seychelles (Indian Ocean), and Tok Pisin and Hiri Motu in Papua New Guinea, all of which are now recognized as (co-)official languages of the territories where they are spoken (often holding co-official status with a second, European language, for example English or French). However, there is certain variation in the ways that creoles declared as official languages actually come to be used in official domains in everyday life, and the declaration that a creole has official language status does not always mean that it is used in the same ways that another co-official language such as English or French is. The case of Bislama in Vanuatu is a good illustration of this, and underlines how attitudes toward creoles and longer-established languages are often quite different, with pidgins and creoles being treated as lower in prestige and pragmatic value than European languages of wider communication/LWCs such as English, Spanish and French, even when creoles are given official or national language status.

Vanuatu is an island state in the South Pacific which has a population of 250,000 but as many as 105 different Oceanic languages.[6] Prior to achieving independence in 1980, Vanuatu was governed jointly by both a British and a French colonial presence, and both English and French were used in schools as mediums of education. Among the common people, a pidgin known as Bislama arose, lexified with English words, and was used as a common language between people from different language groups. This resulted in the establishment of a situation of triglossia, with Bislama serving regular L functions, and English and French both being H varieties used in formal domains. When the Vanuatu nationalist movement began campaigning for independence in the 1970s, the decision was taken to use Bislama to try to unite the population politically, as Bislama was the most widely known language in the territory (then still known as the New Hebrides), and it soon became symbolic of the indigenous people's struggle for self-rule, stimulating new feelings of nationalism and unity (Devonish 2008). When independence was attained, Bislama was recognized as the state's single national language, and also as an official language, along with English and French. However, despite being recognized as an official language, Bislama was not made use of in formal domains during the post-independence period, and the other two official languages,

---

6. Devonish (2008) notes that this represents the largest number of languages per head of population anywhere in the world.

English and French, continued to dominate these domains. After it had served its purpose as a rallying-point for independence and as a symbol of anti-colonial feelings, the new leadership largely discarded it in favor of the use of English and French as languages to develop the new state. Devonish (2008) suggests that this is a common pattern—pidgins and creoles may be welcomed at a nation-building stage, when their symbolic, unifying function can be exploited, but are less desired (in formal domains) when it comes to state-building and the practical growth of new infrastructures, as people regularly think that standard European languages provide more resources and opportunities for the development of a modern state than could ever be offered by a pidgin or creole. The deeply ingrained negative attitudes that people hold toward pidgins and creoles as potential H domain equals to LWCs seem likely to hold back the ways that the former may come to be used as genuine official languages and oust European languages in these functional roles.

A similar lack of confidence in the value and potential of pidgins and creoles also frequently hinders their more widespread use in the area of education. The great majority of creoles are spoken in territories where some other, European language (very often the lexifier of the creole) has enjoyed a long-term presence and is still the language of choice in higher education, as knowledge of English, French, Portuguese, or Dutch opens up access to advanced written materials in these languages, and facilitates international connections. Because there is a common belief that the lexifier of a creole (or some other language of wider communication) must be used in higher education, for practical purposes, little effort is made to develop good-quality teaching materials in pidgins and creoles, even for earlier levels of education. Parents typically focus on having their children learn standard English or standard French in order to maximize their opportunities for better-paid employment after leaving school, and this prioritization of the lexifier languages works against the use of pidgins and creoles as mediums of education, especially at the secondary level. Time spent using a pidgin or creole in school is broadly perceived to be wasted time, which could be better used in mastering skills in English, French, or some other language that offers special advantages to its speakers.

Interestingly, teachers polled in a survey carried out in Papua New Guinea (reported and commented on in Siegel 2009) all felt that using Tok Pisin (the national pidgin/creole) would improve communication between teachers and students and students' general academic performance, yet over 90% of teachers taking part in the survey were still in favor of using only English as a medium of education in schools. There is consequently a Catch 22 situation with the potential use of creoles in education. Children beginning school will often have very good oral abilities in a widespread creole and so should be able to use this immediately to good effect in class. However, even teachers who appreciate the likely benefits of creole-medium instruction are distracted by the instrumental power offered by superstrate languages of wider communication. They consequently feel that English or French should be imposed in schools so that children can compete better with others who are learning these languages from an early age. Siegel (2009) notes further that one school in Papua New Guinea did, in fact, experiment with using Tok Pisin as the classroom language in early education, and teaching the skills of reading and writing through Tok Pisin rather than standard English actually resulted in children learning English more effectively and doing better in tests, and led to higher levels of academic achievement. Despite such demonstrations of the ability of creoles to help children make good progress with their studies, the general outlook for the increased use of pidgins and creoles in the classroom remains rather bleak, and while pidgins and creoles may be perceived to have great value as markers of solidarity and to be the preferred languages of self-expression, the attitudes that people commonly hold toward them as languages suited to formal activities and domains such as government administration, legal matters, higher education, and business are much less positive, and are likely to hinder their spread into these areas of life in a genuinely meaningful way. This may furthermore seem to be a long-term condition that will continue to plague pidgins and creoles for as long as they are felt to be mixed languages and poor copies of the superstrate languages which have long dominated domains such as (secondary and higher) education and state administration.

So, while official language status and increased use in education are further potential developments for creole languages, and applications which have been experimented with in certain states, such moves to extend the use of creoles may often involve a difficult battle with prejudices held toward new languages of this type, and fall short of elevating them into roles traditionally reserved for 'prestige' standardized languages of western Europe.

Re-creolization

A final phenomenon to mention here is the occasional occurrence of 're-creolization', a patterning in which people deliberately adopt (or re-adopt) creole speech at some point in their lives, substituting creole patterns for non-creole speech. Re-creolization has been observed to occur in the language used by many young people of Afro-Caribbean origin living in large cities in England, such as London and Birmingham. Around the age of 14–15, young black teenagers who showed no signs of having used any form of creole in their earlier years have been found to adopt Jamaican creole patterns from the films they see and the music they listen to. It is noted that the parents of these teenagers mostly do *not* speak creole, because a major process of de-creolization took place in the 1950s in England, in which the creole speech of immigrants from the Caribbean became increasingly like British English. Young people who re-creolize their speech are therefore not simply taking up the language patterns of their parents, and Romaine (1988) observes that young people whose parents come from elsewhere in the Caribbean are using patterns which are specifically characteristic of Jamaican creole, rather than the creoles spoken on the islands of the Caribbean where their parents grew up. Additionally, young people whose parents speak French-based creoles are also adopting Jamaican creole, which is lexified with English words. Observers of the ways that Afro-Caribbean teenagers in the UK are changing their speech and converting it into creole forms take this to be a deliberate outward assertion of a shared group identity: being young and black and faced with the challenges of inner city life and potential prejudices from other segments of British society. Jamaican creole is adopted as a way to express solidarity with other young people from the same ethnic and social background and to indicate pride in an Afro-Caribbean cultural identity.

Sometimes re-creolization may also occur later in an individual's life. In the USA, a creole known as Gullah is still spoken on eastern coastal areas between northern Florida and North Carolina (though among many speakers it has been undergoing de-creolization due to increased contact with speakers of standard and local forms of English). Young people who do grow up as Gullah speakers frequently abandon the creole when they move out of the Gullah community to seek job or educational opportunities in other areas, and typically switch to use either standard American English or African American Vernacular English during their professional lives. However, it has been noted that many of these speakers ultimately come back to their original communities to spend their retirement, and when they do, they re-creolize their speech, re-adopting Gullah patterns that they had not made use of for many decades (Nichols 2004). In such cases, too, re-creolization seems to serve a clear identity-related purpose and emphasizes a person's reconnection to their original social and ethnic group.

The study of pidgins and creoles thus leads to a wide range of interesting questions and phenomena relating to language and social identity, the development of new languages and attitudes held to such languages, and how languages may evolve rapidly through different forms along a life cycle with different stages and final outcomes. In the current chapter, we have provided a very broad introduction to some of these issues, but there is still much more to explore and learn about pidgin and creole languages. For some suggestions on further readings and activities, see the range of listings provided in what follows.

Suggestions for further reading and activities

1. Explore the online *Atlas of Pidgin and Creole Language Structures (APICS)* at: http://apics-online.info/
Pick one of the many pidgins and creoles documented there, and create a brief profile of the pidgin/creole. Try to supplement what you can find at APICS with information about the pidgin/creole that you can locate elsewhere on the internet.
2. Try to find out more about the use of Tok Pisin as an official language in Papua New Guinea. What functions can Tok Pisin be used for, and to what extent does Tok Pisin now occur in the educational system?
3. Learn about the origins and attitudes held toward the Sierra Leone creole Krio in the following reading:

    Oyetade, Akintunde, and Victor Luke. 2008. Sierra Leone. In Andrew Simpson (ed.), *Language and national identity in Africa*. Oxford: Oxford University Press, 122–140.

    How well suited is Krio to being a national and official language in Sierra Leone, and what challenges might hinder its success in these roles?
4. Read more about the development of a pidgin and creole-like sign language in Nicaragua in Kegl (2002), and how this seems to be an occurrence of abrupt creolization:

    Kegl, Judy. 2002. Language emergence in a language-ready brain. Acquisition issues. In Gary Morgan and Bencie Woll (eds.), *Language acquisition in signed languages*. Cambridge: Cambridge University Press, 207–254.
5. Watch the first two segments of *The Empire Strikes Back*—part of the DVD series *The Story of English*, produced by Films for the Humanities and Sciences (www.films.com).

The first segment shows you how Tok Pisin is spoken in rural areas of Papua New Guinea, and follows a British animal doctor who uses Tok Pisin in his visits to the villages of different language groups. The second segment focuses on Sierra Leone and Krio. Both Tok Pisin and Krio were originally lexified with English words. How much of these creoles can you understand when you listen to speakers in the film?

6. Use the internet to find out about the new mixed language 'Tsotsitaal', spoken by young South Africans. What are the roots of Tsotsitaal, and how important are its connections to gangsterism? Compare Tsotsitaal in South Africa with the new mixed urban language 'Sheng' which has developed in Kenya. To what extent are these new languages similar or different?
7. What is Hip-Hop Creole and who creates this kind of music?
8. It has sometimes been suggested that English arose as a creole language in the Middle Ages. What can you find out about this idea?

6

The Globalization of English

Introduction

In chapter 2, we considered languages which have acquired large numbers of speakers as national and official languages and have been more successful in their expansion across populations than other local languages and varieties. In the current chapter, we are going to examine the phenomenal spread of knowledge of the English language around the world, resulting in English being called the world's first 'global language', understood and used by more speakers than any other language present or past. In addition to a large population of native speakers of English located in different countries in different continents, there is now an extremely large number of second-language speakers of English with a global distribution, growing daily at a very fast rate and in some places developing new forms of English—'new world Englishes'. The language is now used by German tourists visiting Japan, by politicians and businessmen from different linguistic backgrounds in meetings taking place in Europe, Asia, and Africa, and young people in schools all over the world are now regularly learning English from an early age. In this chapter we will examine a range of topics and questions relating to the global explosion which has occurred in the use and learning of English, among which are the following:

- How has English come to be so widespread in its use around the world?
- Are there any negative consequences resulting from the emergence of a global language?
- What can be predicted about the future of English as a global language? Is there any chance it might be overtaken in this role by some other language, or be replaced as a means of shared communication by new technology?
- If English continues to be globally dominant during the 21st century, how might the language change, and what will be the forces influencing and shaping English in the future?
- What attitudes do people who speak English as a second language have toward it, and how do such attitudes potentially affect the ways they speak 'global English'?

We will begin with some general facts and figures about who currently knows and uses English, and how three broadly different types of English-speaking groups can be identified.

What makes English a global language, and who speaks English?

English can be classified as a truly global language in virtue of four prominent properties, which are not combined together with any other language to the same striking degree:

- **Total numbers of speakers**. It is generally estimated that at least a quarter of the world's population is now able to speak English with some level of proficiency, ranging from a native speaker ability through very advanced second-language skills to more basic levels of competence.
- **Global distribution of speakers of English**. The 1.75 billion first- and second-language speakers of English are widely distributed across the continents of the world, throughout the Americas, Europe, Africa, Asia, and Australasia, resulting in English being understood and spoken in almost all regions of the planet.
- **Extensive recognition and use of English as an official language by states around the world**. English has now been recognized as an official or co-official language in 55 countries. It is used for all official language functions in a further four countries which have not actually declared it an official language (the USA, the UK, Australia, and New Zealand), and is made use of in typical co-official language functions in seven other states. Consequently, English effectively serves as an official or co-official language in over a third of the world's 195 countries.
- **Widespread learning of English in schools and other educational establishments**. English is being learned by more young people in more countries than any other language of wider communication. Governments all over the world are giving English a high priority in their educational systems, and English has become the most widely taught foreign language in both public and private schools. The huge increase in English-learning which has occurred in recent decades is creating new generations of proficient second-language speakers and a massive growth in the numbers of young people who are able to communicate by means of English.

The new recognition of English as the world's first ever global language is consequently a *combination effect* resulting from the preceding four properties being taken into account together, and no other language can compare with English when all four measurements of global development are considered. For example, Mandarin Chinese, the second most commonly known language in the world, is spoken by over a billion people, but almost all of this very large population is located in China, hence Mandarin is not 'globally' widespread in the same way that English is (and Mandarin is also not a commonly adopted official language, nor is it being learned as a foreign language anywhere nearly so extensively as English is at the moment).

The extensive spread of English around the world is often visually presented in terms of three circles representing the different ways that the language has been acquired and is currently used, following a model proposed by the linguist Braj Kachru (Kachru 1988, 1992). This distribution of English across three different kinds of population is schematized in Figure 6.1.

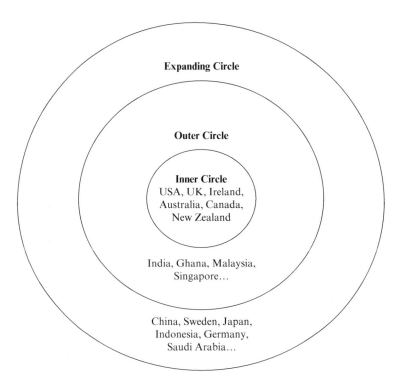

FIGURE 6.1. Kachru's Three Circles of English (as adapted from Kachru 1988, 1992 in Crystal 1997: 54).

A first, '**inner circle**' contains those countries where English is spoken as a *mother tongue* (first language/L1) by the majority of a country's population. These are the countries where English has been established as a language for a long time and continues to be heavily dominant in all domains of life: the UK, Ireland, the USA, Canada, New Zealand, and Australia. There are relatively few countries in the inner circle, but as almost all of their inhabitants are speakers of English (and most of these are native speakers), they represent a significant proportion of the world's English-speaking population.

A second '**outer circle**' includes countries where English is mostly known and used as a *second language* by speakers who have a different mother tongue, but where this 'L2' presence of English is nevertheless quite widespread and important in formal domains such as government administration, often being recognized as an *official* or *co-official language* of a country. Many of the states in the outer circle are territories that were originally colonized by Britain and that retained English in official roles following independence. These countries generally have an established tradition of English-learning and use, many very advanced second-language speakers, and in various instances have developed new, distinctive local forms of English. India, Malaysia, Nigeria, Ghana, and Singapore are all considered to be parts of the outer circle of English, along with many other ex-British colonies in Asia, the Caribbean, and Africa, making up a total of over fifty states.

The third component of Kachru's three circles of English is known as the '**expanding circle**'. This is made up of countries where English has now been established firmly in the education system, being taught as the primary foreign language, often from a quite early age, but English is not recognized as an official language and is generally not used in any (non-educational) formal domains of life, though it may sometimes occur in the media, pop culture, advertising, and some business interactions. English is typically *a new presence* in outer circle countries and it is learned and spoken as a second, foreign language. The expanding circle represents the most dynamic area of growth of the English language and is estimated to have as many speakers as the inner and outer circles combined. Countries in the expanding circle include China, Japan, Indonesia, the Netherlands, Sweden, Germany, and Saudi Arabia.

With this general background to the current state of English around the world, we will now examine *how* English has come to be so widespread, both geographically and in terms of its use in different domains—what has actually caused English to become a global language? Considering the dramatic expansion of English from an initially small and rather insignificant nation of speakers in western Europe to all corners of the globe and a quarter of the world's population, it will be useful to outline some of the history of English and see how it came to be spoken in such faraway places as the South Pacific, Africa, and the Indian subcontinent.

Principal causes of the development of English as a global language

The special growth of English as the most widely spoken language in the world today can be attributed to three very broad, historical causes and sets of forces, as well described in Crystal (1997) and Jenkins (2003):

1. The dominance of England as a maritime, trading, and (finally) industrial power, establishing colonies and settlements in the Americas, Africa, and Asia from the 17th century to the 19th century.
2. The growth of the USA as an economic power and force of cultural influence during the 20th century.
3. Rapid and varied advances in technology made during the second half of the 20th century, regularly linked with English in different ways.

We will first consider the historical spread of English around the world as a result of England's overseas colonial expansion, and then turn to developments in the 20th century, when English expanded further via other, non-militaristic routes.

Overseas settlement and the establishment of English-governed colonies

The English language originally came into existence as Anglo-Saxon when England was repeatedly invaded by Germanic tribes during the 5th and 6th centuries, the Angles, the Saxons, and the Jutes. This established the beginning of Old English, which was then further influenced by incursions from Vikings speaking Old Norse, and by Norman invaders who subjugated England in the 11th century and imposed French as the language of the ruling class for several hundred years. From all this mixture, Middle English emerged, and then developed into Early Modern English in the 16th century, the language found in Shakespeare's plays and poetry. It was this form of English which accompanied early explorers sailing from England to discover new lands and plunder the ships of other nations such as Spain and France, as five major maritime powers developed in Europe and regularly vied with each other for the control of trading routes and the establishment of new overseas settlements and territories: Portugal, Holland, France, Spain, and England.

From the 17th century onward, England became increasingly successful as a naval power, and ships setting sail from its ports took speakers of English to many uncharted lands far away from Europe. The transmission of English to the Americas, Africa, Asia, and the South Pacific is commonly described as having taken place in two rather different ways, referred to as the two 'dispersals' of English. The **first dispersal** of English involved large-scale settlement of English speakers in new territories claimed for England. Starting in the 17th century, and continuing through the 18th century, parts of **North America** were settled by immigrants from England seeking new opportunities and religious freedom away from the mother country, and this resulted in the thirteen original colonies which became the United States. As immigrants from other European countries were much fewer in number, English naturally became the dominant language in the thirteen colonies. Following the division of North America into the **USA** and **Canada**, and the movement of significant numbers of English-speaking 'loyalists' into the latter, English also spread further north into areas that had previously been solely under French control.

In a quite different part of the world, the territories of **Australia** and **New Zealand** were seized and settled by English-speakers. This occurred in Australia from the end of the 17th century onward, as large numbers of prisoners were transported to the new colony, served out a custodial sentence, and then generally stayed on to work as laborers, and in New Zealand principally during the 19th century as immigrants sought a better life away from the misery experienced in overcrowded industrial cities in England. Elsewhere in the southern hemisphere, South Africa also saw the arrival of settlers from England during the 19th century, building up a population of English-speakers alongside other immigrants from Europe who spoke Dutch.

The second dispersal of English was rather different in character from the first, and was characterized by the relocation of smaller numbers of English-speakers to territories in Africa and Asia, initially for the purposes of overseeing trade with England and establishing and then guarding trade monopolies. Over time, this typically led to the annexation of lands in Africa and Asia as colonies governed by the British with the help of local administrators trained in English. Those territories occupied by British forces and trading companies during the second dispersal mostly did not attract significant numbers of settlers from the British Isles, as Europeans often found it difficult to adapt to the different hot and humid climate in much of Asia and (equatorial) Africa, and the worrying presence of diseases they had little immunity to, unlike the much more familiar and welcoming conditions settlers found in destinations such as New Zealand and much of North America. English nevertheless gained an important status in countries of the second dispersal as the language of government and economic upward mobility, and though it was not spoken by very large local populations (in contrast to countries of the first dispersal which were actually re-populated by native speakers of English), the access which knowledge of English provided to better-paid employment and Western learning created a new tradition of learning English among the ambitious and more prosperous levels of local society.

In Africa, English became established as the language of British colonial administration in **Nigeria**, **Gold Coast** (Ghana), **Sierra Leone**, **Cameroon**, and **Gambia** in the west, in **Uganda**, **Kenya**, and **Tanzania** in the east, and in **Zimbabwe**, **Zambia**, **Botswana**, and **Malawi** in the south. In many instances, due to the extreme ethno-linguistic complexity of these territories, English was retained as an official language following independence, being viewed as an ethnically neutral (though foreign) language giving no special advantage to any language group (see chapter 2), and so has retained an important position and economic value in these 'Anglophone' countries through into the post-colonial, modern period.

South Asia served as a useful trading partner for Britain from the 17th century onward, and became part of the British Empire in the mid-19th century. During the time that the Indian subcontinent was governed by British forces, English came to have an increasing presence in official administration and commercial activities, and was the language stipulated for use by local government employees. English was also taught extensively in schools serving the indigenous elite and upper classes, who then frequently had some professional involvement with the British colonizers, either in business or as mid- and senior-level civil servants. When independence came to South Asia in the 20th century, and it ultimately split into the new states of India, Pakistan, Bangladesh, Nepal, and Sri Lanka, English continued to play a significant role in many areas of public life, and was heavily retained in government administration and the educational system. In the 1960s, there was much conflict between the supporters of Hindi as a national language for India, and speakers of other regional languages. In many states, this led to a strengthening of the official use of English as an alternative to Hindi, especially in the south of India, where there were considerably negative feelings toward Hindi. English now continues to be used in the domains of government, business, law, education, and commerce, and also has a major presence in the media. It is characterized as playing a useful ethnically neutral and unifying role in an area where there are many different regional languages, and is firmly embedded as the medium of international communication in South Asia, in interactions between representatives of India, Pakistan, Bangladesh, Nepal, and Sri Lanka. Due to the very large population in India (1.2 billion), and the historical embedding of English among those receiving education beyond the primary level, India is now estimated to have the second-largest number of speakers of English anywhere in the world—125 million—and a distinctive form of English has developed over time.

Further east in Asia, English has also taken root in the Southeast Asian states of Myanmar (Burma), Malaysia, Singapore, and the Philippines. The former three territories were established as British colonies during the 19th century, and English is still widely known, long after independence was achieved, particularly in Singapore, where it is an official language (see chapter 2), and somewhat less so in Malaysia, where it is used alongside Malay in parts of the educational system. In Myanmar, English has no official use and was discontinued as the language of higher education in 1964, but is nevertheless known by many people. Finally, the Philippines is home to a very large English-speaking population, largely due to the establishment of English in schools and government administration during the period of control of the Philippines by the USA, from 1898 to 1946. Owing to the unsuccessful promotion of Pilipino as a national language following independence, English continued to be used as a lingua franca between speakers of different Filipino languages and in many other domains, including higher education, business, and parts of national and local government.

Taken together, the first and second dispersals of English created a very wide foundation for the development of English as a global language, with English being transplanted to countries all over the world, and new populations of English-speakers coming into existence far away from the original homeland of the language in England. However, it should also be noted that English was actually not the only language to be spread away from Europe in a significant way between the 17th and 19th centuries. While Britain seized a large number of overseas territories as colonies and protectorates during this period, and introduced English in these areas, France was also highly active in spreading its influence and language to new colonies established in Africa, Asia, and the South Pacific, resulting in French being almost equally distributed relative to English in Africa and Southeast Asia. Thus while a global *distribution* had been established for English by the end of the 19th century, the *number of speakers* of English at this point was nowhere near as high as it now is, relative to the world's population. What caused this major rise in speaker numbers and caused English to accelerate past French and other competitor languages was the occurrence of further developments relating to English which took place in the 20th century.

Emergence of a new world superpower: the USA

The successful growth of English as a global language clearly has its roots in the expansion of British colonial power, which peaked toward the end of the 19th century. Throughout the 19th century, industrial innovation and the creation of new machinery and forms of transportation produced a massive increase in the output of goods made in Britain, and these needed new markets to be sold in. The empire of overseas colonies established in Asia and Africa provided the perfect trading partners for the sale of British goods and brought great wealth back into Britain for most of the 19th century. However, at the beginning of the 20th century, this international ascendancy enjoyed by Britain began to go into decline as the country became financially crippled by conflicts in which it became involved in different parts of the world. Yet just as Britain was experiencing a flagging of its strength on the international stage, a new force was emerging vigorously in the form of the United States, and this (predominantly) English-speaking nation began to exert an increasing economic, political, cultural, and also linguistic influence over the way that the 20th century would unfold. With regard to the effects on global language use that the rise of the USA would end up having, these have manifested themselves in a variety of ways, many of which are inter-related with developments in new technology. These will be discussed later. In addition to these communications and media-related domains which have fed off advances in the transmission of information, the arenas of commercial and official international relations have increasingly taken advantage of English as a potential lingua franca since new international organizations began to be formed in ever-greater numbers during the 20th century. The growth of the USA as a military, economic, and political power, combined with the remaining influence maintained by Britain, ensured that English would regularly be a language used in international meetings and by international organizations as these became more common in the 20th century. Every time branches of the United Nations, the World Bank, the International Atomic Agency, the World Health Organization, and other new international groupings met to discuss issues affecting multiple countries, English would inevitably be one of the set of languages sanctioned for use by participants, and English often came to be used by representatives at such meetings more frequently than any other officially approved language.

Technology and the spread of English in the modern world

David Crystal (1997: 61–62) makes the following important observation about the growth of English and raises an interesting question:

> ... what is impressive is not so much the grand total [of speakers], but the speed with which the expansion has taken place since the 1950s. In 1950 the case for English as a world language would have been no more than plausible. Fifty years on, and the case is unassailable. What happened in this fifty years—a mere eye-blink in the history of a language—to cause such a massive change of stature?

The answer, Crystal suggests, lies heavily in the ways that modern society has come to make use of English, in many instances utilizing new technology developed or significantly refined during the second half of the 20th century. Six important technology-related developments which dramatically increased the speed at which English has spread and acquired new speakers can be mentioned here, following discussion in Crystal (1997: 82–94).

As the result of improvements in motion picture technology, there was a huge growth in the **film industry** in the post-World War II decades of the 20th century and a rapid spread of movies made in English all over the world, with the dominance of Hollywood in film-making being largely responsible for the popularity of English-language films. Television shows produced in the USA have also been very popular globally in recent decades and have brought an increasing amount of English to audiences in other countries, as programs are subtitled rather than dubbed.

Advances in broadcasting and the transmission of radio signals have resulted in **short wave radio programs** being easily available in English throughout the world, for example the Voice of America, the British BBC World Service, and Radio Moscow (which significantly broadcasts in English in order to reach a larger audience than one which would understand Russian).

Technological developments have also helped the global spread of English in the **music industry**, with popular music from the USA and Britain being widely listened to in many countries, first via records and cassette tapes, later through the use of CDs, and more recently via digital recordings and the streaming of music and music videos. American and British pop, rock, soul, and hip-hop groups have been very successful in attracting fans—for example, the Beatles, Elvis Presley, the Rolling Stones, Madonna, Michael Jackson, Bob Dylan, and U2, to name just a few groups and individual artists. This dominance of English-sung popular music has created a fashion in which aspiring musicians from other countries and other language backgrounds often choose to sing in English, too, rather than their mother tongue, as a way to increase international sales.

The late 20th century has also seen a massive increase in **newspapers**, **magazines**, and **journals**, helped by improvements in printing methods, and in areas such as science and education, journals have increasingly come to be written and printed in English, with a majority of academics and scientists now believing that it is necessary to publish their research in English in order for this to be widely read and appreciated.

A major technological innovation in the late 20th century which has had a huge influence on the spread of English as a global language is the development of **computers** and **the Internet**. A very significant portion of information publicly made available on the worldwide web occurs in English. In addition to materials one might naturally expect to be in English, called up by search terms inputted in English, the use of search terms in other languages often results in entries being retrieved that are also written in English. For example, a search using German 'Frankfurt Hauptbahnhof' ('Frankfurt main train station') actually produces a majority of initial webpages written in English, and where pages occur in German, there is the option for these to be translated automatically into English. Additionally, while there is certainly much information available on the internet that is written in the major languages of the world, smaller languages are much less well represented, and speakers of these languages, who increasingly have access to the worldwide web, may now access the Internet frequently through English.

Finally, another area where scientific progress has indirectly resulted in the spread of English as a global lingua franca is the expansion of **international air travel**. As relatively low cost air travel is now widely available to all parts of the world, global tourism has increased at a very fast rate from the final decades of the 20th century into the 21st century. In order for communication to be possible between tourists and local people involved in the tourist industry, English has developed as a natural default lingua franca which can be used in a large number of overseas destinations.

All of the preceding developments have conspired to facilitate the spread of English very swiftly across a much larger population of speakers than in earlier times, stimulating new domains of use and creating ever-greater demands for English-learning, as discussed in the following.

'Nothing succeeds like success': how the growth of English also produces further growth

As English has become so widespread around the world, knowledge and use of English in many countries has become associated with being educated, successful, and well-connected with the modern world.[1] These positive associations have led to the increased use of English in marketing, as a way to enhance the appeal of products, and it is now quite common to see advertisements partially or sometimes even wholly in English in countries where most people speak other languages. In many cases, it is clear that using a local language to create advertisements in place of English would help communicate information about a product in a much more transparent and comprehensible way, but the eye-catching value of using English words is often felt to outweigh the desire to convey product details in a maximally intelligible way. A related phenomenon is the adding of often nonsense English phrases to personal accessories and items of clothing as a way to give them a cosmopolitan, international flavor. This is a regular occurrence with t-shirts, bags, and other personal items purchased and used by teenagers in many countries in Asia. Manufacturers feel that adding smatterings of English to products principally targeted at younger buyers will help increase their attractiveness, and the actual English words used do not really need to make sense (or, perhaps, only little attention is paid to ensuring that they make sense and are grammatical)—it is their presence and identifiability as English which will convey a young, trendy image upon the owner of such products—essentially English simply for the sake of English and its associations. The following samples of 'English' were all attested on t-shirts being sold in Japan and are very typical of the 'ornamentation' use of English in Japan.

Let's go where You've never been
Find your stay place.
You will find your possibility, if you try it what your new things
MUCH

TORTOISE CLUB
always and anyway
I want to be
quick response

WE RUN
A EIGHT SHIP HERE!

BASIC AND EXCITING
Refreshed and foppish sense and comfortable and flesh styles
will catch you who belong to city-groups

---

1. 'Nothing succeeds like success' is a saying from Alexandre Dumas, 1854, originally in French: 'Rien ne réussit comme le succès.'

> Standing to the ovation for myself.
> You are luck if you are luck
> thinking what you think
> we can see things that hate and heart
> if you change another one
> please not changed sold out man or woman
> they are bores............
>
> Amiably Regrettable
> Fall coming rain. He is trembling for a cold and loneliness,
> While grasping and closing a cold can coffee I defend a wet body.
> I wish a good luck and success of back all persons
> who take from my heart for this cross...

The growth of English produced by the range of factors described thus far has also given rise to the newer, more serious phenomenon of the heavily increased use of **English as a Lingua Franca (ELF)**, which has attracted a lot of interest from linguists studying the language's ongoing development. English has for a long time served as a lingua franca, but in the past this function as a common 'link language' was most typically made use of when speakers of one or more other languages communicated with a native speaker of English. Hence, for example, a business meeting in Hong Kong with invitees from Malaysia, Vietnam, Japan, and Thailand might have been held in English when chaired by a businessperson from Britain. Now, however, such meetings frequently take place in English in the complete absence of native speakers of English, and English is increasingly being used among L2 speakers of English when no L1 speakers are present. This growth in the use of English as a common language among L2 speakers is particularly noteworthy in the expanding circle of English, where no long tradition of speaking English has been established, but new speakers are becoming more and more confident in their abilities in English. In addition to the spontaneous use of English among individuals who are all second-language speakers in ad hoc meetings and informal encounters, English has also been formally recognized as the official common language of many international organizations and multinational companies which do not include representatives or workers from L1 English countries, for example the Association of South East Asian Nations (ASEAN), the Organization of Petroleum Exporting Countries (OPEC), Samsung, Nokia, Daimler-Chrysler, Lenovo, and Renault. English has been instituted worldwide as the official language of air traffic control, used everywhere between pilots and ground controllers who are L2 speakers of English, and English has come to be the default lingua franca used at sea, between ships of all international flags, very regularly when no L1 speakers are involved in acts of ship-to-ship communication. English is therefore coming to be used at a much higher rate than before in isolation from native speakers, a practice which may have effects on the global development of English, and may lead to distinctive forms of the language (to be discussed in the section on the future of English).

A further, interesting instance of English often being used just by L2 speakers is the utilization of English as a 'pivot language' in multilingual interpreting and translation in meetings of the European Union (Melchers and Shaw 2011: 192). Because there are now many more member states than in the past, it has been found that the most practical way to provide multilingual translation is to have an interpreter first translate words spoken in one language (for example, Polish) into English, and then have a second interpreter translate this English rendering into a further target language (for example, Romanian). Hence when an EU representative from Poland makes a speech in Polish, an L1 Polish speaker will quickly translate this into English, and a second L1 speaker of Romanian will then translate the English into Romanian.[2] In such a procedure, English is used as a means to convert one language into another without any L1 speaker of English being involved.

A final major domain which has seen tremendous growth in recent years as a direct result of the global expansion of English is the actual teaching of English as a subject and the use of English as a medium of instruction at different levels of education, from pre-school kindergartens to universities and graduate programs offered fully or partially in English. As an ability in English is increasingly felt to be important for personal advancement and professional success, the demand for opportunities to learn English has led to an explosion of English-language tuition in certain places parts of the world, especially in Asia, which now actually boasts the largest number of English speakers in the world (currently estimated to be over 800 million), and in continental Europe, where the role and value of English as a global lingua franca has come to be accepted and exploited much more than in earlier decades.

In South Korea, it is reported that 'English fever' is leading parents to spend almost $15 billion annually on supplementary language services aimed at improving their children's English skills, such as cramming schools, study abroad programs, and private English-language tuition. Kang (2012: 29) suggests that: 'English is perceived by Koreans as the single most important tool they need to have in order to get ahead at school and in society in general,' and such a prioritization on acquiring English leads parents to spend both large amounts of money and much time and effort helping their children become proficient in the language. Park (2009) describes the common new phenomenon of English-focused 'soccer moms' in Korea, who pay for their children to attend expensive English-language immersion schools and evening cramming classes from the age of 5 or 6, and then take them to live and study in an English-speaking country for a couple of years for further heavy exposure to English. Throughout South Korea itself, more and more educational establishments have introduced English-medium teaching, and local governments and private enterprises have set up over thirty 'English villages' partially populated by native speakers of English (the 'villagers'), where an English-language immersion experience can be enjoyed in residential study programs.

In China, too, there has been a massive increase in the learning of English, and young students now regularly begin learning the language as a compulsory subject in elementary schools, whereas previously it was only introduced during secondary education. Among the

---

2. Previously, a single interpreter would have converted words in one language into another without this passing through English. However, with the increase in numbers of languages being used in EU meetings, it became difficult to find interpreters who could switch between all these languages, and so the English-as-pivot system was adopted.

economically more prosperous sections of society in China, English has come to be viewed as the language of social and economic prestige, and a 'defining characteristic of educational progress' (Hu 2007: 120). It is seen as a passport which opens up many economic, social, educational, and professional opportunities, and promotions in various organizations now actually require employees to pass an English-language test. In addition to government-run schools which teach English as a subject, private educational institutions offering bilingual education programs have mushroomed all over the country, both in cities and in rural areas, and parents who have sufficient money often pay high tuition fees and do everything possible to have their children placed in these programs. Hu (2007) describes various instances of the growing craze for bilingual education in which kindergarten and primary schools have been able to boost flagging enrollments hugely through the introduction of bilingual education, and institutes of secondary and higher education have similarly taken to attracting students with the promise of courses taught in English. As the learning of English becomes more and more widespread in China, and speakers make use of their ability in the language in interactions with others, this may now already be creating a distinctive, new sub-variety of English ('China English', Melchers and Shaw 2011: 203). Hence English appears to be establishing itself robustly in China as a result of the rapid growth in opportunities to learn the language, just as it has done among other L2 populations in the past.

In continental Europe, the presence of English in education has also increased dramatically in recent years, in two particular ways. First, over 90% of secondary school students are now learning English as a subject/foreign language, and consequently a broad and effective foundation of English skills is being created among the young and rising generations all over Europe in a way that did not occur in previous times. Second, at the level of higher education, universities in many European countries are beginning to offer courses and programs taught using English as a medium of instruction (EMI). This development, which began in Sweden, Germany, and the Netherlands some years ago and is now spreading vigorously through France, Italy, and a number of other countries, is intended to serve two purposes. One important role for EMI courses is to help a country's own young students improve their abilities in English and increase their chances of competing well in an internationalizing economy where English is the accepted common language. With a high level of English, students have more opportunities to study abroad and also better future job prospects. Salamone (2015) notes that a study carried out by the European Commission in 2014 revealed that young people with international experience had an unemployment rate 23% lower five years after graduation than those who had not studied or trained in another country. Proficiency in English is stressed as often being critical for getting jobs and promotions, and is now viewed as a necessary basic skill that all individuals in the mid- to higher ranks of the workforce should have, whereas previously being able to speak English well would have marked a person out as special. A further study on correlations between English proficiency and professional advancement in Europe published in 2012 indicated that people who had strong English abilities generally earned 30–50% higher salaries.[3] Increasing domestic students'

---

3. This study was carried out by Education First, and is reported in Salamone (2015: 248).

strengths in English through immersion in EMI classes in universities is seen by European governments as a way to help give their young people better access to employment both at home and abroad, more job security when they do find employment, and potentially higher levels of pay.

The second role for EMI classes and programs in European universities is as an important generator of foreign revenue. With the global demand for high quality English-medium education increasing all around the world, countries in continental Europe are racing to attract foreign students through graduate programs in business studies, communications, international relations, and other fields, taught entirely in English. In the past, students in search of such study opportunities would typically travel to inner circle English-speaking countries such as the UK, the USA, Australia, and New Zealand and enroll in classes there. However, more recently, countries from the outer circle, such as India, Malaysia, and Singapore, have been considerably successful in promoting degree programs delivered in English for international students who are not native speakers of English, often at prices which undercut those in the traditional centers of English learning. Now it has come to be the turn of states from the expanding circle of English to try to secure some of the market for foreign students seeking EMI programs in universities, and in Europe there has been steady pressure from the European Commission on states in the EU to prioritize the internationalization of education and set up infrastructure that will attract students from Asia and other parts of the world. This has now been taking place at a very fast rate, and countries in Europe from Scandinavia to the Mediterranean have been establishing wide ranges of EMI programs for mobile international students. As universities everywhere are being required to generate more income from fee-paying students, curriculum expansion through EMI classes is providing significant financial help from foreign students and seems to be setting the tone for how higher education will develop in the future in many European countries.

Pros and cons of the growth of global English

It is clear that there are many advantages to be had from the development of a global lingua franca. With the growth of international travel, speakers of different languages are increasingly interacting with each other for reasons of business, trade, scientific research, and simple tourism, and the possibility that individuals can make use of a single language as a common means of communication almost anywhere they travel in the world facilitates such interactions in a hugely significant way. The establishment of a global language also helps the rapid worldwide dissemination of potentially valuable new research, and provides a way for large amounts of news and information to be accessed on the internet by anyone with a knowledge of English, no matter where they live. Given such obvious pluses, one might not question whether the creation of an internationally known common language is a positive development for the world in general. However, at times it has in fact been suggested that there may also be certain negative consequences arising from the growth of English as a global language, as discussed in the following sections.

Language endangerment

Critics of the growing expansion of English around the world have sometimes labeled English as a 'killer language', 'invading' the territory of smaller languages and causing 'linguicide' and the death of languages spoken by minority groups (Skutnabb-Kangas and Phillipson 2001). In chapter 3 we studied the growing occurrence of language endangerment and death and saw how it is a very worrying problem—for a range of reasons, speakers of smaller languages all over the world are abandoning their ancestral mother tongues and switching to other larger languages, resulting in the loss of many languages and the projection that possibly two-thirds of the world's languages may disappear during the course of the 21st century. English has certainly been involved in triggering language shift and loss in different parts of the world, with language death in North America and Australia being heavily related to the imposition of English on these areas and their indigenous populations. However, language endangerment is a phenomenon which goes much beyond English and its recent development as a global lingua franca, and is found to occur in the modern urbanizing world wherever there are regionally dominant, large languages and economic and social benefits to be had from knowing such languages. In the vast majority of cases, smaller languages are found to be dying out due to the growth in influence of other local languages, rather than increased global knowledge of English. For example, the future existence of Baale and Hozo in Ethiopia is challenged by the growth of Amharic as official language of the country, Nyahkur and Ugong in Thailand are endangered as a result of the expansion of standard Thai as a national language, and Yazva, Nenets, and Yug are dying out because of Russian, not switches to English as a global language. Consequently, most of the ongoing pressure on minority languages is *not* directly coming from the establishment of a worldwide lingua franca, and while English itself may continue to affect the stability and transmission of heritage languages in countries where it is the dominant local language (mostly in states in the inner circle), it is not the development of English as an international language that is causing other languages to go into disuse and die. Furthermore, it has been noted that even when English is in fact given a high status role in countries of the outer circle, typically as an official or co-official language, such an elevation does not necessarily cause other languages to go into decline and disappear, and many populations adopting English as an official language are composed of stable bilinguals/multilinguals who use English for its advantages but maintain their mother tongue/additional languages for other uses, for example India, Tanzania, the Philippines, and Fiji (see discussion in House 2003 and Seargeant and Swann 2012).[4]

---

4. Having noted that English as a global language would generally not seem to be the *direct* cause of language endangerment and loss around the world, it should be added that in some instances the learning of English may have an *indirect* influence on the maintenance of minority languages. In certain states, the introduction of English into education is causing a displacement of other languages that might have been learned, as students find it is difficult to learn multiple languages as subjects in an overcrowded curriculum. For example, the revitalization of endangered Austronesian languages in Taiwan was being aided by the teaching of these languages in schools prior to the introduction of English as a foreign language into secondary schools. Now many ethnically Austronesian students feel they need to make a choice between studying their heritage language or English, and it is common for English to be prioritized, resulting in reduced or minimal learning of the ancestral language (Simpson 2007d).

Language 'downgrading'

While the growth of English as a global language may not be causing other mother tongues to be discarded by their speakers, it has been suggested that increased prominence and focus on the use of English at the international level may nevertheless be having an effect on the continued development of other languages. De Swaan (2001) observes that the speakers of certain languages no longer consider them appropriate for use in domains such as scientific discussion, given the strong domination of English in this area, and therefore little effort is made to update terminology for science and technology, even in languages which previously had a long tradition of use in scientific scholarship, such as German. This is argued to result in a psychological downgrading of languages that once used to be considered prestigious and an unwelcome freezing of their vocabulary growth in various domains which would have naturally developed further had it not been for the global rise of English (Svartvik and Leech 2006; Salamone 2015).

Native speaker laziness in learning other languages

Crystal (1997: 15–16) suggests that people who speak English as their mother tongue may become less keen to learn other languages, as it becomes easier to rely on English as a common means of communication around the world. Crystal argues that on the level of individual, personal development, this may lead to more restricted cultural knowledge and less of an awareness of other ways of life. In business, being monolingual in just English may also have certain adverse effects, as the ability to speak a local language is still considerably helpful for doing business in certain regions of the world, such as East Asia and South America, where proficiency in English is less widespread than other areas (though starting to catch up quickly).

Graddol (2008) additionally notes that L1 speakers of English may soon lose their native-speaker advantage in the language, as people all around the world are now learning English from an early age. This evolving situation may lead to mother-tongue speakers of English actually being at a disadvantage in inter-group communication because they will soon be the only speakers who are monolingual and cannot communicate at all in other languages.

English as a growing marker of social discrimination, or a global equalizer?

Some observers of the growth of English as a global language have argued that knowledge of English is coming to be a new marker of distinctions in social class in countries of the outer

---

A surge toward learning English in the Ukraine and Switzerland is similarly causing a decrease in the learning of Russian and German/French/Italian as second languages in these countries as students feel unable to study more than one additional language in school (Weber and Horner 2012). In Switzerland, English is therefore coming to be the local lingua franca used between L1 speakers of German, French, and Italian, who are no longer learning the languages of the other groups in the country. While Russian, German, French, and Italian are certainly not endangered languages, it is relevant to note that the incorporation of English into school's curricula is causing an 'over-crowding effect' in various places, and languages that used to be almost automatically learned as second languages are now being displaced by English classes.

and expanding circles, where privileged elite classes use English to hold on to positions of power and better employment, while lower classes without skills in English are forced to accept inferior jobs and socially are viewed as being less well-educated if they can only communicate in local languages. Hu (2007: 120) offers the criticism that Chinese-English bilingual education in China 'not only perpetuates the existing unequal and hierarchical distribution of power and access to cultural and symbolic capital, but is creating new forms of inequality and further differentiating Chinese society vertically as well', and Park (2009) has suggested that proficiency in English has now become a class-marker in Korea, too. Quite generally, Phillipson (2009) talks of English 'linguistic imperialism' as the post-colonial promotion of English in former British colonies by English-speaking elites who hope to maintain economic and political power through their mastery and control of the language. The growth of English worldwide is thus perceived by some to result in social discrimination and to be a commodity which distinguishes the rich and educated from the poor and underprivileged.

However, such a negative view is by no means the most prevalent assessment of the effects of global English. Crystal (1997) suggests that the spread of English around the world actually empowers the 'subjugated and marginalized, eroding the division between the "haves" and the "have-nots"', and Coleman (2006)[5] emphasizes that English increases the opportunities open to academics in poorer countries, improving their job prospects and potential mobility, and the chances they have to make their research known to people in other countries.

The crux of the dispute here is really one of *access to English learning*. If people from all socio-economic classes in a country have equal access to English-language instruction, this can result very positively in English becoming an equalizing force, privileging all sections of society in a parallel way, and allowing those from poorer backgrounds to compete for jobs requiring English in ways that might not have been possible in earlier times, when English was not so widely spread in mass education. Teaching English to younger generations in developing countries also raises the potential for increased participation in international commerce and trade, and provides a means to enter the global economy in more effective ways than in the past—and so compete in new areas previously dominated by the more prosperous English-speaking countries of the inner circle.[6] However, if access to English learning is uneven across a society and is restricted to the wealthy classes, this will naturally serve to strengthen class divisions in a discriminatory way. Governments therefore need to help maximize the availability of quality English-language tuition in public school systems as a way to ensure that all segments of society have good chances to learn English and benefit from the advantages that English as a global language potentially can offer.[7]

---

5. Referenced in Salamone (2015: 252).

6. A good example of this is Singapore, which developed very successfully as an international center for banking and commerce in large part due to the English-language skills that its population developed and were able to apply effectively in the workplace, interfacing with trading companies and financial institutions from all over the world.

7. The issue of providing access to good quality English classes discussed here is not different from access to other important subjects such as mathematics. In South Korea, many parents pay for their children to attend evening cram schools to improve their maths skills as well as English, and it might be objected that this provides

Challenges with the development of 'corporate English'

As noted earlier, more and more multinational companies are now adopting English as their official language of internal and external communication and are requiring employees to learn and make daily use of English in interactions with clients and other co-workers, no matter where in the world the offices of such companies are located (as, for example, with the German airline Lufthansa, which made English its official 'world' language in 2011). Companies are developing the use of 'corporate English' because it facilitates communication with a wide range of customers and business partners around the world and enables connections to be made with new areas of the growing global market. It also enables companies to recruit talented new professionals from diverse language backgrounds and allow them to work with other employees using English, rather than having to learn other languages such as Japanese, German, or Norwegian. Additionally, where companies have established branches across many different countries, the common use of English in offices around the world permits effective coordination to occur between teams of workers in geographically distant locations.

While multinational companies may feel that they need to adopt English-only policies, or lose business opportunities and put themselves at a disadvantage to their competitors (who are using English extensively), a variety of negative effects have been observed to occur as consequences of corporate English mandates. Neeley (2012) identifies the following issues as common problems of the institution of 'global business English' within companies. First, employees often worry that promotions will be awarded to those who can demonstrate the best skills in English rather than business expertise, and that job security is weak when an individual's proficiency in English is lower than that of other co-workers. Second, because of worries about job security, employees who feel they have poor language skills often simply stop making contributions in meetings, in order not to stand out as being poorer-than-average speakers of English. This can lead to a decline in performance, as individuals who might have offered useful new ideas or reported errors stop participating in group discussions held in English. Third, it is not uncommon for employees to resist English-only rules and use their own languages because this seems to be a faster and easier way to communicate with other speakers. However, switching into Korean, Danish, or Polish often results in the exclusion of other English-speaking colleagues who may not understand these languages, again affecting work performance. Neeley suggests that there are, in fact, viable solutions to all these potential problems, and that companies can develop and maintain useful English-language practices if they carefully follow the set of steps that she describes in her article, but otherwise the adoption of corporate English has the potential to

---

these children with greater educational advantages than children from poorer families who do not have the financial means to send their children to supplementary cram classes. However, it has not been suggested that a better knowledge of mathematics is a marker of social discrimination and that mathematics consequently might be undesirable for society, as certain critics such as Phillipson have suggested is the case with English. Knowledge of English should therefore not be singled out as a special case having the potential to cause social discrimination— *all* forms of knowledge which may advantage an individual have this potential, and it is critical that fair and equal opportunities be provided to all members of a population to acquire useful tools such as mathematics and foreign-language skills.

be damaging, divisive, and demoralizing in ways that members of senior management may not be aware of.

The preceding range of issues relating to the growth of global English are all areas of concern and are certainly in need of attention. As English develops into the world's first ever global language, there are bound to be consequences for other modes of language use, but are these unsurpassable negative complications which outweigh the obvious benefits of having a worldwide lingua franca? Each person will doubtless have their own view on this, perhaps shaped by personal experience. For those who are supportive of the continued development of a global language, what is necessary is attention to the side-effects of such a novel process and an effort to identify solutions to problems caused by changing patterns of language use, whenever these may arise. As we anticipate that English will continue to spread further around the world in the years to come, an important question is whether this growth will in fact necessarily occur, and, if so, how will it take place? What can be guessed about the future of English as a global language?

Looking to the future

Thinking about the future of global English, we will focus on two major questions:

- Will English actually maintain its dominant position as the lingua franca of the world and develop further in this role?
- If English continues to function as a global language, how might it develop linguistically in future decades? Should we expect that the form of English used internationally around the world will change as a result of the increased growth and influence of non-native speakers in the outer and expanding circles?

Once a global language, always a global language?

English has now spread as a worldwide lingua franca in a way that has never happened with any other language in the past, to the same degree. Is it the case that this special global language status is guaranteed for English in the future, or can any plausible scenarios be imagined in which English ceases to be so dominant as a common means of communication? Here we will consider three possibilities which might result in an upset of the current leading role played by English around the world.

Scenario 1. English is rejected for socio-political reasons.

A clear portion of the global success of English can be attributed to its positive association with popular forms of culture (movies, music, television, fiction-writing), and with general feelings of progress, power, and modernity, linked to the growth of the USA in the 20th century and its frequent leadership in the fields of science and technology. What might happen, however, if the positive associations of English with the modern world somehow turned negative in a serious way, perhaps as a result of global political discord involving the English-speaking countries of the inner circle, and in particular the USA? Might this trigger a widespread rejection of English and a return to the use of other, more local lingua francas?

While it is difficult to gauge the power of socio-political associations in the continued success of English, and whether these are critical for its future buoyancy, a brief reflection on attitudes held toward English in the modern state of Singapore is instructive as it offers some insight into how conflicts between positive and negative feelings toward English may potentially be resolved. An overview of the development of English in Singapore was presented in chapter 2. There it was noted that English has in many ways been very successful for this relatively new state in Asia, helping it thrive economically as well as building cohesion among its multiracial population as a common link language. What was not mentioned in chapter 2 is that the government of Singapore has regularly had ambiguous feelings toward the heavy presence of English in the country. On the one hand, it sees English as necessary for the technological and economic development of Singapore, whose economy relies on its international connections. On the other hand, the government worries that knowledge of English increases the population's exposure to liberal Western ideas, and this may bring unwelcome western values and attitudes into Singapore, leading to a growth in individualism and unwillingness to make personal sacrifice for the good of the community, as well as social decadence. Faced with this conflict between the pragmatic, utilitarian value of English and the negative properties and associations it is perceived to have (from a strongly conservative perspective), what has happened? Significantly, for the purposes of the issue currently under discussion, there has not been any serious consideration of jettisoning English because of its undesired social associations, and the instrumental value and usefulness of English is felt to be so important for Singapore that the government has set out to contain the 'threat' to society posed by English through a range of initiatives designed to strengthen traditional Asian values and culture, among which is the commitment to support the three official Asian languages of the state, alongside English (Simpson 2007b). If the example of Singapore is anything to go by, one might expect that negative attitudes toward English would have to be very extreme in order to cause a widespread rejection of English, and it appears that the utilitarian value of a global lingua franca and the access it provides to knowledge, learning, and international trade and markets is so great that people around the world may be unlikely to stop making use of English, even if it does become entangled with socio-political associations that are sometimes negative.

Scenario 2. Could English be eclipsed by the global growth of some other language?

While English is now very strongly ascendant, for the range of reasons already discussed, is there any possibility that some other language might accelerate past English and become more widely spoken all over the world, displacing English as global language? The two languages which one might consider as potential rivals to English in its role as global lingua franca are Spanish and Chinese, both of which have very large populations of speakers. It is estimated that Spanish is spoken by approximately 500 million people around the world (adding first- and second-language speakers together), and Mandarin Chinese has over one billion L1 and L2 speakers, making these the two most widely spoken languages after English (when both first- and second-language speakers are added together). Could either of these two languages become more dominant than English and take over English's position as the most commonly used language of the world?

Considering Spanish first, this is recognized as an official language in over 20 countries; hence it has a clear formal prominence in many countries, in addition to being widely spoken. However, the geographical distribution of Spanish is largely restricted to the Americas, and western Europe, and it is not spread in any significant way in Asia, Africa, or the Pacific. In order for Spanish to become a truly global language, it would need to be taken up by speakers in many more parts of the world than it is currently used in. Such growth would require a massive increase in economic power and cultural influence from the current set of Spanish-speaking countries (as military conquest colonizing new territories in other continents is no longer an option in the modern, post-colonial world), but presently the economies of Spain and Latin America are not growing at the rate that might be necessary for Spanish to somehow power its way past English. As things stand at the moment, Spanish will remain an extremely important language in the areas where it is currently spoken, but it may not expand significantly beyond these areas, and it is difficult to envision it eclipsing English as the world's most commonly used language.

What, then, about Mandarin Chinese? It has often been found that there is a close link between language use and power, and the success of an international language is tightly connected with the military and economic success of the nation it is associated with. In the 17th–19th centuries, the growth of English was a direct result of Britain's overseas colonial power, and during the 20th century it was the dominance of the USA in the world economy which helped English become a global language. A number of predictions now suggest that the economy of China may eventually surpass that of the USA in the latter part of the 21st century, so one might wonder whether this would help Mandarin Chinese take over the role of global language later in the current century.

Using the information available to us at present to attempt to predict the future, the best guess that can be made about Mandarin Chinese, in the author's view, and that of other observers such as Lu (2008), is that it may actually *not* be very likely for Mandarin to replace English as the world's lingua franca, even if China does out-perform the USA in its economic growth as presently anticipated. The reasons for believing this are of two types: demographic and linguistic. First, although Mandarin Chinese has an extremely large number of speakers already, and this number is set to grow further at a high rate, the geographical location of these speakers is largely restricted to East Asia (specifically, China), and there are no signs of major growth in the learning and use of Chinese in Africa, South Asia, Latin America, the South Pacific, the Middle East, and Europe. In order for Chinese to displace English as the world's most widely used lingua franca, it would need to be adopted as a common means of communication broadly around the globe, and this currently is not occurring.

To some extent, this may be due to the second major reason why Mandarin Chinese is not an obviously natural candidate for global language—the very considerable linguistic difficulties involved in trying to learn Chinese. First of all, Chinese is a *tone language*, meaning that every word has to be pronounced in a special way, with a certain melody or pitch contour, to maintain its meaning. If a slightly different intonation pattern is applied to words in Chinese, the meaning can be radically altered. This makes Mandarin (and all other forms of) Chinese a very challenging language to learn, and an enormous amount of practice with continual correction and coaching from native speakers in one-on-one interactions is required for speakers to communicate successfully. Such an inherent difficulty affecting the acquisition of Chinese could prove to be too great for the large-scale spread of Chinese around the world. Mandarin is not a language that can be picked up easily, and without great effort, and is commonly ranked one of the hardest languages of all to master (see, for example, the ranking of languages by learning difficulty listed by the Foreign Service Institute of the US State Department[8]). A second property of Chinese which makes it one of the world's most time-consuming languages to learn well is its *writing system*. The characters which are used to write Chinese are very many in number—in order to read newspapers and basic literature, it is estimated that a knowledge of over 3,000 different characters is needed. Memorizing and practicing such a large number of different symbols is a process which requires a vast amount of time (normally several years of dedicated study), and the ability to read and write Chinese cannot be acquired in the same rapid way as learning to read and write languages which make use of a smaller alphabet or syllabary, such as English, French, Russian, Korean, or Hindi. Learners of Chinese regularly report that they also forget how to read and write Chinese characters unless these are constantly practiced; hence there is a large 'upkeep cost' to maintaining proficiency in Chinese. It is quite possible that this particular property of Chinese, combined with its use of tones to distinguish words, will make it very difficult for the language to rise to the status of global language, even if China's economic power becomes greater than that of other countries in the world.

Scenario 3. New machines make the need for a global language redundant

A third possibility to consider is whether major advances in technology might result in translation devices that could be used in place of English, as a way for people from different language backgrounds to communicate with each other. There has been considerable progress in the last two decades in the development of software programs that computers can use to automatically translate from one language into another—for example *Babylon, Promt, Linguatec, LEC Power Translator, Word Magic, Google Translate,* and others. If such progress continues to be made in the future, might it then be possible for people of different mother tongues to communicate directly with each other via translation-machines, making the need to learn a global language unnecessary? The short, up-front answer is that it is actually still going to be a long time before any new technology is able to recognize, translate, and reproduce natural human speech from one language to another in a way that is both accurate and swift, and reliable enough to replace the use of a common spoken language. An enormous amount of effort is being devoted to the development of **machine translation**, now a fast-growing lucrative industry, but the difficulties in designing machines which will effectively understand and produce language are also huge, and consequently rapid substantial progress is hard to make for large numbers of languages. Let's briefly describe where the problematic issues lie.

---

8. Reported at: www.atlasandboots.com/hardest-languages-to-learn/ and www.atlasandboots.com/foreign-service-institute-language-difficulty/

All instances of machine translation take input of one form and provide an output of a different type. We are currently using programs that work with either oral input, or written input. The major machine translation programs presently available typically require written input of sentences in one language, and then provide a written translation in another language. We now also increasingly make use of devices that accept oral input and decode this into a written form of the *same* language, which is applied in various ways—we talk to automated machines (including our cell phones), asking for or giving information of different types, and this allows us to carry out a range of useful day-to-day transactions. However, the successful management of oral and written input given to machines is regularly hampered by different challenges which often result in outputs being unsatisfactory.

With oral input, the principal difficulty is accurate *recognition* of speech—machines need to be able to identify the words that are being spoken in order to make use of this data, and the problem is that speech recognition still tends to be accurate to a high degree only when a person speaks relatively slowly, with clear diction, and in the majority dialect of a language (e.g., standard American English). When people produce speech at a normal conversational speed, or use anything but standard language (including accent), the accuracy of speech recognition devices decreases in a significant way. We observe this sometimes when we dictate text messages into our cell phones and see that it is produced incorrectly in written form on the screens of our phones. We also feel the effects of this when other machines that we talk to respond with inappropriate information—they have misunderstood our speech. More work on mechanical speech recognition has been carried out for English than any other language, and yet we are nowhere close to creating devices that will handle anything other than standard forms of English. Yet, in order for machines to be able to act as substitutes for the use of a lingua franca between speakers of different languages of the world, all these languages and their dialects will need a greater amount of work than that already given to English for speech recognition to be carried out accurately and reliably. Such achievements seem very far away at the moment.

Using written input, we can now get machines to translate between a growing number of languages (just over one hundred with *Google Translate* in 2018). The challenge for translation programs is not one of recognition—the words produced in (typed) written input are easy for machines to identify, no matter what script is used—the problem is one of understanding. In order for machines to accurately 'parse' or understand sentences inputted from any language, before rendering them into a second language, extremely complex programs have to be created that will analyze sentences grammatically and also lexically (that is, determine the meanings of words being used—sometimes words are ambiguous and can have different meanings). This is a very difficult task, requiring detailed analyses of all aspects of a language's grammar and vocabulary, and the creation of programs that will be able to make use of and apply this knowledge. Presently, if we test out publicly available free translation software such as *Google Translate*, we find it is possible to get reasonable translations of written input between major European languages such as English, German, Spanish, and French, though when more complicated sentences are used as input, the reliability of the translation regularly falls off. When the language being translated from is not grammatically similar to the language being translated into, there is again a drop-off in performance, and errors and unnaturalness regularly appear in the translations created.[9]

In order for translation machines to replace English as an orally used (i.e., spoken) lingua franca, such machines will have to successfully handle both oral and written inputs in a sequence of operations for each sentence that is spoken. For example, if a person tries to speak Arabic with a speaker of Chinese using a translation device, the device will first need to recognize and decode what Arabic words the person has produced, rendering this into a written form of Arabic. The written form of Arabic will then be used as input for translation between (written) Arabic and (written) Chinese. Finally, the Chinese written output will need to be converted into spoken Chinese. At each point in the Arabic to Chinese translation, there is much potential for errors to be produced, causing mistranslations and misunderstandings to occur.

In addition to the serious problem of mistakes potentially being made by translation machines during the complex process of translating words spoken in one language into an equivalent spoken form in another language, there is a fundamental *time lag* issue that will always affect machine translation in a negative way, no matter how accurate such processes might eventually become. Basically, in order for a translation device to convert speech from one language into another, the machine needs to wait until a speaker has fully completed a sentence before this can be converted into speech in a different language. Let's illustrate this with a simple scenario involving a person speaking Japanese with a speaker of Welsh. Japanese is a language in which the verb occurs at the very end of a sentence (it is an 'SOV' language), whereas in Welsh, the verb is very often the first word in the sentence (it is a 'VSO' language). In order for a machine to produce a sentence in Welsh from a sentence in Japanese, the machine will need to wait until the end of the Japanese sentence, where the verb occurs, in order for it to be able to start the Welsh sentence with a translation of this verb. Similar delays will be caused by many other aspects of the grammar of different languages, and machines will only be able to create maximally reliable translation outputs after a person has finished producing a full sentence. This is very different from the ways that communication occurs when a single language is used, and no translation is involved. As soon as a speaker begins producing a sentence, hearers start to try to understand it and form ideas about how they might wish to respond to its content. This understanding may be adjusted as speakers complete their sentences, but hearers will start on this process as soon as they hear the first words of another speaker, resulting in a rapid rate of communication between speakers. A hearer's understanding of the content of another speaker's sentence will be largely formed before the speaker has finished speaking, and the hearer may have processed this information and be ready to respond as soon as the first speaker

---

9. The more languages that are translated through, the greater the number of errors that occur. This is well-illustrated in a YouTube posting by a group called Collective Cadenza, who translated the lyrics of the song 'Fresh Prince of Bel Air' sequentially through the sixty-four languages that were available in *Google Translate* in 2013, and then translated the final result back into English. What is ultimately produced in English is almost unrecognizable when compared with the original English lyrics, and seems to make no sense, as multiple occurrences of translation have produced so many changes to the meaning of the words. The very entertaining video 'Fresh Prince: Google Translated' can be viewed at: https://www.youtube.com/watch?v=LMkJuDVJdTw.

finishes his utterance. We are all used to this fast rate of communication and exchange of information, and machine translation devices will unfortunately never be able to match this speed and instead will seem laborious, slow, and frustrating when compared with the use of a single common language. In order to appreciate just how different the rate of communication is when full sentences have to be completed before *any* attempt at understanding can begin, imagine communicating with a friend by means of *written* sentences—write out what you mean to say in a sentence on a piece of paper and then hand this to your friend. In order to respond, having read and understood your sentence, your friend should write out a sentence on a piece of paper and then hand this back to you for you to read, and so on. Most people are likely to find that such a slow-down in the process of understanding and communicating is very undesirable, but it is doomed to occur with devices used to translate orally from one language to another.[10]

In sum, it seems improbable that machine translation devices will be widely adopted as replacements for the use of English as a global lingua franca, at least in the immediately foreseeable future. There is still a vast amount of work that needs to be carried out before translation software will be able to provide a reliable and accurate interface between the hundreds (or even thousands) of languages (and their dialects) whose speakers now use English as an international language, and if this can eventually be done, the nature of machine-mediated communication may strike many people as much less satisfactory than use of a lingua franca, due to the necessary time delays and slower speed of communication of the former.

TRANSLATION BLOOPERS

When translation software is applied without supplementary monitoring of the output by anyone with knowledge of the language being translated into, odd and sometimes embarrassing results can occur. The following Chinese-English pairings were seen posted as public signs in China at the time of the Beijing Olympics in 2008, when there was pressure to post a large range of information in English for foreign visitors, and

---

10. Software programs such as *Google Translate* operate somewhat differently when only dealing with purely written input, and attempt to provide more simultaneous translation, offering translational equivalents to written input before sentences are completed. This can be tested out by starting to type a sentence into the input box and specifying which language the input is to be translated into. As you type words in the input language, you will notice that the translation device fairly soon starts to output words in the second language, before full sentences have been finished. You will also notice that the translational output is regularly modified and changed, as more words from the input language are typed and the translation software adjusts its understanding of the input sentence being produced. Try this out with typing an example sentence in English such as 'I think that you will need to carefully reflect on this issue', with the target language being set for German or Japanese, and observe how the German/Japanese words that Google Translate initially produces get changed as the sentence is completed. It would not be possible for this kind of simultaneous translation to occur with an oral output, as once words have been translated and pronounced, they cannot be modified, withdrawn, or substituted for with other words. Hence oral machine translation is bound to involve delays in translation and to deliver communication from one language to another in a way that is slower than communication using a single language.

translation programs were used without careful double-checking of the English being produced.[11]

严禁用自带食物喂鱼
Please do not feed the fishes with your private.

民族园
Racist Park

险区观景，注意安全
Beware of missing foot

衛生紙及雜物，請投入垃圾筒
Please throw anything and
toilet paper into the toilet bowel.

试戴请让营业员协助
Please don't touch yourself,
Let us help you to try out. Thanks!

残疾人专用
Special for deformed.

請勿交談，以防飛沫
Please no conversation, no saliva.

当心落水
Take care to fall into water.

小心碰头
Caution, butt head against the wall.

一旦失窃要报警，切莫姑息又养奸
If you are stolen, call the police at once.

English around the world now and in the future: variation, intelligibility, and change

All languages undergo change over time, and English is bound to undergo further changes during the course of the 21st century, developing new words, new forms of pronunciation (intonation and accenting), and most probably even new grammatical constructions. If English continues to be made use of as a global language, we might wonder whether the

---

11. A further, striking mistake which has regularly been produced by machines translating Chinese into English in recent years is the curious mistranslation of the Chinese word for 'dry' (pronounced 'gan') as the English f-word. This has resulted in eye-catching store signs and listings in restaurant menus such as '干菜类 F*** Vegetables' (indicating the aisle in a store where dry vegetables were displayed), and '干爆鸭子 F*** the duck until exploded' (a dish on a menu which is better translated as 'dry pan-fried duck').

evolving shape of international English will exclusively be determined by native speakers of English in the inner circle, or will be increasingly influenced by the localized forms of English which are emerging and stabilizing among second-language speakers of the outer and expanding circles. Here we will consider some of the variation which is already present in English spoken around the world, and ask how the existence of such variation potentially impacts the maintenance of a mutually intelligible common means of communication and the unity of English as a single broad language.

English in the inner circle: multiple standards

English is a *pluricentric language,* meaning that there are different geographical centers of the language and multiple standard forms. The historical home of English in the British Isles developed the first internationally dominant form of the language, which, in its current standardized form, is now referred to as standard British (or UK) English. Standard American English arose from the interaction of different English dialects in North America and the early standardization efforts of the dictionary maker Noah Webster (1758–1843) and others, who helped craft a distinctive form of English as an intended new national language for the USA. Elsewhere in inner circle countries, alternative standard forms of English were recognized in both Australia and New Zealand toward the end of the 20th century. These different, standardized forms of English exert their influence in different parts of the world and are regularly adopted as models for the teaching of English in outer and expanding circle countries. British English continues to be the primary model for English learning in continental Europe, Africa, and South Asia, while standard American English is the most popular form of English taught in Latin America and East Asia. The major ways that inner circle 'Englishes' vary from each other are mostly: (a) differences in vocabulary, and (b) differences in pronunciation—general accent, stress placement on words, and variation in the way that certain sounds are pronounced.[12] For example, in American English, it is common for the main stress of a word to be placed earlier in the word than in British English in various instances:

US English	British English
I was really FRUstrated when ...	I was really fruSTRATed when ...
Here is my ADdress.	Here is my adDRESS.
Would you like a CIGarette?	Would you like a cigarETTE?
That is really FORmidable.	That is really forMIDable.
His main ADversary is now deceased.	His main adVERsary is now deceased.

Two common instances where there is a systematic difference in the pronunciation of a particular sound in American/British English words are:

(i) the 't' sound between vowels. This is pronounced like a 'd' in US English, but as a 't' in British English in words like: *bottle, butter, daughter*

---

12. There is also some variation in the use of morphology—for example, different past tense forms in US and British English: *He dove* vs. *He dived*—but these are not very many in number.

(ii) the 'u' vowel in words such as *tune, due, enthusiastic,* and *new,* which are all pronounced like the vowel sound in 'do' in many varieties of US English, but like the vowel sound in *few* in most varieties of British English (so *due* and *new* rhyme with *few* in British English).

Some well-known examples of vocabulary differences between British and American English are the following pairs of words which are used to refer to the same object or action in the two varieties of English.

US English	*British English*
sidewalk	pavement
faucet	tap
line	queue
cookie	biscuit
(French) fries	chips
truck	lorry
freeway	motorway
thumb tack	drawing pin
parking lot	car park

Multiple standard forms of English have thus arisen in the inner circle countries populated by native speakers of English, but by and large these are mutually intelligible, as the differences in vocabulary usage are often familiar to speakers of other varieties, owing to the presence of these forms of English in internationally distributed cinema and television.[13]

The outer circle and new World Englishes

In countries of the outer circle, where English is generally used as a second language by native speakers of other languages, differences in the way English is spoken have also come into existence. In many areas, such as South Asia, and former British colonies of West Africa, East Africa, the Caribbean, and parts of Southeast Asia, the consistent use of distinctive, innovative forms of English has led to the stabilization of new varieties of the language which are now referred to as new 'World Englishes'.[14] Two of the most informative introductions to such recently emerged varieties are Jenkins (2003) and Mesthrie and Bhatt (2008), both of which provide many examples and much description of the differences in accent

---

13. In addition to national standard forms of English, there are also many dialectal varieties of English which can at times be quite different from each other, especially in certain regions of the UK. These are often not so easily understandable to outsiders, due to the use of specialized dialect words and different regional accents.

14. These new varieties of English are largely restricted to outer circle countries where English has been spoken for some time by sizable populations, and there is little description of stabilized new varieties having emerged in expanding circle countries, where English has a much more recent presence (though Melchers and Shaw 2011: 203 do mention that there are signs of a new China English coming into existence).

and pronunciation, vocabulary, and grammatical conventions which occur in new World Englishes.[15] Some illustrations of **vocabulary differences** are provided here, with examples taken from both of these works. In these localized expressions, speakers have used words which occur in English in novel combinations to create new ways of referring to a particular object, action, quality, or concept. In other cases, speakers may translate words or expressions which exist in a local language directly into English:

'dry coffee' = 'coffee without milk and sugar' [East African English]
'high hat' = 'a snobbish person' [Philippine English]
'wheatish' = 'light brown color' – a desirable skin tone in India [Indian English]
'next tomorrow' = 'the day after tomorrow' [Nigerian English]
'to by-heart something' = 'to learn something by heart' [South African English]
'to back-answer someone' = 'to answer someone back' [Indian South African English]
'to shake one's legs' = 'to be idle' [Malaysian English]
'to be on the tarmac' = 'to be in the process of seeking a new job' [East African English]
'to be in hot soup' = a mixing of 'to be in the soup' + 'to be in hot water', both of
 which mean 'to be in trouble'; the combination also means
 'to be in trouble' [Singaporean English]
'to add sugar to the tea' = 'to bribe someone' [Nigerian English]

A selection of some of the interesting ways in which new World Englishes may differ in their **grammatical constructions** from inner circle standard forms of English is given in the following examples, all taken from Mesthrie and Bhatt (2008).

'They only shout and stay.' = 'They're always shouting.' [Indian South African English]
'She filled the bottle and left it.' = 'She filled the bottle completely.' [Indian South African
 English]
'You eat finish, go out and play.' = 'When you've finished eating, go out and play.'[16]
 [Singapore English]
'You said you'll do the job, isn't it?' = 'You said you'll do the job, didn't you?'
 [Indian English]
'Who-who came?' = 'Which people came?' [Indian South African English]
Q: 'Didn't you see anyone at the compound?'
A: 'Yes. I didn't see anyone at the compound.' [East African English][17]

A: 'I hope you won't have any difficulty with your fees next term.'
B: 'I hope so.' (= 'I hope what you have said will indeed be true') [East African English][18]

---

15. See also Fillpula et al. (2017).
16. Originally from Platt et al (1983).
17. Originally from Bokamba (1992).
18. Originally from Bokamba (1992).

'Which one I put in the jar, that one is good.' = 'The ones I put in the jar are the good ones.' [Indian South African English]

'Do you know when's the plane going to land?' = 'Do you know when the plane is going to land?' [Indian South African English]

With regard to **pronunciation,** many World Englishes may simplify some of the sounds found in standard inner circle forms of English—for example, reducing the range of vowels used in words, and converting sounds such as 'th' into 't' and 'd' sounds. World Englishes in the outer circle may also be spoken with a different rhythm, intonation, and melody than inner circle English. These differences are well described in Jenkins (2003), Mesthrie and Bhatt (2008), Melchers and Shaw (2011), and Gussenhoven (2017).

Occasionally a new World English may develop so many forms that are different from standard inner circle English that it becomes difficult for others to understand. A good example of this is the situation in Singapore. Currently there are two general forms of English regularly used in Singapore. The first is a form of standard British-influenced English which is learned in school and pronounced with a local, distinctive Singaporean accent, known as Standard Singaporean English. The second is a vernacular learned at home and restricted to informal situations. This spoken form is referred to as Colloquial Singaporean English or as 'Singlish', and has incorporated many non-standard English grammatical features from Bazaar Malay and locally spoken Chinese dialects such as Hokkien. Following is an example of the colloquial form paired with its equivalent in standard English:[19]

Singlish/Colloquial Singapore English
Eh, better do properly, lah. Anyhow do, wait kena scolding. And then, you always ask her for favour, and still don't want to do properly. Must lah. Like that do cannot.

Standard English:
You had better do this properly. If you don't, you may get told off. And since you are always asking her for favours, you should at least do this properly for her. You should! You cannot do it like this.

The government of Singapore has become worried about the popular phenomenon of Singlish. It emphasizes the point that international English has to be intelligible to serve as a lingua franca between peoples of different countries, and is concerned that the use of Singlish may affect a speaker's ability to produce standard Singaporean English, which can be understood internationally. In order to 'protect' the standard variety of Singaporean English, the government actively discourages the use of Singlish, has banned it from television soap operas, and in 2000 instituted a 'Speak Good English Movement' which aims to strengthen the use of standard English forms.

---

19. Example from Alsagoff and Ho (1998).

The ongoing development of variation in new World Englishes spoken in outer circle countries, quite significant in the case of Singlish, raises a question about the sustained unity of English around the world. As an increasing amount of local differences occur in the English used by second-language speakers, and there is growing **divergence** from the standard English of countries in the Inner Circle, is it possible that this divergence could lead to regional World Englishes no longer being mutually intelligible at some point? If this were to happen, such varieties would effectively become new, different languages, and no longer be instantiations of 'global English'. With multiple occurrences of divergence and new forms of English splintering away, English as a global language might considerably weaken as a unified form of international communication and fragment into different mutually unintelligible dialects in the same way that Latin did in the Middle Ages, giving rise to French, Spanish, Italian, Romanian, and other new European languages. Such a pathway of development is an additional scenario in which the current global dominance of English potentially might be threatened.

However, the fatal splintering of English as a global lingua franca is by no means a necessary or even very likely outcome of the development of local variant forms of English, and there are very positive sides to the existence and development of regional varieties of English in different parts of the world. As noted by David Crystal (1997) and others, different varieties of English around the world allow their speakers to express distinctive national identities through the use of different localized forms of English, whether this is signaled by the use of different accents or vocabulary items. Clear variations in accent and also vocabulary have for a long time been present in the English used in countries of the inner circle, distinguishing speakers of American, British, Irish, Australian, and New Zealand English from each other, in ways that speakers of these varieties generally seem to feel proud of, and similar variation also occurs in regional dialect varieties of English spoken within many inner circle countries. Crystal suggests that, just as people from different parts of England or the USA are able to communicate successfully with each other despite having distinct regional forms of English, in the future it can be anticipated that a common global form of English will exist alongside other regional varieties and continue to allow for international communication. Almost everywhere in the world people make use of different formal and informal varieties of the languages they speak, depending on who they are speaking to and where the conversation takes place. The same switching between different dialect forms can be applied to the use of global and localized forms of English, it is suggested—the former can be used as a means to communicate effectively with people from other countries and different parts of the world, while the latter may be reserved for regional and domestic use, where its distinctiveness will reinforce an individual's sense of local and national identity. Global English can therefore have a very successful future without the need for local divergence to be suppressed if speakers simply accustom themselves to the use of more than one form of the language. How the international variety of English actually develops and changes over time is a separate question, and one which will depend on the size of English-speaking populations around the world, their economic and cultural power, and attitudes held toward English as the language continues to expand. In the final sections of this chapter we turn to consider the issue of changing attitudes to English and 'ownership' of the language.

SETTING OUT TO BE MISUNDERSTOOD: COCKNEY ENGLISH RHYMING SLANG

In most instances, divergence leading to unintelligibility in different forms of English arises quite by accident, when influences from local languages affect the way that English is spoken and regional creativity results in the development of new vocabulary items which are not familiar elsewhere. After all, people normally want to be understood by others and it might seem counter-intuitive to make one's language more, rather than less, restricted as a means of communication. However, in some instances, speakers deliberately do develop ways of speaking which are hard to understand. A good example of this is the 'rhyming slang' which occurs in the Cockney dialect of English spoken in the less affluent eastern part of central London, England. In Cockney rhyming slang, speakers make use of a pair of words (sometimes linked with 'and' or 'of') whose second member rhymes with the word they want to communicate. For example, instead of saying simply 'stairs', speakers will say 'apples and pears', as in:

'I'm just going down the apples and pears.' = 'I'm just going down the stairs.'

Similarly, instead of saying 'sun', speakers may say 'currant bun':

'I ain't seen the currant bun in days.' = 'I haven't seen the sun in days.'

This system of rhyming slang frequently becomes more complex, because speakers tend to actually omit the word which rhymes with the word they wish to communicate. Hence 'apples and pears' is shortened to 'apples', and 'currant bun' is shortened to 'currant':

'I'm just going down the apples.' = 'I'm just going down the stairs.'
'I ain't seen the currant in days.' = 'I haven't seen the sun in days.'

This way of speaking is clearly impossible for outsiders to understand if they are not familiar with the system, vocabulary, and omission rules of Cockney rhyming slang. In its origins, Cockney rhyming slang was developed as a secret language that could be used by criminals, but later it was more widely adopted as a fashionable way of speaking, and used to project a local London identity, just as diverging forms of English around the world are now often valued for identity-related reasons. More examples are given in the following:

'He went for a ball up the frog.' = 'He went for a walk up the road.'
derived from: 'He went for a ball of chalk up the frog and toad.'

'Use your loaf, mate!' = 'Use your head, friend!'
from: 'loaf of bread' = 'head'

'I'll just have a butcher's.' = 'I'll just have a look.'
from: 'butcher's hook' = 'look'

> 'Where's your dog?' = 'Where's your phone?'
> from: 'dog and bone' = 'telephone'
>
> 'Where's the trouble?' = 'Where's your wife?'
> from: 'trouble and strife' = 'wife'
>
> 'I just don't Adam it!' = 'I just don't believe it.'
> from: 'Adam and Eve' = 'believe'
>
> 'Mind your bacon!' = 'Be careful of your legs!'
> from: 'bacon and eggs' = 'legs'
>
> 'Don't get too Elephant's/Brahms tonight.' = 'Don't get too drunk tonight.'
> from: 'elephant's trunk' = 'drunk'
> and: 'Brahms and Liszt' = 'pissed' (UK slang for 'drunk').

Attitudes toward English as a global/local language

The feelings that speakers have toward the languages they use may naturally have consequences for their general growth or decline, particularly in the case of non-mother tongue, second languages adopted primarily for their utilitarian value. In countries in Africa and Asia occupied by the British up until the late 20th century, it is relevant to ask whether English is still mentally associated with earlier periods of British colonial domination, or not. If English does still have any negative associations from such times, this certainly might affect the way speakers would willingly use the language.

The evidence available from research into this issue in recent years seems to suggest that English in Africa and Asia is now no longer strongly associated with earlier colonial times, and has come to be viewed as a global, international language with multiple local instantiations, a linguistic system available to everyone, free of past connections. In South Asia, for example, English is now widely accepted as a positive linguistic asset representing educational and economic progress. One large survey in India showed that people regularly preferred English over other Indian languages as a means to gain knowledge and information in television, newspapers, and radio, and a majority of people said that they now consider English actually to be an Indian language. Similar attitudes toward the 'indigenization' of English have been reported in other countries of the outer circle, for example, in Ghana and Nigeria, in West Africa, as aptly captured in the title of an article published about Ghanaian English in 2012: 'I own this language that everybody speaks: Ghanaians' attitude toward the English language'.[20]

As English develops regionally in certain different ways, and in some sense is felt to be a new 'indigenous' language in outer circle countries, this localization of English has not

---

20. Ofori and Albakry (2012).

rejected all new external influence from inner circle countries. However, whereas previously it was British English that served as the primary model and linguistic influence in many African and Asian states, now it is American English that is having a greater effect on the growth of L2 Englishes around the world, above all in the areas of vocabulary and aspects of pronunciation. What should be made of this combination of the local 'customization' of English supplemented with Americanization? It is significant to note that it is actually not only outer circle and expanding circle forms of English which are adopting new words and phrases from American English, but also long-established inner circle varieties of English, too, spoken in the UK, Australia, and New Zealand. What, in terms of identity and attitude, may be signified by this move toward certain forms of American English in both L1 and L2 groups of speakers? Is it a desire to sound more American, due to the attractions of modern American culture and the position of economic and political power held by the USA in the early 21st century?

Studies have suggested that this may not be the case, and that new words and expressions coined in the USA are often not strongly perceived to be *American*, but are felt to relate to a more broadly *international* identity which is up-to-date, fashionable, and dynamic in its character. Speaking English with a range of words incorporated from American English can be viewed as a way that rising generations attempt to project an identity with a modern global component, rather than a directly American one, as teenagers and young adults build complex identities borrowing from a range of sources. Observers have pointed out that speakers of English around the world who adopt new items of vocabulary originating in the USA normally do *not* attempt to convert their speech fully into US English, and so project an image of being American, but typically select certain words and phrases to combine with localized forms of English, adding extra international flavor to distinctively local ways of speaking English, which may also vary according to age and social class. The linguists Miriam Meyerhoff and Nancy Niedzielski refer to such a combination as 'globalization with localization', and show, in an investigation of borrowed Americanisms in New Zealand English,[21] how the use of expressions such as the new quotative 'be like' (as in: '*And she's like: 'Who are you?'*), the emphatic negator 'no way', and other words sourced from US English are combined with an increasingly distinctive local way of speaking English, which makes New Zealand English stand out more and more as different from all other varieties (including Australian English). Speakers thus seem to want to maintain and strengthen the local nature of their identity, and do this by means of speaking English in a very characteristic way (with certain kinds of pronunciation, vocabulary, and slang special to New Zealand), while also adding extra 'international spice' to this with fashionable new words borrowed from the global English market, which currently is supplied heavily with expressions coined in the USA and its vibrant popular culture.

Summing up, one can say that English as now spoken in both inner and outer circle countries shows clear signs of being valued for the way it can help project identity, and it does this is in potentially complex ways. Localized forms of English in inner and outer circle countries are all quite distinctive, whether spoken as a first or second language, and this

---

21. Meyerhoff and Niedzielski (2003).

special character of L1 and L2 new World Englishes allows speakers to express individual and national identities, emphasizing their origins and allegiances in a very positive way. On top of this, the fact that such varieties are all forms of a single, globally shared language adds an extra international component to the identity associated with speaking English, which also seems to be frequently valued by speakers and enhanced by the use of new words and expressions that come into vogue.

Among populations learning English in countries of the expanding circle, such as Japan, China, Russia, Germany, etc., the use of English would seem to play much less of a role with regard to local and national identity, perhaps because distinctive local forms of English have, for the most part, not yet emerged in most territories in the expanding circle. However, certain links between the use of English and the projection of *personal identity* have sometimes been noted to occur among speakers from the expanding circle. For example, Jenkins (2003) points out that the use of English rather than one's mother tongue may allow a person to express a different side of their personality. The following are comments from three Japanese speakers of English, reported in Matsuda (2000: 52–53) which mirror attitudes held in similar ways by other second-language learners:

> 'I think my personality differs in English and Japanese. I'm more *wild* when I speak English ... I mean, more outgoing and not so *conservative*. Yeah, I'm more *conservative* in Japanese. I feel 'this is me' when I can say something in English.' (Chikako)

> 'My personality changes from Japanese mode to English mode. I'm more sarcastic and joking all the time and outgoing and, well, that's when I'm speaking English. In Japanese I'm quieter.' (Eriko)

> 'I use Japanese when I request something, Japanese is softer ... don't you think so? And when I apologize ... well, I might use English if I don't really feel like apologizing. A Japanese apology sounds more sincere.' (Keiko)

Returning to the L2 Englishes of the outer circle, as such varieties stabilize with distinctive local forms and positive attitudes increase toward their use, it might be expected that the domains in which new World Englishes are utilized would gradually extend beyond simple informal conversation, and enter into other areas and modes of communication, for example writing. An interesting, general question is whether it is possible for a non-native speaker to express him/herself in English in a confident and competent enough way to produce works of literature which really communicate the person's feelings? It is sometimes said that we can only achieve this level of communication comfortably and genuinely in our mother tongue.

In South Asia it is found that English has in fact increasingly been used for creative writing, and many international prizes have been won by Indian authors writing in English (for example, the Booker Prize). Such authors defend the use of English in writing and reject claims from others that Indian authors ought to write only in Indic languages (for example, Hindi, Bengali, Tamil, etc.). In 1973, the author Pritish Nandy declared that: 'English is a language of our own, yes, an Indian language, in which we can feel deeply, create and convey experiences and responses typically Indian' (Nandy 1973; 8).

Another author, Kamala Das wrote the following proud words in one of her famous poems:

> I am Indian, very brown, born in Malabar,
> I speak three languages, write in
> Two, dream in one.
> Don't write in English, they said, English is
> Not your mother-tongue. Why not leave
> Me alone, critics, friends, visiting cousins,
> Every one of you? Why not let me speak in
> Any language I like? The language I speak,
> Becomes mine, its distortions, its queernesses
> All mine, mine alone.
> (Kamala Das, 'An Introduction', in *Summer in Calcutta*. 1965. New Delhi: R. Paul))

In Africa, the Nigerian author Chinua Achebe has stated that the national literature of Nigeria and many other countries in Africa could and would be created in English. Concerning the potential difficulty of writing in a second language, he offers the following opinion:

> Let me say straight away that one of the most serious handicaps is not the one that people talk about most often, namely, that it is impossible for anyone ever to use a second language as effectively as his first. This assertion is compounded of half-truth and half bogus mystique. Of course, it is true that the vast majority of people are happier with their first language than with any other. But then the majority of people are not writers. We do have enough examples of writers who have performed the feat of writing effectively in a second language.[22]

Achebe continues:

> What I do see is a new voice coming out of Africa, speaking of African experience in a world-wide language. So my answer to the question: *Can an African ever learn English well enough to be able to use it effectively in creative writing?* is certainly 'yes'. If on the other hand you ask: *Can he ever learn to use it like a native speaker?* I should say, I hope not. It is neither necessary nor desirable for him to be able to do so. . . . English will be able to carry the weight of my African experience—but it will have to be a new English, still in communion with its ancestral home, but altered to suit its new African surroundings.

---

22. Quoted from Jenkins (2003) and the book: *Morning Yet on Creation Day*, New York, Anchor, 1975.

The message is therefore that localized English should be celebrated for its ability to capture different ways of life and thinking around the world, and that rather than reject English as a foreign parasite, English should indeed be embraced as a new indigenous language which can be molded to suit local needs whenever this is useful and helps the creative process of writing.

Creativity, correction, and the ownership of English

Thinking about 'creativity' in English now brings us to reconsider the variation which is found in new Englishes of the outer circle. There are two final, connected questions here:

- When deviations from standard English occur in the varieties spoken as second languages in countries of the outer (and expanding) circle, should these different forms be considered to be *mistakes* (to be corrected and not taught to others) or *legitimate, creative extensions* of the rules of English, which might then be adopted by and even recommended to other speakers?
- Who should be assumed to have the right to judge whether variant forms are grammatical innovations or mistakes—only native speakers of the inner circle, or also second-language speakers of the outer circle who have native-speaker-like competency in English? Who, if anyone, might be assumed to be appropriate 'guardians of the language'?

These issues can best be illustrated with a set of examples. The following are all instances where speakers of English from India, in the outer circle, may produce forms which are different from norms of the inner circle. Are they 'mistakes' or legitimate new developments of the rules of English grammar? If they are considered to be the latter, should other speakers possibly adopt these new ways of speaking?

Example 1: the *be+verb+ing* construction

In South Asian English one might hear the following kind of sentence:

'I think you are knowing my father, isn't it?'

By contrast, speakers of US/British/Australian English would normally say:

'I think you know my father, don't you?'

Is it incorrect for speakers of Indian English to apply the *be+verb+ing* construction in English to 'stative verbs' like 'know', although native speakers don't do this? As we will see in chapter 11, the *be+verb+ing* construction is in fact innovating in the USA and the UK, and being used with stative verbs in certain circumstances, for example, the McDonalds' slogan '*I'm lovin' it*'. Is such creativity only legitimate when it is initiated by native speakers (such as the publicity department working for McDonalds)? That would seem to be unfair. Similarly, there might be criticisms of the use of 'isn't it' in the preceding South Asian English sentence, in place of standard US/UK English 'don't you'. However, again, there are speakers of British English who are starting to use very similar forms, normally contracted as '*innit*' (also reviewed in chapter 11). Is it reasonable to assess this creativity differently in L1 and L2 English?

Example 2: new vocabulary items formed by extensions of principled rules

Consider the words 'postpone', 'depone', and 'prepone'.[23] 'Depone' is a technical legal term (a verb, which is directly related to the noun 'deposition') and so may be considered to be 'respectable' in British/US English, though it is quite uncommon in speech. 'Prepone' is an Indian English word which is common (in India), and was created to contrast with 'postpone', whose meaning is to retard the occurrence of an event and put it back in time. To 'prepone' an event in Indian English simply means to bring it forward in time:

'Lets postpone/prepone the meeting by an hour.'

The creation of 'prepone' follows the logic of word-formation in English, in the same way that 'predate' and 'postdate' do, but significantly, it is a coinage which has been made by non-native speakers from the outer circle. So, how might such a word typically be viewed by native speakers from inner circle countries—as a mistake, not a proper word of English? Are L1 speakers the only ones who can legitimately coin new words in English? This would seem to be an unjustified assumption, and yet it is an attitude which seems to surface in common reactions to new outer circle words such as 'prepone', 'wheatish', 'back-answer', etc.

Example 3: extension of plural marking to non-count nouns

L2 speakers from various outer and expanding circle countries sometimes pluralize nouns in a way that does not reflect standard patterns in L1 countries. Consider the following examples, where the plural marker –*s* is added to the nouns which occur in object-of-verb position.

'He gave me several informations.'
'I need two new equipments.'
'Yesterday the police discovered two more evidences of the crime.'

Native speakers of English from inner circle countries normally combine the nouns 'information', 'equipment', and 'evidence' with the word 'piece' when pluralized in examples such as the preceding, in place of adding an –*s* to these words:

'He gave me several pieces of information.'
'I need two new pieces of equipment.'
'Yesterday the police discovered two more pieces of evidence of the crime.'

This patterning is an exception to the common rule of pluralization with nouns in English. The majority of nouns in English can indeed be pluralized with an –*s* and counted directly without the need for a word such as 'piece':

---

23. Original discussion of these words and their 'grammaticality' status occurs in a 1993 Peter Stevens Memorial Lecture given by Henry Widdowson at the IATEFL International Conference, Swansea, and is reprinted from the *Annual Conference Report* in Jenkins (2003: 162–168).

'He gave me several hints.'
'I need two screwdrivers.'
'Yesterday the police discovered two more clues.'

Words such as 'information', 'equipment', and 'evidence' (dubbed 'non-count nouns') are oddly irregular in requiring the word 'piece' and not accepting the addition of –s. What the speakers of varieties of outer circle English are doing when they add –s to nouns of this type is simply regularization of the general rule of plural-marking in English, and extension of the rule to bring exceptions into line. Such an adjustment might seem to be a positive development and streamline the behavior of words in English in a useful way. However, does it make a difference that it is second-language speakers who are innovating in this kind of way, and is it felt that it should always be native speakers from the inner circle who make adjustments to the language before these are broadly considered to be acceptable?

Changes to English have been constantly made over past centuries by native speakers, and much of the English we produce now would have been considered to be ungrammatical and unacceptable in earlier times, but all the forms of English spoken in inner circle countries have come to be regarded as legitimate because they are L1 varieties. Hence if a speaker of English from some part of the USA is heard to say 'He clumb up a tree' in place of the more common 'He climbed up a tree', it might be thought that 'clumb' is a dialect form which is different from standard English, but not 'ungrammatical', because it is regularly produced by certain native speakers. There is a much more uneven view of the new forms of English which have developed in other parts of the world such as South Asia, and many people may consider that any deviations from standard English which occur in these new World Englishes are simply mistakes and should not be treated as grammatical differences in dialect. The issue raised by feelings of L1 'ownership' of English and legitimate guardianship of changes that occur in the language is one which is likely to have a growing importance as English continues to develop over the decades to come—who has the right to determine how standard world English should be spoken and act as guardians for the shaping of its future? With the massive growth of the numbers of second-language speakers around the world, resulting in the worldwide L2 English population being far greater than the number of native speakers in inner circle countries, there is arguably a need for over-protective, owner-like attitudes toward English held among many mother tongue speakers to be revised, and native speakers should learn to accept that everyone taking part in the expansion of English has a legitimate, potential role to play in the development of this globally shared lingua franca.

Summary

This chapter has considered how English has grown from its origins as the mother tongue of a relatively small and insignificant north European territory to become the language most commonly spoken all over the world, by extremely large numbers of first- and second-language users. We have charted the history of the rise of English as the world's first truly global language, and seen how its use has spread from L1 speakers to large L2 populations, where the language has been adapted in various ways to produce a range of new World Englishes each with special properties. This massive growth and gradual localization of English around the world have been accompanied by the emergence of increasingly positive attitudes toward the language, and a de-coupling of English from its prior associations with colonial domination and imperialist expansion. We also have considered what the future might hold in store for English and whether any currently foreseeable force might topple English from the prominent position it has established as the most widely used link language among speakers of other languages. The general expectation emerging from most contemporary research is that the immediate future of English as a global language looks very good, despite advances in translation technology which pose a threat to the maintenance of a spoken lingua franca, and English is likely to strengthen further over the coming decades, as large new confident L2 populations grow in expanding circle countries. Finally, as globalization comes to partner localization, it can be speculated that L2 English speakers around the world may come to command two varieties of the language and be bi-dialectal, using a distinctive, localized form of English for domestic and regional interactions, and a more general, global variety for international communication, with the latter potentially absorbing more influence from new World Englishes as it continues to evolve.

In the next chapter, we will stay with the theme of English and its growth in ethnolinguistically complex situations, turning our attention to how the use of English came to be so prevalent among the population of the USA, causing heavy language shift and loss among generations of immigrants who brought many other languages to North America. We will also focus on a particular variety of English which has come into being in the USA— African American Vernacular English—and how the existence of different home-spoken forms of the language can pose challenges for achieving success in the educational system when schools are only oriented toward the use of formal, standard English.

Suggestions for further reading and activities

1. Pick a country from continental Europe and create a profile of English-language use and learning in this country, indicating how English occurs in primary, secondary, and higher education, how English is present in the media, and what level of proficiency in English younger and older people typically have.
2. Learn more about the use of English as the language of air traffic control. Is English only used between pilots and controllers from different language backgrounds, or is it also used when both are native speakers of the same language? Do all countries make use of English for ground-to-air communication in the same way? Have there ever been any accidents which have resulted because of poor communication skills in English, causing misunderstandings between pilots and ground controllers?
3. For many centuries, French was very dominant as a language used by the upper classes in Europe, and also spread as a colonial language to many parts of Africa, Asia, and the Caribbean. Find out more about the ups and downs French has gone through as an international language, and how it has competed with English for speakers around the world.

4. Find a work of literature created in a new World English, select a few pages, and try to describe how the English being used there may be different from standard forms of written English in inner circle countries.
5. During the colonial period in India, there was much discussion about whether English or local Indian languages should be used as the medium of education in schools serving the indigenous population. Some British administrators supported the use of local languages, whereas others argued for the imposition of English. What were the arguments for the two positions, and what opinion do you have on whether English should have been used as the medium of secondary education in colonial India?
6. Given that Spanish is very widely known and used in Central and South American countries, is knowledge of English actually growing in Latin America?
7. Try testing out publicly available translation devices such as Google Translate and see how well they perform with oral and written input forms.
8. Read the article by Tsedal Neeley on corporate English and the obstacles to its success:

   Neeley, Tsedal. 2012. Global business speaks English. *Harvard Business Review*. https://hbr.org/2012/05/global-business-speaks-english.

   Select a multinational company which uses English as its working language and try to find out more about how this policy is being implemented. Neeley makes a number of suggestions on how the challenges of instituting corporate English can be overcome. Do you think these will be sufficient to overcome the problems that often arise when English is used as the main language of communication in business meetings among L2 speakers?

7

Language(s) in the United States

Introduction

This chapter focuses on the interplay of linguistic and social forces in the United States, where English has come to have a heavily dominant role in almost all domains of life, despite the presence of many other languages brought to the USA by immigrants building up the population of the country. The chapter is divided into two major parts. In the first part, we examine how English established such a powerful position in the USA relative to other languages, and why the settlement of different ethnic groups in the United States did not result in any widespread bilingualism and the sustained maintenance of other languages. We consider the tensions which continue to exist between movements attempting to promote the official status of English and English monolingualism, and those who attempt to defend multilingualism and encourage the learning of heritage languages as additions to knowledge of English. Such oppositions have increasingly led to legal cases ruling on individuals' rights to language use in the workplace and to changing support for monolingual (English) vs. bilingual education. The first part of the chapter presents arguments that have typically been given in favor of and also against official English monolingualism, and describes the outcomes of various court decisions which have affected people's legal rights to make use of different languages. The second part of the chapter is a concentrated study of the most researched and discussed non-standard variety of English in the USA—African American Vernacular English (AAVE). This variety has regularly been at the center of discussions on how to help young speakers of English which is different from Mainstream American English (MAE) be successful in schools where MAE has been used as the default medium of education, and overcome difficulties often caused by differences between home-spoken dialects of English and MAE-based academic English. We will look at some of the very distinctive linguistic properties of AAVE, ask how this variety may relate historically to other forms of English, and describe approaches that have been proposed to deal with language-related challenges in the classroom, including a discussion of the Ebonics controversy which erupted in 1996 over the linguistic status and educational use of African American language.

  In order to approach these and other related issues, we will first look at the linguistic development of English in the USA from the 17th to 19th centuries and how English came to prevail over the various other languages that were spoken by early settlers and immigrant communities. We will then consider changing attitudes toward multilingualism during the 20th century and what the current situation is in the USA regarding language policy in schools and other areas of daily life. Having seen how linguistic rights are decided by legal means and political ballots, often used to officially 'defend' the pre-eminent position of English in the USA and to impose its use formally within schools and government business, the second half of the chapter will turn to questions raised by the type of English that is being broadly promoted and how speakers of varieties other than Mainstream American English, such as AAVE, may face challenges similar to speakers of other languages in coping with an educational system which is not just (largely) monolingual but narrowly requires the use of a particular dialect of English.

The growth of English as the unofficial national language of the USA

Arriving in America: early immigrants and language use

The first peoples to settle the Americas arrived from northeast Asia, crossing from modern-day Siberia to Alaska by means of a land bridge which connected the two continents many thousands of years ago. This resulted in the establishment of the 'indigenous' population of North, Central, and South America—Native Americans whose numbers had reached approximately 2 million in North America when the first Europeans began to arrive and occupy lands along the Atlantic seaboard (García 2009). It is thought that over 300 different languages were spoken by Native Americans prior to initial contact with any Europeans, belonging to many different language families.

During the early period of European immigration to North America (1500–1800), the majority of new settlers were either English, Spanish, or French.[1] Spanish-speakers occupied Florida and southwestern areas corresponding to modern-day California, Arizona, and New Mexico. Settlers from England spread out extensively along the East Coast and then its hinterland, everywhere from Massachusetts down to Georgia and along the Ohio River valley. Further inland still, and to the north, speakers of French established settlements from Canada down to New Orleans, claiming territory all along the Mississippi valley. Among these three European groups, English-speakers were numerically dominant, embedding the regular use of English across a vast area of land, which became greater still with the Louisiana Purchase of 1803, adding 828,000 square miles of previously French-controlled territory to the United States.

The 19th century brought very large numbers of new immigrants to the USA, as before predominantly from European countries. Due to the devastating famine which occurred in Ireland during the mid-19th century, and accompanying economic challenges, over 4 million Irish immigrants arrived in the United States to boost the population of the country, principally in the Northeast of the USA. German immigrants also came increasingly during the

---

1. Smaller numbers of settlers during this time were speakers of Dutch, in the areas of modern-day New York and New Jersey, and German in Pennsylvania.

19th century and early 20th century, almost 6 million in total, with settlement heavily being centered in the Midwest. The mid-19th century also witnessed the beginning of large-scale immigration from Italy and Greece, and of Yiddish-speaking Jewish people from eastern Europe. Finally, the 19th century attracted considerable numbers of immigrants from Asia as well as Europe, with the Gold Rush of 1849 marking the beginning of significant immigration of Chinese people to California and later the Northeast. Later in the 19th century, considerable numbers of Japanese people also immigrated to the West Coast of the USA.

Between 1500 and the twentieth century, there was consequently a whole range of different languages being spoken by new immigrant communities throughout North America. Given such a multilingual background, it is natural to ask how English came to be so dominant in the USA and what policies and measures were adopted to ensure the position of English in the developing USA.

Early policies toward non-English languages

When the treatment of settler groups in the 18th and 19th centuries is compared with more recent immigration in the 20th and 21st centuries, a broad difference in policy toward the use of languages other than English has been observed. Kloss (1977) notes that a greater level of tolerance was extended by the English-speaking majority—the 'Anglo-Americans', or simply 'Anglos'—toward languages spoken by other early settlers than toward those of later immigrants, and when the very first settlers (the 'pioneers') of a particular territory were not mother-tongue speakers of English, the use and cultivation of their language in the area that had been settled was generally accepted. Consequently, for periods between the 18th and 19th centuries, the following languages all enjoyed a certain tolerance in the territories settled by their speakers:

- German in Pennsylvania
- Dutch in New York and New Jersey
- French in Louisiana
- Spanish in New Mexico and California
- Russian in Alaska.

Certain of these languages were even granted authority in local state laws, though they were never formally recognized at a higher, national level (Schiffman 1996).

After early periods of relative linguistic tolerance, the 19th century saw a significant rise in paranoia among Anglo-Americans about the increase in immigration of other ethnic groups and the use of foreign languages in America (García 2009), and this led to calls for restrictions on both the use and the teaching of 'foreign' languages in the USA (i.e., languages other than English). What really triggered the new paranoia was a change in the pattern of immigration into America from a largely white, Protestant, mostly English-speaking north European source to the immigration of peoples who matched the Anglo-American prototype far less. To many Anglo-Americans this seemed to pose a serious and worrying challenge to the ethnic model which earlier immigration had established as dominant in the USA.

The change in immigration patterns occurred as follows. First, from 1820 onward, immigration ceased to be primarily from Britain and began to come much more from other north European countries such as Germany, Norway, and Ireland.[2] The presence of large numbers of Germans posed a linguistic threat to English in many parts of North America, and the presence of an increasing Catholic population from Ireland was additionally seen by Protestant Anglo-Americans as posing a possible religious threat. Following this, in the second half of the 19th century, there started to be significant immigration from southern and eastern Europe. These immigrants were often Catholic, Orthodox Christian, or Jewish by religious background, and much less like Anglo-Americans in cultural outlook than other settlers from north European countries.

The 'defense' of English in the face of 'foreign invasion' was initiated and continued through legislation relating to the teaching of languages other than English in schools. An important way to potentially control and halt the maintenance of heritage languages is by regulating their use within the classroom. If children are permitted to receive parts or all of their education in a home language which is not the language of the majority, there is a far greater likelihood that this language will be passed on to future generations, as has been discussed in chapter 3. However, if minority languages are banned from use in schools, it is likely that this will influence the linguistic behavior of their speakers and will contribute to the local decline of such smaller population languages. In North America, the end of the 19th century saw the beginning of initiatives to close down schools which offered bilingual education or monolingual teaching in a language other than English. Legislation against non-English instruction was in fact so successful that by the beginning of the 20th century languages other than English were only taught as 'foreign languages' and were no longer used as a medium to teach other subjects (such as history, science, math, etc.). Previously there had been many schools which provided a full range of teaching in German and other languages, but when the 20th century arrived, this type of foreign-language schooling had been effectively eliminated. Furthermore, when the USA entered World War I in 1917, there were almost instantaneous strong attempts to prohibit all use of German in schools throughout the country. The effect of such efforts was that German was discontinued not only as a medium of instruction, but could also no longer even be taught as a 'foreign language'. This ban was extended for many years after the end of World War I, and schools which had previously been German-oriented became fully English-language schools. The children who attended these schools subsequently became largely monolingual in English, despite coming from ethnically German families. When German was eventually allowed back into schools, this came too late for many in the young generation, and most children from German backgrounds had lost too much of their early German ability to become bilingual again.

In the fight to re-establish the right to teach in German during the post–World War I years, one potentially very important legal battle took place: *Meyer vs. Nebraska* (1923). In this courtroom case, a teacher called Robert Meyer engaged in a legal suit with the state of Nebraska which, like certain other states, had imposed a ban on the use of languages

---

2. As already noted, German immigration actually began in earlier centuries, but this increased very heavily in the 19th century.

other than English in all schools, public and private. Meyer was convicted of the 'crime' of tutoring a 10-year-old student in German, teaching him how to read the Bible in German. Meyer subsequently contested the ruling of the Nebraska courts and took the case to the Supreme Court of the United States to appeal it. In a famous linguistic decision, the Supreme Court ultimately ruled in Meyer's favor and declared that the attempt to forbid the teaching of languages other than English prior to the eighth grade was a violation of the Fourteenth Amendment. However, despite the apparent victory in *Meyer vs. Nebraska*, the ruling was criticized by some as not going far enough and not giving children the right to be raised bilingually. All the Supreme Court ruling effectively did was defend the rights of adults to teach 'foreign' languages.

The 19th and early 20th centuries also saw a linguistic assault on Native American languages. Such languages were suggested to be inferior to European languages in terms of their logical structure, and their use was claimed to harm children's opportunities for personal and educational development. In order to suppress the continued transmission of Native American languages, a government policy was introduced which insisted that Native American children be placed in all-English boarding schools away from their reservations. In these schools any use of Native American language or culture was automatically punished, and the children placed in such schools were expected to acculturate completely to American customs and language.[3] One of the language groups affected was the Cherokee. The Cherokee had established a way of writing down their language and, following contact with English-speakers, later set up a successful bilingual education program which enabled members of the group to be able to read in both Cherokee and English (Leibowitz 1980). When compared with neighboring English-speaking populations, the literacy rate achieved by the Cherokee was actually higher than that of most Anglos (Dicker 1996). However, after the children of the Cherokee were sent away to learn English in off-reservation English schools instead of learning it on the reservations from Cherokee teachers, the earlier, impressive literacy rate of the Cherokee decreased very rapidly, and children failed to develop written and also oral skills in their heritage language.

In addition to increased immigration from southern and eastern Europe, the 19th century also saw the beginnings of large-scale immigration into America from Asia, adding further ethnic complexity to the population of the USA. The Gold Rush of 1849 triggered significant numbers of Chinese immigrants to come to California, and then continued immigration from China resulted in large Chinese populations being established in cities such as New York and San Francisco. Immigration also began to come from Japan, mostly to states on the West Coast of the USA where Japanese immigrants took up work as farmers. Later in the 19th century, government policies on Asian immigration and citizenship had indirect negative effects on the maintenance of Asian languages in the USA. From 1870 onward, Asians were not allowed to establish citizenship in the USA, and starting in the 1880s official bans on

---

3. The Indian Peace Commission which was established by the US government to provide policy recommendations for Native American groups reported in 1867 that: "... in the difference of language lies two thirds of our trouble. Schools should be established which [Indian] children should be required to attend: their barbarous dialects would be blotted out and the English language substituted" (quoted in García 2009 from Castellanos 1983).

immigration from Asia were introduced, including the Chinese Exclusion Act, which lasted from 1882 to 1943 (García 2009). During this period, the lack of new immigrants arriving from Asia had impacts on the ability of Asian communities to maintain their languages well. A constant flow of new monolingual immigrants into a community helps other speakers maintain their heritage languages, and when this regular link with the country of origin is broken, language skills often start to deteriorate, as noted in chapter 3.

Following World War I there were further setbacks for the learning of other non-English languages in various ways. First of all, educators and psychologists began to tell the public that the acquisition of two (or more) languages had negative effects on learning for children and so multilingualism should not be promoted. The use of languages other than English was also suggested to be potentially divisive for the population of the USA, hence not to be encouraged at all. Additionally, for a time the USA began to reduce its interactions with the outside world, decreasing contacts with foreign countries and cultures, and increasing restrictions on immigration. Furthermore, despite the official result of the *Meyer vs. Nebraska* case, the teaching of 'foreign languages' was actually banned from elementary schools and only permitted within high schools, as the knowledge of languages other than English was not deemed suitable for young American children. Such a rather bleak linguistic situation, with its antagonism toward the learning and use of other languages, continued until the 1960s, when certain more positive changes began to take place.

Changing approaches to language, 1960–1990

In the 1960s, the long-entrenched attitude of distrust toward multilingualism finally showed signs of starting to change. The lack of serious foreign-language instruction in the USA was brought into focus by developments on the international scene and ongoing competition with the Soviet Union during the Cold War. In 1958 the Soviet Union succeeded in launching its famous satellite *Sputnik,* increasing concerns about possible military threats posed by Russia. This led to a heightened examination of all aspects of Soviet life, and it was found that foreign-language learning was strongly being supported in the educational system. Worried that the USA was significantly behind the Soviet Union in this area, the US government passed the 1958 *National Defense Act*, which made available funding for the study of a wide range of languages that could be used to help improve connections with countries in Europe, Asia, and Africa.

The year 1959 was also important, as many Spanish-speaking refugees arrived in the USA from neighboring Cuba, fleeing the turmoil of the revolution which was taking place on the island. As most of those arriving from Cuba had no knowledge of English, the state of Florida initiated new programs to teach English to the refugee population. What was particularly special about these programs was that they also included teaching in Spanish and aimed to produce English-Spanish bilingualism in children, not simply convert Spanish-speakers into monolingual English-speakers. Furthermore, the new programs of bilingual education were made available not only for Cuban children whose home language was Spanish, but also for young English-speaking Americans in south Florida, and began to produce younger generation speakers who could function effectively in both Spanish and English (Schiffman 1996).

Following the successes of the new programs used in Florida during the 1960s, a proposal for wider use of bilingual instruction was put forward and approved in 1968, as the *Bilingual Education Act (BEA)*. The immediate stimulus for the proposal was a need to address worrying increases in the school drop-out rate of young mother-tongue speakers of Spanish in the state of Texas, which were attributed, at least in part, to the under-development of English-language skills. In 1960, the high school drop-out rate for Spanish background students in Texas reached as high as 89% (García 2009). It was hoped that the structured use of Spanish in schools would help non-English-speaking immigrant children successfully learn to read and write in English, as well as be able to speak the language, and so have better chances of completing their primary and secondary education. Although the focus of the BEA was on the acquisition of academic English, its inclusion of children's heritage languages as part of their schooling facilitated the transition of minority languages in many communities, in particular Spanish, but also other languages, as BEA funding was made use of in ethnically mixed schools throughout the country (Kloss 1977), and between 1968 and 1978 thirty-four states provided support for bilingual programs (Arías and Wiley 2015).

As bilingual education began to help young speakers of languages other than English, a new spotlight was thrown on challenges faced by students whose home variety of English was substantially different from the standard form of English used in schools. In the late 1970s, an important legal battle involving language use in education took place in the city of Ann Arbor, Michigan, leading in 1979 to what became known as the *Ann Arbor Decision*. In this case, the African-American parents of children attending the predominantly white Martin Luther King School in Ann Arbor filed a suit against the school for its 'failure to take into account the cultural, social, economic and linguistic factors that would prevent African American children from making normal progress in the school' (Labov 1982: 168).[4] The children had regularly experienced difficulties in trying to advance into higher grades alongside their peers and were frequently characterized as suffering from learning deficiencies by their teachers.

When the case went to court, the presiding judge ruled that any cultural, social, or economic factors which might distinguish the plaintiffs' children from others in the King School and negatively impact their educational progress were *not* grounds for the award of special services to help these children improve their performance. However, the judge conceded that language-related factors potentially did have relevance, if it could be shown that the home language of the plaintiffs' children was significantly different from the English used by educators in the classroom. If there were major differences between these varieties, the school might be required to take action to prevent negative effects arising from language barriers in the classroom, according to the law.

Expert linguists were called into court to provide testimony on the properties of African American Vernacular English[5], and how these varied in a systematic way from those of Standard American English (SAE). Some of the very distinctive syntactic and

---

4. Quoted in Schiffman (1996).
5. At the time, this variety was referred to as 'Black English', or 'Black English Vernacular' (BEV).

phonological rules made use of in AAVE will be described in the second half of this chapter. When details of these properties were presented in a clear way, the judge was convinced that AAVE and SAE were sufficiently different from each other to constitute a potential barrier to classroom communication and to necessitate attention, and he ruled in favor of the plaintiffs, rendering the Ann Arbor Decision, which required teachers in the school to learn more about AAVE and utilize this knowledge in their teaching of SAE reading skills to African American students. The Ann Arbor Decision was an important point in American legal linguistic history as it formally recognized that linguistic 'barriers' to advancement in education were not always the result of children speaking foreign languages, but might also arise from the interaction of substantially different dialect forms of a single language.

A further potentially important official declaration on language, which was made by the US government in 1990, was the *Native American Languages Act*. A key passage from the Act pledges support for the preservation and use of Native American languages, and recognizes that Native Americans should be free to maintain and pass on their languages to rising generations as they wish:

> It is the policy of the United States to preserve, protect, and promote the rights and freedom of Native Americans to use, practice and develop Native American languages.. (*Native American Languages Act, 104*)

The *Native American Languages Act* clearly reverses the official policy directed toward these languages and their speakers during the late 19th and early 20th centuries, when government and state initiatives attempted to suppress the use of Native American languages. The Act is therefore a very positive development and has helped stimulate a change in public opinion toward Native American language and culture, which in earlier times was biased by negative portrayals of Native Americans and official attempts to inhibit the transmission of their languages. Critics of the Act, however, suggest that it will have few practical effects because the declaration has simply come too late—Native American languages are currently dying out at a very rapid rate, as described in chapter 3, and most will probably disappear in a short period of time even if they are accorded help by means of the new Act.

Renewed, organized defense of English

From the 1960s onward, for at least a couple of decades, developments relating to language policy in the USA showed signs of being less restrictive than earlier in the 20th century. There was greater openness to the use of different languages in public domains of life, and foreign- and heritage-language learning was encouraged in schools and universities. However, the 1980s also saw a hostile reaction to the increased presence of languages other than English in education and government services from people who thought that official attitudes toward language in the USA were becoming too permissive and were not giving sufficient support to the status of English in American society. The new backlash against government assistance for multilingual programs which began during the 1980s was led by and centered around a new organization called *US English*, founded in 1983 by Samuel

Hayakawa, a senator from California, and Dr. John Tanton. The principal goals of the US English movement were:

a. to have English be recognized as the official language of the USA and the only language of all government and public offices;
b. to have state and federal governments discontinue the funding and operation of all bilingual education programs;
c. to cause the termination of all other governmental bilingual services wherever possible (e.g., bilingual ballots and voting material, the use of languages other than English in any governmental activities, etc.).

The US English movement managed to raise considerable amounts of money, and widely publicized its view that bilingual education and the official support of languages other than English was harmful for individuals and society in the USA, claiming that multilingualism had negative effects on national unity and cohesion, that bilingual education impeded children's cognitive development and ability to learn English well, and that governmental sponsoring of services in different languages was unnecessarily costing tax-payers large amounts of money. Originally the organization hoped to achieve constitutional recognition of English as the single official language of the USA. However, attempts to have the constitution amended in such a way continually proved to be unsuccessful. The leaders of US English consequently turned their attention away from the national level to that of individual states, and vigorously campaigned for the recognition of English as the official language of states throughout the country. This widespread lobbying for official English was initially focused on states with large immigrant populations, such as California, Florida, and Arizona, where US English perceived that the 'menace' posed by other languages was at its greatest and where disgruntled voters might be persuaded to give their support to proposals to establish English as the sole official language of a state.

By means of advertisements placed in newspapers and propaganda mailed directly to people's homes, US English sought to convince people of its opinions on the dangers of multilingualism, bilingual education, and rising immigration, and the need for change to occur in order to protect stability, prosperity, and the fundamental nature of American society. In its pressure on the voting public, claims have been repeatedly made by representatives of US English that new immigrants, unlike those of earlier times, are often unwilling to assimilate to the American way of life and integrate well into society. Crucial for such blending is the learning and adoption of the English language, and it is suggested that recent immigrants in many parts of the USA are refusing to learn English and substitute it for the language they have brought with them from other countries. According to many within the US English movement, the maintenance of a second, non-English mother tongue prevents new residents from developing an American national identity and feelings of loyalty to the USA.

In California and various other states, US English has targeted the Spanish-speaking population more than other immigrant groups with criticisms that new Spanish-speaking immigrants are not assimilating as they should, and not learning English (Fillmore 2004). Reacting to the view that US English was being over-critical of Spanish-speaking immigrants, the organization appointed a woman of Mexican descent as its president. However, this woman, Linda Chavez, also showed herself to be openly critical of immigrants from Spanish-speaking countries, in statements such as the following:

> Most Americans support immigration with one condition—there is the expectation that immigrants adapt themselves to the language, values and mores of this nation. It is a social contract between the person welcomed into the home and the host: when in Rome, do as the Romans do. When Hispanics insist that they do not have to follow the same rules as every group before them, they threaten this contract. (Chavez 1991: 94)[6]

In the same publication, Chavez adds that:

> The real fear of many Americans is that Hispanics will one day be a group which is so large and powerful that it will insist that the United States adopt a bilingual policy. That fear is not so far-fetched, as the example of Canada demonstrates. French-Canadians make up only about one-quarter of the Canadian population, but they have succeeded in forcing the entire country to recognize and use French as an official language. Will something similar happen with Spanish, when nearly one third of the US population is Hispanic? The mere possibility drives some Americans to make sure that day will not come. (Chavez 1991: 88–89)

Supporters of US English adhere to the idea that speaking one (and often *only* one) language is the only way that an ethnically mixed nation can exist in a united way. In his article 'Preserving the primacy of English', Norman Shumway, a member of US English, writes that:

> English has been the common language of the United States as a result of historical tradition. That common tradition has been the 'glue' which has held us together, forging strength and unity from our rich cultural diversity. (Shumway 1988: 121)

Commenting on such a view, Susannah MacKaye, an observer of language-related political developments in the 1980s and 1990s has suggested that:

> Language is seen as the only common bond among Americans, as the only factor in the attainment of the American dream, and as the only clue to ethnicity. Enormous power is ascribed to language, making it the great equalizer, without considering any of the other societal and cultural factors in play. In each of these beliefs there is truth and error, history and myth, and the weight of tradition, both real and invented. Consequently, legislation concerning language issues is not the simple matter it may appear to be. (MacKaye 1990: 146)[7]

---

6. The two excerpts from Chavez (1991) here are quoted from Dicker (1996), as are the statements from Shumway (1988) and Dole (1996), initially reported in Broder (1995).

7. Quoted in Schiffman (1996: 273).

Another prominent figure, the Republican politician and presidential candidate in 1996, Robert Dole, echoed these same feelings in a public speech given in 1995 (reported in the *Washington Post*):

> With all the divisive forces tearing at our country, we need the glue of language to help hold us together.... If we want to ensure that all our children have the same opportunities in life, alternative language education should stop. (Broder 1995: A1)

US English has accordingly fought for the dismantling of educational programs which support bilingualism, along with calls for English to be recognized as the official language of states within the USA. The movement has argued that all bilingual programs should be replaced by 'immersion'-type programs in which immigrants are immersed in English-only education and not taught in any language other than English. As justification for such a switch in pedagogical approach, US English claims that earlier immigrant generations learned English through simply being immersed in an English-speaking environment, and modern immigrants should also be able to learn successfully in a similar way, without the need for any bilingual programs. In fact, pushing its position on monolingual language learning further, US English has publicized a view that bilingual education actually *impedes* the learning of English. Such an assessment of the demerits of bilingual education is expressed in the following excerpt from a *New York Times* editorial in 1981:

> Teaching non-English-speaking children in their native language during much of their school day constructs a roadblock on their journey into English. A language is best learned through immersion in it, particularly by children.... Neither society nor its children will be well-served if bilingualism continues to be used to keep thousands of children from quickly learning the language needed to succeed in America. (*New York Times*, October 10th, 1981)[8]

As a result of large amounts of negative publicity sponsored by US English in newspapers and television, the general public in many places came to accept its claims that bilingual education is bad for children's linguistic development and may result in a child failing to learn English.

Other specialists in language dispute such negative views of bilingualism and argue that there are many important misconceptions in propaganda disseminated by the US English movement. What follows is a summary of points which have commonly been made in defense of bilingualism and bilingual education by various educators and linguists in the USA and other countries.

[1] First, concerning the value of bilingual education, modern research into second-language acquisition has shown that the acquisition of literacy skills in a second language

---

8. Quoted in Cummins (1991: 187).

is considerably helped by learning to read and write first of all in one's mother tongue. Hence a child whose home language is, for example, Spanish, is likely to be more successful in mastering English literacy if the child has the opportunity to learn reading and writing in Spanish before attempting to acquire academic English.[9] Consequently, bilingual programs do have considerable positive value, despite US English claims that bilingual education is not effective and even detrimental to linguistic development.

[2] Second, Schiffman (1996) notes that the 'sink-or-swim' immersion programs of the past, where immigrants were taught only in English, actually resulted in many immigrants 'sinking' and not acquiring English well at all. Those who were unable to make any progress in monolingual immersion education simply dropped out of school and had no other choice but to work as unskilled laborers (see also Fillmore 2004 on this point).

[3] Third, it has been found that recent immigrants are generally not following a different linguistic path from earlier generations with greater retention of heritage languages. In immigrant families there still is regular transition from the dominant use of a heritage language to the increased use of English. As noted in chapter 3, this typically happens over the course of three generations, and sometimes even faster. While certain ethnic groups may succeed in maintaining bilingualism in their heritage languages and English more successfully than others, there is continual language loss in all immigrant groups, and pressures to know and use English have actually became stronger than in the past.

[4] Fourth, it is not correct that there is reluctance among immigrants to learn English. The opposite is actually found to be the case, and English-language programs everywhere in the USA are over-subscribed and desperately insufficient in number for the huge demand there is for English tuition. All over the country new immigrants regularly seem to be very keen to participate in English-learning programs, as they quickly realize that any kind of even moderate economic success in the USA requires a knowledge of English. This was not so in the past—immigrants with little or no English knowledge could easily get employment in the agricultural or industrial sector, but nowadays much of the job market demands higher-level English skills than before. Unfortunately, the English as a Second Language programs that have been made available are often too few to cope with the demand for learning among new immigrants. For example, back in 1986 when US English was campaigning to make English the official language of California, in Los Angeles County it was estimated that 40,000 people were stuck on waitlists for English classes.

Concerning the preceding points [3] and [4], a number of critics have argued that the US English Movement has attempted to create and exploit the image of a golden age of immigration in earlier centuries, where immigrants quickly and voluntarily relinquished their native languages and cultures to assimilate to the language and culture of America. This is linked to the 'melting pot' image of the USA as a country where a wide range of different ethnic groups have met and combined to form a harmonious new culture. Critics have

---

9. This observation will be discussed more in chapter 8, which focuses on bilingualism.

argued that this picture may largely be a myth, and that early immigration was not so idyllic in nature (Dicker 1996: ch. 2). It is claimed that immigrants in previous centuries actually did not voluntarily give up their language, culture, and ties to their homelands for the sake of assuming a new American identity, that immigrants held on to their culture and language as long and as strongly as they could, and that each new wave of immigrants was generally viewed with distrust by those who had arrived in earlier immigration cycles, rather than being welcomed in as new arrivals to the 'melting pot'. Where new immigrants did assimilate or 'acculturate', it is suggested that this was largely due to intense social pressure to conform to patterns of life established by previous generations of immigrants.

Furthermore, in modern times there are indeed very positive attitudes toward the learning of English (as mentioned earlier), especially among the children of those who have immigrated to America. In surveys carried out among various immigrant groups, a significant majority of children from different heritage language groups said they actually preferred speaking English to their parents' languages.

[5] Fifth, the principal goal of the majority of bilingual programs established in schools in the USA has not been to help speakers maintain their heritage languages, contrary to claims made by opponents to bilingual education. Rather, the regular goal of such programs has been to simply help speakers make use of their mother tongue to develop academic and literacy skills which will then facilitate the learning of English as a second language. Following the acquisition of English, skills in the heritage language often fall into decay and are not supported by the educational system. There has been much harmful confusion over this point in media discussions and portrayals of bilingual education, which have regularly claimed, incorrectly, that bilingual education is focused on helping immigrants maintain their heritage languages. This is simply not correct. For the most part, bilingual education programs in the USA have been *transitional* in nature, helping students make a transition from the dominant use of a heritage language to the development of proficiency in English. Such programs use immigrants' native languages as temporary bridges to assist in the acquisition of English, and then generally abandon attention to the former, once sufficient foundations in English have been established.

[6] Sixth, it has often been claimed that bilingual education is extremely expensive and that schools and state governments cannot afford such a major financial burden.[10] However, this assessment has been challenged in Fillmore (2004), who notes that the cost of bilingual education is much less than the cost of other compensatory or special education

---

10. A similar point about the expense of support for languages other than English has been made by US English with regard to the costs of providing governmental information in languages other than English, such as voting, health, and employment information. As illustration, it has been suggested that the Department of Motor Vehicles wastes millions of dollars printing driving tests in Spanish and other languages in the state of California (and 39 other states in the USA; Diack and Berry 2007). However, the logic behind such accusations of wastage is very questionable. Each person taking a driving test makes use of one test booklet, and whether this is printed in English, Spanish, or some other language does not affect the cost of printing the booklet. If a Spanish-speaker does not take a driving test printed in Spanish, that person will take one printed in English, and the cost to the taxpayer is essentially the same (once initial translation costs have been paid, and these are minimal when compared to the cost of printing millions of driving tests each year).

programs which are needed for students who have difficulties acquiring English. Fillmore quotes a study reported in Parrish (1994) which estimated that the annual, supplemental cost of bilingual education for one student was $60, compared to $875 for compensatory education and $2,402 for special education programs. Bilingual education programs might therefore seem to be the cheaper alternative for students from other home language backgrounds who are faced with difficulties acquiring academic English.[11]

[7] Finally, Wiley (2004) and various others have emphasized that it is a fundamental mistake to think that choices must be made between English and other languages (and their associated cultures). The view of assimilation which members of the US English Movement have often promoted is that new residents adapting to American culture and language should replace their original language and culture with that of the USA.[12] It assumes that it is generally not possible for a person to be genuinely bicultural and bilingual. However, there is much evidence that this is not true, and both bilingualism and biculturalism are globally widespread phenomena.

With regard to language, a majority of the world's population is actually thought to be bilingual or multilingual, and there is no reason why multilingualism should not be able to develop effectively within the USA. The importance of knowing English in the USA is not disputed, and all sides agree that new immigrants to the USA will have much greater opportunities open to them if they are able to learn English. However, the successful acquisition of English does not require the abandonment of a person's initial mother tongue, and it is perfectly possible for an individual to learn a new, additional language without having to discontinue the use of his/her first learned language and substitute one for the other.

Related conclusions hold for biculturalism and identity. It is over-simplistic to assume that a person is only able to enjoy a single set of cultural forms and maintain a monolithic identity. Even within monolingual societies, people regularly have complex identities which involve feelings of belonging to different groups and physical places, but these do not necessarily conflict with each other. For example, a monolingual speaker of English from South Carolina might pride himself on being a Southerner as well as an American, feel loyalty to a particular sports team, a political party, and other groups that he has membership in, and be drawn to aspects of a distinctively Southern way of life as well as more general American culture.

The situation is entirely similar for people with backgrounds relating to different languages and cultural traditions. A person can take advantage of one particular culture as well as participate in the common practices of another tradition—for example, a person of

---

11. The US English Movement would most probably suggest that no supplemental education is needed for speakers of other languages and that simple immersion in regular classrooms where English is used should be sufficient for the mastery of English. However, the high failure rate of students in such environments indicates that some special supplemental tuition is necessary, and bilingual education may well be much cheaper than other options that have been tried.

12. Such a view has long been held by proponents of English only, both in the present and in past years. For example, in 1915 President Theodore Roosevelt proclaimed: "We have room for but one language here, and that is the English language" (quoted in García 2009: 165).

Chinese ethnic background can celebrate the Chinese lunar New Year as well as Christmas, July 4th, and Martin Luther King Day. Bi-culturalism is a greatly enriching phenomenon, and within the USA there are many in the population who designate themselves proudly and patriotically in a bicultural way as Italian-Americans, Greek-Americans, Korean-Americans, and so on. Feelings of belonging to a certain ethnic group, for example that of the Japanese-Americans, who are distinct in many ways from Japanese living in Japan due to their experiences of living in the USA can co-exist and thrive healthily with the cultivation of loyalty to the nation, and ethnic, regional, and religious identities are not mutually exclusive with the maintenance of national identity.

Despite the existence of such valid counter-arguments to negative portrayals of multilingualism, bilingual education, and immigrant attitudes toward the learning of English, the US English Movement has managed to achieve a number of its goals through forcefully pressing its opinions on the voting public in many states. Although the primary objective of the organization to get English recognized at the national level as the official language of the USA was not successful, similar campaigns did succeed at the state level, and to date, thirty states in the USA have established English as the sole official language of the state. In some instances, however, the practical consequences of such decisions may not be particularly far-reaching. For example, in California, when voters approved Proposition 63 in 1986 making English the official language of the state, this was taken to be an important victory for the Californian chapter of the US English Movement, yet the effects of Proposition 63 for everyday life in California have not been very significant, and California continues to provide an extensive range of programs for non-English speakers, making use of other languages. Schiffman (1996: 273) notes that '. . . all written materials explaining government services must be made available in a language other than English when that language is spoken by more than 5% of the people served by a local office', and quotes the California Bilingual Services Act declaration that:

> Every state agency . . . directly involved in the furnishing of information of the rendering of services to the public whereby contact is made with a substantial number of non-English-speaking people, shall employ a sufficient number of qualified bilingual persons in contact positions to ensure provision of information and services to the public, in the language of the non-English-speaking person.[13]

Consequently, California governmental agencies actually do provide considerable amounts of information in languages other than English, and the success of Proposition 63 was, to a certain extent, just a symbolic, 'moral victory' for US English rather than the cause of drastic change in the official use of language in the state.

More concrete and measurable effects on language use have been achieved by initiatives aimed at eliminating bilingual education programs around the country, and once again, California with its very high immigrant population was a key early battleground in this

---

13. The Dymally-Alatorre Bilingual Services Act, California Government Code §7290.

campaign. At the time that new anti-bilingual education legislation was proposed in 1998, one out of every four people resident in the state of California had been born outside the USA, resulting in California having a third of the total foreign-born population of the country. A large proportion (25%) of children in California's schools were also recognized as having 'Limited English Proficiency' (LEP), with 1.4 million young people from immigrant families not being able to speak English well enough for educational purposes—as much as 43% of the total of LEP students in all the USA (Fillmore 2004). This heavy concentration of LEP students and the difficulties such young people were experiencing in schools were highlighted in publicity soliciting voter support for a new Proposition 227 which was sponsored by a Californian businessman, Ron Unz, and presented as an 'English for the children initiative'. Prop 227 asked voters to approve the replacement of all bilingual education programs with English-only instruction, and recommended that all LEP students be restricted to having a maximum of one year of special language support ('structured English immersion') to help in the learning of English.[14] Propaganda distributed by Unz and his group made the claim that bilingual education programs were failing to produce competent speakers of English, that students in such programs were not successfully learning to read and write, and also were doing poorly in other subjects such as math. Additionally, materials sent out to voters suggested (incorrectly) that bilingual education meant monolingual Spanish-only education (in Hispanic neighborhoods) for at least four years, with no learning of English, and that the children of immigrants were not transitioning into mainstream education as fast as they should in order for them to catch up with their peers.

Largely as a result of the intensive advertising efforts of Unz and his supporters, Prop 227 was approved by a majority of voters (61%), who were convinced that bilingual education was not beneficial for the state and its young people and therefore should be discontinued. Observers and critics of the outcome have suggested that the pro-227 movement was able to gather so much public support for its proposals because of a lack of knowledge about second-language acquisition and bilingualism among the general population. While much research into bilingualism had been carried out since the 1970s, the positive results of this had not been well-communicated in the media, and misconceptions about bilingual education were widely present in newspaper and television reports.

The passing of Prop 227 caused a very drastic decrease in the presence of bilingual education programs in schools in California, although it did not succeed in entirely eliminating all such programs. Due to the way the proposition was written and presented, a loophole was available for schools to continue to operate bilingually if parents requested *waivers* from English-only instruction for their children, and petitioned for bilingual education instead. In various cases this did indeed occur. However, the ten years following the approval of Prop 227 generally saw a plummeting in the number of bilingual programs being maintained. In 1998, approximately 29% of California's LEP students (also frequently referred to as 'English Language Learners', or ELLs) were receiving some form of bilingual education. By 2007, this had dropped to 6%. Many schools and district authorities made little effort to inform parents

---

14. Structured English immersion programs required teaching to be all in English, with a curriculum and method of teaching focused on children who need to learn the language (Salomone 2010).

of their rights to request waivers from English-only education, and certain school boards even instructed teachers explicitly not to grant waivers (Salomone 2010: 155). Prop 227 also instilled fear among teachers that they could be sued for damages by dissatisfied parents and the state if they used languages other than English in the classroom, on grounds of not complying with the ruling of the new legislation. All of this consequently conspired to drastically reduce the range of bilingual instruction that had previously been available to ELLs in California.

Spurred on by the apparent successes of Prop 227 in California, but determined to build improvements into the stringency of similar, future propositions, Unz and his team drafted a much tighter anti-bilingual education proposition for consideration in the neighboring state of Arizona, with more restrictions on its potential application. Prop 203 was approved in Arizona in 2003, by a majority of 63% of voters, and criminalizes any teacher use of a foreign language as a medium of education, and mandates that children must read and write only in English. The proposition allows teachers and schools to decline waiver requests without offering any kind of explanation, and has resulted in waivers from English-only instruction being almost impossible to get (García 2009). Further instances of legislation outlawing the use of bilingual education have been enacted in other states by means of voter ballot, and the general picture which unfolded through the first decade of the 21st century was a rolling back of earlier educational initiatives utilizing languages other than English for transitional teaching purposes.

Positive moves: defending multilingualism

Although there have been vigorous attempts to discourage and delimit the public presence and use of languages other than English by prominent individuals and organizations such as Ron Unz and the US English Movement, there have also been initiatives in recent years to defend and support the maintenance of non-English languages in the country. First, it can be noted that there are actually states in the USA which have official policies of bilingualism. In *Hawai'i*, a state constitutional amendment has recognized both English and Hawaiian as official languages. The state motto is written in both English and Hawaiian, both languages are made use of in state governmental acts and transactions, and both occur on official symbols of Hawai'i. *New Mexico* is also a bilingual state. After an initial period in the state's history which enforced the dual presence of both Spanish and English in the description of all state laws, the government now remains empowered to make use of Spanish alongside English in any ways deemed helpful for the state. Spanish is regularly used in a broad spectrum of official activities (elections, dissemination of legal information, records of public meetings) and in bilingual education, and the state song is sung in both English and Spanish versions (Dicker 1996). Two further bilingual states are *Alaska* and *Louisiana*. The former has designated 20 Native American languages as official state languages together with English, and the latter promotes the use of French in addition to English in a number of domains, including bilingual education, the economy, tourism, and cultural activities. The maintenance and increased use of French in these areas of life is overseen by the *Council for the Development of French in Louisiana (CODOFIL)*, an organization incorporated within an office of the state government.

In terms of active public resistance to the influence of the US English Movement, smaller groups have emerged in various places dedicated to the protection of multilingualism and multiculturalism. Following voter approval of Proposition 63 in California in 1986, a civil rights group based in Florida, the *Spanish-American League Against Discrimination (SALAD)* issued a statement calling for 'English Plus', which subsequently received support from other groups all over the country.

> We won't accept English Only for our children. We want English plus. English plus math. Plus science. Plus social studies. Plus equal educational opportunities. English plus competence in the home language.[15]

SALAD and other organizations subsequently formed a new coalition group which called itself *English Plus Information Clearinghouse (EPIC)*. EPIC's mission statement made it clear that it recognized the importance of English as the nation's dominant language and that all individuals needed to develop proficiency in English for reasons relating to national integration and personal success. The group also stressed that the USA should support the learning and use of languages other than English so as to better participate in the global economy and help with international relations. Salomone (2010) notes that the careful wording of EPIC's statement managed to offer a different perspective on the heated issue of multilingualism and bilingual education. It cleverly shifted the discussion away from the view that languages other than English might be *problems* for the progress of American society, to the more positive view that such languages constitute a valuable *resource* for the country. As a result of EPIC's attempts to provide better information about multilingualism to the public and its emphasis on the potential value of other languages, the states of Rhode Island, Washington, New Mexico, and Oregon all declared their support for English Plus resolutions, and both multilingualism and multiculturalism. One statement issued by the state of Oregon indicated that its leaders would set out 'to welcome, encourage and protect diverse cultures and use of diverse languages in business, government, and private affairs',[16] and New Mexico pledged protection for its multicultural tradition of 'diversity with harmony' against potential threats posed by English Only policies. Other national organizations have also adopted resolutions supporting multilingualism and multiculturalism. These include the *National Council of Teachers of English,* the *American Psychological Association,* the *Linguistic Society of America,* and the *National Association for Bilingual Education.*

Challenges to the imposition of English Only legislation have become a further feature of resistance to the US English Movement and the policies it promotes, with a range of organizations attempting to defend the legal use of languages other than English in the workplace. Issues relating to language rights are now increasingly being decided in cases taken to court, as both pro- and anti-Official English supporters explore the legality of restrictions

---

15. Spanish-American League Against Discrimination Education Committee, 'Not English Only, English Plus!' unpublished manuscript, October 4, 1985.

16. Quoted in Salomone (2010: 150) from Tatalovich (1995: 18).

on language use in states which have adopted English as their sole official language. As illustration of this, one successful legal challenge to a state official-English law was the case of *Yniguez vs. Mofford 1990* in Arizona, as described by Dicker (1996) and summarized here. In 1988 Arizona adopted English as its official state language, requiring that it be used in a range of areas of life, from education to government activities. Two years later, two individuals jointly filed a suit against the state of Arizona which challenged the legality of the Official English law, claiming that it violated their constitutional right to freedom of speech. One of the plaintiffs was a senator for the state, Jaime Gutierrez, the other a state insurance-claims manager, Maria-Kelly Yniguez. Both Gutierrez and Yniguez had regularly used Spanish to communicate with certain of their constituents and clients before 1988, when the Official English law was implemented in the state. Following this, Yniguez stopped interacting with her clients in Spanish for fear she might be sued by members of US English for contravening the new law requiring that English be used in official government business. Gutierrez continued to speak Spanish with his constituents, but was also worried that his behavior might be claimed to be illegal. Yniguez and Gutierrez therefore decided to contest the Official English restrictions on language use and get legal clarification on whether such regulations did indeed violate the First Amendment. The judge presiding over the case in 1990 ultimately ruled in favor of the defendants, Yniguez and Gutierrez, and declared that the English Only law was unconstitutional. In further discussion of the case by the state attorney general, it was added that the Official English regulations only constrained official acts of the state government itself, as an organization, and not the daily activities of its employees. Individuals such as Yniguez and Gutierrez were consequently free to use Spanish or any other appropriate language in their interactions at work. This case interestingly tested how deeply an Official English law might be able to interfere with the language used by government workers representing the state, and resulted in a ruling which was widely received as positive (though criticized by pro-English-only factions).

A second 'workplace' case which can be mentioned here concerns the use of languages by workers in a privately owned company rather than government offices, in another state with an official-English state law—California.[17] In *Garcia v. the San Francisco Spun Steak Company*, two employees of a meat products factory, Priscilla Garcia and Marcela Buitrago, filed a suit against their employers for imposing a ban on languages other than English on the factory floor in 1990. Prior to this, many Hispanic workers in the factory had spoken Spanish with each other while working in the factory. However, in 1990 other non-Spanish-speakers submitted complaints to the factory management about the use of Spanish, claiming that Garcia, Buitrago, and others had been making derogatory remarks in Spanish about other co-workers. As a response to these complaints, an English-only rule was introduced by the management for all communication between workers. The justification given for such a new regulation was that it should help eliminate tension between Hispanic and non-Hispanic workers, and also improve safety in the factory, as some non-Spanish-speaking workers

---

17. This case is also described at some length in Dicker (1996), and depicted in a segment of the film *English Only in America?* (Diack and Berry 2007), which includes interviews with one of the plaintiffs and a senior representative of the factory management.

suggested that it was distracting to hear Spanish being spoken when they operated potentially dangerous machinery. The new language rule required only English to be used by employees when they were working, with Spanish being restricted to lunch and other breaks from work occurring during the day.

When the two employees, Garcia and Buitrago, continued to speak to each other in Spanish while working, the management sent them warning letters and separated them from each other within the factory. Garcia and Buitrago subsequently took the Spun Steak Company to court, contending that it had no right to impose language restrictions on its employees and that its actions were discriminatory. In 1991 when the case was heard, a district court ruled in favor of the plaintiffs, stating that the imposition of English caused inequality among workers in the company. A case against an Official-English-based rule was therefore again apparently successful. However, the case was subsequently appealed, and the appeals court overturned the decision of the district court and ruled in favor of the English-only restriction introduced by the factory's management.

It can therefore be seen that language disputes caused by the introduction of English as an official state language will not necessarily all be decided in a unique way, and some may result in a ruling which permits the continued freedom to use languages other than English in the workplace, whereas others may actually condone the introduction of English-only type rules. How such cases will continue to be ruled on will be interesting to see. For the moment, however, it is not easy to discern any obvious trend or advantage for either side of the English-only debate in disputes over language rights at work.

Interestingly, with regard to the use of languages other than English in the classroom, 2016 saw a significant return to earlier practices allowing and even supporting multilingual programs in California, nearly two decades after Proposition 227 enforced English-only education throughout the state. Proposition 58, sponsored by a Democratic state senator, Ricardo Lara, and presented to voters in November 2016, advocated a repeal of measures requiring English-only instruction in the absence of school-approved waivers and renewed freedom for schools to develop and offer bilingual programs as they wished. To the dismay of Ron Unz, the initial sponsor of Prop 227 and continual supporter of English-only education, Prop 58 was approved by voters with a striking majority of 74% and was widely endorsed by community and educational organizations all over California.

What caused such a turnaround in public support for bilingual education between 1998 and 2016? Ricardo Lara and others attribute the endorsement of Prop 58 to important changes in attitude that have grown among the mixed population of California during the first two decades of the 21st century. In the 1990s, Prop 227 was supported from within the Hispanic community by parents who were frustrated with the slow progress of their children in inner-city bilingual education programs and their apparent failure to acquire good levels of academic English. Such parental anger did not accompany discussions of multilingual education when these occurred in 2016, and the debate had a quite different character when Prop 58 was being tabled. Studies of waiver-permitted bilingual programs in the years leading up to Prop 58 showed that these programs were actually very successful. For example, an investigation of the academic performance of 18,000 ELLs carried out by Stanford University in 2014 demonstrated that by the fifth grade, ELL students who had received waivers to remain in small bilingual programs were just as proficient in English as those in those in English-only programs, they did equally well on state tests, and they mastered literacy in a second language as well.[18] In the second decade of the 21st century, more and more parents requested waivers to enroll their children in successful dual-language immersion programs, waiting lists for places in such programs have grown considerably, and interest in multilingual education appears to have re-emerged all over the USA. Now, parents (especially from the upper middle class) increasingly see that knowing more than one language is an asset for their children ('language as a resource, not a problem') and recognize that biliteracy and bilingualism are skills that will give their offspring significant advantages in competition with others. Ricardo Lara, himself a product of a bilingual education program, emphasized that a change in perspective on bilingual programs and the opportunities they open up for students had resulted in a voting public that was quite different in its orientation in 2016 than that back in 1998, and that Californians had come to value and understand the importance of having their students be multilingual and multiliterate. With bilingual instruction being reconceived of as a form of academic *enrichment* rather than just a transitional form of education for the development of English skills, a positive new mentality is becoming associated with the use of other languages in many American schools, and if this is sustained further, it may contribute to the growth of more stable, genuinely valued multilingualism in the USA. This new direction of development is now very promising and is working to help dispel negative perceptions of languages other than English and their place in American society which were publicly stimulated during earlier campaigns for the establishment of Official English.

Summary

The first part of this chapter has considered how English came to have such a dominant role in the USA, despite the presence of many other languages brought to America by early settlers and later immigrants. We have seen how English-speakers adopted policies which made it difficult for other language groups to maintain their heritage languages at times, and we have described attempts to establish English as the official language of nation, state, and education. We also noted that a more relaxed, positive attitude toward languages other than English has existed in the USA in various periods, most recently in the 1960s and 1970s, with hints that the 21st century might perhaps witness a revival of 'foreign' language learning through immersion programs aimed at the young, which are now becoming more and more popular, especially with middle-class families looking to give their children educational advantages. In much of the discussion relating to language use in society and schools in the USA, national integration, and the status and learning of English, one other language (and its speakers) has often figured prominently—Spanish, the heritage language of the largest minority group in the USA. As reference to Spanish and Spanish-speakers is so commonly made in dialogues between organizations such as US English and English Plus, the first part of this chapter will close with an extended sidebar on Spanish in the USA, providing

---

18. Noted in a Southern California Public Radio report broadcast on October 26, 2016 (author: Claudio Sanchez). Available at: http://www.npr.org/sections/ed/2016/10/26/498291619/the-return-of-bilingual-education-in-california

more background on its speakers, the current state of the language in the USA, knowledge of English among the Hispanic community, and attitudes held by Spanish-speakers toward both Spanish and English, according to recent research. The second part of the chapter will then go on to focus on the nation's second-largest ethnic minority group—African Americans—and issues associated with a variety of speech used by a portion of this group, African American Vernacular English, which have also caused much discussion in considerations of language use in schools.

SPANISH IN THE USA: AN OVERVIEW

Americans of Spanish-speaking descent, officially termed Hispanics in US Census Bureau information, make up the largest ethnic group in the USA after the category of English-speaking Americans of European origin. In 2014 it was estimated that there were 55 million Hispanics in the USA, making up 17% of the national population, and it was projected that by 2050 this proportion would rise to 25%. Of the Hispanic population, 60% live in the southwestern states of California, Arizona, New Mexico, Colorado, and Texas, where they comprise 18% of the local population. The large Spanish-speaking population of the Southwest was established many centuries ago, before this area became part of the USA, unlike the Hispanic presence in the Northeast of the USA, which is much more recent in origin. The area of greater Los Angeles has the largest proportion of Spanish speakers in the Southwest, with 37% of the population of L.A. county identifying itself as Hispanic in official surveys, the great majority of these being of Mexican ancestry. Over half of the very large Hispanic population present in L.A. county were born outside the USA and are therefore first-generation immigrants whose mother tongue is Spanish (Silva-Corvalán 2004).

In the Northeast of the USA there are over 8 million Hispanics, equaling 15% of the total Hispanic population in the USA. While there are many more Hispanics in the Southwest, there is more diversity of origin in the Northeast, and the Hispanic population comes from a wider range of different countries and territories. The largest group are the Puerto Ricans. In New York City, there are over 2 million Hispanics, making up 27% of the city's 8 million inhabitants, and 36% of these are Puerto Ricans (Zentella 2004).

According to research summarized in Silva-Corvalán (2004), the presence of a large Hispanic population in the Southwest does not mean that there will continue to be a high percentage of Spanish speakers in these areas in the future, because language shift into English is occurring at a high rate, and proficiency in Spanish is being lost. It is estimated that 90% of Hispanics in the USA can speak English, and that knowledge of Spanish is being lost a lot faster in the 21st century than earlier immigrants lost their abilities in other languages in the first half of the 20th century. In the Northeast of the USA, it is observed that second-generation Hispanics increasingly cannot speak Spanish and that two-thirds of first-generation settlers are shifting to English as their dominant language after only fifteen years in the USA (Zentella 2004). Those settling in the Northeast from other Spanish-speaking countries who are the most likely to maintain their proficiency in Spanish are middle-class Hispanics who learned to read and write in their native country and then found these skills in Spanish useful for employment in the USA.

In L.A. county, Silva-Corvalán reports that only 30% of those who use Spanish in the home were born in the USA; hence the majority of those who speak Spanish with their family are in fact Generation 1 immigrants from other Spanish-speaking countries. Furthermore, 65% of those who use Spanish in the home also speak English either well or very well, and only 35% do not report themselves as speaking English well. This indicates that 'a substantial proportion of those who were born outside the USA ... do learn English well enough to participate adequately in American society, and probably will not pass a fully functional variety of Spanish on to their offspring' (Silva-Corvalán 2004: 214). Rather than being a growing 'threat' to English, knowledge of Spanish is therefore not inhibiting the acquisition of English, and the buoyancy of Spanish itself is only maintained by regular in-migration of new native speakers of Spanish from other countries. Proficiency in English among Hispanics, by way of contrast, is very widespread, in particular among those born in the USA, but also increasingly among first-generation immigrants. As for attitudes held toward Spanish and English, Silva-Corvalán reports that there are strongly positive attitudes toward both languages through almost all of the Hispanic community. Spanish has significant symbolic value, marking shared ethnic identity, while English is seen as important for the access it provides to better-paid employment and broader participation in American society. Bilingualism in English and Spanish is very much desired by Hispanics, but in reality it is likely that young Hispanics born in the USA will become English-dominant and not develop strong Spanish skills, especially in the area of reading and writing.

African American Vernacular English

African American Vernacular English (henceforth AAVE) is a form of speech used among the African American community in the USA which is generally considered to be a variety of English with very distinctive properties, differing from standard American English (SAE) in its vocabulary, pronunciation, and grammar in many striking ways.[19] AAVE is spoken by a large number of African Americans spread throughout the USA, and is therefore characterized as an *ethnic dialect*, rather than a *regional dialect*.[20] As in other ethnic groups, socio-economic divisions exist within the African American population, and these relate to differences in individuals' language. African Americans from middle-class backgrounds

---

19. What is here termed AAVE is also sometimes referred to simply as 'African American Language (AAL)'—see the volume edited by Lanehart (2015). In earlier decades, AAVE was also called 'Black English Vernacular (BEV)'.

20. While there are some regional differences in the way AAVE is spoken around the country, for the most part speakers from different regions share the same core properties of AAVE in grammar and vocabulary (Winford 2015).

with higher levels of education and socio-economic status are more likely to be speakers of SAE (perhaps accented in a distinctive way), while AAVE is typically produced by speakers from lower socio-economic backgrounds, and used in informal situations.[21] As a very colloquial form of speech different from SAE, AAVE has often been highly stigmatized in the past and negatively described as an illogical, substandard form of English lacking rules. Psychologists such as Carl Bereiter and Siegfried Engelmann developed a view that the divergence of AAVE from SAE was an indication of serious cognitive deficiency among its speakers, and that AAVE was 'not merely an underdeveloped version of standard English' but also 'a non-logical mode of expressive behavior . . . lacking the formal properties necessary for formulating cognitive concepts' (Bereiter and Engelmann 1996: 112–113).[22] The first part of this consideration of AAVE will be devoted to a study of the 'irregularities' found in AAVE and will show that the significant differences which exist between AAVE and SAE are not due to any random, rule-less failure to produce standard English by cognitively deficient speakers, but instead result from the application of very clear grammatical and phonological rules, which simply happen to be different from those which produce SAE. The conclusions from this overview of properties of AAVE will be that AAVE most certainly needs to be recognized as significantly different from SAE, but this divergence occurs in very principled ways, which simply reveal the workings of a different system of rules, not an inability to master the rules of SAE.

Such conclusions will feed into questions relating to language use in education. Specifically, it will be asked what kind of English should be taught and used in classrooms where the majority of students speak AAVE. Many young African American children experience difficulties in bridging the gap between their home language, AAVE, and the variety required for use in school, SAE (or other terms used for this variety: 'mainstream American English', 'general American English', 'mainstream classroom English', 'academic English'). As AAVE and SAE are different in many ways, despite having an underlying similarity, how can young speakers of AAVE be most effectively taught to read and write and develop learning skills which will be of benefit to them in later life? What useful role, if any, might AAVE have in the classroom, and how can young speakers of this variety acquire a proficiency in SAE and so compete with their peers who grow up with SAE (or a close, regional approximation of SAE) as their home variety? To a significant extent, the consideration of AAVE will illustrate attitudes and issues that affect non-standard varieties of English more generally, so the problems discussed with regard to AAVE are actually of a wider relevance, being concerns for any ethnic or regional group whose speakers use a dialect which is regarded as being 'substandard' English. Finally, we will also examine different theories of the *origins of AAVE*, and how claims of English-origin and African-language-origin were stressed for different political purposes during the 1996–97 Ebonics controversy.

---

21. Labov (1972) characterizes this form of speech as: '. . . the relatively uniform dialect spoken by the majority of black youth in most parts of the United States today, especially in the inner city areas of New York, Boston, Detroit, Philadelphia, Washington, Cleveland, Chicago, St. Louis, San Francisco, Los Angeles and other urban areas.'

22. Quoted in Smitherman (2015).

To begin, we will look at a selection of features typical of AAVE in its pronunciation and grammar, how these differ from SAE, and how they often relate to SAE rules in a very systematic way.

Properties of AAVE: pronunciation
Consonant cluster simplification

Speakers of AAVE regularly pronounce consonant clusters (i.e., sequences of consonant sounds) in a reduced way when these sequences occur at the ends of words. The following sequences all 'lose' the second of their consonants, so that the words are pronounced as if spelled in the way following the arrows:

st	best	→	bes'
ld	old	→	ol'
nd	end	→	en'
pt	slept	→	slep'
ft	left	→	lef'
ct	fact	→	fac'

Such a process of reduction and simplification is actually found in some form in *all* dialects of English. In standard English spoken at a normal speed, when two or more consonants occur at the end of a word *and* the next word begins with a consonant, speakers regularly reduce the cluster in the first word by eliminating the final consonant, hence *old man* is pronounced as *ol' man*, and *best place* is pronounced as *bes' place*. The simple difference between speakers of AAVE and SAE is that the former also modify word-final clusters when these occur: (a) at the ends of sentences, and (b) when the next word begins with a vowel (Green 2002). Speakers of AAVE thus extend a phonological process already present and at work in standard varieties of English to an increased range of environments, and the simplification of consonant sounds in AAVE is not random, but conditioned in a slightly different way from similar reduction in SAE.

Consonant cluster simplification at the end of a sentence in AAVE
AAVE: *She wen' out wes'.*   *Jim jus' lef'.*
SAE: *She went out west.*   *Jim just left.*

Consonant cluster simplification before words beginning with vowels in AAVE
AAVE: *Mary lef' already.*   *She gonna sen' a letter.*
SAE: *Mary left already.*   *She's going to/gonna send a letter.*

This process of cluster reduction can produce complex words in AAVE which sound quite different from their SAE counterparts. Take, for example, the word *test*. The plural form of *test* in SAE is *tests*, but in AAVE it is pronounced as *tesses*. People unfamiliar with the properties of AAVE may think that speakers of AAVE are producing ungrammatical English when they use words such as *tesses*, but *tesses* and other related forms are created by the principled application of AAVE phonological rules, as follows. The singular form *test* is reduced to *tes'* in normal AAVE consonant clusters simplification, and then pluralized. When plural *'s* is added to words ending in *–s* in both SAE and AAVE, an extra vowel is added in, hence *dress* and *caress* become *dresses* and *caresses*. Applied to AAVE *tes'*, this general adjustment of adding an extra vowel to link a noun ending in *–s* with a following plural marker *'s* consequently produces *tesses* in AAVE. *Tesses* may sound quite different to SAE *tests*, but it is formed in a fully rule-governed way.

'th' substitutions

In standard varieties of English, many common words contain the letter combination *th*, but in AAVE, most occurrences of *th* sounds are pronounced in different ways, by using one of the following sounds: *d, v, f, t*. Hence the SAE words in the left column in the following are often pronounced in AAVE as if they were spelled in the way represented in the right-hand column:

SAE	AAVE
this	*dis*
smoothe	*smoov*
birthday	*birfday*
mouth	*mout*
mother	*muver*

Although there are several different sounds that seem to substitute for *th* in AAVE, the way substitutions are made is very systematic. In SAE, the letters *th* actually represent two different sounds: (a) a 'voiced' sound in which a speaker's vocal folds are made to vibrate when the sound is produced—as heard in words such as *this, the, there, thou, bathe, father*; and (b) a 'voiceless' sound which does not involve vibration of the vocal folds, as occurs in words like *thin, thick, bath, thirty, pithy*. AAVE speakers are found to replace *th* sounds which are voiced in SAE pronunciation with alternate voiced sounds—*d* and *v*: *d* is used at the beginnings of words, hence *this → dis, they → dey*, and *v* is used at the ends of words and in the middle of words, hence *smoothe → smoov, father → faver*. The voiceless sounds *f* and *t* are never used as replacements for voiced *th*, and are only substituted for voiceless *th* sounds, where these occur in the middle of words or at the ends of words: *birthday → birfday, mouth → mout*. Where a voiceless *th* occurs at the beginning of a word (for example in *thirty, thin, thick*), AAVE speakers actually use the a voiceless *th* sound and pronounce words in the same way as SAE speakers. Examining the ways that AAVE speakers replace certain sounds which occur in SAE reveals that such adjustments are made according to a very clear linguistic logic, and not haphazard mispronunciations of SAE words (Green 2004).

Properties of AAVE: syntax
Omission of 'copula' <u>be</u>

Many of the special, distinct features of AAVE relate to differences in the grammar of standard, mainstream varieties of English and that of AAVE. As with AAVE phonology, a consideration of syntactic properties leads to the conclusion that differences between AAVE and SAE are not the result of random, illogical 'mangling' of standard English, but are due to a different systematization of syntax in AAVE, which is clearly principled and used by speakers of AAVE in highly constrained ways. Here we will look at three syntactic phenomena as illustrations of differences between the grammars of AAVE and SAE.[23] The first of these relates to variation in the use of the copula verb '*be*'. A well-observed characteristic of AAVE is that speakers often omit the copula verb *be* in the present tense, but speakers of SAE do not (DeBose 2015):

SAE: *She is really skinny.* AAVE: *She _ real skinny.*
You are crazy! *You _ crazy!*
Jim is at home right now. *Jim _ at home right now.*
We are having a party. *We _ havin' a party.*

A very interesting observation made by Labov (1969) is that AAVE speakers do not omit copula *be* in *all* environments and that there are rules governing when it may or may not be omitted. For example, if copula *be* occurs in an 'exposed' position at the beginning or end of a sentence, it must be pronounced and cannot be left out in AAVE. Speakers of AAVE judge the forms in the right-side column in the following to be ungrammatical (this being indicated with a star symbol *) and always pronounce *be* in its various forms in such cases, as represented in the left-side column.

AAVE: *I wonder what it is.* **I wonder what it _*
Is she really? **_ She really?*
How wet you are! **How wet you _!*

This indicates that AAVE-speakers do indeed have a present tense copula in their vocabulary (i.e., they do make use of *be* sometimes), and that they simply omit it from sentences under certain circumstances. Labov (1969) made a further interesting discovery about this phenomenon, working out that copula *be* in AAVE can only be omitted (or 'deleted' from sentences) in those environments where standard English allows copula *be* to be contracted and reduced to -'*s*, or -'*re*. Consider the following examples. It can be seen that when SAE speakers use reduced forms of *be*, AAVE speakers omit *be*, and when contracted forms are unacceptable in SAE, *be* omission is not possible in AAVE:

SAE: *She's really skinny.* AAVE: *She _ real skinny.*
You're crazy! *You _ crazy!*
Jim's at home right now. *Jim _ at home right now.*
We're having a party. *We _ havin' a party.*

SAE: **I wonder what it's.* AAVE: **I wonder what it _*
**How wet you're!* **How fine you _!*
**I forgot where we're.* **I don't know where we _.*
**Tell me where it's.* **Tell me where it _.*

---

23. For discussion of other grammatical differences, see Rickford (1999) and Green (2002).

The generalization, therefore, is that wherever SAE permits *be* contraction, AAVE permits *be* deletion, and where SAE bans *be* contraction, AAVE similarly disallows *be* deletion. Both rules appear to be governed by the same logic and show a complex interaction between syntax and phonology. One way of analyzing the patterns is to suggest that AAVE speakers allow copula *be* to be reduced in a specific set of environments, just as in standard English, and then take the further step of fully deleting the output of this reduction. Such deletion may possibly be driven by the general tendency toward simplification of syllable/word-final sounds in AAVE which has already been seen in patterns of consonant cluster reduction. The reduction of copula *be* often results in a final sequence of consonants—for example, *what's* and *Jim's* which end in *ts* and *ms* clusters as the result of *be* contraction—so AAVE may simply opt for the deletion of the final consonant in such sequences of consonants, establishing a general process of *be* deletion/omission. If this is so, then copula deletion in AAVE is neither haphazard nor symptomatic of any deficit in language abilities, as earlier suggested by certain psychologists. Rather it is governed by a complex interaction of rules which relate directly to principles of syntax and phonology in standard varieties of English.

'Invariant' *be*

A second distinctive patterning in AAVE we will consider here is the use of so-called 'invariant' *be*—the occurrence of *be* with subjects of all person and number combinations:

AAVE: Lou usually <u>be</u> here around 8.   SAE: Lou <u>is</u> usually here around 8.
        Sometime she <u>be</u> mad with me.   Sometimes she <u>is</u> mad with me.

This use of *be* in AAVE might seem to be similar to the use of an invariant *be*-form in certain British dialects of English, for example:

British Westcountry English: I *be in the garden right now.*
Standard English: I *am in the garden right now.*

However, there is an important difference between the AAVE use of invariant *be* and that found in other dialects of English (Trudgill 1974a). Interestingly, AAVE invariant *be* only occurs when the verb refers to some action or state which is a habitual occurrence, and *be* may not be used when there is a description of a temporary condition or non-repetitive action. The British Westcountry English example in the preceding would therefore not be acceptable in AAVE because it describes a temporary condition—the speaker is momentarily in the garden. If a sentence describes a passing state in AAVE then invariant *be* is not used, and the omission of *be* typically occurs instead:

AAVE: She _ busy right now.   Not: *She be busy right now.

As already noted in chapter 5, there is a special linguistic term for verbs and certain other items which emphasize that the action of a verb is (a) ongoing, (b) completed, (c) a long time away in the future or past, or (d) a habit. This term is 'aspect'. Invariant *be* in AAVE is therefore said to mark '*habitual aspect*', as it always occurs with descriptions of repeated actions.

AAVE has other markers of aspect, too, in addition to invariant habitual *be*. These aspect markers are not found to occur in standard English. They make use of familiar English words which have been reanalyzed in novel ways in AAVE, as described in the following.

AAVE 'COMPLETIVE' ASPECT
Use of the word '*done*' as an aspect marker emphasizes that an action has been completed:
    Marcus <u>done</u> finish up his food.   (SAE: Marcus has already finished his food.)
    He <u>done</u> sol' all the good ones.   (SAE He's already sold off the good ones.)

AAVE 'REMOTE' ASPECT
Use of the word '*been*' pronounced as '*bin*' signals that an event took place a long time ago, in the remote past:
    He <u>bin</u> write to Joe.   (SAE: 'He wrote to Joe a long time ago.')
    I <u>bin</u> talk with her about that.   (SAE: I talked with her about that a long time ago.)

AAVE 'CONTINUATIVE' ASPECT
Use of the word '*steady*' in AAVE indicates that an action occurs continually and intensely:
    Bruce jus' <u>steady</u> tellin' her lies.   (SAE: 'Bruce just keeps on telling her lies.')
    Rick <u>steady</u> makin' a pile of wood.   (SAE: Rick is making a pile of wood without stopping for a break.')

These aspect markers occur *in addition to* equivalents to standard English past tense forms such as '*have*' and '*had*' combined with a participle form of the verb, as in: '*I had <u>left</u> by then.*' In AAVE, such a sentence can be expressed as: '*I <u>had</u> done <u>left</u>.*' or '*I <u>had</u> bin <u>left</u>*', stressing either the completion or the remoteness of the action (or even stressing both with: '*I <u>had</u> bin done <u>left</u>*'). AAVE thus has a rich inventory of aspect markers which are used in very specific ways to emphasize different perspectives of actions being described. Although the words used to mark aspect in AAVE also occur in SAE, and speakers of SAE who are not very familiar with AAVE might think that words such as *done, steady*, and *been/bin* are being used incorrectly in AAVE speech, studies of the patterning of these words reveals they make up a complex system of event-description with very well-defined properties.

Auxiliary verb inversion in questions
A third patterning that can be mentioned much more briefly relates to the use and positioning of 'auxiliary' verbs such as '*have*', '*be*', or '*do*' in AAVE and SAE. In both SAE and AAVE, auxiliary verbs are placed at the beginning of a sentence, before the subject, to signal that a sentence is a question:

    <u>Have</u> you seen John?
    <u>Is</u> John helping you?
    <u>Do</u> you have the time?

However, in more complex sentences, speakers of AAVE also put the auxiliary verb *have/ be/do* before the subject in lower clauses which have the meaning of questions. This does not occur in SAE, which maintains a subject > verb order, as seen in the following sets of sentences (where the relevant sequencing of the subject and the verb in the embedded clause is underlined):

SAE: *Lou asked his wife if she did it.*
I *wanna know what he bought.*

AAVE: *Lou ask his wife did she do it.*
I *wanna know what did he buy.*

What this contrast shows is that AAVE is actually *more* consistent in its ordering of subjects and verbs in clauses which semantically are questions, and SAE is rather inconsistent, inverting subject and auxiliary verbs in main clause questions but not in embedded clause questions. SAE is therefore the 'illogical' variety here. In this paradigm and various others discussed in research on AAVE, it appears that AAVE patterns in a more regular, clearly principled way than standard varieties of English, with syntactic rules being fully general in their application rather than subject to exception.

Many more illustrations of differences between AAVE and SAE could be given as a result of investigations of AAVE carried out over many years, and in each case it could be shown, as in the preceding, that what may appear to be deviant linguistic 'irregularities' to outsiders and non-speakers of AAVE are actually fully rule-governed, logical features of language, and are similar in many ways to patterns found in other, non-stigmatized languages. Careful research into AAVE by linguists since the late 1960s has consistently led to two conclusions which are important for practical issues relating to language use in education and the social treatment of non-standard dialects and their speakers. First, the study of a wide range of linguistic phenomena in AAVE has shown that, contrary to the early opinions of certain psychologists with little expertise in African American language, AAVE is not a randomly created, substandard form of mainstream American English used by people who cannot master the complexities of SAE. Rather, AAVE is found to be a variety of language which is governed by exactly the same type of complex rules that occur in all other human languages, and that the particular properties found in AAVE simply result from the use of a different subset of formal rules, enriched by a distinctive vocabulary. Second, because AAVE does make use of different grammatical and phonological rules and combines these with special elements of vocabulary, the result is that AAVE is indeed quite different from SAE in many *principled* ways. Consequently, young L1 speakers of AAVE should not be expected to be able to function with SAE in schools without some form of assistance and training from their teachers, as was recognized in the Ann Arbor Decision.

The final part of the chapter will consider how educators have attempted to help African American students bridge the gap between their home variety of language and academic English, and the kinds of attitudes that have surrounded the use of AAVE in education. Before going on to this much-discussed and sometimes hotly contentious topic, we will digress for just a moment and reflect on the historical roots of AAVE—where have all the special properties of this variety come from, and what might be known about the origins of AAVE?

Theories of the emergence of AAVE

Among linguists engaged in the study of AAVE, the question of how this variety initially came into existence has generated much debate and there is still a lack of full agreement on how AAVE developed in earlier centuries. Broadly speaking, two different perspectives on the origin of AAVE have been argued for—an 'Anglicist Hypothesis', and a 'Creolist Hypothesis'.

The Anglicist or English Origins Hypothesis suggests that African slaves brought to America from the 17th century onward acquired English from regular, direct contact with white settlers who spoke different regional varieties of the language, including many dialectal forms that were not inherited by SAE. The distinctive features present in modern-day AAVE and not shared by SAE are attributed to properties of regional British English spoken by Anglo-Americans living in the Southern colonies prior to the American revolution, and later on to influence from Southern (white) US English, as it developed differences from English spoken in other parts of the USA. Linguists pursuing the Anglicist Hypothesis have pointed out that a large number of the special features of AAVE can also be found in dialects of English that still exist in Britain and in Southern US English, or in records of dialects presumed to be have been spoken by settlers at the time that slaves were first brought to America from Africa and the Caribbean. AAVE is therefore taken to be an offshoot of the way that English was spoken in different dialectal forms by early white settlers that African slaves had contact with from the 17th century onward, and to contain many relics of these regional forms of English which are not present in modern SAE (Van Herk 2015; Winford 2015).

The Creolist Hypothesis in its first incarnation suggested that the speech of black slaves in America from the 17th to the 19th centuries was actually a widespread creole language, with English as its primary lexifier, and West African languages as important substrate languages (Stewart 1967; Dillard 1972). Noting that the majority of slaves brought to colonies such as South Carolina and Georgia initially came from the Caribbean rather than Africa, and that slaves coming from Caribbean would have most likely been creole speakers, it is suggested that an early creole spread throughout the slave population in America and provided many of the characteristic properties of current AAVE. As support for such a creole origins hypothesis, linguists have shown that various morphosyntactic features found in AAVE can also frequently be observed in creoles around the world. Because AAVE is presently not fully creole-like, however, the Creolist Hypothesis suggests that a process of *de-creolization* subsequently affected the creole, as African Americans increasingly interacted with white Americans following the end of slavery. De-creolization (discussed in chapter 5) would have changed the original creole into a variety much closer to general American English, accounting for why some creole features are still present in AAVE, and also for why AAVE is no longer as strongly creole-like as languages such as Tok Pisin, Kamtok, and Krio, which are mutually unintelligible with their erstwhile lexifier, English. A later, rather weaker version of the Creolist Hypothesis has suggested that the formation of early speech patterns among black Americans was only *influenced* by creole speech, and that there was variation in the predecessor forms of modern-day AAVE according to area, social group, and century, caused by other influences (for example, by regional varieties of English; see Rickford 2015).

The balance of the evidence and argumentation would currently seem to favor the Anglicist position over the strong Creolist Hypothesis, but the issue is far from being fully settled. A major problem affecting the strength of support for either position is the absence of good historical records of the way African Americans actually spoke during the 17th and 18th centuries when pre-modern AAVE was first being formed. This means that most theorizing about early African American language is based on socio-historical and demographic data rather than on clear linguistic data—for example, whether population conditions favored creole formation or not, and what kinds of regional English can be assumed to have been locally present in earlier centuries as models for African slaves to have copied (Winford 2015). Unfortunately, we do not know for sure how slaves in the 17th and 18th centuries spoke, and whether they really developed creole forms or simply adopted features of regional English dialects. This means that the question of the origins of AAVE cannot, in fact, be conclusively resolved for lack of decisive evidence. While the origins issue might not seem to be one that would have much consequence for contemporary African Americans, we will shortly see that it can be given significance, as we come to discuss the Ebonics controversy and whether African American language should be considered to be a form of English (as suggested by the English Origins Hypothesis), or a direct descendant of African languages and not a form of English (as would be more supported by a Creolist Hypothesis attributing heavy influence to African substrate languages).

AAVE and education

Because of the many differences between AAVE and SAE, children whose home language is AAVE generally have a much harder time mastering English literacy skills than children who speak varieties of mainstream American English—the way that SAE is written often does not correspond closely to the way that AAVE-speaking children would naturally express themselves. In some instances the problems arise because the pronunciation of AAVE and standard English are different, and this affects children's ability to learn spelling well, if their regular home language is AAVE. Other problems may arise from differences in the grammatical conventions used in AAVE and SAE. Trudgill (1974a) provides useful illustrations of basic difficulties that may occur when young African Americans set about learning to read and write in the medium commonly used in schools in the USA, Standard American English, drawing on original work by Labov (1972). In the area of pronunciation, it is noted that sounds which are distinct in certain words in SAE may sometimes be pronounced in the same way in AAVE. For example, many AAVE speakers will pronounce the vowel sounds in words such as *pin* and *pen, tin* and *ten* in an identical way, so that the words sound the same. As a result of such pronunciation forms, AAVE-speaking children may tend to misspell words containing the vowels *i* and *e* more often than speakers of mainstream American English and have greater difficulties in following standard spelling conventions in their writing. Because English spelling often does not reflect actual pronunciation in a consistent way, this might not be thought to be a special problem. Teachers are normally aware of the problems of pairs of words in standard English which are pronounced the same but spelled differently ('homophones'), for example *ate/eight, flea/flee, bare/bear, cell/sell, days/daze*, and so on, and therefore warn children of the potential confusions they may make in their spelling in these cases.[24] However, if teachers are not aware of AAVE to the same degree, they will probably not be able to help AAVE-speaking children in the same way. Special knowledge of AAVE among teachers would clearly help in such instances.

Elsewhere there are problems which could perhaps either be phonological (to do with pronunciation) or grammatical, and it is not immediately obvious which aspect of language is causing a problem. Consider the following sentence, which might be produced by an AAVE-speaking child.

'*I pass by the school yesterday.*'

Because the adverb *yesterday* is used, the event which the speaker is describing is situated in the past. One would therefore naturally expect the verb to occur with the past tense marker *–ed*, and be pronounced as *passed*, but young AAVE speakers may often not do this. Labov (1972) and Trudgill (1974a) note that there might be three different reasons why *–ed* is frequently not heard on verbs referring to past time events in the speech of African American children. Any one of the factors described in A–C in the following could potentially be the cause of this difference from standard English.

A. Young AAVE-speaking children might have no clear concept of past tense (i.e., they might not understand that language can specify explicitly that an event occurred in the past rather than some other point in time).
B. AAVE-speaking children may be aware of what past tense is, but not employ *–ed* as a marker of past tense.
C. Maybe *–ed* is understood to be a past tense marker, but it is not pronounced on verbs in AAVE for phonological reasons, because this would result in a final sequence of consonants on most verbs, and AAVE tends to avoid word-final consonant clusters. We have already seen that there is an active process of consonant cluster reduction which occurs in AAVE. Possibly this applies to simplify *passed*, which ends in two consonant sounds (*s* and *d*, not separated by any pronounced vowel, as the spelled, intervening *e* is silent), so that speakers actually produce *pass* in place of *passed*. The form *pass* ends in only one consonant sound.

Hypothesis A can easily be discounted because in other instances young AAVE speakers do in fact produce past tense forms which are used in a normal way to contrast with present tense forms. When a verb has an *irregular* past tense form and is not combined with *–ed* (for example, *went, ate, began, bought, came, chose,* etc.), such past tense forms regularly occur in AAVE speech.

24. For a list of 479 homophones present in American English, visit: http://l-lists.com/en/lists/rqq8n9.html. For British English, see the 441 homophones listed at: http://www.singularis.ltd.uk/bifroest/misc/homophones-list.html.

One way of trying to find out whether either hypothesis B or C is correct involves having AAVE speakers participate in a pronunciation exercise which probes whether they understand –*ed* as indicating past tense, or whether they do not register this suffix as meaning anything at all. In a series of tests, AAVE-speaking children were asked to pronounce sentences such as the following (having first read the sentence to themselves in order to understand it):

When I passed by the notice-board, I read the posters.

It is expected that an AAVE-speaking child will not pronounce the –*ed* suffix on *passed*, but if the child understands this marker as indicating past tense, the child should give the second verb *read* a past tense pronunciation (as if spelled *red*, rhyming with *bed*). If, however, the child simply does not pay any attention to the –*ed* inflection and does not register it as encoding past tense, the child might be anticipated to pronounce *read* as a present tense form, as if spelled *reed* (rhyming with *feed*). Test results showed that most AAVE-speaking children pronounced the verb *read* in such sentences as a present tense form, indicating that they actually do not understand the –*ed* suffix to signal past tense. This is an interesting discovery, because it demonstrates that this particular problem has to do with reading and with linking the form –*ed* to the notion past tense, and is not due to phonology and consonant cluster simplification—which would have been an alternate, quite plausible explanation. It would be beneficial if the results of this kind of research could be used by teachers to improve their understanding of AAVE and the difficulties faced by young African Americans in acquiring literacy in standard English, and thus lead to the creation of strategies to help AAVE speakers overcome these difficulties. However, during much of the 20th century, little real attention was given by educators to AAVE itself, and attempts to teach literacy skills took a quite different approach.

For many decades toward the end of the 20th century, a dominant classroom strategy adopted by teachers in schools with African American students aimed for the actual *elimination* of students' home language, through suppressing its use within schools and presenting AAVE as substandard, incorrect English which students should ideally abandon (Smitherman 2015). Standard English forms were regularly promoted as the 'correct' way to speak, and teachers would continually pressure young black students to switch from AAVE patterns to those of mainstream American English, believing that AAVE was preventing students from making progress in school and therefore should be replaced by use of SAE.

Such an elimination-and-substitution type approach has been criticized for various reasons. Language is used by speakers in ways to identify and define themselves socially, so when young African Americans use AAVE, they express solidarity with their friends and family, and identify themselves as being members of the same ethnic group. When teachers tell children that the way they speak is incorrect and substandard, this can be interpreted in a very negative way as characterizing *all* speakers of children's home language as linguistically incompetent on account of their 'substandard' speech. In turn, such a characterization of AAVE may cause hostility toward the learning of standard English, as children feel that SAE and its promotion represents an attack on the integrity and standing of their home social group. Most young speakers may therefore not want to abandon their AAVE speech in favor of SAE. Because AAVE serves to identify them with their peer group and friends, schoolchildren will not want to risk losing their friends by changing the way that they regularly speak.

After many years in which failed attempts were made to eliminate AAVE from children's speech in school, educators reached the conclusion that the best way to help African American children overcome difficulties created by differences between AAVE and SAE is not to attempt to replace AAVE with SAE. Such an approach was consistently rejected by speakers of AAVE and did not lead to the successful learning of reading and writing in school. A better solution therefore needed to be found to help AAVE-speaking children acquire literacy skills, which would not involve the full loss of their home variety of speech.

The challenges faced by African American students in making satisfactory progress in schools were first significantly highlighted in the Ann Arbor trial and decision in Michigan in 1974, as discussed earlier in the current chapter. The judge in the Ann Arbor case ruled that AAVE had the potential to constitute a barrier to educational success whenever standard English was used in the classroom and teachers did not adjust their teaching in any way to compensate for the differences between SAE and AAVE. Schools in Michigan were accordingly told that they should create training programs for teachers to help them acquire better knowledge of AAVE as a way to improve their teaching of literacy skills to African American students. However, the Ann Arbor initiative was ultimately not as successful as initially hoped, as many teachers were confused about how to use the information they had gained about AAVE in the classroom. The program was subsequently abandoned after just two years.

Twenty years later, the educational problems in inner city schools with large numbers of African American students had not been solved, and many African American students were still making much slower progress than other groups of students, often being held back from proceeding into higher grades or being categorized as learning disabled and assigned to special schools. Educators commonly blamed the lack of achievement of African American students on aspects of their AAVE speech and their lack of understanding standard classroom English.

Frustrated by this general situation, and encouraged by the earlier legal decision that had been given in the Ann Arbor case (despite its lack of conversion into any major practical success), in 1996 teachers in the Oakland District School Board, California, proposed a new initiative to use AAVE in the teaching of standard English. The proposals were set forth in a resolution publicized in December 1996, and then modified in an important way in January 1997. The first version of the resolution caused tremendous public debate and heated reactions from many segments of society, including many prominent African Americans. Modification of the resolution and its restatement in a less radical and 'inflammatory' way in 1997 were not enough to quell the uproar that the wording of the first resolution had brought about, and the high level of negative public reaction to the proposals ultimately led to the abandonment of the initiative. In order to appreciate what caused the controversy, referred to as 'one of biggest linguistic brouhahas in the USA in the twentieth century' in Baugh (2004: 305), it is necessary to understand the way the first resolution was stated, and its use of the word 'Ebonics.'

The term 'Ebonics' was first coined in 1973 from a combination of 'ebony' and 'phonics', and used to refer to the range of speech patterns found among African Americans. 'Ebonics' was considered useful as an alternative to the term 'Black English', as it did not make use of the word 'English', and so could be used to refer to the speech of African Americans without implying that this was necessarily a form of English. When the Oakland school board distributed their first resolution, it significantly made use of the term 'Ebonics' and 'African Language Systems' as a way to refer to the language spoken by African American students in the school district, and stated that Ebonics was *not* to be considered a form of English but a *different language* system, one primarily related to the Niger-Congo language group in Africa. This important part of the Oakland proposal caught the attention of people throughout the USA and led to enormous public debate on television and radio. The Oakland school board proposed that special funds be allocated and used for bilingual education in Oakland schools, so that students speaking Ebonics could receive special classes in English and become bilingual in English and Ebonics, their mother tongue.

The characterization of African American students' speech as a different language from English, and the proposal to institute bilingual education, caused heated reactions from many quarters. One important consequence of the classification of Ebonics as a distinct language, genetically unrelated to English (i.e., not a dialect of English), was financial. If Ebonics were to be considered a distinct language and qualify for bilingual education support, this might mean that schools throughout the USA with African American students would be eligible to apply for government funds to pay for new bilingual programs. Reacting to such a possibility, the Secretary of Education at the time, Richard Riley, immediately denied that Ebonics was a distinct language, and declared that government funds set aside for bilingual education support could not be used to assist African Americans, whom Riley referred to as speakers of Black English, hence a dialect of English:

> Elevating Black English to the status of a language is not the way to raise standards of achievement in our schools and for our students. The administration's policy is that Ebonics is a nonstandard form of English and not a foreign language. (Richard Riley, Secretary of Education).

Among the African American community, there was also much aggravated criticism of the Oakland school board's reference to African American speech as a separate language and its apparent proposal to make use of 'Ebonics' in the classroom. Jesse Jackson and other well-known, high-profile African Americans argued that it would be disastrous for the development of African American children if they were to be schooled in 'Ebonics' and taught that it was a different language from English.

To some extent, the outrage voiced by Jesse Jackson and others may have been caused by misunderstandings of the Oakland proposal which were spread in the media. For example, opponents of the resolution claimed that children would be taught to read, write, and speak AAVE/Ebonics and not be taught to communicate in standard English, but this was not the intention of the Oakland school board at all, and a primary goal of the Ebonics resolution was to help young African Americans learn standard classroom English. However, mischaracterizations of the Ebonics proposal were very frequently presented in TV talk shows and on the radio, and their sensational value served to inflame the situation further. A more accurate description of issues relating to the Ebonics proposal was issued by the *Linguistics Society of America*, but not much attention was paid to it in the media, and the spread of incorrect information in the media caused great public antipathy toward the Oakland school board and its Ebonics proposal.

As a result of the extreme reactions caused by the December 1996 resolution, the Oakland school board changed some of the more controversial aspects of its wording, and shifted its position to what it hoped would be a less provocative and more acceptable stance. The differences in the December 1996 and January 1997 versions of the resolution are clearly illustrated in Baugh (2004: 312–313). The new, 1997 resolution clarified that its primary goal was to 'move students from the language patterns they bring in to school to English proficiency', and impart 'the acquisition and mastery of English language skills'[25] rather than to teach Ebonics itself, hence transitional use of Ebonics and not the maintenance and development of Ebonics. In fact, the reworded version of the proposal was also much more vague about the kinds of ways that Ebonics would be made use of, and instead of stating that Ebonics would be the primary medium of education in the classroom, it simply called for a recognition of language differences in the home speech of African American students as a way to help improve their proficiency in English in school.

Despite this move to a less controversial stance in the revised resolution, the degree of negative public reaction to the Oakland educators' initiative had become so acute that not much attention was paid to the rewording of the resolution in January 1997, and the initiative was ultimately shelved by the Oakland board. Baugh (2004: 315–16) writes that 'Stung by hostile reactions to their efforts by blacks and whites alike, Oakland educators eventually dropped all reference to Ebonics in their educational plans.' The Ebonics initiative thus unfortunately failed to activate and test any new pedagogical approach to AAVE in schools, and for some time after 1997 most educators hesitated to attempt further innovations with AAVE-techniques.

Positive approaches adopted in the 21st century: bi-dialectalism, contrastive analysis, and code-switching

In the first two decades of the 21st century, new programs focused on helping children whose home language is AAVE have been established in various parts of the USA and positive progress has been made, implementing and developing further ideas that were actually discussed through the 1990s—bi-dialectalism and the positive valuation of AAVE alongside mainstream American English, using contrastive analysis and code-switching as techniques for the learning and use of standard classroom English. *Bi-dialectalism* is an approach which promotes respect for both AAVE and standard English, and emphasizes that both varieties of English have value and are useful for different kinds of interactions and areas of life. Children are taught to take pride in their home language and are encouraged to continue using AAVE

---

25. Resolution No. 9697-0063 of the Oakland Board of Education, January 15, 1997.

with their family and friends, but standard English is presented as being the language form appropriate for use in reading and writing and in formal communication with people who are not speakers of AAVE. Thus rather than attempting to eliminate AAVE from a child's speech, bi-dialectalism helps children supplement their home language with a proficiency in mainstream American English for use in certain domains, and the result aimed for is that children can control both AAVE and SAE and *code-switch* between the two varieties when necessary.[26]

As a way to assist the learning of standard English, teachers compare and contrast differences between AAVE and standard English in grammar and pronunciation in a technique known as *contrastive analysis*. For example, variation in the use of the words '*it*' and '*there*' in presentational sentences in standard English and AAVE will be highlighted, and children will be made aware that AAVE/African American language (AAL) uses *there* in situations that standard English uses *it*, as in the following sentences:

Mainstream American English	AAL/home language
There's a store near my house called 'Bogo'.	*It's a store near my house called Bogo.*
There's a dog barking in the yard.	*It's a dog barking in the yard.*

Students are taught how to identify which features of language are specific to their home language, which are different in standard English, and how to translate accurately between the two varieties. Hollie et al. (2015) provide an illustration of a classroom activity that involves the discussion of grammatical differences between AAVE and standard English which precedes 'code-switching' translation from one variety into the other. The following teacher-student exchanges took place in a third grade classroom in South Central Los Angeles, filmed in 2005. One portion of the class was a discussion of multiple negation, which occurs in AAVE but not standard English. The first three AAVE ('home language') sentences with instances of multiple negation were written on the board, and then discussed by the teacher and the class. Following this, students were asked to translate/code-switch the sentences into standard English ('school language').

(Sentences written on board)
1. My sister don't never share with me.
2. I don't have no pencil.
3. Grace is bold because she don't take nothing from nobody!

Teacher: 'Who can explain what multiple negation is?'

Student: 'Multiple negation is when we use more than one negative word in a sentence.'

Teacher: 'When we use more than one negative word in a sentence, are we using school language or home language?'

26. Children growing up in countries such as Germany, Italy, Thailand, and China often become bi-dialectal in a regional dialect of German/Italian/Chinese/Thai, which they use at home and in informal interactions with local people, and standard German/Italian/Thai/Mandarin Chinese, which is learned in schools and used for academic purposes and communicating with people from outside the local region. Bi-dialectalism is very common around the world, and consequently a feasible goal to aim for in AAVE communities in the USA.

Class: 'Home language!'

Teacher: 'Today, we are code-switching instead of proofreading. Can someone tell me the difference between code-switching and proofreading?'

Student: 'Proofreading is to correct mistakes, but code-switching doesn't have any mistakes because it's our home language.'

Teacher: 'That's right, it's not mistakes. The sentences you see on the board are examples of sentences that we can use in our home language. There's nothing wrong with our home language at all. We just have to make sure we know how to code-switch our home language when we are speaking and writing in situations that call for school language. Before we code-switch these sentences, let's read them.'

The use of contrastive analysis and training in code-switching/translation has proved highly effective in making young AAVE-speakers aware of the differences between standard English and their home language, and how to transition from one to the other when this is required by the social situation. An early pilot study carried out in the Chicago area in (1989) compared instruction using contrastive analysis with traditional techniques (Taylor 1989). African American students from inner city Chicago who used significant amounts of AAVE in their writing in Aurora University were divided into two sets, an 'experimental' group who were instructed in standard English writing through the use of contrastive analysis, and a 'control' group who received instruction in standard English by means of conventional teaching methods.

After 11 weeks, students in the experimental contrastive analysis group showed a 59% decrease in their use of AAVE in their writing, demonstrating the benefits of the technique, whereas students in the control group, taught via traditional techniques, actually registered an 8.5% increase in their use of AAVE in writing. With regard to one particular feature, the omission of third person singular agreement –s from present tense verbs in AAVE (AAVE: *He help me every day* vs. SAE: *He help̱s me every day*), students who had received contrastive analysis demonstrated a huge drop in their use of the AAVE form when writing standard English, almost 92%. Carefully drawing attention to specific differences between AAVE and SAE and practicing translation thus heightens students linguistic awareness of SAE and AAVE and enables them to separate the two varieties better in writing and speech (Rickford 1999).

The use of contrastive analysis and code-switching in programs emphasizing bi-dialectalism has now spread further around the USA, and is helping students acquire literacy skills successfully in many inner city areas.[27] A good example of a school which took up the bi-dialectal contrastive analysis approach in 2003 was a charter school in Los Angeles called the Culture and Language Academy of Sciences (CLAS). Hollie et al. (2015: 600) note that:

---

27. For further discussion of code-switching between AAVE and mainstream American English, see Mills and Washington (2015).

CLAS has become a national model for culturally and linguistically responsive teaching and for having success with African American students. At CLAS, we validate and affirm AAL [African American language] starting at kindergarten, where students learn about their linguistic heritage as Africans in America. Students then learn the dimensions of SE [standard English] through the lens of their home languages. Contrastive analysis is a primary teaching strategy as well. CLAS has maintained high achievement data according to the California Standards Test and the Academic Performance Index API), specifically in English Language Arts, when compared to the local district and the state.

The bi-dialectal contrastive analysis approach not only seems to help children learn to read and write in standard English more effectively than traditional techniques, it also has important psychological effects for students' attitude toward their home language as well as standard English. As students are encouraged to continue using AAVE with friends and family, and regular classroom discussion of the differences between AAVE and standard English is carried out in a very positive way, this builds important respect for the value of the home language, and helps avoids many of the problems which result from stigmatizing AAVE and attempting to eradicate it from children's speech. Dialect awareness programs, Wolfram (1999: 53) stresses, must 'combat the stereotype that vernacular varieties are nothing more than imperfect attempts to speak the standard variety', and this is being done successfully in schools which have switched to this kind of approach. There would consequently seem to be cause for new hope in addressing the educational challenges which have long been faced by speakers of non-standard varieties such as AAVE, and helping these speakers achieve linguistic equality with their peers. Now that effective teaching strategies for AAVE-speakers have been shown to be available, hopefully the news will spread and schools will increasingly incorporate these techniques and the positive perspectives on AAVE which bi-dialectalism promotes.

Summary

In the first part of this chapter on language issues in the USA, we followed the evolving historical relation of English to other languages, and the dominance of the former in government, education, and the workplace. The second half of the chapter has discussed how significant differences between standard English and other dialect forms of the language can lead to problems in the area of education, focusing on AAVE as a representative of the latter due to the degree to which it shows differences from SAE and the attention its potential use in schools has drawn from educators, politicians, and the general public. AAVE-speaking children (and all children who speak varieties of English markedly different from SAE) face considerable challenges when attempting to master academic English and to learn how to read and write. Educators need to find ways to solve these problems and give young African Americans the same opportunities for success in school that SAE-speaking children have. The chapter has noted that attempts to simply eliminate children's AAVE and replace it with standard English should be avoided for social and psychological reasons and have also been found to be ineffective, just as immersing children who are mother-tongue speakers of other languages in monolingual English classes does not result in them learning English without special, additional tuition. Other pedagogical strategies therefore need to be tried to provide dialect speakers with good, equal opportunities for educational advancement. One initiative attempted in Oakland, California, in 1996, proposed increased use of AAVE/Ebonics in schools as part of bilingual education programs which also supported the learning of standard English, but it did so in a way that unfortunately alienated much of the African American community and caused heavy criticism from other sections of the public.

Finally, just as there has been new growth in the popularity of dual language immersion in different parts of the country, with AAVE there are now also signs of positive new developments, inspired by creative, energetic individuals and schools which are trying out and succeeding with new teaching methods in public charter schools around the nation. The hope is that this time these efforts will be sustained and supported by the general population and will facilitate greater educational success among children whose home language is not a form of mainstream/standard American English, the language which has long been dominant in the USA.

Suggestions for further reading and activities

1. Find out about the legal case *Lau vs. Nichols*, 1974. What was the importance of this case, what triggered the lawsuit, and what were the consequences of the Supreme Court's ruling?
2. If you live in the USA, select a minority language spoken in your area and try to find out what government services are made available in this language, and also what private sector support there is for the language. For example, is it used on local radio and TV, are there local newspapers in the language, are there private schools offering instruction in the language, is the language used in places of worship for sermons and prayers, etc.? If you live in another country which has linguistic minorities, try to find out what services and information are provided for speakers of minority languages in this country, and compare the level of support with what you know about the USA.
3. Read the following article about making English the official language of the USA and discuss the potential consequences of giving English this role. What positive and negative effects might there be?

    Wiley, Terrence. 1998. What happens after English is declared the official language of the United States? Lessons from case histories. In Douglas Kibbee (ed.), *Language legislation and linguistic rights*. Amsterdam: John Benjamins, 179–195.

4. Watch the 2007 movie *English Only in America?* produced by Anne Diack and Julie Berry for the Films Media Group (length: 25 minutes). How do the interviews and discussion in the film affect your understanding of the Official English debate?
5. Access the internet sites of *US English* (www.us.english.org) and *English First* (www.englishfirst.org), to gather more current information on the campaign to make English official in different states and in different areas of life. Also access the website of the

Institute for Language and Education Policy (http://www.elladvocates.org/), for discussion of language issues in the USA from a very different perspective, supporting the maintenance of heritage languages and bilingual education.

6. Read the following article which emphasizes the need to maintain languages other than English in the USA. Do you agree with the points made by the author?

    Fishman, Joshua. 2004. Multilingualism and non-English mother tongues. In Edward Finegan and John Rickford (eds.), *Language in the USA*. Cambridge: Cambridge University Press, 115–132.

7. For further, detailed discussion of the contentious issue of bilingual education up until the mid-1990s, consult the following volume:

    Crawford, James. 1995. *Bilingual education: history, politics, theory, and practice*. Los Angeles: Bilingual Education Services.

8. Read John Baugh's article on using the linguistic analysis of AAVE to help teach literacy and other educational skills to young African Americans. What suggestions does Baugh have for improving the success of African American students?

    Baugh, John. 2001. Applying linguistic knowledge of African American English to help students learn and teachers teach. In Sonja Lanehart (ed.), *Sociocultural and historical contexts of African American English*. Amsterdam: John Benjamins, 319–330.

9. View the first half of the movie *Do You Speak American? Out West* [volume 3 of a three-part series produced by Films for the Humanities and Sciences] to learn more about Chicano English, AAVE, 'Valley Girl' speech, and 'Surfer Dude' English spoken in California. The section on AAVE demonstrates the classroom use of contrastive analysis and code-switching in the teaching of mainstream American English in an inner city school in Los Angeles. How effective do you think the use of these techniques seems to be?

10. Read the article 'Ebonics and Its Controversy' by John Baugh, and research more about the Oakland Ebonics initiative via the internet. From what you learn, why do you think the Ebonics proposal caused so much heated public discussion, becoming the number one story featured on television and attracting more viewers than other sensational stories of the time, such as the O. J. Simpson murder trial?

    Baugh, John. 2004. Ebonics and its controversy. In Edward Finegan and John Rickford (eds.), *Language in the USA*. Cambridge: Cambridge University Press, 305–318.

8

Bilingualism

Introduction

Previous chapters have described many kinds of situations in which multiple languages come into contact with each other, and there are people who use more than one language in their daily life—for example, bilingual members of minority groups, code-switching in multilingual societies, international commerce carried out in English as global language by second-language speakers. The ability to communicate in two or more languages is very widespread around the world, and it is often said that over half of the world's population may indeed be either bilingual or multilingual, knowing more than two languages. This chapter considers the important phenomenon of bilingualism in greater depth, focusing on how the knowledge of two languages is actually established in individuals and how bilingualism may provide benefits to speakers in different ways as they navigate their way through life. Topics to be examined in the chapter include the following:

- How do children, adolescents, and adults become bilingual?
- How are the two languages spoken by a bilingual mentally stored and accessed when spoken?
- Are all bilinguals alike in the way they learn and use different languages?
- What are the advantages of being bilingual? Are there any potential disadvantages or dangers to result from early exposure to two languages, for example 'language confusion'?
- How can research into bilingualism help shape language policy in education?

What does it mean to be bilingual?

The first task in our study of individual bilingualism is to clarify exactly what is meant by use of the term '**bilingual**' and to explain how it is understood and applied in the current chapter. In some descriptions of bilingualism, a very broad definition of the term 'bilingual' is used, and any person with even a basic knowledge of two languages is classified as bilingual, including new second-language learners who have only just begun to study an additional language in school or university. Here, however, we will make use of the term 'bilingual' in a more restrictive and traditional way, reserving it for individuals who have a significantly more advanced proficiency in two languages and the ability to switch between two languages without difficulty or hesitation in a range of different situations, as noted in the following definition:

Application of the term 'bilingual'
A person should be considered to be bilingual if he/she can communicate in two different languages fluently and effectively and without hesitation in a wide variety of common situations in everyday life.

Being bilingual means that a person can interact easily with other speakers of the languages he/she knows and talk confidently about any of the kinds of non-specialist topics that might come up in regular daily conversation—for example, social relations with family and friends, aspects of a person's work, items of popular culture, and current news events. A person is *not* considered to be bilingual if they can communicate effectively in a second language only within certain very restricted contexts and not in other common situations, for example an air traffic controller who has mastered the technical vocabulary necessary to interact with airline pilots and provide information about landing conditions in airports, but who would not be able to use this 'second language' to engage in simple conversation about other, personal matters, or a Japanese high school student who has learned how to translate very specific grammar points from written Japanese into written English, but would find it difficult to communicate orally in English in a spontaneous way if visiting an English-speaking country.

We also need to clarify how we will refer to the two languages spoken by bilinguals. Throughout the chapter, these will regularly be referred to as L1 and L2 ('language one' and 'language two'), but our use of L1 and L2 here should be noted to be somewhat different from the use of these terms in earlier chapters, where L1 typically represents a person's mother tongue and L2 is often a second language learned later in life and not to the same high level as the mother tongue. With bilinguals, it is possible that two languages may be acquired at the same time and to a broadly similar level of advanced proficiency—young bilinguals may become successful native speakers of two languages, and in this sense have two 'mother tongues'. The use of L1 and L2 in the current chapter should therefore not be taken to imply any *necessary* difference in the status (time of learning, level of proficiency) of a person's two languages. As we will see, a number of different outcomes may result from significant exposure to two separate languages. During the course of the chapter, 'L1' and 'L2' will simply be used to refer to the pair of languages involved in a person's bilingual experience, no matter when and how this unfolds over time and what level of linguistic achievement is ultimately attained.[1]

---

1. In some studies of bilingualism, the terms L1 and L2 are avoided because they may lead readers to suppose that L1 is acquired before L2 and to a higher level. In place of L1 and L2, the terms 'language A' and 'language Alpha' are sometimes adopted (avoiding use of the term 'language B' as this might suggest an ordering of acquisition relative to language A). As 'language A' and 'language Alpha' are a little clumsy to use, the chapter will stick to use of the shorter forms 'L1' and 'L2', which nevertheless do occur as terms in many works on bilingualism.

> **INDIVIDUAL VS. SOCIETAL BILINGUALISM**
> The term 'bilingual' is often used to characterize both individuals and societies, but it is important to understand how the term may be applied in different ways. Countries which are officially bilingual, such as Canada, Belgium, and Cameroon, may have populations in which two languages are commonly spoken and have special recognized roles as official languages, but may not contain large numbers of individuals who are bilingual. For example, in Canada, where English and French are both official languages and are widely used, it is estimated that only 17.5% of the population can actually speak both languages (2011 Census). Referring to a society (or a country, or a region) as being bilingual or multilingual does not necessarily mean that individual bilingualism/multilingualism is widespread among the members of its population. In fact, research has suggested that individual bilingualism may actually be more common in territories which are *not* officially bilingual.

Factors affecting the successful establishment of bilingualism

In approaching the study of bilingualism and the investigation of individual bilinguals, a number of important questions need to be considered, as a way to classify bilinguals and understand and compare their linguistic behavior.

How is bilingualism first established?

Where do people come into contact with the two languages they acquire over time? Is bilingualism primarily achieved in the home through linguistic contact with family members and relatives who speak two languages, or is one language acquired at home and a second language learned in interactions which take place elsewhere, either in school or in the local neighborhood with same-age friends who speak a different language?

When is bilingualism established?

Some bilinguals grow up hearing two languages in their immediate environment, often the home, and develop an ability in both languages at the same time. Such individuals are known as *simultaneous bilinguals*. Other bilinguals, however, may have a different experience, and come into contact with two languages in a sequential way, acquiring one language first before being exposed to and learning a second language. This route to knowledge of two languages is referred to as *successive* or *consecutive bilingualism*. With such a sequencing of exposure to two different languages, it is relevant to consider how far apart in time the L1 and L2 are acquired, as this potentially has consequences for how successful the process of acquisition is achieved, and how an individual's two languages may mentally be stored in certain instances, as we will later see. When a young child is exposed to two languages simultaneously in an appropriately structured and sufficient way (more on this soon), a native-like ability in both languages can develop, and parallel results may also be achieved when there is sequenced contact with two languages, providing this occurs at an early age, ideally before adolescence. If, however, an individual only begins to acquire a second language at a later age, the level of bilingualism attained may be lower than that of early consecutive bilinguals. Research into age-of-acquisition and L2 proficiency will be discussed later on in the chapter.

Why are the two languages being learned/acquired?

Various situations lead individuals of different ages to come into contact with and acquire two languages, and the social background to a person's bilingual exposure can affect its outcome in various ways. In many cases, clear socio-economic factors may trigger bilingualism, as, for example, when children grow up speaking a minority language in the home, and then learn a more widely spoken majority language when they enter school or pre-school classes. In other instances, parents who are native speakers of different languages may want their offspring to learn both the mother's and father's language as a way of connecting to the cultures associated with those languages. Later in life, certain individuals may themselves decide to acquire a second language for professional or cultural reasons. In all cases of bilingual acquisition, personal motivation and others' encouragement and positive valuation of both L1 and L2 are important factors which will help the successful establishment and maintenance of bilingualism.

Are both languages acquired and maintained at the same advanced level?

A distinction can often be made between *balanced bilinguals* and *non-balanced bilinguals*. The former type of bilingual establishes and maintains an identical high level of ability in two languages, whereas the latter is fluent in both languages and can use both languages without hesitation in common everyday situations, but is nevertheless stronger in one of the two languages, and weaker in the other. Fully balanced bilinguals are quite uncommon, because bilinguals tend to use their two languages in different kinds of interactions and with different people—one language may more often be used in informal interactions with family and friends, and the other may more commonly be used in schools, spoken at work, and occur in other more formal acts of communication. The regular use of a language in a particular domain of interaction naturally leads to an expansion of its vocabulary with new specialized terms, and such vocabulary growth may not occur evenly in a bilingual's two languages. The result is that an individual's knowledge of words in their L1 and L2 may often not be balanced, and a person may be more confident and find it easier to speak about certain topics in one of their two languages.

Two kinds of non-balanced distributions of L1/L2 vocabulary may occur. In one situation, it is possible that all of the words known in L1 are also known in L2, but L2 additionally contains other vocabulary items never learned in L1. For example, a bilingual who grows up learning and using both L1 and L2 in the home may develop a large, parallel vocabulary for interacting with family members about informal, personal and everyday issues, but then expand the vocabulary of L2 further through using this in school, university, and the workplace. Many words learned in L2 will therefore not be known by the bilingual in L1. In another situation, L1 and L2 may share a very large core of words, but both L1 and L2 may contain certain additional items of vocabulary that have not been learned in the other language. Hence both L1 and L2 may be used for various specialized kinds of interaction, as well as being regularly spoken in everyday informal communication. For example, an adult bilingual working as a motor mechanic in an ethnically Chinese part of Los Angeles might use Mandarin to talk about technical aspects of car repair with his customers, but switch to English to discuss aspects of his child's education with teachers in a school environment, and the bilingual's vocabulary will contain words in one language which are not known (or not so easily accessed from memory) in the other.

Frequency of use may in certain cases also lead to an established *dominance* relation between L1 and L2. Although a person may have learned how to talk fluently about everyday topics in both L1 and L2, if one of these languages tends to be used more often in day-to-day life, this can result in it becoming easier and more automatic for a bilingual to use—a 'practice effect'—and as this reinforcement of the language increases over time, an individual may establish a dominance in a particular language and use it in most of the situations where either L1 or L2 could in fact be used. For example, supposing a person who is bilingual in French and German uses both these languages in the home with family members but only speaks German when at work, over time, such a bilingual may well become dominant in German, and start to use German more and more in the home, bringing the language home from work. As German is so regularly activated in the mind of this person and is used in communication during the day, it becomes the default, first language the speaker tends to use when he/she knows that others around will understand it, even if the speaker's other language could also naturally be used in the same linguistic contexts. When a bilingual is dominant in one of the languages they are fluent in, this language is normally listed first when referring to the bilingual's two languages; hence a German-French bilingual would be someone who is dominant in German, and a Swedish-English bilingual would refer to a person dominant in Swedish.[2] During the development of bilingualism in children, it also occurs quite frequently that one of the two languages being acquired becomes dominant (perhaps only temporarily) and is used more automatically than the other, especially when the child receives more input in this language.[3]

---

2. In instances where a bilingual is not obviously dominant in one language, the two languages are simply listed alphabetically, for example English-Swedish, and French-German. Such alphabetically listed pairs of languages are actually ambiguous in the information they provide, and could be used to refer to someone who is not dominant in either of the languages he/she knows, or is dominant in the first-listed language, so sometimes more explicit information needs to be provided.

3. Is language dominance the same as 'strength' in a particular language? In other words, if we say that a person who is bilingual in French and German is dominant in German, does this mean that such a person is necessarily stronger in German and has a greater proficiency in German than in French? The answer here is 'no', because our definition of bilingualism presumes that a bilingual is fully fluent in both the languages he/she knows. Being dominant in one of these two languages simply means that a bilingual tends to use this language more than the other language he/she speaks. In other approaches to bilingualism which define bilingualism more loosely as having some functional knowledge of two languages (but not necessarily fluency and the ability to use both languages confidently in most everyday situations), the term 'dominance' may be used somewhat differently, and may refer to the language a person knows best and is strongest in, normally the mother tongue.

Are there differences in the bilingual's attitude towards the two languages?

Bilinguals may often maintain different attitudes toward the two languages they know, and sometimes these attitudes can undergo change during the course of a person's lifetime. Various bilinguals may have a *preference* for speaking one of their two languages. In many instances a person may feel a greater personal attachment to one particular language and may feel more comfortable using this language in close, emotional interactions with family and friends. Such a situation is common with consecutive bilinguals who acquire one language in the home and a second language in school. The home-acquired language may have strongly positive associations with family, security, caring, and a person's ethnic culture which the school-acquired language does not, and so remains a bilingual's preferred language, even if the requirements of daily communication cause the school-acquired language to become the bilingual's dominant language (hence a bilingual's preferred language is not necessarily his/her dominant language—the latter may simply be used more frequently due to the kinds of interactions the bilingual has in everyday life).

Interestingly, it is also found that children who are consecutive bilinguals may sometimes develop a preference for their school-acquired language, rather than the language acquired in the home. This may occur when the former is highly valued by others the child comes into contact with, and the latter, home language is regularly stigmatized. In such situations, children from minority groups may increasingly wish to identify with other majority-language speakers around them though use of the school-learned language, and simultaneously distance themselves from the language they first acquired within the home.

Finally, children who grow up as simultaneous bilinguals may experience different preferences for L1/L2 as they mature and develop new connections with speakers of the two languages. The positive associations which cause a particular language to be a bilingual's preferred language may therefore change over time as young bilinguals are exposed to different influences during their childhood and adolescence. The results of language preference may also be significant for the long-term maintenance of bilingualism. If children developing a bilingual competence establish a strong preference for one of the two languages they are acquiring/have acquired, this may ultimately lead to decreased use of the other language and an eventual loss of competence, threatening the continuation of bilingual proficiency in an individual.

Is the development of bilingualism stimulated with sufficient, varied input from both L1 and L2?

In order for children to successfully become bilingual, they must be exposed to a significant amount of linguistic input from both target languages on a daily basis throughout their childhood years. This input should ideally be provided by multiple, different speakers of the L1 and L2, and should be presented in a contextually consistent way (soon to be described) in order to avoid potential confusion in learning. Children themselves must also actively engage in interactions with those speaking to them in both L1 and L2, and must be constantly encouraged to make use of and practice the two languages they are acquiring.

Simultaneous bilingual acquisition is a process most commonly initiated with children in the home environment from a very early age, when two different languages are spoken natively by close family members, normally the parents of a child, and it is hoped that the child will pick up and become fluent in both languages as the result of regular linguistic stimulation with L1 and L2. One method often used to maximize the success of children's early exposure to two different languages has become known as the *'one parent, one language'* principle (OPOL). Many studies have shown that children are best able to separate out the potentially confusing input of two different languages being spoken to them if they can associate each language with a different person, learning that one person always speaks in a certain way, while another speaks in a second, different way. Within the family unit, this separation of languages by speaker naturally works well if mother and father decide to speak to their child exclusively in different languages. For example, if the mother is a native speaker of Italian, and her husband's mother tongue is English, the one parent, one language strategy would suggest that the mother speak to her child only in Italian, and that the father consistently use just English.

In order for the one parent, one language approach to be successful in stimulating simultaneous bilingual growth, it is important that parents stick to the use of their designated language with and in front of their child. This not only provides the child with a reliable, contextual separation of the two linguistic systems it is being confronted with, helping the child figure out that two distinct languages are being spoken, each by a different person, it also supplies critical *motivation* for the child to learn both languages. If the child believes that it will only be able to communicate with its mother using Italian, and that the father only understands English, the child will feel the need to use both languages in order to interact with its parents and to convey desires and other emotions to them. If, however, the child comes to realize that its mother speaks English as well as Italian, the child may naturally be tempted to use English with both parents and ignore the development of the second language. The need for language consistency clearly presents a challenge for parents, as they will have to communicate with each other in front of the child in some language, and if both languages are used in exchanges between mother and father, this may trigger suspicions in the child that its parents are actually not monolinguals and that they understand each other's speech. Some parental ingenuity is therefore required to make the OPOL method work long enough for early bilingualism to be established.

It is also important that *multiple speakers* are involved in giving children linguistic input from each language. If a child hears one of the two target languages only from one speaker (its mother or father), this may not be sufficient for the child to develop a solid foundation in the language, if the child is also being exposed to a second language. Parents consequently need to enlist the help of relatives and friends wherever possible to interact with their child in just one of the two languages being acquired, and expand the monolingual coverage from just 'one parent, one language' to 'one person, one language' with multiple speakers of L1 and L2. In many instances, one of the parents' languages may be the language spoken by most people in the local population—the local majority language—and the child will receive additional input in this language whenever trips are made outside the home. The local environment will thus help strengthen the development of this language, but also will create a potential imbalance in the strength of the child's emerging L1 and L2, and the child's second language needs to be given careful extra attention and support through contact with as many speakers as possible.

Such care is needed not only in the initial stages of bilingualism, to help both languages be successfully acquired at the outset of language development, but should also be provided when children later enter school, as linguistic contact in schools is likely to reinforce one of the child's languages but not the other. While the *establishment* of bilingualism in children is important and requires considerable effort and nurturing from parents and other surrounding family, the *maintenance* of bilingualism throughout childhood and into adolescence also necessitates much care, especially when one of the two languages being acquired by a child is widely spoken in the local area. Raising a child to be a broadly balanced bilingual therefore benefits both from parents consistently following the one parent, one language approach, and from regular monolingual contact with other speakers of L1 and L2 throughout the period of childhood. The latter may serve as important motivators for children to continue to practice both their languages after they inevitably realize that their parents are not monolinguals and one language can potentially be used to communicate with both mother and father (the language children see their parents speaking to each other). If visiting relatives and parental friends continue to appear to speak only one language, either the child's L1 or L2, then good natural opportunities will be provided for children to maintain both their languages, in order to talk with grandparents, aunts, uncles, and other family friends.

Before summarizing some of the terms and concepts introduced so far, we will present a selection of commonly occurring scenarios in which children are exposed to two or more different languages as they grow up, either simultaneously or consecutively. Differences in the combination of languages spoken in the home and by the local majority population typically lead to different challenges and potential outcomes for households attempting to raise children as speakers of two languages. Each example described in the following is intended to be representative of similar situations involving other languages in other geographical locations.

Situation 1
Mother and father have different mother tongues. One of these is the language spoken by the local majority.

Example: Mother, father, and child live in Los Angeles.
Mother is a native speaker of Armenian.
Father is a native speaker of English.
Their child was born in the USA.

Likely outcome for bilingual acquisition:

The child will acquire English easily and well, due to the availability of abundant English input locally and later in school.

However, the mother will have to work hard with relatives to stimulate the acquisition and maintenance of Armenian.

As English is almost certain to develop well, the child should not experience any language-related difficulties in school.

Situation 2

Mother and father have the same mother tongue, which is not the local majority language.

Example: Mother, father, and child live in Frankfurt.

Both mother and father are native speakers of Turkish.

Their child was born in Istanbul and grew up there to the age of 5 before the family relocated to Germany.

Challenges for bilingual acquisition:

The child will acquire Turkish very naturally before the family moves to Germany. When the child begins school in Frankfurt and has to learn and use German in the classroom, this may cause difficulties for the child and affect its progress in school, unless some kind of special help is provided. Without special help, the child may develop only a weak proficiency in academic German and have difficulties learning to read and write well.

Situation 3

Mother and father have different mother tongues. Neither of these is the language spoken by the local majority.

Example: Mother, father, and child live in Tokyo, where the mother and father met and got married.

Mother is a native speaker of Chinese.

Father is a native speaker of Korean.

Their child was born in Japan.

Likely outcome for the attempted acquisition of both parental languages and Japanese:

The child will most probably acquire Japanese well, as soon as it has regular contact with other Japanese-speaking children in the neighborhood, pre-school, and school. If the common language spoken by the mother and father to each other in the home is Japanese, rather than Korean or Chinese, this will help stimulate the child's Japanese further.

If the one parent, one language strategy is followed, the child will pick up Chinese early on, due to regular daily contact with its mother. If there is less intensive daily contact with the father, it may be difficult for the child to efficiently acquire Korean, unless there is much interaction with other local Korean relatives (for example, a grandmother regularly communicating with the child in Korean).

Over time, the child will almost certainly become Japanese-dominant, and much effort will be needed to help the child maintain its early proficiency in Chinese and an interest in developing this further. Korean will probably not develop well, despite good intentions of the parents.

As the child's strongest language will normally be Japanese, and local schooling makes use of Japanese, the child should not experience any language-related difficulties in education.

Various other scenarios are of course possible, but the situations described in the preceding give a flavor of some of the more frequent situations that arise in mixed marriages and among immigrant families when the learning of two or more languages is encouraged among their children. While the acquisition of bilingualism is a common phenomenon around the world, certain circumstances and strategies adopted by parents clearly help bilingualism develop to native speaker or near-native speaker levels. How young children manage to make use of input from two languages, separate this mentally, and learn to use two linguistic systems will the subject of the next part of the chapter. Before this, a brief interim summary is provided below.

Interim summary of terms introduced

Bilingual. A person is *bilingual* if able to communicate in two different languages fluently and effectively and without hesitation in a wide variety of common situations in everyday life.

Simultaneous bilingual. Someone who becomes bilingual while being exposed to L1 and L2 simultaneously, from a very early age.

Successive/consecutive bilingual. Bilingualism is established in a sequential way, through acquisition of L1 before exposure to and acquisition of L2.

Balanced bilingual. The speaker's knowledge of L1 and L2 is fully parallel in vocabulary and proficiency.

Non-balanced bilingual. There is a difference in the words known by a bilingual in L1 and L2. Although a bilingual may be a fluent speakers of both languages, some words known in L1 may not be known in L2, and vice versa.

Language dominance in bilinguals. A bilingual fluent in two languages, L1 and L2, may make use of one of these languages more regularly and more automatically than the other.

Preferred language. A bilingual may have a stronger personal attachment to one of their languages. A bilingual's preferred language is not necessarily their dominant language.

One parent, one language principle. Each parent speaks to the child in a different language, in order to promote bilingualism.

The development of bilingualism from early childhood onward

We will now begin to examine aspects of the actual process of bilingual language acquisition and how young language learners manage to cope with and mentally organize linguistic input they receive into two distinct language systems and then develop this further. As we will see, a potentially important feature of young bilingual speech is that children at a certain age are found to *mix* languages in their speech in various ways, making (short) sentences with words from both of the languages they are learning, and creating new words with mixtures of L1 and L2 elements. How to analyze and understand this language mixing has been a major question for studies of bilingual acquisition and has led to two different theories of early bilingual language learning, one in which children initially construct a single hybrid language system composed of input from both L1 and L2, and a second model which posits that children build two separate language systems from the beginning, but mix elements from these two systems together for other reasons. We will also consider later L2 learners—adolescents and adults—and the much-discussed question of whether L2 learning after a certain age is carried out in a different way from early bilingual acquisition and might be responsible for the typical failure of late L2 learners to achieve native-speaker levels of proficiency in their second language (the so-called 'Critical Period' debate, applied to second-language acquisition). Finally, we will discuss research on the mental storage of L1 and L2 words in bilinguals, and review evidence suggesting that different modes of mental representation may evolve and undergo change in certain bilinguals, distinguishing advanced consecutive and simultaneous bilinguals from L2 learners in earlier stages.

Early simultaneous acquisition of two languages

Before we consider infants' simultaneous acquisition of two languages, it will be useful to provide a brief overview of the typical steps of language acquisition found with children who have a monolingual experience when young, with exposure to only one language. The process of language acquisition observed among such children typically follows a regular, sequenced pattern of development.

It has been discovered that when children are born, they may already be able to distinguish the language spoken by their mother from other languages they hear, suggesting that certain linguistic development has taken place in the womb, prior to birth, with the sounds and intonation of mothers' speech being perceived and distinguished by pre-natal children. Between the ages of 6–8 months, babies begin to 'babble' and produce sequences of consonants and vowels which are experimental and have no obvious meaning ('a-ba-ba', 'ga-ga-ga', etc.). At around the age of 10–12 months, infants then start to make sounds which clearly converge on the language produced by adults who interact with them. They also produce their first meaningful words, and react as if they understand the speech of others (for example, they respond to commands and offers from their caregivers, especially when these are reinforced by gestures). Half-way through their second year, many children begin to make two-word sentences from their small vocabulary of 20–30 words, indicating the onset of syntactic knowledge in their language. Toward the end of the second year, the acquisition of new words accelerates in a very clear and impressive way, growing to around 200–300 words, and this leads to the production of multiple word utterances some time during the beginning of their third year (Owens 1992; Guasti 2002). Thereafter, children learn more and more about the syntax, semantics, and pragmatics of the language they are regularly exposed to, but already have a significant amount of this language robustly in place as they enter into their fourth year.[4]

---

4. There is a certain amount of variation among children with regard to exactly when transitions are made from one early learning stage to the next, and there are even some children who only begin to speak in their third or fourth year, but subsequently develop fully normal abilities in language. However, all children appear to follow the same sequence of developmental steps in the acquisition of language, whenever these actually take place during their early childhood.

For children being exposed to *two* languages, the process of acquisition is more complicated, as children have to figure out that the linguistic input they receive belongs to two distinct systems, to be used with different individuals. When children exposed to two different languages come to the point where they actually produce words and then short sentences, most frequently in the second year of their life, two features of their speech have often caught the attention of parents and researchers observing their linguistic development. First, it is found that many young children who are spoken to in two different languages produce words and sentences which combine elements from both the L1 and the L2. At the word level, children may create brand new words not used by any adult speakers which are blends of L1 and L2 words, or which combine morphological affixes from one language with words from the other language. Examples of this kind of novel word creation are given in what follows, from patterns observed with young children simultaneously exposed to English and French, English and Norwegian, and English and Swedish.

L1/L2 word blends formed by young children

Mixing of English and French. French *chaud* (pronounced like English *show*), meaning 'hot', was mixed with its meaning equivalent in English, *hot*, to form a new word using the consonant sound of the beginning of the French word ('*sh-*') and the vowel and final consonant of the English word ('*-ot*'). The result, intended to mean 'hot', was pronounced as '*shot*'. (Grosjean 1982)

Mixing of English and Norwegian. The first part of the English word *horse* was combined with the final consonant of the Norwegian equivalent *hest* to produce the new blended word *hort*, meaning 'horse'. (Lanza 2007)

Combinations of words and affixes from L1 and L2

Mixing of English and Norwegian. The Norwegian verb ending *–e* was added to English verbs, resulting in *looke, walke,* and *helpe*, meaning 'looks', 'walks', and 'helps'. The Norwegian affix *–et*, which has the same meaning as the English word 'the', was added to English words such as *hair*, resulting in novel mixes such as *hairet*, meaning 'the hair'. (Lanza 2007)

Short sentences made by young children with words from both L1 and L2

Mixing of English and French. The French verb *manger* 'to eat' and the noun *bonbon* 'candy' were combined with the English subject pronoun *they*, resulting in the sentence: '*They manger bonbon*', meaning 'They eat candies.'

Mixing of English and Swedish. The English noun *horsie* (i.e., 'little/dear horse') was added to the Swedish verb *sova* 'sleeps', producing the sentence '*Horsie sova*', meaning 'The horse is sleeping.' (Arnberg 1987)

A second common property of early child language is that children regularly hearing two different languages rarely seem to learn pairs of words from L1 and L2 with the same meaning, and instead just acquire and use one word, either from the L1 or L2, for each object they are introduced to. For example, a child who is spoken to in English and Spanish on a regular basis might learn the word *dog* but not the Spanish equivalent *perro*, and if the same child learns *gato* 'cat' first, it will typically not learn and use the English word *cat* for some time, but will use *gato* to refer to all cats, in all linguistic contexts. This lack of translational equivalents in L1 and L2 has been reported as a feature of early child language which lasts for several months, even when input from adult speakers in L1 and L2 is relatively balanced and includes the words for everyday objects in both languages. It seems that once children master a word for a particular object in either L1 or L2, they may consider this item of vocabulary sufficient for all further references to the object—hence, if *dog* and *gato* are learned, then their translational equivalents *perro* and *cat* are not felt to be necessary, even though adult speakers may sometimes make use of these words. Linguists studying the development of early child vocabulary have found that sometimes L1/L2 equivalents do seem to occur, but that these words are actually used by children in different ways, and so are not direct equivalents of each other in L1 and L2. Observing a child exposed to Italian and German, Volterra and Taeschner (1978) noted that the child appeared to have learned words meaning 'there' in both Italian and German—*là* and *da*. However, close attention to the way that *là* and *da* were used by the child showed that they were not fully equivalent in meaning—German *da* was used to refer to objects which were visible, while Italian *là* was only used for objects which could not be seen by the child at the time of speech (often temporarily being hidden behind other objects).

These two general patterns—the mixing of words and parts of words from L1 and L2, and an absence of L1/L2 translational equivalents—may generally occur in young children's speech in bilingual environments for an extended period of months sometime between the ages of 2 and 3. It often creates concern among parents who worry that their children are linguistically confused as the result of being spoken to in two different languages and will be unable to develop a 'normal' proficiency in either language when compared to same-age children with a monolingual learning experience. In various instances, parents may even decide to discontinue the attempt to raise their children bilingually because of such patterns, fearful that language-mixing will become a permanent feature of their children's speech and will disadvantage their development.

What do these characteristics of early child language tell us about the way that language skills develop in bilingual children? Two different interpretations have been given to the patterns observed, resulting in two major hypotheses about the way language is mentally represented in young, emerging bilinguals—a one-system and a two-system analysis.

Proposals made in Volterra and Taeschner (1978) and Redlinger and Park (1980) have suggested that when children are first exposed to two different languages, they assume that all of the input they receive from speakers of the L1 and L2 is actually part of a single linguistic system—one language—and it is only after a certain amount of time (several months) that children manage to develop separate mental representations for L1 and L2 and realize that two distinct linguistic systems/languages are being used by speakers in their environment. In the earliest stage of acquisition and language production, it is assumed that children construct a unitary, hybrid model of L1/L2 words and grammatical conventions, and believe that everything they hear belongs to this single 'language'. Support for such a '*Unitary Language System Hypothesis*' is argued to be both the occurrence of creative language-mixing found among young children and the typical absence of synonymous L1/L2 words. If children interpret all L1/L2 words and patterns of grammar as belonging to one language system, they may naturally feel free to draw on all such elements in the utterances they produce and randomly mix properties of the two languages within single sentences. With regard to the development of vocabulary, if L1/L2 pairs such as *perro/dog* and *gato/cat* are believed to be fully synonymous words present in a single language, children might be anticipated to be economical in the efforts they make to add new words to their limited active vocabulary and only make regular use of one member of the L1/L2 pair, this accounting for the lack of translational equivalents in early 'bilingual' speech—if a child has learned one word to refer to an object in his/her single language system, why bother to learn a second word with the very same meaning?

In the approach presented in Volterra and Taeschner (1978), it is suggested that young children simultaneously exposed to two languages will typically pass through three significant stages of development on their way to becoming truly bilingual, moving from an initial unitary language system to the successful full separation of L1 and L2 within a two-system mental model paralleling adult bilingual knowledge. The three stages posited by Volterra and Taeschner involve a gradual step-by-step disentangling of the words and grammar of L1 and L2, as described in the following.

> **Stage I.** A child hearing two languages, L1 and L2, develops a single lexical system composed of words from both languages, and a single set of grammatical rules adopted from both languages, which are uniformly applied to combinations of L1/L2 words. This mixed form of language is used with all adult speakers, regardless of whether the adults use L1 or L2 with the child.
>
> **Stage II.** The child realizes that L1 and L2 words belong to different lexical systems, and separates the use of L1 and L2 words—(short) sentences are now much more consistently created either with L1 or with L2 words, and there is significantly reduced or no mixing of L1 and L2 words in a single sentence. The child learns to use sentences made with L1 words to L1 adult speakers, and sentences made with L2 words to L2 adult speakers, correctly adjusting its use of vocabulary to the language used by the person speaking to the child. However, in Stage II, a single set of grammatical rules sourced from both languages continues to be used with both L1 and L2 words. Consequently, during Stage II it is hypothesized that the vocabularies of L1 and L2 have been mentally separated into two distinct systems, for use with different individuals, but there is not yet any clear separation of L1/L2 grammar, and a hybrid grammatical system is made use of as in Stage I.[5]

---

5. Volterra and Taeschner's claims that children use a single hybrid set of grammatical rules drawn from L1/L2 during Stage II originates from their observations of early child Italian and German, where constructions which are syntactically different in adult Italian and German (for example, word order patterns with adjectives and nouns, negation, and possessors) were produced uniformly in the same way in early 'bilingual' speech, whether L1 or L2 words were being used. This led Volterra and Taeschner to argue that a single mixed syntax was being applied in Stage II to sentences which were lexically either Italian or German.

Stage III. The child comes to realize that there are two different sets of grammatical rules for the use of L1 and L2, and applies these appropriately when speaking with L1 and L2 words. Stage III represents the successful separation of both L1 and L2 vocabulary and syntax and results in the establishment of two distinct language systems which will increasingly converge on adult L1/L2 speech norms as the child's language skills develop further.

If we illustrate the progression from Stage I to Stage III with a representative pair of languages, English and Greek, a child being spoken to regularly in both languages is expected to show the following pattern of development:

Stage I. The child has a vocabulary consisting of English and Greek words. If the English word for an object has been learned, its Greek equivalent will not be used by the child, and vice versa. For example, if English *cow* has been acquired, it will be used for all references to cows, and the Greek word *agelada* will typically not occur in the child's speech. The child uses its mixed English-Greek vocabulary with all adult speakers, whether they are addressing the child in English or in Greek. Syntactic constructions, such as they exist in the child's early language, are produced by a single set of rules taken from English and Greek.

Stage II. The child separates out English from Greek words in its speech and produces sentences with either English or Greek words, in response to adults speaking English or Greek. However, there is no difference in the syntactic way that these sentences are created, and the child continues to use a hybrid set of grammatical rules.

Stage III. The child learns that there are different grammatical rules for English and Greek, resulting in a full separation of English and Greek words and syntax. Apparent initial confusion about the distinctness of the two languages is resolved, and the child begins to use English and Greek regularly as two discrete linguistic systems.

A second prominent approach to early child bilingualism argues for a different view of language competence when 2-year-old children first begin to produce short sentences with words from both L1 and L2. Instead of concluding that bilingual children during the mixing stage are making use of a single, hybrid language system, the '*Separate Development Hypothesis*' claims that bilingual children from a very early age are in fact able to differentiate and make use of two linguistic systems (Padilla and Liebman 1975; Bergman 1976; de Houwer 1990).[6] Whereas the Unitary Language System Hypothesis argues that children succeed in separating adult L1/L2 input into two different systems only over a period of time, passing through the three stages just described, the Separate Development Hypothesis posits

---

6. The Separate Development Hypothesis is also sometimes referred to as the Independent Development Hypothesis.

that young children mentally establish a two-system model from a very early age, and know that two different languages are present in adult L1/L2 speech before and during the phase when they engage in language-mixing. Two principal arguments are given in support of such a two-system view, one from children's phonological development in bilingual environments, the other from mixing itself.

First, regarding phonology, while there is evidence that children may mix up words and basic grammar from L1/L2 at an early stage, when one considers speech perception and children's pronunciation, no linguistic 'confusion' between the L1 and L2 is found—children seem to show a remarkable ability to distinguish and later reproduce adult L1/L2 phonology in distinct ways from a very early age, with the ability to perceive two languages as different being present before children actually start to produce their own first words.[7] Proponents of the Separate Development Hypothesis argue that if children show clear signs of being able to perceive and use two different *phonological* systems from a very early age, they must have a broader awareness that there are two linguistic systems underlying the L1/L2 input they receive *in general*, this extending from phonology to include morphology, the lexicon, and grammatical conventions (i.e., syntax), hence that *all* aspects of adult L1/L2 speech belong to two different systems/languages.

Second, it is suggested that the phenomenon of language mixing among young children may in fact *not* constitute strong evidence for a single, hybrid language combining words and grammar from both L1 and L2, contra what has been suggested by advocates of the Unitary Language System Hypothesis. The reason for doubting the support that patterns of mixing give for a one-system approach is that mixing of L1/L2 elements actually continues for some time *after* children become clearly aware that there are two distinct linguistic systems in their environment. At a certain point in their development, bilingual children show very clear signs of knowing that they are being spoken to in two different languages, and children themselves use their L1 and L2 appropriately with different adults. However, children reaching this stage still occasionally mix words and phrases from L1 and L2 together in a single sentence or utterance. This suggests that mixing may not necessarily occur because children assign all L1/L2 words in the input to a single undifferentiated language, as mixing is found to take place even when children have realized that others around them are speaking two distinct languages (though the rate of mixing at this later stage is typically less than at earlier points).

The Separate Development Hypothesis proposes that language mixing in early bilinguals may arise for different reasons. At the earliest stage of bilingual development, when children's vocabulary is very restricted, it is suggested that they *code-switch* between their two languages when a word has been learned in one language but not the other. For example, if a child is trying to speak its L2 to a particular adult who regularly addresses it in this language, but the child has not learned the word in L2 for a certain item, the child may use an equivalent word in its L1, if the latter has already been learned. Hence *horsie sova* ('the horse is sleeping') might be produced when a young English-Swedish bilingual tries to speak its L2 Swedish but has not yet learned the Swedish equivalent to English *horse/*

---

7. Children in their first year have even been found to phonologically distinguish languages that are closely related, for example Spanish and Catalan—see Bosch and Sebastián-Gallés (2001).

horsie. In order to express the desired meaning, the child simply code-switches into English, borrowing the English word and embedding it in a Swedish sentence directed to a Swedish-speaking adult. Mixing at such an early age is consequently attributed to a lack of L1/L2 vocabulary, necessitating switching between the two languages, and is not seen as a sign of a single fused L1/L2 language.

Somewhat later, when children have learned the words for various objects in both their L1 and L2, mixing may still occur, it is argued, because of differences in the relative strengths of L1/L2 synonyms within children's bilingual vocabulary—the words for certain objects may have been learned earlier and may be more frequently used in one of a child's two languages, making these words more accessible than their translational equivalents in the second language. For example, if a young English-Chinese bilingual has learned the word *cookie* before its Chinese equivalent *binggan*, and uses *cookie* more frequently than *binggan*, the child may use *cookie* in a sentence that is otherwise in Chinese because *cookie* is simply more accessible and easy for the child to use than its Chinese equivalent.

A third 'explanation' of young children's language mixing given by proponents of the Separate Development Hypothesis is that such patterns may sometimes occur because adults speak to children with both L1 and L2 and provide children (inadvertently) with mixed language input, which children then simply copy as a way of speaking. Although adults may make efforts to follow the one parent, one language principle in interacting with their children, it has often been observed that mothers and fathers may be inconsistent in their speech and may use every possible means to communicate with their children when the children don't seem to understand. This may often include language mixing and L1-L2 code-switching, which encourages children themselves to engage in mixing.[8] Significantly, children who have been raised more consistently according to the one parent, one language principle show less language-mixing behavior than children whose parents talk to them in two languages, and are more effective in selecting the appropriate language to use with each parent—hence their language patterns are much less random than those found with other bilingual children. This is taken to indicate that they successfully establish a two-system model of language from early on and manage very well at mentally keeping their two languages separate.

Considering the two hypotheses of early child bilingualism—the Unitary Language System Hypothesis and the Separate Development Hypothesis—both offer good arguments and evidence in their favor, and both models of language development are inherently plausible, so it is difficult to be sure whether children begin their bilingual competency with a single, fused language system and gradually separate this into two distinct languages as the Unitary Language System Hypothesis suggests, or whether two differentiated but imperfect language systems are mentally in place from a very early stage, before children start to combine words into sentences, as argued in the Separate Development Hypothesis. It might even

---

8. For example, Lanza (2007) describes the language habits of the mother of a young English-Norwegian bilingual Tomas in her interactions with her son. Lanza notes that when Tomas' mother thought that he didn't understand her when she spoke Norwegian, she would simply switch to English and say the same thing again in this language, hoping that this would be more effective. Tomas thus regularly received a mixture of languages from a single parent as he grew up, and this seems to have encouraged the habit of language-mixing in Tomas' own speech.

be the case that both theories of language development are correct for different situations, with children raised according to the one parent, one language principle quickly establishing two linguistic systems incorporating formally distinct rules of grammar, phonology, and morphology, while children who are exposed to more mixed linguistic input assume a single hybrid system at the outset, and then gradually extricate the grammar and vocabulary of L1 and L2 in a series of steps.[9] Currently, opinions among language researchers are still divided (though there is a tendency to favor the Separate Development Hypothesis), and what is needed to really settle the issue is a much broader database than that available at the moment, with more precise comparisons of children of the same age exposed to the same pairs of languages under contrasting conditions of input—either consistent use of one language by adult speakers, or mixed, inconsistent use of L1/L2 by multiple speakers interacting with children. Hopefully such data will be collected by research projects carried out in the coming years.

Explicit signs of L1/L2 distinction in early children

However bilingual competence does develop in children's earliest years, it is well documented that children spoken to regularly in two languages at some point start to demonstrate a clear awareness that these forms of speech comprise different systems, which are subsequently identified with actual language names. Hoffman (1991) presents a good sampling of these 'manifestations of language awareness' among emerging bilinguals, drawing on her own work and that of others, and a number of Hoffman's examples will be reproduced here.

In a study of her own child Cristina, Hoffman found that around the age of 2 her daughter began noting that her mother and father gave the same objects different names. For example, in the presence of her German-speaking mother, Cristina banged on a table and said '*Papa mesa*', meaning that her father would use the (Spanish) word *mesa* for a table, rather than the (German) word *Tisch*, which she would normally hear from her mother. Cristina additionally showed she was aware of being spoken to in two different languages by using phrases like: *como dice papá* (like Papa says (it)) and '*so wie Mama*' (as mother (says)). At such an early age, it is common for emerging bilinguals to refer to their L1 and L2 in an indirect way as other individuals' special way of speaking, and not to use explicit language labels such as 'German' and 'Spanish'. Such indirect reference to different languages is also seen in the following example in which a boy named Pascual tells his mother off in German for speaking to a Spanish-speaking friend in the wrong way (with English words). No language names are used by Pascual, but he is clearly able to distinguish different ways of speaking through the examples he gives to his mother.

    Pascual: *Mami, nicht so mit Carmen sprechen!*
                   'Mami, don't speak to Carmen like that!'
    Mother: *Wie denn?*
                   'How should I speak then?'

---

9. Indeed, de Houwer's (1990) defense of the Separate Development Hypothesis pointed out that it was primarily focused on accounting for children raised by the one parent, one language principle, and that it was not clear that it would necessarily be the correct model for children exposed to more inconsistent, mixed L1/L2 input in their early years.

Pascual: 'So, "*hola, como estas?*", *nicht* "hello"!'
             'Like this: "hello, how are you" [Spanish], not "hello" [English].'

Similar manifestation of L1/L2 awareness can additionally be found in the ways that young children actually *use* their two languages, before they know that these languages have different names. Kessler (1984) provides the following example of a girl named Lita at age 2.4. Lita's mother offers her some juice, speaking Spanish, but Lita declines the offer and instead asks for candy, using the English word *candy* in her Spanish sentence. When a second request for candy is unsuccessful, Lita switches to use of the correct Spanish word for candy—'*dulce*'. This switch indicates that the young girl is aware that one way of speaking (Spanish), which she uses with her mother, operates with a specific set of words which are different from a second way of speaking (English) used with other people. Lita replaces English *candy* with Spanish *dulce* in the hopes that this will increase her chances of being given what she wants.

Mother: *¿Quieres jugo?*
           'Do you want juice?'
Lita: *No jugo,* candy, *mami.*
           'Not juice, candy, mama.'
Lita: Candy! (with emphasis, followed by a long pause) . . . *Dame dulce,* please.
           'Candy!   . . . Give me candy, please.'

The same girl at a slightly later age, 3.6, learned the words for the two languages she speaks and openly acknowledges that she speaks both Spanish and English, as seen in the following example (again from Kessler 1984):

Mother: *Y oye, Lita, ¿a ti te gusta hablar el inglés, o el español, o los dos?*
           'Tell me, Lita, do you like speaking English, or Spanish or both?'
Lita: '*Dos*' ('two' - holds up two fingers). 'That's *inglés* ('English' - points to one finger). 'And that's *español*!' ('Spanish' - points to another finger)

It is interesting to note that in both of these examples, Lita clearly knows that she speaks two different languages (though at age 2.4 she can't yet name them), but *still* mixes these languages up in a single utterance to her Spanish-speaking mother. In the first example the English word *please* is still inserted in her Spanish sentence even after the correction of *candy* to *dulce* has been made, and in the second exchange Lita mixes in English 'That's/And that's' when giving the names of Spanish and English in Spanish. This is the kind of data that is presented as support for the Separate Language Hypothesis, because it shows that language mixing may occur even when a speaker knows that there are two different languages; hence mixing is not necessarily evidence for a single undifferentiated system.

Hoffman (1991) notes that are three other ways in which children frequently display their awareness of two distinct types of speech. First, when the one parent, one language principle is used in the home, children sometimes act as translators for their parents who, for some time, they believe to only know one language. So, if both parents are present with the child and the mother or father talks to it in one language, the child may translate these words into its second language for the benefit of the other parent. Second, it has been found that the practice of one parent using only one language in the home creates such a strong expectation in children that they will hear a certain language from each parent (for example, French from the mother, German from the father) that children may fail to respond in any way if a parent uses a different language, even if the child understands that language when it is spoken by the other parent. It is very much as if young bilingual children mentally switch themselves into a specific language frame when interacting with a close family member and fully shut out the second language that they know, so that the latter fails to be recognized and understood when heard from someone who normally uses a different language. Third, children may sometimes complain if parents use what seems to be an inappropriate language with others, as seen in the earlier example with Pascual, who criticizes his mother for speaking English to his Spanish-speaking friend.

Consequently, a whole range of patterns observed with children exposed to two languages in their early years show that a clear, conscious awareness of the distinctness of these languages comes to children after some time and is explicitly manifested in their linguistic behavior. Many of the patterns found not only testify to children's bilingual awareness but also emphasize the importance of specific individuals in the development of infant bilingualism. In children's earliest years, languages are very strongly associated with people in their immediate environment, and the consistent use of a particular language by each adult interacting with children provides an extremely important anchor for children to focus on as they acquire two (or more) languages. The regular association of different ways of speaking with different people/parents seems to allow children to construct robust mental representations of the languages they hear over time and to establish a solid foundation for the growth of bilingual competence.

Languages may sometimes also become associated with different places that young bilinguals regularly spend time in, quite frequently with one language being used inside the home and another dominating interactions in other, public places outside the home. Such L1/L2 separation determined by physical location can be a useful supplement to the linking of languages to specific people and can help children develop different language modes that are activated by either personal or physical context.[10] The more children find themselves in predictable, recurring situations with individuals and places associated with distinct languages, the more they are able to separate the linguistic input they receive and build this into two, largely self-contained systems, and eliminate unintentional mixing.

Having focused so far on how two languages may first be established as distinct systems in young children receiving either simultaneous or consecutive bilingual input, the chapter will now turn to later stages in the acquisition of two languages, and consider interactions

---

10. At a rather later age, typically when children have attended school for some time, young bilinguals' L1 and L2 may additionally become associated with and triggered by different kinds of conversational *topics*, as often occurs with adult language switching. For example, school and study-related topics might result in the use of one language and family-related issues may be discussed in another (with certain individuals). However, the role of topic in determining language use is much less important in pre-school bilinguals than the effect of person spoken to and the place where an act of communication occurs.

between L1 and L2 after early childhood, examining how L1 and L2 may exert influences on each other (the phenomenon of 'interference'), whether second-language learning initiated later in life can be as successful as infant bilingual acquisition (the Critical Period Hypothesis), and how vocabulary items from two languages are mentally stored and related to each other and the concepts they represent in early and late bilinguals ('lexical storage').

L1/L2 interference

When a person learns two languages, this requires that the L1 and L2 are established as two separate systems of words, grammar, and phonological rules, which can be accessed independently, allowing a person to speak either language. Although successful L1/L2 learning therefore necessitates functional separation of the different language systems, it has nevertheless been found that there is some interaction between the properties of speakers' L1 and L2, and multiple languages stored in an individual's brain are actually not fully isolated from each other. When L1/L2 interactions take place with some effect on speech, this is known as 'interference', 'language transfer', or 'cross-linguistic influence'. For people who become bilingual at an early age, the effects of interaction are often subtle, but do still occur, and will shortly be discussed in a section focusing on lexical storage, the linking of concepts and words, and bilingual language processing and production. For others who learn a second language later in life, either during late adolescence or in adult life, the effects of interference can, however, be quite considerable, and are often much more obvious and pronounced than with young bilinguals. Here we will concentrate on these more salient effects of L1/L2 influence found in later learners, which tend to affect all speakers in certain ways. In turn, this will lead to questions about the relation of language learning to age, and discussion of the Critical Period Hypothesis.

L1/L2 interference most commonly involves properties of the language a speaker is stronger in affecting the speaker's weaker language, when there is an imbalance in ability between L1 and L2, as often occurs when a second language is learned later in life. Sometimes, if an L2 is learned in adult life but is used more frequently than a person's original mother tongue, it is also possible for the 'weaker' language which is not spoken natively to affect the way a person's mother tongue is used. Additionally, when speakers have a high level of ability in both L1 and L2, it is possible for there to be influence and transfer going in both directions—aspects of the L1 can affect the way the L2 is spoken, and vice versa. The interactions that occur typically take place in the areas of L1/L2 phonology, syntax, and vocabulary, as discussed in the following.

When there is **phonological interference**, and a speaker's L1 influences his/her L2, this is informally referred to as speaking 'with a foreign accent'. Transfer of some of the phonological properties of a person's stronger language to a weaker language is particularly common in people who learn their second language in their mid-teens or later. Here we will give four examples of this process.

First of all, *individual sounds* can be affected by phonological transfer when there are differences in the inventory of vowels and consonants present in two languages. For example, when speakers of English attempt to learn various languages from India such as Malayalam, Bangla, and Hindi, they often have considerable difficulty hearing and reproducing many of the 'plosive' consonant sounds which involve the tip of the tongue coming into contact with the roof of the mouth or teeth, as these can be made in many more positions than in English ('dental', 'alveolar', and 'retroflex'), with or without voicing, and with or without aspiration. Where English has two consonants 't' and 'd', a language like Bangla has eight different contrasting sounds. The greater phonological simplicity/paucity of the English plosive system regularly affects the way Bangla and other Indian languages are spoken as a late-learned L2, and L1 English speakers will generally produce all of the dental, alveolar, and retroflex stops in a language such as Bangla as if they were either English 't' or 'd'. L1 English phonology thus dramatically affects L2 Bangla pronunciation, causing speakers to sound very 'English' when they attempt to produce the language.

Second, *groups of sounds* made in one language may prove difficult for speakers of another language to pronounce, and cause changes to occur in L2 speech. English, for example, has various consonant clusters (sequences of consonants) that never occur in Japanese. When L1 Japanese speakers produce English words such as 'Egypt', with a final 'pt' sequence, Japanese phonology alters this with the insertion of extra vowels between and after the final consonants, resulting in its pronunciation as 'Egyputo'. Similar adjustments occur with all other English words containing consonant clusters, giving rise to a very distinctive Japanese-sounding English among many speakers.

Third, the *rhythm* given to speech may be different across languages, and in certain languages speakers produce all syllables equally long ('syllable-timed' languages, such as French and Spanish), whereas in other languages speakers vary the length of syllables according to the stress pattern of words ('stress-timed languages', such as English). When an L1 speaker of a syllable-timed language such as French speaks a stress-timed language such as English as a late-learned L2, the rhythm may sound quite different from that of native speakers of English, as French phonology influences the production of L2 English.

Finally, many of the world's languages make use of *tones* and *intonation* in special ways. All syllables in Thai, for example, are pronounced with one of five tones, so there is much variation in the pitch given to words. When Thai speakers come to learn and speak a non-tone language such as English, they often transfer aspects of Thai tone to English words, and pronounce them with much greater fluctuation in pitch than native speakers of English would.

With regard to **syntactic interference**, grammatical rules present in one of a speaker's two languages, normally the mother tongue, may be used to produce sentences in the speaker's second language, especially when this L2 is learned after mid-adolescence. For example, when speakers of Spanish or Italian learn English, they may apply the '*subject-drop*' patterning of Spanish and Italian to their L2 English, producing sentences such as:

'John is not British. Is from the USA.' (meaning: '<u>He</u> is from the USA.').

The same speakers may also allow *word order patterns* in their L1 to influence the production of their L2, resulting in incorrect L2 sequences such as:

'Has visited Sue the university?' (in place of: 'Has Sue visited the university?')
'Where are the boxes blue?' (in pace of: 'Where are the blue boxes?')

Where the use of *verbal tense forms* in one language differ from those in another, the conventions present in a speaker's stronger language may become imposed on their L2. One distinctive property of English, which is different from many other western European languages, is that reference to an ongoing action in the present is expressed with the verb *be* and a verb combined with the suffix *–ing*, for example 'He is running.' In German, French, and other European languages, ongoing action in the present is simply expressed with a present tense verb. If this aspect of German and French interferes with a person's English speech, it will give rise to unnatural forms such as:

'Look outside. It rains.' (instead of: 'It's raining.')

Sometimes a grammatical word is present in two languages and very often is used in the same way, leading speakers of one language to assume that it is always used in the same way in a second language they are learning, but there is actually some *mismatch in grammatical form*. For example, the English word *a* (the 'indefinite article') has an equivalent in closely related languages such as French, and this word is used in many of the same ways as in English, but not when the name of a profession such as 'doctor' or 'soldier' follows the verb 'to be'. In such instances, *a* occurs in English but most commonly does not in French. This non-correspondence in use of the indefinite article in English and French regularly results in transfer of the French pattern to L2 English, and similar transfer of the English pattern to L2 French, in both cases producing very unnatural sentences:

'He is doctor.' (L2 English from an L1 French speaker)

'*Il est un médecin.*' ('He is a doctor'. L2 French from an L1 English speaker)

The third area in which there is often L1 interference on a person's L2 speech relates to the meaning of apparently similar words present in L1 and L2, and instances of the incorrect understanding, use, and translation of such words, which are known as 'false friends'. In patterns of **lexical interference**, a speaker of one language may come across a word in a second language, realize that it looks very similar to a word in the speaker's L1, and so make the assumption that it has the same meaning as the L1 word. In many cases, such an assumption may be more or less correct, as there are many words in related languages such as English, German, Dutch, and Swedish (all Germanic languages) which do have parallel or close-to-parallel meanings across the languages they occur in. However, in other instances, L1 and L2 words which look very similar actually have quite different meanings. For example, an English learner of French might naturally think that the French words *librairie* and *sensible* have the same meaning as the English words *library* and *sensible*, yet this is not correct. The word *librairie* actually means *bookshop*, and *sensible* in French is equivalent to the English word *sensitive*. Where lexical interference occurs, and the meaning of words in a person's L1 are applied to those encountered in an L2, this often leads to misunderstandings. An L1 speaker of French learning English might produce incongruous sentences such as: 'I'm going to the library to buy some books', if English *library* is taken to mean the same as French *librairie*, and an English L1 speaker learning French might say '*Jean* *est très sensible*' in the incorrect belief that he/she is communicating '*Jean is very sensible*', but a French speaker will understand such a sentence to mean '*Jean is very sensitive*.'

Sometimes it occurs that similar-looking words in two languages do have a common meaning, but in one language an *additional* meaning has developed, making it ambiguous in one language but not the other. For example, the Spanish verb *asistir* can be used with the same meaning as the English verb *to assist* (i.e., to provide help to someone). However, Spanish *asistir* can also mean '*to attend (a meeting)*'. This meaning difference between Spanish and English is represented as follows:

A Spanish speaker whose L1 lexicon/vocabulary interferes in the production of L2 English might assume that English *assist* can in fact be used with the second meaning of Spanish *asistir* and may create sentences such as '*I am going to assist at the meeting*', believing this to communicate that the speaker will simply be present at the meeting, whereas English speakers will understand it to mean that the speaker will provide some help ('assistance') at the meeting.

Lexical interference also occurs when the basic, core meaning of a word in one language can be translated with a word in a second language, but these L1/L2 words have additional, unpredictable extensions of the core meaning, which are different. A good illustration of this is the English word *full* and its normal translational equivalent in French *plein*. In most everyday circumstances, where English *full* can be used, French *plein* can also be used (reference to containers being full, etc.). However, English has a colloquial use of *full* which refers to a person having eaten substantially/to satiation (literally being 'full of food'). Hence a common way to decline the offer of further food during a meal is to say 'No, thank you, I'm full already.' L1 English learners of French frequently translate *full* into *plein* and use it in similar circumstances, with this extended meaning, when speaking French, but this often causes much confusion as French *plein* does not have the same extension of meaning but a different colloquial use. If used by a woman, '*Je suis pleine*' communicates that the speaker is actually pregnant (full with a baby). Such a difference in the extended meanings of words may regularly lead to misunderstandings which sometimes go undetected for much time, not being as obvious as clear grammatical errors which result from syntactic interference.[11]

Related mistakes occur when idiomatic expressions are translated by speakers of one language into another. For example, a speaker of English and Spanish might translate the English phrase '*run for president*' directly into Spanish with '*correr por presidente*', but this does not make sense in Spanish and would not be understood by monolingual Spanish speakers.

---

11. In connection with this particular example, two further pairs of false friends which seem to involve 'pregnancy' in European languages can be mentioned. In Romanian, the word *pregnant* does not mean '*with child*', but rather '*brief and informative*', and in Spanish the word *embarazada* means *pregnant*, but English speakers often wrongly assume it means *embarrassed*.

Finally, it can be noted that the majority of cases of L1/L2 lexical interference involve a speaker's stronger language influencing use of the weaker language, but in situations where a person has lived for a long time in a society which predominantly uses the second language acquired by a person—for example, when immigrants come to use the majority language of a local population more frequently than their mother tongue, after many years in a new country—it is not uncommon for the second, learned language to interfere lexically with use of the mother tongue. Hoffman (1991) mentions a Spanish woman who lived in England for many years with the result that her English came to influence the way she occasionally spoke Spanish. An example of her speech is given in the following sentence, which is a direct translation into Spanish of the English words '*How well you look today!*'.However, the sentence sounds very odd in Spanish, as the Spanish verb *mirar* can only mean '*look at (something/someone)*' not '*appear/look (well/ill/happy etc)*.

'Que bien miras hoy!'
how well you-look today
Intended meaning: 'How well you look!'

In conclusion, the phenomena of phonological, syntactic, and lexical interference are regular, recurring indications of speakers' failure to acquire native-like competence in a second language they attempt to learn. Frequently, a person's mother tongue will exert influence over certain aspects of the way they speak their second language so that this is produced in various ways that are different from native speakers. Patterns of interference may, to some extent, be found with speakers who acquired a second language either when very young, by means of simultaneous or successive bilingual exposure, or at a later age, but such effects are most obvious and pronounced among late L2 learners, who regularly struggle to mimic native speakers' pronunciation when the phonology of L1 and L2 do not coincide, and also make syntactic and lexical errors in their speech. This naturally raises questions about speaker age and language-learning outcomes. Specifically, is there a strong connection between a person's age of exposure to a language and his/her ability to develop native-like proficiency in an L2, and what accounts for common differences in L2 performance among young bilinguals and later learners? Approaching this issue, we will consider the much-discussed Critical Period Hypothesis and how it may or may not apply to second-language acquisition and the development of bilingualism.

The Critical Period Hypothesis

> Perhaps no other domain in second language acquisition has generated so much public attention, debate, and controversy as the critical period hypothesis. Li (2013a: 146)

The Critical Period Hypothesis (CPH) suggests that there is a limited period of time during which humans can successfully acquire a language to normal, native-like levels (Birdsong

1999b). In its original formulation in Lenneberg (1967), the critical period was believed to extend from the age of 2 until puberty, when it was thought brain lateralization was completed, causing language functions to be largely settled within the left hemisphere (Li 2013). During the critical period, it is suggested that native-speaker command of language can be acquired, but when attempts to acquire language begin after this special 'window of opportunity', language-learning will proceed more slowly and ultimately will be less successful, not reaching regular, native-like levels. Subsequent research led to the conclusion that brain lateralization actually occurs quite a bit earlier than previously assumed, and a modified view of the CPH was proposed in which the important peak of the critical period for language acquisition ends much sooner than initially thought, around the age of 5. Language-learning between the ages of 6–10 was then hypothesized to take place during a gradual 'offset' of the critical period and to be less effective than between ages of 2–5, though still allowing for higher levels of achievement than language acquisition attempted after the offset period.

The CPH was originally proposed as a theory to explain the failure of language development to regular, native-like levels in various children who were found not to have had any normal exposure to language in their early years, and whose process of acquisition only began after early childhood. Despite significant input and instruction provided by linguists and psychologists, children with such backgrounds were often only able to develop quite basic language skills and regularly failed to achieve native-speaker proficiency. In other behavioral studies of animals and humans, it has frequently been noted that stimulation and experience of an appropriate type must occur within a particular time frame—a critical period—in order for certain properties and traits to develop fully and in a normal way. Critical periods have been posited as temporal constraints for a wide range of phenomena, for example the development of sociability and territoriality in canines, imprinting in various birds (ducks, Japanese quails, gulls), masculinization-feminization in turtles, species-normal song development in birds, among other patterns (Eubank and Gregg 1999: 71). In humans, there is a critical period for the development of normal vision, found to extend from birth to around the age of 6. With such abundant empirical support for the existence of critical periods in the natural world, linguists argued that it would be plausible to attribute major failures found in late childhood/adolescent language-learning to the effects of a critical period constraining the acquisition of human language. The CPH therefore emerged as a potential explanation for instances of unsuccessful *first* language acquisition, when adequate linguistic input and interaction are not made available to children at a certain age.

Whether the CPH may also apply to occurrences of consecutive *second* language acquisition (SLA) in the same way it is assumed to constrain *first* language acquisition (FLA) requires some careful thought and investigation, as there are differences in the two language learning conditions. The principal similarity between FLA and SLA which leads one to suppose the CPH as a constraint on both such processes is the observation of lower than native-speaker levels of ultimate attainment when acquisition is delayed until adolescence or later in both FLA and SLA. However, when FLA begins after the critical period, the result is found to be extreme and sometimes catastrophic. Children who try to acquire their first language only when reaching puberty typically experience great difficulties in mastering the grammar of adult language and often end up speaking in chaotic ways, without the structure imposed by syntactic rules regularly governing the target language (Pinker 1994). When SLA is initiated in adolescence or adulthood, by way of contrast, the level of linguistic achievement that can be reached is qualitatively far higher than with late FLA, and although speakers generally fail to reach native-levels of proficiency, they nevertheless can become very competent speakers. Late SLA would therefore seem to benefit significantly from the fact that speakers have already developed a first language in their early years, this somehow facilitating the learning of further languages later on in life, while late FLA operates entirely without such a foundation and seems to suffer badly as a result. These similarities and differences between first- and second-language acquisition need to be borne in mind when assessing the potential relevance of the CPH for SLA as well as FLA. In considering the CPH relative to SLA, we will first briefly review arguments and evidence which support the assumption of the CPH as a constraint on second-language learning, and then present common arguments given against such a view, along with alternative suggestions and approaches to SLA.

Positive evidence for the CPH in second-language acquisition has been provided by studies of young bilinguals and later L2 learners which show that there are differences in speakers' performance in language tests which relate to age of acquisition. Johnson and Newport (1989) report on a linguistic experiment carried out with 46 Chinese and Korean learners of English who had all lived in the USA for at least five years, but who had arrived in the USA at different ages. Participants in the test were asked to judge whether a set of 276 English sentences were grammatical or not. Half of these sentences were grammatical, but the other half contained different morpho-syntactic errors relating to verbs and nouns, for example:

Every day our neighbor wash the car.
The farmer bought two pig at the market.
A bat flewed into the attic last night.

The results of the experiment showed that those who had arrived in the USA and had begun to learn English between the ages of 3–7 performed as accurately as monolingual native speakers, but those who arrived later, between the ages of 8–10, failed to demonstrate native-like abilities. Johnson and Newport argued that the distinctions in proficiency they found should be attributed to the CPH, and showed that the key factor in test performance was indeed age of arrival and not any other influence such as length of residence, motivation, or cultural factors. A similar study of grammaticality judgments by Chinese children described in Liu, Bates, and Li (1992) also concluded that age 6–7 was important for the attainment of native-level L2 skills. Immigrant children beginning their learning of English before this time performed like native speakers, while those who started learning English later typically made non-native-like errors in their judgments. In the area of phonology, other research has shown that native-like accents and pronunciation are most likely to be achieved by speakers who begin learning an L2 at a young age, in DeKeyser and Laron-Hall (2005) this being found to be age 6.

A second area of investigation which has added support for the CPH in SLA is the development of *neuro-imaging* studies which provide information about the areas of the brain that are involved in language production and understanding. The broad observations to come out of many fMRI (functional magnetic resonance imaging) and ERP (event-related potential) studies is that early bilinguals, who have learned their L2 within the hypothesized critical period, show differences in brain activity during speech events (speaking and listening) from late bilinguals, who have learned their L2 in adolescence or adulthood. Early bilinguals show a markedly greater involvement of areas in both the left and right hemispheres of the brain, whereas in late second-language learners it is clearly the left hemisphere which dominates speech production and processing and the right hemisphere plays very little role for language (Birdsong 1999b; Neville et al. 1997; DeKeyser and Larson-Hall 2005; Hull and Vaid 2005). This observation that early SLA makes use of different neural systems from late L2 learning is naturally explained if there is a critical period for second-language learning and post-critical period SLA is carried out in qualitatively different ways from the establishment of bilingualism in early years.

Arguments which have been given *against* the assumption of a critical period for SLA have principally come in two forms. The first of these highlights a prediction of the CPH that L2 learning should be fully native-like during the peak of the critical period, be *somewhat* less successful during the offset period of the critical period, and then show a clearly marked downturn when the end of the critical period is reached. SLA investigations which consider speakers who began L2 learning at different ages, from early childhood through adolescence and into adulthood, should expect to find a point at which learning outcomes start to decline very significantly, this marking the end of the hypothesized critical period. However, studies of various phenomena have reported that L2 learning abilities seem to decline in an even way as speakers' age of acquisition increases, and there is evidence of a steady downward progression at more or less the same rate rather than any sudden, sharp drop-off, as might be expected by the CPH. For example, Flege, Munro, and MacKay (1995) tested the English pronunciation skills of 240 native speakers of Italian who had immigrated to Canada between the ages of 2 and 23 and had lived in Canada for over thirty years. When native speakers of Canadian English were asked to judge the level of the L1-Italian speakers' English accents (when pronouncing five short sentences, such as *The red book was good*), the results showed that those who arrived in Canada earlier regularly achieved a more accurate pronunciation of Canadian English than those who arrived later, and none of the late learners in the study was judged to be native-like in their pronunciation, which initially seemed to support the CPH. However, when the rate of decline was mapped according to age, it was found to be very even and without any sudden drop-off indicating the end of a special, critical period for learning. The lack of a sharp age-related discontinuity in L2 learning found in this and certain other investigations seems to go against the expectations of the CPH.

A second aspect of the CPH which has been investigated experimentally and disputed is the prediction that native-like ability in an L2 should not be achievable if learning begins after the hypothesized critical period, in adolescence or adulthood. With regard to the attainment of native-like pronunciation of an L2, Long (1990) explicitly suggests that for most people this should only be possible if L2 acquisition begins before the age of 6, though a few speakers may still be able to sound native-like if they start to speak an L2 between the ages of 6–12. When exposure to the L2 only begins after the age of 12, according to Long, it will be impossible for learners to acquire a native accent. Such claims were argued to be too strong by Bongaerts (1999) in a study which examined very advanced Dutch speakers' pronunciation of L2 English and French. The participants in Bongaerts' research had learned a little English/French in high school from the age of 12 onward, but then had intensive input and training in English/French when they began university at age 18. When asked to read a series of sentences in English and French, recorded and judged for their accent quality by L1 speakers of English and French, some of those taking part in the experiment were judged to be indistinguishable from native speakers. Bongaerts concluded from this that there is no absolute age-related barrier to the achievement of a native-like accent in a second language, contra assumptions of the CPH. Bongaerts added, however, that the attainment of native-like pronunciation skills in late L2 learners was nevertheless still quite exceptional as a phenomenon, so some explanation for the uncommon success of the exceptional speakers in his study was necessary. Bongaerts suggests that this was due to the speakers' very high level of motivation, the large amount of L2 input they received from native speakers when entering university, and special, intensive training they were given, making them aware of subtle differences in the sounds of Dutch and English/French and how to accurately reproduce these in their L2 speech. With a certain, few individuals, such highly focused training and the richness of their linguistic environment appears to have led to native-speaker levels of L2 accent performance, at least in reading exercises, which is unanticipated for the CPH.

When researchers challenge the suggestion that there is a biologically determined critical period for L2 acquisition, alternative hypotheses need to be provided for the common failure of late L2-learning to be as successful as early bilingualism often is. One idea proposes 'automatization' and 'entrenchment' of individuals' language learning abilities as a possible explanation for age-dependent differences in L2 achievement. The suggestion is that if children receive input from just a single language during their early years, the brain may adapt itself in a significant way to accommodate the linguistic properties of this language and in doing so become very rigidly structured. The L1 input will result in 'automatization' of the language faculty and will make later changes and adjustments necessary for the addition of a second language quite difficult to bring about. Otherwise put, the brain gets so used to dealing with one type of language over several years (the initial L1), that it cannot easily switch to incorporate a different linguistic system later. However, if two different languages are learned sequentially at an early age, this may occur before the first language fully automatizes the brain, and so allow for successful native-like acquisition of the second language. Other suggestions offered up to explain age-related acquisition differences highlight social factors which may impact learning. Adolescents and adults typically attempt to learn second languages in quite different environments from those enjoyed by children and generally have much less time for L2 interactions, greater stress and pressure in their lives, and receive less attention from language instructors than children normally receive from their parents and other caregivers (Bialystok and Hakuta 1999). All this is suggested to make late

L2 learning more difficult for speakers and to result in lower outcomes than with infant and early child bilingualism.

Quite generally, with such conflicting ideas and evidence being present in the literature, there is still no consensus of opinion about the CPH. Some researchers are convinced that it plays a role in constraining second-language acquisition, while others remain skeptical and believe that differences in ultimate attainment between early and late L2 learning should be attributed to other factors. A few final comments can be made here. First, despite attempts to prove the CPH incorrect by identifying late L2 learners with apparent native-like skills in certain areas, it has not been possible, to date, to find any individual who has mastered native-level skills in all areas of language, i.e., syntax, semantics, morphology, as well as phonology, and the best 'counter-examples' to the CPH are late learners who have developed native-like pronunciation, and have not been tested for their abilities in L2 grammar and word meaning. DeKeyser (2005) stresses this important point, saying: 'It is doubtful whether there is any evidence that anyone has learned a second language perfectly in adulthood.' Second, the evidence presented for native-speaker levels of phonological proficiency in works such as Bongaerts (1999) is possibly less conclusive than has been suggested. Native-like pronunciation of the speakers' L2 has only been demonstrated in very constrained tasks involving the reading of short, pre-prepared sentences. It is not at all clear whether speakers who are judged native-like in their reading of sentences would still be rated native-like if asked to produce instances of unscripted, spontaneous speech. Indeed, in another study, Patkowski (1990) failed to find native-like levels of phonological performance in any of the advanced speakers whose pronunciation was judged from recordings of more natural speech and conversations. Such observations might seem to bolster the case for the CPH, despite the lack of critical period cut-off effects found in studies like Flege, Munro, and MacKay (1995).

To the extent that cut-off effects and age-related discontinuities have indeed been observed in other pieces of research, these seem to lead to the view that a critical period exists which has a peak spanning ages 2–5, when native-levels of ability are reached by all children receiving sufficient L2 input, and an offset period ending at some point between the ages of 6–10. During the latter portion, L2 learners can still develop *near-native* skills and sound very similar to native speakers in many ways, but can generally be distinguished from native monolinguals in other, sometimes subtle ways, by means of careful testing. In the post-critical period stage, a steady decline in learning ability continues further, making it more and more difficult for a second language to be learned easily and well. Two complications make this picture still an ongoing hypothesis which is very much in need of further exploration and substantiation. First, there is considerable variation in individuals' levels of achievement when learning is initiated in later years—some speakers are much better late learners than others. Second, it is possible that the critical period for development of native-like *pronunciation/phonology* may not coincide fully with the timespan enabling native-like *syntax* and *morphology*; hence the window of opportunity for achieving native-like language skills may shift just a little, depending on the linguistic skill being considered. The addition of these confusing properties to an already contentious area of research will certainly keep arguments over the CPH alive and on the agenda as one of the most contested issues in the theoretical study of L2 acquisition.

Going into reverse: language loss

Our discussion of the CPH has focused on how languages are learned. A rather less-studied, but intriguing phenomenon is the occurrence of language loss. It has been found that languages once acquired can (disappointingly) be lost, a process technically known as *'language attrition'*. Most cases of such attrition occur when an L2 has been partially learned, but not used or reinforced on a regular basis, and speakers gradually forget what they may have struggled hard to learn. In other cases, changes in a person's life situation may also affect their L1 abilities and cause these to decline, with potentially dramatic effects in younger speakers. Children have sometimes been reported to lose their first language at an amazingly fast rate if they are immersed in an environment where the first language is no longer spoken at all. One study of a 6-year-old Spanish girl who was suddenly placed in a completely French-speaking environment showed that her abilities in Spanish disappeared in just three months, and were quickly replaced with a native-speaker knowledge of French.

Although personal language loss might often seem to be almost total if a language is no longer used for a significant period of time, with speakers having only very dim memories of languages they once spoke, there is also certain evidence that linguistic knowledge, once established, may not be fully lost when attrition occurs, but simply stored away in some dark corner of the brain where it is temporarily inaccessible to speakers. Studies of second-language acquisition have compared the performance of first-time learners—complete novices, who have no prior knowledge of a target language—with that of second-time learners, who had previously studied a language but then apparently lost all knowledge of the language due to long-term attrition. It was found that second-time learners make much faster progress (re-)learning a language than those who have never studied it before, suggesting that earlier linguistic knowledge does not get eliminated when attrition occurs, and can be re-activated successfully with appropriate stimulation.

There are also frequent interesting anecdotes of individuals who have suddenly regained an ability to speak a language they have not used for a very long time, when some event triggers its reactivation. A particularly striking case of this kind involved a lady called Adelina Domingues, who was born in the Cape Verde Islands, where she grew up speaking Portuguese. At the age of 17, she emigrated to the USA as a young bride, and spoke English exclusively from this point on, as she raised five children in her new home. At the age of 108 she suffered a minor stroke, which had few non-linguistic effects, but completely eliminated her ability to speak English to anyone. At the same time that her English was abruptly disabled, rather bizarrely she simultaneously regained her earlier lost proficiency in Portuguese, a language she had not spoken for almost a century.[12] Languages which have undergone heavy attrition therefore somehow seem to remain subconsciously embedded in the brain for very long periods of time.

---

12. Sandra Disner, personal communication. Commentary on this case appeared in a CNN interview posted at: http://newsroom.blogs.cnn.com/2014/06/03/did-bowe-bergdahl-forget-english/. See also the case of a woman who lost her ability to speak English following a bicycle accident, but regained an earlier knowledge of German in its place: https://www.bbc.com/news/disability-45804613.

Lexical storage: how a bilinguals' two vocabularies are represented in the mind

A further topic which has attracted much attention in discussions of bilingualism is the way that words in a speaker's L1 and L2 are mentally stored and accessed, and how a bilingual's two vocabularies may interact with each other. Here we will consider three models of 'bilingual lexical storage' that have been posited, each of which attempts to capture new data and insights that have come to light about the ways that bilinguals' brains organize words from L1 and L2.

The words that we know in a language are linked to mental *concepts* which encode the meanings of words—ideas we form in our minds about what a 'bicycle' or a 'chair' or 'windsurfing' is. With monolinguals, the linking of words to concepts can be assumed to be straightforward, and hearing a particular word will directly call up the concept associated with the word, as schematized below, where capitalized words are used as convenient, simple representations of concepts (hence BICYCLE is shorthand for what we understand by the word 'bicycle'—a means of transportation with two wheels, handlebars, a saddle, brakes, etc.).

Word – concept linking in monolingual speakers

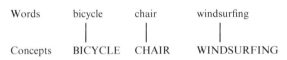

When a person knows two languages, the linking of words to concepts may potentially occur in different ways. A prominent early modeling of bilingual vocabulary organization in Weinreich (1953) and Ervin and Osgood (1954) proposed that there are three ways in which a person's L1 and L2 words may link up with the concepts in the mind. 'Compound bilinguals' are suggested to be speakers whose mental concepts are typically each linked to two words, one in the L1 and one in the L2. Hence, for example, English 'house' and Spanish '*casa*' would both be directly linked to a single concept representing the meaning of such objects ('HOUSE-*CASA*').

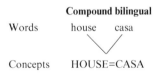

'Coordinate bilinguals' are hypothesized to have a different mental organization of words and concepts, with distinct concepts being present for each word in the L1 and the L2, rather than shared conceptual representations occurring with words in both languages. As diagrammed below, English 'house' would be associated with its own concept 'HOUSE', and Spanish '*casa*' linked to a separate concept '*CASA*'

A coordinate bilingual organization of words and concepts is suggested to arise in situations where an individual learns two languages sequentially in different environments, for example Spanish is learned by a child as its L1 in Puerto Rico and then English as an L2 in the USA, or Spanish is first acquired in the home and English is learned in pre-school and school. Where the L1 and L2 are acquired in different places, from different people and in different contexts, the concepts associated with L1 and L2 words are assumed to be independent of each other, and there may be slight differences in the meaning of typical translation pairs such as 'house' and '*casa*' (Heredia and Brown 2012). A compound structuring of words and concepts, by way of contrast, is assumed to result from a simultaneous bilingual learning experience, in which both L1 and L2 are regularly used by the same people in the same situations. Words in the two languages are taken to have the same meaning, and consequently are linked to a single conceptual form. These hypothesized differences between compound and coordinate bilinguals have been supported by tests which show that compound bilinguals rate common translational pairs of words as being more similar in meaning than coordinate bilinguals do, when the latter have learned their two languages in different environments (Lambert 1961). For compound bilinguals, such pairs are indeed equivalent in meaning, whereas the independent word-concept structure of L1 and L2 words in coordinate bilinguals allows for L1/L2 word pairs to vary in their meaning.

The third type of bilingual lexical organization posited by Weinreich (1953), and assumed in much following work, is referred to as 'subordinate bilingualism'.[13] Subordinate bilinguals are typically speakers whose L2 has been learned through their L1 by associating words in the L2 directly with L1 translation forms. Such speakers have a much less advanced proficiency in their L2 than in their L1 and less of a balanced L1/L2 ability than compound or coordinate bilinguals. Because of the dependency of L2 words on L1 translations, it is suggested that words in the L2 are not directly linked to concepts in the mind, but have to access concepts indirectly, passing through L1 words, as schematized below. As both L1 and L2 words are linked to a single store of concepts, words in L1 and L2 are taken to be fully equivalent in meaning.

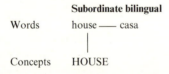

Two important points need to be made about Weinreich's three types of word-concept organization. First, these structures may undergo change over time. Most commonly, as speakers increase their proficiency in an L2 and use L2 words with increased frequency, a subordinate mode of organization may transition into a compound structure, as L2 words become directly linked to their associated concepts and no longer need to access the latter

---

13. Elsewhere, in Potter et al. (1984), Weinreich's subordinate and compound bilingual models have been recast, with different titles, as the 'Word Association Model' and 'Concept Mediation Model'.

indirectly through L1 forms.[14] Second, it is quite possible that bilinguals' vocabularies are not entirely structured by a single mode of organization, and it may be, for example, that some words are linked to concepts in an independent coordinate fashion, while others share a single conceptual form in a compound structure. Culture-specific words and abstract words (for example, for emotions) which vary quite significantly across different societies may be natural candidates for an independent coordinate-style word-concept linking, whereas words for culturally invariant concepts such as 'triangle', 'fire', and 'water' are expected to have a compound structure.[15] As new words are sometimes learned by means of translation rather than direct personal experience of their meaning, these may additionally be introduced in subordinate structures. The three forms of lexical organization described here can therefore be taken to allow for their application to individual words rather than the entirety of a bilingual's vocabulary—there certainly may be a dominant organizational style in each bilingual's mental lexicon, but also some variation, as speakers' knowledge of words and their relations to concepts changes over time.

An important refinement of Weinreich's original compound and subordinate models of bilingualism was later proposed in Kroll and Stewart (1994), in order to capture the results of various experiments into connections between words and concepts in sequential bilinguals. What Kroll and Stewart discovered is that there is very frequently an asymmetry in the speed of translation between words in L1 and L2 when L1 is a person's mother tongue and L2 a second language learned some time after the L1. Most sequential bilinguals are significantly faster at translating a word from their L2 into L1 than doing the opposite and translating from their mother tongue into the L2. Kroll and Stewart took this as evidence that there are two unidirectional links between L1 and L2 words, and that each link is of a different strength. A strong connection from the L2 lexicon to words in L1, represented by the bold line in the schematization of the Revised Hierarchical Model on page 298, allows for easy and swift movement from an L2 word to a translation equivalent in L1, while a weaker link going in the opposite direction from L1 to L2 words causes L1-to-L2 translation to be slower. The strong L2-to-L1 connection is established by the ways that L2 words may often be learned, as translations of L1 words, and the weaker L1-to-L2 link is due to the fact that L1 words are learned directly as names for concepts and are not frequently practiced as translations for L2 words.

An asymmetry in connection strength is also posited to occur between L1/L2 words and a shared set of concepts, with the L1 word-to-concept linking being strong, and the L2 word-to-concept store connection being weak. This difference in connection strength is supported by experimental evidence which reveals that sequential bilinguals are often faster at naming objects in their L1 than in their L2. The L1 word-to-concept connection

---

14. It is possible that a subordinate structuring could also undergo reorganization into a coordinate bilingual system, but this is less likely to happen than conversion into a compound structure, given that the meaning of L2 words is first established on the basis of L1 words (hence L1 and L2 words are equivalent in meaning and associated with identical conceptual forms).

15. We will consider the topic of cross-cultural variance in word meaning a lot more closely in the next chapter, on 'linguistic relativity'.

is strong and allows fast access of L1 words when associated concepts are activated, while the naming of objects with L2 words is slower, as a weaker link is assumed to connect the L2 lexicon and concepts (and object naming with L2 words may even be carried out in a two-step fashion, via L1 words, which will also make it slower than the speed of L1 naming).

The Revised Hierarchical Model (Kroll and Stewart 1994)

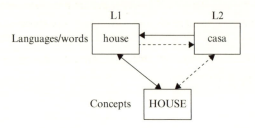

The Revised Hierarchical Model is well placed to capture the interconnections of L1/L2 words and concepts in bilinguals who have a clearly dominant language, normally their mother tongue.[16] A further minor refinement of this model, known as the Re-revised Hierarchical Model (Heredia 1997), substitutes the terms 'most dominant language' and 'least dominant language' for L1 and L2 in the Revised Hierarchical Model, as a way to allow for situations in which increased use of an L2 may actually make the L2 more dominant than the mother tongue. In such cases, the connections of L2 words to the shared store of concepts may then become stronger than the L1 word-to-concept link.

In addition to the models of bilingual lexical organization proposed by Weinreich and Kroll and Stewart, an influential hypothesis about variability in word-concept connections in bilinguals has been proposed in De Groot (1992), as the 'Distributed Conceptual Feature Model'. The goal of this modeling is to capture the degree of similarity that exists between L1 and L2 words that are common translation equivalents. The model posits that concepts corresponding to words can actually be broken down into 'semantic features' which are quite basic in their meaning and are available to form complex concepts and words in every language. Such features are therefore sometimes referred to as universal 'semantic primitives', and the analysis of words in terms of a set of more basic semantic features is often known as 'lexical decomposition'. Take the word 'woman', for example. This can be analyzed as a complex concept built up by the conjunction of three semantic features: female + human + adult, and represented in the following way.

---

16. In order to model simultaneous bilinguals, and early sequential bilinguals who have learned their two languages to the same level in the same environment, the Revised Hierarchical Model would need to be adjusted so that all links between L1/L2 words and concepts occur with broadly equal strength, as in Weinreich's compound bilingual model.

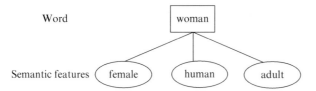

When words that are commonly taken to be close translation equivalents in two languages are analyzed in terms of basic semantic features, it is suggested that the more features shared by an L1/L2 pair, the closer they will be in meaning to each other. Words representing *concrete objects* may often be extremely similar or even identical in meaning in two languages. For example, English 'chair' and Dutch '*stoel*' are taken to share the same set of semantic features, as seen in the following representation.[17]

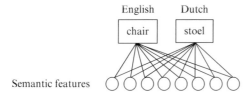

However, abstract nouns may have a significant overlap in meaning but not share all of the same semantic features. This is seen with a representation of English 'fear' and its closest equivalent in German '*Angst*'.

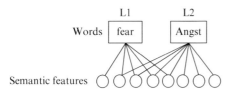

A useful prediction of the Distributed Feature Model is that the degree to which L1/L2 words share the same semantic features should determine how long it takes speakers to translate words from one language into the other, or to recognize that a word in one language is a close/direct translational equivalent of a word in another language. This prediction has been demonstrated to be correct in a number of different psycholinguistic experiments (Kroll and Tokowicz 2005). For example, words such as English 'chair' are translated into Dutch '*stoel*' more quickly than English 'fear' typically gets translated into German '*Angst*' or recognized as a translation equivalent to '*Angst*'. The Distributed Feature Model is thus able to provide a more fine-grained analysis of concepts than other approaches and contributes to our understanding of how L1/L2 words may sometimes be very similar in their basic meaning but still exhibit certain differences.

---

17. We do not attempt to give the identity of the semantic features here. What is important is the claim that the *same set* of features characterize both English 'chair' and Dutch '*stoel*'.

The interaction of L1 and L2 in speech production and processing

One of the most amazing properties of bilingualism, which is often just taken for granted, is speakers' ability to keep their two languages apart when they speak and produce sentences with words from just one language. How do stable bilinguals manage to consistently select and use words from one particular language without accidentally producing equivalents from their second language, as young children sometimes do in an early period of mixing? Speakers must have some kind of mechanism allowing them to successfully *inhibit* the selection of words from the non-target language (the language not in use), so as to avoid inadvertent mixing of L1 and L2. For some time, linguists hypothesized that bilinguals regularly developed a neural linguistic 'switch' which would allow for any language not being used to simply be turned off at will (Macnamara and Kushnir 1971). More recently, questions have been raised as to whether such a switch mechanism is completely 'foolproof' and whether speakers' inhibition of a non-target language is really always 100%. The fact that bilinguals can indeed produce unmixed sentences with words from only one of their two languages might seem to suggest that inhibition of the non-target language is completely effective. However, it is also possible that a second, non-target language might still be switched on subconsciously to some extent and have hidden effects on our understanding. Here we will consider some interesting work which has been carried out on bilinguals' language 'production' (of speech and writing) and 'processing' (comprehension of others' speech and writing). The conclusion of these studies is that bilinguals' second language may in fact be switched on 'in the background' at times when their other language is being spoken and this has the potential to cause various (subtle) interference effects. We will first look at what has been found to occur in bilinguals' speech production and then turn to consider processing, drawing on summaries of a number of revealing experiments well-described in Grosjean (2013a/b).

Hermans et al. (1998) is a study of Dutch-English bilinguals which sets out to probe the question of whether language production is 'selective' or 'non-selective' in nature. If speech production is an entirely selective process from start to finish, this means that only words (and grammar) from the target language are considered and selected for the construction of sentences, and a bilingual's second language plays no role at any point in sentence planning. If, however, speech production may be non-selective, this would mean that, at a certain point in sentence planning, properties of the non-target language might come into play and 'interfere'. For example, the construction of sentences begins with speakers having an idea that they wish to express, and this requires the use of various concepts. As the concepts present in a bilingual's brain may be linked to two different vocabularies, it might be that at an early planning stage the activation of a concept may cause words in both of a bilingual's languages to be considered as candidates for use, not just words from the target language. This would constitute a non-selective step in the planning of speech, if it did occur, and one might expect to find certain signs of lexical interference if one were to look carefully enough.

Hermans et al. (1998) used a picture-naming task to investigate the selective/non-selective issue with their Dutch-English bilinguals. Participants in the experiment had to name pictures viewed on a computer as swiftly as possible in their L2 English, at the same time as hearing words from their L1 Dutch, added in as deliberate interference. Some of the Dutch words played during the experiment were phonologically related to (sounded like) the Dutch word for the object seen in the picture. For example, when seeing a picture of a mountain, participants might hear the Dutch word '*berm*' which sounds like the Dutch word for 'mountain', which is '*berg*' ('*berm*' actually means 'verge'). The researchers wanted to see if the playing of such words might cause speakers to slow down and hesitate in providing their answers, and this is indeed what happened. Participants' naming of pictures in English was significantly slower when Dutch words phonologically related to the correct English word were heard than when participants were played phonologically unrelated Dutch words. The conclusion drawn from this was that participants were accessing their Dutch vocabulary when they were attempting to produce English words. Hearing the Dutch word '*berm*', for example, was suggested to activate similar-sounding Dutch words including '*berg*', and as '*berg*' has the same meaning as English 'mountain', this made it harder for participants to select 'mountain' as their response, resulting in delays in naming the picture—in order to overcome the 'temptation' to use words from the non-target language, speakers had to inhibit use of their second language with deliberate effort. This consequently provides evidence that bilinguals' two vocabularies do interact with each other in speech production, and that word selection in a target language is subject to possible interference from speakers' second language, which is not fully switched off during the planning of speech.

However, further experiments argued for a more nuanced conclusion. A criticism of the Hermans et al. study was that both English and Dutch were activated in the minds of participants when they began the experiment, due to various factors (for example, interactions with the researchers taking place in Dutch as well as English), and this might have had an effect on their performance in the picture-naming task. Quite generally it has been claimed that situations which involve use of both of a bilingual's languages will activate both, and may heighten the potential for L1/L2 interference. To have a more complete picture of the ways that a non-target language might be switched on and interfere with target-language production, experimental conditions should ensure that the non-target language is not activated by any aspects of the experiment (so all interactions and instructions should be given in the target language alone). In such a situation, does a speaker's non-target language still have the power to intrude in L1 production? Hermans et al. (2011) set out to investigate this with a different experiment, in which only English was used with Dutch-English bilinguals. In the experiment, participants viewed pictures of objects on a computer followed by a letter and had to indicate whether the letter they saw was part of the English name of the picture. In some cases the letter clearly was a sound in the English name of the picture, for example, a picture of a 'bottle' was presented followed by a 'b'. In other cases, the letter was not a sound in the English name of the picture, but it was a prominent sound in the Dutch word for the object seen in the picture, as, for example, when an 'f' followed a picture of a bottle—the Dutch word for 'bottle' is '*fles*'. The goal of the experiment was to see if the picture plus letter combination might activate Dutch words as competitor candidates for naming the pictures and cause a slow-down in decision time. However, no hesitations occurred in this experiment, leading to the conclusion that participants' non-target language (Dutch) was fully suppressed and was not causing interference, unlike in the experiment in Hermans et al. (1998).

A follow-up experiment reported in Hermans et al. (2011) added a further twist to the unfolding story of background L2 interference. The additional experiment carried out by Hermans' group replicated the picture-naming + letter experiment with special pairs of words known as 'cognates'. Cognates are words which have the same meaning in two languages *and* have a similar sound, e.g., Spanish *nación* and English *nation*, German *Brot* and English *bread*. In the new trial of the experiment incorporating cognate words, a significant slow-down effect was noticed to occur. So, when a picture of the moon was presented with a following 'm', the fact that the Dutch word for 'moon' is the cognate '*maan*' did interfere with participants' reaction time, revealing that the non-target language was activated and intrusive in lexical decision tasks when words in a bilinguals' two languages were similar in form and meaning (i.e., cognate pairs).

The global conclusions to result from these investigations, and other similar studies, are that L1/L2 interference may occur despite speaker attempts to inhibit a non-target language, and is generally dependent on the activation level of L1 and L2. When situational factors cause a speaker's non-target language to remain switched on while their other language is prioritized for speech production, the former may have various effects on the way the latter is made use of, and certain stages of production would seem to be non-selective, accessing information from both a person's languages. However, when a bilingual's second language is not activated by aspects of the speech situation (for example, recent use of the L2, or knowledge that others present are also speakers of the L2—see Grosjean 2013: 58 for a list of relevant factors), full inhibition of interference from the non-target language seems to be possible for speakers to achieve, except in the special case where words in the L1 and L2 are closely related in both sound and meaning, as pairs of cognate words.

Similar conclusions have also been reached in experimental studies of language processing—how individuals understand sentences. One experiment carried out by Spivey and Marian (1999) made use of eye-tracking technology to investigate language comprehension in bilinguals. Russian-English bilingual test participants wore a head-mounted eye-tracker which allowed researchers to see and record where the participants were looking during the processing of speech. In front of each participant was placed a board with four objects on it, and an instruction was given in Russian to move one of the objects to another position on the board. In various instances, one of the non-target objects had an English name which sounded like the name of the target object in Russian. This was done in order to see if it would cause participants to look to the non-target object more than in other cases and perhaps be slower to move the correct target object, due to a competition effect and the temptation to move the non-target object. Results showed that when one of non-target objects did indeed have an English name which sounded similar to the name of the target object in Russian, participants looked toward it significantly more than in other cases. The conclusion was therefore drawn that bilinguals' second language does have an effect on the processing of speech in their other language, and that inhibition of a speakers' non-target language is not fully successful in comprehension tasks.

As with the production studies, however, others noted that interference from the non-target language might have been assisted by artificial activation of the second language during the experiment, due to the way that the experiment was carried out. Marian and Spivey

(2003) consequently ran the same experiment taking special care not to trigger any activation of English, and found that interference no longer occurred—participant looks to the non-target object whose English name resembled the target object's name in Russian were no longer than to other objects on the board. It therefore appears that interference occurs specifically when a person's second language is in a state of activation during processing, as with production, and that full inhibition of a non-target language is generally possible only when it has not been recently stimulated. Bilinguals can suppress subconscious interference from a non-target language when they speak and listen to others, but only when this language is temporarily dormant and has not been 'woken up' by different forms of attention given to it.

Finally, it needs to be added that L1/L2 proficiency level also seems to play a role in any interference that occurs, and when a person is processing speech heard in their stronger language, there will be less activation and interference from the weaker language, but when a speaker listens to others' speech in their weaker language, the stronger language may naturally be more active and intrusive in comprehension (Weber and Cutler 2004). Interactions of various types thus occur between bilinguals' two languages both in speech and listening, and have a range of dynamic effects on the ways that speakers are able to make use of each of their languages.

Bilingualism and its effects on children's cognitive and educational development

Having looked at a range of different theoretical aspects of bilingual learning and representation, the last part of the chapter will now consider certain practical consequences which bilingualism may have for children's cognitive development and how the learning of two languages may impact educational success, either positively or negatively. Specifically, we will be asking whether the exposure of children to two languages from an early age is potentially beneficial for children, or, alternatively, whether it could be harmful in any way.

In earlier centuries, and right up until the mid-20th century, it was often suggested that bilingualism actually had undesirable effects on children's mental development and might impede its normal progress, as speculated in the following statements made by prominent intellectuals in the 1920s:

> ... the use of a foreign language in the home is one of the chief factors in producing mental retardation. . . . (Goodenough 1926: 393)

> ... the brain effort required to master (the) two languages instead of one certainly diminishes the child's power of learning other things. (Jesperson 1922: 148)

The idea was broadly disseminated that learning a second language takes up vital space in the brain that is needed for the full development of a person's first language and possibly other cognitive functions, and therefore causes these abilities to be significantly reduced in efficiency. Such a view has sometimes been referred to as the 'Balance Theory' (Baker 1988: 170). In many instances, the claims that were made about the negative effects of bilingualism had no foundation in actual research but simply corresponded to intuitions and feelings that social scientists had about bilingual behavior. However, later there did seem to be some empirical evidence supporting such general views, and bilingual children in various communities studied in North America and Scandinavia were noted to perform poorly in certain cognitive and linguistic tasks, and less successfully than monolingual children tested in other communities. Such results were presented as a warning to parents and educators that bilingualism comes with a worrying cost for children's general progress in school and puts them at a disadvantage in relation to their monolingual peers.

More recently, from the 1950s onward, the validity of these early intelligence-testing experiments and their conclusions was called into question in two inter-connected ways. First of all, it was objected that the bilingual children who were identified in earlier studies as having lower levels of intelligence and weaker linguistic abilities were all children who came from poor immigrant families facing a range of socio-economic problems and that there was no testing of bilingual children from more stable backgrounds. It was therefore suggested that the reportedly poor cognitive and linguistic performance of the immigrant children might well be due to other socio-economic factors and might not be directly attributable to their exposure to two different languages. Secondly, when research was carried out with other, different groups of children in the 1950s, it was found that there were no negative effects of bilingualism on the children's linguistic and cognitive development, and that, when children from similar family backgrounds were compared, there was no obvious variation in IQ levels among children having a bilingual vs. a monolingual experience.

From the 1960s onward, interesting studies then started to reveal that there actually might be positive effects from continued exposure to two or more languages. This began with studies in Canada which assumed that bilingual children were in fact less linguistically and cognitively able than monolinguals and tried to identify what the causes of such deficiencies might be. The studies made sure that the children compared all came from similar family-background types, in many initial cases being middle-class children attending French schools in Montreal. Instead of finding that bilingual children were indeed behind monolingual children in their general performance, the research projects instead found that bilinguals actually scored higher than monolinguals in tests designed to measure both verbal skills and general intelligence. As the positive results of these more balanced investigations were confirmed by further studies carried out in different countries, researchers became increasingly convinced that bilingualism had the potential to be beneficial for children and to help them linguistically and also cognitively in various ways (which will soon be described). The trend of later research has consequently pointed much more toward positive rather than negative effects from bilingual exposure.

Where beneficial effects were found to emerge from an exposure to two languages, this advantage came to be referred to as '*additive bilingualism*', while a second term '*subtractive bilingualism*' was applied to cases which still seemed to show certain negative effects of bilingual exposure. Much attention then focused on trying to understand how and why children's bilingual experiences could apparently have such differing results, so that instances of subtractive bilingualism could be prevented in the future and could be replaced with the benefits of additive bilingualism.

Researchers found that subtractive bilingualism most frequently occurred among children from low-income minority groups with poor L2 skills in the majority language used in schools, and concluded that the phenomenon of subtractive bilingualism occurs for two basic reasons, one linguistic and the other attitudinal/psychological.

Linguistically, an important obstacle to academic progress for minority group children occurs when their mother tongue is not developed well enough (with the acquisition of skills in reading and writing) before they are required to learn and use the language of the local majority of speakers for classroom activities in school. Quite generally, the degree to which education carried out in an L2 may be successful or fail often depends on the level of formal proficiency children are helped to achieve in their L1 before attempting to learn and use an L2 in school. Specifically, it is argued that children should first be allowed to learn how to read and write in their mother tongue before being asked to learn a second language and to become literate in this L2. If children enter school with little or even no knowledge of a local majority language and have to learn such a new language at the same time as learning how to read and write for the first time with this language, the double learning burden often seems to be too great and causes failure.

Children also need to be taught how to use language 'as a cognitive tool' in a range of analytic tasks in school. If children are able to develop use of their L1 in analytic reasoning before facing the challenge of learning and using an L2 regularly in the classroom, this will help them cope with new learning tasks which require the L2. However, if children do *not* develop their L1 to the point where it can naturally be used for analytic reasoning and argument before confronting an L2 in school, severe difficulties may be experienced as they face the triple task of: (a) rapidly learning a second language for use in school, (b) simultaneously learning literacy skills with this new L2, and (c) learning for the first time how to develop linguistic reasoning skills through the vehicle of the second language. There is consequently much agreement that literacy should first be taught through a child's mother tongue, wherever possible, and children should also learn how to use their L1 in academic-type discussion, before the attempt is made to acquire and use these skills in a second language.

Psychologically, subtractive bilingualism may be caused in part by the expression of negative attitudes toward minority children's home languages both in school and in other daily interactions. If a child's mother tongue is stigmatized and devalued when it is different from that of the local majority, the child may not develop use of its L1 properly outside the home environment and may even develop negative attitudes toward using the L1 in the home itself. This may then negatively impact the child's ability to successfully learn the L2 of the local majority, as L2 learning often benefits from the transfer of certain linguistic skills initially developed in a speaker's first language. It is also found that negative attitudes toward the L1 may lead children to actually reject their mother tongue and try to replace it with use of a second language that is perceived to be more prestigious. However, if such a second language is not learned well, this can leave the child without an advanced level of proficiency in either of the languages it has been exposed to.

When negative attitudes are publicly expressed toward the languages of minority groups and the cultures associated with these languages, this frequently has further effects on the *cultural identity* of emerging bilingual children. A child may come to develop negative feelings about the culture associated with its mother tongue, as well as the language itself, leading to attempts to identify fully with the local majority culture. For example, young, ethnic Koreans born in Japan in the mid-20th century often chose not to embrace any of their Korean heritage language and culture and instead began to identify completely as Japanese, both culturally and linguistically. Another common result in such situations is that children from minority groups may feel mentally lost between the two cultures they are raised in. Children feel external pressure to reject their heritage culture because it is not valued in any positive way, but do not feel well enough integrated into the L2 majority society to be accepted as full members of that society. Faced with such a conflict, children often develop feelings of social disconnection, alienation and confusion, a condition referred to as '*anomie*'.

Subtractive bilingualism is therefore a complex phenomenon caused by the interaction of different social and linguistic factors. Young individuals exposed to two languages are sometimes unable to develop either of these to the advanced level necessary for academic success, leading to difficulties in school and other psychological conflicts relating to L1/L2 cultural identity. Attempting to prevent the future occurrence of subtractive bilingualism is an important task for educators and linguists and will require a better structuring of young people's bilingual learning in schools, as well as careful attention to the social attitudes expressed toward heritage languages and their speakers. Exposing children to two languages from an early age is not inherently perilous, but needs planning and care in certain situations in order to be successful. And when bilingualism is well established and allowed to flourish in children, interestingly it can lead to all kinds of personal advantages, as will now be described.

'The bilingual advantage'

Investigations have continued to probe the linguistic and cognitive abilities of bilingual children and adults since the 1960s and have frequently found that certain skills may be developed by bilinguals to a higher level than typically occurs with monolinguals, as well as levels of general intelligence and academic performance that equal or sometimes surpass those of monolinguals.

On the linguistic side, studies have found that young bilingual children show *greater verbal fluency* than their monolingual peers, as demonstrated in their ability to relate complex stories containing a greater number of distinct ideas than monolinguals, despite the fact that young bilinguals appear to have a smaller total vocabulary in each of their languages than monolingual children (Doyle et al. 1978). It is concluded that being able to communicate well may actually not relate to the size of a person's vocabulary but rather to the way that a person uses the words they know. Many investigators believe that bilingual children are more creative in their language use and more flexible in their thinking because of their familiarity with more than one linguistic system, this providing them with an ability to see things from different perspectives (Peal and Lambert 1962; Bialystok 2005). Evidence has also been found that learning a second language can actually have positive effects on the improvement of a person's first language. In one study, children whose first language was Swedish were found to improve their L1 abilities quite significantly after they started to learn English, and subsequently performed at a more advanced level in their mother tongue than other, monolingual Swedish children.

On the general cognitive side, Peal and Lambert (1962) posited that bilingualism provides 'a positive boost to cognitive functioning', and much research carried out since this work has confirmed that bilingualism does appear to have a beneficial effect on the stimulation and enhancement of abilities known as the *'executive function'*. This is the set of cognitive skills used in processes of selection, inhibition, multi-tasking, and switching and sustaining attention. Three principal abilities are assumed to be at the core of the executive function: (i) *working memory* (the ability to mentally maintain and process information), (ii) *cognitive flexibility* (the ability to efficiently adjust to situational changes and new information), and (iii) *inhibitory control* (the ability to ignore potentially interfering information) (Bialystok and Barac 2013). Bilinguals of all ages have been found to show high levels of command of executive function processes, and demonstrate greater *'executive control'* than monolinguals. Among children, executive control is known to be important for academic achievement, which in turn is related in a positive way to long-term health and well-being (Duncan, Ziol-Guest, and Kalil 2010; Best, Miller, and Naglien 2011; Bialystok, Craik, and Luk 2012).

Experimental research has shown that bilinguals are particularly good at solving problems which require a person to ignore misleading clues and suppress and *inhibit* distracting information which may interfere with finding the correct solution to a puzzle. Bilingualism naturally improves levels of *inhibitory control* because such a mental process has to be applied by bilinguals every time they speak—using one of a pair of languages requires a bilingual to constantly inhibit words from the other language in order to avoid inadvertently mixing the L1 and L2. Young bilinguals get practice in this executive function from an early age, and the use of inhibitory control with language seems to carry over beneficially into other, non-verbal cognitive tasks (Bialystok 2005). In simple terms, learning how to keep two languages apart helps a person be able to focus their attention more selectively in non-linguistic tasks and concentrate better on just a sub-part of the information present in a situation, even when other, irrelevant information is contextually very prominent.[18]

---

18. Two examples of the kinds of experiments used to probe inhibitory control with young bilingual children can be briefly mentioned here. In Bialystok and Codd (1997), children were shown two towers made of either Lego or Duplo blocks and told that each Lego and Duplo block represented an apartment where one family could live. Bilingual and monolingual children had to say which tower housed the greater number of families. The misleading clue in the experiment was that the Duplo blocks were twice as large as the Lego blocks, so a tower of four Duplo blocks (housing four families) was taller than a tower of six Lego blocks (housing six families). While monolingual children regularly indicated that a four-block Duplo tower housed more families that a six-block Lego tower, distracted by the height of the tower, bilingual children were able to ignore the irrelevancy of the tower height and answered more correctly than the monolingual children.

In Frye, Zelazo, and Palfai (1995), monolingual and bilingual children were given two containers, each marked with a colored shape, for example a blue circle or a red triangle. The children had to distribute a set of cards with colored shapes into each container, and in one test were asked to do this according to shape, hence a red circle should have been added to the container marked with a blue circle, and a blue triangle should have been put in the container bearing the red triangle. Monolingual children participating in the experiment were distracted by the salient color of the cards and regularly sorted the cards according to their color, not their shape (hence a red circle was added to the red triangle container). Bilingual children were able to ignore the color distraction and focus only on the shapes on the cards and consequently sorted cards correctly according to shape. Elsewhere, bilinguals have also regularly been noted to perform better than monolinguals in applications of Stroop Tests and Simon Tests (Bialystok, Craik, and Luk 2012).

Early bilingualism stimulates the growth of inhibitory control and other cognitive abilities, and the maintenance of bilingualism allows a person to retain these skills at a higher level than monolinguals through adult life and into older age, when they seem to bring further advantages of a rather different type, offering helpful protection against cognitive decline with age. General studies of aging have often highlighted the importance of participation in stimulating mental and social activities as a means to help counter the effects of cognitive deterioration in old age, this providing individuals with valuable *cognitive reserve* (Stern 2002). Bilingualism helps speakers build up and maintain cognitive reserve in a similar way, due to the mental exercise which is regularly involved in switching between different languages and inhibiting the language currently not being spoken (Bialystok and Barac 2013). As a result of this extra boost in cognitive protection, it has been found that bilinguals frequently retain good mental health for longer periods of time than monolinguals. On average, aging bilinguals experience the onset of Alzheimer's type dementia several years later than monolinguals, and seem better able to cope with the disease when it eventually does develop (Bialystok, Craik, and Luk 2012). Additionally, older bilinguals have been observed to maintain their powers of attention more effectively and with less decrease than many same-aged monolinguals.

One final area of 'bilingual advantage' which can be noted here concerns social identity. If a child's home language is not stigmatized and devalued by speakers of other languages, research shows that there can be very positive *cultural effects* arising from exposure to two languages. A bilingual experience may not only increase a child's general cognitive powers, but also broaden children's cultural perceptions and allow them to see people from other linguistic groups in a more positive way than monolinguals may, on average, due to bilinguals' interaction with and more advanced knowledge of two different ethno-linguistic groups. Such a constructive effect on attitude may arise even when a bilingual's two languages are spoken by groups which are distinct but culturally not very far apart. For example, English-French speaking children in Canada have been shown in certain tests to have much more positive opinions of people from the other language community than monolinguals had—hence bilingual children from dominantly French-speaking families displayed better attitudes about English-speaking people than monolingual French-speaking children did.

Bilingual children can also develop very positive bi-cultural identities when neither linguistic/cultural group is negatively valued. In place of developing *anomie* from the apparent conflicts of an imbalanced two-culture situation, children can instead come to feel that they belong to two different cultural groups in a very enriching way. This has been reported in investigations of second- and third-generation speakers of various heritage languages in the USA, who indicate clear feelings of pride in their heritage background, and identify themselves as following and benefiting from both American and Chinese/Korean/Hispanic/Italian cultural traditions. Such rewarding biculturalism is a phenomenon which is suggested to be comparatively recent in the USA, and did not seem to exist in the same way before World War II. In the first half of the 20th century, it was reported that bilingual children in the USA frequently did suffer from cultural alienation because they felt that they were not genuine members of their parents' heritage culture nor that of the dominant American society. However, with gradual changes in public attitude toward the value of other cultures in the USA, conditions enabled the growth of confident new generations of bi-cultural Americans proud of their origins and their abilities in the heritage language of the group. When given appropriate support from outside society, a bilingual environment can therefore have very positive results for the development of personal identity, helping stimulate open-mindedness and tolerance in culturally well-balanced individuals.

In sum, far from being a threat to cognitive development and efficiency, much evidence now indicates that bilingualism can bring considerable benefits to individuals in a broad variety of ways relating to language, cognitive processes, and cultural identity, this being collectively referred to as the 'bilingual advantage'. Researchers have also arrived at a better understanding of the conditions necessary to promote such additive bilingualism and simultaneously avoid the kinds of negative educational outcomes which have been termed 'subtractive bilingualism' in the past. Such advances in our knowledge of bilingualism lead to the hope that there may now be greater encouragement for people of all ages in monolingual societies to engage in a bilingual experience and reap the rewards of the acquisition of two languages which bilinguals elsewhere have long been enjoying (whether they were aware of this or not).

Suggestions for further reading and activities

1. Use the internet and libraries to find out what is meant by the controversial term *semilingualism* and the *Threshold Model*, which references semilingualism as one possible outcome of bilingual exposure. Try to find different views on semilingualism and discuss how they diverge in their opinions of semilingualism. What is meant by BICS (basic interpersonal communicative skills) and CALP (cognitive academic language proficiency) in Jim Cummins' work on the Threshold Model?
2. Watch the first half of the award-winning film *Speaking in Tongues* by Marcia Jarmel and Ken Schneider (2010), a Patchworks Production. This film shows you how immersion bilingual (dual-language) education works, by following four young aspiring bilinguals in schools in San Francisco. After watching the film, discuss both the children's and the parents' different attitudes toward bilingual education.
3. Read the following article to learn more about educational achievement levels in children attending dual language immersion schools:

    Lindholm-Leary, Kathryn. 2016. Bilingualism and academic achievement in children in dual language programs. In Elena Nicoladis and Simona Montanari (eds.), *Bilingualism across the lifespan*. Berlin: De Gruyter Mouton, 203–223.

4. Read sections 8.1–8.3 in chapter eight of *Bilinguality and Bilingualism* by Josiane Hamers and Michel Blanc (2000, Cambridge: Cambridge University Press). These sections deal with bilingualism and bi-cultural identity. Find out what is meant by the terms *enculturation, acculturation*, and *deculturation* and how cultural and linguistic identity develops.
5. Use the internet and the following reading to find out more about *language attrition*.

    Montrul, Silvina. 2016. Age of onset of bilingualism effects and availability of input in first language attrition. In Elena Nicoladis and Simona Montanari (eds.), *Bilingualism across the lifespan*. Berlin: De Gruyter Mouton, 141–161.

6. Read about bilingualism and language-mixing in advertising around the world in the following article by Tej Bhatia and William Ritchie. If you have experience of the mixed use of two languages in advertising, is this similar to what is described in the article?

   Bhatia, Tej, and William Ritchie. 2004. Bilingualism in the global media and advertising. In Tej Bhatia and William Ritchie (eds.), *The handbook of bilingualism*, Oxford: Blackwell, 513–546.

7. Chapters 23–31 of *The Handbook of Bilingualism*, edited by Tej Bhatia and William Ritchie (Oxford: Blackwell, 2004), each focus on bilingualism in different parts of the world (Europe, Latin America, South Asia, etc.). Arrange for each member of your class to select one of these chapters and present its principal findings in class. What kinds of similarities and differences seem to be found in bilingualism around the world, as described in these chapters?

8. Some researchers studying age-of-acquisition effects in bilinguals have proposed that the term *sensitive period* be used in place of *critical period*. Try to find out what the intended difference is between these two terms.

9. Find out more about *cognitive reserve* and how bilingualism can help prevent the onset of dementia in aging populations in the following reading:

   Duncan, Hilary, and Natalie Phillips. 2016. The contribution of bilingualism to cognitive reserve in healthy aging and dementia. In Elena Nicoladis and Simona Montanari (eds.), *Bilingualism across the lifespan*. Berlin: De Gruyter Mouton, 305–322.

9

Language and Thought
The Linguistic Relativity Controversy

Introduction

Chapter 8 included some discussion of how words link up with concepts in the minds of speakers, and how these connections may be organized in people who know more than one language. In chapter 9 we are going to consider how language in general relates to thought, and whether it can be concluded that the language we speak may cause us to see the world in certain pre-determined ways, influencing our way of thinking and aspects of our behavior. Studies of the world's many languages show that there are many ways that languages may be different from each other in the structure of their vocabularies and grammar. If language has the power to affect the way we think and experience the world, does this mean that speakers of different languages will have different ways of thinking and perceptions of the world to some extent, and how might we be able to detect this? How might the effects of language-mediated perception potentially manifest themselves in a person's behavior, differently in different societies? This is the much argued-over topic of '*linguistic relativity*', which has been examined, defended, and criticized by linguists, philosophers, and social anthropologists for many decades now, a high-stakes hypothesis which speculates that language may create more subjectivity in our thought than most speakers are normally aware of.

The first part of the chapter will introduce ideas about linguistic relativity as they evolved during the middle of the 20th century in the work of Edward Sapir and Benjamin Lee Whorf. We will then note various criticisms raised at early approaches to linguistic relativity which caused a downturn in interest in the theory during the 1970s–1980s. Research into linguistic relativity bounced back again from the 1990s to the present, as new techniques were developed to probe in a more rigorous way how language may influence non-verbal behavior and to provide better empirical support for the hypothesis. The third part of the chapter will look at some of the key experiments linguists have carried out on the ways that languages express spatial location, object categorization, quantity, and color variation in different ways, and how events may be remembered differently through language—all phenomena which are argued to show the effects of language on perception. Finally, the chapter will consider the interaction of linguistic relativity and bilingualism and how an individual's way(s) of thinking may be impacted by knowledge of two different languages, linking us back to the theme of chapter 8.

The Sapir-Whorf Hypothesis

The core idea of linguistic relativity that language exerts an influence on the way we perceive the outside world has also been referred to as the Sapir-Whorf Hypothesis, named after Benjamin Lee Whorf and Edward Sapir. The latter was a professor of linguistics and anthropology at Yale University. The former was a student of his, who by profession was a chemical engineer and a fire prevention officer. Whorf became deeply interested in trying to understand differences between what he called 'Standard Average European' (English, French, German, Spanish, and other languages of western Europe), and Native American languages, and was jointly inspired by Sapir's teachings and his own investigations of Hopi and other Native American languages. Both Sapir and Whorf shared the view that language constrains people's experience of the world, and that different languages will provide different access to and perception of outside 'reality'. A good sense of Sapir and Whorf's ideas about the connections of language with thought can be gained from the following oft-cited quotations from their work.[1] First of all, Sapir proclaims, quite dramatically that:

> Human beings do not live in the objective world alone . . . but are very much at the mercy of the particular language which has become the medium of expression for their society. It is quite an illusion to imagine that one adjusts to reality essentially without the use of language. . . . The fact of the matter is that the 'real world' is to a large extent built up on the language habits of the group. . . . We see and hear and otherwise experience very largely as we do because the language habits of our community predispose certain choices of interpretation. (Sapir 1929: 209–210)

Whorf develops this line of thought further in a well-known piece of work originally written in 1941 (note that the first term used in this passage, 'background linguistic system', means the grammar of a language):

> The background linguistic system of each language is not merely a reproducing instrument for voicing ideas but rather is itself the shaper of ideas. . . . We dissect nature along lines laid down by our native languages. The categories and types that we isolate from the world of phenomena we do not find there because they stare every observer in the face; on the contrary, the world is presented in a kaleidoscope flux of impressions which has to be organized by our minds—and this means largely by the linguistic systems in our minds. We cut nature up, organize it into concepts, and ascribe significances as we do, largely because we are party to an agreement to

---

1. Also quoted in Wardhaugh (1998), Swoyer (2011), and various other overviews of Sapir and Whorf's famous writings.

organize it in this way—an agreement that holds throughout our speech community and is codified in the patterns of our language. The agreement is of course an implicit and unstated one, but its terms are absolutely obligatory; we cannot talk at all except by subscribing to the organization and classification of data which the agreement decrees. . . . This fact is very significant for modern science, for it means that no individual is free to describe nature with absolute impartiality but is constrained to certain modes of interpretation even while he thinks himself most free. . . all observers are not led by the same physical evidence to the same picture of the universe, unless their linguistic backgrounds are similar, or can in some way be calibrated (be made similar). (Whorf 1956: 214)

Consequently, for both Sapir and Whorf, people experience the world in distinct ways because of differences present in their languages, which act as filters on the world, highlighting and obscuring different physical phenomena like a special lens fitted to a camera. This selective, filtering effect is taken to be a function of variation in the meaning and availability of words across different languages, and differences in their grammar, as will now be illustrated.

Differences in words and concepts across languages

Many language groups develop specialized vocabularies which appear to relate to aspects of the environment they live in. The following are some frequently mentioned examples:

- *Sami* (Finland) has 10 distinct terms for reindeer which have different physical properties (Thomason 2015).
- *Pintupi* (Australia) has 10 different words corresponding to the English word 'hole' (Salzmann et al. 2014).
- *Shona* (Zimbabwe) has very large numbers of words for 'walking' carried out in different ways (Comrie et al. 2003).
- *Hanunóo* (the Philippines) has dozens of words for rice (Conklin 1957).
- *Inuit* (Alaska, Greenland) is reported to have a variety of distinct words referring to different kinds of snow.[2,3]

---

2. Salzmann et al. (2014) note six different words for 'snow' in Yup'ik Eskimo which have fully distinct morphological shapes: *qanuk, natquik, nutaryuk, muruaneq, utvak,* and *pirtuk*. Following Whorf's original statement that Inuit had multiple words for 'snow' and accordingly a more differentiated perception of snow, claims about the number of Inuit words for 'snow' became significantly inflated in the popular press, which eventually drew heavy criticism in Pullum (1989). Harrison (2010) presents a recent vindication of Whorf's original claims with detailed discussion of words for 'snow' and 'ice' among Inuit languages.

3. More humorously, the 2014 film *Paddington Bear* notes that there are over 200 different ways of saying 'it's raining' in British English, due to the ever-frequent occurrence of rain in Britain. This is (deliberate) exaggeration, though there certainly are many ways to refer to rainfall in British English, and people in Britain often do talk about the weather.

Here are the actual words for 'holes' in Pintupi, together with their fine-grained meanings (from Crystal 1987):

pirti	a hole in the ground
yulpipa	a shallow hole where ants live
nyarrikalpa	a hole inhabited by small animals
pirnki	a hole formed by a rock shelf
kartalpa	a small hole in the ground
pulpa	a rabbit hole
makarnpa	a goanna hole
katarka	a hole left by a goanna after hibernation
yarla	a hole in an object
mutara	a hole in a spear

It has been suggested that the existence of such specialized vocabularies will result in the speakers of these languages paying more attention to differences in reindeer, rice, snow, and types of hole, etc., and that speakers of other languages without such a wide range of words for these categories will not pay attention to and perceive the distinctiveness of the relevant physical phenomena, leading them to different perceptions of the same 'reality'.

Additionally, it is well known that all languages have certain words which are difficult to translate into other languages. A colorful sampling is provided here, from collections posted online by Khodorkovsky (2008), Echevarria (2009), and Wire (2010). The descriptions of the meanings of these words given by the three authors here are noted to be quite approximate in several instances, and not able to entirely capture the special properties of abstract terms such as *wabi-sabi, toska,* etc.

Wabi-Sabi (Japanese)
A word which refers to a way of living that emphasizes finding beauty in imperfection, and accepting the natural cycle of growth and decay. (Echevarria 2009)[4]

Mamihlapinatapei (Yagan, Argentina)
A wordless yet meaningful look shared by two people who both desire to initiate something but are both reluctant to start. (Khodorkovsky 2008)

Ilunga (Tshiluba, Democratic Republic of Congo)
This word refers to a person who is ready to forgive any abuse the first time it occurs, to tolerate it the second time, but to neither forgive nor tolerate a third offense. (Khodorkovsky 2008)

Tartle (Scottish English, Scotland)
A verb meaning to hesitate while introducing someone due to having forgotten his/her name. (Khodorkovsky 2008)

---

4. See also more discussion of *wabi-sabi* at: https://www.altalang.com/beyond-words/2009/04/13/wabi-sabi-translating-the-beauty-in-imperfection/.

Prozvonit (Czech and Slovak)
A word which refers to the action of calling someone on a cell phone causing it to only ring once so that the owner of the phone will call back, helping the caller save money on his/her minutes. (Khodorkovsky 2008)

Toska (Russian)
A word described by the author Vladmir Nabokov in the following way: 'No single word in English renders all the shades of toska. At its deepest and most painful, it is a sensation of great spiritual anguish, often without any specific cause. At less morbid levels it is a dull ache of the soul, a longing with nothing to long for, a sick pining, a vague restlessness, mental throes, yearning. In particular cases it may be the desire for somebody of something specific, nostalgia, love-sickness. At the lowest level it grades into ennui, boredom.' (Wire 2010)[5]

Tingo (Pascuense, Easter Island)
This word refers to the act of taking objects one desires from the house of a friend by gradually borrowing all of them. (Khodorkovsky 2008)

The existence of words with very special meanings which are difficult to translate suggests that speakers of different languages have different sets of concepts established in their minds. For example, the Russian concept of *toska* is assumed not to be present in the minds of speakers of other languages as no direct translational equivalent for *toska* can be found in other languages. Consequently, speakers of Russian have a system of concepts which is distinct from that of speakers of other languages and therefore a partially different worldview. The more a language has words of this type, without direct equivalents in other languages, the greater this may affect speakers' perception of the world and make it different from speakers of other languages.

Often words which are difficult to translate refer to objects, patterns of behavior, and institutions which are culture-specific and do not occur in other societies. English has many such words, linked to different sub-cultures present in the English-speaking world, for example the following terms linked to different aspects of college life in the USA:

fraternity/sorority house
hazing
tail-gating
rush week
frontload
dead week

---

5. This quotation is also posted at: http://www.goodreads.com/quotes/309633-toska---noun-t--sk---russian-word-roughly-translated-as.

Cultures need not even be dramatically different for there to be words which cannot be simply translated. For example, Hudson (1996) argues that the following common English words have no direct single word equivalents expressing the same concept in French:

brown   monkey   chair   jug   carpet

Hudson concludes that different languages do not just provide different words to refer to the *same* cross-cultural concepts, but the set of concepts associated with each language and its words is actually different, a kind of lexical and conceptual variability he terms 'semantic relativity' (Hudson 1996: 82). The question is then raised as to whether there are any obvious cross-linguistic limits on semantic relativity and whether different languages may vary greatly in the range of concepts associated with words in their vocabularies. If languages might differ very significantly in their inventories of concepts (linked to words) and cause largely different conceptual systems, this should have major consequences for speakers of different languages and should regularly result in a non-aligned perception of the world and people's relations within it. While serious attempts to quantify semantic relativity have not been made, a fairly widespread view is that speakers of different languages most probably share a core set of concepts relating to the physical world (or, at least, concepts that may not be identical but are relatively close to each other in meaning) and that culture-specific lexical variation such as that highlighted here represents more of a periphery of speakers' vocabularies with less real significance than the core.

Hudson also notes that it is possible that all of the complex concepts encoded by culture-specific words in a language might actually just be different combinations of a smaller number of more basic concepts shared by speakers of every language. For example, German makes a distinction between verbs of eating and uses the word *essen* when humans are engaged in eating and *fressen* when it is animals who are eating. Although these words might be taken to represent two distinct concepts, they can also be broken down into the subparts [human + agent + eat] and [animal + agent + eat], and as English clearly has the concepts [eat], [human], [animal], and [agent] (referring to the person/animal deliberately carrying out an action), it could be suggested that German is not really different from English in any fundamental way and doesn't have any special concepts which are not present in English— German simply combines the common basic concepts in a way which doesn't occur in English to produce two verbs where English has developed only one.[6] Supposing all apparent differences in the range of concepts present in different languages could be explained in such a way, semantic relativity might in fact be suggested to be very limited. Languages could be taken to share a universal stock of basic concepts used to construct additional, more complex concepts.

In recent years this possibility has led certain linguists, such as the semanticist Anna Wierzbicka, to try to identify what these universal concepts might be, and how they can

---

6. Another simple example of this kind of 'lexical decomposition' is the concept [woman], which can be analyzed as being built from the more basic concepts (or 'semantic features'—see chapter 8) [+female], [+human], and [+adult].

be used to provide definitions of complex concepts in all languages. Such an approach to semantic relativity is still programmatic, however, and is not accepted by all researchers as a realistic account of speakers' mental processing and production of complex concept/word pairs. Indeed, certain psycholinguistic experiments have found evidence that complex concepts are accessed 'holistically' by speakers, without showing signs of being broken down into sets of more basic concepts. Hence even if it might be possible to analyze complex words as combinations of basic concepts, it is not clear that speakers actively do perform such an analysis every time they hear such words—once complex concepts have been formed in the brain and labeled with a word, they seem to be used and understood without any major process of lexical decomposition of the type needed to reduce them down again to sets of simple concepts. Consequently, once speakers of Russian have learned what *toska* means and have established it as a mental concept, this word will not subsequently be 'unpackaged' (fully) in everyday language use, and instead represents a concept that is constructed and present in the minds of Russian speakers but not those of other languages. Semantic relativity, as it occurs with such culture-specific concepts, therefore most likely needs to be accepted as an area of genuine variation across languages and across the conceptual systems of their speakers—though the question of how much of a language's vocabulary is taken up by culture-specific terms and how much is shared across cultures still remains.

Differences in grammar across languages

For Benjamin Lee Whorf, it was actually systematic differences encoded in the *grammar* of a language, rather than the existence of individual, culture-specific words, which have the greatest potential to cause differences in perception and worldview among speakers. In his discussion of the linguistic relativity principle, he emphasized that:

> ... users of markedly different grammars are pointed by their grammars towards different types of observations and different evaluations of externally similar acts of observation, and hence are not equivalent as observers but must arrive at somewhat different views of the world. (Whorf 1956: 221)

Grammar involves distinctions which are both very general and which are used very regularly. For example, the use of singular vs. plural encoding in nouns in English is a general distinction which is made *every time* a speaker of English uses a (count) noun—*dog/dogs, car/cars, book/books*, etc. Whorf suggested that distinctions found in the grammar of a language may have effects on speakers' non-verbal thought, causing speakers to see and pay attention to related distinctions in their general, non-linguistic perception of the world. For example, as speakers of English regularly make a singular/plural distinction in speech, they can be taken to perceive objects in the world in terms of the concept of singular vs. plural quantity, Whorf hypothesized. Because grammar-based distinctions are also made very regularly in our speech, they will constantly be reinforced by this high-frequency use and have a much more significant potential effect on our perception than individual, conceptually complex words such as *toska, wabi-sabi, fairness,* and *frustration* which speakers may use much less frequently.

Whorf himself was very interested in the structure of Native American languages and found that various of these languages did not have any extensive system of tense markings encoded on the verb, unlike European languages such as Spanish and Italian. However, many Native American languages do have verb endings which indicate how the speaker has come to know the content of the statement he/she makes. For example, different endings will indicate whether an action has been actually seen by the speaker, whether he has just heard (from a reliable source) that it took place, or whether it is just rumor that the action occurred. Such verb affixes are often called 'evidentials' as they indicate the type of evidence a speaker has for a statement. Observing such morpho-syntactic differences between Native American and many European languages relating to tense and evidentiality, Whorf argued that speakers of Native American languages may be more concerned with the status of the truth of a statement than with the notion of time and tense, when compared with speakers of European languages. For Whorf, the frequent absence of tense endings on verbs in languages such as Hopi has the result that speakers of these languages *pay less attention* to the notion of time, and consequently may develop a quite different perception of time than speakers of languages with regular tense endings on verbs, as occurs in the languages of western Europe. Such a view is supported further by an additional observation relating to the linguistic structuring of time. In European languages, time can be broken down into units which can be counted, for example: *four weeks, two hours, five minutes*. However, such a segmentation of time into discrete, countable units is described as not being possible in the Native American languages Whorf was investigating in anything like the way it occurs in European languages, which readily allow for divisions of time into easily countable portions of past, present, and future. The special structuration of time words found by Whorf in Hopi and the differences between Native American and European languages in use of these words is again consistent with speakers of these languages having developed different ideas of time.[7]

Criticisms of early linguistic relativity

While many people found the Sapir-Whorf Hypothesis fascinating and inspiring when it was developing in its early years, during the 1970s and 1980s others began to level criticisms at it and claim that it was both theoretically flawed and empirically unproven. These criticisms of the initial stages of the Sapir-Whorf Hypothesis caused various changes to be made in the ways that linguistic relativity came to be investigated from the 1990s onward, when interest in linguistic relativity grew again. Here we will mention five points often raised as arguments against the Sapir-Whorf Hypothesis as it was originally conceived (or portrayed—sometimes critics of the theory were rather free in attributing claims to Whorf that he had actually not made).

---

7. See Pavlenko (2005: 443) for further discussion.

Linguistic diversity does not always imply major differences in worldview and perception

A central assumption of linguistic relativity is that different ways of perceiving the world regularly arise as a result of differences in language. Consequently, it might be expected that when languages are found to be quite different from each other, this should cause the occurrence of correspondingly different worldviews and different ways of thinking. However, it has been pointed out that the languages spoken by culturally similar neighboring societies may often show many linguistic differences without there being obvious major differences in the worldview (apparently) held by their speakers. For example, English and German, or Burmese and Thai, are pairs of languages which are linguistically quite different from each other in many ways, but there would not seem to be equivalently large differences in cultural orientation among speakers of these language pairs. Therefore, it would appear that significant differences in the structure of languages do not necessarily cause profound differences in worldview.

The lesson to be drawn from such observations, for those attempting to defend the principle of linguistic relativity, should be that *not all linguistic differences* can be assumed to cause differences in perception, hence that languages may vary grammatically in a number of major ways without this structuring thought and perception in any particular way. For example, whether a language employs case-marking with its nouns or not, whether it creates questions via the fronting of question words such as 'who' and 'what' or not (*wh*-movement vs. *wh in situ*), whether it has clitic pronouns, dominant SVO, SOV, or VSO word order, etc.—these are all common linguistic parameters of variation which would not be expected to produce differences in ways of thinking for any analysts, either relativist or anti-relativist. The fact that languages may be quite different in certain aspects of their grammar without this causing major differences in worldview is therefore ultimately not a strong argument against linguistic relativity, as only certain kinds of grammatical variation can naturally be expected to have potential consequences for perception.

Not all our concepts arise from language

The Sapir-Whorf Hypothesis holds that speakers learn about aspects of the world, establish concepts, and structure their perception of reality by means of the language they learn to speak, which results in a highlighting of certain features of the world and a shadowing of others, as each language imposes an idiosyncratic filtering effect on people's perception of reality. Such an approach emphasizes that concepts arise in our minds as a direct result of the language we acquire, with its particular vocabulary and grammatical properties. However, critics of the Sapir-Whorf Hypothesis have frequently noted that mental concepts can arise without any direct stimulus from language, quite independently as the result of personal experience and interaction with our environment. For example, pre-linguistic children are strongly believed to entertain concepts and develop a perception of the world around them, but this is not driven by knowledge of language at an early age. The same conclusion applies to other animate species—animals interact with their environment as they mature and arrive at a perception of the physical world, but not as the result of any linguistic system. When language does become available to us as children, adolescents, and adults, we also continue to form many concepts without having any names/linguistic labels for these, encountering objects in our daily life and building corresponding mental concepts for these objects without being able to name them correctly. Any adult who has had to carry out repairs to a household appliance (for example, some plumbing component) will probably have had the following experience—you know the 'bit' that needs replacement and have a clear picture of it in your mind, but when you go to the local hardware store to buy it, you are only able to describe it in a clumsy way to the storekeeper as the technical name of the item is unknown to you (and turns out to be a 'back-flow preventer', a 'vacuum-breaker', a 'pipe escutcheon', or some type of 'flange'). Concepts can clearly arise and be entertained in the mind without this necessarily being mediated by language.[8]

This being so, it might be argued that the Sapir-Whorf approach is entirely wrong, and that *all* concepts come to us from our direct experience of the world, hence that language plays no role in the selective establishment of our concepts and the structuring of perception. However, this would also not seem to be right, as many complex concepts clearly do not result from simple interaction with the world around us. Words such as *politics, anthropology, atom, heaven*, and *interstellar* are all terms which we will learn through language, and it is unlikely that we will have a concept formed for these items before we learn the words themselves. Normally we will hear such words first and then gradually develop a corresponding concept as we learn more clearly what the words are commonly used to refer to.

The general conclusion from the preceding is that some of the concepts which underlie our perception of the world may be established directly from experience, without language, but others are language-dependent and cannot be the result of simple interaction with our environment. This means that two basic 'routes' to the formation of concepts are in operation as we expand our conceptual systems. The fact that some concepts do come to us without the assistance and interference of language means that a particularly strong version of the Sapir-Whorf Hypothesis, claiming that thought only results from the manipulation of concepts sourced from language, cannot be maintained.[9] The additional observation that some concepts cannot be the result of simple non-linguistic experience means that language does impinge on the formation of our conceptual system, as suggested by Sapir and Whorf.

---

8. See also Schaller (2012: 44–45) for description of the case of a deaf Mexican man named Ildefonso who grew up without instruction in any systematic sign language. At the age of 27, in California, the author Susan Schaller attempted to teach Ildefonso American Sign Language, but realized that he could make no connections of the signs she made to their intended referents. In other words, he had not realized that objects in the physical world were associated with names of any type (in the case of deaf people, manual signs being used as names). After many days of trying to teach Ildefonso the link between the sign for 'cat' and real cats or pictures of cats, suddenly Ildefonso realized that the signs Schaller was making performed a symbolic function and that all objects had commonly agreed-upon names. He then became very excited at this discovery and wanted to know and learn the signs for everything he was familiar with. The important point here is that prior to learning signs at the late age of 27, Ildefonso showed very clear indication that he had established concepts for all the entities he regularly found around him but simply had no names for any of these concepts. Concepts can therefore become established in the mind and be maintained for long periods of time without being associated with any linguistic label.

9. In fact, neither Sapir nor Whorf suggested that all our thinking is carried out by means of language and that thought = language.

The big question not resolved here is how much of a person's conceptual system comes from direct experience and how much results from the influence of language and the categories and words that exist in particular languages. To what extent does language affect the way we build up concepts structuring our perception of the world?

Linguistic relativity vs. linguistic determinism

Many commentaries on the Sapir-Whorf Hypothesis have focused on a distinction in the degree to which language may be suggested to exert an effect on our thinking, the two terms *linguistic relativity* and *linguistic determinism* being used to represent a weaker and a stronger interpretation of the Sapir-Whorf Hypothesis.

Linguistic relativity

Language has a *tendency to influence* thought. It points us toward different types of observation and predisposes certain choices of interpretation and particular ways of thinking (Montgomery 1986; Cook 2011).

Linguistic determinism

Language *fully determines* thought, it forces speakers to think in a certain pre-set way.

Critics of the Sapir-Whorf Hypothesis have regularly argued that the strong version of this approach, linguistic determinism, cannot be correct, because not all thought involves language, and we can also learn new perspectives and mental concepts beyond those commonly given to us by our mother tongue by acquiring other languages (more on this shortly). Researchers who continue to work on the relativistic program initiated by Sapir and Whorf and who have positive views of linguistic relativity now all seem to agree with this assessment, and the deterministic view that language constrains our perception in a totalitarian way is not held among the majority of practicing 'neo-Whorfian' linguists (Montgomery 1986: 253; De Groot 2011: 373). As Swoyer (2011: 34) puts it: 'Extreme versions of the linguistic relativity hypothesis (i.e. linguistic determinism) are dead, and good riddance', and a similar general sentiment is expressed by Gentner (2007: 193): 'The neo-Whorfian debate should not be on whether language forces one unique conceptual system on its speakers (i.e. linguistic determinism) but on whether it privileges some systems over others (the linguistic relativity view).'[10] In assessing the legacy of the Sapir-Whorf Hypothesis, it is therefore important to realize that it is the so-called 'weaker' version of this approach that is commonly investigated by linguists now, linguistic relativity, and not the more exotic possibility that language functions like an absolute strait-jacket on thought, imposing a view of the world that cannot be escaped from by any means (linguistic determinism).[11]

---

10. Quoted in Everett (2013: 107).

11. Despite some of the rhetoric in Whorf's writings, it is likely that Whorf himself did not uphold an absolute deterministic view of language, though he is sometimes represented (rather unfairly) as advocating such a position.

The need for non-verbal evidence of the influence of language on perception

This is an important point. Whorf actually presented no non-linguistic evidence for his assertions about the effects of language on perception, and all his suggestions about correlations between differences in language and differences in ways of thinking were essentially educated guesses rather than the result of scientific experiment. Whorf made the assumption that if people could be shown to speak in different ways, it could also be concluded that they think in different ways. He would typically highlight certain distinctions present in two or more languages and claim that these must lead to differences in modes of thought. However, the fact that people speaking one language describe physical phenomena in a way that varies from people speaking a second language does not mean that these groups necessarily conceptualize the relevant phenomena in different ways. This effect on cognition must be shown, with experimental tasks that probe speakers' non-verbal behavior, where it can be seen that people really *act* differently when there are differences in their languages. Having more words for plants or dogs or cloudy skies in a particular language does not, by itself, demonstrate that its speakers perceive plant-life, clouds, and canines in a finer way than those who speak other languages, and connections between specific linguistic diversity and variation in thought need to be carefully proven rather than just asserted.

This criticism of the early Sapir-Whorf Hypothesis has been well taken to heart by researchers interested in examining Whorf's program further, and has led to a much stronger emphasis on experimental evidence for linguistic relativity and the use of appropriate methodology to investigate links between language and cognition, making testable behavioral predictions beyond linguistic data.

Additionally, where controlled experiments do appear to reveal significant correlations of language differences with non-verbal behavior and perception, it needs to be carefully shown that it is indeed specifically the differences in language which are causing cognitive differences and not some other coincidental factor relating to culture or the environment. Otherwise it might be argued that aspects of a people's culture and environment have a direct effect on their cognition, causing them to behave in certain ways, and language itself is not the cause of differences in perception, just an additional (non-agentive) reflection of such differences. Recent experimental investigations of linguistic relativity have also attempted to confront this challenging issue wherever possible and wherever culture/the environment could provide a plausible alternative explanation of certain aspects of behavior.

In considering the various criticisms that were raised against the Sapir-Whorf Hypothesis in its early stages, quite generally, it can be said that these have had a beneficial, corrective effect on the investigation of linguistic relativity and the claims which arise from studies of language variation. Shortly we will see some of the results of experiments designed to test linguistic relativity in more rigorous ways with different patterns of language, carried out by neo-Whorfian researchers who have taken on board the range of points just made. Before we do this, we will first consider a number of other conceptual issues and questions relating to linguistic relativity discussed in an interesting book written by the linguist George Lakoff.

Lakoff (1987) on Whorf and linguistic relativity

In his (1987) book *Women, Fire and Dangerous Things: What Categories Reveal about the Mind*, the linguist George Lakoff revisits some of the important themes raised by Whorf and the idea of linguistic relativity. Lakoff makes a number of useful, insightful points and raises many further questions about the systems of concepts that speakers of different languages have and how these may differ from language to language.

Lakoff points out that there are varied reactions to the idea that different cultures might understand the world in different ways. Some people may be concerned that communication between different groups will be hampered by underlying differences in ways of thinking. Others find it very interesting that there may be different worldviews and perspectives on life held in different societies. Still others are sure that the idea of linguistic relativity must be wrong and that everyone sees the world in the same way whatever language they happen to speak. Lakoff then points out that there may be different views of linguistic relativism, depending on the answers that are given to thirteen very broad questions relating to concepts and conceptual systems, including the following selection of six.

Questions about relativism and concepts (Lakoff 1987: 307)

- How much variation is there across conceptual systems?
- How deep is the variation?
- Do conceptual systems that are organized differently count as different systems?
- Do systems that are used differently count as different systems?
- Do you behave differently if you have a different conceptual system?
- Do you have control over which concepts you use?

Fundamental concepts

Relating to the questions of the depth and breadth of variation in conceptual systems, certain kinds of concepts may play a greater role and have a greater importance than others in potentially causing widespread, significant differences between languages—'fundamental concepts', such as those relating to space and time, rather than 'isolated concepts' which don't connect with other concepts to any significant extent.[12] Fundamental concepts involving spatial and temporal relations may often be used to establish other kinds of concepts and so have considerable effects on the conceptual system of a language. Hence if the fundamental concepts present in different languages show variation, then other concepts which depend on them will also vary (as suggested by Whorf with regard to the perception of time and space in Native American languages). Also, fundamental concepts tend to get incorporated into the actual grammar of a language (for example, time is often understood in terms of spatial relations, and tense-markers may therefore arise from words relating to relative physical location), so such concepts tend to be used with very high frequency, increasing their effects on a language and its conceptual system.

---

12. Lakoff (1987: 308) actually refers to isolated concepts as 'superficial concepts', but this term seems less suited to capturing the key property of such concepts—that they do not create strong connections with other concepts.

Isolated concepts such as Russian *toska* or Japanese *wabi-sabi*, by way of contrast, may be extremely interesting from an anthropological point of view and are not found in any other language, but their high degree of semantic specialization means that they are unlikely to affect much else in an individual's conceptual system and are unlikely to be used as building blocks to create other new concepts.

Consequently, when approaching the issue of the amount and depth of variation between conceptual systems with different languages, attention needs to be given to the kinds of concepts that appear to show variation. When fundamental concepts exhibit differences across languages, this will cause much wider variation through their conceptual systems. However, if the primary variation found in a language is just the existence of different isolated concepts such as *toska* which are not connected to other concepts, then its general conceptual system might not be so unlike that underlying other languages which lack these isolated concepts (hence although French lacks a direct equivalent to English '*fairness*' and various other isolated concepts, it may not be so fundamentally different from English in terms of its total conceptual system).[13]

The ability to form concepts

Every individual has the ability to form new concepts and generate new ideas. Because of this, there is an important distinction to be made between what occurs as an individual's currently formed *conceptual system* and the *conceptual capacity* (ability) of an individual.

A person's conceptual capacity. The ability each individual has to form new concepts. The same ability is present in all individuals.

A person's conceptual system. The set of concepts a person has at a particular point in time, different (to some extent) for each individual.

Given that people share the same basic conceptual capacity, what results in the existence of different conceptual systems is often the exposure to different experiences that people have in different societies (including exposure to language). Lakoff notes that a number of different outcomes may result from the interaction of our experience and our conceptual capacity.

Different experiences produce different concepts/conceptual systems

The Cora people of Mexico live in a mountainous area, and their daily interaction with this physical environment heightens their awareness of the summits, slopes, and bottom parts of hills. As a result of this, spatial geography relating to their surroundings has now

---

13. Similarly, the fact that speakers of Inuit might have multiple words depicting different occurrences of 'snow' should not affect much else in their conceptual system. In fact, it has been noted that many English-speaking skiers may also have a variety of words for snow (*powder, slush*, etc.), but the conceptual system these people have will *generally* still be very much like other English-speaking people because the existence of highly specific concepts such as *powder-snow*, etc., does not affect other parts of an individual's conceptual system.

come to be a salient part of the grammar of their language (Casad 1982). Although Cora people are born with the same conceptual capacity as speakers of other languages such as English, their particular experience of living in a mountainous area has led them to conceive of the location of objects in a way which is different from English-speakers, and they have formed a different set of positional concepts. In many instances, it may be concluded that exposure to different experiences leads to the establishment of (partially) different conceptual systems.

Parallel experience occurs, but different concepts evolve from this experience

It is also found that the *same* experiences may sometimes give rise to *different* concepts, because experience does not force one to conceptualize in any fixed way. Experience just provides the input necessary to form some type of concept. Pavlenko (2005: 115) describes a difference in the concept 'back' as it occurs in English and the West African language Hausa, as reported in Hill (1982). This term is initially established from the rear side of a person's body, and then often extended metaphorically to other objects, but possibly in different ways in different languages. In English if you are looking at an undifferentiated object such as a bush, the 'back' of the bush is the side which is furthest from view, however in Hausa the opposite is true and the back of the bush is the side of the bush which faces toward you. A speaker of Hausa will therefore describe the location of a bush between him/herself and a house as being 'behind/at the back of the house', and a tree visible on the other side of the bush as being 'in front of the bush', while English speakers would say 'in front of the house' and 'behind the bush' in these cases. Here the same conceptual capacity and the same basic experience leads to different ways of conceiving of space, and contributes to the creation of a different conceptual system.

Similar experiences occur, but certain concepts fail to be formed in some languages

A third scenario of note is where the same conceptual capacity and the same experience cause a concept to occur in one language/conceptual system but fail to trigger it in another. One interesting example of this quoted by Lakoff relates to the Tahitian people who, according to Levy (1973), have no word for 'sadness' and also no concept of 'sadness'. It is reported that Tahitians do indeed experience what appears to be sadness and depression, but they view this emotion as related to sickness, tiredness, or the attack of an evil spirit. Tahitians thus seemingly lack a concept which other languages have, although they have the same conceptual capacity and the experience necessary to give rise to the concept.

Translation and understanding

Scholarly debate on linguistic relativity has frequently focused on questions relating to translation and understanding, and how the availability or absence of translational equivalents for words in certain languages bears on hypotheses of linguistic relativity. Lakoff again provides useful insight into some of the key issues involved here, commenting on the four following claims which have often been made by different commentators (slightly adjusted from Lakoff 1987: 311):

1. If two languages have markedly different conceptual systems, translation from one language into the other will be impossible.
2. If translation is impossible, then speakers of one language cannot understand the other language.
3. If two languages have different conceptual systems, someone who speaks one language will be unable to learn the other language because he/she lacks the right conceptual system.
4. Because people *can* learn radically different languages, those languages can't have different conceptual systems.

Lakoff remarks that differences in conceptual systems may make translation difficult at times, and perhaps even impossible in certain cases (claim 1), but this does mean that *understanding* is impossible (claim 2). Supposing there are two languages A and B which have developed different sets of concepts in broadly the same kind of situation (outcome 2 described in the preceding), *direct* translation (i.e., word for word) between A and B is likely to be impossible. However, because a speaker of language A has the same conceptual capacity as speakers of language B, and (in the scenario envisaged) similar experiences to speakers of B, a speaker of A would still be able to *learn* language B by developing the different concepts associated with language B and linking these to the words of this language. The speaker of A can come to *understand* language B and learn to speak it even if he/she cannot *translate* all the words from B into A. For example, with sufficient effort, a speaker of English can learn Chinese along with all its special vocabulary items and different concepts, but still may not be able to create fully accurate, direct translations from Chinese into English in all instances. Direct *translation* necessitates that the concepts associated with words in two languages actually mirror each other, whereas *understanding* only requires that speakers' experiences of the world are broadly similar and that they have the same conceptual capacity (i.e., the same ability to form concepts).

So, while claim 1 above may be correct, claims 2 and 3 are not. Variation in the concepts present in two languages does not cause understanding and learning to be impossible. Even if a speaker of English does not make the considerable effort to learn Russian, a Russian-speaker could carefully explain the concept underlying *toska* to the English-speaker, using English words, and this description could then establish the concept of *toska* in the mind of the English-speaker. A linguistic label/name for this newly added concept can then be added for use when speaking English, and the most natural way to do this is to simply borrow the original word *toska* and incorporate it into English sentences (just as speakers of English have borrowed and use other emotional terms such as German '*Angst*' into English). In such a way, understanding can come about where direct translation is typically difficult. Claim 4 is also not supported—the fact that we can learn quite different languages does not mean that these languages must have the same conceptual system as our m other tongue—making use of our conceptual capacity, we can acquire new concepts and add these to the inventory of concepts we already have.[14]

Lakoff makes an additional relevant point about the flexibility of conceptual systems in general. Critics of the linguistic relativity hypothesis sometimes express skepticism at the suggestion that different languages may offer, privilege, or impose different views of the world and different modes of perception, and assert instead that speakers of all languages must interpret the world in the same basic way. It is assumed that conceptual systems provide speakers of all language with a *single* shared worldview and a single way of making sense of reality. Hence, for each area of experience the assumption is made that our conceptual system allows us only a single way of understanding that experience. However, Lakoff points out that the availability of different ways of thinking is actually quite common even within individual languages, and all speakers have a variety of ways of conceiving of their experiences just by means of the resources of a single conceptual system and language. It is therefore not true that we are constrained to think in a single way and perceive the world in a unique and uniform manner. For example, in trying to understand love, anger, friendship, and misfortune, speakers of English regularly make use of different means of conceptualization—'love' can be understood in terms of physical force (*attraction, electricity, magnetism, being drawn to someone*) or in terms of health (a relationship can be seen as *healthy, sick, dying, on its last legs;* Lakoff 1987: 306). This being so, it should not be so surprising that people speaking other languages develop different ways of conceptualizing experience and different interpretations of reality, and that these alternating perspectives have some relation to language, as suggested by the linguistic relativity hypothesis.

Summing up, Lakoff's discussion of linguistic relativity, as outlined here, is useful in its clarification of a number of issues relating to the Sapir-Whorf Hypothesis and the consequences of a relativistic position. He shows that differences in ways of thinking brought about by the development of different conceptual systems do not constitute insurmountable barriers to communication and understanding, because humans share the same ability to form concepts and can exploit this creativity when the situation requires. Cross-linguistic differences in modes of thought and perception are furthermore to be expected, given that such differences may also exist within individual languages, and will be greatest when they involve variation in fundamental concepts. Finally, Lakoff makes us aware of how experience interacts with speakers' conceptual capacity in different ways to produce (or fail to produce) concepts corresponding to the physical and psychological world and our interpretations of these 'realities'.

---

14. Bassetti and Cook (2011: 153) refer to an experiment carried out by Casasola, Bhagwat, and Burke (2006) which shows how young children can quickly acquire a new word-concept pair that is not in their parents' language. Using videos of events which ended up with two objects coming into close contact with each other, Casasola and her colleagues taught a group of 18-month-old infants a new word '*toke*' that was intended to mean 'being in close contact/in a tight fit' (similar to the Korean word *kkita*). This concept is not represented in English by any word, but was acquired by the young children very quickly after watching the video recordings. When requested to do so, the children could put two objects in a '*toke*' position (i.e., in close contact with each other). Young children, like adults, can use their conceptual capacity very effectively to generate new concepts associated with words and extend the range of their language's conceptual system with concepts imported from other languages.

> ### A TRIBUTE TO WHORF AS A RESEARCHER
> Whorf's writings served as an important catalyst for subsequent research in the area of language and perception, in which Whorf's ideas were refined and developed further with advances in research methodology and a better understanding of the consequences of linguistic relativity as a hypothesis. Lakoff (1987: 330) also pays tribute to the integrity and courage of Whorf's research, which presented ideas quite at odds with mainstream sociological attitudes of the time. Whorf carried out his work when fascism was spreading widely in Europe and there was also considerable Anglo-centered chauvinism in North America. White people were seen as more intelligent than non-Caucasians and Western civilization was viewed as superior to other cultures. It was also thought that European languages were far more advanced than non-Western languages and that the latter were primitive in many ways. Consequently, the general idea put forward by Whorf that the languages of 'savage' Native Americans were as developed and complex as European languages was both radical and bold for the times, and Whorf's work helped increase an awareness of the sophistication of Native American languages at a time of continued general antipathy toward Native American groups and their cultures. His careful description of languages such as Hopi and Navajo showed that these languages simply highlight and express the experiences of their speakers in ways which are different from European languages, and that no linguistic interpretation of the outside world can be said to be superior to others. All are subjective and individualistic ways of describing our different interactions with the world. Lakoff writes that: 'Whorf was not only as pioneer in linguistics. He was a pioneer as a human being. That should not be forgotten' Lakoff (1987: 330).

Testing out the linguistic relativity hypothesis

Having seen how the linguistic relativity hypothesis initially developed and was subsequently critiqued, we will now consider how the hypothesis has been defended by means of experiments which have attempted to probe the effects of language on speakers' non-verbal behavior and thus avoid the criticism, which was leveled at some of Whorf's early speculations, that differences in language must be *shown* to affect perception, not simply be assumed to do so. Here we will review work carried out on the domains of *color terminology, quantity, object categorization,* and *space*, highlighting how the results of different kinds of tests provide support for the linguistic relativity hypothesis.

Color

One area of cognition in which language clearly has the potential to interact with perception is the realm of color. The central question of interest is whether the existence of specific color terms in a language has an effect on speakers' perception of the broad spectrum of color and creates a special sensitivity to variation in hue which might vary from language to language. As different languages have developed different sets of color words, the possibility arises that speakers might see color divisions in distinct ways as a result of the vocabulary they have at their disposal, supporting a relativist position. This has now been extensively investigated in studies which began in the 1950s and then became increasingly numerous and sophisticated as interest in color terms grew rapidly, following a landmark discovery described in Berlin and Kay (1969).

In order to compare and contrast color terminology across languages, and the way this may affect perception, researchers have regularly set out to establish what the set of *basic color terms* (BCTs) are in each language. A word is taken to count as a BCT if it satisfies the following four criteria. First, the word must be 'monolexemic' and linguistically unanalyzable, meaning that it contains no isolatable sub-parts, hence terms such as *greenish, blue-green*, and *coffee-/salmon-colored* are not BCTs. Second, a BCT must permit its application to a fully wide range of objects and not be restricted in the way it can be used. Consequently the adjective *blond* is not classed as a BCT, as it is normally only applied to describe hair (and less frequently wood). Third, if there is a productive way of modifying color terms in a language, such as adding *–ish* in English, or the words *light/dark*, BCTs must allow for this process. 'Red' is a BCT, allowing for *reddish* and *light/dark red*, but *crimson* is not, as *crimsonish* and *light crimson* sound odd. Finally, BCTs should not be the names of substances, such as *gold* and *silver*.

Berlin and Kay (1969) carried out a study of BCTs in approximately 100 languages, in the anticipation that significant variation would be found. Interestingly, both cross-linguistic differences and striking regularity in the sets of BCTs present in languages were found. Variation is clearly present in the number of BCTs which occur in different languages, with this ranging from a minimum of two to a maximum of twelve. English, for example, has eleven: *white, black, red, green, yellow, blue, brown, purple, pink, orange*, and *grey*, while Dani, spoken in New Guinea, only has two, equivalent to English *black* and *white*. Other languages occupy different positions on the scale from two to twelve, lacking various of the BCTs found in English. The unexpected regularity which Berlin and Kay discovered intersecting with this variation is the heavy predictability of the kinds of BCTs that will occur in a language once the total number of BCTs is known. If a language has two BCTs, these will be (equivalents to) *black* and *white*. If it has three, the third term will be *red*, if four, *green* or *yellow* will be added, and a five-BCT language will add both *green* and *yellow*. Following this, languages sequentially add in *blue*, then *brown, pink* and/or *orange*, and/or *purple*, and finally *grey*.[15] Languages around the world thus show an amazing uniformity in the way that sets of color terms evolve, suggesting some kind of universal basis for the BCT divisions which are found.

However, it is actually the variation in BCTs across languages which is investigated most in studies concerned with linguistic relativity. An experiment devised by Kay and Kempton (1984) asked speakers of English and Tarahumara (spoken in Mexico) to look at sets of three colored chips arranged in a row, and say whether the middle chip B seemed more like the leftmost chip A or the rightmost chip C. Chip A was greenest in color, chip C bluest, and chip B somewhere between green and blue. The critical difference between English and

---

15. A twelve-term language such as Russian has twelve BCTs due to having two words for the range of hues referred to by *blue* in English.

Tarahumara is that English has two distinct color terms for the blue-to-green ranges of hues, *blue* and *green*, whereas Tarahumara has only one term for this range *siyóname*. Kay and Kempton wanted to see if this difference in the availability of color terms would affect the way that English and Tarahumara speakers perceived differences between the triads of chips, a non-verbal task that only involved observation and pointing.

The results of the experiment showed that English and Tarahumara speakers did indeed behave differently in the ways they saw similarity among the chips when the color of chip B was approximately mid-way between that of chips A and C. When chip B would still have been categorized as a shade of green by typical speakers of English, the English speakers consistently indicated chip B was more like chip A, but Tarahumara speakers were much more varied in their judgments and often grouped it with chip C, and when chip B would have been categorized as a shade of blue by typical speakers of English, the English speakers regularly grouped it with chip C (close to 100% of the time), but the Tarahumara speakers were again more varied in their groupings, frequently (50% of the time) saying it was more like chip A.[16] This strongly suggests that English speakers' perception of the range of colors presented was influenced by the existence of two color words representing the end points of the spectrum of colors seen, whereas for speakers of Tarahumara, all of the chips seen would have been categorized as shades of a single color. A second task involving only speakers of English confirmed this interpretation of the results, and significantly demonstrated that the sorting behavior of English speakers should be directly attributed to properties of language rather than any other factor (see Kay and Kempton 1984 for details).

Other grouping experiments with different languages have found parallel results. One described in McWhorter (2014: 7–9) compared speakers of English and Russian who were asked to judge similarity among triads of blue-colored squares. In these two languages, Russian has the more extensive color vocabulary and has two BCTs for 'blue'—*goluboy* (light blue) and *siniy* (dark blue)—and this seemed to impact the way they judged similarity among blue-colored squares, causing them to produce different reactions from those found with English speakers. A second experiment sought to eliminate the effects of language on the judgment task, and required Russian participants to recite memorized sequences of numbers while they engaged in the task. The mental effort required to constantly recall and reproduce the number sequence was anticipated to block the processing of language, and, sure enough, it was found that when Russian participants had to perform the secondary number-reciting task, their judgments changed and were no longer different from those of English speakers. The conclusion from this, as in the Kay and Kempton experiment, is that vocabulary differences between two languages affect the perception of the color spectrum in non-verbal tasks, and that when access to language is temporarily blocked (or otherwise confused), speakers' behavior predictably undergoes change.

---

16. Note that the ways that speakers of a language generally classify shades as belonging to one color or another is discovered by showing speakers a 300-chip array of different shades of the BCTs present in their language and asking them to indicate which chips instantiate which colors, as well as which chip is the 'best' example of each color. This establishes the divisions between color terms and prototypical, focal centers for every color.

A third, interesting psycholinguistic experiment carried out by Gilbert, Regier, Kay, and Ivry (2006) has provided evidence for the influence of language on color perception from a different angle. Gilbert and her colleagues designed an experiment which makes use of the fact that linguistic abilities, for most adults, are located in the left hemisphere of the brain, and visual information processed by the left hemisphere is channeled from a person's right visual field; hence what we see with our right eye regularly connects up with language much more directly than what is presented to our left eye/left field of vision.

In Gilbert et al.'s experiment, participants were asked to visually fixate on a small cross on a computer screen which was surrounded by twelve colored squares at a certain distance from the cross. The instruction to fixate on the central cross causes squares on the left side of the cross to be perceived in the left visual field while those on the right appeared in the right visual field. Among the twelve squares, eleven were identical in color, a uniform shade of blue. A twelfth square was always slightly different, and was either a somewhat different shade of blue, or a shade of green close to some shades of blue, but one which would still commonly be identified as green by speakers of English. The task for English-speaking participants in the experiment was to judge whether the odd square was on the left or the right of the fixation point, doing this without moving their eyes from looking at the cross. The experiment showed that when the different square appeared on the *right* of the cross *and was green*, subjects were quicker to confirm this location of the twelfth square than when it was on the left, or when it occurred on the right but was a different shade of blue rather than being green. This neatly demonstrates that the perception of color is related to the existence of words for color and the application of language to the processing of visual information. When slight differences in similar shades of color are presented to the right visual field and a connection to language in the left hemisphere of the brain is established, people perceive differences which correspond to the division of these shades into the categories 'blue' and 'green'. However, parallel differences are not perceived in the same way when the same visual information is fed to the left visual field and its subsequent connection to the right hemisphere of the brain, as this part of the brain is not heavily involved in the processing of language among most adult speakers.

Further confirmation of the crucial role of language in the perception of color differences was provided by the introduction of a verbal interference task in the experiment. Participants were asked to carry out the same experiment simultaneously recalling a sequence of eight numbers, a task which was anticipated to block the accessing of language abilities during the course of the experiment. When this interference task was added, participants performed quite differently, and there were no longer any differences in their ability to discern the oddly colored square when this occurred to the right or the left of the fixation point. The conclusion of the study was that speakers make use of language in the processing of visual color information whenever language can be accessed, and this causes people to perceive distinctions in color that fail to be noticed when access to language is temporarily unavailable.

These experimental investigations of the role of language in color perception offer positive support for the linguistic relativity hypothesis and the view that language influences the way we interpret certain phenomena in the world. Other experiments considering memory recall of different colors (Davidoff et al. 1999) and the description of paintings by speakers of different languages (Pavlenko 2014) provide additional evidence of the intrusion of language into speakers' processing of visual information, and collectively have established a substantial body of work on this area of language and thought, approached in interestingly different ways and with insightful results.

Quantity/number

A second topic linguists have engaged with in attempting to detect the effects of language on ways of thinking is quantity and number. An initial, ground-breaking study was carried out by Lucy (1992), who compared differences in the ways that nouns are marked as being singular or plural in English and Yucatec Maya, a language spoken in Mexico, with potential differences in the perception of number among speakers of these languages. Quite generally, Lucy noted that plural number-marking occurs more regularly and with more types of nouns in English than in 'Yucatec', and wanted to examine whether this linguistic difference might cognitively affect how speakers pay attention to singular/plural distinctions in their perception of everyday life.

There are two broad ways in which English and Yucatec vary in their use of plural marking with nouns. First, in English the use of plural-marking (normally the addition of –s to the ends of nouns: *cat—cats, book—books*) is obligatory with any noun that refers to more than one occurrence of the entity picked out by the noun—plurality *must* be encoded in English if a noun is understood to be plural in number, and if no plural marker occurs, a noun such as 'cat' or 'book' is automatically understood to be singular in English.[17] In Yucatec, by way of contrast, a simple noun such as *wàakaš* meaning 'cow' can refer to either one cow or more than one cow without the need for any explicit plural-marking—plural-marking is not obligatory in Yucatec, unlike English. Yucatec does have a plural-marker which can be added to the end of nouns, the suffix *–óob*, so 'cows' can be expressed by either *wàakaš* or *wàakaš–óob*, but the plural-marker is not used as much as plural-marking in English. Lucy notes that if the much more common use of plural-marking in English than in Yucatec is a linguistic difference which affects non-verbal cognition, then English speakers should pay more attention to the number of entities in the world than Yucatec speakers do, i.e., whether 'one' or 'more than one' entity is being perceived.

Second, speakers of English use plural-marking with a *wider range* of nouns than do Yucatec speakers. In English, plural *–s* is added to nouns referring to humans, animals, and all kinds of objects, though not to substances and other mass and 'non-count nouns' (hence we don't say *muds or *evidences). In Yucatec, the plural marker *–óob* is only added to animate referents (humans and animals) and a very few inanimate nouns such as 'car'. If this second difference also affects non-verbal cognition, it might be expected that speakers of English would pay attention to singular/plural distinctions with a wider range of referent types than Yucatec speakers. Specifically, English speakers should attend to differences in

---

17. Hence there is an automatic difference in the way the following noun phrases are interpreted as responses to the question 'Who ate all the sausages I left on the table?': (a) 'Some dog.' (b) 'Some dogs.' The former can only be understood as referring to one dog, and the latter can only refer to more than one dog.

number for humans, animals, and inanimate objects, but Yucatec speakers should pay attention to number primarily with humans and animals and not (most) inanimate objects.

Lucy investigated these possibilities by means of several tasks involving pictures of everyday life in Yucatecan villages and farmlands. Groups of English- and Yucatec-speaking subjects were presented a series of pictures in which there were people, animals, inanimate objects such as farming tools, water jars, etc., and also substances such as piles of corn dough. The animals, objects and substances occurred in different groupings in the various pictures (e.g., two dogs or cows together in one picture, a dog or cow alone in the second, two shovels in one picture, a single shovel in the second, etc.). In one task, participants were asked to look at the pictures and describe what they saw while they viewed the pictures. A second task required participants to look at each picture and then report what they had seen after a short pause, without the use of the picture, making use of their short-term memory of the image. Lucy was interested to see how much attention the English and Yucatec speakers paid to the single/plural grouping of animals, objects, and substances (in piles) as indicated by their mentioning of singular/plural distinctions when they referred to what they saw and recalled from memory.

The results of the experiment turned out as would be expected if the linguistic differences in English/Yucatec number-marking have effects on perception. Overall, English speakers made significantly more mention of differences between singular and plural groups than Yucatec speakers did. Furthermore, English speakers consistently referred to (and recalled) singular vs. plural distinctions with both animals *and* inanimate objects, whereas Yucatec speakers mentioned such distinctions with animals much more than with inanimate objects. Additionally, as expected, reference to the singular/plural occurrence of amounts of substances was far less than number reference with animals and inanimate objects with both sets of speakers.

Consequently Lucy concluded that the obligatory marking of number in English does seem to make speakers pay more attention to whether all kinds of entities (except for substances) occur singularly or in groups, and the restriction of optional number marking to animate entities in Yucatec appears to make its speakers pay attention to singular/plural groupings with animate entities much more than with inanimate objects. This is a positive result for the linguistic relativity hypothesis again—language is seen to show clear signs of affecting the way people think and causes speakers to pay particular attention to properties of the physical world which are encoded in their grammar.[18]

---

18. Lucy's (1992) experiments with Yucatec and English have also been replicated in a comparison of Japanese and English carried out by Athanasopoulos (2006), with parallel results. In similar picture-related tasks, English speakers were found to demonstrate significantly more sensitivity to number differences with animals and inanimate implements than speakers of Japanese, who seemed to pay attention to singular/plural distinctions with animals much more than objects, just like speakers of Yucatec. Linguistically Japanese resembles Yucatec in its use of number-marking, having an optional plural-marker which is only applied to animate nouns. The similar patterning of Japanese and Yucatec in Lucy (1992) and Athanasopoulos (2006) is therefore fully in line with the linguistic parallels present in the two languages, offering additional good support for a relativistic position.

The categorization of objects across languages

A third area of language and cognition that has stimulated much relativistic research in recent decades is the way that speakers of different languages perceive and categorize objects, and how certain grammatical properties of languages may cause people to see similarities and differences among objects in varied ways. Here we will first consider an early, influential study by Carroll and Casagrande (1958) which compared English and Navajo, and then a group of later studies on various other languages which develop this work further.

Carroll and Casagrande were intrigued by a linguistic difference between English and Navajo which is present with verbs of 'handling' in the latter language. When speakers of Navajo make use of a verb of handling such as 'give' or 'place', the verb must occur in a form which provides certain information about the *shape* or some other important property of the object which is being handled. For example, if the object of the verb to 'hand/pass (something to someone)' is long and flexible, such as a piece of string or rope or a snake, it will be inflected as *šańléh* (for example, in commands meaning 'Pass it here'); if the object is long and rigid, such as a stick, the verb form will change to be *šańtííh*, and if the object is flat and flexible, the form *šańłcóós* must be used. Carroll and Casagrande hypothesized that this feature of Navajo might increase speaker's sensitivity to the shape of objects and attempted to test whether this might be so by investigating children's perception of objects in Navajo and English. Psychologists researching the cognitive development of children had established that children at a certain early age often distinguish objects on the basis of their relative *size* and *color*, and only later come to see and use *shape* as a salient, distinguishing property. Carroll and Casagrande wondered whether the special inflections used with verbs of handling in Navajo might have an effect on young Navajo-speakers' perception of shape in the comparison of objects and potentially cause shape to emerge as a sorting concept earlier than with same-aged speakers of other languages such as English.

In order to examine this possibility, Carroll and Casagrande invited a group of young Navajo children to participate in an experiment which involved comparing objects and indicating which two of a set of three objects were felt to be most similar. When the objects in a set differed in their color and shape, two objects would have the same color but be different in shape, and two would have the same shape but be different in color, as illustrated in the following examples.

Object 1: yellow rope	Object 1: yellow stick
Object 2: blue stick	Object 2: blue cylinder
Object 3: blue rope	Object 3: blue stick

The researchers would first place objects 1 and 2 together in front of the participants and then show the participants object 3 and ask which of the first two objects it went best with (i.e., whether it seemed most similar to object 1 or object 2). The choice made by the participants provided information on whether they found color or shape to be most salient as a categorizing property.

The 135 children participating in the experiment were all ethnically Navajo living in the same environment on a Navajo reservation in Arizona. Their lifestyle was parallel, but they differed significantly in their linguistic abilities. Some had been brought up speaking Navajo and were either monolingual or heavily dominant in Navajo. Others had been primarily exposed to English and knew little or no Navajo language. The expectation of the researchers was that if the grammar of Navajo forces its speakers to pay more attention to the shape of objects not just in language but also in non-linguistic reasoning and thought, then the Navajo-speaking children might perceive the objects having a common shape as being most similar, rather than those with a common color, but the English-speaking children might pair objects on the basis of their color rather than their shape (as established in a similar experiment with young English-speaking children in Brian and Goodenough 1929). The test results showed that the Navajo-speaking children did indeed most frequently pair up objects that were similar in shape rather than color, whereas the English-speaking children predominantly selected objects on the basis of color. This suggests that aspects of language may exert an effect on speakers' perception of the world and cause people to pay particular attention to certain properties of natural phenomena, when these are regularly highlighted in the use of language. Language, therefore, does have the power to affect ways of thinking, as proposed in the linguistic relativity hypothesis.

The Navajo project initiated by Carroll and Casagrande also produced a further important result bearing on the Sapir-Whorf Hypothesis when they extended their study to include an additional, control group of English-speaking children living in the Boston area. Somewhat to the surprise of the researchers, the Boston group of children paired up objects in the same way as the Navajo-speaking children, apparently using shape as the primary sorting criterion in a way that was different from previous studies of English-speaking children which had found color to be more important (Brian and Goodenough 1929). The explanation offered for this unexpected patterning was that the children in the Boston group all came from middle-class homes where playing with toys of certain types (jigsaw puzzles, building blocks, etc.) may have helped develop the concept of shape at an accelerated rate. Hudson (1996: 99) notes that when English-speaking children from poorer backgrounds (where expensive shape-based toys might be presumed not to be available) were tested in New York, they performed like the English-speaking Navajo children and unlike the middle-class children from Boston. Carroll and Casagrande consequently amended their conclusions and claimed that language does have the ability to affect cognition, but that there may also be other non-linguistic influences on our perception of the world and the way we think. Specifically, in the phenomenon being investigated by Carroll and Casagrande, practicing with toys of certain types is hypothesized to have a similar effect to speaking Navajo and increases children's attention to the shapes of objects. A general consequence of this study is therefore that the strongest interpretation of the Sapir-Whorf Hypothesis, linguistic determinism, would seem to be incorrect. While there is evidence that language can direct our thinking in various interesting ways (hence linguistic relativity is supported), it is perhaps just one of a variety of different forces that may influence perception.

The importance of the concept of shape in the classification of objects has also been investigated from another angle, comparing 'noun class' languages like English and Spanish with 'classifier' languages such as Japanese and Chinese. In the former type of language, nouns occur in two broad types: (a) 'count nouns' such as *dog, car,* and *book* which can be directly combined with numerals to indicate a group of referents, for example *two dogs, five cars, fifteen books*, and (b) 'mass nouns' such as *water, mud*, and *glue* referring to substances, which need to be combined with a 'unitizer' in order to be measured out and occur with numerals, as for example *two cups of water, three piles of mud,* and *five drops of glue*. Unitizers allow for the substances referred to by mass nouns to be portioned out and 'individuated' as specific, countable amounts of the noun. Count nouns do not require unitizers and are inherently individuated—perceived as discrete entities without the need for any other word to specify an instance of the noun.

In classifier languages, *all* nouns must occur with some kind of unitizer, commonly referred to as a classifier, before they can be combined with a numeral. Grammatically, it is therefore as if nouns in classifier languages are all mass nouns and need a unitizer to provide an individuated measure of the noun which can be counted and refer in a specific way. Depending on the unitizer added to the noun, different meanings may be communicated, as the unitizer specifies different kinds of shapes or weights of the mass/substance referred to by the noun, as seen in the following examples from Mandarin Chinese from Zhang (2007: 49).

yi pian mianbao = one unit bread: 'a slice of bread'
yi kuai mianbao = one unit bread: 'a chunk of bread'
yi tiao mianbao = one unit bread: 'a loaf of bread'

yi duo hua = one unit flower: 'a flower'
yi shu hua = one unit flower: 'a bunch of flowers'
yi cu hua = one unit flower: 'a cluster of flowers'

In noun class languages, a very large proportion of nouns—the 'count nouns'—refer to objects which are intrinsically individuated, and it has been suggested that the critical property of count nouns which regularly provides such individualization is the *shape* of objects referred to by such nouns—count nouns are predefined in terms of their shape, and so do not need additional individuation via the use of unitizers. Nouns in classifier languages, by way of contrast, are suggested to be semantically underspecified with regard to individuation (Boroditsky 2003) and simply denote amorphous *material* which always needs the application of a unitizer specifying some kind of shape or weight to enable reference.

Considering these linguistic differences between noun class and classifier languages, Lucy (1992) hypothesized that if they were to have more general cognitive consequences, it might be expected that speakers of noun class languages would show a greater sensitivity to the *shape* of objects, while speakers of classifier languages would have their attention drawn more to *material* in the comparison and categorization of objects. Lucy consequently set out to test this hypothesis and designed a similarity judgment experiment in which adult speakers of English, a noun class language, and Yucatec Maya, a classifier language, were presented triads of objects and asked to indicate which two in each set were more similar to each other. The goal was to see whether speakers might perceive object similarity as being primarily related to the shape or material composition of the objects in the triads. Sets were therefore constructed in which an 'original' object had shape and material attributes that were repeated in two 'alternate' objects, the shape property being shared by one alternate object and the material property being present in the other, as illustrated in the following example triads.

original	shape alternate	material alternate
sheet of paper	sheet of plastic	book
stick of wood	candle stick	block of wood
ceramic bowl	metal bowl	ceramic plate
strip of cloth	strip of paper	shirt

Participants in the experiments were requested to say which of the alternate objects seemed most like the original in each set.

When data from both languages were collected and compared, the results showed that speakers of English regularly picked out the shape alternates as being closest to the original object, while Yucatec speakers selected material ones. This distinct patterning in behavior is entirely as anticipated if the grammatical differences between nouns in noun class and classifier languages do indeed have a broad effect on speakers' perception and cause them to pay primary attention to different aspects of nouns' meanings. Speakers of the noun class language English prefer to classify objects on the basis of their shape, whereas speakers of the numeral classifier language Yucatec Maya see similarity across object types as resulting from the material they are composed of. The properties of object shape and material thus seem to have a different cognitive saliency for speakers of different languages which can be attributed to the linguistic patterning of their nouns. Note that the heightened sensitivity to shape found by Lucy among English-speaking adults is not inconsistent with Carroll and Casagrande's (1958) conclusions about English—the latter work was focused on English-speaking Navajo *children* who had not yet developed the concept of shape to the same level of saliency as that of color and size. For all speakers of English (and other languages), the concept of shape develops strongly and fully by at least the age of 10, and Lucy's experiment on object categorization examined the behavior of *adult* speakers, who could all be expected to have shape well-established as a potential sorting concept. An anecdote from a later study of Yucatec speakers carried out by Lucy and Gaskins (2001) is also worth mentioning. As the researchers conducted a parallel follow-up experiment on the categorization of objects in Yucatec and English, they noticed that the way the Yucatec speakers approached the test was visibly different from the English speakers, and demonstrated a very obvious interest in the material of the objects they were being asked to compare:

> The Yucatec speakers were constantly evaluating the material composition of the test items before sorting them: feeling how heavy they were, poking their nails into them to test for malleability, scraping the surface to see what the material under the paint was, smelling and tasting the objects, and generally questioning or commenting on their material properties.... The English-speaking Americans showed none of this sort of reaction—they could get all the information they needed by sight alone. (Lucy and Gaskins 2001: 271–272)[19]

---

19. Quoted in Everett (2013: 205).

Significantly, the findings from Lucy (1992) drawn on the basis of English and Yucatec have been confirmed by a range of investigations of other noun class and classifier languages, including Spanish, Korean, Chinese, and Japanese (see Imai and Gentner 1997; Imai and Mazuka 2007; and further references in Pavlenko 2005: 66). These additional studies provide further support for Lucy's original conclusions, with one modification which recognizes that as objects become increasingly complex in their properties, this may influence the similarity judgments given by speakers of classifier languages. In Imai and Gentner (1997) and other recent works making use of triad sorting tasks, participants were presented with three different kinds of objects to compare: *substances* (for example, sand heaped into a certain shape), *simple objects* (for example, a pyramid or cube made from a certain material), and *complex manufactured objects* with specific functions (for example, a lemon squeezer or a paper clip). Two examples of these object triads are given here. The first makes use of a substance (wax), the second utilizes a complex object as the original object (a clear plastic clip).

original	*shape alternate*	*material alternate*
kidney-shaped piece of wax	kidney-shaped piece of plaster	a number of irregular-shaped pieces of wax
clear plastic clip	metal clip	clear piece of plastic

As with Lucy (1992), it was found that speakers of noun class languages favor *shape* as a way to categorize simple objects, while speakers of noun classifier language favor *material*, and these strong preferences also manifest themselves with substances molded into different shapes. However, when the original object to be compared with the two alternates is complex in design and has a particular use, speakers of classifier languages seem to frequently shift their categorization criteria and perceive the function or shape of such objects as being more salient than their simple material make-up. In the second triad shown in the preceding, speakers of both English and Japanese therefore regularly indicated that the metal clip was more similar to the plastic clip than the piece of plastic was. This tells us that the effects of language on object categorization involved are a little intricate when investigated in an extensive way. At the basic level of simple objects and accumulations of substances, speakers of noun class and classifier languages regularly perceive different physical properties as most striking (shape vs. material), and so the grammatical differences present in these languages do appear to exert effects on speakers' cognition. However, in certain instances, these language-induced, default sorting preferences can apparently be over-ridden by other salient factors such as the specialized function of objects being presented, so that object complexity also needs to be taken into account as a potential influence on the perception of similarities and differences among objects. The linguistic relativity hypothesis receives support from object categorization tasks, but reveals that there are also certain limits on the ways that language may influence perception.

Space

A fourth broad area of cognition that has been suggested to show signs of the influence of language is the perception of space, and how speakers think of the location of objects relative to each other. Research into over forty languages has revealed that there are three different ways in which speakers typically describe spatial relations when giving directions or specifying the location of physical objects. These modes of description are known as 'frames of reference' (Levinson 2003). A 'relative' or 'egocentric' frame of reference locates other objects relative to the speaker or some other person viewing a particular scene, and results in the regular use of terms such as 'on the left/right'—for example: 'The post office/the car is on the left/on your left'. English, Dutch, and Japanese are languages which strongly favor the use of a relative frame of reference in talking about spatial location. An 'absolute' or 'geocentric' frame of reference, by way of contrast, makes use of fixed points of cardinal direction rather than the speaker's body to describe where objects are located, so that 'north', 'south', 'east', and 'west' are used in place of 'left/right' to give information about the position of objects which may even be very close by and in proximity to the speaker or hearer, hence one may hear equivalents to 'There's a spider on your north arm' in a language which predominantly utilizes an absolute frame of reference. Many languages have been found to favor an absolute frame of reference for the everyday description of spatial locations, including Balinese (Indonesia), Tzeltal (Mexico), Belhare (Nepal), and Warwa (Australia), and some languages seem to utilize this mode of description almost exclusively, never making use of relative terms such as 'left side' or 'right side' (Pederson et al. 1998). The third frequently attested patterning used to specify location is an 'intrinsic' frame of reference, in which the position of objects is described in relation to other objects in a person's field of vision, as for example in: 'The cup is next to the book.' This strategy may sometimes be combined with a basic relative frame of reference, as in English, or with an absolute frame of reference, but there are also languages which seem to use only an intrinsic frame of reference, such as Mopan (Belize, Guatemala) and Totonac (Mexico) (Pavlenko 2014: 116).

The different modes of spatial description dominant in a language have often been observed to correspond to differences in general sensitivity to location. Speakers of languages using an absolute frame of reference have regularly been noted to be highly aware of geographical direction and can easily point to north, south, east, and west at any given moment, whereas typical speakers of relative frame of reference languages generally lack this ability and would often not be able to spontaneously point out where north or south are during most of their daily life. The special importance of cardinal direction for speakers of absolute frame of reference languages is well brought out in the following description given by the linguist Nicholas Evans as he grappled to learn the Kayardild language in Australia. Evans reports that he felt he had to radically reprogram his mind to force it to pay attention to the points of the compass:

> I suddenly had to add a whole new channel of ongoing attention to how I thought about space. I needed to use "absolute reckoning", orienting to the points of the compass for every waking moment, if I was to follow what was being said, and talk in a way that people would understand. . . . [The Kayardild] virtually never think, imagine, or even dream without orienting their mental scenes to the compass. . . . One aspect of speaking Kayardild, then, is learning that the landscape is more important and objective than you are. . . . It is not that I never thought by compass before

learning Kayardild. Sometimes I had needed to do it, in occasional boy-scout mode, when orienteering, or navigating a city with a grid layout. . . . But the experience of speaking Kayardild was something quite different—an incessant need always to know the compass directions, and always to attend to them, or face an embarrassment equivalent to not knowing my wife's name, or not noticing whether you are male or female. (Evans 2010: 163–165, quoted in Pavlenko 2014: 300–301)

A common correlation between a feature of *language use* (an absolute vs. a relative frame of reference) and an aspect of *cognition* (focus vs. lack of attention to cardinal direction) has therefore repeatedly been found, raising the relativistic possibility that language use affects speakers' perception in the domain of spatial awareness. A person develops the habit of talking about the location of objects in certain ways due to the language they are exposed to, and this linguistic practice may be suggested to have an influence on speakers' ways of thinking about space and their perception of the relations of objects to each other. In order to try to test the apparent link between language and spatial perception, the linguist Stephen Levinson and other researchers constructed a number of non-verbal experiments involving the memorization of object layouts, the memorization of routes, and tasks requiring the completion of routes through pictorial mazes. Here we will briefly describe two of these experiments and discuss how their results potentially bear on linguistic relativity.

One experiment, which has been reproduced with many languages, presents participants with a row of different objects placed on a tabletop, and asks participants to memorize the order of the objects. Normally there are between three and six objects, and these have sometimes been figurines of animals (a rabbit, a cat, a dog, etc.), causing this experiment to be casually known as the 'animals-in-a-row' memorization task. Participants are then made to turn around 180° to face another table and reproduce from memory the ordering of objects they have in their minds. Speakers of relative frame of reference languages like English or Dutch typically memorize the sequence of objects they have seen in terms of a left-to-right distribution, so if a [cat • rabbit • dog] ordering was initially presented, with a cat figure on the left and a dog figure on the right, when participants are rotated 180°, they reproduce a [cat • rabbit • dog] sequence with the cat figure on their left and the dog on their right. However, absolute frame of reference speakers regularly seem to memorize the same sequence of objects as an orientation in terms of points of the compass, so if the row of objects had a west-to-east orientation, with 'cat' initially being the furthest to the west and the 'dog' on the eastern end, the reproduction of the cat/rabbit/dog ordering would maintain the original west/east alignment when a 180° rotation of the speaker is made. The result will be that the 'cat' on the second tabletop will be to the speaker's right, and the 'dog' to his/her left (though the participant will actually see the positioning as being constant—'cat' to the west, 'dog' to the east). These two contrasting placement patterns are illustrated on page 341. The results of animals-in-a-row experiments with different languages support the assumption that spatial language has an influence on spatial cognition, because relative and absolute frame of reference language produces different results in this non-linguistic object memory and placement task.

Object placement with relative frame of reference speakers

| CAT | RABBIT | DOG |

Initial view ↑

↓ View after rotating 180°

⟵ WEST

| DOG | RABBIT | CAT |

Object placement with absolute frame of reference speakers

| CAT | RABBIT | DOG |

Initial view ↑

↓ View after rotating 180°

⟵ WEST

| CAT | RABBIT | DOG |

A second experiment, of a similar nature, asks participants to consider a series of arrows which represent a partial route beginning at a point A and ending in a point B, and commit this image to memory. Participants then have to rotate 180° and inspect three images, each of which contains two arrows. Participants are told that if one of these pairs of arrows is added to the initial series of arrows, it will lead from point B back to the original point A (so, if each arrow represented a step of movement through a maze, the final two steps would return a person back to his/her starting point in the maze). This is illustrated in the following diagram, based on Everett (2013: 85):

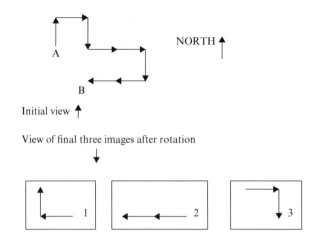

Speakers of relative frame of reference languages generally select image 3 as the way to connect point B with point A; however, speakers of absolute frame of reference languages commonly select image 1. This strongly suggest that different modes of memorization are carried out and applied in the maze route completion task, and absolute frame of reference speakers embed the first image in their minds in terms of north/south/east/west orientation of the image and its arrows, and also see the three secondary images as being arrows pointing in particular directions of the compass. Image 1 will therefore be the natural way to solve the puzzle for such speakers. For speakers of relative point of reference languages, the initial image will be memorized as a left/right/nearer/further orientation of arrows, and the secondary three images will also be viewed in the same way, causing the continuation in image 3 to be seen as the way to complete the route. As with the animals-in-a row experiment, language seems to have an effect on the performance of speakers in a non-linguistic task.

Everett provides useful discussion and assessment of these results. The broad observation is that the ways speakers of different languages carry out the animals-in-a-row and maze tasks shows a strong correlation with the default frame of reference used in each language, which suggests that the way people think about spatial location is a reflection of their language use. Some caution in assuming this conclusion is nevertheless still in order here. As others have noted, it may be natural to wonder whether it is language which necessarily affects the perception of space, or whether it could be that a person's lifestyle in a particular environment leads to the development of a way of thinking about spatial location, which in turn might manifest itself in the use of a certain default frame of reference when using language. For example, it might be hypothesized that speakers of languages with absolute frames of reference and a heightened sensitivity to compass directions, such as speakers of the Australian languages Guugu Yimithirr and Kayardild, could have first developed a strong awareness of directionality due to their daily interactions with their rural landscape and then incorporated this into their speech. The language-thought relation in such a view would then be that a particular mode of perception arises first and then affects the development of language, and not that language is responsible for the occurrence of certain ways of thinking.

Plausible as such a hypothesis might initially seem, it does not appear to be well borne out by the actual distribution of absolute vs. relative frame of reference languages around the world. Pavlenko (2005: 116) notes that while in certain cases there may well be an influence from geography and ecology on the adoption of an absolute frame of reference system, the cross-linguistic variation that is found with regard to dominant frame of reference does not seem to be fully reducible to such language-external factors, and an analysis of twenty languages in Majid et al. (2004) shows that lifestyle and environment are not the primary causes of different frames of reference. The latter arise in a way that often seems independent of differences in culture and daily life among language groups. Everett's personal summation of this complex issue is that language *and* other factors may influence the development of different ways of thinking about location and the strength of individuals' sense of spatial orientation. He notes, for example, that the frequent use of maps and map-reading among speakers of relative frame of reference languages can cause a heightened awareness of cardinal direction, and that speakers of absolute frame of reference languages can learn to use a relative frame of reference when this is necessary. Consequently, language cannot be said to absolutely *determine* ways of thinking about space, but it does seem to be a potentially important factor that can *influence* speakers' perception of the spatial world around them. As with researchers' investigations of other cognitive phenomena, support is found for linguistic relativity but not linguistic determinism, and language may sometimes conspire with additional non-linguistic forces to affect cognition.

Finally, it is interesting to observe that different, language-influenced modes of thinking about space may occasionally affect the way speakers think in other domains such as time. Boroditsky and Gaby (2010) investigated how speakers of Pormpuraaw (Australia) and English perceive the flow of time to occur, and how this relates to their different perceptions of spatial location. English is a relative frame of reference language using body-related terms such as 'left' and 'right', while Pormpuraaw utilizes an absolute frame of reference with frequent reference to the cardinal points of the compass. In thinking about *time*, experiments consistently show that speakers of English construct a mental representation of time as flowing linearly from left to right. When speakers of English are given randomly shuffled sets of images which relate to each other as points along a single temporal progression, such as a picture of a person as a young child, as a teenager, in middle-age, and in later life, and are asked to sequence these, they automatically place the picture of the earliest point in the temporal progression to their left, and the final point to their right, so that the left-to-right ordering corresponds to the passage of time: left = earlier in time, right = later. As such a left-to-right sequencing is an egocentric relation, and English employs a relative/egocentric frame of reference for referring to spatial location, Boroditsky and Gaby became interested in finding out whether there might be a connection between speakers' conception of space and time/temporal ordering. In order to explore this possibility, they conducted a comparative experiment with speakers of Pormpuraaw, an absolute frame of reference language, to see what kind of sequencing speakers of this language would impose on parallel sets of pictures. The intriguing discovery made by Boroditsky and Gaby was that Pormpuraaw speakers behave as if they conceive of time as flowing from east to west. Images depicting the earliest point in a temporal sequence were always positioned to the east, and those later in the temporal progression were added linearly toward the west. Such an east-to-west ordering was applied to the sets of images no matter what the orientation of the participants was. When speakers were made to face south, they would place the earliest image to the east, on their left, and when they were asked to face north (tested on a different day), they would again place the earliest image to the east, this time to their right. English-speaking participants in the same rotation experiment did not adjust the way they laid down the sets of images, and always ordered these temporally from left to right, regardless of the cardinal direction they were facing. It therefore seems that thinking about space in a certain way can directly affect thinking about other phenomena such as time, and the use of a spatial frame of reference of a particular type can be extended to structure other kinds of mental representation in a similar way.[20]

Conclusions

Having seen a range of recent empirical studies of the relation of linguistic phenomena to cognition, what can we conclude about linguistic relativity in general? The way that putative connections between language and thought are now investigated among 'neo-Whorfian' researchers is markedly different from the earlier Whorfian approach, when it was simply assumed, rather than shown, that differences among language affect perception. Responding to well-founded criticisms of the early Sapir-Whorf Hypothesis, researchers interested in linguistic relativity have realized that their investigations need to be more rigorous than in the past and should focus on the construction of controlled, non-verbal experiments which take into account the possible interfering role of culture and environment. This more careful approach has helped clear away certain confusions which beset the presentation of linguistic relativity at its outset. What remains can be broadly summarized as follows.

Languages clearly do vary with regard to the set of linguistically encoded concepts they contain at any particular point in time. This variation occurs most obviously with single words as distinct language-particular concepts (e.g., Russian *toska*, Japanese *wabi-sabi*), but grammatical differences also occur and are potentially more important because they are used

---

20. Studies of possible connections between language and thought often lead to additional unexpected discoveries as by-products of investigations with specific targets. In considering the connection between spatial frame of reference and the perception of temporal progression, it has been remarked that the English left-to-right representation of the flow of time is not only an egocentric ordering made relative to a speaker's body, it also coincides with the *direction of writing* which occurs in English. This led researchers to investigate whether there might be a further correlation between the direction of writing in a language and the way speakers mentally represent the flow of time, and there is now some preliminary evidence supporting a possible, though not necessary, connection here. Tyversky et al. (1991) and Fuhrman et al (2010) report that speakers of Arabic and Hebrew represent time as flowing from right to left, which accords with the direction of writing in these languages, and Chan and Bergen (2005) find some convergent evidence of a similar kind for Chinese (written in different horizontal/vertical directions in mainland China and Taiwan).

The fact that there may be a connection between direction of writing and the linear perception of time for speakers of relative frame of reference languages such as English does not mean that Boroditsky and Gaby (2010) are incorrect in positing a connection between spatial thinking and the mental representation of time—the direction of writing in English is still an egocentric phenomenon, just one which can potentially influence the *use* of an egocentric/body-relative representation of time, in stimulating a left-to-right directionality on this relation.

much more frequently in speech. The presence of different concepts encoded via language results in the establishment of different conceptual systems among speakers, and sensitizes speakers to certain distinctions, stimulating an awareness (or a heightened awareness) of various phenomena in the world and perspectives on our interactions with others. Lexically, the word-related component of our conceptual system plays a role in building up knowledge of the world, and contributes to the interpretation of our experiences of life. Differences in grammar also have cognitive effects, as increasingly revealed in experimental studies of contrasts in different languages, and have been found to exert specific influences of various kinds on speakers' actual behavior.

With regard to the way that new concepts are formed and added to a person's conceptual system, in many instances the conclusion is that this occurs through language, causing knowledge to be partially dependent on the language a person comes into contact with. Other concepts, however, are acquired without language, and so language is certainly not the only influence on our thinking. The regular *use* of language is also important in the way it may distinguish conceptual systems which are otherwise similar in a certain area. Speakers of two languages may have at their disposal a parallel set of words/concepts in one domain of reference but habitually differ in their selection of these items in everyday patterns of communication, increasing the cognitive prominence of those concepts which are utilized with greater frequency. Speakers of English, Dutch, and Japanese, for example, all have words for 'north', 'south', 'east', and 'west' as well as 'left' and 'right', but privilege the use of the latter terms in reference to immediate spatial location, unlike speakers of a language such as Balinese, who do the opposite and more frequently specify spatial location via cardinal points of the compass rather than the words for 'left' and 'right'. This leads to different frames of reference being prominent in these languages, with various ensuing effects.

Taken together, the insights and research reviewed here lead to the conclusion that language does indeed have the power to influence thought, to help introduce and heighten the salience of various concepts, and to lead speakers to make use of certain ways of thinking which have an impact on their non-verbal behavior. As the result of work carried out in recent years, there is consequently now a broad range of support for the linguistic relativity hypothesis understood in its neo-Whorfian form that language can and does affect cognition, in ways ranging from the holding of different language-specific concepts, such as German *Gemütlichkeit* or Czech *litost*, to the attention speakers give to similarities in shape, material, and color among objects and the spatial location of objects. More refined empirical investigation has therefore led to the linguistic relativity hypothesis acquiring much firmer foundations than in previous years as a scientific program of research.

At the same time that such a neo-Whorfian view of linguistic relativity has become more strongly established, the possibility that language might fully determine thought (i.e., linguistic determinism) has been widely discarded as a hypothesis.[21] It has frequently

---

21. However, linguistic relativity is sometimes still incorrectly portrayed as implying a deterministic view in articles in the popular press, creating bad publicity for the hypothesis (as linguistic determinism is implausible). McWhorter (2014) is a recent monograph which takes aim at instances of such 'popular linguistic relativity', propagated by poorly informed journalists seeking to publish eye-catching stories on the Sapir-Whorf Hypothesis.

been noted that non-linguistic factors may also influence perception and structure behavior in the same way that language can in various instances, and that speakers are able to think past their native languages by acquiring new concepts from other languages and life experiences. A person's mother tongue contributes in various ways to their perception and interpretation of the world, but does not always cause other modes of thinking to be inaccessible.

From an anthropological point of view, it is interesting to discover cross-linguistic differences in language and ways of thinking, as a complement to other kinds of research on differences in society and culture around the world. Work on linguistic relativity thus broadens the information we have available about the ways in which distinctive modes of perception may arise and vary across language groups. The study of linguistic relativity also has a practical value in highlighting how our actions and views may be influenced in ways that we are not aware of by aspects of the language we grow up speaking. In many instances this influence may not have harmful effects and may simply lead speakers to a different perspective on certain physical phenomena such as the color spectrum or the relative salience of inanimate objects. However, there are also times when language use inherited from others may subconsciously shape the attitudes we hold toward different groups and practices in society, and may do this in ways which ultimately have negative consequences, as when sexist or racist views are kindled by the words used to refer to differences in gender and ethnicity, or when euphemistic terminology is used to reduce attention to the negative effects of conflict and war. As with other cognitive phenomena, language can predispose us to adopt certain modes of thinking with our social and political relations, and we should try to understand how we may be influenced toward different beliefs by the language we have acquired. Some further consideration of this 'social' side of linguistic relativity will feature in the next chapter, which is focused on the interaction of language and gender and differences which exist in gender terminology.

With the growth of studies on linguistic relativity in recent years, there are many topics we have not been able to cover in the current chapter, which has had to be selective for simple reasons of space, and a number of interesting additional topics are listed in the suggestions for further reading. Here, in closing the chapter, we will briefly consider one final area of investigation which has started to attract the attention of many researchers in the field of linguistic relativity. How does the widespread phenomenon of *bilingualism* interact with the linguistic relativity hypothesis, and how do people think and perceive the world if they speak two (or more) languages?

McWhorter's book sets out to highlight the exaggerations often found in such articles while attempting to recognize the seriousness of more scientific investigations of language and cognition. However, sometimes it is not clear that the criticism in McWhorter's book is indeed of popular 'mythical' claims about language and thought rather than linguistic relativity in general. It is therefore advisable that reading of this volume is preceded by a consideration of Anthony Webster's 2014 review of the book in the *Journal of Linguistic Anthropology*. This review points out how McWhorter sometimes criticizes a position or view that has actually not been explicitly expressed by any particular researcher:

> Webster, Anthony. 2014. Why the world doesn't sound the same in any language and why that might matter. *Journal of Linguistic Anthropology* 25:1: 87–104.

Linguistic relativity and bilingualism: what happens when you're bilingual?

The key idea of the linguistic relativity hypothesis is that a person's ways of thinking are potentially affected by the language they speak, hence a speaker of English and a speaker of Japanese may perceive aspects of the world in different ways due to certain linguistic differences between the two languages. An interesting question is what happens when a person speaks two languages—what effects on cognition may result from knowledge of two different linguistic systems?

There are three broad outcomes that might hypothetically be anticipated to occur. A first theoretical possibility is that the modes of perception established by the learning of a person's first language continue to dominate exclusively when subsequent languages are learned, so that an L1 English speaker who later learns Japanese will continue to exhibit the typical cognitive patterns of other monolingual English speakers, and these patterns will not be affected by learning Japanese as a second language. Such an outcome will, of course, only potentially be applicable to consecutive bilinguals who learn one language after the other, and not to simultaneous bilinguals, who really do have two mother tongues. A second possibility is that bilinguals might develop two modes of perception, which would operate differently, depending on the language that the speaker makes use of at any particular moment. In such a scenario, a Japanese-English bilingual might be expected to think in Japanese ways when speaking Japanese, and in an English way when communicating in English. A third possibility is that bilinguals develop cognitive patterns that are unlike those of monolinguals of either of the languages they know, hence a Japanese-English bilingual would show signs of language-related cognition somewhere between those typically found with monolingual speakers of Japanese and English.

So, which of these three outcomes do we seem to find occurring, from research that has been carried out to date? The answer is that most of the investigations attempting to clarify this issue provide support for the third possibility just described, and the common finding is that bilinguals exhibit a single cognitive patterning in experiments which is frequently somewhere between those of monolingual speakers of the L1 and L2, in qualitative or quantitative terms. So, for example, the perception of color terms among speakers of Russian, Greek, and Korean who also speak English has been found to be different from monolingual speakers of Russian, Greek, and Korean, and seems to regularly be affected by color distinctions made in English. This results in a patterning among bilinguals that is part-way between monolingual speakers of these languages and not exactly like monolinguals of either the L1 or the L2 (Bassetti and Cook 2011: 157; de Groot 2011: 368–371; Athanasopoulos and Aveledo 2012: 239–240). The categorization of objects among bilinguals has been similarly found to be affected by both of a speaker's languages and gives rise to patterns that do not correspond with those of monolingual speakers of either the L1 or the L2. Japanese-English bilinguals consequently make use of both material and shape as ways to judge the similarity of triad sets of objects, in ways that are unlike either typical Japanese or English monolinguals (Cook et al. 2006; Athanasopoulos and Aveledo 2012: 243). The general conclusion coming from these and other studies is that bilinguals often develop language-related cognitive patterns in thinking about color, space, time, and object categorization that are different from those of monolinguals and seem to show a merging of the modes of perception otherwise associated with speakers of a bilingual's L1 and L2 (Bassetti and Cook 2011: 179).

What has not been extensively found in experiments so far is evidence for the second possibility noted earlier, and the active presence of two distinct modes of perception, each linked to a different language. However, this may perhaps be due to the nature of the experiments now used to test linguistic relativity. In order to show that language may affect cognition, experiments need to be designed which focus on speakers' non-verbal behavior rather than their use of language (otherwise such tests may just show that language affects language use, not a person's non-linguistic perception). The judgments that participants are asked to give therefore do not involve language, and it may consequently be difficult to know which of a bilingual's two languages might be underlyingly 'responsible' for his/her reactions to non-verbal stimuli, and whether a person could make use of two different language-related modes of perception in a non-linguistic experiment.

One possible way around this problem is to manipulate the *language of instruction* used in experiments, and have bilinguals participate in the same experiment twice, on different days, and receive instructions for the experiment in their L1 on the first day of testing, and in their L2 on the second day. This might have the potential to activate different languages and their modes of thinking among bilinguals on separate tests, while maintaining the important non-verbal property of the experiment itself. A variant of such an approach would be to divide a bilingual test group into two sub-groups and have each instructed in a different language prior to participation in the same experiment. Two studies have actually attempted such an alternation in language of instruction, and interestingly the results showed that in these cases the bilinguals tested did indeed exhibit two different patterns of behavior. Barner et al. (2009) examined object categorization with Mandarin Chinese-English bilinguals and found that participants grouped objects according to material when given instructions in Chinese, and on the basis of shape when instructed in English. Boroditsky et al. (2002) similarly manipulated the language of instruction with Indonesian-English bilinguals in tests relating to tense and the perception and memory of scenes viewed in pictures. It was found that those instructed in Indonesian performed like Indonesian monolingual speakers, while those who were given instructions in English performed like English monolinguals. This suggests that the language of instruction used with experiments may sometimes play a significant role in experiments with bilinguals and may trigger the mental activation of a particular language and an associated mode of thought. The results of these two studies provide support for the possibility that bilinguals may indeed maintain two distinct ways of thinking with regard to various phenomena, each established and maintained by a different language, as might be anticipated by the linguistic relativity hypothesis as a potential foreseeable outcome of bilingualism. Such a possibility also accords with non-experimental testimonies frequently given by bilinguals that they have different conceptual experiences when communicating in their two languages (see Wierzbicka 1985, 'The double life of a bilingual'; also Hunt and Agnoli 1991).[22]

---

22. However, some caution is needed here, as a third experiment carried out by Athanasopoulos (2007) did not find variation according to the language of instruction given to bilinguals, and participants exhibited a cognitive patterning midway between L1 and L2 monolinguals regardless of the language they were instructed in prior to testing.

Investigations into the interaction of bilingualism and linguistic relativity have thus resulted in somewhat divergent results. A number of studies, the majority so far, have reported that bilinguals appear to think differently from monolinguals of either of the languages they speak when tested in a variety of areas such as color perception, object categorization, spatial reference, etc., and exhibit a patterning that is part way between the typical modes of perception associated with monolingual speakers of bilinguals' L1 and L2. Other research has found that two different modes of cognition may in fact be maintained by bilinguals, corresponding to typical L1 and L2 ways of thinking, and that each distinct perspective can be activated and (temporarily) made dominant by means of stimulation with the relevant language. Although these experimental studies thus report different effects of bilingualism on cognition, they are all highly interesting and encourage further research into this fascinating area of language-thought interactions. Future research will be able to build on the foundations laid by recent pioneering work in this domain and, who knows, might even lead to the conclusion that more than one outcome of bilingualism on cognition is actually possible.

AUTOBIOGRAPHICAL MEMORY AND THE LINGUISTIC ENCODING OF EVENTS

'Autobiographical memory' is an expression used to refer to the memories that individuals have of events which have taken place in their past, often with some personal involvement. The interesting, language-related observation about autobiographical memory is that people's memory of events seems to regularly be 'coded' in some way for the language which was spoken when the events were experienced. So, if an event takes place in which there is communication in some language, the memory of the event appears to remain associated with that language when it is stored. One consequence of this which has regularly been observed with speakers of two languages is that the retrieval of memory is richer when a person is asked to describe an event in the language in which it actually 'took place' (i.e., the language which was spoken when the event occurred). This was first noticed and analyzed in some detail in a memory recall experiment carried out by Javier et al. (1993). Bilingual participants in the experiment were asked to describe events from their lives, and it was found that these were reported more vividly and in greater detail when the participant used the language in which the experience had initially occurred. Language thus serves as a powerful mechanism for accessing memories (Altarriba and Morier 2012).

A particularly practical consequence of this is that psychiatrists who interview bilingual patients and ask them to talk about past events are advised to pay special attention to the language used in interacting with their patients. It may be that repressed and difficult memories can only easily be retrieved (or be retrieved more accurately) through the language associated with them. Alternatively, in certain instances, using the patient's other language in interviews can allow the latter to maintain a certain emotional distance and detachment from an earlier memory they are asked to describe, and can reduce the psychological pain that might otherwise arise if the event is reported more vividly in the language it took place in.

> How does all this link up with our discussion of the linguistic relativity hypothesis? Is it the case that that experiencing an event 'through' (or 'with') a particular language causes it to be perceived in a different way than if it had been experienced through a different language that a speaker knows? Possibly, but not necessarily so. The more important point here is that in *reliving* an event that is in memory, the choice of language used to recount it is significant and seems to impose a filter on memory and recall, so that using a different language (i.e., not the language of the event) will produce a different description of the same event and its memory. Language affects the way we can retrieve and describe parts of our memory, and not all languages allow the same kind of access to past events that have been mentally stored.
>
> For more discussion of autobiographical memory in general, see Pavlenko (2005: 463–468); Knickerbocker and Altarriba (2011); Altarriba and Morier (2012).

Suggestions for further reading and activities

1. Read chapter 1 (Introduction) of Anna Wierzbicka's *Understanding Cultures through Their Key Words* (1997, Oxford University Press) to learn more about the ways that languages differ from each other in their vocabularies.
2. A number of studies have considered how speakers' memory of events shown to them in video recordings may be influenced by grammatical properties of the languages they speak. This is manifested in the ways these events are described by participants in experiments, using their short-term memory. Read how eye-witness accounts which are affected by language may lead to interpretations of events that can have significant, real-world consequences, such as the attribution of blame to those involved in events, in the following two papers:

    Fausey, Caitlin, and Lera Boroditsky. 2010. Subtle linguistic cues influence perceived blame and financial liability. *Psychonomic Bulletin and Review* 17:5: 644–650.

    Fausey, Caitlin, and Lera Boroditsky. 2011. Who dunnit? Cross-linguistic differences in eye-witness memory. *Psychonomic Bulletin and Review* 18:1: 150–157.

3. Bassetti and Cook (2011: 171–172) use a simple internet experiment to probe meaning differences between words that are taken to be translational equivalents in different languages. In order to gain a preliminary understanding of how English 'lunch' and Italian '*pranzo*' signify different types of midday meals to their speakers, they googled images of both words and compared the items that appeared in the pictures of 'lunch' and '*pranzo*' they found. Use the same methodology to investigate other pairs of common translation equivalents in any two languages and discuss the differences you observe from such an experiment.

    Bassetti, Benedetta, and Vivian Cook. 2011. Relating language and cognition: the second language user. In Vivian Cook and Benedetta Bassetti (eds.), *Language and bilingual cognition*. New York: Psychology Press, 143–191.

4. Many languages incorporate a gender system in which nouns are assigned to two or more gender classes. For example, in German, nouns are all either grammatically classed as being masculine, feminine, or neuter. In various cases, the gender of a noun is semantically 'natural'—'man' will be a masculine noun, and 'woman' a feminine noun—but many other words seem to be assigned to different genders quite arbitrarily, hence 'table' is a feminine noun in Spanish but a masculine noun in German, and 'bridge' is masculine in Spanish but feminine in German. It might seem unlikely that the assignment of nouns to different genders would have any semantic consequences when these nouns are inanimate—how could a bridge be considered feminine in German but masculine in Spanish? However, studies which have attempted to probe this possibility have found some intriguing results which suggest that speakers may in fact metaphorically transfer aspects of real semantic gender to inanimate nouns depending on their grammatical gender. Read about this in the following two papers:

   Sera, Maria, Chryle Elieff, Diane Dubois, Melissa Burch, James M. Forbes, and Wanda Rodriguez. 2002. When language affects cognition and when it does not: an analysis of grammatical gender and classification. *Journal of Experimental Psychology: General* 131: 377–397.

   Boroditsky, Lera, Lauren Schmidt, and Webb Phillips. 2003. Sex, syntax, and semantics. In Dedre Gentner and Susan Goldin-Meadow (eds.), *Language in mind: advances in the study of language and thought*. Cambridge: Cambridge University Press, 61–78.

5. Differences in the ways speakers may perceive *motion* in English and Spanish have been suggested to relate to differences in the ways these languages use verbs to depict movement. Spanish is known as a 'verb frame language', and English as a 'satellite language'. In English, verbs regularly refer to the manner of motion, and particles are used to represent the direction of the movement, as in 'He ran in/out', whereas in Spanish, the main verb represents the direction of movement and a secondary verb is used to add information about the manner of motion, hence a speaker of Spanish would say the equivalent of 'He entered, running' for English 'He ran in.' Read the following article to learn more about how such differences may have cognitive effects:

   Gennari, Silvia, Steven Sloman, Barbara Malt, and W. Tecumseh Fitch. 2003. Motion events in language and cognition. *Cognition* 83: 49–79.

6. Try to understand what is meant by Dan Slobin's phrase 'thinking for speaking' and how this relates to the linguistic relativity hypothesis, making use of the following paper by Slobin:

   Slobin, Dan. 1995. From 'thought and language' to 'thinking for speaking'. In John Gumperz and Stephen Levinson (eds.), *Rethinking linguistic relativity*. Cambridge: Cambridge University Press, 71–96.

10

Language and Gender

Introduction

The final two chapters in this book are going to look at variation that occurs *within* individual languages, rather than *between* different languages. Chapter 11 examines aspects of variation that are associated with *changes* occurring within languages, while the focus of the current chapter is on how there may be differences in the ways that men and women speak the 'same' language, and why this variation may have arisen. We will begin by looking at some simple examples of differences that have been observed in male and female speech in various cultures, first of all cases where men and women speak in quite different ways and then other situations where women and men use certain forms of speech with different degrees of frequency. This will lead us to a discussion of the possible causes of differences in men's and women's speech, when such differences are observed, and what these patterns may tell us about men's and women's relation to each other and to society in general. We will see that there are interesting, contrastive interpretations of observations made about men's and women's speech, and different theories of the use that men and women make of language. The chapter will also consider the presence of sexism in language, and the issue of variation within men's and women's language. While much of the first part of the chapter will be concerned with gender-related language use in the West, and in particular the many studies made of male and female speakers of English in the UK, the USA, Canada, New Zealand, and Australia, the latter part of the chapter will add a special focus on gendered language use in Japan.

Speech differences between men and women

One frequently mentioned example of obvious differences present in the speech of men and women living in a single community is the case of the **Carib** people in the West Indies. In this group, men use many expressions which women do not use, and women use a whole variety of words which are not found in men's speech. Historically this is due to the fact that long ago an army of Carib warriors invaded an area inhabited by Arawak-speaking people and killed all the Arawak men. The women who remained then continued to speak Arawak while their new husbands spoke the (related) Carib language. Nowadays the Carib and Arawak languages have become largely mixed, but there are many words of Arawak origin which just occur in the speech of women, and many words of Carib origin which are only used by males.

In other groups one finds that there are regular distinctions in the forms of words used by men and women speaking the same language. For example, in **Yana**, a Native American language from northern California, the form of women's words is sometimes shorter than men's words due to the presence of different endings in men's speech (Sapir 1923):

	men's word	women's word
'grizzly bear'	t'en'na	t'et
'Yana'	Yana	Yah
'deer'	ba	ba-na
'see me'	diwai-dja	diwa-tch

In **Karajá**, from Brazil, the opposite patterning occurs, and women's words regularly include extra syllables or sounds not heard in the same words pronounced by men (Talbot 2008):

	men's word	women's word
'house'	heto	hetoku
'Sunday'	nobiotxu	nobikutxu
'turtle'	otu	kotu
'bicycle'	bisileta	bisikreta

Women speaking **Yanyuwa** in Australia similarly add extra syllables to certain words in their speech, making it sound quite distinctive from the way that men talk. For example, the phrase 'this short initiated man' in men's speech would be *jinangu wukuthu rduwarra* and in women's speech is *nya-ja nya-wukuthu nya-rduwarra*, with the element *nya* added on to each word (a special noun class marker; Bradley 1998).

Sometimes there are sound substitutions rather than additions in men's and women's speech. In **Koasati**, a Native American language from Louisiana, men's words substitute a final *–s* sound when women's words end with either an *–l* sound or a nasalized vowel. This small adjustment makes men's and women's speech sound quite distinctive, and it would not be appropriate for men to use the women's forms, or vice versa (Haas 1944):

	women's word	men's word
'we peel it'	molhil	molhis
'I lift it'	lacawwil	lacawwis
'he will lift it'	lakawwa^n	lakawwas

In **Zulu** (South Africa), there are also sound substitutions which affect the ways that women pronounce various words. In traditional Zulu society, a married woman is not supposed to mention the name of her husband, her father-in-law, or his brothers and must also avoid the use of syllables which occur prominently in the names of these male relatives. Rudwick (2013) notes that if the name of a woman's husband were to be *Mandla*, for example, the wife should not pronounce words with either of the syllables *man* or *dla* occurring in them.

In order to comply with this linguistic taboo, women typically substitute other syllables for the syllables they are expected to avoid. Consequently, the regular word for 'water' *amanzi*, containing the syllable *man*, may be converted to *amadambi*, avoiding *man* with the use of *madam*, and the word for 'food' *ukudla*, containing *dla*, might be pronounced as *ukumaya*, substituting the sequence *maya* for the syllable *dla*. This special way of speaking among Zulu women is known as *hlonipha* ('respect language') and also occurs in the neighboring *Xhosa* language group (Finlayson 1978). It is additionally found in a similar form in South Asia in traditional Hindu families. In order to demonstrate respect for her husband and his male relatives, a wife speaking *Hindi* (and other regional languages) should not pronounce the name of her husband or his father and uncles, and should also avoid using syllables that occur prominently in their names. For example, if the name of an elder brother-in-law were to be *dhanii raam*, a wife should not use words such as *dhaniyaa* ('coriander') which sound quite like the male relative's name. Instead, some other way of referring to 'coriander' must be found, such as the substitution of a different phrase like *harii botal waalaa masaalaa* 'the spice in the green bottle' (Valentine 2008).

In other languages, one finds that specific words which have relational meanings are quite different in men's and women's speech, not just different forms of a single basic 'root', and pronouns and kinship terms may vary depending on whether these are being used by male or female speakers. For example, in **Thai** and **Burmese**, the word for 'I/me' is different for men and women:[1]

Thai 'I/me'		**Burmese** 'I/me'	
men's form	women's form	men's form	women's form
phom	*dichan*	*janaw*	*jama*

Concerning terms used for family members, in **Korean** it is found that the way of referring to an older brother or sister varies according to the sex of the speaker. A female speaker will refer to her older brother and older sister as *oppa* and *onni*, while a male speaker will use the words *hyong* and *nuna*. Sometimes words and expressions used to refer to the establishment of a new kinship relation such as 'marry/wed' also vary depending on whom such terms refer to. In **Chinese**, two different verbs occur with the meaning 'marry/wed', one used only by males—*qu*—and the other reserved for females—*jia*—as illustrated in the following:[2,3]

---

1. Thai male and female speakers also use different politeness particles at the ends of their sentences—males use the element *khrap* to signal respect to the person they are talking to, and females use *kha*.

2. The Chinese characters corresponding to these two words for 'marry/wed' have pictorial components which conjure up different images. *Jia*嫁, used for female subjects, symbolizes the subject (a new wife) going to someone else's house, whereas *qu*娶 which occurs with male subjects represents a woman being fetched by her ear.

3. In some languages, such as *Kinyarwanda* (Rwanda) and *Setswana* and *Ikalanga* (Botswana), only one word for 'marry/wed' occurs, and it can actually only be used with a male subject, hence it is not possible for women to say 'I married him' (Atanga et al. 2013).

Male speaker:	*wo **qu**-le yi-ge hen you qian de ren.*
	'I married a very rich person.'
Female speaker:	*wo **jia**-le yi-ge hen you qian de ren.*
	'I married a very rich person.'

Differences in the words used by men and women have also been observed in English. Up until the 1970s (but perhaps not so strongly any more), Lakoff (1975) reported that women in Britain and North America used various terms and patterns that did not occur in men's speech and were felt to identify speakers as being women if occurring in written or spoken language. These include various specialized color terms and emphatic expressions, such as the following,

mauve, aquamarine, magenta, lavender
charming, adorable, divine, exquisite

One *phonological* difference which commonly exists in men's and women's speech in communities around the world is that men speak in a lower/deeper pitch than women. This natural difference in pitch may, however, often be deliberately exaggerated to some extent by speakers of both sexes, and linguists have suggested that men frequently lower their pitch and women sometimes raise their pitch in order to emphasize a masculine or feminine identity. For example, women in Japan have been recorded as using a pitch level which is often significantly higher than in other countries. This is especially striking among women working in certain jobs, such as: (a) elevator operators in department stores (who announce the goods sold on each floor in artificially high-pitched voices), (b) sales assistants in department stores, (c) train station announcers, (d) TV commercial narrators. The special high pitch of women workers heard in these environments is sometimes referred to as the 'service voice', and was measured in an experiment described in Loveday (1986). Loveday asked a group of American, European, and Japanese women to produce a number of common 'formulaic' expressions (greetings, expressions of thanks, etc.), and when these were recorded and analyzed, it was noted that the American and European women averaged a level of 240 hertz in their pitch production, while the Japanese women reached highs of up to 310–450 hertz. A pronounced, high pitch level is also found among many women who are not professionally involved in public announcement or customer service, and is associated with certain ideas of stereotypical femininity in Japan. As there are no inherent physical reasons for such elevated pitch levels, and women everywhere are born with the same basic vocal apparatus, the higher average pitch level used by many Japanese women is concluded to be an aspect of intonation which is deliberately adopted.

In other countries, too, men and women from an early age have been noted to exaggerate either low or high pitch levels in their speech, to some extent. For example, young pre-adolescent males have often been observed to adopt a lower pitch in their voice several years before there is any physical change in their bodies which might cause them to have a genuinely deeper voice. Among adults, it has also been documented that the average pitch level used by American and British men is lower than that found with many other language groups, leading to the conclusion that males in the USA and UK artificially produce a lower than normal pitch when they are speaking, perhaps subconsciously, as a way to emphasize masculinity.

A well-known example of a woman in later life deliberately altering her vocal pitch is Margaret Thatcher, the first female prime minister of the UK (in power from 1979 to 1990). When Mrs. Thatcher was campaigning to be elected, she was advised to cultivate a lower vocal pitch, because Britain had previously only had male prime ministers and most people might expect someone with so much authority to have a male-like, deeper voice. Margaret Thatcher's pre-election regular voice was actually like that of other typical British women, and so, in order to sound more authoritative, like a man, she began to speak more slowly and monotonously and with a lowered pitch, resulting in a speaking style that subsequently became a strong characteristic of most of her public addresses.[4]

When there are differences between men's and women's speech and certain patterns are only used by male speakers or by female speakers, these are referred to as *sex-exclusive* differences. The cases of lexical variation and sound substitution described earlier for Carib, Yana, Zulu, English, etc., are all reported to be instances of such sex-exclusive, or 'qualitative' differences between men's and women's speech, and the cultivation of exaggerated high or low pitch is also typical of either women or men, hence has the same property of being a qualitative difference in male and female speech (Margaret Thatcher being an odd exception here). There are also other cases of variation in male and female speech in which the same patterns are used by both men and women, but in different amounts—either men or women use certain forms with a higher frequency than members of the other sex. Such instances of variation are known as *sex-preferential* patterns, or 'quantitative differences' between male and female speech. They are actually more common than sex-exclusive differences, and in certain ways are more intriguing and revealing, leading to interesting theories concerning *why* men and women may prefer different forms.

With regard to English, a range of sex-preferential, quantitative differences in men's and women's speech have been found in aspects of pronunciation and the use of other more vernacular forms of speech. Three examples can be given here as illustration. First, in casual speech in many parts of Britain and the USA, the *-ing* ending on verbs may get reduced to *-in'*, as in the following examples:

I *was walkin'/walking down the road when* . . .
I *was watchin'/watching it closely* . . .

It has been repeatedly found that both men and women use the contracted/shortened form *-in'* in colloquial speech, but women typically use this form *less often* than men do.

Second, speakers of British English from various parts of the UK frequently pronounce words beginning with *h* without an *h* sound, dropping it in casual speech, hence *half an*

---

4. Learn more about this and hear examples of Margaret Thatcher's changing vocal patterns at:
   (a) www.telegraph.co.uk/news/politics/11251919/From-shrill-housewife-to-Downing-Street-the-changing-voice-of-Margaret-Thatcher.html
   (b) www.youtube.com/watch?v=Tetk_ayO1x4

hour becomes *'arf an hour*, *Henry* is pronounced as *'Enry*, and *happy* is modified as *'appy*. As with the colloquial reduction of *–ing* to *–in'*, the non-standard h-less pronunciation of words in Britain has been found to occur more frequently in the speech of men than in women's speech.

Third, in the area of grammar, there are quantitative differences in men's and women's speech, and vernacular forms such as double-negation (the use of two negative elements with the meaning of a single instance of negation) are used both by men and women in certain groups in casual speech, but are found to occur more frequently in male speech:

Double negation: I *ain't got nothin'*.
Standard English equivalent: I *haven't got anything*.

In early, much-referenced work considering interactions between language and gender, Peter Trudgill (1974a/b) set out to try to explain why there might be such differences between men's and women's patterns of speech. Considering first male/female phonological variation in Chukchi (Siberia) and Koasati, Trudgill notes that in both languages the distinctive forms used by women are mostly *older* historical pronunciations. Importantly, male speakers as well as female speakers also reported that they felt the female forms were *better* than the men's pronunciations. Trudgill then points out that in many other cases where women tend to use a vernacular form such as *-in'* or double negation with significantly less frequency than men, such forms are generally perceived as being 'lower in style' than the non-colloquial equivalent. Trudgill takes this as indicating that women may have a general tendency to avoid forms of speech which are considered to be low-status, colloquial forms, preferring instead more conservative 'correct' speech. In Chukchi and Koasati, female speakers retain the older pronunciations of their languages, and in English-speaking communities in the UK and North America they also show a greater tendency than men to use more standard forms.

Many more studies have subsequently confirmed this tendency, and in Britain and the USA it has been matched against the social class/socio-economic background of speakers (measured in terms of levels of education, income, profession/job, and domicile location). When a range of different pronunciations and grammatical phenomena were compared, it was found that in the lowest and highest social classes, men and women's speech showed no major variation, but in socio-economic groups in the middle range, the speech of women often differed from the speech of men from the same social class, and was more similar to the speech of men in a higher social class. Thus, women from an upper-working class background were found to speak more like men from a lower-middle class background, and women from a lower-middle-class background produced patterns more like those of men from the upper-middle-class. The linguist Jennifer Coates concludes from this that in the lowest and highest classes women adopt the same level of speech as the men from the same socio-economic background, and that women from these classes are therefore primarily concerned with identifying themselves as members of the same social class as the men, hence showing *solidarity* with the men. In the other intervening class levels, it is hypothesized that women act linguistically in a more class-conscious way, attempting to speak like men from a higher class level and favoring *overtly prestigious* standard forms of language more than men do. By way of contrast, where men use a particular form more often than women, it often turns out to be a vernacular form which is not admired by the society as a whole.[5]

Trudgill was one of the first linguists to offer potential explanations for these frequently observed differences between male and female speech. He argues that they may be due to different pressures which Western societies (in particular) often exert on men and women. Women, he suggests, may be unable to achieve social prestige in the same ways as men, due to unequal access to higher levels of employment, and so use other means to claim social status, including dress/appearance and the use of 'educated' standard forms of language. Men, on the other hand, are viewed as being under a rather different pressure in society, emphasizing the need to appear masculine and identify one's genuine class background. Working-class vernacular speech is therefore suggested to be highly valued by many men as it expresses masculinity and identifies speakers with their social group. Such a positive view of colloquial, non-standard language has been termed '*covert prestige*' by linguists, because speakers themselves may often not openly admit that they find vernacular forms better than standard language, and non-standard patterns are not regularly promoted in schools.

The effects of covert prestige on attitudes toward language have been revealed in linguistic experiments which asked people to evaluate their own speech and then compared these self-evaluations with the ways that participants actually did speak in separate, recorded interviews. For example, words might be read aloud with two or more different pronunciations, and speakers would be asked to indicate which form they used themselves. Often such studies have shown that there are marked differences between what people actually say and what they think they regularly say (or what they claim to be their regular patterns of speech). The results from one experiment carried out in Norwich (England) showed that as many as 40% of people reported that they spoke in a more colloquial way, with more vernacular forms, than they actually did. These people '*under-reported*' their speech, as they claimed to be using less statusful forms that they did in reality (as revealed by recordings of their speech in interviews). Sixteen percent of people also '*over-reported*' themselves, claiming that they spoke with more statusful forms that they did. Significantly, all of those who over-reported themselves as using more prestigious higher-class forms were female informants (Trudgill 1974a: 91). Trudgill suggests that this is:

> . . . presumably because they wish they did use them or think they ought to and perhaps, therefore, actually believe that they do. Speakers, that is, report themselves as using the form at which they are aiming and which has favourable connotations for them, rather than the form they actually use. (No *conscious* deceit is involved, it seems). (Trudgill 1974a: 91)

---

5. Interestingly, the tendency for various women to use forms which are judged to be more prestigious may develop from an early age, and children as young as six have been shown to pattern in this way, with girls avoiding the vernacular forms used more commonly by boys from the same social background.

Considering people who under-report themselves as using more vernacular, less prestigious/standard forms than they really did, this has been found to be a common feature of men's self-evaluations (with over half the males participating in one experiment described in Trudgill 1974a: 92 under-reporting their speech). Trudgill interprets this as suggesting that, at a sub-conscious level, males are very favorably disposed to non-standard speech forms, and so claim to use these forms more than they really do. Men may therefore seem to be equally as concerned with acquiring prestige as female speakers, but what male speakers can be said to aim for is covert prestige and identification with the image of masculine working-class speakers who heavily use vernacular speech.

Linguistic change in men and women's speech

Trudgill also observes that where there is some kind of change in speech in a community toward a high-class or national form, this change is very frequently led by women. For example, in North Carolina in the 1970s, women led a change from an older prestige form to a newer one becoming established elsewhere in the USA. Previously the prestige pronunciation form of words ending in *r* in most of the USA was to omit the *r*-sound (as in British English). However, this general pattern changed in the northeastern USA and a new prestige form emerged in which speakers began to pronounce the *r*-sound in words such as *car* and *farm* (more about this change will be described in chapter 11). In North Carolina, it was noted that the first people to start following the new prestige pronunciation from further north in the USA, significantly, were female speakers, and men were slower to join in the change.

Another change led by women toward a new prestigious form was observed in the Austrian town of Oberwart (Gal 1979). This town originally belonged to Hungary but later became part of Austria as the result of a border adjustment following World War I. Originally, all the inhabitants of the town used to speak Hungarian in all domains of life, but then German was introduced into the schools and later became dominant in industry and commerce. For some time Hungarian continued to be used by all speakers at home and socially with friends. However, with the increased association of German with economic success and business and the association of Hungarian with peasant working-class life, younger women in Oberwart began to switch more and more to the use of German in all social domains as well, while men frequently stuck to Hungarian. Thus women led a change to a higher-status variety of speech, while men continued to favor a form of speech which gave them covert prestige and identified them as members of the working class.

Trudgill's general conclusion is that men and women speak as they do because they feel certain language is appropriate to the projection of different male and female identities, which are constructed by a range of forces and pressures in society. Trudgill also adds that in many Western countries people have been changing the way they feel about differences between men and women in modern society, and that the change in attitudes and the gradual erosion of sexual stereotypes may explain the observation that linguistic differences between younger men and women are rather less prominent than they used to be with older speakers.

Holmes' views on the differences in women's speech

Holmes (1992) reviews Trudgill's initial descriptions of women's speech, and notes that there are four common explanations of the observation that women seem to use more standard forms of language than men in Western societies:

Social status

Women are sometimes suggested to use language as a means to claim social status. It is often noted that women in many societies may not have the same opportunities as men to obtain senior-level, prestigious jobs, and so use other means to assert the high social status that professional advancement often provides for men. The use of standard language is regularly associated with speakers who have higher levels of education and socio-economic success, while non-standard speech is more commonly linked to membership of the lower classes. The deliberate adoption and increased use of standard language forms by women in the middle classes has been interpreted by various linguists as a mechanism that women may exploit to enhance their personal image and project a desired, statusful identity.

Woman's expected function as role models in society

Holmes notes that a second explanation for women's use of more standard speech sometimes given in the past is that 'society tends to expect "better" behavior from women than from men' (Holmes 1992: 172). Among children, boys are often granted more personal freedom than girls and are punished for misbehavior much less frequently than girls, and in adult life, women tend to be criticized for any negatively perceived aspects of their conduct more severely than men are. Women are regularly expected to serve as models of 'correct' behavior in society, and linguistically this means that women should refrain from coarse, vernacular language and instead make use of standard language, which can then be copied as a model by children learning to speak through interaction with their mothers.

Differences in power between men and women

A third common explanation for women's more careful speech is that the hierarchical structure of many societies imposes a power imbalance between men and women, which results in women being expected to show deference and respect to men. This is particularly evident in various more traditional, non-Western communities, where women are relegated to clearly subordinate positions in society, but is also sometimes a force affecting male-female relations in modern, Western states as well. Where such differences in power are present in any community, women frequently experience pressure to adopt patterns of behavior which symbolically recognize the dominant position of men. In the domain of speech, this typically results in the use of polite, standard forms of language rather than very casual, colloquial forms.

Masculinity is communicated by non-standard speech

A fourth rationale for male/female speech differences given by Trudgill is that women avoid the use of vernacular, non-standard speech forms because these communicate an image of masculinity and toughness, often highly valued by men, but dispreferred by women who may not wish to be perceived as having qualities of this type. The common association of non-standard speech with masculinity has been confirmed in experiments where people were asked to listen to different voices on a tape and indicate who they thought were the 'toughest' speakers in the group. The common result in such experiments is that informants pick those speakers who use colloquial speech, clearly showing the mental correlation of vernacular non-standard forms with masculinity and machismo. While women may not necessarily wish to cultivate an image of exaggerated femininity, they may equally not desire to be labeled masculine and tough-sounding, and this can be achieved by a reduction in the use of non-standard forms of language in their speech.

A different perspective: Holmes (1998b)

While the preceding explanations all have a certain plausibility and have regularly been influential in discussions of male/female language differences, criticism has also been directed by some analysts at the social status account of women's speech, especially as it was originally formulated by Trudgill with the rather contentious claim that *women are more status conscious than men* and more concerned with establishing a statusful position in society than male speakers.[6] Graddol and Swann (1989) and Holmes (1998b) provide many interesting insights into these issues, and the upcoming sections will draw significantly on these works. Holmes (1998b) proposes an interesting reinterpretation of the range of patterns which led to early hypotheses about why men and women make use of different patterns of speech, and does this with four 'dimensions of analysis' which have been successfully applied to other aspects of language and society, the notions of *function, solidarity, power,* and *status*. Each of these properties of speech is associated with a question which Holmes uses to approach the phenomenon of male/female language differences (slightly adjusted from Holmes 1998: 462):

Function: What is the purpose of each conversational act?
Solidarity: How well do the people talking relate to each other?
Power: Who's in charge of the conversation?
Status: How does speech indicate social status?

As we will see, Holmes uses these questions to develop a series of new 'universal' statements about men's and women's speech which offer possible alternative explanations of the differences frequently observed in male and female language habits.

---

6. The influential sociolinguist William Labov made similar assumptions about the role of social status in affecting women's choice of speech: 'Women in our society are more status-conscious than men, generally speaking... and are therefore more aware of the social significance of linguistics variables' (i.e. they know that that a person's speech is often interpreted as an indicator of social class) (Labov 1972: 182).

Function

Acts of communication may be carried out for different purposes. One major function of speech is simply the exchange of new pieces of information. This is sometimes termed the *referential use* of language. Most instances of speech convey some amount of referential information; however, we also frequently use language for another, more social purpose, to establish, maintain, and strengthen our personal relations with others. This aspect of communication is referred to as the *affective use* of language. Frequently, our interactions with others are combinations of both the referential and affective use of language wrapped up together, as we give and receive information in ways that simultaneously encode the social relations we have with our friends, family members, colleagues, and other acquaintances. Our language is phrased in various ways that express how friendly and close we may be to those we are speaking with. There are also some special acts of communication which are primarily, or fully focused on the affective function of language, for example the greetings we exchange when we meet and leave other people—there is no real referential information in expressions such as 'Good morning', 'Hi', and 'Bye for now', and even the standardized questions we use as greetings often do not genuinely ask for or get answered with any explicit information; hence "Sup, man' can be 'answered' with just 'Hey, dude', and 'How are things?' is frequently responded to with an automatic 'Fine' rather than an informative description of one's present living state. Conversely, some forms of communication are almost exclusively referential in nature, and have no, or very little affective component, for example news broadcasts, conference presentations and lectures, and the language style used in instruction manuals for cars, furniture assembly, product use, and the like.

In considering the ways that men and women make use of language, it has been suggested that there is an imbalance in the emphasis placed on referential and affective communication by men and women, and that men's speech may on average contain a higher proportion of referential information than women's talk, while women may make use of the affective function of language more frequently than men. If casual conversations between men and women (or just between male speakers, or female speakers) are analyzed for their referential and interpersonal content, male speakers may often appear to prioritize the communication of factual information and be less concerned with using language to explore their hearers' feelings, whereas female speakers introduce more affective themes into their conversation and frequently use language in a largely social way, to build and strengthen bonds with others, express their emotions, and understand how others may be feeling. The affective use of language is therefore argued to be dominant among women, and more commonly added into conversation, alongside referential information, than with male speakers. In recognition of such a distinction between highly typical male and female language use, observed in Western societies, Holmes proposes the following generalization as a possible first 'universal' statement:

Women tend to focus on the affective functions of an interaction more often than men do.
(Holmes 1998: 463)

One of the examples Holmes gives as illustration of the different approaches to conversation attributed to men and women is the following exchange heard by Holmes in a camp-site in New Zealand where a man was adjusting a radio and a woman passed by with some laundry:

Woman: You've got a radio there then.
Man: Yes (pause) I'm trying to get the weather.
Woman: I've been trying on mine but I can't get a thing.
Man: mm
Woman: We really need to know before we leave (pause) we're on bikes you see.
Man: mm
Woman: I've got a young child with me too. (pause) We're from Hamilton and we're cycling to Taupo. (pause) Where are you going then?
Man: Taupo.

After the interaction, the man told Holmes he thought that the woman really wanted to find out about the weather conditions and that was why she stopped to talk to him—in other words, she wanted to gain some information. However, Holmes, who had heard the conversation, felt sure that the woman was not really concerned about getting any information on the weather and had just used this topic as a friendly excuse to break the ice and initiate a new social contact and chat casually with the man.

Holmes notes that such apparent differences in male and female speakers' approach to conversation have the potential to give rise to misunderstandings between men and women. Sometimes for women the goal of talking with someone may be the sharing of a personal problem in the hope that this will help the speaker feel better, as hearers respond sympathetically and with emotive understanding. Yet such a focus may be largely missed by male speakers as they simply scan the speaker's speech for information and use referential rather than affective language as reply forms, offering strategies to deal with problems but not emotional support. The following is a representative exchange which took place between a husband and wife at dinner, reproduced by Holmes (1998: 464):

Ann: That meeting I had to go to today was just awful.
Bob: Where was it?
Ann: In the NLC building. People were just so aggressive.
Bob: Mm. Who was there?
Ann: Oh the usual representatives of all the government departments. I felt really put down at one point, you know, just so humiliated.
Bob: You should be more assertive dear. Don't let people trample all over you and ignore what you say.

Here we have a situation in which the wife, Ann, has had a bad experience at her place of work, and she wants to tell her husband, Bob, about what happened, in order to elicit some sympathy from him as her closest, most intimate partner in life. Bob, however, reacts to her laments by asking questions in order to try to find out more information about the situation, as a way to construct advice for his wife on how to avoid such trauma in the future. Bob's good intentions are sincere, and he wants to help his wife, but he reads the situation in a typically masculine way, believing that Ann is giving him information so as to get further information in return, specifically a solution to the problem she is describing. Ann, on the other hand, was actually not looking to find practical advice on dealing with her colleagues in the future. Instead, she was hoping to receive kind, supportive words from her husband as a form of emotional comfort after the difficult day, not the rather cold analysis he provides, which most likely makes her feel worse as it implies she ought to have behaved more confidently in the circumstances described. The husband has focused on the informational content of the interaction, while the wife was actually talking with her husband for an affective purpose.

Holmes points out that misunderstandings of this kind have often been highlighted in descriptions of male-female interactions in Western countries, which present the frequent association of men with information-heavy speech and women's greater attention to social relations as key distinguishing features of archetypal male and female modes of engagement in communication (see, for example, the bestselling books by the author and sociolinguist Deborah Tannen *That's Not What I Meant* (1986) and *You Just Don't Understand* (1990). There is consequently substantial support for the first generalization that Holmes proposes, that women tend to focus on the affective functions of an interaction more often than men do, as a characteristic property of Western societies. Whether it may be a real sociolinguistic 'universal' and apply in the same way in all cultures and societies around the world is not yet clear, due to lack of research, but the observations made in Western countries at least provide a foundation and hypothesis for the examination of similar phenomena elsewhere.

Solidarity

'Solidarity' is a term used to refer to the degree of familiarity and closeness (or distance) that exists between individuals, and the ways that people relate to each other. Close friends and family members will share a high degree of solidarity, while less intimacy and lower degrees of solidarity will typically occur between people who meet and interact with each other less often, for example a customer and a sales assistant in a large department store, or a patient and a doctor who is visited once a year, and, of course, between people who have never previously met each other. Linguistically, solidarity can exert various effects upon the language we make use of in our communication with others. In languages such as French, Italian, and German, speakers use one form of the pronoun 'you' when they know someone well (*tu* in French and Italian, *du* in German) and a different form for 'you' when the addressee is someone who is less familiar (*vous* in French, *Lei* in Italian, and *Sie* in German). In Japanese the degree of solidarity which exists between speakers and hearers is reflected in special verb endings, one type used for people one is close with and a different set of endings for strangers and people one is less familiar with (hence 'understand' is *wakar-u* among people that are close with each other, and *wakar-imasu* when there is a low degree of familiarity/closeness/solidarity). In Holmes' (1998) re-examination of male and female speech patterns, the significance of a number of the differences observed to exist in women's and men's speech is given a new interpretation, as will soon be described, and attributed to solidarity as a cause, rather than other factors suggested in earlier analyses. Similar conclusions are also reached by the linguist Jennifer Coates in her book *Women Talk* (1996).

Lakoff (1975) describes a variety of linguistic patterns which she asserted were more common in women's than men's speech and typical of female speech style. Various of these patterns were suggested to reveal that women generally lacked confidence when they spoke, were hesitant, weak, and unassertive, 'characteristics associated with conventional femininity' (Coates 1996: 171). Lakoff argued that this was to be expected 'because they are socialized to believe that asserting themselves strongly isn't nice or lady-like, or even feminine' (Lakoff 1975: 54).[7] The features signaling such a lack of confidence and tentativeness, for Lakoff, included devices known as '*hedges*' and '*boosts*' (or hedging and boosting devices), a higher rate of the use of questions than men, and the use of question intonation patterns in statements (rising intonation at the end of sentences, making declarations sound like questions, hence expressing statements with some uncertainty). Hedging devices include lexical hedges like the expressions '*sort of*', '*kind of*', '*I suppose/guess*', '*it seems like*', and 'tag-questions' in which sequences like '*isn't it*' are added to the ends of sentences to make them into questions, as illustrated in the following.

Its sort of nice.
Steve's kind of/kinda cute, right?
I guess they shouldn't do that.
It seems like he was wrong.
Mary's upset, isn't she?

Boosting devices include elements called 'intensifiers', such as '*really*', and '*so*', and the use of emphatic stress, often in combination with each other:

It's a REALLY good film.
That's SOO nice of you.

Overall it has been confirmed in subsequent studies that women do indeed use hedges and boosts more than men. However, careful research has shown that these forms do not always signal uncertainty or a lack of confidence, and in fact may be used for a variety of other purposes. Holmes (1998b) and Coates (1996) argue that what is communicated through women's use of hedges and boosts is actually *solidarity* and close, considerate *connections* with others being spoken to, and the general maintenance of good social relations. Here we will focus on how women's questions are frequently used for such social reasons rather than being markers of uncertainty.

Coates (1996: 201) notes that questions can be categorized into two broad types, according to the person who may benefit from their use. Questions which genuinely ask for certain information ('information-seeking questions') are viewed as being primarily

---

7. Quoted in Coates (1996: 171).

speaker-oriented—the speaker will benefit from acquiring information provided in answers to the question. The second type of question which often occurs is characterized as being *other-oriented*—someone other than the speaker (typically the addressee—the person spoken to) accrues some benefit from the use of the question, as we will shortly see. Other-oriented questions help maintain the flow of conversation, build and strengthen connections with other speakers, and facilitate relations with others in a number of different ways. While self-oriented information-seeking questions are made use of by all speakers as the need arises, other-oriented questions are much more common in women's than in men's speech and regularly serve to heighten solidarity. Some of the ways these questions are utilized will now be illustrated with examples from casual speech.

Coates (1996: 201) suggests that three particular trends in the talk of women friends motivate the use of many of their other-oriented questions. First, it is argued that 'the establishment and maintenance of a shared world [i.e., shared values and opinions] is a crucial aspect of women's friendship', and that questions are a useful device for checking that other people in a group do indeed hold the same views and are therefore closely 'connected' with each other. This gives rise to questions such as the following, which are often rhetorical and not given any answer, but nevertheless offer the opportunity for others to add a different opinion and disagree if they wish. Note that the question component in some of the upcoming examples is in some cases a tag inserted mid-way in a sentence.[8]

> *It's strange, isn't it?, the life some people lead.*
> *It was dreadful, wasn't it?, what happened. How could anyone do that?*
> *Marrying Jim was a mistake, wasn't it?, Sue will never be independent now.*
> *Can you imagine having a son who is accused of murder?*

Second, Coates adds that the collaborative aspect of conversation is highly valued by women when talking to each other as friends, and questions are useful ways of stressing the collaborative nature of an interaction when one person is speaking—questions signal an explicit awareness of others, acknowledging their presence, and indicate the speaker's desire to stay connected with others in the group. This often results in the insertion of small question tags midway within sentences, such as the following:

> *And they had a very accurate picture of him, didn't they?, they roughly knew his age.*
> *Well, we were in the library, right?, and we were in that corner where all the picture books are.*

In such conversation collaborations among women, it is felt that the group should naturally take precedence over the individual, and the frequent use of questions encourages the interaction of everyone in the group. Quite often questions can also be directed at specific individuals and can be used to invite someone in a friendly way to participate in a conversation, as for example in:

---

8. The examples presented here all come from Coates (1996), in some instances being a little adapted.

Last week you bought a new Toyota, didn't you, Tammy?
That's not what Brad told us, is it, Lindsey?

Coates refers to the use of tag questions in this way as 'facilitative tags', as they offer a means to include others in a conversation, who might perhaps be somewhat hesitant to speak.

A third underlying characteristic of women's conversational exchanges, according to Coates, is the tacit wish not to act or come across as an 'expert' imposing authoritative information on any topic of discussion, as this has the potential to undermine close, friendly connections with others. The use of questions allows a speaker to avoid sounding like an expert, and so stimulates cohesiveness in a group and minimizes social distance. Questions can be used to introduce information known by the speaker in a way that suggests this information is also familiar to others, even when this is not the case, for example:

In Austria they speak German, don't they?

In addition to the use of other-oriented questions in the ways already described, as mechanisms to emphasize connections and collaboration, Coates and Holmes identify three further situations in which women are frequently found to use other-oriented questions. Often these occur when female speakers are engaged in discussing *sensitive topics*, for example child abuse or incest, leading speakers to ask each other for their views and insights, as in:

I mean, I think it was your theory, wasn't it? that it runs in families.
I mean is it—is it to do with the mother?

Talking about sensitive topics is sometimes felt to be too difficult if speakers simply make blunt statements, and the use of questions and other hedges help mitigate the force that subjects of this type may otherwise exert in a conversation.

Self-disclosure—the revealing of confidential personal information, our hopes and fears and private behavior and experiences—is also an activity that regularly gives rise to cautious language and the use of hedges and question forms, as information is presented carefully to people a speaker trusts. The following is an example of this kind of talk, which occurs more frequently among female speakers, who confide in each other more often than men typically do:

I mean, I just fell for him, didn't I?, he was so charming. Was I wrong to sleep with him so soon? I don't know.

Finally, questions may be used as useful ways to soften criticism, as in the following example from Holmes. The context here is a wife looking at a flooded kitchen floor, which she attributes to the husband's failed attempt to fix their leaking sink:

Well, that wasn't the best bit of plumbing you've ever done, was it?

In summary, a closer consideration of the ways that questions are used by female speakers results in different conclusions from those originally suggested by Lakoff. Rather than being indications of uncertainty and weakness, questions are used by women as an effective and powerful means to express mutual connection and solidarity with other speakers. The same is true of women's use of hedges, as discussed at length in Coates (1996, chapter 7). Consequently the common occurrence of these forms in women's speech does not indicate that women are continuously under-confident speakers, but rather that they are more concerned with the feelings of the people they are talking to and regularly make efforts to build beneficial connections within groups. Fishman (1977) also reaches this conclusion based on her study of conversational interactions, arguing that women do more than their fair share of keeping mixed, male-female conversations going with small talk, questions, and new topics, which she indignantly calls 'doing the conversational shitwork'.

Finally, linguistic patterns of two additional types provide further support for the view that women are more oriented toward the maintenance of positive social relations than men often are—studies have shown that women make more *compliments* to others than men do, and also offer *apologies* with greater frequency than male speakers, both actions which help build cohesiveness among social groups.[9] With such broad-based evidence of women's use of language to stimulate solidarity, Holmes proposes the following, second generalization:

Women tend to use linguistic devices that stress solidarity more often than men do.

As there are also signs that women in other, non-Western cultures utilize language in similar ways, Holmes tentatively suggests that her second generalization may perhaps be universally true—i.e., it may hold widely across different linguistic groups in different parts of the world.

Finally, it is worth noting a speculation offered at the end of Coates' (1996, chapter 7: 172) study of hedges and how such devices are used especially skillfully by female speakers. Coates invites readers to consider the possibility that this expertise with hedges (and the same could be said of other-oriented questions):

'... does not arise by chance, but stems directly from our experience as a subordinate group. It is one of the keys to survival for members of less powerful groups in society

---

9. For interesting discussion of the structuring and use of compliments, see Holmes (1998a). This article points out that men and women not only give compliments to others in different amounts (women compliment others much more than men), men and women also tend to compliment others about different things. Women very frequently compliment other women on aspects of their appearance, while men tend to compliment other men (when they do this) about their possessions (their cars, tools, etc.) and compliment women about their appearance and their abilities (e.g., 'You did that really well, honey.'). Additionally, the ways that compliments are linguistically structured is typically different with male and female speakers. The latter often make use of a sequence of the word 'what' followed by an adjective and a noun, with expressive intonation, as in 'What lovely shoes!', but such forms are avoided by men, who instead frequently use a simple adjective + noun sequence with a flat intonation, for example 'Great shoes.' Women may also make use of the verb 'love' in compliments, but men do not. Hence a sequence such as: 'I love those socks. Where did you get them?' would only normally be heard from a female speaker, not a male. The very strong degree to which these different structures are only used by either males or females makes them modern sex-exclusive differences for most speakers, not just sex-preferential patterns.

that they pay close attention to the face needs of the powerful.[10] As a group with little power, women have had to develop extraordinary interpersonal sensitivity, to anticipate the needs and desires of more powerful others—that is, men.'

An advanced linguistic ability with elements such as hedges and questions is therefore hypothesized to have arisen among women out of some necessity, due to male/female power differences in society, and continues to have an important function as a skill allowing women to facilitate collaboration and the open discussion of topics that may otherwise be difficult to approach.

Power

We will now consider how *power* and *dominance* may figure in men's and women's use of language and their participation in conversations. Holmes (1998) points out that many societies maintain a stereotypical idea about women's speech, which may be quite inaccurate, that women talk a lot more than men and dominate the 'talking time' in mixed groups of men and women to such an extent that men hardly get a chance to talk. This view is found in proverbs and sayings present in a broad variety of cultures, as illustrated in the following (from Coates 1993, Holmes 1998, and Sunderland 2006):

- *A woman's tongue wags like a lamb's tail.* [English proverb]
- *The North Sea will sooner be found wanting (lacking) in water than a woman at a loss for words.* [Jutland proverb]
- *Women are nine times more talkative than men.* [Hebrew proverb]
- *Nothing is so unnatural as a talkative man or a quiet woman.* [Scottish proverb]
- *Three women make a market.* [Sudanese proverb]
- *A woman's tongue is the last thing about her that dies.* [English proverb]
- *The tongue is the sword of a woman and she never lets it become rusty.* [Chinese proverb]
- *Three women together make a theatrical performance.* [Chinese proverb]

It is natural to ask what leads to such a widespread stereotype of women's talking, and whether there is any truth to the idea that women dominate conversations between men and women. Serious investigation of mixed-sex conversations has now been carried out with studies of male-female interactions in a range of public and private domains, and the results of this research are revealing and interesting. What investigators have found is that men and women tend to talk different amounts in different situations, and in a variety of contexts it is actually men who typically dominate talking time and do not allow women to speak so

---

10. According to Brown and Levinson (1987), individuals have two kinds of needs relating to the notion of 'face'—positive face requirements and negative face requirements. The former reflect the desire every person has to be accepted, approved of, and admired, while the latter relate to the desire every person has not to feel coerced, pressured, or hindered in any way. People often structure their behavior with different strategies of politeness to satisfy others' face requirements.

easily. This occurs particularly in public interactions such as town hall meetings, audience-involved discussions on television shows, and company board meetings—all situations, it is noted, where holding the floor and talking may increase an individual's status (James and Drakich 1993; Johnson 2008). This suggests that public speaking may be used by males as an opportunity to establish and increase their personal standing, and so be linked with power and status, apparently more so than is the case with women, who frequently talk much less in such visible, open discussions before large groups of people. Women tend to talk more in smaller, intimate groups, and in private with their partners, where it is found that men talk significantly less.

Interestingly, the observed dominance of men in 'public' speech seems to develop at an early age and has been observed to occur in school classroom situations, with boy students dominating talking to teachers much more than girl students (Elliot 1974; French and French 1984; Graddol and Swann 1989). One study of over a hundred classes in both arts and science subjects (Sadker and Sadker 1985) found that boys spoke three times as much as girls on average, and that they were eight times more likely to call out answers than girls were. There is evidence that this dominant behavior is also encouraged by teachers and that teachers pay more attention to boys, give them more praise, and are also more indulgent toward them when they misbehave (Kelly 1988; Swann and Graddol 1988). When girls call out answers before teachers invite them to answer, they may be reprimanded for this, whereas boys are not criticized for the same behavior. Boys also use clear strategies for demanding attention and dominating class discussions, such as being quicker than girls when raising their hands to answer questions.

Graddol and Swann (1989) note that men have in general been found to have a range of techniques which allow them to dominate conversations when they wish to, while women are commonly more supportive and non-dominant in mixed-sex interactions. This can be seen in the use of interruptions, minimal responses, and the ways that topics introduced by men and women are more or less successful and sustained in conversations, as discussed in the following sections.

Conversational support

Research into the flow of conversation has uncovered significant differences among men and women in the way that new topics of conversation are introduced and subsequently supported (or not). An important set of studies by Fishman (1978a/b) found that topics introduced by men consistently survive in conversations much better and longer than topics introduced by women. Consider the following exchange from Fishman (1978a):[11]

Man: I just saw in the paper where Olga Korbut . . .
Woman: Yeah
Man: . . . went to see Dickie.
Woman: You're kidding (pause). What for?

---

11. Adapted in Graddol and Swann (1989: 75).

Man: I don't know (pause).
Woman: I can't imagine what she would go to see Dick Nixon for. I don't get it (pause).
Man: I think she's on a tour of the United States (pause).
Woman: Has he sat down and talked to her?
Man: (shows the woman a picture in the paper)

The topic of the conversation here was introduced by the man and then enthusiastically supported by the woman, who asks the man questions to keep the conversation going. This can be contrasted with a second exchange from Fishman (1978a), where a topic is unsuccessfully introduced by a woman. In this interaction, the man whom the woman is talking to (her partner) does not give her any obvious encouragement to continue talking about the topic she attempts to introduce into the conversation.

Woman: They have this many publications in women's studies received every month. It's one of these. In oth-
Man: Uhm.
Woman: In other words—about um (pause) well at this rate (pause) you know about (pause) two thousand a year.
Man: It's a lot.
Woman: And Carol said that they found out that there were four hundred applications from graduate students doing PhDs in women's studies.
Man: Hmh.

The difference in the amount of support the men and women give each other in the previous two sequences is typical of what was reported for the range of conversations recorded and analyzed by Fishman (1978a/b). While expressions known as 'minimal responses' (instances of *'uhm/ah'* and other short phrases uttered in the middle of a conversation) were used by both women and men, male and female speakers used them in different ways. Typically, men would just produce a minimal response after a woman had been talking for some time, but women would add words like *uh-huh, mmh, ah*, and *oh* at much more regular intervals when men were speaking, indicating that they were paying attention to the men and being cooperative and sensitive conversational partners (Fishman 1978b). Furthermore, in Fishman's (1978a) study, women were found to raise 62% of all the topics in the conversations, and men 38%, yet almost all of the men's topics were encouraged by the women they were talking to, but only 35% of the topics brought up by women were successful.

Interruptions and delayed minimal responses

The use of *deliberate interruptions* is a way in which a person can attempt to dominate a conversation, cutting a speaker short and not letting them complete their point, sometimes abruptly contradicting what a speaker is trying to say or imposing a new direction of discussion, as in the following two examples, where a # symbol indicates the location of an interruption:

Speaker A: I think that the customers are unhappy because they paid for our product and- #
Speaker B: -# NO, the customers are NOT unhappy, you're wrong about that, you're just not getting through to them right!

Speaker C: I'm planning on sending a letter to-#
Speaker D: -#Where's the camera? Did you put it somewhere? I can't find it anywhere.

The ability to deliberately interrupt a conversation (and get away with it, without censure) indicates clear *power* in a person, because those in subordinate positions are not permitted to interrupt their 'seniors'—junior company employees do not interrupt their bosses, lower-ranking soldiers do not cut short the speech of officers when they are talking, and children are often told by their parents not to interrupt them. When conversations take place between men and women of supposedly equal status (husbands and wives, male and female friends, etc.), studies have shown that interruptions are regularly made by men rather than women (96% of the time in one study of 'natural' conversations by Zimmerman and West 1975, and 75% of the time in a later experimental study of young male and female undergraduate students who had only just met, in laboratory conditions, carried out by the same researchers, West and Zimmerman 1983[12]). This heavily disproportionate occurrence of interruptions made use of by male speakers is taken to indicate that men constantly exert power and dominance in mixed-sex conversational situations, and are less co-operative and less considerate conversational partners than their female counterparts.

Male speakers have also been observed to make use of '*delayed minimal responses*' as an additional way to control conversations (Graddol and Swann 1989: 78). Listeners normally use words such as *oh, ah, uh-huh*, etc., as minimal responses to show that they are paying attention to the speaker and interested in what this person is saying. However, if such expressions are delayed and not given immediately, they can clearly communicate that the listener is bored and not paying attention. This may naturally discourage the speaker from continuing to talk; hence the use of delayed minimal responses can be deliberately employed as a power device. This kind of language use is found almost exclusively in men. An example of the occurrence of delayed minimal responses in a conversation is given in the following.

Woman: Yesterday I went to a talk about gender relations.
   3-second silence
Man: Uh-huh. (spoken with low, disinterested intonation)
Woman: It was really interesting. There were two speakers from Holland.
   2-second silence
Man: I see. (flat, intonation again)

---

12. It is expected that the interruption rate might be somewhat less among students, whose social status and level of education can be assumed to be the same for both males and females. It is surprising that there is still a very high rate of interruptions by males in the 1983 study of undergraduate students carried out by Zimmerman and West. One might have anticipated that confident, educated females would interrupt males with the same frequency that males interrupted females, but this was not the case.

Further investigations have shown that men may also tend to exert power and to dominate speech situations regardless of the professional status of women they may be talking to. In a study of interactions between doctors and patients (West 1984), it was found that male doctors regularly interrupt female patients, and, more interestingly, that male patients frequently interrupt female doctors. Although having the status of a doctor might be expected to result in a woman being accorded higher respect, it seems that men still attempt to dominate conversations in such situations.

Single-sex group interactions

Finally, we can briefly mention conversational tendencies found to occur in single-sex rather than mixed-sex groups of people. In a study of all-boy and all-girl groups who were given instructions to carry out various tasks (Goodwin 1980), a natural power hierarchy among boys was observed in the all-boy groups which resulted in boys with greater power issuing orders to those with less authority, for example:

Gimme the pliers! Get away from my tools! Take this one!

In parallel all-girl groups, no obvious power hierarchy was found to be present and tasks were approached with much greater co-operation. This was reflected in the type of language used by the girls, which consisted not in commands, but more often in suggestions and 'we'-forms, such as:

Let's do it this way. We could try fixing it like this. Maybe this will work.
We need to find more bottles. Let's look around. See what we can find.

Similar patterns have been found in other studies, for example Austin, Salehi, and Leffler (1987) and Cook, Fritz, McCornack, and Visperas (1985). Females' language is therefore again found to be friendly and co-operative and not oriented toward the display and use of power, unlike the language of males, who often seem to focus on 'establishing the self as dominant, maintaining the attention of others, and asserting the self when others are the focus of attention' (Maltz and Borker 1982).

Conclusions concerning power, talking time, conversational support, and interruptions

For Holmes (1998), the broad conclusions relating male/female language use and *power* are as follows. Men and women participate in conversations in different ways because they have different goals in their acts of communication. Women view talk as an activity which can strengthen social bonds and build cohesion in a group or with single partners. They are regularly found to act supportively in their interactions and show sensitivity to the face desires (see footnote 10) of the people they are speaking with, and when conversations are informal and intimate, women tend to talk more than men, using language as a way to develop new social relations and strengthen existing friendships. Men, by way of contrast, often seem to approach communication with others from a rather different perspective and see public speaking as an opportunity to assert personal status and power, while private and casual interactions are valued less as they contribute less clearly to an individual's hierarchical standing. Male emphasis on the use of language for power-related ends results in men speaking more than women in various public contexts, and communicating less than women in private situations. Holmes summarizes her consideration of language use and power as follows:

> Overall then, what seems to be apparent from studies of the ways women and men interact is that women focus more often on the solidarity dimension, while men are more concerned with power and status. Women behave in ways that indicate concern for the feelings of their addressees and attention to the positive face needs of their addressees, while men tend to use linguistic strategies which reflect a greater concern with their own presentation of face. (Holmes 1998: 472)

Holmes then offers a third 'universal' generalization:

> *Women tend to interact in ways which will maintain and increase solidarity, while (especially in formal contexts) men tend to interact in ways which will maintain and increase their power and status.*

Interestingly, these patterns would also seem to hold across other cultures, too, as far as investigations have been made.

LANGUAGE, GENDER, AND ELECTRONIC COMMUNICATION

The connections between language, power, solidarity, and gender which Holmes and others have described for oral communication have also, intriguingly, now been observed in studies of on-line communication. At one point there was an expectation that communication via the internet and the anonymity it in theory allows might make the gender of communicators invisible and eliminate the dominance that males often bring to face-to-face interactions, resulting in greater gender equality on-line. However, research into language use in chat rooms, instant messaging, discussion lists, emails, and various other on-line forums of communication has shown: (a) that gender is still strongly visible in electronic forms of communication, and (b) that traditional gender-related differences in the use of language to exert power and to emphasize solidarity among men and women have replicated themselves in mixed-sex and single-sex on-line exchanges.

Investigators such as Susan Herring and her colleagues (see Herring 2005 for an excellent summary) have found that men's and women's gender regularly becomes visible in computer-mediated communication (CMC) through the use of different styles which individuals may not be aware of and not be able to switch off, and these differences typically reveal the gender of communicators to others interacting with them on-line.

> Males regularly post longer messages, are more assertive in what they write, use more criticisms, crudity, and insults, and are frequently more confrontational in their interactions, whereas females often post shorter messages, are more likely to offer apologies, gratitude, and appreciation, and are more cooperative and supportive toward others than male communicators. The potential for the internet to neutralize gender differences in electronic communication consequently seems not to have been realized, and male and female styles of language in CMC seem to be as frequently linked to power and solidarity as they often are in face-to-face acts of communication.

Status

Having considered the roles that *solidarity, power*, and the *function of speech* may have in influencing the forms of language adopted by men and women, Holmes returns to Trudgill's (and others') early claims that *social status* is a significant factor affecting the development of women's speech. It has been widely reported that women in Western societies use more standard forms in their speech than men from the same socio-economic background, and it is also commonly recognized that standard forms of language are associated with higher levels of education, personal affluence, and social prestige. Given that female speakers proportionally use a greater amount of such symbolically prestigious forms than men from similar social backgrounds, Trudgill had proposed that women were more focused on projecting a higher social status than men through the use of 'educated' language forms. However, such a conclusion seems to be contradicted by Holmes' new arguments (considered in the preceding pages, and echoed in other work by Jennifer Coates and Deborah Tannen) that it is actually men who seem to be more concerned with status and power, and that women are primarily concerned with solidarity and consequently act in supportive ways which do not obviously enhance their power or prestige. Holmes therefore needs to provide some additional explanation for the higher frequency of standard language in women's speech, one which does not attribute it to desires for higher social status.

The interesting and novel suggestion that Holmes makes is that the observation of substantial differences in the use of standard forms in male and female speech may in fact relate to the ways that data on men's and women's speech has often been collected in the past. Most typically, this has been done in interviews in which researchers have talked to men and women about the kinds of language they (believe they) use. Holmes suggests that the social status of the researchers and the formality of the speech situation may have exerted an influence on the language used by men and women participating in these interviews in different ways, due to the phenomenon of *linguistic accommodation*. The term 'accommodation' is used to refer to the ways that people sometimes modify their behavior and make it more similar to that of other people they are interacting with. In the area of language, this manifests itself very often in the acquisition of a different accent if a person moves to a different region or country where his/her native language is spoken with certain different pronunciations. For example, when young English-speakers from the USA or the UK spend a year studying or working abroad in Australia, they may gradually adopt some of the inflections and special words common in Australian English and end up speaking with an accent that sounds Australian in various ways—they 'accommodate' their original speech patterns to those of the people around them in their new environment.[13]

Holmes suggests that women who are interviewed by educated, middle-class academics for the purposes of research may adjust their typical speech patterns and accommodate them to the standard forms used by the interviewers, as women may perceive such accommodation to be a way of expressing friendly (temporary) solidarity with those talking to them. Male speakers, by way of contrast, who frequently focus less on presenting themselves in supportive ways in their interactions and are more attuned to hierarchies and power, might well be expected not to accommodate their speech in the same way.

Such a putative difference in accommodation among male and female participants in their interactions with researchers could well account for the difference in standard language forms noted and recorded in linguistic interviews—more standard patterns being found in the speech of women than with men from the same social group. In a similar way, it is proposed that the formality of the interview situation may have affected the language used by women in particular. Quite generally, people tend to use more standard speech when they find themselves in formal contexts and are not familiar with the person they are speaking to. The interviews which occur in sociolinguistic experiments are interactions of just this kind. It is therefore possible that women might use more standard forms of speech because of the perceived formal nature of the interview situation and the presence of a stranger (the interviewer). Men, by way of contrast, are suggested to be less sensitive to context and any pressure to adjust their language, and so are hypothesized not to alter their speech in formal situations as much as women do.

Additionally, it is noted that women may perhaps have a greater acquired *ability* than men to change the way they speak in different situations; hence this advantage can be utilized effectively by women when they feel a certain kind of language is appropriate for a particular exchange. Holmes quotes Chambers' (1992) remarks in the following excerpt, which notes that women have been documented as commanding a broader range of language forms and linguistic styles than men, for use in different interactions:

> The empirical evidence clearly shows women as much more able performers than men in the whole spectrum of sociolinguistic situations ... they command a wider range of linguistic variants ... they have the linguistic flexibility to alter their speech as social circumstances warrant. (Chambers 1992: 199)

---

13. Accommodation also occurs with non-linguistic behavior in certain instances. For example, there is cross-cultural variation in the distance that people regularly maintain between each other when engaged in conversation, and speakers of Arabic may often stand closer together than speakers of English. As English-speakers learning Arabic and living in an Arabic-speaking country adjust to the different cultural norms they experience in the Middle East and North Africa, they may come to stand closer to others when they talk to them than they would have done in their home countries. Similar patterns occur with variation in the time a person holds the gaze of another person they are speaking to, and in automatically making gestures of greeting and respect such as bowing in Japan and putting one's palms together to 'wai' (ไหว้) someone in Thailand in place of shaking their hand.

This leads Holmes to posit a further 'sociolinguistic universal tendency' as part of a new account of men's and women's observed differences in speech:

Women are stylistically more flexible than men.

Finally, Holmes approaches the general question of why it might be that women show a greater sensitivity to their addressees than men and feel a desire or need to be co-operative and supportive in their linguistic interactions with others. Three possible explanations are briefly considered. First, it is suggested that males and females may traditionally be *socialized in different ways*—brought up to have different expectations about the ways they should behave as boys and girls and men and women, acquiring gender and gendered identities through patterns of cultural learning which accord with the practices established in a society. Males may be encouraged to develop individual power and status, while females may be taught a different style of behavior emphasizing instead the value of social relations and support for others in one's group. Such a cultural explanation ascribes differences in the ways that men and women speak simply to the ways they have been taught to use language differently, following the traditions present in a population of speakers.

A second possible explanation of such differences links them directly to imbalances in male/female power in many societies around the world. Where men occupy dominant positions in patriarchal societies, they are free to adopt a rather unrestrained way of speaking with women which does not set out to attend to others' face desires and permits the regular use of linguistic power strategies to control conversations. However, women as relative subordinates in male-dominated populations must learn how to use facilitative, supportive speech and develop non-confrontational behavior to help them best survive and prosper in the face of an unfair power disadvantage. The more cooperative, solidarity-focused styles of speech found with many women and the flexible use of different styles would be female speakers' 'solution' to the imbalanced nature of society and their way of coping with male/female mismatches in power and sex-based status.

A third hypothetical explanation of the different orientations that men and women often show in their linguistic interactions attributes these to *biology* and suggests, controversially for some, that women may have an *innate* linguistic advantage over men, providing them with greater linguistic skills. Researchers such as J. K. Chambers argue that differences in brain lateralization in males and females may give women a neurological advantage over men in the area of language, allowing them to develop a variety of linguistic skills more easily than men. Chambers (1992) (quoted in Holmes 1998: 478) writes:

> There is, in the psychological literature, a long record of evidence of female verbal superiority. Over many years, women have demonstrated an advantage over men in tests of fluency, speaking, sentence complexity, analogy, listening, comprehension of both written and spoken material, vocabulary, and spelling. (Chambers 1992: 201)

Other, recent research (Kung et al. 2016 and references therein) has shown that sex-related differences in linguistic ability may relate to levels of testosterone, normally higher in males. Kung et al. (2016) measured early post-natal testosterone levels in 1–3-month-old infants and tracked the linguistic development of these children between the ages of 18–30 months. It was found that children with higher post-natal levels of testosterone, typically boys, developed a smaller expressive vocabulary than girls who regularly had lower levels of testosterone. The researchers note that this difference between girls and boys is significant because a small early vocabulary has often been found to correspond with later difficulties in language, which occur more commonly with boys than with girls.

Holmes adds that a combination of all three explanations is also possible and even likely to be correct, in her opinion. A small but significant biological advantage might help females who are socialized in stereotypical gender-biased ways within male-dominated societies develop more advanced abilities in language than average males, and this provides them with the means to effectively negotiate their way in society. She summarizes as follows (Holmes 1998: 478):

> Overall, then, it seems possible that biology, power relationships, and the acculturation process all contribute to accounting for gender-differentiated patterns in communities where women demonstrate more context-sensitive pragmatic skills and a wider sociolinguistic repertoire then men. (Holmes 1998: 478)

The development and current trajectory of research into language and gender

The hypotheses developed in Holmes (1998) which we have just considered provide a new perspective on 'classic' observations coming out of early research into men's and women's language and offer up generalizations that are supported by more recent investigations of a range of different languages and their speakers. In positing a set of 'universal' generalizations or tendencies about male and female language styles, Holmes stresses the need for more cross-linguistic comparative research to help confirm or question the cross-cultural validity of the connections between language and gender that she and other linguists such as Jennifer Coates and Deborah Tannen suggest are significant. This sets up an interesting agenda of research for the future, with more investigation of gendered language use in non-Western societies being particularly necessary and potentially valuable and informative.

As work has been carried out in the area of language and gender since it was seriously initiated in the 1970s, it has at times been characterized by different themes or orientations which have partly colored the ways that linguistic data has been collected and interpreted. In early stages of investigation associated with Robin Lakoff's ground-breaking study *Language and Women's Place* (1975), women's language was sometimes characterized as being weak, and less assertive than men's, an assessment which has subsequently been referred to and criticized as the '*deficit*' view of female speech. Later, a theme of '*dominance*' became prevalent in descriptions of men's and women's language patterns and explanations offered for the differences in male and female speech, with certain properties of women's speech being understood to be reactions to the dominance of men in many social groups. Other work, well-represented by Deborah Tannen's series of books, stressed the notion of '*difference*' in men's and women's approaches to communication, arguing that male and female speakers simply have different conceptions of the primary social functions of linguistic interactions, and that misunderstandings between men and women often arise because of fundamentally different orientations toward the affective vs. informative uses of language.

Most recently, work and theorization on language and gender have emphasized the importance of studying variation *within* men's and women's speech and frequently employ the term *discourse* and its plural form *discourses* in its description of language use. It is suggested that in order to understand men's and women's speech, it is necessary to take into account the discourses associated with each act of speaking, where 'discourses' broadly refers to ideas that speakers hold about the topic of conversation, the person they are speaking to, and all other background information speakers have in mind when they engage in any act of communication.[14] A key idea in current research is that such *contextual information* plays a critically important role in influencing the language that speakers choose to make use of in each of their interactions with others and causes *variation* in the ways that men and women speak at different times. In such a broadly 'variationist' approach, modern studies of language and gender emphasize the need to consider ethnicity, social class, age, religious identity, and culture as factors that will interact with a person's sex in affecting language use; hence men and women of different ethnicities may perhaps develop different patterns of speech when using the 'same' language (English, French, etc.). Broad statements about 'women's language' or 'men's language' should therefore always be cautious and not assume that speech patterns identified as common in one particular ethnic or socio-economic group will necessarily hold in the same way in other groups in a single language community.

While there have certainly been considerations of variation within men's and women's speech in past work—for example, Trudgill's observations that women in the lowest and highest socio-economic classes share the same speech patterns as men from these classes, unlike women in intervening class levels—the current increased interest in looking at differences among female or male speakers and across different cultures and ethnicities is opening up a new understanding of some of the complexities of language and gender and

---

14. Clear, easy-to-understand definitions of the term 'discourse' used in relation to language and gender are rather elusive. Goddard and Meân (2000: 111) suggest that Vivian Burr's (1995) description is a useful 'starting point', but her characterization of the notion 'discourse' and Goddard and Meân's commentary on it are not particularly transparent, especially given the fact that Godard and Meân (2000) is intended to be an introductory textbook. They write that:

> She [Vivian Burr] says that a discourse is 'a set of meanings, metaphors, representations, images, stories, statements and so on that in some way together produce a particular version' of people, events or objects (Burr 1995, p. 48). Discourses provide people ways of describing and framing cultural objects or categories that construct or influence how we understand them. There are many discourses available, each of which frames an object within a system of related references and associated understandings.' (Godard and Meân 2000: 111).

Baker (2008), in a rather more accessible way, notes that discourses are influences on the way we interpret the world and interact with others, and such information comes to us from a wide range of sources, including movies, pop songs, fashion magazines, sports events, holiday brochures, advertisements, and social media—basically every platform that sends out some kind of message to those who come into contact with it, either consciously or subconsciously.

is allowing for the resolution of certain apparent contradictions in generalizations that have previously been proposed about men's and women's language.

Following the general spirit of this new trend toward comparative studies of men's and women's language in different cultures, contexts, and ethnicities, the chapter will presently feature an extended study of the interaction of language and gender in *Japan*. Some of the good reasons for including such a focused profile on Japan are: (a) much of what has been discussed thus far in the chapter has been primarily driven by research on language and gender in Western societies; (b) men's and women's language issues have been quite extensively researched in Japan; (c) there are many interesting results of studies of language and gender in Japan; (d) a consideration of men's and women's language use in Japan provides nice illustrations of within-sex variation relating to a speaker's age, social background, relationship with the addressee, and individuals' variation along a stereotypical male-to-female cline of style.

Before we begin our description of men's and women's language in Japan, we will first give a brief illustration of how the study of variation within same-sex speakers can help resolve a contradiction that seems to be present in statements already made, earlier in the current chapter, following generalizations offered by Trudgill and assumed by others. In discussing differences in the ways that men and women speak Chukchi and Koasati, Trudgill noted that the special forms used by women were *older* historical pronunciations, and that women therefore seem to prefer the use of more conservative speech, while men's speech may undergo change away from earlier historical forms and may not be admired as much as the way women talk because of this. However, shortly after noting Trudgill's comments on Chukchi and Koasati, we added another of his observations, that 'where there is some kind of change in speech in a community towards a high-class or national form, this change is very frequently led by women.' This seems to suggest a contradiction—in one instance, women are presented as being the guardians of tradition in society and resisting change, yet elsewhere they are characterized as being innovators and embracing and leading language change. How can these two different patterns of women's language use be understood without there being any contradiction? Are women traditionalists or innovators? The interesting answer is that they may be both, and whether they maintain old forms of their language or lead changes to new forms depends on where they live and how they relate to the rest of their social group. To see this, we will look at language change and use and its relation to gender in certain countries in Africa.

The **Kera** language is spoken in southern Chad and Cameroon. One of its important features is a system of tones which distinguish words in the language, as in other tonal languages such as Chinese, Thai, and Vietnamese. Recent research into Kera described in Pearce (2013) has shown that the tonal system is undergoing change, and the changes that are occurring are linked to gender and location. In urban areas, women are innovating and changing the ways tones are pronounced, with the result that women's urban use of tone is distinct from men's speech, and women are leading a change to new forms. In rural areas, however, there is again a difference between men's and women's use of tone in Kera, but women in the countryside are actually found to be more conservative than men and to maintain older tonal forms of the language. Female speakers are consequently found to be at both ends of the spectrum of variation which occurs in the pronunciation of Kera, and are more 'extreme' than men in both urban and rural areas, either being more traditional and conservative in their speech, or more innovative and forward-moving. There is consequently clear variation in the ways Kera women speak, meaning that a single generalization about the speech patterns of female speakers of Kera is not possible and a greater complexity needs to be recognized, and language use is affected by context—whether women stand out as traditionalists or modernizers relates to where they live, in towns or in the countryside.

In South Africa, among **Zulu** speakers, two special types of language related to 'pure' Zulu are made use of by many speakers. As described at the beginning of this chapter, women speakers often use a very traditional way of speaking known as *hlonipha*, which is derived from standard Zulu via sound modifications made to avoid pronouncing syllables that are prominent in the names of a woman's husband's name and the names of his male relatives. However, Zulu women are not uniform in the way they make use of language, and an increasing number of women do not use *hlonipha* and have begun to use a new language form called **Tsotsitaal** which is a mixture of Zulu and English, with words from both languages being given new meanings and used in novel ways. The older, women's way of speaking, *hlonipha*, encodes respect for males and is an important symbol of traditional, submissive femininity in Zulu society, which helps sustain the patriarchal system of this ethnic group. Use of the new mode of speech, Tsotsitaal, communicates a quite different image, and is felt to be modern, and to help project a 'streetwise' identity in speakers. Women who speak Tsotsitaal are viewed as rejecting traditional Zulu culture and embracing a new self-empowered, liberal femininity (Rudwick 2013). As with speakers of Kera, we therefore find that some women from a particular ethno-linguistic group are acting in a very conservative way, maintaining traditional ways of speaking, while others are changing their patterns of speech and adopting new forms of language, and as with Kera, this conservative/innovative division among women speakers is again heavily geographical in nature, *hlonipha* being strongly kept up by women in rural areas, while Tsotsitaal has been taken up by women in urban environments. The gendered use of language is context-dependent, varying according to location, and there is both marked conservatism and clear innovation among women speakers from the same ethnic group.[15]

A third example, from North Africa, emphasizes the same message that women living in a particular country may not constitute a uniform linguistic group and may exhibit clear variation in the language patterns they make use of, which may also be significantly different from those used by men in the same area. Morocco has an interesting and complex language situation in which four languages have a strong, general presence, but are used differently and with distinct symbolic values by male and women speakers: **(Modern) Standard Arabic**, **Moroccan Arabic**, **Berber**, and **French**. Standard Arabic is characterized by Sadiqi (2003) as a 'male language' because it is spoken much more commonly by men than by women, and

---

15. Here it should be noted that urban Zulu women are not innovating in the *creation* of new language forms, as Tsotsitaal was originally developed by male speakers as a 'gangster' language in cities, and continues to be used by many young males in towns. The innovation that is occurring with Zulu women in urban areas is their novel *adoption* of forms that were not previously used by women in the past.

men express negative attitudes toward women who use Standard Arabic, as the language symbolizes male cultural identity and power in Moroccan society. When women occasionally make use of Standard Arabic (symbolically, as a form of protest in the media), this is seen as threatening the male-based status quo and having a destabilizing effect on society. Deprived of the opportunity to speak Standard Arabic without public censure, women make use of three other forms of language as a means to empower themselves. Many women in Moroccan towns speak French, and engage in code-switching between French and Moroccan Arabic, and these two forms of language are viewed as being predominantly female 'styles' which are used much less frequently by men. French is associated with modernity, open-mindedness, and higher levels of employment, and is suggested to be an attractive linguistic option for 'women who wish to break through social barriers and develop themselves both socially and economically' (de Ruiter 2008: 105). French-Moroccan Arabic code-switching is an innovation, and as a new way of speaking, it also symbolizes modernity, and individual determination (Sadiqi 2008).

In rural areas, where women are again essentially excluded from the use of Standard Arabic, the language they make use of to empower themselves and mark their presence in the community in acts of story-telling and the singing of folk songs is Berber (Ennaji and Sadiqi 2008). This language is seen as representing a significant component of Moroccan cultural identity linked to family and the home, and its use by women is positively viewed as helping perpetuate traditional values and stability in society.

As in South Africa, Chad, and Cameroon, we therefore find two apparently different tendencies in women's speech—a traditionalist use of old language forms which appears to suggest that women are conservative in their use of language, and an innovative move toward the use of French and the development of French-Moroccan Arabic code-switching, which shows women as the adopters of new forms of speech. As in our previous two examples, both patterns of linguistic behavior occur with female speakers in a single cultural society, indicating that women's use of language is not monolithic and may incorporate multiple ways of speaking, and women's language choice is also context-sensitive and a function of the resources made available to women and valued in different locations—innovation is found in women's language in urban areas, while conservatism, which also critically results in forms that are distinctive from men's use of language, is characteristic of women's language patterns within rural areas. Women can thus regularly be both innovators and traditionalists, and both styles of expression may have symbolic value and may be importantly different from men's ways of speaking.

Language and gender in Japan

Highly distinctive forms of women's language (*nyooboo kotoba*) first arose in Japan during the Kamakura Period (12th–14th centuries), in the speech of women in the imperial court. Over 500 special words came to be used by such women to refer to everyday aspects of their life. For each of these words, there was a different male equivalent, as illustrated in the following sampling, from Shibamoto (2005: 181).

	MALE	FEMALE
rice	*meshi*	*gugo*
carp	*koi*	*komozi*
paper	*kami*	*kumo*
illness	*yamai*	*o-mooki*
salt	*shio*	*shiromono*
paper	*kami*	*kumo*
fever	*netsu*	*o-nuruke*

These words created and used by women of the court gradually spread to women of other classes in Japanese society. In the course of such a process, they became strongly linked with an image of feminine elegance and refinement. Later, further distinctions in women's speech were added and became seen as characteristic of refined women's language, as we will shortly see. In modern times, there is still a widespread belief in Japan that 'women's language' is a national tradition that is culturally important and should be maintained. All educated and socially refined women in the middle and upper classes are expected to make use of polite-sounding 'womanly language/speech' (*onna-rashii kotoba*). The kinds of features that now typify such 'womanly language' are listed in the following bullet points and will subsequently be described, one by one.

- a distinctive pitch range and use of intonation
- special nouns, verbs, and pronouns
- special sentence-final particles and exclamatory words
- clipped, incomplete sentences
- avoidance of Chinese-origin words ('Sino-Japanese' words)
- a high rate of use of respect language.

Intonation and pitch

As noted earlier in the chapter, women (but not men) working in certain jobs (elevator operators in department stores, sales assistants in department stores, train and bus station announcers) make use of a markedly high pitch in their voices, termed the 'service voice'. A significantly high pitch level is also found among many other women who are not professionally involved in public announcement or customer service, and is associated with the idea of stereotypical femininity in Japan. Interestingly, research has shown that this high pitch is applied by speakers only when they speak Japanese, and Japanese-English bilinguals have been observed not to use the same high pitch when speaking in English. This indicates that Japanese women's higher pitch levels are not due to any inherent biological factor but are the result of cultural influence. Many women in Japan may seem to adopt a high pitch level when speaking Japanese due to a belief that it is *desirable* for women to speak in such a way, but such a constraint does not extend to the speaking of languages other than Japanese. The use of higher pitch levels in Japanese speech has also been experimentally shown to be associated with the properties of 'cuteness', 'kindness', and 'politeness', while lower levels of pitch are felt to signal a speaker who has the more negative personal qualities of 'selfishness' and 'stubbornness' (Loveday 1986). Additional studies of female sales assistants have found that a high pitch level is typically used in their speech when they address customers, but that they often switch to a lower level of pitch when they talk with friends, indicating that their professional high pitch level is deliberately 'turned on' in situations which require speakers to express politeness and respect to others.

Special lexical items

As in women's *nyooboo kotoba* language in earlier centuries, there are certain nouns and verbs which occur typically in the speech of women, and others that are used by men. Following are some example pairs given by Shibamoto (2005).

	MALE	FEMALE
stomach	*hara*	*onaka*
pickles	*tsukemono*	*okookoo*
water	*mizu*	*ohiya*
delicious	*umai* or *oishii*	*oishii*
eat	*kuu* or *taberu*	*taberu*

Note that with the words used for 'delicious' and 'to eat', the common female form may also used by males, but the male forms *umai* and *kuu* are avoided by female speakers. Quite generally, while male speakers may often be able to use common female forms, female speakers are much less able to use male forms. There is consequently an imbalance in the way that typical male/female terms can be used by members of the opposite sex. In addition to nouns and verbs, there are also differences with pronouns, and certain forms of the pronoun meaning 'I' or 'me' are restricted in their use according to the sex of the speaker. The forms *atakushi*, *atashi*, and *atai* can only be used by women, while *ore* and *washi* are only used by men, and *boku* is a predominantly male pronoun (more on the use of *boku* among younger speakers will be added later).

Sentence-final particles (SFPs) and exclamatory words

Sentence-final particles (SFPs) are small words used at the ends of sentences to add in some extra meaning, such as the conversion of a sentence into a question or a command, or the communication of some aspect of the speaker's assessment of the content of the sentence (doubt or confidence that what it describes is true, etc.) or his/her attitude toward the hearer. SFPs are very common in Japanese, and there are a great number of such elements. Certain of these are characteristically used by women, so that a speaker sounds typically feminine if they occur in her speech. Others are typical of males' speech and would almost never be used by a woman. The seven sex-exclusive SFPs found in women's and men's speech are as follows:

SFPs characteristically used by women
wa   no   te   kashira

SFPs characteristically used by men
ze   zo   na

Women's SFPs express femininity and are used for various purposes. *Wa* is said to have a softening function and to help create a relaxed atmosphere as well as communicate respect. *No* in declarative sentences emphasizes shared knowledge and common ground between speaker and hearer. *Kashira* is described as signaling the speaker's uncertainty about what is being described and softens the force of a sentence (Ide and Yoshida 2000; Shibamoto 2005). Men's SFPs, by way of contrast, are felt to be much more assertive and authoritative, and a particle such as *zo* can only be used by a speaker who has greater power than the hearer (whether the hearer is female or male).

Men and women also make use of various 'exclamatory words', similar to English expressions such as 'wow', 'gosh', etc., and different forms are used by male and female speakers:

MALE	FEMALE
hoo	*Ara*
oi	*maa*
yai	*choito*

Incomplete sentences

Female speakers of Japanese may often feel a societal pressure to speak in ways that are not strongly assertive, and one way of doing this is to produce sentences that appear to be unfinished. This has been noted to occur in both speech and writing and is a typically feminine style, common in women's magazines. In various instances it may involve the use of a verb in the so-called 'continuative' form ending in *–te*, a bit like verbs in the *–ing* form in English. Normally, verbs ending in *–te* must be followed by another verb, but sometimes such sentences are simply left incomplete, similar to the English translation given in the following:

Hanahira-ga harahara-to chirikakatte . . .
'The petals beginning to flutter down to the ground, . . .'

Another way that incomplete sentences occur is for a 'sentence' to consist in just a 'because'-type clause, and for the consequence of the because-clause to be omitted, as in:

Jikan-ga nai kara,...
'Because I don't have time, . . .'

One common 'explanation' for such incomplete sentences in women's speech is that such a style expresses a feminine, non-assertive preference to leave the conclusion of a sentence unstated if it is already understood from context. Hence in the second example just presented, if the addressee understands that the speaker cannot visit the hearer due to the speaker's lack of time, then explicit reference to this consequence can be omitted and left unsaid (hence 'Because I don't have the time, . . .' is used as an abbreviation for 'Because I don't have the time, I cannot accept the invitation to come to your house.'). It is also suggested that incomplete sentences are used to encourage others to enter into a conversation, similar in some ways to tag-questions in English, and so are facilitative devices which stimulate solidarity.[16]

The avoidance of Chinese-origin words and vulgar expressions

Two further properties of female speech that have often been noted in studies of Japanese are (a) the avoidance of words of Chinese origin, and (b) the avoidance of vulgar expressions. The second property might seem to be typical of feminine speech patterns in many cultures, and in Japan results in women generally not using 'coarse' masculine expressions such as *chikishio* ('damn'), or *dekai* ('big') (Ide and Yoshida 2000). With regard to words originally sourced from Chinese—Sino-Japanese words/*kango*—it has been noted that women may feel pressured to use fewer Sino-Japanese words than men, for the (clearly sexist) reason that use of such words tends to signal technical knowledge, and academic expertise, and the expression of scientific knowledge is perceived to be a masculine characteristic that women should not exhibit (or at least, not exhibit 'too much').

Use of polite language and honorific forms

One of the most commonly noted gender-related differences in the speaking of Japanese is that women are generally noted to use more polite forms of language than men—more words and expressions which encode respect and deference both toward people who are being spoken to and people who are being spoken about. This has regularly been observed in natural conversation and also confirmed by means of linguistic experiments which have probed male and female speakers' attitudes toward the level of speech they thought they should use with hearers of different types. In one such experiment, described in Ide and Yoshida (2000), men and women were presented with simple sentences (e.g., Japanese equivalents to: 'Good morning, how are you?') with different amounts and levels of honorific speech and respect/humbling language,[17] and asked which form would be appropriate for the speaker to use with the following types of addressee, where there are ascending degrees of social status and distance (hence, more respect language would be expected to be used with addressees higher in the list):

---

16. For further discussion of the various ways that sentences can be left incomplete, and their general prevalence in speech, see: www.japantimes.co.jp/life/2016/05/09/language/complete-japanese-speaker-leave-sentences-incomplete/#.WYTR4lXyuUk

17. Honorific speech is the use of special language forms to encode respect for someone of higher status, normally either the hearer or the subject of a sentence. A speaker can also use special humbling forms to increase the respect shown to others of higher status. Additionally, polite forms of verbs will be made use of when a speaker interacts with someone from outside his/her own group of intimates (where 'intimates' will include family, friends, fellow players on sports teams, and some familiar co-workers).

children > spouse > delivery person > friend > workplace junior > same-status colleague > neighbor > spouse's friend > parent at PTA meeting > child's professor > workplace superior

The investigations consistently showed that women use (or at least think that they/women should use) forms with a higher politeness level than men to addressees of the same type.

Such male-female differences in attitudes toward and use of honorifics have been discussed at length by linguists and social anthropologists. One frequent cause of the differences is suggested to be that women in Japan are expected to be 'modest' in their language and behavior even when there is no difference in status between themselves and other participants in a conversation, and because of this they may feel obligated to use more polite and formal speech. In addition to the property of modesty, other socially desirable properties may be signaled by the use of respect language and politeness in Japanese. In experiments where people were asked to judge the qualities of others they heard speaking, simply based on their language, it was found that users of honorifics were judged to be more intelligent, more educated, were expected to be more wealthy, and generally more capable than those who did not use honorifics (Ide and Yoshida 2000). This suggests that many Japanese people associate the use of honorifics with education, higher class, intelligence, and other positive characteristics. For those wishing to claim the status that such properties attach to people in Japanese society, it is common to place an emphasis on the use of honorific speech. In connection with this association of respect language with the higher socio-economic levels of society, films, TV dramas, novels, and cartoons in Japan all frequently show female characters, especially middle-aged women in the middle and upper classes, using more honorifics than male characters, supporting an important stereotype of women in these classes.

The importance of using 'correct' polite forms and honorifics is also frequently emphasized in education and the media in Japan, and there are numerous, widely read 'self help' books, magazine articles, and other materials on how to use honorifics 'correctly', this being emphasized as an essential ability for sophisticated women in Japan.[18] Such works stress that women will present an attractive and beautiful image if they speak correctly, and also warn that without careful attention, women's speech will become corrupt.[19] Two sample titles of the many wide-selling books on this topic noted in Okamoto (2004) are (translated from the original Japanese):

'To make yourself nice: women's beautiful ways of speaking.'[20]

'Women's attractiveness depends on how they speak.'[21]

---

18. In fact, books of this general kind, proscribing the correct way for women to speak in polite, refined ways, have been produced and made use of since the 17th century in Japan.

19. Indeed, nationwide opinion polls in Japan are regularly conducted on whether 'women's language' is becoming 'corrupted', and how much so. People in older generations in particular feel that younger women's ability to use polite language is in decline, in comparison with earlier decades.

20. '*Suteki-na anata-o tsukuru: josei-no utsukushii hanashi-kata*' by Kenji Suzuki, 1989, Tokyo: Goto Shoin.

21. '*Onna-no miryoku-wa hanashi-kata shidai*' by Yoshiko Kanai, 1994, Tokyo: Yamato Shuppan.

Other books focus on how men and women should write letters in different styles and provide sample letters in female and male versions. Significantly, the female versions are normally longer and use more honorifics than the male versions.

One explanation for the more frequent occurrence of polite language and honorifics in women's speech is that women use such forms in order to project a socially desired image (at least, among the middle and upper classes) of a person with good demeanor. Such a view is supported by other observations that have been made. In one study of language used within companies in Tokyo, it was found that women in higher positions actually used higher-level honorifics than female junior employees when they communicated with each other. This quite puzzling patterning seemed to go against fundamental rules of politeness in Japanese, because it is normally subordinates who are required to use honorifics toward people in higher positions, not the other way around. The researchers, Sachiko Ide and Fumio Inoue, suggested that the reason why the opposite pattern sometimes seems to occur might be that women in higher positions use exaggeratedly polite language to project the image of being educated and refined. Similar considerations may underlie the observation that certain female customers may use extra polite language and honorifics when speaking to sales persons even though it is the customer who has the greater power in such a situation (and so need not use honorifics toward a sales person). It is suggested that this is again a 'strategic' use of honorifics by female customers, to portray themselves as educated, refined persons. Quite generally, then, the knowledge of honorifics and how to use them may be viewed as a mechanism which can improve one's social identity (or harm it, if polite language is used 'incorrectly' or clumsily), and there is considerable pressure from society on women to use more polite and respect language than men, in order to conform to patterns of stereotypical femininity.

Variation in women's speech

Many recent studies of women's speech in Japan have highlighted variation that occurs within the speech of female speakers and how this may lead to patterns that do not conform with those of *onna rashii kotoba*, stereotypical womanly speech. Reynolds' (2000) article 'Female speakers of Japanese in transition' describes a number of interesting cases where women are now speaking in different, sometimes new ways, as changes occur within Japanese society and these affect the use of language. Reynolds begins by pointing out that even with regard to traditional men's and women's speech, there are some forms which are sex-exclusive (or virtually sex-exclusive) and others which are sex-preferential, used by both men and women, but to different degrees, resulting in areas of overlap in male and female speech with certain forms. This distribution is diagrammed on page 389, where V stands for a 'variant form'. V_i at the top of the diagram is intended to represent very masculine, strongly forceful forms not used by female speakers (e.g., blunt imperative or question forms such as: '*Totte kure*' 'Get it for me', and: '*Itta ka?*' 'Did you go?'). V_n at the bottom represents highly feminine forms, not used by male speakers (e.g., use of certain SFPs such as '*wa*' and '*kashira*'). Between these two extreme points there are forms which are masculine or feminine to differing degrees, and in the middle area V_k to V_m there are forms that are often used by both men and women.

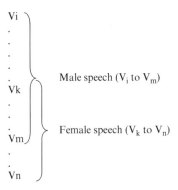

Reynolds (2000: 301) writes that:

> ... women are supposed to choose a style closer to the least assertive end, which men are supposed to avoid. Also, it seems that the risk of stepping into the overlapping area of V_{k-m}) is greater for females than for males. A woman using a style in this area may be considered impolite in more situations than a man talking in the same way. If we limit ourselves to informal speech . . . , the option for a style is much narrower in the case of a female speaker.

Reynolds then discusses a number of instances where female speakers are noted to diverge away from the stereotypical range of forms characteristic of *onna rashii kotoba*, involving women occupying new positions of authority, working-class women, and young women in rising generations.

Women in authority

Changes in work patterns in Japan in recent decades have had consequences for the style of language some women produce. In traditional, feudal Japanese society, women commonly held subordinate positions and consequently had no opportunity or need to express themselves in an authoritative way. This resulted in the emergence of *onna rashii kotoba* and its association with the properties of being polite and non-assertive, while men's speech was frequently forceful and commanding. As Japan underwent rapid modernization and industrialization in the twentieth century, and particularly since the end of World War II, it has become increasingly common for women to take up jobs and work together with men. In recent decades, women have also acceded to positions of professional authority in the workplace, and have begun to experience new needs to speak in ways that command respect, requiring the use of styles of language that dispense with traditional, stereotypically soft, deferential feminine forms. Reynolds describes the conflicting pressures which arise as follows:

> In order to be accepted as a "good woman", a female speaker of Japanese should choose to talk non-assertively, indirectly, politely, and deferentially: but in order to function as a supervisor, administrator, teacher, lawyer, doctor, etc or as a colleague or

associate, she must be able to talk with assurance.... A woman in a superior position is expected to signify her authoritative power in her language,... but female speech does not provide a means to this end. (Reynolds 2000: 302)

In many instances, women currently faced with this difficult situation are adopting more and more typically male/forceful patterns of speech, and defeminizing their speech to a certain extent, adopting more forms found in the V_{k-m} area and less of those typical of the V_{m-n} region. This helps establish their position of seniority, but simultaneously attracts criticism from conservative elements in society who complain that women's language is being seriously eroded by the new ways of speaking taken up by professional women.

Reynolds notes that female teachers in junior high schools often find themselves in a dilemma with regard to the language they should use in interactions with students. Such teachers have to display both friendliness and authority toward their classes, and it is informal male speech that can satisfy these two requirements simultaneously. There is also evidence that some students prefer female teachers who talk a little bit more like male teachers than those who talk very formally. However, women teachers who make use of male styles of speech in the classroom are often criticized by parents and other outsiders, and there is consequently pressure not to adopt such pragmatically useful patterns. Reynolds adds that: 'The social expectation that women, regardless of their roles, should talk *onna-rashiku* [like women] is so strong that women teachers themselves often view de-feminization negatively.' The tension between conforming to traditional ideas of womanhood and being effective in the workplace is therefore very challenging for women in professional roles in Japan, as patterns of employment change but societal attitudes toward women remain stubborn and are resistant to departures from tradition.

Women in the market place

It has been observed that *onna rashii kotoba*/womanly language is a model of linguistic behavior which is predominantly adopted by women from the middle and upper classes, and there is less difference between men's and women's speech in the lower and working classes in Japan (as in Western countries).[22] Studies of exchanges between salespersons, vendors, and customers in department stores and market places are a further good illustration of contrasts that exist between use of the idealized sophisticated women's style of speech and the occurrence of less 'adorned' language in women's speech. In department stores, there is a clear, strong emphasis on the use of honorifics with customers, who are often assumed, by default, to be members of the middle and upper classes and who must be treated with great respect in virtue of their customer status no matter what socio-economic group they actually belong to, according to department store policies. In market places, however, individual sellers act as independent agents and are free from any constraints on their behavior imposed by employers, and this, together with the relaxed, informal atmosphere of markets,

---

22. It has also been noticed that gender distinction in speech style is more of an urban phenomenon than a rural one—women in the countryside tend to use less 'feminine' forms and make more use of 'masculine' or neutral forms.

results in the use of different forms of language. Despite the fact that in both market places and department stores the same customer–sales person relation exists, female vendors in market places use honorifics much less frequently than sales women in department stores, and instead make use of a more informal style of speech and interaction, with familiar rather than distant/polite forms of language. It is suggested that the non-use of honorifics by market vendors may occur so as to try to convey greater friendliness in the casual atmosphere of market places, in contrast with the more formal atmosphere which is deliberately cultivated in large department stores.

Changes in young women's use of language

A number of studies have shown that middle-aged and older women tend to use more 'feminine' forms than younger speakers, who may sometimes add in more typically male forms to their speech. With regard to the use of honorific words, it is found that many young people may now omit honorifics when talking about people who should be accorded respect but who are not present when they are being mentioned—for example, when students talk about one of their professors in his/her absence. Older women typically would use honorific words in the same situation. Younger women also now use certain 'male' SFPs in intimate, informal interactions with close friends. Researchers have suggested that younger speakers who know each other well avoid the use of honorifics, strongly feminine SFPs, and formal language because this can be construed as signaling a lack of closeness with the hearer. Younger female speakers concerned with emphasizing friendship with other same-aged people consequently avoid using very formal, ultra-feminine language, and may even substitute heavily masculine forms as new symbols of solidarity with their friends.[23]

The use of different pronoun forms by young men and women in junior high schools has also resulted in some interesting findings which show that language patterns are undergoing change among the young. As noted earlier in the chapter, in addition to the formal sex-neutral pronoun *watashi* meaning 'I/me', male speakers have long used a special pronoun *boku* to refer to themselves, while female speakers have used *atashi*. Recently, however, both boys and girls in schools in Tokyo and other urban environments have been switching to different forms, and high school girls have been adopting the 'male' pronoun *boku*. Girls interviewed about their use of *boku* say they feel that they cannot compete with boys in classes, games, or schoolyard fights using the very formal and feminine-sounding pronoun *atashi* or the sex-neutral but formal *watashi*, and so make use of the masculine pronoun *boku* when they are at school. However, because the use of *boku* by females is generally censured in daily life in Japan, the same young women switch to use *watashi* when outside school, and so have two distinct ways of speaking in different domains. Furthermore, most girls stop using *boku* when they leave school and take up jobs, and so the temporary 'deviant' use of *boku* in schools has come to be tolerated more than the use of masculine forms by adult women, which is seen as posing a greater threat to Japanese traditions.

---

23. Young speakers of other languages have been noted to exhibit similar phenomena. For example, the use of slang and swear words may sometimes be used by young women in Western societies to emphasize closeness with friends of the same generation in intimate contexts.

Doing *burikko*

Finally, at quite another extreme in female speech is a recent phenomenon of girls 'doing *burikko*'. Miller (2004) describes *burikko* as a derogatory term used to refer to women who exhibit 'feigned naivety' and 'bogus innocence'. It is formed from the verb *buru* meaning to 'pretend, act', and a suffix *-ko* 'child/girl', and the combined meaning is suggested to be something like 'fake child' or 'phony girl'. Linguistically, typical *burikko* behavior is signaled by the following properties during the *burikko* 'act'.

(a) The *burikko* 'voice'. Deliberate use of a very high, falsetto voice, well above the range used by female speakers on other non-*burikko* occasions. This is supplemented with intonation patterns that swoop up and down a lot, though always basically high, and the heavy use of nasalization.
(b) Special *burikko* words. Use of 'baby-talk' words and 'cutesy' expressions, frequently formed by onomatopoeia and reduplication (for example, *wanwan* 'bow-wow' for dog, in place of *inu* 'dog', and *chu chu* 'little birdy' for 'bird' in place of *kotori*, etc.), other specially coined slang words, the full avoidance of Chinese-sourced words (which signal learning and knowledge), heavy use of the honorific prefix *o-* attached to words.
(c) The frequent use of incomplete sentences or sentences that seem to drift off into inaudibleness, signaling non-assertiveness and timorousness in an artificial way.
(d) In writing, distinctive 'round characters' *maru moji* may be used in place of more traditional angular forms. For example, the character on the left below is a stylized *burikko* form of the standard character on the right. Such roundness is intended to look 'cuter' than the regular square-like way of writing various characters.

Burikko form   *Standard form*

The *burikko* voice and behavior is most commonly thought to be put on in the presence of powerful males. Miller (2004: 152) suggests that:

> It announces that the speaker is unsure, weak, or less powerful. . . . A woman who takes on the role of *burikko* is asking to be given the same lenience and indulgence accorded to an unschooled child. . . . She is consciously placing herself in the role of the innocent, reflecting traditional cultural expectations that women not be knowledgeable about certain cultural domains.

Although women who perform *burikko* may do this to project an attractive image which solicits special attention, reactions to *burikko* are actually often negative, sometimes extremely so. Surveys carried out among young men indicate that they frequently find the *burikko* style annoying and unattractive, and other young women also seem to find it very fake and irritating. It is also not clear that the *burikko* stance appeals to those powerful older males who are thought to be its primary targeted audience. Nevertheless, as a specialized style among a section of young women, it continues to be practiced and adds a further interesting dimension of variation to women's language in Japan,

As has been seen in this overview of studies on language and gender in Japan, men's and women's use of Japanese may show many striking differences, due in significant part to pressures arising from traditional culture and the hierarchical organization of Japanese society. This has led to the development of highly specialized ways of speaking among many women which emphasize a stereotypical image of non-assertive, deferential, refined femininity. The linguistic patterns which have long supported such an image are, however, now starting to undergo certain change as the structure of society changes in modern, 21st-century Japan, resulting in new ways of speaking and some women's adoptions of more assertive, forceful forms previously only used by men. It has also been noted that not all women in Japanese society have always aspired to use traditional *onna rashii kotoba* and that this has principally been favored by middle- and upper-class women, and more so in urban areas than in the countryside. In addition to changes in speech found among women in positions of authority, innovations are also occurring among the young and in different directions, some taking young female language more toward common masculine speech in various ways, while new ultra-feminine patterns have emerged in the *burikko* style which exaggerates differences between male and female speakers. The interaction of language and gender in Japan is both fascinating and dynamic, and offers a rich area for research and comparison with men's and women's language patterns in other societies around the world.

Challenging 'essentialist' links between language and gender

As highlighted in the preceding section on Japan and also previous examples drawn from Africa, the relationship between a person's gender (biological sex) and the language he/she makes use of is not a necessarily direct and invariant one, with all women and men in a particular society and language group speaking in the same, fully predictable ways. Male and female speakers often do not constitute neat, homogeneous groups, and a whole range of factors may give rise to variation within women's and men's linguistic practices and a greater richness of patterns than was sometimes assumed in early work carried out on language and gender. In recent years, a new 'social constructionist' approach to gender has also become prominent, in which individuals' identities are no longer assumed to be static and immutable but rather ever-developing, as the result of acts of linguistic and other behavior that people regularly engage in. Rather than assuming that the way we speak is determined by a fixed identity we have established, social constructionists argue that our speech is 'one of the ways that people *shape* their identities, (and) *construct* themselves as (certain kinds of) women and men' (McConnell-Ginet 2011: 8). Whenever speakers make use of language which conventionally indexes a particular gendered identity, people are *doing identity work* which builds up and reinforces an evolving personal image. Gender is viewed as the accomplishment and product of social interaction, emerging and changing over time through personal contact and communication with others (Holmes and Meyerhoff 2005). Individuals are taken to 'perform' and create their own gendered identities in an ever-dynamic way, rather than acting in pre-assigned ways determined by their biological sex.

One of the major early influences on the development of the new social-constructionist, post-modern approach to gender in the 1990s was the work of Judith Butler, in her two books *Gender Trouble: Feminism and the Subversion of Identity* (1990), and *Bodies That Matter* (1993). As noted in Baker (2008), in much of the 1970s and 1980s, linguists frequently made the assumption that people spoke in different ways because of who they were, an 'essentialist' view positing a direct causal connection between gender-based identity and a person's speech. Butler, however, argued for a fully different perspective on the relation of identity and behavior and proposed that people construct identities for themselves through the way they speak and act, promoting the theory of 'gender as *performance*'—language (among other things) is used to performatively *construct* our gendered identity in a continuous process, and gender is 'something that we do rather than who we are', 'the repeated stylization of the body, (through) a set of repeated acts' Butler (1990: 33).

The new, post-modern approach to gender and language initiated in the 1990s also vigorously emphasized that people's gender identities are often not straightforward, fixed, and predictable, and there may be considerable fluidity in gendered identity across individuals and society. Men and women may 'performatively subvert or resist the prevailing codes of gender' (Cameron 1997: 334), breaking away from established gender stereotypes and their anticipated linguistic behavior with creative performances of language and gender in sometimes unexpected ways. Baker (2008: 88) adds that frequently it may indeed be studies of speakers 'who do *not* conform to society's expectations of the way gender should 'correctly' be performed . . . that we can ascertain that all gender is performative.' Such strongly visible acts of departure from commonplace stereotypes of language and gender may be effected in a variety of interesting ways which clearly demonstrate the performative aspect of language use and its role in the construction of gendered identity. Here we will briefly mention three insightful studies of the adaption of gendered language patterns by groups attempting to establish new identities which simultaneously challenge traditional assumptions about the nature of gender.

Barrett (1999) describes the use of language to index a range of identities performed by African American drag queens. As African American Vernacular English (chapter 7) is often perceived as a strong marker of masculinity and commonly associated with heterosexual men, gay members of the African American community sometimes make use of different, non-AAVE ways of talking, in order to signal a gendered identity which is not that of the heterosexual stereotype. Barrett suggests that, in general, people may not have just a single, set 'identity', but 'something closer to what Paul Kroskrity (1993: 206 ff.) has called 'a "repertoire of identity", in which any of a multiplicity of identities may be fronted at a particular moment' (Barrett 1999: 318). The new term 'polyphonous identity' is proposed by Barrett to refer to this complex phenomenon. Barrett observes that African American drag queens may make use of language in a very fluid way to index different components of their polyphonous identity—their status as African Americans, as gay men, and also specifically as drag queens: 'Through style-shifting, the linguistic variables associated with each aspect of identity may co-occur, creating a voice simultaneously associated with several identity categories' (Barrett 1999: 318). The primary linguistic means made use of to emphasize and perform the drag queen category is the adoption of speech patterns used by affluent, middle-class white women, and the projection of a highly exaggerated feminine persona. This stereotypically feminine speaking style may, however, sometimes be interrupted by switches into a masculine voice (AAVE or gay male speech), as a means to stress the ambiguous nature of speakers' polyphonous identity and highlight the fact that the white-woman style is a performed identity that does not correspond to the biological identity of the speaker. Barrett points out that while 'drag queens use language to signal female "gender", typically they do not see themselves as "women" but maintain a basic "male" gender identity.' The language patterns made use of by drag queens such as those documented by Barrett thus lead to the conclusion that 'performed gender may differ from self-categorized gender identity', and that language can be used in a variety of ways to perform aspects of a speaker's complex self-image.[24]

A second study illustrating the non-homogenous nature of gender as a social category, and the use of language to index a gendered identity, is Besnier's (2003) investigation of the speech of '*fakaleiti*' in the South Pacific kingdom of Tonga. The *fakaleiti* are Tongan men who regularly act like women in a range of ways, as they perform gender in their daily interactions with others.[25] Linguistically, the *fakaleiti* borrow an important component of women's speech in Tonga to construct their particular gender identity, just as African American drag queens do. What is interesting and distinctive about the way this is done in Tonga is that it involves the manipulation of multilingualism and code-switching, rather than the use of stereotypically feminine speech patterns from within a single language. In Tonga, heterosexual men emphasize the speaking of the national language, Tongan, while women may often make use of English as well as Tongan. English is a strong symbol of cosmopolitanism and modernity, associated with higher education, white collar employment, and women's hopes for upward mobility and escape from the restrictions of traditional culture.[26] It therefore features commonly in educated, aspiring women's speech, either in code-switched form together with Tongan, or on occasion monolingually without any Tongan words. While the use of English among women is often positively evaluated, men who use too much English in their daily lives (outside of the domains of higher education and business) are often felt to be less masculine than other men who communicate predominantly with Tongan. Such a stereotypical gender association of English with female speakers is deliberately exploited by the *fakaleiti*, who code-switch Tongan and English as a way to project a non-masculine image, even when they have a relatively low degree of proficiency in English due to lack of formal education. What 'counts' is the symbolic value of English appearing in a person's speech, however

---

24. See also Mann (2011) for an extension of Barrett's investigation of the speech of drag queens and its relation to the indexing of polyphonous identity.

25. The word *faka* means 'in the way of', and *leiti* is derived from English 'lady', hence *fakaleiti* literally means 'in the way of/like women'.

26. In this way, English and code-switching with English in Tonga has a similar value to the use of French and code-switching with French among educated women in Morocco, as mentioned earlier in the chapter.

'correctly' used, and when this occurs frequently in a man's language it signals a rejection of masculine identity and the declaration of a different gendered orientation.

A third revealing investigation of gender-challenging language patterns now often referenced in post-modern work on language and gender is Kira Hall and Veronica O'Donovan's (1996) description of 'Shifting gender positions among Hindi-speaking *hijras*'. Most of the individuals known as '*hijras*' in India were raised as boys, but in adolescent and adult life they see themselves as neither man nor woman, and belonging to a third sex, at the same time 'deficiently' masculine and 'incompletely' feminine. *Hijras* frequently wear feminine clothing and jewelry, but sometimes may also wear items of clothing traditionally worn by men. In their speech, they use both feminine and masculine forms of speech, including the morphological marking of gender on adjectives and verbs, and alternate between feminine and masculine styles of speech on different occasions for clearly identifiable reasons, to convey different social meanings relating to solidarity and power.

The variable linguistic and social behavior of *hijras* is illustrated in Hall and O'Donovan (1996) with details of the language habits of an individual referred to as Sulekha. When the *hijra* Sulekha has the physical appearance of a woman, through the use of feminine dress and make-up, she also walks, laughs, and talks like a woman. However, at other times, Sulekha wears masculine clothing, and then speaks like a man, using masculine inflections. Sulekha's choice of linguistic gender varies according to the context she finds herself in. Hall and O'Donovan state that her choice of language depends on the social role she is performing at the time of any interaction, and the gendered identity of the person she is speaking to— talking to men or women or other *hijras* results in Sulekha adopting different gendered ways of talking, broadly: 'when she converses with a woman, she speaks as a woman; when she converses with a man, she speaks as a man' (Hall and O'Donovan 1996: 245). Additionally, in emotionally charged moments, when Sulekha wishes to strongly emphasize a particular statement, she regularly adopts masculine forms, even when otherwise performing a feminine role. She finds that anger and the criticism of others is most effectively expressed by means of male rather than female speech forms, and her general use of both female and male speech allows her to switch from one to the other quite easily when the situation favors such alternations. *Hijras* such as Sulekha are said to be very aware of the social meanings conveyed by their varying feminine and masculine speech, and make use of different forms of gender-inflected speech as a socio-linguistic resource, much like the adoption of different styles of speech by other speakers.

Hall and O'Donovan suggest that the kind of 'gendered negotiations' which characterize *hijra* speech are not restricted just to communities associated with an alternative gender identity, but actually have a much wider application in society, with women and men from many different backgrounds able to 'manipulate linguistic expectations of femininity and masculinity in order to establish varying positions of solidarity and power' (Hall and O'Donovan 1996: 258). They emphasize that the *hijra* study adds further strong support for the post-modern view of language and gender that 'speaking styles recognized culturally as "women's speech" or "men's speech" are not determined by the sex of the speaker, but rather constructed in social interaction.' Critically, the language often stereotypically associated with masculinity and femininity in a society can be used to index more than simple biological sex and may be adopted across genders to express important relations such as power and solidarity. In the case of the *hijras*, masculine speech is made use of at times where the expression of power or social distance is felt to be necessary or appropriate, while feminine speech is adopted to encode solidarity. Interestingly then, while the *hijras* clearly challenge standard binary ideas of gender with their changing language, dress, and actions, the switches that they make between masculine and feminine styles of speech are also influenced and guided by traditional cultural meanings of power and solidarity linked to masculine and feminine ways of speaking. What Hall and O'Donovan's linguistic portrait of the *hijra* shows is that both masculine and feminine forms of language can be effectively used by individuals regardless of their gender identity, and so these interactional styles should not be taken to be restrictively anchored only to male or female speakers.[27]

Language and sexism

In this final section, we now turn to consider the issue of whether and how language might be sexist. As the language we use often conveys our attitudes toward others, it is clearly possible for aspects of language to convey sexist attitudes which stereotype a person negatively according to their gender. The existence of sexism in language has indeed been claimed in a broad range of research on different languages, which has generally concentrated on ways in which language: (a) may support the prejudiced view that men have a greater, more central importance in society than women, (b) portrays women in generally negative ways, and (c) fails to provide women with the same linguistic resources available to men for the description of their experiences and for reference to members of the opposite sex. The study of sexism in language has also been noted to potentially link up in an important way with the linguistic relativity hypothesis described in chapter 9. Hudson (1996) and Graddol and Swann (1989) both point out that if our thinking may be influenced by the language we make use of, sometimes in ways that we may be unaware of, it is possible that certain gender-related vocabulary and expressions may help promote the continuation of sexist attitudes, even in cultures which have attempted to confront practices of sexual discrimination and create greater equality between men and women. In this overview of the linguistic expression of sexist attitudes, we will first consider patterns which have been argued to discriminate against women's position in society and to encode the primacy and centrality of men, and then examine imbalances in the words which speakers of different languages have available to them for the representation of men and women and their actions in life.

Two simple patterns which attracted the attention of early campaigners against language-related sexism in English-speaking societies are the typical sequencing of male terms before female terms in related pairs of words such as *men and women, boys and girls, husband and wife*, and *sons and daughters*, and the replacement of a woman's family (maiden) name with her husband's surname upon marriage (causing 'Mary Smith' to officially become known as 'Mrs. Mary Croft' when marrying a man whose surname is Croft).

---

27. See also Gaudio 1996, Ogawa and Smith 1996, and Livia 1996 for similar points made on the basis of studies carried out among Hausa-, Japanese- and French-speaking communities.

It was objected that the regular placement of male terms before female forms presents males as having greater importance than females, and that the imposition of male surnames on married women accords greater public value to men in the union of marriage. There is one well-known exception to the former pattern—*ladies and gentlemen*. Interestingly, when this phrase was translated into Korean and Japanese, the tendency to have male terms precede female terms was so dominant in these languages as well that speakers actually reversed the order of *ladies* and *gentlemen*, producing *sinsa swuknye yelepwun* in Korean and *shinshi shukujo* in Japanese ('gentlemen (and) ladies'; Kim 2008: 151).

In other languages, such as French and Italian, where nouns are all grammatically either masculine or feminine, it is found that certain nouns referring to professions traditionally dominated by men have only evolved a masculine form and no feminine form exists. Hence in French, the word for a 'minister' only has a masculine form *un ministre*, complicating its use when a minister is actually a woman. Similarly, in Italian, until recent years there were only masculine noun forms for the following professions/positions: 'lawyer' *avvocato*, 'mayor' *sindaco*, and 'minister' *ministro*. Following pressure from campaigners, female forms were created (*avvocatessa, sindachessa, ministra*) but then not widely adopted as they were perceived to be 'forced' and somehow unnatural (Mills 2008). Elsewhere, in Hindi, it is found that the feminine form of various professional terms is not equivalent in meaning to the male term, and may sometimes just mean the wife of a man having the named profession, hence *guruani* means 'wife of a teacher' (male term: *guru*), not female teacher, and *vakilni* means 'wife of a lawyer', not female lawyer (Valentine 1987: 43). Related 'sexual asymmetries in the lexicon' have been observed in many of the world's languages.

French, Italian, Spanish, Arabic, and other languages in which gender is encoded in nouns, adjectives, and some verb forms also often have a morphological 'agreement' rule which heavily biases male referents over females. In cases where the subject of a sentence is a combination of male and female referents, for example 'Two men and three women arrived', the agreement-marking which appears on adjectives and verbs is always masculine (plural), even if the number of female referents outnumbers the male referents. This is neatly illustrated in the following Spanish example from Mills (2008: 31), in which the subject is 'two million women and a mouse'. The 'mouse' is masculine in gender, and forces the verb to show masculine gender. Despite the verb's reference to two million women, the masculinity of the 'mouse' is accorded more importance in the agreement rule and outweighs the force of any number of feminine referents:

Dos millions de mujeres y un ratón fueron atropellados por un camion.
'Two million women and a mouse [masc.] were run over [masc.] by a truck.'

English does not have any morphological gender-marking on verbs and adjectives, but it did develop the suffix *–ess* for attachment to nouns to signal a female referent of the type of the noun, for example:

host – hostess	*actor – actress*	*emperor – empress*
sorcerer – sorceress	*hunter – huntress*	*governor – governess*

Feminist critiques of this process of converting a male noun to a female form by adding a suffix have objected that it represents the male form as the core, foundational member of the pair and female forms as derivative, being created from the male form. As the result of campaigns to redress this perceived imbalance in words referring to male and female occupations and positions, female terms ending in *–ess* have mostly been dropped, and either a single term is now used to refer to both males and females, as is the typical use of *actor* and *author* for male and female referents, eliminating *actress* and *authoress*, or a new sex-neutral term has been coined to replace earlier pairs, as in the substitution of *flight attendant* for *air hostess* and its use to refer to males in this occupation as well as females. Other vocabulary changes responding to pressure to eliminate occupational nouns ending in *–man*, such as *watchman* and *foreman*, have similarly led to new replacements which are sex-neutral, for example:

fireman → *firefighter*
watchman → *guard*
foreman → *supervisor*

Many of these new terms have been successful and are now in common use. However, some have encountered unexpected difficulties. For example, when *chairperson* was coined to replace *chairman* as a sex-neutral term, in practice it has often come to be used to designate a female referent or a low-status male, with either *chairman* or simply *chair* being used for males performing such a role in more high-status committees. Again, an imbalance in male and female terms has emerged.

There has additionally been much discussion relating to use of the terms '*man*' and '*he*' which have often been used with intended 'generic' reference, in the case of *man*, to refer to all humans in general statements such as the first of the following examples, and, with *he,* to refer in a gender-neutral way in more specific statements where the gender of a particular referent is unknown and could be either male or female, as in the second example.

Man is constantly faced by challenges.
Every visitor to the Grand Canyon feels that he has an unforgettable experience.

The important question is whether these terms really are gender-neutral or whether they conceal a male component of meaning. If they aren't genuinely gender-neutral, then it may be objected that a male term is being used to represent both sexes generically in an imbalanced way that specifically supports the primacy and visibility of males (Spender 1985).

A number of commentators have pointed out that *man* cannot be used in a gender-neutral way in many instances, unlike the sex-neutral terms *person,* and *people* and *human(s),* as illustrated in the following examples. These are all unacceptable or extremely odd when *man* is used (as represented with the addition of a * symbol), but would be fully acceptable if a different sex-neutral term is employed.

*She is the best man for the job. (Valentine 1987)
✓ *She is the best person for the job.*

*Mary Brown was the first man to have a baby in that ward. (Hudson 1996)
✓ Mary Brown was the first person to have a baby in that ward.

*One of the men on the farm is a beautiful French woman. (Graddol and Swann 1989)
✓ One of the people on the farm is a beautiful French woman.

*The only man to survive the pandemic was Mary Smith.
✓ The only human to survive the pandemic was Mary Smith.

This suggests that the word *man* is not a true sex-neutral generic expression. Because of this, there has been pressure for *man* not to be used in expressions which are intended to be sex-neutral, leading to word replacements and substitutions of the types already mentioned, and others such as the following, noted in Graddol and Swann (1989):

man-made	→	*artificial, synthetic*
prehistoric man	→	*prehistoric people*
man a post	→	*fill a post*
manpower	→	*workforce*

With regard to the pronoun *he* (and *him, his*), this has often been used in contexts which are meant to be sex-neutral, but it has again been objected that *he* 'feels' very masculine and so seems to unfairly privilege the use of a male form as a representation for both males and females, emphasizing the primacy of males. Attempts to avoid the use of *he* have sometimes involved coupling *he* with *she*:

Every applicant should state whether he or she has been trained in CPR.

However, this pairing of male and female pronouns often sounds clumsy, especially when repeated over several sentences, as for example in:

Every student should make up his or her mind. He or she should decide whether to attend and whether to bring along his or her parents.

In colloquial speech, people often use a third person plural *they/their* in place of *he/his*, even if there is no intended plural referent:

Someone just left the room but I didn't notice who they were.
Did anybody forget their laptop? I found one in the classroom.
No one thinks they will lose in this kind of game.

This way of avoiding the use of *he* in sex-neutral contexts sounds better to most people than using *he or she*, but it is sometimes felt to be stylistically too casual for use in formal written materials, and it is quite inconvenient that English has failed to develop a genuinely sex-neutral third person pronoun for use in both speech and writing, unlike languages such as French and German.

We have already mentioned that languages sometimes have morphologically related pairs of words referring to males and females which might be expected to be equivalent in meaning, differing only in the gender to which they apply (for example, Hindi *guru* and *guruani*), but which actually are significantly different in meaning, with the male form referring to a position or occupation which is more socially valued than the female form (hence male *guru* is a teacher, while *guruani* is the wife of a teacher). This imbalance in the meaning of male and female terms also occurs in pairs of words that are quite different in their shape, but are used with men and women in the same, common contexts. For example, in Japanese, a wife will refer to her husband as *shujin*, which literally means 'master', while her husband will refer to his wife as *kanai* meaning 'the one inside the house', or as *uchi-no-yatsu*, again meaning 'the one inside the house', but making use of the word *yatsu* which is otherwise only applied to people of lower status, emphasizing the subordinate role of married women (Kim 2008). In addition to the frequent occurrence of semantically non-equivalent male/female word pairs of this type, research into sexist language patterns has regularly highlighted the existence of '*lexical gaps*', which involve the *absence* of certain expected words relating to men and women and their experiences in life. In Japanese, for example, there are multiple terms available for men to use to refer to women in clearly negative, derogatory ways, such as the following: *busu* 'ugly woman'; *urenokori* 'older, unmarried woman' lit. 'unsold merchandise'; *gusai* '(my) stupid wife'; *oorudo misu* 'old maid' 'old miss'—which conveys disdain for women who remain single after a certain age. However, there are no equivalent terms for women to refer to men in parallel, negative ways—there are thus significant gender-related gaps in the lexicon/vocabulary.[28]

The occurrence of lexical gaps which disadvantage women in their speech has been found to be a common cross-linguistic phenomenon. In English, it has been noted that there are various words which can be used to refer to sexually promiscuous men in a positive way, for example words such as *stud* and *virile*, but no obvious positive equivalents for women (*fertile* and *nubile* are not used in the same kind of way), hence women do not have the lexical means to refer to their experiences and behavior in the same way as men. While there are, in fact, a large number of words which refer to sexually promiscuous women, these are almost all negative and pejorative. One study on North American English carried out in 1977 identified as many as 220 words for a sexually promiscuous woman (Stanley 1977), but almost all of these were negative in connotation. As a result of this, whereas men have a large vocabulary potentially available for insulting women, women generally have much fewer words available to insult men.

There are some indications that this situation is now finally undergoing change in certain parts of the population. In recent years, it has been observed that female college students in North American have begun using sexual terms to refer negatively to male students, sometimes adopting terms that were originally used by males in pejorative ways toward females. For example, the *UCLA Dictionary of Slang Vol. 3* (1997) includes entries such as: 'He's such a slut.' However, such changes are quite restricted in nature when compared to the vocabulary

---

28. Japanese men also have special first and second person pronouns which they can use to encode power in interactions with women—*ore* 'I' and *omae* 'you'—but no strong pronouns of this type are available for women.

available to men, and not occurring in other cultures or groups where similar lexical gaps are present in the same form—for example, Zulu, where there is a highly positive term to refer to sexually active men with multiple partners—*amasoka* 'man highly favored by girls'—but only negative terms for women with the same pattern of behavior—*isifebe* 'a loose woman', and the very derogatory *unondindwa* 'woman with multiple sexual partners' (Atanga et al. 2013).[29]

The kind of lexical gaps noted in the preceding, which result in multiple negative terms being available for reference to women but not men, have been called instances of the '*semantic derogation of women*', following an influential article by Muriel Schulz published in 1975. Schulz described at length a disturbing pattern of *lexical change* in English, subsequently reported to occur in other languages, too, in which words referring to women easily and frequently acquire pejorative meanings over time, often negatively linked to sexual behavior. The English words *mistress* and *whore* are good examples of this process. Both words started off as neutral in meaning, with no negative connotations. *Mistress* was simply the female equivalent of *master*, but over time it came to mean a female partner for extra-marital sex illicitly kept by a man. The word *whore* originated as a sex-neutral term meaning 'a lover of either sex'. It then became more restricted and was only used to refer to a female lover, and finally came to designate a prostitute and to be used as an extremely negative way of referring to a woman with multiple partners (Kim 2008). Other words developing in the same way in English, which are less common nowadays, are *hussy* which originally was a neutral term for 'housewife' and *wench* which initially meant 'girl'. Like *mistress* and *whore*, both such words acquired negative meanings in the course of time.

Similar examples occur in other European languages. In Portuguese, the word *ramariga* was once a neutral term for a young woman, but now has a secondary meaning 'prostitute', and the same is true of Spanish *muerzela*, while in French the word *grace* has changed its meaning from simply 'girl' to 'a loose woman' (Kim 2008). Significantly, all three of these words originally had neutral, male equivalent terms, but the male terms never developed negative meanings (Portuguese *rapaz*, Spanish *hombrezuelo*, and French *garcon*, all meaning 'young man/boy'). Related patterns have been described in Asian languages, and most probably occur in other parts of the world. Kim (2008) reports an ongoing change occurring with Korean *akassi* and Chinese *xiaojie*. The former term was originally used to refer to daughters of noble families before they married, and then became broadened in its use, being applied to young women in general. However, the term *akassi* is now being avoided because 'it has come to have strong sexual connotations, including the meaning of "women in the sex trade"' (Kim 2008: 155). A similar negative sexualization of Chinese *xiaojie* 'miss, girl' is argued to be taking place in mainland China, and many young Chinese women indicate that they feel offended when addressed as *xiaojie* due to its sexual implications, the term having come to be increasingly used with female sex workers in China (Kim 2008: 159).

---

29. A further example of a sexist lexical gap which was mentioned earlier in the chapter in footnote 3 is the absence of a verb meaning 'to marry' in *Kinyarwanda, Setswana*, and *Ikalanga* which can be used by women to describe their getting married to a man. Hence although these languages provide the lexical means for men to say 'I married her', there is no verb which will permit a woman to say 'I married him.'

It can thus be seen that sexism continues to infuse itself into language in a range of ways among different linguistic groups, and new discriminatory patterns are coming into existence, despite an improved awareness of the force of sexist language in many parts of the world. Quite generally, the presence of gender-related imbalances and biases in language has the potential to affect attitudes toward men's and women's status and behavior in society in ways that may be very negative and may contribute to the maintenance of old prejudices and harmful stereotypical images, particularly of women, even as society is developing more equal opportunities for men and women in other domains of life. While advances have been made in dealing with many obvious instances of lexical sexism in certain languages, attention still needs to be given to other more subtle patterns of sexism that may persist in language, as discussed in Mills (2008), and to newly developing areas of language use that support gratuitous and pernicious differentiations between the sexes.

Suggestions for further reading and activities

This chapter has provided an introduction to a broad selection of issues relating to language and gender, many of which are assumed as foundational knowledge by those carrying out new research in the area of gendered language use. There are many more interesting topics that can be explored in the interaction of language and gender. Some directions for further study are described here.

1. Deborah Tannen's article 'I'll explain it to you' discusses how men's and women's talking and listening styles may be affected differently by the degree to which the person speaking is knowledgeable about the topic being discussed. Read this article to find out how a person's 'expert' or 'non-expert' status affects the way they may be listened to by men and women.

   Tannen, Deborah. 2008. "I'll explain it to you": lecturing and listening. In Virginia Clark, Paul Eschholz, Alfred Rosa, and Beth Lee Simon (eds.), *Language: introductory readings*. Boston: Bedford/St. Martin's, 531–544.

2. Watch the movie *War of the Sexes: Language*, distributed by Films for the Humanities and Sciences (2005). Some parts of the film discuss the 'nature vs. nurture' controversy—whether gender differences arise as a result of our natural sex ('nature'), or are learned as part of the process of socialization children and adults go through in different cultures ('nurture'). What opinions on the 'nature vs. nurture' controversy are voiced by different people interviewed in the film?

3. Find about more about language and gender differences as they develop in children, by reading chapter 9 of Jennifer Coates' book:

   Coates, Jennifer. 1993. *Women, men, and language*. Harlow: Longman.

4. Computer programs have been created that claim to identify the sex of the author of any piece of writing or speech based on the words and style they use. For example, Baker (2008) reports that a computational study of 45 linguistic features in the International Corpus of English allowed researchers to predict the sex of a speaker correctly 88% of the

time for females, and 86% of the time for males in same-sex conversations. Try testing out the *Hacker Factor Gender Guesser* to see how well this kind of program performs, and whether it is accurate in guessing the sex of a speaker in different styles of prose (letter-writing, extracts from novels, written conversations etc).

http://www.hackerfactor.com/GenderGuesser.php

5. Learn more about the idea that men and women frequently misunderstand each other when communicating in the following two well-known works.

   Maltz, Daniel, and Ruth Borker. 1982. A cultural approach to male-female miscommunication. In J. Gumperz (ed.), *Language and social identity*. Cambridge: Cambridge University Press, 196–216.

   Tannen, Deborah. 1990. Asymmetries: women and men talking at cross-purposes. Chapter 2 of *You just don't understand*. New York: Ballantine Books.

6. Select a country other than the USA, the UK, or Japan that you are interested in and use the internet and library resources available to you to research studies on language and gender in this country. To what extent do the patterns you discover match up with the findings that have been described in the current chapter? Are there any significant differences in language and gender interactions reported in the works that you are able to access?

7. Sally McConnell-Ginet (2011: 237) states that: 'Different meanings promote the pursuit of different kinds of social action, cultural values, social inquiry.' She then probes the social meanings of the words 'queer', 'gay', and 'lesbian', and the politics associated with these terms. Read chapter 11 of McConnell-Ginet's book *Gender, Sexuality and Meaning* and try to understand how the shaping of word meanings relates to the shaping of social and political practices.

   McConnell-Ginet, Sally. 2011. 'Queering' semantics: definitional struggles. Chapter 11 of *Gender, sexuality and meaning*. Oxford: Oxford University Press, 237–262.

8. Mills (2008) describes instances of 'indirect sexism' in language, and suggests that these less blatant occurrences of sexism should be the focus of new research and action, now that campaigns for political correctness have helped eliminate more obvious sexist words. Read chapter 5 of Mills' book to find out what she means by 'indirect sexism' and where it may occur.

   Mills, Sara. 2008. *Language and sexism*. Cambridge: Cambridge University Press.

9. While there may often be a correlation between a certain style of speech and speakers of a particular gender, Deborah Cameron (1997) makes the point that exceptions and counter-examples to broad generalizations about men's and women's language can often be found, and generalizations of the type 'men use language this way and women use it that way' may frequently simplify a rather more complex set of linguistic practices. In analyzing the casual conversation of male college students, Cameron demonstrates that (at least some) young men engage in *gossip* and also co-operate in building up a shared identity through their linguistic interactions, patterns

which other researchers had suggested were typically female. Read Cameron's paper 'Performing Gender Identity: Young Men's Talk and the Construction of Heterosexual Masculinity' and see how the male students' speech is used to stimulate group involvement, build consensus, and affirm group solidarity in ways otherwise attributed to the use of language among female speakers. Do you find Cameron's analysis and conclusions surprising, and what impact do you think they have on Holmes' suggested generalizations about patterns of language and gender observed among male and female speakers?

Cameron, Deborah. 1997. Performing gender identity: young men's talk and the construction of heterosexual masculinity. In Sally Johnson and Ulrike Hanna Meinhof (eds.), *Language and masculinity*. Oxford: Blackwell, 47–64.

11

Language Variation and Change

Introduction

The final, major topic we will consider in this introduction to language and society is the significant occurrence of *language variation and change* in speech communities around the world, and the sociolinguistic causes and consequences of such change. By tradition, up until the 1960s, language change was primarily studied from the perspective of *historical linguistics*, with researchers documenting and analyzing major linguistic changes observed across large stretches of time. When modern-day English, French, or Chinese is compared with the kind of English, French, or Chinese used many hundreds of years ago, it is easy to find striking differences in many aspects of language, such as grammar, morphology, and vocabulary. In English, for example, the basic word order of the language changed dramatically from an object-before-verb pattern in the Old English period to a verb-before-object pattern in Middle English; the Great Vowel Shift from late Middle English to Early Modern English altered the ways that vowels were pronounced in all English words, causing much of the current mismatches between spelling and pronunciation in the language; and the vocabulary of English developed in important ways over the centuries, as the result of successive early invasions of the British Isles: Celtic words were first overrun and largely replaced by Anglo-Saxon words, which were then supplemented by words from Viking invaders and large amounts of French vocabulary following the Norman conquest of England. Latin words subsequently flooded into English during the Middle Ages. Due to such major changes in the language, Old English and Middle English are very different from Modern English as spoken in the 21st century, and linguists are able to make use of rich historical records to chart the progress of linguistic developments over time, showing very clearly how Chaucer's English changed into Elizabethan English and then into the language of the modern period.

Historical linguists focusing on studying language change in the past have often made the assumption that a certain distance in time is necessary for changes to be first detected and then analyzed, and that occurrences of current, *ongoing change* cannot be observed, because the range of variation found among speakers at any single point in time may often be confusing, and the direction of change cannot easily be predicted. Well-established changes which have taken place over the course of centuries are much easier to examine in many ways, as they frequently appear to be more clear-cut, with identified starting points and end points and obvious transitions from the use of one pattern to the adoption of another. However, ongoing variation and the initiation of changes in language are an area of study that can actually be extremely rewarding, if carefully carried out, because the sociological motivations for such variation and change can often be detected better than with earlier, historical patterns of development, and it is also possible to investigate the effects of ongoing change on members of society and the attitudes held toward new occurrences of variation in speech. The present chapter provides an overview of ground-breaking and important research of this type, looking at current and very recent innovations in language, and highlighting some of the interesting results which have come from new, sociolinguistic investigations of language change and the techniques these studies have involved. We will begin with a consideration of two classic, pioneering studies of language variation carried out in the 1960s, which set the scene and standards for much subsequent work on ongoing change, and then move on to examine a diverse set of more contemporary projects, each of which brings into focus a different aspect of language change and its relation to society, ranging from '*uptalk*' and '*vocal fry*', through the international spread of quotative '*be like*', to very recent lexical creativity in forms such as '*big-ass car*' and the question-marker '*innit*'.

Investigating sound change in New York City: Labov (1966)

William Labov, from the University of Pennsylvania, is a sociolinguist who has been at the center of research into language variation and change for many decades. Labov developed very effective new methods for the study of everyday speech, and many of his investigations became landmark inspirations for later generations of researchers. One of his most referenced early studies was centered in New York City, and examined differences in the ways that many people in New York were pronouncing certain sounds in their words. One of these was the /r/ sound which occurs at or toward the ends of words, such as *far, cart, door, near*, and *pearl*. When this sound is clearly heard in word-final/pre-final positions, it is referred to as a '*rhotic*' pronunciation. In New York City in the 1950s and on into the 1960s, it was observed that speakers seemed to regularly fluctuate in their use of rhotic pronunciations, sometimes pronouncing the *r* sound at the ends of words, and sometimes leaving it unpronounced in these environments—an obvious case of ongoing language variation. To many people, it appeared that the variation was quite random and unpredictable, as noted in an assessment made by the linguist Alan Hubbell in 1950 (cited in Labov 1966):

> The pronunciation of a very large number of New Yorkers exhibits a pattern . . . that might most accurately be described as the complete absence of any pattern. Such speakers sometimes pronounce /r/ before a consonant or in final position and sometimes omit it, in a thoroughly haphazard fashion. (Hubbell 1950;48)

However, Labov suspected that there was an explanation for the alternation between rhotic and non-rhotic pronunciations, and that speakers did attach some significance to the use of the /r/ sound, both in their own and in others' words. Labov guessed that this was connected with the projection of social status and that rhotic patterns were gradually becoming a new prestige form of pronunciation in New York City, initiated by those in higher class levels, and slowly spreading down into other socio-economic groups. Historically, rhoticism had in fact been widespread in American and British speech, but then disappeared from many parts of the United States and Britain during the 18th and 19th centuries, remaining absent from the South and East of the USA through until the middle of the 20th century, when it started to resurface in the alternating patterns commented on by Hubbell and other linguists. Labov was convinced that this modern reintroduction of /r/ must have some social motivation, and he also believed that he could find ways to analyze ongoing language variation in systematic and revealing ways. For the study of New York /r/, these convictions led to the creation of a set of experiments designed to probe different aspects of the use and perception of rhotic speech and the connections this might have with the projection of social identity.

The first, major component of Labov's research into varying sound patterns in New York was a novel 'fieldwork' study of the occurrence of /r/ in the speech of sales assistants working in three department stores in Manhattan: Saks Fifth Avenue, Macy's, and Klein's. These stores critically differed in the kinds of customers they would typically attract. Saks Fifth Avenue was an upmarket store in an expensive part of town, Macy's was more of a middle-priced store frequented by middle-income clientele, and Klein's was a much cheaper store in a less expensive part of Manhattan, where shoppers regularly came from lower-income groups. Labov thought that the /r/ sound might be occurring more frequently in speakers from higher socio-economic groups, going to stores such as Saks, and that it might be found less in the speech of those from lower socio-economic backgrounds visiting stores like Macy's and Klein's. He also wondered whether such hypothetical differences might be mirrored in the speech of sales assistants interacting with their customers as the result of *accommodation*, the phenomenon that people sometimes modify aspects of their behavior (language, gestures, etc., as discussed in chapter 10) and make it closer to that of others they are regularly in contact with. If sales assistants in Saks, Macy's, and Klein's were indeed to mimic the speech of their customers to some extent, it might be expected that they would make use of different amounts of /r/ when assisting customers, more /r/ use being anticipated in Saks, and less in Macy's and Klein's.

In order to find out whether his hunches about /r/-related variation might be correct, Labov went to each department store to gather data from the sales assistants working there, posing as a regular customer. Labov wanted to get the sales people to produce words which had /r/ sounds at their ends without explicitly asking them to do so or giving away his identity as a linguistic researcher, which might have caused the sales assistants to speak in an unnatural way. To do this, in each store Labov consulted the store directory listing the location of different goods items and looked for a section of goods located on the *fourth floor*. This allowed him to approach sales assistants in the store and ask where the relevant goods were located, with questions such as: 'Excuse me, where is the men's shoe department?' The answer would then regularly come back as: '(*It's on*) *the fourth floor*', and Labov would hear how two words containing word-final /r/ were pronounced by sales assistants to a 'customer' in that store. Following this exchange, Labov pretended that he had misheard the sales assistants' answers, and asked for the information a second time, saying: *'Excuse me?'* or *'Where was that?'* The second question would normally cause the sales person to repeat the words *'fourth floor'* more slowly and with a more careful pronunciation. Labov then thanked the sales assistant, moved aside, and wrote down the pronunciations he had heard, together with information about the approximate age of the sales assistant, his/her gender and ethnicity.

Analyzing the data he was able to gather from hundreds of interactions with sales assistants in the three department stores, Labov found that his intuitions had been correct, and there were very clear correlations between the nature of each store (i.e., the kind of clientele it attracted) and the amount of rhotic speech used by assistants working there. The use of /r/ by sales assistants in Saks was higher than in Macy's, and those working in Macy's pronounced /r/ sounds significantly more frequently than sales assistants in Klein's. Labov's suspicions were therefore satisfyingly confirmed and /r/ use was not found to be random and unpredictable, and instead showed clear signs of being directly linked to social class. Differences in the speech of sales assistants in the three department stores suggested they were regularly accommodating their language to reflect speech patterns of their customers, and the higher the socio-economic background of the latter, the more frequent /r/-insertion this caused in the language of the former.

The patterns noted by Labov in his interactions with sales assistants also offered evidence that a linguistic *change* was underway. A significant difference occurred in the pronunciations Labov heard in the answers to his initial question, often given in a casual, automatic way, and the more careful pronunciations which were given to Labov's second question when he pretended to have misheard and the sales assistants repeated their words more slowly and clearly. In Klein's, this was noted to lead to a much higher rate of /r/ use in the repetition of *'fourth floor'*. Labov interpreted such patterns as showing that /r/ would be used when speakers had the time to reflect on the production of their speech and deliberately inserted an /r/ sound in their 'ideal way' of speaking—rhotic pronunciations appeared to be desired by speakers and became a feature of their careful, planned speech, while /r/-less forms appeared as variants when they found themselves speaking faster and without conscious reflection.

Labov's conclusion that patterns of /r/-variation represented an ongoing change toward increased use of rhotic speech was later well-supported by a replication of Labov's department store investigation carried out twenty years later, by the linguist Joy Fowler, who used the same methods employed by Labov again in 1986, in Saks', Macy's, and a newer lower-cost department store, as Klein's had disappeared. As predicted by Labov, it was found that /r/ insertion in the speech of sales assistants had further increased with time, though it remained higher in Sak's than in Macy's, and more frequent in Macy's than in the lower-cost department store, mirroring the proportional differences originally found in the 1960s. This growth of rhotic speech in New York City during the late 20th century showed that variation was leading to an overall change in the way people spoke, and that the renewed use of /r/ was coming to be an increasingly widespread prestige form of speech.

A second component of Labov's study of English speech patterns in New York consisted of interviews he held with a large number of speakers from different socio-economic backgrounds, grouped as members of the lower class, the working class, the lower middle class, and the upper middle class, on the basis of their occupation, education, and income. Labov gathered information about the speech of members of these groups in five different ways. He observed his subjects engage in *casual speech* when they interacted with other family members in their home environments. Interviews were carried out with these speakers, and this normally resulted a less spontaneous way of speaking and examples of more *careful speech*. Subjects were also asked to read stories out loud, as well as lists of isolated words, and pairs of words which sounded similar but differed in the presence of an /r/ in one word vs. its absence in the other—'minimal pairs' such as *sauce* and *source*. The three reading tasks were expected to produce increasingly more formal levels of pronunciation from the subjects, as they concentrated on speaking 'correctly'.

There were three significant, general results from this set of studies on the use of /r/ among New Yorkers from different social backgrounds. First, it was confirmed that members of different social classes used different amounts of /r/ in their speech, this being highest, in general, among members of the upper middle class in their casual and careful speech, and when they read stories out loud. Such a general patterning verified the assumption that rhotic speech was a property of speakers from higher socio-economic backgrounds and an indicator of ascribed social status and prestige. Second, it was found that speakers from all groups changed their pronunciations in the different contexts observed by Labov, increasing their use of /r/ in the more formal pronunciation tasks they were asked to perform. Thus speakers who did not use much /r/ in casual and even careful speech added /r/ sounds in their reading tasks and the pronunciation of lists of words and minimal word pairs. Labov concluded that this resulted from speakers' awareness that /r/ was a new general norm to be aimed for, and that they were trying to add this sound when given the time to produce words more carefully. Third, when speakers' use of /r/ was compared in the word list and minimal pair reading tasks, the interesting discovery was made that speakers from the lower middle class actually inserted the /r/ sound much more frequently than speakers from the upper middle class. Labov called this a 'crossover' pattern of '*hypercorrection*'—speakers from the lower middle class seemed to want to sound like members of a higher class level, the upper middle class, and exaggerated their use of /r/ as a way to do this, ironically using the sound more than members of the upper middle class actually did. Labov suggested that this phenomenon of hypercorrection was a further sign of ongoing linguistic change—speakers were switching to new pronunciation patterns and over-exaggerating the use of these forms when given the opportunity, in careful reading tasks.

A third experiment carried out with speakers from New York aimed at probing *attitudes* toward rhotic speech and finding additional support for the claim that /r/ sounds were linked with higher social status. In the third experiment, the speech of five female speakers was first recorded and then rearranged in special ways. Sentences in which the speakers had produced no /r/ sounds were grouped together as an /r/-less speech recording. Other sentences in which the same speakers had in fact produced /r/ sounds were isolated in a second recording of 'consistent' /r/ use. Finally, a third set of recordings was created with a mixture of /r/ and /r/-less pronunciations for each of the five speakers. The recordings were then played to listeners from different social backgrounds without telling the latter that only five women had been involved in producing the voices they heard on the tapes. The listeners were asked to pretend that they were personnel managers and to rate the voices according to the speaker's suitability for certain jobs varying in their relative prestige, on the following scale ranging from high to low: *television personality > executive secretary > receptionist > switchboard operator > salesgirl > factory worker*. The results of the experiment demonstrated an amazing uniformity of assessment from listeners of all social groups. Speakers with voices using /r/ consistently were judged to be better suited to the higher occupations, /r/-less voices were associated with lower status jobs, and voices using mixed /r/ and /r/-less speech were linked to middle-level jobs. Because the tapes had been carefully created using each of the five speakers' /r/ and /r/-less pronunciations, and listeners did not know they were hearing the same speaker more than once, in many instances the five speakers were judged to be suitable for different jobs, and the only difference in their speech which could have caused such variability in assessment was the presence vs. absence of /r/ among their words. This showed very clearly that New Yorkers from all different backgrounds mentally linked rhotic speech with higher social status, as established in part by occupation level.

The three major components of Labov's study of variation in the pronunciation of word-final /r/ in New York during the 1960s all converged neatly on the same conclusion that /r/ sounds at this time were becoming a new prestige form, and that variations among individual speakers and across the community in New York were indications that a linguistic change was currently in progress. As he characterized the nature of this change and how it was working its way through different groups, Labov stressed an important feature of the change—the evidence available suggested very strongly that speakers were *conscious* of the social value of /r/ pronunciations and that their development of these forms constituted a *conscious change* toward a new statusful pattern of language. Hypercorrection and the increased use of /r/ in careful speech showed that speakers were very much aware of the social value of rhotic speech and were deliberately aiming to adopt this style of pronunciation as a way to claim social status. Other linguistic changes, we will shortly see, may occur below the level of speakers' conscious awareness, as subtle adjustments are made subconsciously by speakers and have a different character and pattern of development. Subsequent investigations of variation and change have benefited considerably from Labov's insight that certain changes may be consciously made by speakers, while others may be subconscious and display a different social orientation. We will return to and expand on this point shortly when we consider another of Labov's well-known studies carried out in rural Massachusetts.

Finally, the fieldwork aspect of much of Labov's early work, including the New York project, led him to the realization that the collection of certain kinds of linguistic data was inherently difficult and needed special strategies. While formal speech was easy to record and document, and could be gathered simply by asking speakers to read passages of text or lists of words, casual, informal speech was much more difficult to capture because of the 'Observer's Paradox'—when people become aware of the presence of an outside observer among them, they frequently alter the way they speak, and if the observer is a well-educated academic researcher, they may tend not to use their most casual forms of speech. Instead, speakers may partially accommodate their speech to the style of the linguists who interview them and produce rather more formal language. In order to try to elicit casual, informal speech from his informants, Labov developed a particularly effective method, and asked his interviewees to talk about any time in the past that they thought they might have lost their life, either due to some natural accident or as the result of the actions of others. Talking about such 'near death' experiences often causes people to become so involved in vivid memories of the past that they forget they are being interviewed and they revert to a much more casual form of speech of the type they would use on a daily basis with close friends and family. Other good opportunities Labov sometimes found for hearing 'real' informal speech were on occasions that an interview in someone's home was interrupted by other family members or there were incoming phone calls. On such occasions the interviewee would often switch to a quite different, more casual style of speech talking to the family member or friend. By such means, Labov was able to gather sufficient amounts of colloquial speech to compare with other, more formal language, and successfully established methods of sociolinguistic research that have been widely adopted up until the present day.

ARBITRARY r

Labov's study of New York /r/ shows that rhotic speech was acquiring new social meaning in New York City in the 1960s. It has since very clearly become the 'prestige' pronunciation of words with a final /r/ in their spelling throughout the USA. However, as noted earlier, rhotic speech was *not* common in the 19th and early 20th centuries in the East and South of the USA, and pronouncing word-final /r/ sounds was looked down on and stigmatized at this time. Speakers who did use /r/ pronunciations were said to sound like people from western parts of the USA and would be unlikely to achieve a high level of social and economic success in the East with such an accent. Rhotic speech in the USA has thus fluctuated in its social value, going from being stigmatized to being desired as a linguistic status symbol. This fluctuation in the valuation of a single sound underlines the arbitrary connection between many properties of language and the social meaning they are given—rhotic speech is not inherently pleasing or displeasing to the ear, but has been assessed in different ways at different times, depending on current fashion. In much of England, the opposite situation to the USA holds at the moment with regard to rhotic speech—the dominant prestige pronunciation is presently /r/-less, and pronouncing word-final /r/ is felt by many to be a sign of unsophisticated, rural speech in the southwest of England, and is avoided by those hoping to be socially successful in other parts of the country.

The arbitrary association of /r/ with social meaning is also highlighted by the way rhotic and non-rhotic speech is now distributed in the South of the USA. Wolfram (2004) notes that /r/-less pronunciations were once the prestige forms in the South, but then this situation changed, and upwardly mobile young speakers started to pronounce their /r/-s, following a general, national re-adoption of rhotic speech as prestigious once again. This has left two quite disparate groups in the South still leaving their /r/ sounds unpronounced: *working-class* speakers in the countryside, whose non-rhotic speech distinguishes them negatively as not belonging to the more affluent middle class, and older members of the *upper classes*, whose retention of /r/ sounds

> distinguishes them positively as belonging to a higher class level than those in the middle classes who have taken up rhotic speech again. Wolfram (2004: 71) comments that these development have united these two groups in their use of non-rhotic speech 'but with quite different meanings associated with the *r*-lessness'—for the one group, it is viewed as a non-prestigious form signaling membership of the working class, for the other it is perceived as a prestige form indicating membership of the most affluent social class. The meaning projected by this quirky sound has thus been pushed around and given all kinds of social interpretations which do not result from its purely linguistic sound properties, but its association with different groups in society, at different points in time.

Martha's Vineyard

A second, important piece of work carried out by William Labov in his early years of sociolinguistic research was a study of ongoing language changes on the scenic New England island of Martha's Vineyard in Massachusetts, published as Labov (1963). When Labov visited Martha's Vineyard in the 1960s, the island had a relatively small fixed population of around 6,000 inhabitants, but because of the beauty of the beaches on its eastern shores in the area known as 'Down-island', large numbers of tourists come to Martha's Vineyard during the summer months, swelling its population hugely, so that at the height of summer, approximately 7 out of every 8 people on the island are visitors on vacation. This summer 'invasion' from the mainland provides much-needed economic support for permanent residents on the island, as there is otherwise little industry on Martha's Vineyard, and fishing and farming have gone into decline. However, many of the older inhabitants of the island are unhappy with the dramatic rise in tourism, as this has resulted in outsiders buying up large amounts of property on Martha's Vineyard, especially in the Down-island area. Away from the beaches and further west on the island there are rural areas which extend into 'Up-island' and the former center of the fishing industry in the region of Chilmark and the port town of Menemsha, where many of the original Vineyarder families still live.

Between 1939 and 1943, the speech patterns of people on Martha's Vineyard were described by linguists as part of the *Linguistic Atlas of New England/LANE* project (Kurath et al. 1939–45). When Labov came to the island thirty years later, he compared the LANE descriptions with the way he heard people speaking, and realized that there were differences in the ways that some inhabitants were pronouncing their vowels, in words such as *white, life, night,* and *house, out,* and *mouse.* Interested in finding our more about this recent change, Labov interviewed a large number of residents from different backgrounds and areas on the island and learned that the new vowel pronunciations were not evenly spread across Martha's Vineyard and its inhabitants. The new sounds were most common among people aged between 30 and 45, and those under the age of 30 did not seem to use them much, which seemed a little odd, as when new patterns of speech evolve, it is often young people who develop these and adopt them early on. Among the older generation, the new vowels were also strongly found among fishermen on the island. In terms of their geographic distribution, the new pronunciations were more frequently heard in the rural areas of Up-island, in particular around Chilmark, and were used much less in the heavily populated beach areas of Down-island where the tourist trade was centered. Finally, Labov ascertained that speakers were largely unaware of differences in the ways that people pronounced the vowel sounds in question—the change was taking place below the level of speakers' consciousness—and there was little variation in the way that each individual spoke—either a person consistently made use of the new vowel sounds, or they didn't use them at all. This was unlike the situation with the growth of rhotic speech in New York City, where speakers made the 'new' /r/ pronunciation only some of the time, and would also produce words without sounding out a word-final /r/.

It seemed to Labov that the ongoing change had probably originated among the older fishermen in the western part of Martha's Vineyard and then had spread to speakers in the 30–45-year-old age group, but had not been taken up by younger or other older people, for some unexplained reason. In fact, much about the change appeared to be puzzling, at first. It was not initially clear where the new vowels had come from to begin with in the fishermen's speech, nor why other people aged between 30–45 would subconsciously copy the way the fishermen had started to speak.

As Labov approached these questions, he became aware of more information that bore on the ongoing change. Interestingly, it turned out that the 'new' pronunciations were actually older ways of pronouncing certain vowel sounds that had been common in New England in preceding centuries but which had subsequently gone out of fashion and had declined during the 20th century, continuing to survive as linguistic 'relics' in the speech of certain isolated, small groups. Labov hypothesized that the Martha's Vineyard fishermen had actually retained these old forms in their speech to some extent, and then 'reactivated' them more vigorously in recent times. But why? And why did others begin to imitate the fishermen's 'new' way of speaking?

The answers to these questions, Labov believed, lay in understanding the economic situation and social dynamic in Martha's Vineyard, as the fortunes of the island had experienced much change in the post-war period. The economy of Martha's Vineyard had taken a significant downturn as the traditional pursuits of fishing and farming were no longer able to sustain families on the island well, and Martha's Vineyard eventually became the poorest county in the state of Massachusetts. The tourist trade then grew significantly and began to provide employment for many in the service industry, but it also brought new challenges for the social identity of residents on the island, which had previously been founded on an older lifestyle and inherited tradition, not the modernism they increasingly saw among visitors from the mainland. As the latter began to take over much of the eastern portions of Martha's Vineyard, displacing local inhabitants, many Vineyarders came to be unhappy with the way that Martha's Vineyard was developing, despite the economic benefits that tourism was bringing to the island. Among those who most objected to the presence of the summer visitors were the older fishermen in Chilmark, who continued to pursue a way of life disconnected from the heavy consumerism of the 1960s, which seemed to govern the behavior of the tourists. Labov observed that others on the island who had similar negative views of the tourist trade held a strong sense of admiration for the Chilmark fishermen, seeing them as symbols of the old Martha's Vineyard which they still identified with and felt loyalty toward. Labov suggested that this caused many Vineyarders to take the fishermen as an important reference point for resistance to the growth of tourism and all its undesired effects on life on the island. Seeing the defiant fisherman as the preservers of indigenous old values, other like-spirited residents started to copy the speech patterns of the fishermen, as a way of proclaiming a genuine Martha's Vineyard identity and their proud feelings of belonging to the island. Use of the special vowel pronunciations therefore marked speakers as connected to Martha's Vineyard and made them sound different from those with accents similar to mainland New England speech and the pronunciations of the tourists.

Labov's interesting interpretation of the spread of the 'new' vowel patterns was given further strong support from investigations of attitudes toward Martha's Vineyard and the summer visitors. People interviewed by Labov were asked about how they felt toward the tourist industry and the changes it had brought to Martha's Vineyard. They were also asked whether they had a positive attachment to the island and were happy to continue living on Martha's Vineyard, or whether they were considering a move elsewhere for educational or professional purposes. The answers to these questions revealed that there was a very high correlation between adoption of the fishermen's vowel sounds and a desire to stay on Martha's Vineyard, as well as strong feelings of disapproval relating to the waves of tourists visiting the island and buying real estate in the Down-island area. Those who had such feelings used the 'new' vowel sounds, and were predominantly in the 30–45 age group, having decided that they wanted to stay on Martha's Vineyard, while younger speakers still uncertain about their future and whether they might leave the island at some future point had not changed the way they spoke, and still used pronunciations like those on the mainland in New England. The linguistic innovation among 30–45-year-olds and the heavy concentration of the distinctive speech patterns in Chilmark and among older fishermen consequently had a very natural explanation, with an ongoing change in speech being made for social reasons as the expression of solidarity and local islander identity.

Labov concluded his Martha's Vineyard study with a summary of the way that change had occurred among the islanders, as noted in the following remarks (somewhat adjusting Labov's original wording and filling in some gaps):

1. A language feature used by a group A is marked by contrast with another standard dialect. In Martha's Vineyard, the vowels used by the fishermen were different from standard American English vowels common at the time.
2. Group A is adopted as a reference group by group B, and the feature is adopted and exaggerated as a sign of social identity in response to pressure from outside forces. In Martha's Vineyard, many in the 30–45-year-old age group began to copy the fishermen's vowels, as the fishermen were seen as positive symbols of a way of life in Martha's Vineyard that was coming under threat.
3. Increased use of the feature leads to its generalization and the establishment of a new norm, adopted by neighboring and succeeding groups for whom group B serves as a reference group. This predicts a continuation of the spread of the 'new' vowel sounds on

Martha's Vineyard, and such a patterning has essentially been reported in a study carried out four decades after Labov's initial survey, Pope et al. (2007) 'Forty Years of Language Change on Martha's Vineyard'.

Commenting on Labov's investigations in both Martha's Vineyard and New York, and comparing the changes which occurred in the two locations, Aitchison (2001) highlights key similarities and differences in the two occurrences of change. First, neither of these changes was a complete innovation, coming fully 'out of the blue'. The rhotic patterns which developed in New York City in the 1960s were forms which had always been made use of somewhere in the USA, and the 'new' vowel sounds adopted by many on Martha's Vineyard in the 30–45-year age group had long been present in the speech of the fishermen on the island. Secondly, both changes occurred when one social group began to pattern its linguistic behavior on that of another group. In New York rhoticism was adopted among lower socio-economic groups when it was taken to be a signal of prestige in upper-middle-class speech, and in Martha's Vineyard, 30–45-year-olds took to copying the speech of the Chilmark fishermen as symbols of islander identity.

There are also two potentially significant differences in the ways that the New York and the Martha's Vineyard changes took place. The evidence available suggests that the change in New York was to a large extent made *consciously*, whereas that in Martha's Vineyard was not. Such a difference may perhaps be a function of how long a change has been underway—new changes just appearing in a language may not be perceived very distinctly, and speakers may only become aware of certain innovations after they have been present and spread for a certain amount of time. A second salient feature of the changes in New York and Martha's Vineyard which is different is the orientation of the change relative to more widespread, standard forms of the language. In New York, the adoption of /r/ pronunciations was a move toward a new socially prestigious form indexing high social status, whereas the Martha's Vineyard change led speakers away from standard pronunciations to the use of non-standard forms. Aitchison notes that there may be a connection between these two properties, and changes which occur above the level of consciousness ('changes from above') may frequently (though certainly not always) move toward wider socially accepted norms and patterns indexing overt prestige, while changes which are made subconsciously ('changes from below') may often move away from standard forms.

Attitudes toward conscious vs. subconscious changes

We have just noted that certain changes in language use may be conscious and known to speakers, whereas other differences in speech may actually go unnoticed and may be subconsciously adopted patterns. When people are aware of variation and change in the speech of others, and this change is *not* toward a socially prestigious form, we find that there is frequently criticism of it as sub-standard or 'sloppy' speech. Two good examples of negative attitudes to such conscious (vs. subconscious) changes can be noted here from Aitchison (2001) for British English, and Zentella (2004) for Latin American Spanish.

In British English, many people pronounce words which end in /t/ with a 'glottal stop' sound when such words occur before another word, for example in sequences such as '*Does i(t) fi(t) well?*', where a glottal stop replaces a /t/ sound which precedes another word beginning with a consonant. People tend not to know they are making this change, and they are also generally unaware that others pronounce /t/ as a glottal stop in similar sequences—it is a subconscious change. However, a growing number of speakers in certain parts of the country (particularly in the London area) also pronounce /t/ as a glottal stop in the middle of words between vowels, for example in *bi(tt)er* and *bu(tt)er*, and before other words beginning with vowels, as in '*Wha(t) a mess!*' and '*a bi(t) of cake*'. This change of /t/ to a glottal stop in other positions comes to be noticed much more by other speakers and often attracts criticism. Ironically, then, speakers who themselves make the /t/-to-glottal stop change *subconsciously* in some environments stigmatize the same adjustment when it is *consciously* heard in other environments. The conscious/subconscious difference is important, and sometimes it is only when a change is consciously perceived that people react to it in negative ways and label is as undesirable, 'sub-standard' speech which speakers should preferably correct.

A similar patterning has been remarked on in Central and South America. Zentella (2004) notes that in Spanish, a written /s/ has a standard pronunciation as an /s/ sound, but when it occurs at the end of a syllable or word, it is also sometimes 'aspirated' and pronounced like an /h/ by speakers from Cuba and Puerto Rico, or simply deleted by speakers from the Dominican Republic. Hence '*estos costeños*' ('those coastal people') may be pronounced as /ehtoh kohteñoh/ or /eto koteño/. Speakers of Spanish from other areas of Latin America frequently criticize this loss of /s/ and /h/ substitution quite harshly. Columbians, in particular, have been noted to call /s/ deletion or substitution with /h/ a sloppy, low-status habit, and argue that words should be pronounced entirely as they are written—if an /s/ occurs in a word, it should be pronounced as an /s/. Such a criticism of word-final /s/ substitution and deletion seems odd and unjustified when coming from Columbians because Columbians themselves also substitute an /h/ sound for /s/ when the latter sound occurs at the *beginning* of a syllable or *between vowels*. This tends to occur in the speech of the central highlands of Columbia, and even highly educated people from this area regularly say /pahamos/ in place of /pasamos/ 'we pass', and /ahesino/ instead of /asesino/ 'assassin'. This shows that certain speakers criticize 'deviations' from spelling pronunciation in other speakers in some instances, but ignore their own similar deviations in other environments. Hence, just as with the use of glottal stops in place of /t/ sounds in British English, when certain speakers of Spanish become *consciously* aware of a non-standard sound change being made (/s/ substitution/deletion in word-final position), this leads to negative attitudes and stigmatization of the change, although, ironically, the same speakers *subconsciously* make an identical change in other parts of their speech (/s/ conversion to /h/ in syllable-initial and intervocalic positions).

Language changes linked to developments in social identity: two further cases

Labov's research in Martha's Vineyard showed how important it may be to consider aspects of the social background of a population where language change is taking place, in order to understand what may be causing variation and change to occur. In understanding differing attitudes toward the summer visitors on Martha's Vineyard and the traditions symbolized by the older fisherman on the island, Labov was able to arrive at a good explanation of the pronunciation changes he observed, and why they were largely restricted to a certain portion of residents on the island. Two other, more recent studies of variation in communities in North America have found similar explanations of changes that are taking place, linking newly adopted ways of speaking with the emphasis of solidarity with a revived local identity in a new socio-economic atmosphere. The first of these, carried out by Sylvie Dubois and Barbara Horvath (2000), looks at the adoption of a broad new style of pronunciation among younger generation members of the Cajun community in Louisiana, and leads us to a more general discussion of the perception of different accents and their social meaning. The second study, by Becky Childs and Gerard Van Herk (2014), focuses on a salient morphosyntactic change in Newfoundland English which has reappropriated a traditional linguistic form as a strong new symbol of belonging to modern Newfoundland society.

Cajun English in Louisiana

Toward the end of the 20th century, Dubois and Horvath (2000) observed that younger members of the Cajun community in Louisiana were changing their speech from standard Southern English to different, non-standard forms, and set out to investigate what kinds of changes were going on, and why they had been occurring. The authors' research shows that the 'new' patterns of speech could be causally linked to a sequence of changing socio-economic conditions which occurred in the state of Louisiana during the 20th century, and changes in attitudes toward the use of language as a symbol of ethnic identity. Previously, French had been the linguistic symbol of belonging to the Louisiana Cajun community, but now in rising generations it has come to be English, spoken in a distinctive way. How has this transition from one symbolic group language to another been triggered and accepted in Cajun society?

For many centuries, Cajuns were monolingual speakers of French, living a traditional way of life in the countryside of Louisiana. From the 1930s onward, this way of life was increasingly affected by new state policies, and in the area of language, English was imposed as the medium of education in schools. Coming to school as monolingual French speakers, young Cajuns' home language influenced the way they learned to speak English and eventually led to the development of a highly distinctive form of Cajun English. Following World War II, Dubois and Horvath (2000: 305) note that an increase in urbanization and industrialization 'destroyed the economic order on which Cajun ethnic identity was built' and caused the Cajun community to collapse. The speaking of both French and Cajun English became stigmatized, and caused language shift into more standard forms of Southern English, and a massive reduction in the transmission of French to new generations, as well as having clear effects on ethnic identity. Young people who grew up in the post-war period were less confident in their Cajun identity and began to assimilate both linguistically and culturally into Anglo society in Louisiana. English came to replace French as the language of the home because French was perceived to be a hindrance to individuals' chances to improve their economic and social status. As English replaced French, it was also spoken with far fewer Cajun English features, as speakers endeavored to blend in more with non-Cajuns in the state.

The 1960s, however, saw important changes toward Cajuns and French in Louisiana, and the beginning of a 'Cajun Renaissance' which has continued strongly to the present. In 1968 state laws were passed to encourage the use of French, and Louisiana declared itself to be officially bilingual, with both English and French recognized as official state languages. French was reintroduced as a mandatory subject in schools and featured more in television. The effect of such changes on ethnic identity was extremely positive. Young Cajuns learned to become proud of belonging to the Cajun community and regularly celebrated traditional forms of Cajun life and culture, including Cajun music and cuisine. Accompanying these developments, the long-important language component of Cajun identity then underwent a major change. In previous, older generations there was a strong belief that it was necessary to speak French as one's primary language in order to be considered Cajun. However, in the years between the decline of the earlier French Cajun community and the revival of Cajun pride from the 1960s onward, knowledge of French had been drastically lost, and could no longer serve (immediately, at least) as a common marker of Cajunness—young people didn't have the skills necessary to use French to communicate with other Cajuns. The widespread loss of French in Louisiana is consequently what triggered changes in young Cajuns' English. Unable to easily acquire French as a linguistic symbol of being Cajun, rising generations in the late 20th century modified the ways they spoke English, and attempted to convert their standard Southern English into the distinctive pronunciations of early Cajun English, which their grandparents had developed by accident and 'error' when first learning English.

The special characteristics of the English spoken by younger Cajuns in Louisiana today, and the changes which these speakers have introduced into their language, can therefore only be well understood and appreciated when the broad socio-historical context in Louisiana is added into the picture. Young speakers have gone back to the use of old forms of language previously widespread in the community as a means of signaling renewed pride in membership of that community, and for practical reasons have changed the linguistic symbol of Cajun identity from one language to another, spoken in a particularly distinctive way. In doing so, they are showing that different forms of language can be utilized as markers of ethnic identity, and, when speakers have insufficient knowledge of their heritage language, they may be able to adapt the language of the local majority as an effective, substitute symbol of group identity.[1]

The ongoing variation and change in contemporary Cajun speech also turns out to be quite similar in nature to the changes reported in Martha's Vineyard. In both cases, a portion of the population has adopted older speech patterns from within the community and changed their speech from standard regional American forms to vernacular patterns commonly used in earlier times by a particular group with strong, local traditions. Research has shown that this kind of change actually occurs quite frequently when ethnic pride is reasserted among minority groups and local communities. However, linguistically there are certain differences in the ways that older forms of language are recycled by new generations of speakers, as we will soon see in a study of recent language change taking place in eastern

---

1. Similar observations have been made about the use of Scottish and Irish English as markers of national identity in Scotland and Ireland, as knowledge of Gaelic and Irish has been lost.

Canada which involves morphology rather than distinctive pronunciations and specially accented forms of English. First, though, we are going to dwell a little further on the topic of accent, which is so often an important marker of group identity and autonomy.

What's in an accent?

The studies of variation in New York City, Martha's Vineyard, and Louisiana have all emphasized the fact that the way a person sounds in his/her speech is very important and that attempts to project a certain identity can lead to changes in pronunciation. We have also seen that the social meaning of sounds may fluctuate quite regularly. For example, rhotic speech was initially prestigious in Britain and America, then stigmatized in much of both countries, but later re-adopted as an educated, high-status form of pronunciation in the USA, and in Martha's Vineyard a pair of older vowel sounds which were originally very common came to be viewed negatively and were abandoned for much time, but more recently were taken up again as markers of covert prestige. This raises the question of whether any sounds or accents are perceived to be more attractive and pleasing to the ear in virtue of their inherent sound qualities, or whether attitudes toward different pronunciations are conditioned purely by social facts rather than objective linguistic properties. Such issues were neatly investigated in an experiment carried out in the 1970s by Howard Giles and Peter Trudgill[2] which tested people's reactions to different regional accents of English in the UK. The experiment was able to show, very convincingly, that people's 'aesthetic' evaluations of accents are indeed socially conditioned and are not made simply on the basis of the sounds that are heard in different accents.

The Giles and Trudgill experiment consisted in two parts, each involving different participants. In the first part, people from Great Britain were asked to listen to recordings of ten different accents from around the UK and to rate the speakers on a number of properties, including whether their speech sounded pleasant and attractive or not. The listeners were also asked to guess where in the UK the speakers came from.

Nearly all the listeners involved in the experiment correctly recognized the accents they heard and which part of the country the various speakers were from. There was also a high level of agreement in the listeners' evaluations of the qualities of the ten accents. The ordering of the accents given for the quality of most pleasant to least pleasant is represented as follows (most pleasant highest):

1. 'BBC' accent
2. Welsh accent
3. Yorkshire accent
4. Irish accent
5. Geordie accent
6. West Country accent

---

2. Published as 'Sociolinguistics and linguistic value judgments' in Peter Trudgill's (1983) volume *On Dialect*, Oxford: Basil Blackwell.

7. Glasgow accent
8. Liverpool accent
9. Birmingham accent
10. London (Cockney) accent

Given that there was clear agreement on which accents sound more attractive, it might be concluded that some forms of English are in fact *inherently* nicer to listen to than others. However, the investigators Giles and Trudgill argued that this is not the case and suggested that there may well be social reasons for the rankings produced by the first part of the experiment. They point out that the accents at the bottom of the ranking in positions 7–10 have in common that they are all from large urban areas, while those placed higher in the ranking, in positions 2–6, are rural accents. At the top of the list is a non-regional accent, the well-known BBC accent used extensively in television and radio at the time. Giles and Trudgill suggest that the preference for rural accents over urban accents comes from the mental associations people have for these varieties. British people may dislike urban accents because they think of the negative properties of cities when they hear such accents—dirtiness, heavy industry, work, and the prevalence of crime. Rural accents, by way of contrast, have quite different positive connotations and are associated with clean air, nature, vacations, and an older, simpler lifestyle free of modern worries, and this may lead to these accents being rated as more pleasant than those from urban areas. Finally, it is proposed that the BBC accent is ranked highest for a different reason, due to having an association with higher levels of education, social status and personal power.

The second part of Giles and Trudgill's investigation added good support for their hypothesis about British speakers' social assessment of the ten UK accents. In the continuation of their project, Giles and Trudgill played the same tapes of the ten different accents to listeners from outside the UK, people who would be able to understand the English they heard, but who would be unlikely to recognize which part of Britain the accents actually came from. Giles and Trudgill's idea was that if listeners could *not* identify where the accents were from, they would not be confused by rural/urban-type associations and would judge the attractiveness of the accents on purely linguistic grounds. This would then show whether some accents really were inherently more pleasant than others. The recordings were played to groups of native speakers of English in Canada and the USA, and, when questioned, it was clear that the listeners did not know where the speakers they heard came from—for example, the Scottish speaker was in several instances misidentified as being Mexican, and the Welsh speaker was thought to be from Norway.

There were two common exceptions to the misidentification of the accents—the North American listeners did all correctly identify the BBC accent and the London accent. This resulted in the BBC accent being placed first in their ranking of the accents, just as the British listeners had placed it first. Giles and Trudgill suggest that the BBC accent is so well-known that North American listeners placed the BBC accent first for the same reasons that the British speakers did—its associations with prestige and power. Concerning the London accent, which was also correctly identified, surprisingly the North American speakers placed this *second* in the ranking, not tenth as British speakers had done. Giles and Trudgill suggest this is because a London accent does not have the same associations for North American speakers as for British people—for North Americans, London may be associated with the thought of spending a pleasant vacation in an interesting, historical, and vibrant city.

Concerning the rest of the accents, there was no agreement at all among the North American listeners as to which were more attractive, and they were all ranked in an unpredictable, chaotic way. Consequently, there was no correspondence with the ranking provided by the British listeners. This indicates very clearly that the ten accents were *not* judged and ranked for objective, inherent linguistic reasons by the British listeners, or this should have produced a similar ranking with the North American participants. Rather, the common ranking of the ten accents by British listeners can be concluded to have been made for *social* reasons connected with the places associated with each accent, and assumptions held by listeners about people living in these places. When we maintain positive ideas about a particular geographical location and its inhabitants, it seems that we may also perceive accents from such a place to be pleasant to the ear, and when we hold negative opinions about a place and people connected to it, interestingly we may find the way people talk in such a location to be unattractive as well. Such conclusions have been borne out by other studies carried out since the 1970s, and it has also been shown that people are willing to attribute a broad range of personal characteristics to speakers heard on tape recordings based entirely on their accent (for example, whether a speaker might be assumed to be honest, friendly, educated, etc.—see Preston 2004 for attitudes expressed about different accents of American English). Accents and the sounds of our speech are at times very important, but they gain their value not from any intrinsic linguistic properties, but from the social meanings variously given to them as they are used by speakers in different situations of life.[3]

Newfoundland non-standard –*s*

Social identity is often signaled by a person's pronunciation of words in distinctive ways, but it can also be communicated by special patterns of grammar and morphology, and even relatively small deviations from standard forms of grammar can become strong markers of group identity if the relative patterning is sufficiently salient to other speakers. One such identity marker has emerged in recent times in Newfoundland, Canada, with the addition of a non-standard –*s* inflection on verbs with a first person subject, as in '*I loves it*', researched by Childs and Van Herk (2014). Making use of Childs and Van Herk's study, we will see how this salient pattern has come out of the linguistic background present in Newfoundland and find that young speakers are taking a form with very old roots and using it in new ways, changing some of its linguistic properties for complex reasons of identity.

---

3. And because there are no necessary connections between the quality of sounds and their aesthetic perception by listeners, the social attributes of sounds and accents can naturally shift around, and the same sound may be valued differently at different times.

The use of a non-standard –s inflection has been a characteristic of the English spoken in Newfoundland for much time, and used to be particularly common in sentences referring to habitual activities/habits, as in the following example:

I *always goes up to M's cabin on the weekends.* (Childs and Van Herk 2014: 635)

In the second half of the 20th century, use of this patterning went into sharp decline, especially in towns and cities, and was only retained strongly in rural areas. However, the 21st century has seen a new growth in the use of non-standard –s among the younger generation and it is once again being heard regularly in urban areas. What has caused this change of a feature that seemed to be disappearing from urban speech?

Childs and Van Herk see the resurgence in non-standard –s as being closely connected with an increase in local pride and a renaissance of traditional culture and music which celebrates the special character of Newfoundland and its inhabitants. This may make the linguistic change in Newfoundland appear similar to those we have already seen occurring in the Cajun community in Louisiana and among the permanent residents of Martha's Vineyard. In both of these situations, we found that a portion of the population is modeling its language on patterns used by another group which symbolizes past traditions (the fishermen in Martha's Vineyard and older generation members of the Cajun community), and this is caused by renewed identification with local ways of life and ethnic culture. Is this also what is happening in Newfoundland, as younger people in the cities are adopting patterns from speakers in the countryside as part of the local, cultural renaissance? Not exactly. Childs and Van Herk show that there is a quite special 'flavor' to the way that the Newfoundland change is occurring, as the result of three important properties associated with non-standard –s more broadly within Canada.

First, the use of non-standard –s is a patterning which is very striking and salient—everyone who hears it is very aware of its occurrence, unlike the use of special older vowels in Martha's Vineyard, which are not noticed so obviously by other listeners. Second, non-standard –s is felt to be very 'Newfoundlandy' and a stereotypical property of traditional Newfoundland English. Given the regrowth of local pride among the rising generation, these two properties might seem to make non-standard –s an ideal pattern to adopt to emphasize support for Newfoundland's culture and traditions and membership of a collective Newfoundland identity. However, the potentially positive attributes of Newfoundland –s are perceived to be counter-balanced by a third, more negative property which complicates its simple adoption by young city-dwellers. Non-standard –s, along with other distinctive features of Newfoundland English, has been stigmatized and viewed in a negative way by people from other parts of Canada because such forms have long been associated with rurality, the speech of old-fashioned farmers, and a general lack of education—not the image sought by young people pursuing a modern, sophisticated, city life. So, what might young, aspiring, urban Newfoundlanders do in such a situation, and how might they be able to 'buy the positive social capital of local-ness without the negative capital of appearing uneducated' (Childs and Van Herk 2014: 649)?

The 'solution' which has emerged in this situation is that younger speakers in towns and cities have incorporated non-standard *–s* in their speech in novel ways that distinguish them from those in rural areas. In the words of Childs and Van Herk, rather than just being 'recycled' along with its old linguistic patterns, traditional Newfoundland *–s* has been neatly 'upcycled' and made into something new in feeling through changes to the way non-standard *–s* has come to be used by members of the younger generation. The typical patterns of use among rural speakers of Newfoundland English has been to favor non-standard *–s* on verbs which refer to habitual actions, as already noted, and to avoid the use of *–s* on 'stative' verbs such as *know, love,* and *think* (verbs referring to a state of mind). Young urban speakers, by way of contrast, have simply adopted an opposite pattern of use and distinguish themselves from those in rural areas by regularly applying non-standard *–s* to stative verbs and avoiding its use with references to habits.

In fact, for many young speakers, 'New *–s*' is deliberately restricted in its use to just a small group of stative verbs: *loves, hates, knows, thinks, wants, needs, remembers, forgets,* and *hopes,* and is often found only with a subject that is first person singular, either with or without an overt pronoun. Hence, in addition to forms such as '*I loves it*', young speakers also produce simply '*Loves it*' and even just bare '*Loves*', as in '*Taking pictures of me too. Loves*' (Childs and Van Herk 2014: 647).

In creating a distinctive new form out of older non-standard *–s*, young urban Newfoundlanders have refashioned this well-known marker of local identity in a way that manages to avoid the stigmatized image previously associated with it. In place of mimicking the use of *–s* among rural speakers and inheriting the negative associations linked to 'Old *–s*', the use of *–s* in certain linguistic contexts but not others sends a signal to listeners that speakers are choosing to sound local in their own special, new way. New *–s* is now cool and fashionable among the young, a trendy marker of urban 'hipster chic' rather than rural tradition, yet at the same time, it is also critically, quite distinctly a symbol of being from Newfoundland and being very proud of this—a local identity updated and enhanced with innovation.[4]

RECYCLING NON-STANDARD *–s* IN LITERATURE, CINEMA, AND TV

The use of highly salient non-standard forms such as the addition of *–s* to verbs with first person subjects can result in a person's speech sounding very distinctive, and this property of non-standard *–s* (which has occurred in a number of regional forms of English) was taken advantage of by the writer J. R. R. Tolkien when he created a pattern

---

4. Interestingly, non-standard *–s* has also been re-adopted as a special form of speech by young people in certain parts of England. Cheshire (1982) reports that teenagers in the town of Reading (and other parts of the south of England) often use a non-standard *–s* inflection on verbs which do not have third person subjects, resulting in forms such as '*You knows my sister, the one who's small.*' Cheshire also notices that non-standard *–s* is particularly common on verbs which are local slang forms, such as '*bunk (it)*' 'to play truant/hooky' and '*leg (it)*' 'to run', as in '*Then we all bunks it down to Soho*' and '*So, after that, I legs it up to Blagdon Hill.*' Just as in Newfoundland, this non-standard *–s* form seems to be 'lexically restricted' and favors use with a special set of 'carrier' verbs.

of highly stylized speech for his creature Gollum in the *Lord of the Rings* trilogy of novels. Talking to himself in bouts of schizophrenia, Gollum produces very special-sounding words and sentences which enhance the description of his bizarre character and its visual depiction in later cinematic adaptions of the *Lord of the Rings* series. Referring to the powerful ring ('the precious') which Gollum wants to repossess from the three Hobbits he has come across, he cries: '*We wants it, we needs it. Must have the precious. They stole it from us. Sneaky little Hobbitses. Wicked, tricksy, false!*'

Following the great success of the *Lord of the Rings* movies released in 2001–2003, the creators of the popular US television show *South Park* then produced a parody version of *Lord of the Rings*, entitled '*The Return of the Fellowship of the Ring to the Twin Towers*'. The central character in this episode, 'Butters', becomes obsessed about the possession of a particular DVD movie in the same way that Gollum was obsessed about the ring he found, and when Butters finally manages to get his hands on the DVD, he triumphantly says: '*We hasses it!*' producing a hyper-corrected form of the non-standard –*s* pattern—hyper-corrected because speakers who use non-standard –*s* normally do not add it to a verb form which already ends in –*s* such as 'has'. This makes *hasses* stand out even more than 'regular' non-standard –*s* and is a good example of the writing creativity often found in the *South Park* series and the general use of non-standard speech to enhance characterization in works of fiction.

Midway summary of ideas about the spread of linguistic changes

The following summarizes some of the conclusions arising from the studies considered so far.

1. Changes are very often not full and complete innovations but frequently borrow and adapt patterns that have been established in a language in the past and simply have gone out of use or have become restricted to a small part of the population.
2. Changes often occur when certain speakers begin to admire other members of the population for their status in society, their general personal characteristics, or the way they positively symbolize a regional or ethnic identity. This leads the first group of speakers to mimic aspects of the speech of the second group as a way to claim positive social values associated with the latter.
3. Changes may be initiated consciously or occur subconsciously. Where changes are made consciously, individuals' language patterns may fluctuate and show variation between old and new forms as speakers target the use of a new pattern or style of speech, but often revert to their older patterns through ingrained habit. When changes occur below the level of speakers' conscious awareness, much less variation between old and new forms is noticeable.
4. Changes are frequently made toward patterns which have overt prestige and are becoming new standard forms of language among the educated middle and upper classes,

or have covert prestige and introduce non-standard forms valued for solidarity and membership of a particular social or ethnic group or local community.
5. Changes in peoples' speech may either come from a simple, direct copying of forms existing among other speakers, or involve the agentive re-development of other speakers' patterns, converting these into distinctive new forms (as seen with Newfoundland –s).

In the remaining portion of the chapter, we will look at further interesting cases of recent variation and change which have either attracted much attention from the general public, or have been uncovered by careful research carried out by linguists. Each case adds something more to our general understanding of ongoing variation and change and illustrates how new ways of speaking connect with the expression of personal and group identity. We will also see that certain striking new uses of language have attracted considerable criticism from other speakers, for reasons which turn out to have no solid linguistic foundation. This suggests that there is a general inherent resistance to change among much of the population, as it represents a challenging departure from accepted norms of behavior in society.

A mindless linguistic virus? The modern proliferation of *like*

If you ask almost any middle-aged or older person in the USA which new language form in English they are bothered by, it is highly probable that the answer will be the frequent use of *like* by certain younger speakers, as for example in:

> I'm like, 'That's so unfair, because I've told you like a dozen times, and it seems you just wanna, like, ruin my chances to see her.'

Such patterns trigger negative reactions from many older speakers who complain that the repeated insertion of *like* in a person's speech feels like 'verbal litter', *like* being used in a way that seems to be devoid of meaning and to fulfill no linguistic function, making no obvious contribution to the sentences the word is added to, sometimes multiple times. Schourup (1985) says that *like* is 'often considered symptomatic of careless or meaningless speech',[5] while Blyth et al. (1990) found the use of '*be like*' made speakers sound 'vacuous', 'silly', and 'air-headed' to non-users of this expression.

So, is *like* really meaningless, functionless, and a type of word not used by other more sensible speakers? Linguists who have studied the use of *like* by younger speakers have actually concluded the opposite and found that *like* is used with clear systematicity and is neither random nor mindless. Rather, its use is often predictable, is constrained by clear linguistic principles, and serves a range of functions in conversations. 'Ubiquitous' *like* is therefore a complex new linguistic item with a useful versatility which needs careful study in order to be fully understood (Underhill 1988; Tagliamonte and D'Arcy 2004; Buchstaller 2006). Research into *like* has generally divided its use into two primary patterns: (a) the use of *be like* as a new

---

5. Quoted in Dailey-O'Cain (2000: 63).

quotative marker introducing reported speech and thought, and (b) 'bare', non-quotative *like* as a discourse particle, hedge, and sometime focus marker. We will begin by examining the multi-functionality of bare *like* and then turn to the more straightforward quotative use of *be like* and the way it has spread to different English-speaking communities.

Underhill (1988: 238) suggests that bare *like* functions with great reliability as a marker of new information and 'focus', characterizing the latter term as 'the most significant new information in a sentence—often, the point of the sentence', and adding that a word or expression that is in focus usually appears at or near the end of the sentence. Many instances of bare *like* insertion can indeed be naturally attributed to the use of *like* as a focus-marker, as illustrated in the following examples, where the focus of the sentence immediately follows *like* and is naturally pronounced with increased stress. With this focus-signaling use of *like*, there is typically no pause between *like* and the important new information it introduces.

> *And all of a sudden, I see like a* HUGE GUY *with an* AXE!
> *The earthquake this morning was like* REALLY *scary.*
> *That is like* SO *not happening!* (Underhill 1988)

> *For forty cents more, you get like* ALL KINDS *of food.* (Underhill 1988)
> *Well, it's not like* WONDERFUL, *but it's okay.* (Dailey-O'Cain 2000)
> *They drunk like a* WHOLE BOTTLE OF VODKA *in thirty minutes.*

The important connection *like* has with focus in these cases becomes very clear if one attempts to shift the focus of a sentence to a different position, away from *like*. This can be done using the focusing particle '*even*', which attracts focus to the words which immediately follow it. Because sentences typically only have one focus, if this is forced away from *like* by using *even* (or some other heavily stressed item), we expect that it will be odd to include *like* in the sentence—*like* will no longer be able to carry out its function of signaling the focus to its immediate right. Such an expectation is borne out and we find that the following sentences all sound odd when *like* is included, but are fine if it is removed.

> ?*Even* JOHN *like did it.*
> ?*Even* SUE *has like bought one.*
> ?NO WAY *am I like going to go.*

One major use of bare *like* is therefore quite clear—it functions as a particle introducing the focus of a sentence and is not random and meaningless in its presence. Focus-introducing particles are quite common in the world's languages, and so the development of *like* into such a role is not unusual or unprincipled, just not well understood by critics of its occurrence.

A second, observed frequent use of bare *like* is in conjunction with numerals, as illustrated in the following:

> *It's like seven or eight at night and we're all freezing.* (Underhill 1988)
> *It's like a five-six hour climb to the top.*

Underhill (1988) suggests that *like* in such instances means something like 'approximately' and introduces an inexact numeral specification—'roughly five or six hours'. This may well be true for certain co-occurrences of *like* with numerals, but in other instances the numerals combined with *like* can reference a very exact amount, hence not mean 'approximately', as seen in the following two examples.

> *Dan's got like* THREE *Maseratis.*
> *The Russian gymnast got like a 9.5 on the floor routine.*

Such cases sound particularly natural if the number refers to an amount or a score that is somehow impressive and the numeral is stressed. They are therefore most probably best treated as instances of focus particle *like* which coincidentally involve numerals.

A third application of bare *like* is as a 'hedge' politeness marker, used to make requests or suggestions to others sound softer and less of an imposition, as in:

> *Could I like borrow your sweater?* (Underhill 1988)
> *I just think we should like tell her, so she knows what's going on.*

In this function, *like* follows in the tradition of many other languages which have developed special lexical items for use in requests and suggestions to soften their imposing force, for example Korean *chom*, Japanese *chotto*, and Thai *noi* (all literally meaning 'a little' but used to decrease the directness of commands and other 'face threatening acts'[6]).

Finally, the fourth use of *like* is as a marker of hesitation when sentences are not fully well-planned. *Like* is used to fills gaps and pauses as speakers consider what to say next, and in this role *like* functions as a younger generation version of older generations' *um* and *er*. Hesitation marker *like*, similar to *um* and *er*, is often followed by a pause, unlike focus-marker *like,* or the use of *like* to introduce approximate numerals and as a softener in requests:

> *So, then I'm gonna like . . . finish this up and leave.*
> *Lee's probably like . . . already gone, I expect.*

Schourup (1985) makes the observation that '*like* . . . occurs with the greatest frequency in positions of great lexical indecision'[7], where a speaker is not sure what his/her next words should be. Because of this property, 'hesitation *like*' will sound odd in positions where speakers are unlikely to pause in their speech, for example when the next words in a sentence can be easily predicted as parts of idioms and other frequent multi-word expressions. The following examples from Siegel (2002) all illustrate this—hesitation *like* sounds very unnatural between the parts of commonly used expressions:

---

6. See chapter 10, footnote 10, for reference to the notion of 'face'.
7. Quoted in Siegel (2002).

?They were always keeping, like . . . , tabs on me.
?I can't, like, . . . stand him.
?Tony is looking the number, like . . . , up.

Siegel (2002) has also shown experimentally that young speakers often produce hesitation *like* when they are temporarily not sure how to continue unplanned sentences, just as older speakers use *um* and *er*. Siegel had high school students talk about a difficult topic, which would be likely to cause hesitations in their speech. The students were asked the question: 'What is an individual?', and typically started off hesitatingly in the following kind of way:

'Someone that doesn't . . . I don't know. It's like . . .'

The study demonstrated that more planning time results in less use of hesitation *like*, and that both male and female high school students use *like* more when they are not given enough time to plan their sentences well before they begin to speak.

Bare *like* is therefore a complex, multi-functional innovation among younger speakers and is used in at least four different ways, each associated with linguistic constraints: (a) focus *like*, (b) approximate numeral *like*, (c) softener *like*, and (d) hesitation *like*. Far from being mindless 'verbal litter', younger generation *like* is the creative adaptation of a highly versatile element which can now be used for a variety of purposes to structure sentences and highlight information in different ways, all of which can be described and analyzed and are found to correspond with longer-established functional words in other languages as well as English. Instead of being vilified as a random aberration, new *like* should perhaps be celebrated for the many inventive ways it can now contribute to contemporary colloquial speech.

What, then, about the new quotative form *be like*, which has also become very widespread among younger speakers in the USA, Canada, Britain, and other L1 English-speaking populations? *Be like* is simpler in its linguistic function than its relative, bare *like*, and therefore much less needs to be said about how it is used by speakers. *Be like* introduces instances of reported speech, 'quoting' what was originally said, as illustrated in the following exchange from Dailey-O'Cain (2000), where each occurrence of *be like* could simply be replaced with *said*:

She's sitting there and she's like, 'Oh my god!'
She's like, 'That's your boyfriend?'
And I'm like, 'Yeah.'
She's like, 'Oh, he was a cool one at Lawrence.'

In this use as a new quotative expression, *be like* offers an alternative to the verb *say*, and is one of several new expressions which have developed this function, '*go*' and '*be all*' being two further adaptions of a similar type:

> *So then Chris goes: 'No way, man, I'm not doing that!'*
> *And Bob's all: 'Yeah, dude, you gotta do it, seriously!'*

Unlike '*go*' and '*be all*', *be like* can also be used to report thoughts that the speaker has had but not actually spoken out loud, just directed to him/herself—instances of 'first person internal dialogue':

> *And that really worried me. I was like: 'Whoah, get yourself out of here, man, its dangerous.'*

Despite the fact that the function of *be like* is quite transparent and is easy to understand, speakers who do not use *be like* often voice objections to its occurrence in younger people's speech and also have negative opinions about speakers who produce *be like* in place of standard quotative verbs such as *say* and *reply* (or *thought* for internal dialogue). In the USA, we have already noted that *be like* users were branded as sounding 'vacuous', 'silly', and 'air-headed' when *be like* originally began to become popular (Blyth et al. 1990). Negative attitudes to *be like* have continued to be strong in the USA, and are well reported in a number of pieces of research, such as Dailey-O'Cain (2000). As it cannot be objected that *be like* is meaningless or without any obvious linguistic function, one might wonder why older speakers have consistently reacted negatively to its use in the USA. Such attitudes may appear to show that older speakers are simply opposed to any striking changes in speech introduced by the younger generation. If so, such a stance would seem to be unfair, as innovations are also made by older speakers and these are not regularly censured in such a way. For example, Eckert (2004: 366) provides the following patterns as instances of innovations made by adult speakers which seem to go unnoticed and do not attract criticism.

(a) Insertion of 'okay' with rising intonation to highlight parts of a discourse and guide the listener to the important points. This pattern does not seem to be used by teenagers.

'We need to make a presentation, okay(?), and that will make it absolutely clear, okay(?), that we're the only people who can do this kind of work.'

(b) Increased use of nouns in a new way as verbs:

   to 'impact' the market
   to 'access' a web-site
   to 'team' on some project

(c) Use of empty phrasings:

   'What we have here is a situation where . . . the market is unpredictable.'
   'What it is is that the market is unpredictable.'

Eckert notes that the phrases in (c) don't seem to have any real meaning and are just used to allow the speaker to keep hold of the conversation while working out what he/she wants to say. In this sense they are like extended versions of the hesitation marker 'uuhh' and no more meaningful than 'like'. However, because they come from the mouths of older speakers, they attract much less negative attention than younger generation 'like' or 'be like'. With regard to the use of nouns as verbs, as in (b) in the preceding, Eckert has the following to say:

> I am willing to bet that if it were adolescents introducing these forms, we would see a considerable negative public reaction, with claims that adolescents were unwilling to go to the trouble of using the longer forms *have an impact on*, *gain access to*, *work as a team*. Eckert (2004: 366)

The new use of 'okay' similarly seems to go under the radar as a change, Eckert, argues, because it is used by business people as a way of asserting their authority.

Concerning *be like*, the level of negative reaction to this form found among adult speakers in the USA seems to be heightened by the associations it has with a certain group of younger generation speakers, who are assumed to be responsible for the creation of *be like* and behind its spread in the USA—'valley girls' in southern California. Because such young women are perceived to be frivolous in their behavior by more conservative members of older generations, distinctive new patterns of speech originating from this group have regularly attracted criticism. The stigmatization of forms such as *be like* has then stuck with these patterns as they have spread further among younger generation speakers elsewhere in the USA, and the latter are held to be 'guilty by association' with the language of girls from the San Fernando Valley. Not only is *be like* a frequent, salient, new phrase created by members of the younger generation, its originators have a negative image in conservative society, and so the widespread use of *be like* comes across as a major affront to older users of standard English.

The importance of *be like*'s association with 'valley girl' speech for its vilification in the USA has been neatly shown in an investigation of attitudes towards *be like* among speakers of British English. Quotative *be like* is now used significantly in the UK, mostly by younger speakers, as in the USA, but when Isabelle Buchstaller (2006) examined people's attitudes toward this new form, she found that the great majority of people in Britain had no idea where the expression had originated from and did not associate it with any specific group or country. Interestingly, the attitudes held toward *be like* were also discovered to be different from those in the USA, and were frequently more positive, with speakers using *be like* being characterized as 'lively', 'cool', and 'carefree'.

This finding emphasizes two important points. First, when new forms of speech spread from one population to another, they may be adopted as linguistic innovations without simultaneous adoption of any negative attitudes that exist toward such forms in the community of origin. In the UK, *be like* has been borrowed from speakers in the USA without the set of negative attitudes linked to this expression in the USA. *Be like* seems to have been borrowed simply for its novelty value, and not any symbolic associations, showing that new attitudes can be established toward items appropriated from other populations. In this sense, the adoption of *be like* in Britain significantly seems to be almost the opposite of changes seen in Martha's Vineyard and New York City, where 'new' forms were adopted precisely for the social symbolic value associated with these forms (higher social status with New York /r/, and a shared islander identity with the Martha's Vineyard vowels).

Second, Buchstaller's study confirms the assumption that negative reactions to *be like* in the USA must be attributed in large part to *be like*'s association with its assumed 'valley girl' creators, not any inherent linguistic properties—otherwise one would expect these properties to result in the same kind of negative attitudes wherever *be like* were to be taken up, for example in the UK, yet the perception of *be like* is clearly different there. Just as in Giles and Trudgill's study of the perception of British accents of English in the USA and the UK, we find that attitudes toward language variation are often closely linked to attitudes to the speakers who make use of different forms, and not the actual linguistic items used by speakers.[8]

Changing the meaning of old words and developing new words

One very common process of language change involve shifts in the meaning of words over time, as successive generations of speakers make use of words in different ways. This can result in the original meaning of a word being significantly changed, or even completely lost, as people extend the initial, literal meanings of words in other creative ways. When this kind of change happens swiftly, and younger generation speakers are perceived to use words in ways which differ from those in older generations, this can often trigger criticism from the latter, and claims that innovations in meaning are 'illogical' and contributing to the decline of language standards. What is ironic is that each generation seems to repeat this pattern of behavior and to uncritically accept instances of meaning change that have occurred in the past, but react negatively to new changes that are occurring, especially when initiated by those who are younger.

A simple illustration of this process can be given with a comparison of the development of the adverbs *hopefully* and *literally* in English. Up until the 1960s, it was still common to hear some people complain about the new ways in which speakers were using 'hopefully' which departed from its established meaning and use as a word meaning 'full of hope'. A sentence such as '*John arrived hopefully*' originally could only mean that '*John arrived full of hope*', and it can indeed still have this meaning. However, 'hopefully' also came to be used in a second way, frequently positioned at the beginning of sentences, as in '*Hopefully, John has arrived*', and here the meaning of 'hopefully' is '*I hope that . . .*' or '*We should hope that . . .*'. The sentence '*Hopefully, John has arrived*' is therefore commonly used to mean '*I hope that John has arrived*'. This shift in the meaning of 'hopefully' struck many language purists as 'wrong' in the past, and they objected that sentences of the type '*Hopefully, John has arrived*' should only be used to mean '*John has arrived full of hope*'. If we fast forward to the present, it is unlikely that any older generation members will now object to the new use of 'hopefully' and this has become very widely accepted and is used by all speakers nowadays. However, a

---

8. Hence, when North American speakers evaluated British accents but did not know where their speakers came from, they gave random value judgements of the accents they heard, whereas British listeners who knew which part of the UK each accent belonged to were consistent in their assessment of the speakers' voices—knowledge of the population using a particular form of language affects how speakers react to such a patterning.

new target of a similar type has now loomed into sight, in the form of '*literally*', and shifts in the use of this adverb are currently attracting many negative comments from older generation speakers (the same people who changed 'hopefully' when they were younger and were criticized by their seniors).

McWhorter (2016) notes that 'literally' originally meant 'by the letter' and would be used with this meaning in sentences where some act of written communication was involved, for example:

He followed the instructions literally.
He meant it literally.

In recent generations, the use of 'literally' has changed quite considerably and has been extended to describe situations in which no writing is involved.[9] 'Literally' is now used very frequently in a metaphorical way to express simple vividness and exaggerated emphasis in the description of a situation, as in:

We were all literally dying of boredom, but he just wouldn't stop talking.
When I told him that, he literally exploded with anger.

In such common uses, 'literally' no longer communicates 'in actuality, by the letter' and in fact means 'figuratively'—the opposite of the original 'true' meaning of 'literally'. In examples like those given in the preceding, the subject of the verb is not in fact 'dying' or 'exploding', and 'to die of boredom' and 'explode with anger' are metaphors which do not allow any literal meaning, yet we often do find such expressions combined with 'literally' in modern, colloquial speech. Such a somersault in meaning has enraged many older speakers who claim that it violates the inherent semantics of 'literally' and so is blatantly incorrect, ungrammatical, and a sign of low intelligence among people who use 'literally' in such a way. The meanings of words should not permit reverses of this contradictory kind, where they come to signify the opposite of their original 'true' meaning.

Given the patterning that has been observed across generations, however, it is likely that 'literally' will come to be widely accepted in its new figurative use as time goes on, and the apparent logical conflict between its meaning as 'exactly, in reality' and 'metaphorically' will no longer cause excitement and indignation among speakers, as people accept this quirk of meaning over time and come to focus on other outrageous changes that may be beginning to ruin the language. In fact, there are many cases in the past where words seem to have developed contradictory meanings, and these have all gradually been accepted and now are used without any objections from speakers, as seen in the following examples of 'contronyms':[10]

---

9. Metaphorical uses of 'literally' have, in fact, been noted since the 19th century, but their frequent use is a much more modern phenomenon in English.

10. For more examples of potential contronyms in English, see the set of 75 words listed at: https://www.dailywritingtips.com/75-contronyms-words-with-contradictory-meanings/

sanction: (a) 'a penalty for disobeying a law' (b) 'official approval for an action'

transparent: (a) 'invisible/see through' (b) 'obvious'

seed (something): (a) 'remove seeds from something' (b) 'to add seeds to a place, a field etc'

lease a property: (a) offer a property for rent (b) obtain the rental of a property

custom: (a) a common practice (b) uncommon, special ('a custom car')

hold up: (a) to support someone (b) to impede someone

fast: (a) moving at a speedy rate (b) not moving anywhere, stuck ('hold fast')

The generalization is, therefore, that words regularly seem to shift about in the meanings they are given by speakers at different times, and semantic change appears to be both a natural and unstoppable process in language, despite the attempts of critics to reverse it. In many cases, semantic change increases the possible use of words by broadening their meaning, and so adds to speakers' expressive power in useful and often interesting ways. Such innovations are welcomed by a majority of speakers as they represent an expansion of the options available to people in their speech, and often allow us to describe situations and events in a wider range of ways.

While contronyms and words like 'hopefully' are semantically ambiguous and retain their original meanings as possibilities while developing new uses, in other cases of lexical development we find that a word loses its original, literal meaning when occurring in a new linguistic context, though the word may still be used with the original meaning in other contexts. A colorful example of such an innovation which is currently working its way into colloquial English in the USA is the combination of 'ass' with an adjective in positions preceding nouns, for example 'a bad-ass squirrel', 'a big-ass gun', 'a crazy-ass preacher', 'a lame-ass excuse'. In this new patterning, the word 'ass' no longer retains its original slang meaning 'posterior' and is becoming a new suffix added to adjectives which serves to intensify the meaning of the adjective. Hence a 'big-ass gun' makes no reference to any person's backside but indicates that the firearm in question is impressively large. In fact, McWhorter (2016) argues that the new adjectival suffix *-ass* does not just mean 'very' but also adds in an extra component of meaning '*surprisingly*', hence a 'big-ass pot' is used to refer to a pot that is not just very big but one whose large size is unexpected, and 'Sally married some broke-ass lawyer' would be appropriate in a situation when speakers typically expect lawyers to be affluent but the particular lawyer being referred to is surprisingly poor (i.e., broke). The technical term for a word used in such a way is that it helps communicates a 'counter-expectational' meaning—something runs against people's normal expectations. Many languages have words dedicated to express such a notion, and English itself has words such as 'surprisingly' and 'unexpectedly', so the new adjective-*ass* construction is not extremely unusual in the meaning it has developed. What the 'appropriation' of *–ass* into *big-ass, rich-ass, stupid-ass*, etc., importantly does is to create a new means to express counter-expectational situations and properties in a very informal style of speech in English where 'surprisingly' and 'unexpectedly' would sound much too formal and out of place—contrast: 'That's a surprisingly/unexpectedly large gun, man' with: 'That's a big-ass gun, man'. The adjective-*ass* innovation thus fills a gap and increases the breadth of speakers' vocabulary in colloquial interactions, and has done this by co-opting an existing word, *ass*, and bleaching it of its original meaning in the new construction.[11] Words can creatively be assigned quite new meanings in the development of language and there is no need for concern when a literal meaning is jettisoned in the process. Such a 'sloughing off' of early meanings is, again, a very common phenomenon found in historical change.

So, alongside words which *add* new meanings while retaining their original meaning as a possible use (*hopefully, literally*, etc.), we have words which morph semantically from one meaning to another—the *bad-ass* pattern and many other lexical changes where words are given a fully new interpretation and completely lose their old meaning in the new linguistic context they occur in. A third type of change which frequently takes place is for words to lose their original physical shape as they develop new, broader uses, often as grammatical words, in a process known as 'grammaticalization'—the creation of new grammatical forms from original descriptive words. This kind of change can be briefly illustrated with a new patterning which is now spreading in southern British English, the development of '*innit*'.

Teenagers in parts of London have recently been noted to make increasing use of the word *innit* in questions and also statements such as the following, from Palacios Martínez (2014):

It was good innit?
I better get my jacket innit.

The origin of this word is the phrase *isn't it?*, which occurs as a common question tag used to check that listeners' have understood and agree with what the speaker is saying, or confirm a piece of information, as in:

It's a nice day, isn't it?
This is the right way, isn't it?

Over time, among younger speakers in London, *isn't it* has undergone a phonological change to produce the new form *innit*, and at the same time it has broadened its use and lost the grammatical restrictions originally imposed by *isn't it*, which can only be used as a question tag when the verb of the main portion of the sentence is '*is*'. With the newly adapted, grammaticalized *innit*, the verb in the main portion of the sentence can now in fact be any of the following: *is, are, was, were, has, had, can, will, might, would, must, should*, and *could*, as (partially) illustrated in the following examples:[12]

---

11. An additional new use of 'ass' which plays with the literal meaning of the word is its occurrence in expressions such as '*Jeb saved his brother's ass last night*.' Here '*ass*' is used to represent the whole of the person this portion of anatomy is attached to, and does not correspond simply to 'ass' in its localized meaning 'posterior'. The use of a part of a person, animal, or inanimate item to represent the whole person/animal/thing is known as 'synecdoche', and is a common feature of language, occurring, for example, in '*three <u>head</u> of cattle*', and '*They hired three new <u>hands</u> to help with plowing the fields*'.

12. All examples here and in the rest of the section are taken from Palacios Martínez (2014).

You forgot your book, innit?   ['innit' stands for 'didn't you?']
They must have the wrong place, innit?   ['innit' stands for 'mustn't they?']
You like Coronation Street, innit?   ['innit' stands for 'don't you?']
You can have it for Friday, innit?   ['innit' communicates 'okay?']
[oh my god] I would just die, innit!   ['innit' communicates 'for sure!']

Grammaticalized *innit* has furthermore developed more functions than the simple question tag *isn't it*. In addition to the original functions of checking listeners' understanding and agreement, it is used as an emphasizer equivalent to '*Too right!*' or '*Of course/For sure!*', as a device to keep the listener's attention, and as a means to show surprise toward or confirmation of something said by another speaker. In the latter use, it may occur as a single word sentence, not tagged on to any preceding sentence produced by the speaker:

A: *Your school is quite near.*
B: *Innit? You have to go miles!*
[Meaning: That's right! YOU, by way of contrast, have to go a long way to your school]

Socio-linguistically, the use of *innit* also performs an identity function and makes younger speakers who use it sound different from others around them, especially adult speakers. In sum, *innit* is a good example of a new grammatical word which has changed from an early recognizable source (*isn't it*) via a process of grammaticalization into a quite different item which is highly distinctive, extremely versatile, and a salient marker of belonging to a particular social group. New functional words may spring out of more transparent lexical sources and quickly develop an independent life and special character of their own.

Finally, we can note that sometimes completely new words seem to be coined which have no obvious connection to other, existing words (though in some cases, an etymological dictionary might perhaps suggest a link). A nice illustration of a word whose use has recently increased quite dramatically, and which typically fails to be mentally connected up by modern speakers with any earlier source is the colloquial term '*dude*', as documented in Kiesling (2004). Although *dude* feels like a very modern expression, which many older speakers will associate with an origin in the surfer subculture of the 1970s in California, *dude* was actually used as a word to describe a 'sharp dresser' already in the late 19th century, and in the 1930s and 1940s was popularized as an address term among groups of young Mexican Americans ('*pachuchos*') and African Americans who were known for their use of flamboyant dress. From such groups, *dude* then spread into young, non-conformist, white American speech in the 1970s via black music culture, like many other prominent words of slang (such as, for example, '*cool*'). *Dude* then began to expand its functional use, and young people oriented toward a laid-back lifestyle in the 1980s started to use *dude* not only as a term of address ('*Hey, dude, what's going on?*'), but as an exclamation signaling delight, as in '*Dude!! That's amazing!*'

While much slang which was fashionable in the 1970s has now disappeared (for example words such as '*groovy*'), *dude* (and '*cool*') has made a major comeback, and *dude* is now very popular again among young white speakers in the USA. As *dude* has reappeared and grown in use, it has also undergone further change in the way it is used. Originally, *dude* was just used by young males to each other as a greeting and then an exclamation. Now, it has spread to young female speakers, and between males it has a more complex patterning than before. The overall effect of *dude* is as a marker of solidarity, indexing a shared, masculine, heterosexual identity among white male speakers under the age of 30, with the flavor of a relaxed, 'chilled-out' attitude to life. Its functional use is as an address term to other males in greetings, as a component of exclamations ('*Whoah, dude!*'), and as an addition to warnings and criticisms to soften the force of such potentially confrontational occurrences of language (in technical linguistic terms—a 'positive politeness' strategy used in situations of threat to a listener's 'face'—see footnote 5), as illustrated in the following:

Dude, that's not cool.
Dude, relax!!
Dude, you just ran a red light, man.
Gimme the controls, dude!

Dude now also regularly occurs in the speech of young women, especially when they talk with other women. Kiesling (2004) notes that *dude* is not often used in greetings among females, but frequently occurs in situations where speakers who feel close to each other are talking about negative experiences they may have had ('*Dude, that's awful!*', '*Dude, what a total pig!*', or even just '*Dude!*' alone, said with a falling tone signaling disgust and disbelief). The use of *dude* conveys empathy toward the hearer and a close connection in the suffering which results from unpleasant circumstances, which may sometimes be experienced by both the hearer and the speaker, as in '*Dude, this class is soooo boring*.'

Just as with *innit*, and *like*, innovation with *dude* has resulted in a multi-functional element that is continuing to evolve and develop new uses which many speakers may not be consciously aware of but nevertheless apply very effectively in their daily interactions. And just like *innit* and *like*, *dude* contributes to communication with other speakers on two different linguistic levels—it has an important *social* role, stressing solidarity among speakers (though, significantly, not intimacy—*dude* is used by male speakers to close female friends but not to intimate girlfriends and lovers), and also a set of more specific, situational uses and functions, for mitigating criticism, emphasizing commiseration, exclamation, and greetings. The broad take-home message from considering lexical change and innovation with words such as *dude, like, literally,* and *innit* is that words' meaning and use are continually on the move and frequently lead to many enhancements of language that critics of change are often unaware of. Rather than view semantic change and the development of new words by younger speakers as signs of language decay, a more positive perspective is to simply accept change as an inevitable property of language and to embrace the value that innovations commonly bring to our general power of expression.

Changing sounds: identity-marking and discourse-intonation in the speech of teenagers and young adults

New patterns of pronunciation and intonation are often used by speakers to signal membership of a particular group or social class, and may also be adopted for innovative functional purposes, as alternatives to older patterns. We have already seen how changes in the pronunciation of certain sounds can index a desired identity in Labov's important studies of the adult working population in New York City and Martha's Vineyard. Younger speakers in high schools and college have also frequently been observed to develop and use new modes of pronunciation as linguistic symbols of identity, or as stylistic forms with functional applications, and here we will highlight a range of such sound-related changes, either innovated by or most prominent among younger generation speakers.

Uptalk

In considering changes in the use of lexical elements, it was noted that the surge in everyday use of 'like' among younger speakers has most probably attracted more criticism from older speakers in the USA than any other recent innovation in language. If one were to ask what pattern might be ranked second to 'like' as an attractor of negative public attention in public discussions of ('bad') language in the USA, it is likely that it would be wide-scale adoption of 'uptalk' among younger speakers. Technically referred to as a 'High Rising Terminal Contour', uptalk involves the use of a high rising intonation pattern at the ends of sentences which are statements, making them sound, to some speakers, as if they actually were questions, which frequently also end in a high rising pitch. This is illustrated in the following exchanges, where an upward pointing arrow indicates final high rising intonation. In the second example, the speaker uses a high rise at several points as she continues to talk:

A: *So, what did you buy in the farmer's market?*
B: *A pound of that nice goat's cheese you like* ↑*.*
Pam: *and um he just stood there . . . and I've got a real phobia for big moths* ↑ *I hate them flying around me and that* ↑ *and as I was sort of nodding off to sleep I could hear a um . . . like what I thought was a moth* ↑ *banging on the window* ↑ *and I just remember thinking ooh yuck you know . . .* (Britain 1998: 214)[13]

The reason why uptalk seems to trigger negative reactions from non-users of this pattern is its apparent borrowing of question intonation into sentences which are not questions. Critics complain that it is simply 'wrong' and confusing to listeners to pronounce declarative statements as if they were questions, with a final high rise. Additionally, when uptalk intonation was first noticed and commented on as a characteristic of female speech in the mid-1970s, the use of a high rise, question-like intonation in statements was described as signaling uncertainty and a lack of assertiveness—women were suggested to be hesitant

---

13. Quoted in Coates (1993: 184).

to make clear, direct statements in their interactions with certain male speakers, and so attempted to make their declarative sentences sound like questions, in order to reduce their assertive force (Lakoff 1975). Since the 1970s, uptalk has increased tremendously in its use among younger speakers and has spread geographically from the USA to Australia, New Zealand, and the UK (and the second example given in the preceding is actually from New Zealand). On account of its striking prominence and the negative assessments it has attracted in public discussions of language, a number of linguists decided to carry out studies of uptalk patterns to see whether this intonational 'habit' appears randomly in users' speech, or whether uptalk might actually be used for specific linguistic purposes. Several interesting conclusions and proposals have now resulted from these studies.

First, it has been established that one function of the final high rise intonation which occurs in uptalk is to draw attention to and highlight new information that is being communicated by the speaker. One of the studies noting this role of uptalk was carried out in a student sorority group in the University of Texas, by Cynthia McLemore (1992). In house meetings, it was observed that uptalk intonation patterns were consistently used to announce new information as opposed to reminders about 'old' information that members attending the meeting were assumed to know already. While mentions of regular events scheduled in the sorority's calendar were given with a falling intonation, McLemore found that special, one-off events were produced with a final rising intonation, drawing listeners' attention to the newness of the information. This use of uptalk to put special emphasis on the informational focus of the sentence has been found in other investigations considering differences in the presentation of old vs. new information, and may often be heard in everyday life when people state their names to others in certain situations, as for example when ordering a drink in a café such as Starbucks where the barista regularly writes the customer's name on the cup of a special order. Younger customers can often be heard to give their name, which is clearly new information (unknown to the barista), with the uptalk 'question' intonation:

Barista: *And your name?*
Customer: *Jennifer* ↑.

The focus use of uptalk intonation also bears an interesting relation to another intonational pattern that is very common in English, the use of 'nuclear stress' to focus the new information component of a sentence, most typically in sentence-final position (Zubizarreta 1998). Whereas nuclear stress adds a high rising intonation pattern to a single, prominent syllable in a final, focused word (for example, 'Yesterday John bought a BOOK-case'), the uptalk equivalent tends to stress all syllables in a final word (for example, 'Yesterday John bought a BOOK-CASE'). Otherwise, uptalk and the more widespread nuclear stress rule seem to be very similar and have the same function of highlighting new information through final rising intonation.

A second, functional feature of uptalk that has been suggested by a number of analysts is that sentences pronounced with such a stress pattern are both statements and questions at the same time. Consider, for example, the following exchange, in which a wife responds to her husband's question about dinner with the words 'six o'clock' pronounced with a final rise (from McConnell-Ginet 2011: 118):

Husband: *When will dinner be ready?*
Wife: *Six o'clock ↑.*

McConnell-Ginet (1975) suggests that the wife uses uptalk, question-like intonation because she is both stating certain information about the planned time of the evening meal and adding an implicit question 'Is that okay for you, do you want to eat earlier?' Uptalk may thus be used to communicate something extra when a statement is being made, in this instance that the time of dinner could perhaps be adjusted if desired. If the answer 'six o'clock' had instead been pronounced with falling rather than rising intonation, it would sound as if the time were firmly fixed and not open to any adjustment. Uptalk consequently adds in a useful versatility to statements of certain types and may communicate much more information than just the bare words present in a sentence or an answer-form.

A third discourse function of uptalk often commented on (see, for example, Ladd 1980), is its use by a speaker to communicate to listeners that the speaker has more to say and wishes to continue talking. The final high rise tone therefore conveys non-finality or incompleteness, and signals that the speaker has not finished saying what he/she wants to say—there is still more to come. In this function, uptalk intonation provides a helpful clue to listeners about when they should join in the conversation and respond to what the speaker has been saying.

Uptalk has additionally been attributed a fourth role in discourse, used by speakers to communicate a solidarity-like connection with the people they are talking to, similar to the use of phrases such as 'you know' and 'right?' in sentences like 'He's a nice man, you know, always helping other people'. Expressions like 'you know' are typically inserted by speakers when they want to establish that they are 'in tune with' and 'on the same page' as the listener, sharing the same kinds of views. Uptalk is taken to be an intonational version of such phrases, used to emphasize the existence or assumption of common ground between the speaker and the hearer.

The two general conclusions of studies of uptalk usage are that (a) uptalk is not a random, meaningless or 'incorrect' use of intonation but has regular linguistic uses which help structure discourse and communicate extra information to speakers, of a range of types, and (b) the question-like intonation present in uptalk patterns should not be interpreted as signs of hesitation, and lack of assertion in the female speakers who often use such forms. In the University of Texas sorority study in McLemore (1992), those who used uptalk as a focus device in their public addresses to other sorority members were actually very assertive young women in positions of responsibility within the sorority, and their speech was authoritative in quality, not timorous or insecure in feeling. On closer examination, uptalk is therefore neither an inappropriate, senseless use of intonation, nor an indication of lack of self-confidence among young female speakers. As with many other cases of linguistic innovation made and adopted by the younger generation, uptalk seems to have attracted unfair criticism which stems from a simple lack of understanding and appreciation of the ways that new forms are put to use in acts of communication.

Vocal fry

While uptalk has seen negative discussion in the public arena for some time, there is a second intonation-related pattern recently adopted by many young female speakers which has begun to catch similar levels of negative attention in the USA—'vocal fry'. This is a kind of very low pitch 'creaky voice' produced by slowly fluttering the vocal cords, most often at the ends of sentences, so that the vocal cords make a rattling, cracking type of sound, samples of which can easily be found online.[14] Vocal fry has experienced a rapid growth in use in the second decade of the 21st century in large part due to its increased occurrence in popular music and TV by well-known figures such as Britney Spears and Kim Kardashian. The speech patterns of these and other icons of modern pop culture have been copied and have spread rapidly among other young women in the USA, particularly in the college-going population, and was found to be used by as much as two-thirds of young women in one US college study carried out in Long Island University, Brookeville, New York.[15]

Attitudes toward vocal fry are very mixed. While many users of vocal fry have positive opinions of its sound and the image projected by its use (as reported in a survey described in Yuasa 2010), other non-users often have strong negative reactions toward vocal fry and those who produce it. Comments such as the following are frequent in articles posted online which discuss the rise of this relatively new phenomenon:

'. . . much to the dismay of those they interact with, young American women can't stop speaking in vocal fry.'[16]

'Like many young women in the US, my girlfriend has vocal fry, a speech pattern that annoys lots of people and . . . makes some people want to go on murder sprees. . . . Can she be cured?'[17]

It has also been pointed out that a person's use of vocal fry may potentially harm their chances of getting employment. A study carried out at the University of Miami and Duke University showed that young women who use vocal fry were perceived to be less trustworthy, competent, and hirable than those who did not use this patterning. Anderson et al. (2014) devised an experiment in which multiple speakers were recorded producing the phrase 'Thank you for considering me for this opportunity' both with and without vocal fry. The recordings were then played to 800 men and women of different ages, who gave their opinions of the voices they heard and whether the speakers sounded educated, trustworthy, and might have a

---

14. For example, at: https://www.today.com/video/new-speech-pattern-of-young-women-vocal-fry-44540995528 and: https://www.theatlantic.com/business/archive/2014/05/employers-look-down-on-women-with-vocal-fry/371811/.

15. Referenced at: http://www.sciencemag.org/news/2011/12/vocal-fry-creeping-us-speech?ref=hp.

16. From a June 4, 2014, article in *Time* magazine by Maya Rhodan, '3 Speech Habits That Are Worse Than Vocal Fry in Job Interviews', posted at: http://time.com/2820087/3-speech-habits-that-are-worse-than-vocal-fry-in-job-interviews

17. https://www.vice.com/en_us/article/8gknwp/i-took-my-girlfriend-to-a-speech-therapist-to-cure-her-annoying-vocal-fry-988

good competitive chance as a job candidate. For each quality, the opinion of the listeners was that the 'normal-toned' voice seemed clearly preferable, and that speakers who used vocal fry had less chances of making a good impression in job interviews than those who did not use vocal fry. These negative evaluations of voices heard with vocal fry were also noted to be stronger when the listener themselves were women.[18]

Vocal fry is consequently an emerging new intonational pattern which, like uptalk before it, is generating 'spirited' reactions from other speakers as it embeds itself among female members of the younger generation in the USA (vocal fry is not made use of by male speakers). Given the apparent popularity of this new speech form among its users, it is natural to wonder whether vocal fry may spread out further in the population, to somewhat older speakers in their 30s and 40s, and, with time, be felt to be more 'acceptable' among this generation (though perhaps not with older speakers). This is what seems to be happening with uptalk, which is now occurring more frequently in the speech of middle-aged adults (though still strongest among adolescents and young adults, and still censured by members of older generations). It is never easy to predict how linguistic changes will unfold, as so many factors affect the development of new ways of speaking, especially when these are 'fashionable' new ways of speaking, and it is not clear that vocal fry will have the broad success of uptalk, which has spread from the USA to other English-speaking countries and is also gradually being taken up by older speakers. One important difference between uptalk and vocal fry is that uptalk is an intonational pattern which performs a range of useful linguistic functions, as described, as well as indexing a younger identity, whereas vocal fry is simply a general style of speech and does not have specific functions. Vocal fry communicates the image of successful young women in 'cool California' (to those who have positive feelings about the way vocal fry sounds), but it does not contribute further to the structuring of discourse in any obvious way, unlike other recent innovations we have considered here, such as uptalk, *like*, *innit*, and *dude*, all of which have both social, identity-related and special linguistic functions. Perhaps the restriction of vocal fry's role to just identity projection may have an effect on its spread to broader categories of speakers (males, older speakers, and populations in other countries) and not give vocal fry the potential for growth that uptalk and *like* have both enjoyed. It will certainly be interesting to revisit vocal fry in another decade and see whether it has developed significantly further or alternatively has fallen out of fashion as a dated style of speech.

Reinstating British aspirated /t/ in northern California

While vocal fry is a new style of pronunciation used to project a modern, young, southern Californian identity oriented toward popular culture, a different kind of innovation in pronunciation has interestingly been observed among certain young female speakers in northern California as a signal of their rejection of the 'cool Californian' image. Bucholtz (1996) investigated the speech patterns of female students in a northern California school who celebrated having a 'geek' identity. These girls deliberately shunned all aspects of fashion, language, and social behavior strongly associated with popular Californian teenage culture,

---

18. See also 'Employers Look Down on Women with Vocal Fry', published in *The Atlantic*, May 29, 2014, posted at: https://www.theatlantic.com/business/archive/2014/05/employers-look-down-on-women-with-vocal-fry/371811/

and instead emphasized an identity linked to independence of thought and intelligence. Bucholtz found that this special orientation of the 'geek girls' surfaced in distinctive patterns of language use, marking their separate identity. One clear manifestation of this was the use of a British-like pronunciation of /t/ sounds between vowels in words like 'butter' and 'bottle', which were made with 'aspiration' so that they sounded like /t/s at the beginnings of words. This use of British intervocalic /t/ contrasts very clearly with the standard American English pronunciation of /t/ between vowels, which is more like a /d/ (hence 'butter' often sounds more like 'budder').

The northern Californian 'geek girls' studied by Bucholtz are thus changing their /t/ sounds to an older pronunciation which has special, social value due to its association with common stereotypes of British people and their speech which are held in the USA, southern British 'BBC' English being perceived to be 'articulate' and a sign of speakers' education. Changes in intonation and pronunciation among high school students in California are therefore being used to claim different types of identity which seem to be in direct opposition to each other, one embracing pop culture and modernity, the other acquiring status through its explicit rejection of 'trivial adolescent concerns' (Eckert 2004: 372). Language and the ways that words are pronounced in different ways offer useful vehicles for the projection of personal and group identity, and as image-creation has a particularly special importance during late adolescent years, high schools come to be natural, rich environments for the occurrence of linguistic experimentation and change.

Extreme variation: language use among female jocks and burnouts

The oppositions which exist between different social groups coalescing in high schools often lead to special, exaggerated forms of speech as symbols of the membership of a particular group and distance and distinction from other rival groups. One investigation of such variation carried out in a high school near Detroit has shown how the symbolic value of differences in language may be used as a resource in a more 'extreme' way by female speakers than by males from the same social group.

Penelope Eckert (1989) studied the speech patterns of two groups of students which have a presence in many high schools in the USA—the so-called 'jocks' and 'burnouts'. Members of the jock group are typically studious, well-behaved, and participate with enthusiasm in a wide range of school activities and sports, and often have plans to continue their education in college, while 'burnouts' display little interest in their studies, are more focused on life outside the high school, and are likely to get a local low-paid job rather than attend college, and generally reject the set of middle-class values and ambitions which are often encouraged in school. Jocks and burnouts frequently engage in inter-group conflict and use differences in language to stress their belonging to either the jock or burnout group.

One of the primary linguistic markers of being part of the burnout group noticed by Eckert was the use of new pronunciations of certain vowel sounds, which had been developing in Detroit, as part of a broader change in pronunciation known as the 'Northern Cities Vowel Shift'. Whereas the burnouts had adopted the new urban vowel sounds heard widely in the cities of Detroit, Chicago, Buffalo, and Cleveland, members of the jock group were found to be more conservative and retained more of the older pronunciations of vowels. Eckert also became aware of an important difference in use of the old vs. new sounds that related to the sex of the speaker—in both the jock and burnout group, female speakers used the sounds symbolizing their group significantly more than male speakers did. The interpretation Eckert gave to this difference is as follows. Boys, it was argued, were able to establish status in their groups directly through their *actions*—for example, jocks earned respect among their group for prowess in sports, and burnouts did so by demonstrating an ability to fight well with others. However, girls' membership of the jock and burnout groups was not recognized in the same kind of way, and even if a jock girl were to perform well in sports, or a burnout girl prove herself to be a strong fighter, these skills did not result in the same high level of admiration as occurred when the same skills were manifested by male jocks and burnouts. Instead, girls tended to be valued as members of the jock and burnout groups by virtue of the way they dressed and spoke. Commenting on Eckert's study, Cameron (2008: 147) describes Eckert's conclusions as follows:

> Eckert's argument is that girls are impelled by their more marginal position in the group to make more intensive use of symbolic resources generally. They cannot assert their status as 'good jocks' and 'good burnouts' in the same way as boys, through action: consequently they are driven to display their commitment to the group through close attention to the symbols of jock or burnout style, such as clothing styles and vowel pronunciations.

The result of such pressures to make use of language differences to signal membership of the jock or burnout groups was that jock girls used more of the older vowel sounds than all other speakers, and burnout girls appeared to be the most innovative speakers and had the highest rate of use of the new vowel sounds. In both jock and burnout groups, the female speakers consequently used a more extreme version of the speech typical of the group than was found among males as a way to display their strong commitment to the group. This observation bears interestingly on the debate about whether female speakers are the leaders of linguistic change or, conversely, are more traditional in their speech, as discussed in chapter 10. Summarizing Eckert's findings in the Detroit study of burnouts and jocks, Cameron emphasizes that:

> The real generalization is not 'women are more conservative than men' or 'women are more innovative than men', but 'women carry the tendency of their group, be that conservatism or innovation, to greater lengths than men. (Cameron 2008:v148)

In such an assessment, changing language patterns, when they occur, may be expected to be more striking and extreme among female speakers, particularly in situations where women are judged more by style than by accomplishments in life. This is an interesting conclusion which is well worth bearing in mind when considering how identity-related variation and change becomes established and spreads within different social groups. Is language change always more striking and advanced in women when it serves as a marker of loyalty to a group?

Crossing

In the preceding examples, we have seen how adolescents are making creative use of variation in their speech as signals of personal identity and belonging to a particular social group. The final patterning we will consider here is a further, very special kind of identity-related personal speech innovation which connects teenagers from different social and ethnic groups—the phenomenon of 'crossing' (or 'language crossing'). The term 'crossing' refers to 'the use of language varieties associated with social or ethnic groups that the speaker does not normally "belong to"' (Rampton 1995: 14).[19] Speakers take up and use distinctive patterns that are used by members of a quite different group which is not part of the speakers' own community. For example, in certain urban settings in the USA, certain patterns of African American Vernacular English (AAVE) have been incorporated into the speech of young people from other ethnic backgrounds, and in the UK, young white teenagers have been observed to make use of features of Afro-Caribbean 'Creole' speech, 'crossing' from the language they have grown up using into patterns associated with a very different group. Fought (2006: 197) stresses the rather unexpected nature of crossing behavior as follows:

> . . . people generally speak like the people they want to be like . . . (and) . . . for the most part we want to sound like those around us. . . . So why would someone use a speech variety associated with another group altogether?

She then raises a number of important research questions about the recent emergence of crossing found among younger speakers in different environments, including the following:

- Why might an individual choose to do it? Does crossing indicate a desire to be a member of the other ethnic group?
- How 'extensive' is crossing linguistically? What linguistic areas (lexicon, phonology) are individuals who cross most likely to use?
- What is the attitude toward crossing among members of the ethnic group whose code is being borrowed?

In order to get to some provisional answers to these questions, and to better appreciate what occurs in language crossing, we will briefly describe the results of four different studies which have highlighted properties of this new mode of language use, one carried out in the UK, and three in the USA.

The term 'crossing' originates from an in-depth investigation of language variation among teenagers in a town in the South Midlands area of England, published as Rampton (1995). Rampton found that younger, white and also South Asian speakers frequently borrowed features of the 'Creole' speech patterns used by members of the Afro-Caribbean population, and did this for a variety of reasons relating to the symbolic value of Creole and its speakers, who were perceived to be 'tough', 'streetwise', and 'cool'. In temporarily appropriating

---

19. Quoted in Fought (2006).

the 'toughness' associated with Creole speech, one common use of crossing into Creole was to present an image of rebellion and opposition against authority, as represented by teachers and adults in other positions of power. In classrooms, for example, Creole was sometimes used to address teachers in a way that sought to undermine their authority, as young speakers knew their teachers would not be able to understand what was being said in Creole, and would therefore be embarrassed by not knowing how to respond. However, other crossing uses of Creole were not so self-assertive or deliberately disrespectful and challenging in nature, and instead occurred for largely humorous purposes, Creole being used by white and South Asian teenagers in a joking way, to increase solidarity with their peers. One important interactional constraint was regularly followed by white and South Asian adolescents in their use of Creole speech—it was not made use of when males from the Afro-Caribbean community were present, as there was a worry that male native speakers of Creole would take offense at the appropriation of their language. Negative reactions from young Afro-Caribbean men to others' crossing into Creole were particularly strong when this involved the copying of Afro-Caribbean pronunciation of Creole words, and so this was especially avoided in the presence of the former (but sometimes used in their absence). Rampton concluded that the crossing use of *words* from another group's language may be viewed as acceptable and tolerated as a sign of peer group 'affiliation', but not the borrowing of distinctive forms of *pronunciation*, because phonology functions as a stronger symbol of in-group ethnicity not open to outsiders, at least in certain communities. Quite generally, Rampton argued that the crossing behavior he observed in the UK was *not* part of an attempt by speakers to take on a new ethnic identity and be accepted as members of the Afro-Caribbean group. Rather, crossing was carried out by speakers to project an image with just some of the properties attributed to native Creole speakers—their masculinity, confidence, and positive associations with street culture—and not the entirety of their ethnic identity.

Cutler (1999) is a detailed study of a single individual, named 'Mike', a white middle-class teenager, and his developing relation with African American language and popular culture in New York City. The description of Mike's attitudes and linguistic behavior over a period of years offers useful insights into connections between crossing and identity, and leads to the conclusion, as in Rampton's work, that speakers who engage in crossing are not trying to claim a new ethnicity when they adopt the language patterns of another group. In Mike's case, a clear interest in African American youth culture began in his early teens, when he began to listen to hip-hop music, dress in certain ways like his African American peers, and started to change the way he spoke with the use of AAVE words and expressions. At this initial stage, between the ages of 13 and 14, Mike showed signs of wanting to identify closely with young African Americans, but after he changed his school at the age of 15, this attraction seemed to change and Mike began to talk negatively about African Americans, resenting the fact that they apparently did not wish to socialize with white teenagers like himself. By the age of 16, this sense of rejection led Mike to be frequently critical of the young black community and lose any sense of shared identity with African Americans. However, even though Mike no longer had thoughts of trying to adopt a black identity, he regularly continued to engage in crossing and used AAVE heavily in his speech. Cutler interprets this as showing that for Mike (and others) crossing into AAVE serves a very general identity-related purpose, indexing membership of a broad, anti-establishment, urban youth culture which has roots in the African American community but is no longer restricted to this ethnic group. Various features of AAVE have, in this, sense become 'public property', and are being appropriated by a wider population of modern youth as symbols of a trans-ethnic hip-hop identity.

Following on from Rampton (1995) and Cutler (1999), Angela Reyes and Lane Igoudin have documented the spread of AAVE further into portions of the Asian community in the USA, the so-called 'model minority' stereotypically associated with industriousness, educational and economic success, and exemplary behavior. Reyes (2005) considered crossing among (mostly) second-generation Vietnamese, Cambodians, and Laotians living in poorer multi-ethnic neighborhoods in Philadelphia which also had significant populations of African Americans. Reyes found that young Asians present in these areas felt more in common with local, low-income African Americans than with the white mainstream community elsewhere in the city, and as a result engaged themselves in the same youth cultural forms as their African American peers—hip-hop music, clothing styles, and often strongly assertive behavior. Linguistically, they used aspects of AAVE to build up an identity as belonging to a new 'problem minority' group of Asian Americans which substituted toughness and aggressive behavior for the 'typical' Asian properties of conservatism, meekness, and the prizing of intelligence, hard work, and contributions to society. Reyes claims that '... rather than trying to "act black", ... the teens used African American slang to fashion their own identities as the 'Other Asian' and break away from the stereotype commonly associated with the Asian community in the USA' (Reyes 2005: 527).

Igoudin found something similar, but in a different kind of young Asian community. While most investigations of crossing with AAVE have looked at male teenagers, Igoudin's (2013) study documents AAVE crossing among Asian girls in a suburban southern California high school. Igoudin, like Reyes, notes that teenagers in the USA of Asian descent face greater difficulties than other ethnic minorities in establishing a distinctive and acceptable modern young identity. First of all, there is no special accented form of English or vocabulary of slang which distinguishes Asian Americans from other groups. Second, Asian Americans are regularly considered to be the 'model minority' often stereotyped as 'mild-mannered and socially incompetent nerds ... whose intelligence and industriousness is counter-balanced by social ineptitude' (Bucholtz 2004: 128).[20] Igoudin argues that crossing with AAVE was used by the teenage girls he studied as a way to help them disassociate themselves from other young Asian Americans and break away from the 'smart but uncool' Asian American stereotype which has developed in many parts of the USA (Bucholtz 2004: 128), in a way similar to the use of AAVE by male teenagers in Philadelphia. As in Philadelphia, there were no signs that AAVE crossing among Asian American girls in California was part of an attempt to adopt an African American identity in any way. When students interviewed by Igoudin were asked if they thought their speech made them sound like African Americans, they replied that they simply spoke 'ghetto', the language of the young, rather than 'African American'. Igoudin's concludes from this that a reduced version of AAVE was being used by the Asian American teenagers in order to 'join a distinctive teenage subculture in which class and race lines are blurred' (Igoudin 2013: 52) and that AAVE is taking on a new function in various urban

---

20. Quoted in Igoudin (2013: 52).

environments in the USA as a cross-ethnic linguistic marker of contemporary youth identity not just restricted to the African American community, but facilitating cross-cultural socialization among young people from a range of different ethnic backgrounds.

While there are clear similarities in the identity-related use of AAVE in Reyes' and Igoudin's studies, helping young Asian Americans escape from the prototypical image associated with their ethnicity and connect with teenagers from other groups, there is also a significant difference in the way that crossing was found to occur in Philadelphia and California. While young Asian males in Philadelphia exploited the associations that AAVE potentially has with 'toughness' and masculinity to project a 'dangerous' and aggressive image at times, such a confrontational use of AAVE was quite absent from the behavior of the Asian high school girls observed in California. Igoudin found that the teenagers he interviewed did not use AAVE to contest or 'rebel' against authority, and generally had positive attitudes toward school, saying that they cared about their academic success. They also indicated that speaking with adults required a different linguistic style, and they would switch out of 'ghetto' into more standard forms when they felt it was appropriate to be serious and speak 'proper English' in a respectful way. Crossing into a strongly vernacular form of speech such as AAVE consequently may be used to communicate an anti-authoritarian, anti-establishment stance, but it can also occur without such attitude simply as a modern, youthful style of speech shared with others in casual interactions.

Returning to the questions raised by Fought (2006) at the outset of this section, research into the relatively recent phenomenon of crossing seems to allow for the following conclusions. First, concerning the issue of whether crossing indicates a desire to be a member of the ethnic group whose speech styles are borrowed—the 'source group'—the answer to this appears to be 'no'—crossing is used to construct a separate new identity. This may take advantage of some of the associations linked to speakers of the source group but may not correlate with a wish to be recognized and accepted as a member of this population of speakers. In this sense, crossing is very different from the changes in individuals' speech noted earlier in the Martha's Vineyard and Louisiana Cajun communities, where new forms of speech were adopted to stress solidarity and identification with a particular group.

Second, it has been observed that there is actually much variation in the amount and frequency of crossing. Some speakers use crossing just a little (for example, white teenagers using Creole in Rampton's UK study), while others may 'cross' more frequently, but only for a few sentences each time. At a higher level still, the female students in Igoudin's study made use of the crossing 'style' quite regularly in speaking with their peers, and so crossing in this group has established itself with a particularly high frequency and is now an accepted norm in many situations. Where crossing does occur, in different groups, the generalization is that lexical items (words, expressions) are most frequently adopted from another group, distinctive phonology is borrowed less, and special grammatical constructions are the features which are least commonly copied (perhaps because they are the most difficult to learn and reproduce).

Finally, what do we know about attitudes toward crossing by members of groups whose language patterns have been borrowed? To date there has still not been much research directly probing this question, but certain indirect evidence on the issue is provided by observations in Rampton's work that British speakers regularly avoid crossing into Creole in the presence of Afro-Caribbean males. This concern about using Creole patterns in front of male native speakers, particularly Creole phonology, allows one to infer that male members of the source group do not approve of crossing among members of other ethnic groups, especially in the area of pronunciation. While the borrowing of lexical items is tolerated somewhat more, and might be interpreted by members of the source group as an acceptable sign of 'homage' to their way of speaking, from the evidence available it would appear that ethnic group accent is a much more personal feature of language that is not willingly offered to outsiders for casual use. Further studies will be necessary to confirm this as a recurrent patterning. It may also be interesting to consider cases of pure 'accent-appropriation' without other lexical and grammatical aspects of crossing, and attitudes that speakers have toward such linguistic behavior. For example, how might speakers of a strongly-accented form of English such as Newcastle (UK) English or Brooklyn (New York) English feel toward outsiders putting on a Newcastle or Brooklyn accent in their presence—flattered or defensive? One could guess that there would be similar feelings of 'protection' in such cases and negative reactions to the borrowing of these strong markers of local group identity by others. Perhaps one only earns the 'right' to use a strong local accent by being born and raised in its place of origin, and local identity cannot simply be borrowed by outsiders. Questions arising in the 'exotic' context of crossing may therefore have a broader relevance and may lead to other useful questions about borrowing in general, which is cross-linguistically a very widespread phenomenon, and whether different attitudes may perhaps exist toward the borrowing of lexical and grammatical vs. phonological features. As with investigations of other patterns of linguistic variation and change, observations about one aspect of language innovation can help frame useful new questions for additional areas of research and open up paths for fresh discoveries relating to the use of language in society.

Studying language variation and change in society: recurrent themes, issues, and final remarks

This chapter has considered a range of case studies of variation in colloquial speech as a way to uncover and highlight properties of language change and the social significance of linguistic variation. As the general focus of the book is on interactions between language and society, the emphasis in the current chapter has been on changes in speakers' language which are caused by or have effects on individuals' connections to others in society, and we have not attempted to examine instances of change which appear to occur for purely linguistic rather than sociolinguistic reasons.[21] The chapter has also concentrated on recent or current, ongoing variation and change rather than past, historical patterns of change. This is because it

---

21. As an example of change which is not a response to purely societal factors, in chapter 6 we saw that pidgin languages regularly undergo significant changes as they develop into creoles. Such changes are due to the increasing use of such languages as primary forms of communication by speakers, which causes dramatic growth in morphosyntactic complexity and vocabulary, and are not caused by social factors such as the projection of personal identity and speakers' relations to others. For a good, non-specialist introduction to purely linguistic aspects of change, see Aitchison (2001) chapters 6–9.

is potentially easier to identify the social causes and consequences of change as innovations are actually taking place, due to the rich availability of data that can be carefully examined. In attempting to investigate changes in language which have occurred long ago in the past, the same level of detail and information is not available for analysis, and it is often not easy to be sure if changes have occurred for social reasons or not. Finally, we have restricted our attention mostly to patterns of change in the English-speaking world, for the simple reason that readers may find it easier to appreciate these examples and in some cases may have opinions and intuitions about the actual patterns themselves and an understanding of the attitudes that commonly exist toward speakers using them.

In considering the different case studies, a number of prominent themes have surfaced and recurred, some of which were already mentioned in the midway summary. Throughout the chapter, in many of the individual studies, we have seen a clear link between language variation and change and the *expression of identities* of various kinds. The first four case studies we looked at all had this property, and occurred to express speakers' desired membership of groups of different types. Variation in New York City with word-final /r/ was used to project an image of belonging to a *higher socio-economic class*. Newly adopted vowel patterns in Martha's Vineyard occurred to express a *local identity*, and in Newfoundland non-standard –s was part of the projection of a modern, new local identity. In Louisiana, the kind of identity projected by the adoption of Cajun English forms was an *ethnic identity*. It can be added that the changes in peoples' speech in Martha's Vineyard, Newfoundland, and Louisiana had a further property in common—they all occurred as responses by individuals to changing social and economic situations. Following these four studies, the set of cases of language variation and change we looked at in the second portion of the chapter all showed links with the formation and projection of identity among adolescents, as teenagers stake out new identities during their formative high school years, and develop these identities further as young adults in college and beyond. Innovation and variation in language were used to express an individual's belonging to a specific group (jocks, burnouts, geeks/nerds) or a broader youth-centered group identity relating either to urban hip-hop culture or to pop music icons and imagery from a televised young southern Californian lifestyle. Language regularly serves as an important symbol of personal and group identity, and the innovation of and adoption of new ways of speaking are powerful ways to signal both an individual's distinctness from other speakers and a close association with a select group of peers.

A second, broad observation about many of the instances of variation and change featured in the chapter is that changes in an individual's speech often result from the adoption of patterns of language that are already used by certain other speakers. This was the case in Martha's Vineyard with special vowel sounds, in New York City with the increase in rhotic speech, in Louisiana with younger speakers' adoption of the English forms used by older members of the Cajun community, in occurrences of crossing, and with the adoption of British /t/ by northern Californian high school girls. Consequently, in such instances, the patterns are not completely new in a fully global sense, but they are novel ways of speaking for the people who start to make use of them, and so constitute a change locally in these speakers' language. We also find that there may be 'adoption with innovation' and some adjustment made to forms copied from others, as in the case of Newfoundland non-standard –s, or the partial copying of Creole and AAVE in occurrences of crossing in the UK and the USA. In addition to the adoption of existing patterns used by others, either with or without modification, there are also instances of change which are genuinely innovative in nature, and this we saw with the largely new patterns of uptalk, vocal fry, and newly developed words and phrases such as 'innit' and 'broke-ass lawyer', as well as with the use of new meanings with old, existing words (e.g., 'literally'). A key property of a range of cases of change is that speakers reinterpret the symbolic or semantic value of an item or a general pattern, a process which highlights the unfixed, arbitrary nature of many linguistic forms. A prime example of such fluctuation in the meaning ascribed to a particular pattern is the changing social value of rhotic speech in the USA and the UK, where the pronunciation of word-final /r/ has been both a prestige form and stigmatized at different times and in different places. We also saw that non-standard –s has been assigned a new significance by younger speakers in Newfoundland, and that distinctive forms of English spoken by older members of the Cajun community have taken on a new symbolic use as markers of Cajun identity among younger speakers not proficient in French or Louisiana Creole. Linguistic symbols of social identity may thus be old and borrowed or newly innovated, and are often given different values over time.

The chapter's consideration of a good range of cases of variation and change has noted that speakers' innovations may lead to elements and patterns which are either *general new styles of speech* for the individuals who adopt them, helping project some targeted aspect of identity (as with vocal fry, the use of 'new' vowels in Martha's Vineyard), or they may have *specific functional uses* (such as the highlighting of new information with 'like', or the quotation of speech and thoughts with 'be like'). In various cases, new linguistic forms may actually serve both purposes—they can be part of a general style of speech associated with a particular group, and can fulfill a specific discourse function (as with uptalk, 'dude', and 'innit'). It is only careful research which leads to the appreciation of how these innovations may be functionally made use of, and to many non-users it may appear that innovations are often random and senseless patterns, contributing nothing more than empty novelty value to a person's speech. This common, superficial perception of many changes in language contributes to a phenomenon which has been noted to occur frequently when changes take place and bring deviations from mainstream forms of speech—the public expression of *negative attitudes* toward new patterns of colloquial speech and the younger generation speakers who make use of them. Each new generation makes innovations in its ways of speaking, is typically criticized for this by older generations, and then, ironically, levels the same kind of criticism at changes made by later generations.

Such patterns lead to a final, general question of whether language change can in any sense be described as constituting either 'progress' or 'decay', a topic discussed in many popular works on language change (Andersson and Trudgill 1990; Aitchison 2001; McWhorter 2016). A very frequent reaction to language change echoed across many centuries and in different populations is that innovation regularly represents decay and deterioration in the ways that a language is being used. Careless speakers change the meanings of words in illogical ways, random new forms of intonation make speech difficult to understand, and grammar is changed in ways that go against long-established rules, undermining the set of linguistic conventions previously held within a society sharing a single language. The targets of complaint change from generation to generation, and are often quickly forgotten as new objects of criticism come into focus and previous innovations are regularized in a language. In 18th-century England, prominent writers and intellectuals voiced their regret that English had lost the extensive set of morphological case and tense inflections it once had in earlier centuries, but such dramatic changes in the language no longer attract the attention of language critics, and currently it is 'like' and uptalk which have come to be the major targets of media debates on language 'abuse'.

So, are the changes which are currently taking place in English genuine signs of linguistic decay, or alternatively, marks of progress? Aitchison (2001) points out that any characterization of language change as representing progress or decay would need to be able to identify an *ideal state of language* that any progress or decay could be said to be moving toward or away from. However, linguistically it is not possible to define what the perfect state of any language actually could be. A language which seems logical and transparent in some ways may be complicated and ambiguous in others, and it is difficult to imagine how a language could be perfectly designed in all possible aspects of its syntax, phonology, and vocabulary. This being so, it is virtually impossible to talk of progress or decay in any realistic, objective way—in Aitchison's words 'languages are ebbing and flowing like the tide, but neither progressing nor decaying, as far as we can tell' (Aitchison 2001: 253). Such ebbing and flowing is nevertheless quite inevitable, the evidence suggests, and languages throughout history have everywhere demonstrated a striking instability in their character, constantly absorbing change and developing new forms. If this very natural property of language can only be accepted by all its speakers rather than resisted and objected to, ongoing changes in our language can in fact be warmly welcomed as clear indications of its vitality, richness, and diversity. As languages undergo change with each new generation exercising its creativity, variation and innovation among speakers should be viewed as a clear cause for celebration—a happy confirmation that the language we speak is still very much alive.

Suggestions for further reading and activities

1. In Milroy (1980), it is argued that a person's *social networks* can play a significant role in the ways that changes are spread through different groups in society. Find out what is meant by the term 'social network' and how social networks may often stimulate language variation. In addition to Milroy (1980), you can find shorter discussions of social networks in Wardhaugh (1998) and Hudson (1996).

    Milroy, Leslie. 1980. *Language and social networks*. Oxford: Blackwell.

    Wardhaugh, Ronald. 1998. *An introduction to sociolinguistics*. Oxford: Blackwell.

    Hudson, Richard. 1996. *Sociolinguistics*. Cambridge: Cambridge University Press.

2. Language change may often occur when people who speak different languages live in adjacent areas and are regularly in contact with each other. Two good examples of such

'contact-induced change' are the Balkan Sprachbund in southeast Europe (Trudgill 1974) and the interaction of languages in south India in the town of Kupwar (Gumperz 1971). Try to learn more about what kinds of changes occur when languages come into contact.

    Trudgill, Peter. 1974. *Sociolinguistics: an introduction to language and society.* Harmondsworth: Penguin.

    Gumperz, John. 1971. *Language in social groups.* Stanford: Stanford University Press.

3. Certain types of linguistic change have been noted to progress through a language at a rate which is described as an 'S-curve' (when plotted on a graph). Use resources you can find on the Internet to identify examples of S-curve changes.

4. Standard forms of languages have been heard more and more widely with the development of cinema and television in the late 20th century. This initially created an expectation that regional dialects and accents would disappear, as speakers adopted the prestige, standard forms of a language. However, various linguists have noted that regional accents in the USA and the UK continue to remain very robust and are not showing signs of dying out, though they may be stronger in certain socio-economic groups than in others (Labov and Ash 1997; Kretzschmar 2004). What can you find out about this issue, and is the situation similar where you live?

    Labov, William, and Sharon Ash. 1997. Understanding bilingualism. In Cynthia Bernstein, Thomas Nunnally, and Robin Sabino (eds.), *Language variety in the South revisited.* Tuscaloosa: University of Alabama Press, 508–573.

    Kretzschmar, William. 2004. Regional dialects. In Edward Finegan and John Rickford (eds.), *Language in the USA.* Cambridge: Cambridge University Press, 39–57.

5. The ways that immigrants and their second-generation children learn and speak a local majority language results in various differences in their speech, and to some extent, the areas of language that will be affected in such situations is predictable. Read about what changes typically occur in first-generation immigrants' learning and speaking of a local majority language in Aitchison (2001, chapter 10), and find out what is meant by the 'substratum theory'. What kinds of over-compensations in their pronunciations of a local majority language are sometimes made by second-generation speakers?

    Aitchison, Jean. 2001. *Language Change: Progress or Decay?* Cambridge: Cambridge University Press.

6. The chapter touched briefly on the phenomenon of *grammaticalization* in its description of British *innit*. Learn more about this process in McWhorter (2016), chapter 3, entitled: 'When Words Stop Being Words. Where Does Grammar Come From?'

    McWhorter, John. 2016. *Words on the move.* New York: Henry Holt.

7. In the UK, a colloquial variety of speech known as 'Estuary English' has been spreading rapidly among younger speakers. Using the Internet, found out what you can about this variety and the attitudes that other, older speakers have toward it.

8. It has been suggested that the meaning and use of the common texting abbreviation *lol* has been changing quite considerably, and *lol* is often used in ways which don't correspond to its original meaning 'laughing out loud'. Read the article 'The Twelve Meanings of LOL' by Katie Heaney, and discuss whether the uses described in this paper are familiar to you or sound odd. From your experience, do you think that there are other texting abbreviations which are changing in meaning too?

   Heaney, Katie. The twelve meanings of LOL. https://www.buzzfeed.com/katieheaney/the-12-meanings-of-lol?utm_term=.dtQA44lPw#.xtbzNN5Xb

References

Aguilaria, D., and M. LeCompte. 2007. Resiliency in Native languages: the tale of three indigenous communities' experiences with language immersion. *Journal of American Indian Education* 46:3: 11–16.
Aitchison, Jean. 2001. *Language change: progress or decay?* Cambridge: Cambridge University Press.
Alleyne, Mervyn. 1971. Acculturation and the cultural matrix of creolization. In Dell Hymes (ed.), *Pidginization and creolization of languages*. Cambridge: Cambridge University Press, 169–187.
Alsagoff, Lubna, and Chee Lick Ho. 1998. The grammar of Singapore English. In J. H. Foley (ed.), *English in new cultural contexts: reflections from Singapore* Oxford: Oxford University Press, 127–151.
Altarriba, Jeanette, and Rachel Morier. 2012. Bilingualism: language, emotion, and mental health. In Tej Bhatia and William Ritchie (eds.), *The handbook of bilingualism*. Oxford: Blackwell, 250–280.
Amritavalli, R., and K. A. Jayaseelan. 2007. India. In Andrew Simpson (ed.), *Language and national identity in Asia*. Oxford: Oxford University Press, 55–83.
Anderson, Rindy, Casey Klofstad, William Mayew, and Mohan Venkatachalam. 2014. Vocal fry may undermine the success of young women in the labor market. *PLOS ONE*. 9(5). Available online at: http://journals.plos.org/plosone/article?id=10.1371/journal.pone.0097506.
Andersson, Lars, and Peter Trudgill. 1990. *Bad language*. London: Penguin.
Anyidoho, Akosua, and M. E. Kropp Dakubu. 2008. Ghana: indigenous languages, English, and an emerging national identity. In Andrew Simpson (ed.), *Language and national identity in Africa*. Oxford: Oxford University Press, 141–157.
Arías, Beatriz, and Terrence Wiley. 2015. Forty years after *Lau*: the continuing assault on educational human rights in the United States and its implications for linguistic minorities. *Language Problems and Language Planning* 39:3: 227–244.
Arnberg, Lenore. 1987. *Raising children bilingually: the pre-school years*. Clevedon: Multilingual Matters.
Atanga, Lilian Lem, Sibonile Edith Ellece, Lia Litosseliti, and Jane Sunderland. 2013. Gender and language in sub-Saharan Africa: a valid epistemology? In Atanga et al. (eds.), *Gender and language in sub-Saharan Africa*. Amsterdam: John Benjamins, 1–26.
Athanasopoulos, Panos. 2006. Effects of the grammatical representation of number on cognition in bilinguals. *Bilingualism: Language and Cognition* 9: 89–96.
Athanasopoulos, Panos. 2007. Interaction between grammatical categories and cognition in bilinguals: the role of proficiency, cultural immersion, and language of instruction. *Language and Cognitive Processes* 22: 689–699.
Athanasopoulos, Panos, and Fraibet Aveledo. 2012. Linguistic relativity and bilingualism. In Jeanette Altarriba (ed.), *Memory, language, and bilingualism*. Cambridge: Cambridge University Press, 236–255.

Austin, Ann, Mahshid Salehi, and Ann Leffler. 1987. Gender and developmental differences in children's conversations. *Sex Roles* 16: 497–510.

Ayres, Alyssa. 2003. The politics of language policy in Pakistan. In Michael Brown and Šumit Ganguly (eds.), *Fighting words: language policy and ethnic relations in Asia*, Cambridge, MA: MIT Press, 51–80.

Baker, Colin. 1988. *Key issues in bilingualism and bilingual education*. Clevedon: Multilingual Matters.

Baker, Paul. 2008. *Sex texts: Language, gender and sexuality*. London: Equinox.

Bakker, Peter. 1994. Pidgins. In Jacques Arends, Pieter Muysken, and Norval Smith (eds.), *Pidgins and creoles: an introduction*. Amsterdam: John Benjamins, 25–40.

Bakker, Peter. 2008. Pidgins versus creoles and pidgincreoles. In Sylvia Kouwenberg and John Victor Singler (eds.), *The handbook of pidgin and creole studies*. Oxford: Blackwell, 130–157.

Baldwin, Daryl. 2014. Oowaaha Myaamiaataweenki: Miami is spoken here. In Terrence Wiley, Joy Kreeft Peyton, Donna Christian, Sarah Catherine Moore, and Na Liu (eds.), *Handbook of heritage, community, and Native American languages in the United States*. London: Routledge, 212–218.

Bamgbose, Ayo. 1991. *Language and the nation: the language question in sub-Saharan Africa*. Edinburgh: Edinburgh University Press.

Barner, David, Shunji Inagaki, and Peggy Li. 2009. Language, thought, and real nouns. *Cognition* 111: 329–344.

Barrett, Rusty. 1999. Indexing polyphonous identity in the speech of African American drag queens. In Mary Bucholz, Anita Liang, and Laurel Sutton (eds.), *Reinventing identities: the gendered self in discourse*. Oxford: Oxford University Press, 313–331.

Bassetti, Benedetta, and Vivian Cook. 2011. Relating language and cognition: the second language user. In Vivian Cook and Benedetta Bassetti (eds.), *Language and bilingual cognition*. New York: Psychology Press, 143–191.

Baugh, John. 2004. Ebonics and its controversy. In Edward Finegan and John Rickford (eds.), *Language in the USA*. Cambridge: Cambridge University Press, 305–318.

Bereiter, Carl, and Siegfried Engelmann. 1966. *Teaching disadvantaged children in preschool*. Englewood Cliffs, NJ: Prentice Hall.

Bergman, C. R. 1976. Interference vs. independent development in infant bilingualism. In G. Keller, R. Taeschner, and S. Viera (eds.), *Bilingualism in the bicentennial and beyond*. New York: Bilingual Press.

Berlin, Brent, and Paul Kay. 1969. *Basic color terms: their universality and evolution*. Berkeley: University of California Press.

Bertrand, Jacques. 2003. Language policy and the promotion of national identity in Indonesia. In Michael Brown and Šumit Ganguly (eds.), *Fighting words: language policy and ethnic relations in Asia*. Cambridge, MA: MIT Press, 263–290.

Besnier, Niko. 2003. Crossing genders, mixing languages: the linguistic construction of transgenderism in Tonga. In Janet Holmes and Miriam Meyerhoff (eds.), *The handbook of language and gender*. Oxford: Blackwell, 279–301.

Best, John, Patricia Miller, and Jack Naglien. 2011. Relations between executive function and academic achievement from ages 5 to 17 in a large, representative national sample. *Learning and Individual Differences* 21: 327–336.

Bhatia, Tej, and William Ritchie (eds.). 2012. *The handbook of bilingualism*. Oxford: Blackwell.

Bialystok, Ellen. 2005. Consequences of bilingualism for cognitive development. In Judith Kroll and Annette de Groot (eds.), *Handbook of bilingualism*. Oxford: Oxford University Press, 417–432.

Bialystok, Ellen, and Raluca Barac. 2013. Cognitive effects. In François Gosjean and Ping Li (eds.), *The psycholinguistics of bilingualism*. Oxford: Wiley-Blackwell, 192–213.

Bialystok, Ellen, and Judith Codd. 1997. Cardinal limits: evidence from language awareness and bilingualism for developing concepts of number. *Cognitive Development* 12: 85–106.

Bialystok, Ellen, Fergus Craik, and Gigi Luk. 2012. Bilingualism: consequences for mind and brain. *Trends in Cognitive Sciences* 16:4: 240–250.

Bialystok, Ellen, and Kenji Hakuta. 1999. Confounded age: linguistic and cognitive factors in age differences for second language acquisition. In David Birdsong (ed.), *Second language acquisition and the Critical Period Hypothesis*. London: Lawrence Erlbaum Associates, 161–181.

Bickerton, Derek. 1981. *Roots of language*. Ann Arbor: Karoma.
Bickerton, Derek. 1984. The language bioprogram hypothesis. *Behavioral and Brain Sciences* 7: 173–188.
Biloa, Edmond, and George Echu. 2008. Cameroon: official bilingualism in a multilingual state. In Andrew Simpson (ed.), *Language and national identity in Africa*. Oxford: Oxford University Press, 199–213.
Birdsong, David (ed.). 1999a. *Second language acquisition and the Critical Period Hypothesis*. London: Lawrence Erlbaum Associates.
Birdsong, David. 1999b. Introduction: whys and why nots of the Critical Period Hypothesis for Second Language Acquisition. In D. Birdsong (ed.), *Second language acquisition and the Critical Period Hypothesis*. London: Lawrence Erlbaum Associates, 1–22.
Bloomfield, Leonard. 1933. *Language*. New York: Henry Holt.
Blyth, Carl, Sigrid Recktenwald, and Jenny Wang. 1990. I'm like, 'Say what?!' A new quotative in American oral narrative. *American Speech* 65: 215–227.
Bokamba, Eyamba. 1992. The Africanization of English. In Braj Kachru (ed.), *The other tongue: English across cultures*. Chicago: University of Chicago Press, 125–147.
Bongaerts, Theo. 1999. Ultimate attainment in L2 pronunciation: the case of very advanced late L2 learners. In David Birdsong (ed.), *Second language acquisition and the Critical Period Hypothesis*. London: Lawrence Erlbaum Associates, 133–159.
Bonvillain, Nancy. 2007. *Language, culture and communication*. Boston: Prentice Hall.
Boroditsky, Lera. 2003. Linguistic relativity. *Encyclopedia of Cognitive Science* 917–921.
Boroditsky, Lera, Wendy Ham, and Michael Ramscar. 2002. What is universal in event perception? Comparing English and Indonesian speakers. Proceedings of the 24th Annual Meeting of the Cognitive Science Society, 136–141.
Boroditsky, Lera, and Alice Gaby. 2010. Remembrances of times east: absolute spatial representations of time in an Australian Aboriginal community. *Psychological Science* 20:11: 1635–1639.
Bosch, Laura, and Núria Sebastián-Gallés. 2001. Evidence of early language differentiation abilities in infants from bilingual environments. *Infancy* 2: 29–49.
Bradley, John. 1998. Yanyuwa: 'Men speak one way, women speak another'. In Jennifer Coates (ed.), *Language and gender: a reader*. Oxford: Blackwell, 13–20.
Brenzinger, Matthias. 2007. *Language diversity endangered*. Berlin: Mouton de Gruyter.
Brian, Clara, and Florence Goodenough. 1929. The relative potency of color and form perception at various ages. *Journal of Experimental Psychology* 12: 197–213.
Britain, David. 1998. Linguistic change in intonation: the use of high-rising terminals in New Zealand English. In Peter Trudgill and Jenny Cheshire (eds.), *The sociolinguistics reader*, Vol. 1: *Multilingualism and variation*. London: Arnold, 213–239.
Broder, David. 1995. Dole backs official English. *The Washington Post*, September 5th, A1.
Brown, Michael. 2003. Language policy and ethnic relations in Asia. In Michael Brown and Šumit Ganguly (eds.), *Fighting words: language policy and ethnic relations in Asia*, Cambridge, MA: MIT Press, 413–448.
Brown, Penelope, and Stephen Levinson. 1987. *Politeness: some universals in language usage*. Cambridge: Cambridge University Press.
Bucholtz, Mary. 1996. Geek the girl: language, femininity, and female nerds. In Natasha Warner, Jocelyn Ahlers, Leela Bilmes, Monica Oliver, Suzanne Wertheim, and Melinda Chen (eds.), *Gender and belief systems*. Berkeley, CA: Berkeley Women and Language Group, 119–131.
Bucholtz, Mary. 2004. Styles and stereotypes: the linguistic negotiation of identity among Laotian American youth. *Pragmatics* 14: 127–147.
Buchstaller, Isabelle. 2006. Social stereotypes, personality traits and regional perception displaced: attitudes towards the 'new' quotatives in the UK. *Journal of Sociolinguistics* 10:3: 362–381.
Burr, Vivian. 1995. *An introduction to social constructionism*. London: Routledge.
Butler, Judith. 1990. *Gender trouble: feminism and the subversion of identity*. New York: Routledge.
Butler, Judith. 1993. *Bodies that matter*. New York: Routledge.
Callahan, Mary. 2003. Language policy in modern Burma. In Michael Brown and Šumit Ganguly (eds.), *Fighting words: language policy and ethnic relations in Asia*, Cambridge, MA: MIT Press, 143–176.

Cameron, Deborah. 1997. Performing gender identity: young men's talk and the construction of heterosexual masculinity. In Sally Johnson and Ulrike Hanna Meinhof (eds.), *Language and masculinity*. Oxford: Blackwell, 47–64.

Cameron, Deborah. 2008. *The myth of Mars and Venus*. Oxford: Oxford University Press.

Cameron, Deborah. 2010. Language, gender, and sexuality. In Janet Maybin and Joan Swann (eds.), *The Routledge companion to English language studies*. London: Routledge, 208–217.

Carmichael, Cathie. 2000. A people exists and that people has its language: language and nationalism in the Balkans. In Stephen Barbour and Cathie Carmichael (eds.), *Language and nationalism in Europe*. Oxford: Oxford University Press, 221–239.

Carroll, John, and Joseph Casagrande. 1958. The function of language classifications in behavior. In E. Maccoby, T. Newcomb, and E. Hartley (eds.), *Readings in social psychology*. New York: Holt, Rinehart and Winston, 18–31.

Carroll, Tessa. 2001. *Language planning and language change in Japan*. London: Curzon.

Casad, Eugene. 1982. *Cora locationals and structured imagery*. PhD dissertation, University of California, San Diego.

Casasola, Marianella, Jui Bhagwat, and Anne Burke. 2006. Learning to form a spatial category of tight-fit relations: how experience with a label can give us a boost. *Developmental Psychology* 45:3: 711–723.

Castellanos, Diego. 1983. *The best of two worlds: bilingual-bicultural education in the US*. Trenton: New Jersey State Department of Education.

Chalmers, Rhoderick. 2007. Nepal and the Eastern Himalayas. In Andrew Simpson (ed.), *Language and national identity in Asia*. Oxford: Oxford University Press, 84–99.

Chamberlain, B. H. 1895. Essay in aid of a grammar and dictionary of the Luchuan language. *Transactions of the Asiatic Society of Japan*, vol. 23 supplement.

Chambers, J. K. 1992. Linguistic correlates of gender and sex. *English World-Wide* 13:2: 173–218.

Chambers, J. K., and Peter Trudgill. 1980. 'Dialectology'. Cambridge: Cambridge University Press.

Chan, Ting Ting, and Benjamin Bergen. 2005. Writing direction influences spatial cognition. *Proceedings of the 27th Annual Cognitive Society Conference*, 32–46.

Chavez, Linda. 1991. *Out of the barrio: toward a new politics of Hispanic assimilation*. New York: Basic Books.

Chen, Ping. 1999. *Modern Chinese: history and sociolinguistics*. Cambridge: Cambridge University Press.

Chen, Ping. 2007. China. In Andrew Simpson (ed.), *Language and national identity in Asia*. Oxford: Oxford University Press, 141–167.

Cheshire, Jenny. 1982. *Variation in an English dialect: a sociolinguistic study*. Cambridge: Cambridge University Press.

Childs, Becky, and Gerard van Herk. 2014. Work that –s! drag queens, gender, identity, and traditional Newfoundland English. *Journal of Sociolinguistics* 18:5: 634–657.

Chinen, Kiyomi, and Richard Tucker. 2005. Heritage language development: understanding the roles of ethnic identity and Saturday school participation. *Journal of Heritage Language* 3:1: 27–59.

Chung, Haesook Han. 2006. Code-switching as a communicative strategy: a case study of Korean-English bilinguals. *Bilingual Research Journal* 30:2: 293–307.

Coates, Jennifer. 1993. *Women, men, and language*. Harlow: Longman.

Coates, Jennifer. 1996. *Women talk*. Oxford: Blackwell.

Coleman, James. 2006. English-medium teaching in European higher education. *Language teaching* 39: 1–14.

Comrie, Bernard, Stephen Matthews, and Maria Polinsky. 2003. *The atlas of languages*. New York: Quarto.

Conklin, Harold. 1957. Hanunóo agriculture: a report on an integral system of shifting cultivation in the Philippines. *United Nations Development Papers* 12, 209.

Cook, Alicia, Janet Fritz, Barbara McCornack, and Cris Visperas. 1985. Early gender differences in the functional usage of language. *Sex Roles* 12: 909–915.

Cook, Vivian. 2011. Relating language and cognition: the speaker of one language. In Vivian Cook and Benedetta Bassetti (eds.), *Language and bilingual cognition*. New York: Psychology Press, 3–21.

Cook, Vivian, and Benedetta Bassetti (eds.). 2011. *Language and bilingual cognition*. New York: Psychology Press.

Cook, Vivian, Benedetta Bassetti, Chise Kasai, Miho Sasaki, and Jun Takahashi. 2006. Do bilinguals have different concepts? The case of shape and material in Japanese L2 users of English. *International Journal of Bilingualism* 10: 137–152.

Crowley, Terry. 1990. *Beach-la-mar to Bislama: the emergence of a national language of Vanuatu.* Oxford: Clarendon Press.

Crowley, Terry. 2008. Pidgin and creole morphology. In Sylvia Kouwenberg and John Victor Singler (eds.), *The handbook of pidgin and creole studies.* Oxford: Blackwell, 74–97.

Crystal, David. 1987. *The Cambridge encyclopedia of language.* Cambridge: Cambridge University Press.

Crystal, David. 1997. *English as a global language.* Cambridge: Cambridge University Press.

Crystal, David. 2000. *Language death.* Cambridge: Cambridge University Press.

Crystal, David. 2004. *The stories of English.* New York: Overlook Press.

Cummins, Jim. 1991. The politics of paranoia: reflections on the bilingual education debate. In Ofelia García (ed.), *Bilingual education.* Amsterdam: John Benjamins, 183–202.

Cutler, Cecilia. 1999. Yorkville Crossing: white teens, hip hop and African American English. *Journal of Sociolinguistics* 3:4: 428–442.

Dailey-O'Cain, Jennifer. 2000. The sociolinguistic distribution of and attitudes toward focuser *like* and quotative *like. Journal of Sociolinguistics* 4:1: 60–80.

Das, Kamala. 1965. *Summer in Calcutta.* New Delhi: R. Paul.

Davidoff, Jules, Ian Davies, and Debi Robertson. 1999. Colour categories in a stone-age tribe. *Nature* 398: 203–204.

de Groot, Annette. 1992. Bilingual lexical representation: A closer look at conceptual representations. *Advances in psychology* 94: 389–412.

de Groot, Annette. 2011. *Language and cognition in bilinguals and multilinguals.* New York: Psychology Press.

de Groot, Annette. 2013. Bilingual memory. In François Grosjean and Ping Li (eds.), *The psycholinguistics of bilingualism.* Oxford: Wiley-Blackwell, 171–191.

de Klerk, Vivian, and David Gough. 2002. Black South African English. In Rajend Mesthrie (ed.), *Language in South Africa.* Cambridge: Cambridge University Press, 356–378.

de Swaan, Abram. 2001. *Words of the world: the global language system.* Cambridge: Polity.

DeBose, Charles. 2015. The systematic marking of tense, modality, and aspect in African American language. In Sonja Lanehart (ed.), *The Oxford handbook of African American language.* Oxford: Oxford University Press, 371–386.

DeCamp, David. 1971. Towards a generative analysis of a post-creole speech continuum. In Dell Hymes (ed.), *Pidginization and creolization of languages.* Cambridge: Cambridge University Press, 349–370.

DeKeyser, Robert, and Jenifer Larson-Hall. 2005. What does the Critical Period really mean? In Judith Kroll and Annette de Groot (eds.), *Handbook of bilingualism.* Oxford: Oxford University Press, 88–108.

Devonish, Hubert. 2008. Language planning in pidgins and creoles. In Sylvia Kouwenberg and John Victor Singler (eds.), *The handbook of pidgin and creole studies.* Oxford: Blackwell, 615–636.

DeVotta, Neil. 2003. Ethnolinguistic nationalism and ethnic conflict in Sri Lanka. In Michael Brown and Šumit Ganguly (eds.), *Fighting words: language policy and ethnic relations in Asia.* Cambridge, MA: MIT Press, 105–139.

Dharmadasa, K. N. O. 2007. Sri Lanka. In Andrew Simpson (ed.), *Language and national identity in Asia.* Oxford: Oxford University Press, 116–138.

Diack, Anne, and Julie Berry. 2007. *English only in America?* Hamilton, NJ: Films Media Group.

Dicker, Susan. 1996. *Languages in America: a pluralist view.* Clevedon: Multilingual Matters.

Dillard, J. L. 1972. *Black English: its history and usage in the United States.* New York: Random House.

Downes, John. 1986. *A dictionary of Devon dialect.* Padstow, Cornwall: Tabb House.

Doyle, Anna Beth, Mireille Champagne, and Norman Segalowitz. 1978. Some issues in the assessment of the consequences of early bilingualism. In M. Paradis (ed.), *Aspects of bilingualism.* Columbia, SC: Hornbeam Press, 13–20.

Dubois, Sylvie, and Barbara Horvath. 2000. When the music changes, you change too: gender and language change in Cajun English. *Language Variation and Change* 11: 287–313.

Duncan, Greg, Kathleen Ziol-Guest, and Ariel Kalil. 2010. Early childhood poverty and adult attainment, behavior, and health. *Child Development* 81: 306–325.

Eastman, C. M. 1983. *Language planning: an introduction*. San Francisco: Chandler and Sharp.

Echevarria, Manny. 2009. 5 more difficult words to translate. https://www.altalang.com/beyond-words/2009/05/01/5-more-difficult-words-to-translate/. Accessed online February 2010.

Eckert, Penelope. 1989. *Jocks and burnouts: social categories and identity in the high school*. New York: Teachers' Press.

Eckert, Penelope. 2004. Adolescent language. In Edward Finegan and John Rickford (eds.), *Language in the USA*. Cambridge: Cambridge University Press, 361–374.

Ennaji, Moha, and Fatima Sadiqi. 2008. Morocco. In Andrew Simpson (ed.), *Language and national identity in Africa*. Oxford: Oxford University Press, 44–60.

Ervin, Susan, and Charles Osgood. 1954. Second language learning and bilingualism. In Charles Osgood and Thomas Sebeok (eds.), *Psycholinguistics: a survey of research and theory problems*. Special issue of the *Journal of Abnormal and Social Psychology*, 139–146.

Eubank, Lynn, and Kevin Gregg. 1999. Critical periods and (second) language acqusition: divide et impera. In David Birdsong (ed.), *Second language acquisition and the Critical Period Hypothesis*. London: Lawrence Erlbaum Associates, 65–99.

Evans, Nicholas. 2010. *Dying words: endangered languages and what they have to tell us*. Malden, MA: Wiley-Blackwell.

Everett, Caleb. 2013. *Linguistic relativity: evidence across languages and cognitive domains*. Berlin: de Gruyter.

Ferguson, Charles. 1959. Diglossia. *Word* 15: 325–340.

Fillmore, Lily Wong. 2004. Language in education. In Edward Finegan and John Rickford (eds.), *Language in the USA*. Cambridge: Cambridge University Press, 339–360.

Finlayson, Rosalie. 1978. A preliminary survey of *hlonipha* among the Xhosa. *Taalfasette* 24:2: 48–63.

Fishman, Joshua (ed.). 1966. *Language loyalty in the United States*. Berlin: Mouton.

Fishman, Joshua. 1967. Bilingualism with and without diglossia; diglossia with and without bilingualism. *Journal of Social Issues* 23:2: 29–38.

Fishman, Pamela. 1977. Interactional shitwork. *Herecies: A Feminist Publication on Arts and Politics* 2: 99–101.

Fishman, Pamela. 1978a. What do couples talk about when they're alone? In D. Butturf and E. Epstein (eds.), *Women's language and style*. Department of English, University of Akron.

Fishman, Pamela. 1978b. Interaction: the work women do. *Social Problems* 25:4: 397–406.

Flege, James, Murray Munro, and Ian MacKay. 1995. Factors affecting degree of perceived foreign accent in a second language. *Journal of the Acoustical Society of America* 97: 3125–3134.

Fought, Carmen. 2006. *Language and ethnicity*. Cambridge: Cambridge University Press.

French, Jane, and Peter French. 1984. Gender imbalance in the primary classroom: an interactional account. *Educational Research* 26: 2.

Fromkin, Victoria, Robert Rodman, and Nina Hyams. 2011. *An introduction to language*. Boston: Wadsworth Cengage Learning.

Frye, Douglas, Philip Zelazo, and Tibor Palfai. 1995. Theory of mind and rule based reasoning. *Cognitive development* 10: 483–527.

Fuhrman, Orly, and Lera Boroditsky. 2010. Cross-cultural differences in mental representations of time: evidence from an implicit nonlinguistic task. *Cognitive Science* 34:8: 1430–1451.

Gal, Susan. 1979. *Language shift: social determinants of linguistic change in bilingual Austria*. New York: Academic Press.

Gambhir, Surendra, and Vijay Gambhir. 2013. The maintenance and vitality of Hindi in the United States. *Heritage Language Journal* 10:2: 328–335.

García, Ofelia. 2009. *Bilingual education in the 21st century*. Oxford: Wiley-Blackwell.

Gardner-Chloros. 2009. *Code-switching*. Cambridge: Cambridge University Press.

Gaudio, Rudolph. 1996. Not talking straight in Hausa. In Anna Livia and Kira Hall (eds.), *Queerly-phrased: language, gender, and sexuality*. Oxford: Oxford University Press, 416–427.

Gentner, Dedre. 2007. Spatial cognition in apes and humans. *Trends in Cognitive Sciences* 11:5: 192–194.

Gilbert, Aubrey, Terry Regier, Paul Kay, and Richard Ivry. 2006. Whorf hypothesis is supported in the right visual field but not the left. *Proceedings of the National Academy of Sciences of the United States of America* 103:2: 489–494.

Goddard, Angela, and Lindsey Meân. 2000. *Language and gender*. London: Routledge.

Gonzales, Andrew. 2007. The Philippines. In Andrew Simpson (ed.), *Language and national identity in Asia*. Oxford: Oxford University Press, 360–373.

Goodenough, Florence. 1926. Racial differences in the intelligence of school children. *Journal of Experimental Psychology* 9: 388–397.

Goodwin, Marjorie. 1980. Directive-response speech sequences in girls' and boys' task activities. In Sally McConnell-Ginet, Ruth Borker, and Nelly Furman (eds.), *Women and language in literature and society*. New York: Praeger, 157–173.

Gottlieb, Nanette. 2007. Japan. In Andrew Simpson (ed.), *Language and national identity in Asia*. Oxford: Oxford University Press, 186–199.

Graddol, David. 2008. English next: Why global English may mean the end of 'English as a Foreign Language.' *Language Problems and Language Planning* 32:2: 203–207.

Graddol, David, and Joan Swann. 1989. *Gender voices*. Oxford: Blackwell.

Green, Lisa. 2002. *African American English: a linguistic introduction*. Cambridge: Cambridge University Press.

Green, Lisa. 2004. African American English. In Edward Finegan and John Rickford (eds.), *Language in the USA*. Cambridge: Cambridge University Press, 76–91.

Greenberg, Robert. 2011. *Language and identity in the Balkans*. Oxford: Oxford University Press.

Grenoble, Lenore. 2011. Language ecology and endangerment. In Peter Austin and Julia Sallabank (eds.), *The Cambridge handbook of endangered languages*. Cambridge: Cambridge University Press, 27–44.

Grenoble, Lenore, and Lindsay Whaley. 2006. *Saving languages: an introduction to language revitalization*. Cambridge: Cambridge University Press.

Grin, François. 1990. The economic approach to minority languages. *Journal of Multilingual and Multicultural Development* 11: 153–173.

Grosjean, François. 1982. *Life with two languages: an introduction to bilingualism*. Cambridge, MA: Harvard University Press.

Grosjean, François. 2013a. Speech perception and comprehension. In François Grosjean and Ping Li (eds.), *The psycholinguistics of bilingualism*. Oxford: Wiley-Blackwell, 29–49.

Grosjean, François. 2013b. Speech production. In François Grosjean and Ping Li (eds.), *The psycholinguistics of bilingualism*. Oxford: Wiley-Blackwell, 50–69.

Grosjean, François, and Ping Li (eds.). 2013. *The psycholinguistics of bilingualism*. Oxford: Wiley-Blackwell.

Guasti, Maria Teresa. 2002. *Language acquisition: the growth of grammar*. Cambridge, MA: MIT Press.

Gumperz, John. 1971. Some remarks on regional and social language differences in India. In A. S. Dil (ed.), *Language in social groups: essays by John J. Gumperz*. Stanford: Stanford University Press, 1–11.

Gumperz, John. 1982. *Discourse strategies*. Cambridge: Cambridge University Press.

Gussenhoven, Carlos. 2017. On the intonation of tonal varieties of English. In Fillpula Markku, Juhani Kelmola, and Devyani Sharma (eds.), *The Oxford handbook of world Englishes*. Oxford: Oxford University Press [accessed online at Oxford Handbooks Online: www.oxfordhandbooks.com].

Haas, Mary. 1944. Men's and women's speech in Koasati. *Language* 20: 142–149.

Hall, Kira, and Veronica O'Donovan. 1996. Shifting gender positions among Hindi-speaking *hijras*. In Victoria Bergvall, Janet Bing, and Alice Freed (eds.), *Rethinking language and gender research*. London: Longman, 228–266.

Hall, Robert. 1966. *Pidgin and creole languages*. Ithaca, NY: Cornell University Press.

Hamers, Josiane, and Michal Blanc. 2000. *Biliguality and bilingualism*. Cambridge: Cambridge University Press.

Harrison, David. 2010. *The last speakers: the quest to save the world's most endangered languages*. Washington, DC: National Geographic.

Harshav, Benjamin. 2009. Flowers have no names. *Natural History* 118:1: 24–29.

Hatcher, Lynley. 2008. Script change in Azerbajian: acts of identity. *International Journal of the Sociology of Language* 192: 105–116.

Hau, Caroline, and Victoria Tinio. 2003. Language policy and ethnic relations in the Philippines. In Michael Brown and Šumit Ganguly (eds.), *Fighting words: language policy and ethnic relations in Asia*. Cambridge, MA: MIT Press, 319–349.

Haugen, Einar. 1966. *Language conflict and language planning*. Cambridge, MA: Harvard University Press.

He, Agnes Weiyun. 2006. Toward an identity theory of the development of Chinese as a heritage language. *Heritage Language Journal* 4:1: 1–28.

Heller, Monica. 1992. The politics of code-switching and language choice. In Carol Eastman (ed.), *Codeswitching*, Clevedon: Multilingual Matters, 123–142.

Heredia, Roberto. 1997. Bilingual memory and hierarchical models: a case for language dominance. *Current Directions in Psychological Science* 6: 34–39.

Heredia, Roberto, and Jeffrey Brown. 2012. *Bilingual memory*. In Tej Bhatia and William Ritchie (eds), *The handbook of bilingualism*. Oxford: Blackwell, 225–249.

Hermans, Daan, Theo Bongaerts, Kees De Bot, and Robert Schreuder. 1998. Producing words in a foreign language: can speakers prevent interference from their first language? *Bilingualism: Language and Cognition* 1:1: 213–229.

Hermans, Daan, Ellen Ormel, Ria Besselaar, and Janet Van Hell. 2011. Lexical activation in bilinguals' speech production is dynamic: how language ambiguous words can effect cross-language activation. *Language and Cognitive Process* 26:10: 1687–1709.

Herring, Susan. 2005. Gender and power in on-line communication. In Janet Holmes and Miriam Meyerhoff (eds.), *The handbook of language and gender*. Oxford: Blackwell, 202–228.

Hill, Clifford. 1982. Up/down, front/back, left/right: a contrastive study of Hausa and English. In Jürgen Weissborn and Wolfgang Klein (eds.), *Here and there: cross-linguistic studies on deixis and demonstration*. Amsterdam: John Benjamins, 11–42.

Hinton, Leanne. 2001. Language revitalization: an overview. In Leanne Hinton and Ken Hale (eds.), *The green book of language revitalization in practice*. San Diego: Academic Press, 3–18.

Hinton, Leanne. 2009. Trading tongues: loss of heritage languages in the United States. In Angela Reyes ad Adrienne Lo (eds.), *Beyond yellow English*. Oxford: Oxford University Press, 331–346.

Hinton, Leanne. 2011. Revitalization of endangered languages. In Peter Austin and Julia Sallabank (eds.), *The Cambridge handbook of endangered languages*. Cambridge: Cambridge University Press, 291–311.

Hinton, Leanne, and Ken Hale (eds.). 2001. *The green book of language revitalization in practice*. San Diego: Academic Press.

Hoffmann, Charlotte. 1991. *An introduction to bilingualism*. London: Longman.

Hoffmann, Fernand. 1981. Triglossia in Luxemburg. In Einar Haugen, J. Derrick McClure, and Derick S. Thomson (eds.), *Minority languages today*. Edinburgh: Edinburgh University Press, 201–207.

Hollie, Sharroky, Tamara Butler, and Jamila Gillenwaters. 2015. Balancing pedagogy with theory. In Sonja Lanehart (ed.), *The Oxford handbook of African American Language*. Oxford: Oxford University Press, 355–370.

Holm, John. 1989. *Pidgins and creoles*. Cambridge: Cambridge University Press.

Holmes, Janet. 1992. *An introduction to sociolinguistics*. New York: Longman.

Holmes, Janet. 1998a. Complimenting: a positive politeness strategy. In Jennifer Coates (ed.), *Language and gender: a reader*. Oxford: Blackwell, 100–120.

Holmes, Janet. 1998b. Women's talk: the question of sociolinguistic universals. In Jennifer Coates (ed.), *Language and gender: a reader*. Oxford: Blackwell, 461–483.

Holmes, Janet, and Miriam Meyerhoff. 2005. Different voices, different views: an introduction to current research in language and gender. In Janet Holmes and Miriam Meyerhoff (eds.), *The handbook of language and gender*. Oxford: Blackwell, 1–17.

Hooper, Simon. 2011. Bretons fight to save language from extinction. CNN report, January 5, 2011, cnn.com/2010/WORLD/europe/12/11/brittany.language/.

House, Juliane. 2003. English as a lingua franca: a threat to multilingualism? *Journal of Sociolinguistics* 7:4: 556–578.

de Houwer, Annick. 1990. *The acquisition of two languages from birth: a case study*. Cambridge: Cambridge University Press.

Hu, Guangwei. 2007. The juggernaut of Chinese-English bilingual education. In Anwei Feng (ed.), *Bilingual education in China: practices, policies and concepts*. Clevedon: Multilingual Matters, 94–126.

Hubbell, Alan. 1950. *The pronunciation of English in New York City*. New York: Columbia University Press.

Hudson, Richard. 1996. *Sociolinguistics*. Cambridge: Cambridge University Press.

Hull, Rachel, and Jyotsna Vaid. 2005. Clearing the cobwebs from the study of the bilingual brain. In Judith Kroll and Annette de Groot (eds.), *Handbook of bilingualism*. Oxford: Oxford University Press, 480–496.

Hunt, Earl, and Franca Agnoli. 1991. The Whorfian hypothesis: a cognitive psychology perspective. *Psychological Review* 98:3: 377–389.

Ide, Sachiko, and Megumi Yoshida. 2000. Sociolinguistics: honorifics and gender differences. In Naoki Fukui (ed.), *Handbook of Japanese linguistics*. Oxford: Blackwell, 444–480.

Igoudin, A. Lane. 2013. Asian American girls who speak African American English: a subcultural language identity. In Inke Du Bois and Nicole Baumgarten (eds.), *Multilingual identities: new global perspectives*. Berlin: Peter Lang, 51–65.

Imai, Mutsumi, and Dedre Gentner. 1997. A crosslinguistic study of early word meaning: universal ontology and linguistic influence. *Cognition* 62: 169–200.

Imai, Mutsumi, and Reiko Mazuka. 2007. Language-relative construal of individuation constrained by universal ontology: revisiting language universals and linguistic relativity. *Cognitive Science* 31:3: 385–413.

James, Deborah, and Janice Drakich. 1993. Understanding gender differences in amount of talk: a critical review of research. In Deborah Tannen (ed.), *Gender and conversational interaction*. Oxford: Oxford University Press, 281–312.

Jarmel, Marcia and Ken Schneider. 2010. *Speaking in Tongues*. Patchworks Films. http://www.patchworksfilms.net/.

Javier, Rafael, Felix Barroso, and Michele Muñoz. 1993. Autobiographical memory in individuals. *Journal of Psycholinguistic Research* 22: 319–338.

Jenkins, Jennifer. 2003. *World Englishes. A resource book for students*. London: Routledge.

Jespersen, Otto. 1922. *Language: its nature, development and origin*. New York: Henry Holt.

Johnson, Fern. 2008. Discourse patterns of males and females. In Virgina Clark, Paul Eschholz, Alfred Rosa, and Beth Lee Simon (eds.), *Language: introductory readings*. Boston: Bedford/St. Martin's, 517–530.

Johnson, J. S., and E. I. Newport. 1989. Critical period effects in second language learning:the influence of maturational state on the acquisition of English as a second language. *Cognitive Psychology* 21: 60–99.

Jones, Eldred. 1968. Some tense, mode and aspect markers in Krio. *African Language Review* 7: 86–89.

Judge, Anne. 2000. France: 'One state, one nation, one language.' In Stephen Barbour and Cathie Carmichael (eds.), *Language and nationalism in Europe*. Oxford: Oxford University Press, 44–82.

Kachru, Braj. 1988. The sacred cows of English. *English Today* 16: 3–8.

Kachru, Braj (ed.). 1992. *The other tongue: English across cultures*. Chicago: University of Chicago Press.

Kanai, Yoshiko. 1994. *Onna-no miryoku-wa hanashi-kata shidai*. [Women's attractiveness depends on how they speak] Tokyo: Yamato Shuppan.

Kang, Hana. 2004. *Heritage language maintenance, acculturation and identity: Chinese and Korean 1.5 generation immigrants in New Jersey*. PhD dissertation, Ohio State University.

Kang, Hyun-Sook. 2012. English-only instruction at Korean universities: help or hindrance to higher learning? *English Today* 28:1: 29–34.

Kay, Paul, and Willett Kempton. 1984. What is the Sapir-Whorf Hypothesis? *American Anthropologist* 86:1: 65–79.

Kegl, Judy. 2002. Language emergence in a language-ready brain: acquisition issues. In Gary Morgan and Bencie Woll (eds.), *Language acquisition in signed languages*. Cambridge: Cambridge University Press, 207–254.

Kegl, Judy, Ann Senghas, and Marie Coppola. 1999. Creation though contact: sign language emergence and sign language change in Nicaragua. In Michel DeGraff (ed.), *Language change and creation: creolization, diachrony and development*. Cambridge, MA: MIT Press, 179–238.

Kelly, Alison. 1988. Gender differences in teacher-pupil interactions: a meta analytic review. *Research in Education* 39: 1–24.

Kessler, Carolyn. 1984. Language acquisition in bilingual children. In N. Miller (ed.), *Bilingualism and language disability*. London: Croom Helm, 26–54.

Khodorkovsky, Maria. 2008. Ten most difficult words to translate. https://www.altalang.com/beyond-words/2008/10/12/ten-most-difficult-words-to-translate/. Accessed online February 2010.

Kiesling, Scott. 2004. Dude. *American Speech* 79:3: 281–305.

Kim, Minju. 2008. On the semantic derogation of terms for women in Korean, with parallel developments in Chinese and Japanese. *Korean Studies* 32: 148–176.

King, Jeanette. 2001. Te kōhanga reo: Maōri language revitalization. In Leanne Hinton and Ken Hale (eds.), *The green book of language revitalization in practice*. San Diego: Academic Press, 119–128.

King, Kendall. 1999. Language revitalization processes and prospects: Quichua in the Ecuadorian Andes. *Language and Education* 13:1: 17–37.

King, Ross. 1996. Language, politics, and ideology in the post-war Koreas. In D. R. McCann (ed.), *Korea briefing*. Boulder, CO: Westview Press, 109–144.

King, Ross. 1998. Nationalism and language reform in Korea: the *questione della lingua* in pre-colonial Korea. In T. Tangherline and H.-I. Pai (eds.), *Nationalism and the construction of Korean national identity*. Berkeley: University of California Press, 33–72.

King, Ross. 2007. North and South Korea. In Andrew Simpson (ed.), *Language and national identity in Asia*. Oxford: Oxford University Press, 200–234.

Kloss, Heinz. 1977. *The American bilingual tradition* Rowley, MA: Newbury House.

Knickerbocker, Hugh, and Jeanette Altarriba. 2011. Bilingualism and the impact of emotion: the role of experience, memory, and sociolinguistic factors. In Vivian Cook and Benedetta Bassetti (eds.), *Language and bilingual cognition*. New York: Psychology Press, 453–477.

Knutsen, Anne. 2008. Ivory Coast: the supremacy of French. In Andrew Simpson (ed.), *Language and national identity in Africa*. Oxford: Oxford University Press, 158–171.

Kramer, Seth, Daniel Miller, and Jeremy Newberger (directors). 2008. *The Linguists*. Garrison, NY: Ironbound Films.

Krauss, Michael. 1992. The world's languages in crisis. *Language* 68: 4–10.

Kretzschmar, William. 2004. Regional dialects. In Edward Finegan and John Rickford (eds.), *Language in the USA*. Cambridge: Cambridge University Press, 39–57.

Kroll, Judith, and Annette de Groot. 2005. *Handbook of bilingualism*. Oxford: Oxford University Press.

Kroll, Judith, and Erika Stewart. 1994. Category interference in translation and picture naming: evidence for asymmetric connections between bilingual memory representations. *Journal of Memory and Language* 33: 149–174.

Kroll, Judith, and Natasha Tokowicz. 2005. Models of bilingual representation and processing. In Judith Kroll and Annette de Groot (eds.), *Handbook of bilingualism*. Oxford: Oxford University Press, 531–553.

Kroskrity, Paul. 1993. *Language, history, and identity: ethnolinguistic studies of the Arizona Tewa*. Tucson: University of Arizona Press.

Kung, K. T. F., W. V. Browne, M. Constantinescu, R. M. Noorderhaven, and M. Hines. 2016. Early postnatal testosterone predicts sex-related differences in early expressive vocabulary. *Psychoneuroendocrinology* 68: 111–116.

Kurath, Hans. 1949. *A word geography of the eastern United States*. Ann Arbor: University of Michigan Press.

Kurath, H., M. Hanley, B. Bloch, and G. S. Lowman. 1939-1945. *Linguistic atlas of New England*. Providence: Brown University Press.

Labov, William. 1963. The social motivation of a sound change. *Word* 19: 273–309.

Labov, William. 1966. *The social stratification of English in New York City*. Washington, DC: Center for Applied Linguistics.

Labov, William. 1969. Contraction, deletion and inherent variability of the English copula. *Language* 45:4: 715–762.

Labov, William. 1972. *Language in the inner city: studies in the Black English Vernacular*. Philadelphia: University of Pennsylvania Press.

Labov, William. 1982. Objectivity and commitment in linguistic science: the case of the Black English trial in Ann Arbor. *Language in Society* 11:2: 165–201.

Labov, William, and Sharon Ash. 1997. Understanding bilingualism. In Cynthia Bernstein, Thomas Nunnally, and Robin Sabino (eds.), *Language variety in the South revisited*. Tuscaloosa: University of Alabama Press, 508–573.

Ladd, Robert. 1980. *The structure of intonational meaning: evidence from English*. Bloomington: Indian University Press.

Lakoff, George. 1987. *Women, fire, and dangerous things*. Chicago: University of Chicago Press.

Lakoff, Robin. 1975. *Language and women's place*. New York: Harper and Row.

Lambert, Wallace. 1961. Behavioral evidence for contrasting forms of bilingualism. In M. Zarechnak (ed.), *Report of the 12th Annual Round Table Meeting on Linguistics and Language Studies*. Washington, DC: Georgetown University Press, 73–80.

Lanehart, Sonja, and Ayesha Malik. 2015. Language use in African American communities. In Sonja Lanehart (ed.), *The Oxford handbook of African American Language*. Oxford: Oxford University Press, 1–19.

Lanza, Elizabeth. 2007. *Language mixing in infant bilingualism*. Oxford: Oxford University Press.

Lao, Ravy, and Jin Sook Lee. 2009. Heritage language maintenance and use among 1.5 generation Khmer college students. *Journal of Southeast Asian American Education and Advancement* 4: 1–21.

Lê Minh-Hằng and Stephen O'Harrow. 2007. Vietnam. In Andrew Simpson (ed.), *Language and national identity in Asia*. Oxford: Oxford University Press, 415–441.

Lee, Jin Sook. 2002. The Korean language in America: the role of cultural identity in heritage language learning. *Language, Culture and Curriculum* 15:2: 117–133.

Lee-Smith, Mei W. 1996. The Hezhou language. In Stephen Wurm, Peter Mühlhäusler, and Darrell Tyron (eds.), *Atlas of languages of intercultural communication in the Pacific, Asia and the Americas*. Berlin: Mouton de Gruyter, 865–873.

Leibowitz, Arnold. 1980. *The Bilingual Education Act: a legislative analysis*. Rossly, VA: InterAmerica Research Associates.

Lenneberg, Eric. 1967. *Biological foundations of language*. New York: Wiley.

Levinson, Stephen. 2003. *Space in language and cognition: explorations in cognitive diversity*. Cambridge: Cambridge University Press.

Levy, Robert. 1973. *Tahitians: mind and experience in the Society Islands*. Chicago: Chicago University Press.

Li, Ping. 2013a. Successive language acquisition. In Grosjean and Li, 145–168.

Li, Ping. 2013b. Neurolinguistic and neurocomputational models. In François Grosjean and Ping Li (eds.), *The psycholinguistics of bilingualism*. Oxford: Wiley-Blackwell, 214–238.

Li, Wei, Lesley Milroy, and Pong Sin Ching. 2000. A two-step sociolinguistic analysis of code-switching and language choice: the example of a Chinese community in Britain. In Wei Li (ed.), *The bilingualism reader*. London: Routledge, 188–210.

Liu, Hua, Elizabeth Bates, and Ping Li. 1992. Sentence interpretation in bilingual speakers of English and Chinese. *Applied Psycholinguistics* 13: 451–484.

Liu, Rong. 2008. Maintaining Chinese as a heritage language in the United States: what really matters? In Robert Cote and Helen Shishkin (eds.), *Arizona Working Papers in Second Language Acquisition and Teaching*. Tucson: University of Arizona, 15: 37–64.

Livia, Anna. 1996. Disloyal to masculinity. In Anna Livia and Kira Hall (eds.), *Queerly-phrased: language, gender, and sexuality*. Oxford: Oxford University Press, 349–366.

Lo Bianco, Joseph. 2008. Policy activity for heritage language: connections with representation and citizenship. In Donna Brinton, Olga Kagan, and Susa Bauckus (eds.), *Heritage language education: a new field emerging*. New York: Routledge, 53–69.

Lo Bianco, Joseph. 2001. Viet Nam, *quốc ngữ*, colonialism, and language policy. In Nanette Gottlieb and Ping Chen (eds.), *Language planning and language policy: East Asian perspectives*. London: Curzon, 159–206.

Long, M. 1990. Maturational constraints on language development. *Studies in Second Language Acquisition* 12: 251–285.

Lothers, Michael, and Laura Lothers. 2012. *Mirpuri immigrants in England: a sociolinguistic survey*. SIL electronic survey report 2012-12, www.sil.org/resources/archives/48007. Dallas: Summer Institute of Linguistics. Accessed 27 October 2016.

Loveday, Leo. 1986. *Explorations in Japanese sociolinguistics* Amsterdam: John Benjamins.

Lu, Dan. 2008. Pre-imperial Chinese: its hurdles towards becoming a world language. *Journal of Asian Pacific Communication* 18:2: 268–279.

Lucy, John. 1992. *Grammatical categories and cognition: a case study of the linguistic relativity hypothesis*. Cambridge: Cambridge University Press.

Lucy, John, and Suzanne Gaskins. 2001. Grammatical categories and the development of classification preferences: a comparative approach. In Melissa Bowerman and Stephen Levinson (eds.), *Language acquisition and conceptual development*. Cambridge: Cambridge University Press, 257–283.

MacKaye, Susannah. 1990. California Proposition 63: language attitudes reflected in the public debate. *Annals of the American Academy of Political and Social Science* 508: 135–146.

Mackridge, Peter. 2009. *Language and national identity in Greece, 1766–1976*. Oxford: Oxford University Press.

Macnamara, J., and S. Kushnir. 1971. Linguistic independence of bilinguals: the input switch. *Journal of Verbal Learning and Verbal Behavior* 10: 480–487.

Majid, Asifa, Melissa Bowerman, Sotaro Kita, Daniel Haun, and Stephen Levinson. 2004. Can language restructure cognition? The case for space. *Trends in Cognitive Science* 8:3: 108–114.

Maltz, Daniel, and Ruth Borker. 1982. A cultural approach to male-female miscommunication. In J. Gumperz (ed.), *Language and social identity*. Cambridge: Cambridge University Press, 196–216.

Mann, Stephen. 2011. Drag queens' use of language and the performance of blurred gendered and racial identities. *Journal of Homosexuality* 58: 793–811.

Mar-Molinero, Clare. 2000. The Iberian peninsula: conflicting linguistic nationalisms. In Stephen Barbour and Cathie Carmichael (eds.), *Language and nationalism in Europe*. Oxford: Oxford University Press, 83–104.

Marian, Viorica, and Michael Spivey. 2003. Competing activation in bilingual language processing: within- and between-language competition. *Bilingualism: Language and Cognition* 6: 97–115.

Markku, Fillpula, Juhani Kelmola, and Devyani Sharma. 2017. *The Oxford handbook of world Englishes*. Oxford: Oxford University Press.

Matsuda, Aya. 2000. The use of English among Japanese returnees. *English Today* 16:4: 49–55.

May, Stephen. 2010. Aotearoa/New Zealand. In Joshua Fishman and Ofelia García (eds.), *Handbook of language and ethnic identity*. Oxford: Oxford University Press, 501–517.

McConnell-Ginet, Sally. 1975. Our father tongue. *Diacritics* 5: 44–50.

McConnell-Ginet, Sally. 2011. *Gender, sexuality and meaning*. Oxford: Oxford University Press.

McLaughlin, Fiona. 2008. Senegal: the emergence of a national lingua franca. In Andrew Simpson (ed.), *Language and national identity in Africa*. Oxford: Oxford University Press, 79–97.

McLemore, Cynthia. 1992. The interpretation of L*H in English. In Cynthia McLemore (ed.), *Linguistic Forum 32*. Austin: University of Texas Department of Linguistics and the Center of Cognitive Science, 127–147.

McNeill, William. 1976. *Plagues and peoples*. Garden City, NY: Anchor Press.

McWhorter, John. 2014. *The Language hoax: why the world looks the same in any language*. Oxford: Oxford University Press.

McWhorter, John. 2016. *Words on the move*. New York: Henry Holt.

Melchers, Gunnel, and Philip Shaw. 2011. *World Englishes*. London: Hodder Education.

Mesthrie, Rajend. 2008. South Africa: the rocky road to nation building. In Andrew Simpson (ed.), *Language and national identity in Africa*. Oxford: Oxford University Press, 314–338.

Mesthrie, Rajend, and Rakesh Bhatt. 2008. *World Englishes: the study of new linguistic varieties*. Cambridge: Cambridge University Press.

Mesthrie, Rajend, Joan Swann, Andrea Deumert, and William Leap. 2003. *Introducing sociolinguistics*. Edinburgh: Edinburgh University Press.

Meyerhoff, Miriam, and Nancy Niedzielski. 2003. The globalization of vernacular variation. *Journal of Sociolinguistics* 7:4: 534–555.

Miller, Laura. 2004. You are doing *burikko!* In Shigeko Okamoto and Janet Shibamoto Smith (eds.), *Japanese language, gender and ideology*. Oxford: Oxford University Press, 148–165.

Mills, Monique, and Julie Washington. 2015. Managing two varieties: code-switching in the educational context. In Sonja Lanehart (ed.), *The Oxford handbook of African American Language*. Oxford: Oxford University Press, 566–581.

Mills, Sara. 2008. *Language and sexism*. Cambridge: Cambridge University Press.

Mkilifi, M. H. Abdulaziz. 1972. Triglossia and Swahili-English bilingualism in Tanzania. *Language and Society*. 1: 197–213.

Montgomery, Martin. 1986. *Introduction to language and society*. London: Routledge.

Morris-Suzuki, Tessa. 1996. The frontiers of Japanese identity. In Stein Tønnesson and Hans Antlöv (eds.), *Asian forms of the nation*. London: Curzon, 46–66.

Mühlhäusler, Peter. 1986. *Pidgin and creole linguistics*. Oxford: Blackwell.

Myers Scotton, Carol. 1988. Codeswitching as indexical of social relations. In Monica Heller (ed.), *Codeswitching: anthropological and sociolinguistic perspectives*. Berlin: Mouton de Gruyter, 151–186.

Myers Scotton, Carol. 1993. *Social motivations for code-switching: evidence from Africa*. Oxford: Oxford University Press.

Nandy, Pritish. 1973. *Indian poetry in English today*. New Delhi: Sterling.

Neeley, Tsedal. 2012. Global business speaks English. *Harvard Business Review*. https://hbr.org/2012/05/global-business-speaks-english.

Neville, Helen, Sharon Coffey, Donald Lawson, Andrew Fischer, Karen Emmorey, and Ursula Bellugi. 1997. Neural systems mediating American Sign Language: effects of sensory experience and age of acquisition. *Brain and Language* 57: 285–308.

Nichols, Patricia. 2004. Creole languages: forging new identities. In Edward Finegan and John Rickford (eds.), *Language in the USA*. Cambridge: Cambridge University Press, 133–152.

Nishimura, Miwa. 1985. *Intra-sentential code-switching in Japanese-English*. PhD dissertation, University of Pennsylvania.

Nishimura, Miwa. 1997. *Japanese/English codeswitching: syntax and pragmatics*. New York: Peter Lang.

No'eau Warner, Sam. 2001. The movement to revitalize Hawaiian language and culture. In Leanne Hinton and Ken Hale (eds.), *The green book of language revitalization in practice*. San Diego: Academic Press, 133–146.

Norris, Mary Jane. 1998. Canada's aboriginal languages. *Canadian Social Trends*, Winter, 51: 8–16.

Ofori, Dominic Maximilian, and Mohammed Albakry. 2012. I own this language that everyone speaks. *English World-Wide* 33:2: 165–184.

Ogawa, Naoko, and Janet Shibamoto Smith. 1996. The gendering of the gay male sex class in Japan: a case study based on *Rasen no Sobyo*. In Anna Livia and Kira Hall (eds.), *Queerly-phrased: language, gender, and sexuality*. Oxford: Oxford University Press, 402–413.

Okamoto, Shigeko. 2004. Ideology in linguistic practice and analysis. In Shigeko Okamoto and Janet Shibamoto Smith (eds.), *Japanese language, gender and ideology*. Oxford: Oxford University Press, 38–56.

Owens, Robert. 1992. *Language development: an introduction*. New York: Macmillan.

Padilla, A. M., and Ellen Liebman. 1975. Language acquisition in the bilingual child. *Bilingual Review* 2: 34–55.

Palacios Martínez, Ignacio. 2014. Variation, development and pragmatic uses of *innit* in the language of British adults and teenagers. *English Language and Linguistics* 19:3: 383–405.

Park, Jin-Kyu. 2009. 'English fever' in South Korea: its history and symptoms. *English Today* 97:1: 50–57.

Parrish, Thomas. 1994. A cost analysis of alternative instructional models for limited English proficient students in California. *Journal of Education Finance* 19: 256–278.

Patkowski, Mark. 1990. Age and accent in a second language: a reply to James Emil Flege. *Applied Linguistics* 11: 73–89.

Pavlenko, Aneta. 2005. Bilingualism and thought. In Annette De Groot and Judith Kroll (eds.), *Handbook of bilingualism: psycholinguistic approaches*. Oxford: Oxford University Press, 433–453.

Pavlenko, Aneta. 2014. *The bilingual mind and what it tells us about language and thought*. Cambridge: Cambridge University Press.

Peal, Elizabeth, and Wallace Lambert. 1962. The relation of bilingualism to intelligence. *Psychological Monographs: General and Applied* 76: 1–23.

Pearce, Mary. 2013. Variation with gender in the tonal speech varieties of Kera (Chadic). In Atanga et al. (eds.), *Gender and language in sub-Saharan Africa*. Amsterdam: John Benjamins, 79–93.

Pearson, Barbara, Sylvia Fernandez, and Kimbrough Oller. 1993. Lexical development in bilingual infants and toddlers: comparison to monolingual norms. *Language Learning* 43: 93–120.

Pederson, Eric, Eve Danziger, David Wilkins, Stephen Levinson, Sotaro Kita and Gunter Senft. 1998. Semantic typology and spatial conceptualization. *Language* 74:3: 557–589.

Petyt, K. M. 1980. *The study of dialect: an introduction to dialectology.* Boulder, CO: Westview Press.

Phillipson, Robert. 2009. *Linguistic imperialism continued.* London: Routledge.

Pinker, Steven. 1994. *The language instinct.* London: Penguin.

Platt, John, Heidi Weber, and Mian-Lian Ho. 1983. *The new Englishes.* London: Routledge and Kegan Paul.

Pope, Jennifer, Miriam Meyerhoff, and Robert Ladd. 2007. Forty years of language change on Martha's Vineyard. *Language* 83: 615–627.

Poplack, Shana. 1980. Sometimes I'll start a sentence in English y termino en espanol. *Linguistics* 18: 581–516.

Poplack, Shana. 1988. Contrasting patterns of code-switching in two communities. In Monica Heller (ed.), *Codeswitching: anthropological and sociolinguistic perspectives.* Berlin: Mouton de Gruyter, 215–244.

Poplack, Shana. 2018. *Borrowing: Loanwords in the speech community and in the grammar.* Oxford: Oxford University Press.

Potter, Mary, Kwok-Fai So, Barbara Von Eckardt, and Laurie Feldman. 1984. Lexical and conceptual representation in beginning and more proficient bilinguals. *Journal of Verbal Learning and Verbal Behavior* 23: 23–38.

Preston, Dennis. 2004. Language attitudes to speech. In Edward Finegan and John Rickford (eds.), *Language in the USA.* Cambridge: Cambridge University Press, 480–492.

Pullum, Geoffrey. 1989. The great Eskimo vocabulary hoax. *Natural Language and Linguistic Theory* 7: 275–281.

Rampton, Ben. 1995. *Crossing: language and ethnicity among adolescents.* New York: Longman.

Redlinger, Wendy, and Tschang-Zin Park. 1980. Language mixing in young bilinguals. *Journal of Child Language* 7: 337–352.

Reyes, Angela. 2005. Appropriation of African American slang by Asian American youth. *Journal of Sociolinguistics* 9:4: 509–532.

Reynolds, Katsue Akiba. 2000. Female speakers of Japanese in transition. In Sally Coates (ed.), *Language and gender.* Oxford: Blackwell, 299–308.

Rickford, John. 1999. *African American Vernacular English: features, evolution, educational implications.* Oxford: Blackwell.

Rickford, John. 2015. The creole origins hypothesis. In Sonja Lanehart (ed.), *The Oxford handbook of African American Language.* Oxford: Oxford University Press, 35–56.

Romaine, Suzanne. 1988. *Pidgin and creole languages.* London: Longman.

Romaine, Suzanne. 1989/1995. *Bilingualism.* Oxford: Blackwell.

Rubin, Joan. 1968. *National bilingualism in Paraguay.* The Hague: Mouton.

Rubin, Joan, and Björn Jermudd (eds.). 1971. *Can languages be planned?* Honolulu: Hawaii University Press.

Rudwick, Stephanie. 2013. Gendered linguistic choices among isiZulu-speaking women in contemporary South Africa. In Atanga et al. (eds.), *Gender and language in sub-Saharan Africa.* Amsterdam: John Benjamins, 233–251.

de Ruiter, Jan Jaap. 2008. Morocco's languages and gender: evidence from the field. *International Journal of the Sociology of Language* 190: 103–119.

Rumbaut, Rubén. 2004. Ages, life stages, and generational cohorts: decomposing the immigrant first and second generations in the United States. *The International Migration Review.* 38:3: 1160–1205.

Ruzza, Carlo. 2000. Language and nationalism in Italy: language as a weak marker of identity. In Stephen Barbour and Cathie Carmichael (eds.), *Language and nationalism in Europe.* Oxford: Oxford University Press, 168–182.

Sadiqi, Fatima. 2003. *Women, gender, and language in Morocco.* Leiden: Brill.

Sadiqi, Fatima. 2008. Language and gender in Moroccan urban areas. *International Journal of the Sociology of Language*, 190: 145–165.
Sadker, Myra, and David Sadker. 1985. Sexism in the schoolroom of the '80s. *Psychology Today*, March 1985: 54–57.
Salomone, Rosemary. 2010. *True American*. Cambridge, MA: Harvard University Press.
Salamone, Rosemary. 2015. The rise of global English. *Language Problems and Language Planning* 39:3: 245–268.
Salzmann, Zdenek, James Stanlaw, and Nobuko Adachi. 2014. *Language, culture and society: an introduction to linguistic anthropology*. Boulder, CO: Westview Press.
Sankoff, Gillian, and Suzanne Laberge. 1973. On the acquisition of native speakers by a language. *Kivung* 6: 32–47.
Sapir, Edward. 1923. Text analyses of three Yana dialects. *American Archeology and Ethnology* 20: 263–285.
Sapir, Edward. 1929. The status of linguistics as science. *Language* 5: 207–214.
Schaller, Susan. 2012. *A man without words*. Berkeley: University of California Press.
Schiffman, Harold. 1996. *Linguistic culture and language policy*. London: Routledge.
Schourup, Lawrence. 1985. *Common discourse particles in English conversation*. Cambridge: Cambridge University Press.
Schulz, Muriel. 1975. The semantic derogation of women. In Barrie Thorne and Nancy Henley (eds.), *Language and sex*. Rowley, MA: Newbury House, 64–75.
Seargeant, Philip, and Joan Swann. 2012. *English in the world: history, diversity, change*. Abingdon: Routledge.
Shibamoto, J. 2005. Women's speech in Japan. In Natsuko Tsujimura (ed.), *Japanese linguistics*. London: Routledge, 181–221.
Shibatani, Masayoshi. 1990. *The languages of Japan*. Cambridge: Cambridge University Press.
Shih, Yu-hwei, and Mei-hui Song. 2002. Code-mixing of Taiwanese in Mandarin newspaper headlines: a socio-pragmatic perspective. In the *Proceedings of the Second International Symposium on Languages in Taiwan*. Taipei: Crane Publishing, 46–74.
Shin, Sarah. 2005. *Developing in two languages: Korean children in America*. Clevedon: Multilingual Matters.
Shumway, Norman. 1988. Preserving the primacy of English. In James Crawford (ed.), *Language loyalties: a source book on the Official English controversy*. Chicago: University of Chicago Press, 121–124.
Siegel, Jeff. 2009. Linguistic and educational aspects of Tok Pisin. In Nikolas Coupland and Adam Jaworski (eds.), *The new sociolinguistics reader*. Houndmills, Basingstoke, Hampshire: Palgrave Macmillan, 512–525.
Siegel, Muffy. 2002. Like: the discourse particle and semantics. *Journal of Semantics* 19: 35–71.
Silva-Corvalán, Carmen. 2004. Spanish in the Southwest. In Edward Finegan and John Rickford (eds.), *Language in the USA*. Cambridge: Cambridge University Press, 205–229.
Simpson, Andrew (ed.). 2007a. *Language and national identity in Asia*. Oxford: Oxford University Press.
Simpson, Andrew. 2007b. Indonesia. In Andrew Simpson (ed.), *Language and national identity in Asia*. Oxford: Oxford University Press, 312–336.
Simpson, Andrew. 2007c. Singapore. In Andrew Simpson (ed.), *Language and national identity in Asia*. Oxford: Oxford University Press, 374–390.
Simpson, Andrew. 2007d. Taiwan. In Andrew Simpson (ed.), *Language and national identity in Asia*. Oxford: Oxford University Press, 235–259.
Simpson, Andrew, and Monica Thukral. 2015. Hindi language maintenance in the USA: focusing on California. Talk presented at the 44th annual conference of the *Linguistics Association of the Southwest* (LASSO), Arizona State University, Lake Havasu, Arizona.
Skutnabb-Kangas, Tove, and Robert Phillipson. 2001. Language ecology: dominance, minorisation, linguistic genocide and linguistic rights. In Marianne Østergaard (ed.), *Images of the world: globalisation and cultural diversity*. Copenhagen: Center for kultursamarbejde med udviklingslandene, 32–47, 206–208.
Smalley, William. 1994. *Linguistic diversity and national unity: language ecology in Thailand*. Chicago: University of Chicago Press.
Smith, Neil, and Ianthi-Maria Tsimpli. 1995. *The mind of a savant: language learning and modularity*. Oxford: Blackwell.

Smitherman, Geneva. 2015. African American language and education: history and controversy in the twentieth century. In Sonja Lanehart (ed.), *The Oxford handbook of African American Language*. Oxford: Oxford University Press, 547–565.

Sohn, Ho-min. 1999. *The Korean language*. Cambridge: Cambridge University Press.

Spender, Dale. 1985. *Man made language*. London: Routledge.

Spivey, Michael, and Viorica Marian. 1999. Cross talk between native and second languages: partial activation of an irrelevant lexicon. *Psychological Science* 10: 281–284.

Spolsky, Bernard. 2004. *Language policy*. Cambridge: Cambridge University Press.

Spolsky, Bernard. 2009. Rescuing Maori: the last 40 years. In Peter Austin (ed.), *Language documentation and description*, Vol. 6. London: School of Oriental and African Studies, 11–36.

Sravanan, V. 1998. Language maintenance and language shift in the Tamil-English community. In S. Gopinathan, Anne Pakir, Ho Wah Kam, and Vanithamani Saravanan (eds.), *Language, society and education in Singapore*. Singapore: Times Academic Press, 155–177.

Stanley, Julia. 1977. The prostitute: paradigmatic woman. In D. L. Shores and C. P. Hines (eds.), *Papers in language variation*. Tuscaloosa: University of Alabama Press, 311–322.

Stern, Yaakov. 2002. What is cognitive reserve? Theory and research application of the reserve concept. *Journal of the International Neuropsychological Society* 8: 448–460.

Stewart, William. 1967. Sociolinguistic factors in the history of American Negro dialects. *Florida FL Reporters* 5: 11.

Sunderland, Jane. 2006. *Language and gender*. London: Routledge.

Suzuki, Kenji. 1989. *Suteki-na anata-o tsukuru: josei-no utsukushii hanashi-kata*. [To make yourself nice: women's beautiful ways of speaking] Tokyo: Goto Shoin.

Svartvik, Jan, and Geoffrey Leech. 2006. *English: one tongue, many voices*. Basingstoke: Palgrave Macmillan.

Swann, Joan, and David Graddol. 1988. Gender inequalities in classroom talk. *English in Education* 22:1: 48–65.

Swoyer, Chris. 2011. How does language affect thought? In Vivian Cook and Benedetta Bassetti (eds.), *Language and bilingual cognition*. New York: Psychology Press, 23–42.

Tagliamonte, Sali, and Alex D'Arcy. 2004. *He's like, she's like*: the quotative system in Canadian youth. *Journal of Sociolinguistics* 8:4: 493–514.

Talbot, Mary. 2008. Language and gender. In Virginia Clark, Paul Eschholz, Alfred Rosa, and Beth Lee Simon (eds.), *Language: introductory readings*. Boston: Bedford/St. Martin's, 507–516.

Tannen, Deborah. 1986. *That's not what I meant*. New York: Ballantine.

Tannen, Deborah. 1990. *You just don't understand*. New York: Ballantine Books.

Tatalovic, Raymond. 1995. *Nativism reborn? The Official Language Movement in the American states*. Lexington: University Press of Kentucky.

Taylor, Hanni. 1989. *Standard English, Black English, and bidialectalism*. New York: Longman.

Thomason, Sarah. 2015. *Endangered languages: an introduction*. Cambridge: Cambridge University Press.

Todd, Loreto. 1990. *Pidgins and creoles*. London: Routledge.

Topan, Farouk. 2008. Tanzania: the development of Swahili as a national and official language. In Andrew Simpson (ed.), *Language and national identity in Africa*. Oxford: Oxford University Press, 252–266.

Törnquist-Plewa, Barbara. 2000. Contrasting ethnic nationalisms: eastern central Europe. In Stephen Barbour and Cathie Carmichael (eds.), *Language and nationalism in Europe*. Oxford: Oxford University Press, 183–220.

Trudgill, Peter. 1974a. *The social differentiation of English in Norwich*. Cambridge: Cambridge University Press.

Trudgill, Peter. 1974b. *Sociolinguistics*. Harmondsworth: Penguin.

Trudgill, Peter. 1983. *On dialect: social and geographical perspectives*. New York: New York University Press.

Trudgill, Peter. 1999. *Dialects of England*. Oxford: Blackwell.

Trudgill, Peter. 2000. Greece and European Turkey: from religious to linguistic identity. In Stephen Barbour and Cathie Carmichael (eds.), *Language and nationalism in Europe*. Oxford: Oxford University Press, 240–263.

Tyversky, Barbara, Sol Kugelmass, and Atalia Winter. 1991. Cross-cultural and developmental trends in graphic productions. *Cognitive Psychology* 23: 515–557.

Underhill, Robert. 1988. *Like* is, like, focus. *American Speech* 63: 234–246.

Valentine, Tamara. 1987. Sexist practices in the Hindi language. *Praci-Bhasa-Vijna Indian Journal of Linguistics* 14: 25–55.

Valentine, Tamara. 2008. Language and gender. In Braj Kachru, Yamuna Kachru, and S. N. Sridhar (eds.), *Language in South Asia*. Cambridge: Cambridge University Press, 429–449.

Van Herk, Gerard. 2015. The English origins hypothesis. In Sonja Lanehart (ed.), *The Oxford handbook of African American Language*. Oxford: Oxford University Press, 23–34.

Veltman, Calvin. 1983. *Language loss in the United States*. Berlin: Mouton.

Vikør, Lars. 2000. Northern Europe: languages as prime markers of ethnic and national identity. In Stephen Barbour and Cathie Carmichael (eds.), *Language and nationalism in Europe*. Oxford: Oxford University Press, 105–129.

Volterra, Virginia, and Traute Taeschner. 1978. The acquisition and development of language by bilingual children. *Journal of Child Language* 5: 311–326.

Wardhaugh, Ronald. 1998. *An introduction to sociolinguistics*. Oxford: Blackwell.

Warner, Sam L. No'eau. 2001. The movement to revitalize Hawaiian language and culture. In Leanne Hinton and Ken Hale (eds.), *The green book of language revitalization in practice*. San Diego: Academic Press, 133–144.

Weber, Andrea, and Anne Cutler. 2004. Lexical competition in non-native spoken-word recognition. *Journal of Memory and Language* 50:1: 1–25.

Weber, Jean-Jacques, and Kristine Horner. 2012. *Introducing multilingualism: a social approach*. London: Routledge.

Weinreich, Uriel. 1953. *Languages in contact: findings and problems*. New York: Linguistic Circle of New York. [Reprinted 1968, The Hague: Mouton]

West, Candace. 1984. When the doctor is a lady. *Symbolic Interaction* 7:1: 87–106.

Whaley, Lindsay. 2002. Can a language that never existed be saved? Coming to terms with Oroqen language revitalization. Paper presented at *Sociolinguistic Symposium 14*, Ghent, April 2002.

Whorf, Benjamin Lee. 1956. *Language, thought and reality*. [Ed. J. B. Carroll] Cambridge, MA: MIT Press.

Wierzbicka, Anna. 1985. The double life of a bilingual. In Roland Sussex and Jerzy Zubrzycki (eds.), *Polish people and culture in Australia*. Canberra: Australian National University, 187–223.

Wiley, Terrence. 2004. Language planning, language policy, and the English-Only Movement. In Edward Finegan and John Rickford (eds.), *Language in the USA*. Cambridge: Cambridge University Press, 319–338.

Wilson, William. 1998. I ka 'ōlelo Hawai'I ke ola, 'Life is found in the Hawaiian language'. *International Journal of the Sociology of Language* 132: 123–137.

Wilson, William. 2014. Hawaiian: a native American language official for a state. In Terrence Wiley, Joy Kreeft Peyron, Donna Christian, Sarah Catherine Moore, and Na Liu (eds.), *Handbook of heritage, community, and Native American languages in the United States*. London: Routledge, 219–228.

Winford, Donald. 2015. The origins of African American Vernacular English. In Sonja Lanehart (ed.), *The Oxford handbook of African American Language*. Oxford: Oxford University Press, 85–104.

Wire, Jason. 2010. 20 awesomely untranslatable words from around the world. http://matadornetwork.com/abroad/20-awesomely-untranslatable-words-from-around-the-world/. Accessed online December 11, 2010.

Wolfram, Walt. 1999. Dialect awareness programs in the school and community. In Rebecca Wheeler (ed.), *Language alive in the classroom*. Westport, CT: Praeger, 47–66.

Wolfram, Walt. 2004. Social varieties of American English. In Edward Finegan and John Rickford (eds.), *Language in the USA*. Cambridge: Cambridge University Press, 58–75.

Wright, Sue. 2004. *Language policy and language planning*. New York: Palgrave Macmillan.

Youssi, Abderrahim. 1995. The Moroccan triglossia: facts and implications. *International Journal of the Sociology of Language* 112: 29–43.

Yuasa, Ikuko Patricia. 2010. Creaky voice: a new feminine voice quality for young urban- oriented upwardly mobile American women? *American Speech* 85:3: 315–337.

Zentella, Ana Celia. 2004. Spanish in the Northeast. In Edward Finegan and John Rickford (eds.), *Language in the USA*. Cambridge: Cambridge University Press, 182–204.

Zhang, Donghui, and Dian Slaughter-Defoe. 2009. Language attitudes and heritage language maintenance among Chinese immigrant families in the USA. *Language, Culture and Curriculum* 22:2: 77–93. DOI: 10.1080/07908310902935940

Zhang, Hong. 2007. Numeral classifiers in Mandarin Chinese. *Journal of East Asian Linguistics* 16: 43–59.

Zimmerman, Don, and Candace West. 1975. Sex roles, interruptions, and silences in conversation. In Barrie Thorne and Nancy Henley (eds.), *Language and sex: difference and dominance*. Rowley, MA: Newbury House.

Zong, Jie, and Jeanne Batalova. 2015. Indian immigrants in the United States. *Migration Policy Institute*: www.migrationpolicy.org.

Zubizarreta, Maria Luisa. 1998. *Prosody, focus and word order*. Cambridge, MA: MIT Press.

Index

accent, 17, 25–26, 132–33, 203, 207, 208–9, 211, 284, 290–91, 375–76, 420–22, 448–49
accommodation, 132–33, 134, 136, 375–76
acrolect, 175
additive bilingualism, 304, 309
affective use of language, 362–64, 378–79
African American Vernacular English/ AAVE, 244–61
Ainu, 13–14, 17, 61–62, 68, 87
Ann Arbor Decision, 228–29, 251, 256
Arabic, 8–9, 11–12, 48, 109–10, 113–15, 381–82
Arabic script, 6–7, 29, 55, 56–57, 118
autobiographical memory, 349
Aymara, 7
Azerbaijan, 56–57
Azeri, 56–57

Balance Theory, 303–4
balanced/non-balanced bilingualism, 267, 271, 273, 275–76, 296
Bambara, 63
Bangla, 35–36, 37–38, 284–85
Bangladesh, 23–24, 35–36, 37–38, 63–64, 186–87
Basilect, 175, 176
Basque, 17, 102
Belarusian, 7, 23–24
bi-dialectalism, 258–59, 260, 261
bilingual advantage, the, 306–9
bilingual education, 41–43, 79, 98–99, 192–93, 196–97, 225, 226, 227, 228, 230, 232, 234, 236–38, 241–42, 257
Bilingual Education Act, 228
Bislama, 156–57, 158–59, 165, 176
boosts, 365
borrowing, 47–49, 50, 51–53, 123–24, 448–49
Bosnian, 11–12
burikko, 392–93

Cajun English, 417–19, 423, 448, 450
California, 68–69, 84, 223, 226–27, 230–31, 236–37, 241, 431, 436, 442–43, 447–48, 450
Cameroon, 32–33, 44, 155, 186, 380–81, 382
Cantonese, 8, 12–13, 76, 77, 127–28, 131–32, 140
Capacity-Opportunity-Desire framework, 82–83, 84, 85
Carib, 352–53
changes from above/below, 416
Cherokee, 226
China, 8, 13, 45, 53–54, 57–58, 74–75, 94, 192–93
Chinese, 8, 12–13, 42, 48, 73, 111–12, 124, 182, 201, 354
Chinese pidgin Russian, 145, 149
Chinook Jargon, 145, 147
circles of English; Kachru's, three, 182–84
classifiers, 335–36, 338
Cockney rhyming slang, 212
code-mixing, 122, 132
code-switching
  alternational, 126
  extra-sentential, 121
  insertional, 125
  inter-sentential, 121
  intra-sentential, 122
  cognitive reserve, 308
color 328–31
  basic color terms, 329
compliments, 368
compound bilingualism, 295, 296
compounds, 154, 164
computer-mediated communication/CMC, 374
conceptual capacity, 324, 325, 326, 327
conceptual system, 316–17, 320–21, 323–27
consecutive/successive bilingualism, 266–67
contrastive analysis, 258–61
contronyms, 433

convergence, 132–34
conversational support, 370–71
Cornish, 102
corporate English, 198
corpus planning, 29, 46, 53
covert prestige, 358, 359, 420
Critical Period Hypothesis, 283–84, 288–93
Croatian, 10–11, 51, 55
Crossing, 445–48
Cyrillic script, 11, 55, 56–57
Czech, 23–24, 51, 315, 345

Danish, 7
de–creolization, 175–76, 178–79, 252–53
Devanagari script, 6–7, 55
dialect, 16–25
dialect continuum, 23
dialect geographer, 20, 23
diglossia; extended, 112
dispersal of English, the first/second, 185
Distributed Conceptual Feature Model, 298
divergence, 52, 134, 211
dude, 436–37

Ebonics, 256–58
embedded language, 125
English as a Lingua Franca/ELF, 191
English as a Medium of Instruction/EMI, 192
English Plus; English Plus Information Clearing House/EPIC, 239
Ethnologue, 15–16
evidentials, 318

frame of reference 338–43
   absolute/geocentric, 338–39
   intrinsic, 338–39
   relative/egocentric, 338–39
French, 44, 52–53, 64–65, 73, 77, 132–33, 146, 223, 290–91, 381–82, 418
functional transfer, 159, 163
fundamental concepts, 323, 324, 327

Garcia vs. the San Francisco Spun Steak Company, 240–41
geek girls, 442–43
Generation 1.5, 85–86, 90–91
Generation 4 Effect, 80–81
German, 9, 23, 109–10, 117–18, 159–60, 189, 196, 223–24, 225, 359, 364–65
globalization with localization, 214
Google Translate, 202, 203–4
grammaticalization, 435, 436
graphization, 29, 53
Greece, 50–51, 109–10, 115–16
Greek 50–51, 115–16, 117–18
   Dhimotiki Greek 109–10, 115, 116
   Katharevousa Greek, 50–51, 109–10
Guaraní, 112, 117–18

hangul, 54
Hawaii, 27, 75, 104–5
Hawai'i Creole, 104
Hawaiian, 104–84
Hebrew, 53, 100
hedges, 365, 367, 368, 369, 426–27, 428
Hindi, 6–7, 9–10, 15, 55–56, 84–85, 186–87, 353–54, 396
historical linguistics, 406
hlonipha, 353–54
Hokkien, 8, 42, 59
hypercorrection, 410, 411

Iceland, 28, 53
idiolect, 5
India, 6–7, 9–10, 15, 27, 44, 186–87, 213, 396
Indonesia, 38–39, 45
Indonesian, 7, 38, 348
inhibitory control, 307–8
innit, 435–36
interference, 284–88
interruptions, 370, 371–72
Invariant System Hypothesis, 3, 5
isogloss, 20–21
isolated concepts, 323–24
Italian, 9, 51, 275–76, 364–65

Japanese, 13–14, 20–21, 30–31, 48–50, 53–54, 58–59, 61–62, 73–74, 80, 119, 382–400
jocks and burnouts, 443–44

Kamtok, 161
Karajá, 353
Kayardild, 339
Kera, 380–81
Khmer, 45
Koasati, 353, 357, 380
Krio, 156

language attrition/loss, 294
Language Bioprogram Hypothesis, 171–72
language documentation, 96–98
language isolate, 17
language nests, 99, 103
language planning, 29–51, 56, 62
language purism/purification, 50
language revitalization, 96, 97–107
language shift, 67–76, 81
leveling, 152
lexical decomposition, 316–17
lexical expansion, 29–30
lexical gaps, 127, 400–2
lexical storage, 283–84, 295–99
lexifier language, 145–46
like; be like, 214, 426–32
Limited English Proficiency/LEP, 236–37
lingua franca, 94, 113, 145, 166–67, 168, 187–88, 189, 191

linguistic assimilation, 58
linguistic determinism, 321, 335, 345–46
linguistic pluralism, 40
linguistic protectionism, 52–53
literally vs. *hopefully*, 432–33
loan words, 47–48
Louisiana, 224, 238, 418–19

Macedonian, 15
machine translation, 202–5
mainstream American English/MAE, 222, 245
Malay, 7, 33, 38, 39–40, 41
Mali, 63
Mandarin, 8, 12–13, 41, 42, 59, 74–75, 182, 201, 348
Martha's Vineyard, 413–16
Master–Apprentice Language Learning Program, 99–100
matrix language, 125
mesolect, 175
Meyer vs. Nebraska, 225–26
Miami, 101–2
minimal responses 371
   delayed minimal responses, 372
Mirpur Pahari, 83–84
monogenetic origin theories (of pidgins), 166–68
moribund, 285
Morocco, 381–82
multi-functionality, 155
munhwao/Cultured Speech, 51–52
Mutual Intelligibility Hypothesis, 6

national languages, 27, 28
Native American Languages Act, 229
Navajo, 334–35
Nepal, 60
Nepali, 60
Newfoundland, 422–24
New Mexico, 224, 238, 239
New York City 'r', 407–11
Nicaraguan Sign Language, 173
North Korea, 47, 51–52
Norwegian, 7, 149, 275
number, 332–33

Observer's Paradox, the, 411
official languages, 27, 28
one parent one language principle, 269–70, 273, 280
onna-rashii kotoba, 383
ornamentation use of English, 190
Oroqen, 95
over-reporting of speech, 358
overt prestige, 416, 425

Pakistan, 6–7, 9–10, 33, 35, 83
Paraguay, 112, 117–18

pidgins
   early, 147, 149, 150
   expanded, 147, 149, 156
   maritime/nautical, 145
   plantation and workplace, 145
   stable, 149, 156
   trading, 145
   warzone/occupation, 145
pluricentricity, 207
polysemy, 155
Pormpuraaw, 343–44
post creole continuum, 175
Punjabi, 55–56, 136, 139

Quechua, 7, 81, 118–19, 167
quốc ngữ, 54–55

reanalysis, 151, 156
re-creolization, 178
reduplication, 161, 392
referential use of language, 362
relexification, 167–68
Revised Hierarchical Model, 297, 298
rhoticism/rhotic pronunciation, 407–11, 420
Roman/Latin alphabet, 29, 53, 55
Russenorsk, 149
Russian, 7, 23–24, 45–46, 224, 302, 330
Ryuukyuan, 13–14, 62

Sabir, 166–67
Sanskrit, 6–7, 10, 48
Sapir, Edward, 312
Sapir–Whorf Hypothesis, 312–13
semantic primitives, 298
semantic relativity, 316
Senegal, 63
sentence-final particles/SFPs, 384
Separate Development Hypothesis (Independent Development Hypothesis), 278–80
Serbian, 10–11, 51, 55
Serbo-Croatian, 10–11, 55
service voice (in Japan), 355, 383–84
sexism, 397, 403
Shanghainese, 8, 12–13
shape vs. material, 336–38
simultaneous bilingualism, 266–67, 269–70, 273
Sindhi, 35
Singapore, 40–43, 64–65, 200, 210
Singlish/Singaporean Colloquial English, 210
Sinhala, 36–37
Slovak, 23–24, 34, 63–64
solidarity, 364–65
South Africa, 7, 43–44, 45–46, 144, 353–54, 381
Soviet Union, 45–46, 56–57
Spanish–American League Against Discrimination/SALAD, 239
Sri Lanka, 36–37

standard American English/SAE, 228–29
standardization, 29
status planning, 29
subordinate bilingualism, 296
substrate language, 146–47
subtractive bilingualism, 304–6
successive/consecutive bilingualism, 266–67, 273
superstrate language, 145–46
Swedish, 7, 275, 279–80, 306

Taiwan, 58–59
Taiwanese, 126–27, 133
Tamil, 36–37, 111–12
three generation pattern of language shift and loss, 69–70
Tok Pisin, 156–57, 176, 177–78
triglossia, 112
Tsotsitaal, 381
Turkey, 56–57
Turkish, 50–51, 115

Ukrainian, 7, 23–24
under-reporting of speech, 358, 359
unilingual language policy, 31

Unitary Language System Hypothesis, 276–78, 279, 280–81
unitizers, 335–36
Universal Grammar, 171
uptalk, 438–40
Urdu, 6–7, 9–10, 33, 35–36, 48, 55

Vanuatu, 156–57, 176–77
Vietnam, 54–55, 76–77
vocal fry, 441–42

Wa, 56
Whorf, Benjamin Lee, 312, 328
Wolof, 63
World Englishes, 208–11

Xhosa, 7, 353–54

Yana, 353
Yanyuwa, 353
Yniguez vs. Mofford, 239–40
Yucatec Maya, 332–33, 336–38

Zulu, 7, 353–54, 381, 401–2

Made in United States
Orlando, FL
05 January 2022

12900863R00293